THE GUINNESS BOOK OF
ANSWERS

General Editor

Norris McWhirter

Associate Editors

Clive Carpenter	Stan Greenberg
Edward Pyatt	Alex E. Reid
Dr James Bevan	Kenneth Macksey
Maurice Burton D.Sc.	John Marshall
Robert Dearling	Patrick Moore O.B.E.
Elizabeth Hogarth	Andrew Thomas

Prof. Kennedy McWhirter M.A., M.Sc.

Dr C. T. Prime M.A., F.L.S. F.I. Biol.

John Arblaster M.I.M., A.I.W.M.

GUINNESS SUPERLATIVES LIMITED

2 Cecil Court London Road Enfield

Middlesex

Contents

The Calendar

Days of the week

ENGLISH	LATIN	SAXON
Sunday	Dies Solis	Sun's Day
Monday	Dies Lunae	Moon's Day
Tuesday	Dies Martis	Tiu's Day
Wednesday	Dies Mercurii	Woden's Day
Thursday	Dies Jovis	Thor's Day
Friday	Dies Veneris	Frigg's Day
Saturday	Dies Saturni	Saternes' Day

Tiu was the Anglo-Saxon counterpart of the Nordic Tyr, son of Odin, God of War, who came closest to Mars (Greek, Aries) son of the Roman God of War Jupiter (Greek, Zeus). Woden was the Anglo-Saxon counterpart of Odin, Nordic dispenser of victory, who came closest to Mercury (Greek, Hermes), the Roman messenger of victory. Thor was the Nordic God of Thunder, eldest son of Odin and nearest to the Roman Jupiter (Greek, Zeus), who was armed with thunder and lightning. Frigg (or Freyja) wife of Odin, was the Nordic Goddess of Love, and equivalent to Venus (Greek, Aphrodite), Goddess of Love in Roman mythology. Thus the four middle days of the week are named after a mythological husband and wife and their two sons.

The seasons

The four seasons in the northern hemisphere are astronomically speaking:

Spring	from the vernal equinox (about 21 Mar.) to the summer solstice (about 21 June).
Summer	from the summer solstice (about 21 June) to the autumnal equinox (about 21 Sept.).
Autumn	(or Fall in USA) from the autumnal equinox (about 21 Sept.) to the winter solstice (about 21 Dec.).
Winter	from the winter solstice (about 21 Dec.) to the vernal equinox (about 21 Mar.).

In the southern hemisphere, of course, autumn corresponds to spring, winter to summer, spring to autumn and summer to winter.

The solstices (from Latin *sol*, sun; *stitium*, standing) are the two times in the year when the sun is farthest from the equator and appears to be still. The equinoxes (from Latin *aequis*, equal; *nox*, night) are the two times in the year when day and night are of equal length when the sun crosses the equator.

Longest and shortest day

The longest day (day with the longest interval between sunrise and sunset) is the day on which the *solstice* falls and in the northern hemisphere occurs on 21 June, or increasingly rarely on 22 June. The latest sunset, however, occurs on 13 or 14 June but the sunrise is still getting earlier by sufficiently large a margin to make the duration of night shorter until Midsummer's Day. At Greenwich (South London) daylight may last up to 16 h 39 min, though the longest duration sunshine is 15 h 48 min, recorded at nearby Kew (West London) on 13 June 1887. The shortest day occurs either on 21 or 22 Dec. when daylight at Greenwich may last only 7 h 50 min. The evenings, however, begin lengthening imperceptibly on 13 or 14 Dec. when the sunset is about 2 s later than the previous day.

Old style (Julian) and new style (Gregorian) dates

In England, until 1752, Lady Day (25 Mar.) was the legal beginning of the year and 25 Mar. is still the beginning of the ecclesiastical year. Dates from 1 Jan. to 24 Mar. in any year were written e.g. 28 Feb. 1659–60 or $16\frac{59}{60}$ indicating the historical year of 1660 but the ecclesiastical, legal and official year of 1659.

Parliament passed in March 1751 the Calendar (New Style) Act, known as Lord Chesterfield's Act (24 Geo II, c. 23), declaring that the following First of January should be the first day of the year 1752 for all ordinary purposes. It was also enacted that Wednesday 2 Sept. 1752 should be followed by Thursday 14 Sept. Thus apparent anomalies of the kind whereby William of Orange, later King William III, left Holland on 11 Nov. 1688 (New Style (NS)) by the Gregorian Calendar and landed in England on 5 Nov. 1688 (Old Style (OS)) by the Julian Calendar were eliminated.

The Julian Calendar, introduced by Julius Caesar in 45 BC, on the advice of the Egyptian astronomer Sosigenes, was in use throughout Europe until 1582 when Pope Gregory XIII ordained that 5 Oct. should be called 15 Oct. The discrepancy occurred because of the Augustinian ruling of AD 4 that every fourth year shall be of 366 days and hence include a Leap Day.

Countries switched from the Old Style (Julian) to the New Style (Gregorian) system as follows:

1582	Italy, France, Portugal, Spain
1583	Flanders, Holland, Prussia, Switzerland, and the Roman Catholic states in Germany
1586	Poland
1587	Hungary
1600	Scotland (except St Kilda)
1700	Denmark and the Protestant states in Germany
1700–40	Sweden (by gradual process)
1752	England and Wales, Ireland and the Colonies, including North America
1872	Japan (12-day lag)
1912	China (13-day lag)
1915	Bulgaria (13-day lag)
1917	Turkey and USSR (13-day lag)
1919	Romania and Yugoslavia (13-day lag)
1923	Greece (13-day lag)

Leap year

Leap years occur in every year the number of which is divisible by four, e.g. 1964, except centennial years, e.g. 1700, 1800, or 1900, which are treated as common or non-leap years *unless* the number of the *century* is divisible by four, e.g. 1600 was (NS) a leap year and 2000 will be a leap year.

The whole process is one of compensation for over-retrenchment of the discrepancy

The four seasons

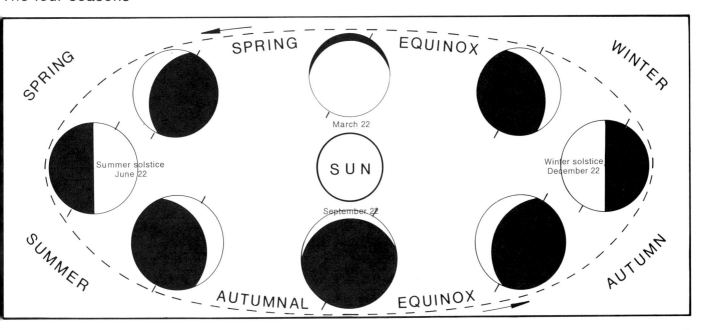

SPRING

SPRING EQUINOX

WINTER

March 22

SUN

Summer solstice
June 22

Winter solstice
December 22

September 22

SUMMER

AUTUMNAL EQUINOX

AUTUMN

between the calendar year of 365 days and the mean solar year of 365·24219878 days. The date when it will be necessary to suppress a further leap year, sometimes assumed to be AD 4000, AD 8000, etc., is not in fact yet clearly specifiable, owing to minute variations in the earth-sun relationship.

The word 'leap' derives from the Old Norse *hlaupár*, indicating a leap in the sense of a jump. The origin probably derives from the observation that in a bissextile (i.e. leap) year any fixed day festival falls on the next weekday but one to that on which it fell in the preceding year, and not on the next weekday as happens in common years.

The term bissextile derives literally from a double (bis) day inserted after the sixth (sextile) day before the calends of March. Thus the Julian calendar compensated (albeit inaccurately) for the discrepancy between its year and the mean solar year.

Public and bank holidays

By English Common Law the days that mark the birth and death of Christ (Christmas Day and Good Friday) are public holidays.

By custom the Bank of England at the beginning of last century was closed on at least 40 saints' days and anniversaries. In 1830 such bank holidays were cut to 18 and in 1834 to only 4.

In 1871 parliament passed the Bank Holidays Act, introduced by Rt. Hon. Sir John Lubbock, MP, 4th baronet—later Lord Avebury—and this statute regulated bank holidays as follows:

England and Wales
  Good Friday (by Common Law)
  Easter Monday (by Statute)
  May Day (from 1978)[1]
  Spring Holiday (last Monday in May)[1]
  Late Summer Holiday (last Monday in August)[1]
  Christmas Day, 25 Dec. (by Common Law)
  Boxing Day, 26 Dec., or St Stephen's Day, unless this falls on a Sunday, in which case 27 Dec. (by Statute)

Scotland
  New Year's Day, 1 Jan., but if this falls on a Sunday, the next day (by Statute) and the day following (by Statute)
  Good Friday (by Statute)
  The first Monday in May (by Statute)
  The first Monday in August (by Statute)
  Christmas Day, 25 Dec. (by Statute)

In addition most Scottish cities and towns have a spring and autumn holiday fixed by local custom.

Northern Ireland
  March 17, St Patrick's Day, or if this falls on a Sunday, the next day (by Statute)
  Good Friday (by Statute)
  Easter Monday (by Statute)
  Easter Tuesday (but note banks in fact remain open on this public holiday) (by Statute)
  12 July (Battle of the Boyne Day), but if this falls on a Sunday, the next day[2]
  Christmas Day, 25 Dec. (by Statute)
  Boxing Day, 26 Dec. or St Stephen's Day, unless this falls on a Sunday, in which case 27 Dec. (by Statute)

[1] It was announced by the President of the Board of Trade in 1965 that in England and Wales the Whitsun holiday would be replaced by the fixed Spring Holiday on the last Monday in May and that the August Bank Holiday would be replaced by the Late Summer Holiday on the last Monday in August from 1967 onwards. This was adopted also in Northern Ireland. New Year's Day also became a Bank Holiday from 1976. On 31 March 1976 a May Day (1 May) Holiday was announced by the retiring Prime Minister, effective from Monday 1 May 1978.
[2] This holiday is proclaimed by the Governor-General of Northern Ireland in the name of the Sovereign by Order in Council.

In addition to the above public and bank holidays the Sovereign has power under Section 4 of the 1871 Act to proclaim a public holiday in any district, borough, town city, county or throughout the whole country. Such an occasion was on her Coronation Day in 1953. If a bank holiday is inexpedient it may be replaced by another date by Proclamation.

Easter Day

Easter, the Sunday on which the resurrection of Christ is celebrated in the Christian world is, unlike Christmas which is fixed, a 'moveable feast'.

The celebration of Easter is believed to have begun about the year AD 68. The English word Easter probably derives from *Eostre*, a Saxon goddess whose festival was celebrated about the time of the vernal equinox.

Easter Days and Leap Years 1964–2000
(Years in bold type are leap years)

1976	18 Apr.	1989	26 Mar.
1977	10 Apr.	1990	15 Apr.
1978	26 Mar.	1991	31 Mar.
1979	15 Apr.	**1992**	19 Apr.
1980	6 Apr.	1993	11 Apr.
1981	19 Apr.	1994	3 Apr.
1982	11 Apr.	1995	16 Apr.
1983	3 Apr.	**1996**	7 Apr.
1984	22 Apr.	1997	30 Mar.
1985	7 Apr.	1998	12 Apr.
1986	30 Mar.	1999	4 Apr.
1987	19 Apr.	**2000**	23 Apr.
1988	3 Apr.		

The date of Easter has been a matter of constant dispute between the eastern and western Christian churches. Almost the entire calendar of the Christian religion revolves around the date upon which, in any given year, Easter falls. The repercussions extend in Christian countries into civil life because, for example, in England the date of the statutory Whitsun bank holiday of course depends on the date of Easter.

According to English Statute Law by Act of 1751 (24 Geo. II, **c**. 23) Easter Day is the *first* Sunday after the full moon, which occurs on, or next after, 21 Mar., but if this full moon occurs on a Sunday, Easter Day is on the Sunday after. The moon, for the purposes of this Act, is not the real moon but the paschal moon which is a hypothetical moon, the full details of which can be found in the *Book of Common Prayer*. Thus Easter may fall on any one of the thirty-five days from 22 Mar. (as last in 1818) to 25 Apr. (as last in 1943) inclusive.

The House of Commons agreed in June 1928, by passing the Easter Act, to redefine Easter as 'the first Sunday after the second Saturday in Apr.'. The date would thus have fallen only between 9 Apr. and 15 Apr. inclusive (i.e. either the second or third Sunday in April). The measure failed owing to the provision that it should require the support of the various international Christian churches, which was, despite the efforts of the League of Nations, not forthcoming.

The United Nations in 1949 considered the establishment of a perpetual world calendar, which would automatically and incidentally have fixed Easter, but the proposals were shelved indefinitely in 1956.

The Vatican Council in Rome in October 1963 approved the resolution to fix the date of Easter, subject to the agreement of other Christian churches, by 2058 votes to nine against.

The boldest scheme for calendar reform,

which is winning increasing support, is that the year should be divided into four quarters of thirteen weeks, with each day of the year being assigned a fixed day of the week. By this scheme it is thought likely that Easter would always fall on Sunday, 8 Apr. For the calendar to conform with the mean solar year a 'blank day' would be required each year.

Summer Time

The device of decreeing that the legal time of day should be one hour in advance of Greenwich Mean Time during the summer months was introduced by Act of Parliament in 1916.

The practice is now governed by the Summer Time Act of 1925. The *statutory* moment for putting the clocks on one hour is at 2 a.m. (GMT) on the day after the third Saturday in April, but if that Sunday happens to be Easter Day (as in 1965, 1976, 1979, 1981, 1987, 1990 and 1992) Summer Time will start a week earlier.

Statutorily, Summer Time always ends at 2 a.m. (BST) on the day after the first Saturday in October.

BUT in practice Summer Time can be extended (at either or both ends of the period) by the Home Secretary by means of an Order in Council, and this was done in 1961, 1962 and 1963 with extensions of three weeks in each direction.

As a matter of record, it may be noted that the 1925 Act operated as prescribed until 1940. Then from 1941 to 1945 and again in 1947 there was Double Summer Time, i.e. Greenwich Mean Time plus two hours. From 1948 until 1952 and since 1961, the period of Single Summer Time was extended while the Act operated normally in the intervening years of 1953 to 1960.

The Union flag

The Union flag, commonly called the Union Jack, is described in a proclamation of 1 Jan. 1801 by authority of the Union with Ireland Act of 1800 as:

'Azure (i.e. blue), the crosses saltire (i.e. diagonal) of St Andrew (i.e. for Scotland) and St Patrick (i.e. for Ireland) quarterly per saltire, counterchanged argent (i.e. white) and gules (i.e. red); the latter fimbriated (i.e. narrowly bordered) of the second, surmounted (i.e. overlaid) by the cross of St George (i.e. for England), of the third, fimbriated as the saltire.'

Every citizen in the Commonwealth may fly the Union Jack.

In the armed forces of the United Kingdom the Union flag is the personal flag of Admirals of the Fleet and Field Marshals.

The Union flag may by custom fly from 8 a.m. to sunset on public buildings.

Variations. It is a nautical custom that if the Union flag (or more practically the Ensign) is flown upside down this is an improvised distress signal.

Half Mast. The Union Jack is flown at half mast in mourning (a) for the death of the Sovereign (from announcement to funeral, except from 11 a.m. to sunset on the day of the Proclamation of the successor); (b) at the funerals of Prime Ministers and ex-Prime Ministers; and (c) by specific Royal Command for the funeral of members of the Royal Family, Foreign Rulers, and on other occasions. If a day for flying flags right up coincides with a half-mast occasion the former will take precedence in case (c) except for the building in which the body may be lying.

Quarter days

(England, Northern Ireland, Wales)

25 Mar. Lady Day (The Annunication of Our Lady the Virgin Mary)
24 June Midsummer (Nativity of St John The Baptist)
29 Sept. Michaelmas (Festival of St Michael and All Angels)
25 Dec. Christmas (Festival of Christ's birth)

Half quarter days are on 2 Feb., 9 May, 1 Aug., and Martinmas (11 Nov.).

Scottish term days

2 Feb. Candlemas (or the Feast of the Purification of the Virgin Mary)
15 May Whit Sunday (from Old English *Hwita Sunnandaeg* or White Sunday because of the white robes of the newly baptised)
1 Aug. Lammas (from Old English *hláf-maesse*, loaf-mass, hence harvest festival)
11 Nov. Martinmas (St Martin's (4th century Bishop of Tours) Day)

The zodiac

The zodiac (from the Greek *zōdiakos kyklos*, circle of animals) is an unscientific and astrological system devised in Mesopotamia c. 3000 BC.

The zodiac is an imaginary belt of pictorial constellations which lie as a backdrop quite arbitrarily 8 degrees on either side of the annual path or ecliptic of the sun. It is divided into twelve sections each of 30 degrees. Each has been allocated a name from the constellation which at one time coincided with that sector. The present lack of coincidence of the zodiacal sectors with the constellations from which they are named has been caused mainly by the lack of proper allowance for leap days. The old order is nonetheless adhered to.

The traditional 'signs' are:
Aries, the Ram 21 Mar.–19 Apr.
Taurus, the Bull 20 Apr.–20 May
Gemini, the Twins 21 May–21 June
Cancer, the Crab 22 June–22 July
Leo, the Lion 23 July–22 Aug.
Virgo, the Virgin 23 Aug.–22 Sept.
Libra, the Balance 23 Sept.–23 Oct.
Scorpio, the Scorpion 24 Oct.–21 Nov.
Saggittarius, the Archer 22 Nov.–21 Dec.
Capricornus, the Goat 22 Dec.–19 Jan.
Aquarius, the Water Carrier 20 Jan.–18 Feb.
Pisces, the Fish 19 Feb.–20 Mar.

Standard time

Until the last quarter of last century the time kept was a local affair, or, in the smaller countries, based on the time kept in the capital city. But the spread of railways across the vaster countries caused great time-keeping confusion to the various railway companies and their passengers. In 1880 Greenwich Mean Time (GMT) became the legal time in the British Isles (but see note re Summer Time) and by 1883 the movement to establish international time by zones was successful.

The world, for this purpose, is divided into 24 zones, or segments, each of 15° of longitude, with twelve that, being to the east, are fast on Greenwich time, and twelve that, being to the west, are slow on Greenwich time.

Each zone is $7\frac{1}{2}$° on either side of its central meridian. The International Date Line—with some variations to suit obvious geographical conditions—runs down the 180° meridian.

A very few countries or divisions of countries do not adhere to the Greenwich system at all and in others no zoning system is used, i.e. the whole nation, despite spanning more than one of the 24 segments, elects to keep the same time. Yet a third group (e.g. India) uses differences of half an hour.

Europe has three zones, part keeping GMT, others mid-European time (i.e. GMT + 1) and the remainder east European time (GMT + 2).

In the United States there are four zones: Eastern, Central, Mountain and Pacific, and these are 5, 6, 7 and 8 hours respectively slow on Greenwich.

The authoritative and complete reference, where the method of time keeping in every place in the world can be found, is *The Nautical Almanac*, published annually by HMSO.

Watches at sea

A watch at sea is four hours except the period between 4 p.m. and 8 p.m., which is divided into two short watches termed the first dog watch and the second dog watch. The word dog is here a corruption of 'dodge'. The object of these is to prevent the same men always being on duty during the same hours each day.

Midnight–4 a.m.	Middle Watch
4 a.m.–8 a.m.	Morning Watch
8 a.m.–noon	Forenoon Watch
noon–4 p.m.	Afternoon Watch
4 p.m.–6 p.m.	First Dog Watch
6 p.m.–8 p.m.	Second Dog Watch
8 p.m.–Midnight	First Watch

Sunrise, sunset and twilight

The *Nautical Almanac* gives the GMT of sunrise and sunset for each two degrees of latitude for every third day in the year. The sunrise is the instant when the rim of the sun appears above the horizon, and the sunset when the last segment disappears below the horizon. But because of the Earth's atmosphere, the transition from day to night and vice versa is a gradual process, the length of which varies according to the declination of the sun and the latitude of the observer. The intermediate stages are called twilight.

There are three sorts of twilight:

Civil twilight. This occurs when the centre of the sun is 6° below the horizon. Before this moment in the morning and after it in the evening ordinary outdoor activities are impossible without artificial light.

Nautical twilight. This occurs when the sun is 12° below the horizon. Before this time in the morning and after it in the evening the sea horizon is invisible.

Astronomical twilight. This is the moment when the centre of the sun is 18° below the horizon. Before this time in the morning or after it in the evening there is a complete absence of sunlight.

Lighting up time for lights on vehicles occurs *half an hour* after the moment of sunset in accordance with the provisions of Section 17 of The Road Transport Lighting Act, 1957.

Lighting up time is later in the west (e.g. at Cardiff) than the east (e.g. at London). Similarly, lighting up time in the north (e.g. at Edinburgh) is also later than in London in summer but earlier in winter.

Wedding anniversaries	
First	Cotton
Second	Paper
Third	Leather
Fourth	Fruit, flowers
Fifth	Wooden
Sixth	Sugar
Seventh	Wool, copper
Eighth	Bronze, pottery
Ninth	Pottery, willow
Tenth	Tin
Eleventh	Steel
Twelfth	Silk, linen
Thirteenth	Lace
Fourteenth	Ivory
Fifteenth	Crystal
Twentieth	China
Twenty-fifth	Silver
Thirtieth	Pearl
Thirty-fifth	Coral
Fortieth	Ruby
Forty-fifth	Sapphire
Fiftieth	Golden
Fifty-fifth	Emerald
Sixtieth	Diamond

Below are given dates of birth and death, where accurately known, of people generally accepted as being famous or infamous, and dates of highly memorable occasions.

January (31 days)

DERIVATION
Latin, *Januarius*, or *Ianuarius*, named after Janus, the two-faced Roman god of doorways (*ianaue*) and archways (*iani*), as presiding over the 'entrance', or beginning of the year.

1 *The Times* founded 1788; Baron Pierre de Coubertin b. 1863
2 Gen. James Wolfe b. 1927
3 Cicero b. 106 BC
4 Isaac Newton b. 1642; Dr Ralph Vaughan Williams d. 1958
5 Edward the Confessor d. 1066; German National Socialist Party founded 1919
6 Joan of Arc *c.* 1412; Jet propulsion invented 1944
7 Sir Thomas Lawrence d. 1830
8 Galileo Galilei d. 1642; Lord Baden-Powell d. 1941
9 Richard Nixon b. 1913
10 Penny Post in Britain 1840; League of Nations founded 1920 (dissolved 1946)
11 Thomas Hardy d. 1928
12 Edmund Burke b. 1729
13 James Joyce d. 1941
14 Albert Schweitzer b. 1875; Charles Lutwidge Dodgson (alias Lewis Carroll) d. 1898; Casablanca Conference 1943
15 Act of Supremacy 1535; Moliere b. 1622
16 Ivan the Terrible crowned 1547; Prohibition in the USA 1920
17 Benjamin Franklin b. 1706; David Lloyd George b. 1863
18 Scott reached South Pole 1912; Rudyard Kipling d. 1436
19 James Watt b. 1736; Edgar Allan Poe b. 1809
20 First Assembly of House of Commons 1265; Edward VIII proclaimed King 1936
21 Vladimir Lenin d. 1924
22 Francis Bacon (Viscount St Albans) b. 1561; Lord Byron b. 1588; Queen Victoria d. 1901
23 Treaty of Utrecht 1579; William Pitt (the younger) d. 1806
24 Frederick the Great b. 1712; Gold discovered in California 1848; Sir Winston Spencer Churchill d. 1965
25 Robert Burns b. 1759
26 General Gordon assassinated 1885; India proclaimed a Republic 1950
27 Wolfgang Amadeus Mozart b. 1756; First demonstration of television 1926
28 Diet of Worms 1521; Sir Francis Drake d. 1596
29 Victoria Cross instituted 1856; Anton Chekhov b. 1860
30 Charles I executed 1649; Franklin Delano Roosevelt b. 1882; Mohandas Gandhi assassinated 1948
31 Franz Schubert b. 1797; *Great Eastern* launched 1858; Anna Pavlova b. 1885

February (29 days)

DERIVATION
Latin, *Februarius* (*februare*, to purify), from *februa*, a festival of purification held on 15 Feb.

1 Victor Herbert b. 1859; British State Labour Exchanges 1910
2 Fritz Kreisler b. 1875; Jascha Heifetz b. 1901; German capitulation at Stalingrad 1943
3 Felix Mendelsohn-Bartholdy b. 1809; Yalta conference 1945
4 Thomas Carlyle d. 1881; Submarine warfare by Germany 1915;
5 Sir Robert Peel b. 1788
6 Charles II d. 1685; Queen Elizabeth II succeeded to throne 1952
7 Sir Thomas More b. 1478; Charles Dickens b. 1812 [see below, *RTHPL*]
8 Mary, Queen of Scots executed 1587; Russo-Japanese War began 1904
9 William Henry Harrison b. 1773
10 Académie Française founded 1635; Charles Lamb b. 1775
11 Thomas Alva Edison b. 1847; Vatican City independence 1929
12 Abraham Lincoln b. 1809; Charles Darwin b. 1809
13 Massacre of Glencoe 1692
14 Captain James Cook d. 1779
15 Japanese captured Singapore 1942
16 George Macaulay Trevelyan b. 1876
17 Molière d. 1673; Thomas Robert Malthus b. 1766
18 Galileo Galilei b. 1564; *Pilgrim's Progress* published 1678
19 Nicolaus Copernicus b. 1473
20 David Garrick b. 1717
21 Cardinal John Henry Newman b. 1801
22 Last invasion of Britain 1797; Frederic Chopin b. 1810; Lord Baden-Powell b. 1857
23 Samuel Pepys b. 1633; George Frideric Handel b. 1685
24 Sir Samuel Hoare b. 1880
25 Sir Christopher Wren d. 1723; Enrico Caruso b. 1873
26 Victor Hugo b. 1802
27 Henry Wadsworth Longfellow b. 1807; British Labour Party founded 1900
28 Relief of Ladysmith 1900
29 Gioacchino Antonio Rossini b. 1792

March (31 days)

DERIVATION
Latin, *Martius*, the month of Mars, the Roman god of war and the protector of vegetation.

1 Battle of Mukden 1905
2 John Wesley d. 1791
3 Alexander Graham Bell b. 1847; Vincent Van Gogh b. 1853
4 US Constitution in force 1789; Comintern formed 1919;
5 Sir Robert Peel b. 1788; Churchill' Iron Curtain speech 1946; Josef Stalin d. 1953
6 Michelangelo Buonarroti b. 1475; Elizabeth Barrett Browning b. 1806
7 Bell's telephone patented 1876
8 Russian Revolution began 1917
9 Amerigo Vespucci b. 1451
10 Arthur Honegger b. 1892; Jan Masaryk d. 1948
11 London's first daily newspaper, *The Daily Courant*, 1702; German troops enter Austria 1938
12 Sun Yat-sen d. 1925
13 Uranus discovered 1781
14 Albert Einstein b. 1879 [see below *RTHPL*]; Karl Marx d. 1883; First Transatlantic broadcast 1925
15 Julius Caesar assassinated 44 BC
16 Long Parliament dissolved 1660; James Madison b. 1751
17 Sir Robert Walpole d. 1745
18 Ivan the Terrible d. 1684
19 David Livingstone b. 1813
20 Sir Isaac Newton d. 1727; Napoleon's 'Hundred Days' begins 1815
21 Johann Sebastian Bach b. 1685; Soviet Republic proclaimed 1919
22 Arab League founded 1945
23 Stamp Act 1765; Alfred, Lord Milner b. 1854
24 Queen Elizabeth I d. 1603; Union of England and Scotland 1603
25 Rome Treaty signed by Six 1957
26 Ludwig van Beethoven d. 1827; David Lloyd George d. 1945
27 United States Navy created 1794; Arnold Bennett d. 1931
28 Crimean War declared 1854; Spanish Civil War ended 1939
29 Sir William Walton b. 1902
30 Vincent Van Gogh b. 1853; Irish peace agreement 1922
31 John Constable d. 1837; Charlotte Bronte d. 1855

April (30 days)

DERIVATION

Latin, *Aprilis*, from *aperire* (to open), the season when trees and flowers begin to open'.

1 Prince Otto von Bismarck b. 1815; Royal Air Force formed 1918
2 Charlemagne b. 742; Hans Christian Andersen b. 1805
3 Pony Express in USA 1860; Johannes Brahms d. 1897
4 North Atlantic Treaty signed 1949
5 Lord Lister b. 1827; Algernon Charles Swinburne b. 1837
6 US Declaration of War 1917; PAYE in Britain 1944
7 Richard Coeur de Lion d. 1199; William Wordsworth b. 1770
8 Entente Cordiale signed 1904
9 Francis Bacon (Viscount St Albans) d. 1626; Vladimir Lenin b. 1870
10 William Booth b. 1829; Algernon Charles Swinburne d. 1909
11 Napoleon abdicated 1814
12 American Civil War began 1861; Franklin Delano Roosevelt d. 1945; Yuri Gagarin orbits Earth 1961
13 Edict of Nantes 1598; Thomas Jefferson b. 1743
14 George Frideric Handel d. 1759; *Titanic* sank 1912
15 Leonardo da Vinci b. 1452; Abraham Lincoln d. 1865
16 Battle of Culloden 1746; Charles Spencer Chaplin b. 1889; OEEC set up 1948
17 John Pierpoint Morgan b. 1837; Nikita Kruschev b. 1894
18 San Francisco earthquake 1906; Eur. Coal & Steel Comm. 1951; Albert Einstein d. 1955
19 Lord Byron d. 1824; Benjamin Disraeli (Earl Beaconsfield) d. 1881; Charles Darwin d. 1882
20 Adolf Hitler b. 1889
21 Foundation of Rome 753 BC; Charlotte Brontë b. 1816; Queen Elizabeth II b. 1926
22 Kathleen Ferrier b. 1912; Yehudi Menuhin b. 1916
23 William Shakespeare d. 1616; William Wordsworth d. 1850
24 Anthony Trollope b. 1815
25 Oliver Cromwell b. 1599
26 Emma, Lady Hamilton b. 1765
27 Gen. Ulysses S. Grant b. 1822
28 Mutiny on the *Bounty* 1789; League of Nations founded 1919; Benito Mussolini d. 1945
29 Duke of Wellington b. 1769; Emperor Hirohito of Japan b. 1901
30 George Washington—1st US President 1789; Adolf Hitler d. 1945

May (31 days)

DERIVATION

Latin, *Maius*, either from Maia, an obscure goddess, or from *maiores* (elders), on the grounds that the month honoured old people, as June honoured the young.

1 Great Exhibition at Crystal Palace 1851; David Livingstone d. 1873
2 Leonardo da Vinci d. 1519; Catherine the Great b. 1729
3 Niccolo Machiavelli b. 1469; Festival of Britain 1951
4 Epsom Derby first run 1780
5 Karl Marx b. 1818; Napoleon Bonaparte d. 1821
6 Sigmund Freud b. 1856; First 4 min. mile by Bannister at Oxford, 1954
7 Johannes Brahms b. 1833; Tchaikovsky b. 1840; *Lusitania* sunk 1915
8 VE-Day 1945
9 Sir James Barrie b. 1860
10 Winston Churchill becomes Prime Minister 1940
11 Irving Berlin b. 1888
12 Florence Nightingale b. 1820 [see below, *RTHPL*]; General Strike ends 1926
13 Sir Arthur Sullivan b. 1842
14 Home Guard formed in Britain 1940; State of Israel proclaimed 1948
15 Pierre Curie b. 1859
16 Modeste Moussorgsky b. 1839
17 Edward Jenner b. 1749; Mafeking relieved 1900
18 Walter Gropius b. 1883
19 St Dunstan d. 988; Anne Boleyn d. 1536
20 Christopher Columbus b. 1506; John Stuart Mill b. 1806
21 Alexander Pope b. 1688; Elizabeth Fry b. 1780; Lindbergh lands in Paris 1927
22 Richard Wagner b. 1813; Sir Arthur Conan Doyle b. 1859
23 Thomas Hood b. 1799; Henrik Ibsen d. 1906
24 Nicolaus Copernicus d. 1543; Queen Victoria b. 1819
25 Ralph Waldo Emerson d. 1803
26 Samuel Pepys d. 1703; Alexander Pushkin b. 1799; End of US Civil War 1865
27 John Calvin d. 1564; Habeas Corpus Act 1679; Jawaharlal Nehru d. 1964
28 William Pitt (the younger) b. 1759
29 Dunkirk evacuation 1940; Mount Everest climbed 1953
30 Joan of Arc d. 1431; Peter the Great b. 1672
31 Pepys' Diary ends 1669; Battle of Jutland 1916

June (30 days)

DERIVATION

Latin, *Junius*, either the goddess Juno, or from *iuniores* (young people), as the month dedicated to youth.

1 Brigham Young b. 1801; John Masefield b. 1878
2 Thomas Hardy b. 1840; Coronation of Queen Elizabeth II 1953
3 Sydney Smith b. 1771; Johann Strauss (the younger) d. 1899
4 Harriet Beecher Stowe b. 1811
5 Adam Smith b. 1723; John Maynard Keynes b. 1883; Marshall Plan 1947
6 D-Day 1944
7 Robert I ('The Bruce') d. 1329; Beau Brummel b. 1778
8 Edward, The Black Prince d. 1376
9 George Stephenson b. 1781; Charles Dickens d. 1870
10 Duke of Edinburgh b. 1921 [see below, *RTHPL*]
11 John Constable b. 1776; Richard Strauss b. 1864
12 Charles Kingsley b. 1819
13 William Butler Yeats b. 1865; Boxer Rising in China 1900;
14 Battle of Naseby 1645; G K Chesterton d. 1936
15 Magna Carta sealed 1215; Edward, The Black Prince b. 1330
16 Duke of Marlborough d. 1722
17 John Wesley b. 1703; Battle of Bunker Hill 1775
18 War between GB & USA 1812; Battle of Waterloo 1815
19 Sir James Barrie d. 1937
20 Battle of Bannockburn 1314; Queen Victoria ascended 1837
21 Inigo Jones d. 1652; American Constitution came into force 1788
22 Niccolo Machiavelli d. 1527
23 Battle of Plassey 1757; Duke of Windsor b. 1894
24 Duke of Marlborough b. 1650; Battle of Solferino 1859
25 Custer's Last Stand 1876; Earl Mountbatten b. 1900; Korean War began 1950
26 Corn Laws repealed 1846; UN Charter signed 1946
27 Charles Stewart Parnell b. 1846
28 End of Napoleon's 'Hundred Days' 1815; Archduke Franz Ferdinand assassinated 1914
29 Peter Paul Rubens b. 1577
30 *Night of the Long Knives*, Germany 1934

July (31 days)

DERIVATION

Latin, *Julius*, after Gaius Julius Caesar (b. 12 July, probably in 102 BC, d. 15 March 44 BC), the Roman soldier and statesman. (Formerly known by the Romans as *Quintilis* (the fifth month.)

1 George Sand b. 1804; Louis Blériot b. 1872
2 Thomas Cranmer b. 1489; Sir Robert Peel d. 1850; Joseph Chamberlain d. 1914
3 Robert Adam b. 1728
4 American Declaration of Independence 1776; Thomas Jefferson d. 1826
5 Cecil Rhodes b. 1853; Britain's National Health Service 1948
6 Last London tram 1952
7 Sir Arthur Conan Doyle d. 1930; Sir Thomas More d. 1535
8 Percy Bysshe Shelley d. 1822; Joseph Chamberlain b. 1836
9 John D Rockefeller b. 1839
10 John Calvin b. 1509
11 Robert I ('The Bruce') b. 1274
12 Julius Caesar b. 100 BC [see below, *RTHPL*]
13 Sidney Webb b. 1859
14 Fall of the Bastille 1789; British Home Guard established 1940
15 Inigo Jones b. 1573; Rembrandt van Rijn b. 1606
16 Sir Joshua Reynolds b. 1723; First atomic explosion Alamogordo 1945
17 Adam Smith d. 1790; Spanish Civil War began 1936
18 William Makepeace Thackeray b. 1811
19 Edgar Degas b. 1834
20 First Moon landing by man 1969
21 Robert Burns d. 1796
22 Battle of Salamanca 1812
23 Haile Selassie b. 1892
24 Simon Bolivar b. 1783
25 Louis Blériot flew Channel 1909
26 George Bernard Shaw b. 1856; Aldous Huxley b. 1894
27 Battle of Killiecrankie 1689; Korean Armistice signed 1953
28 Johann Sebastian Bach d. 1750
29 Spanish Armada defeated 1588; Benito Mussolini b. 1883; Vincent Van Gogh d. 1890
30 William Penn d. 1718; Henry Ford b. 1863; Prince Otto Von Bismarck d. 1898
31 St Ignatius Loyola d. 1556

August (31 days)

DERIVATION

Latin, *Augustus*, after Augustus Caesar (born Gaius Octavius), the first Roman emperor. (Originally called *Sextilis*, the sixth month.)

1 Battle of the Nile 1798
2 William Rufus d. 1100; Thomas Gainsborough d. 1788; Enrico Caruso d. 1921
3 Rupert Brooke b. 1887; Council of Europe 1949
4 Percy Bysshe Shelley b. 1792; Britain declared War 1914
5 Guy de Maupassant b. 1850
6 Alfred, Lord Tennyson b. 1809; Atomic Bomb on Hiroshima 1945
7 British Summer Time Act 1925
8 Battle of Britain began 1940
9 First Atlantic cable 1858; Atomic bomb on Nagasaki 1945
10 Greenwich Observatory founded 1675; Herbert Hoover born 1874
11 Cardinal John Henry Newman d. 1890
12 Robert Southey b. 1774; George Stephenson d. 1848
13 Battle of Blenheim 1704; Florence Nightingale d. 1910
14 India & Pakistan-Dominion Status 1947
15 Napoleon Bonaparte b. 1769; Panama Canal opened 1914; VJ-Day 1945
16 Peterloo Massacre 1819; Sir Alexander Fleming b. 1881 [see below, *RTHPL*]
17 Frederick the Great d. 1786; Berlin Wall erected 1961
18 Earl Russell b. 1792
19 James Watt b. 1819
20 William Booth d. 1912
21 Princess Margaret b. 1930
22 Civil War in England 1642; International Red Cross founded 1864
23 World Council of Churches formed 1948
24 William Wilberforce b. 1759
25 Michael Faraday d. 1867; Paris liberated 1944
26 Battle of Crecy 1346; Krakatoa erupted 1883
27 Confucius b. 551 BC; Sir Donald Bradman b. 1908
28 Count Leo Tolstoy b. 1828
29 Oliver Wendell Holmes b. 1809; Brigham Young d. 1877
30 Lord Rutherford b. 1871
31 John Bunyan d. 1688; Queen Wilhelmina, Netherlands b. 1880

September (30 days)

DERIVATION

Latin, from *septem* (seven), as it was originally the seventh month.

1 Germany invaded Poland 1939
2 Great Fire of London 1666
3 Oliver Cromwell d. 1658; Britai declares War 1939
4 Albert Schweitzer d. 1965
5 Cardinal Richelieu b. 1585
6 *Mayflower* sailed from Plymouth 1620
7 Queen Elizabeth I born 1533; Londo Blitz began 1940
8 Richard Coeur de Lion b. 1157; Firs V2 in England 1944; Richard Strauss c 1949
9 William the Conqueror d. 1087; Battl of Flodden Field 1513
10 Mungo Park b. 1771
11 O Henry b. 1862
12 Herbert Henry Asquith b. 1852
13 Gen. James Wolfe d. 1759
14 Gregorian Calendar in Britain 1752 Duke of Wellington d. 1852
15 James Fenimore Cooper b. 1789 Isambard Kingdom Brunel d. 1859
16 Andrew Bonar Law b. 1858
17 US Constitution signed 1787
18 Samuel Johnson b. 1709
19 Battle of Poitiers 1356
20 Battle of Lexington 1861; Sterling o Gold Standard 1931
21 Sir Walter Scott d. 1832; H G Wells b 1866 [see below, *RTHPL*]
22 Michael Faraday b. 1791; Commercia Television in Britain 1955
23 Sigmund Freud d. 1939; Thoma Robert Malthus d. 1834
24 Horace Walpole b. 1717; Sir Ala Herbert b. 1890
25 Samuel Butler d. 1680
26 T S Eliot b. 1888; *Queen Mary* launche 1934
27 Stockton-Darlington Railway opene 1825; Edgar Degas d. 1917; *Quee Elizabeth* launched 1938
28 Georges Clemenceau b. 1841; Loui Pasteur d. 1895
29 Battle of Marathon 490 BC; Lord Cliv b. 1725
30 First BBC TV Broadcast 1929

October (31 days)

DERIVATION
Latin, from *octo* (eight), originally the eighth month.

1 Paul Dukas b. 1865; Vladimir Horowitz b. 1904
2 Mohandas Gandhi b. 1869
3 St Francis of Assisi d. 1226
4 Rembrandt van Rijn d. 1669; Sputnik I launched 1957
5 Jacques Offenbach d. 1880
6 Charles Stewart Parnell d. 1891; Alfred Lord Tennyson d. 1892
7 Oliver Wendell Holmes d. 1894
8 Henry Fielding d. 1754
9 Universal Postal Union founded 1875
10 Henry Cavendish b. 1731
11 Battle of Camperdown 1797
12 Elizabeth Fry d. 1845; Ralph Vaughan Williams b. 1872; Nurse Edith Cavell d. 1915 [see below, *RTHPL*]
13 Sir Henry Irving d. 1905
14 Battle of Hastings 1066; William Penn b. 1644; General Eisenhower b. 1890
15 Virgil b. 70 BC; Friedrich Wilhelm Nietzsche b. 1844
16 Marie Antoinette d. 1793; Oscar Wilde b. 1854
17 Sir Philip Sidney d. 1586; Frederic Chopin d. 1849
18 Lord Palmerston d. 1865; Thomas Alva Edison d. 1931
19 Jonathan Swift d. 1745; Lord Rutherford d. 1937
20 Sir Christopher Wren b. 1632; Lord Palmerston b. 1784
21 Samuel Taylor Coleridge b. 1772; Battle of Trafalgar 1805
22 Franz Liszt b. 1811
23 W G Grace b. 1915; Battle of El Alamein began 1942
24 Zinoviev letter 1924
25 Battle of Agincourt 1415; Charge of the Light Brigade 1854
26 William Hogarth d. 1764
27 Theodore Roosevelt b. 1858
28 Alfred the Great d. 901; Desiderius Erasmus b. 1466
29 Sir Walter Raleigh d. 1618; John Keats b. 1759; New York Stock Market crash 1929
30 Richard Brinsley Sheridan b. 1751
31 Martin Luther theses 1517; Jan Vermeer b. 1632; Chaing Kai-Shek b. 1886

November (30 days)

DERIVATION
Latin, from *novem* (nine), originally the ninth month.

1 Benvenuto Cellini b. 1500; Hydrogen bomb exploded 1952
2 Marie Antoinette born 1755; George Bernard Shaw d. 1950
3 William Cullen Bryant b. 1794; Karl Baedeker b. 1801
4 Auguste Rodin b. 1840
5 Gunpowder Plot 1605
6 John Philip Sousa b. 1854; Peter Ilich Tchaikovsky d. 1893
7 Madame Curie b. 1867
8 John Milton d. 1674; Munich Putsch 1923
9 Neville Chamberlain d. 1940; Charles Andre Joseph Marie De Gaulle d. 1970
10 Martin Luther b. 1483; H M Stanley met David Livingstone-Ujiji 1871
11 Fyedor Dostoievsky b. 1821; Armistice Day 1918
12 King Canute d. 1035; Sir John Hawkins d. 1595
13 Robert Louis Stevenson b. 1850
14 Jawaharlal Nehru b. 1889; Prince of Wales b. 1948
15 William Pitt (the Elder) b. 1708; William Cowper b. 1731
16 Tiberius b. 42 BC
17 Suez Canal opened 1869; Field Marshal the Viscount Montgomery b. 1887
18 Sir William Gilbert b. 1836; Amelita Galli-Curci b. 1882
19 Charles I b. 1600; Franz Schubert d. 1828
20 Count Leo Tolstoy d. 1910; Wedding of Queen Elizabeth II 1947
21 Voltaire d. 1694
22 Charles Andre Joseph Marie De Gaulle b. 1890 [see below, *RTHPL*]; John Fitzgerald Kennedy assassinated 1963
23 Manuel de Falla b. 1876
24 John Knox d. 1572; Charles Darwin's *Origin of Species* published 1859
25 Andrew Carnegie b. 1835
26 John McAdam b. 1836
27 Teheran Conference 1943
28 William Blake b. 1757
29 Cardinal Wolsey d. 1530; Louisa May Alcott b. 1832
30 Jonathan Swift b. 1667; Mark Twain b. 1835; Sir Winston Spencer Churchill b. 1874

December (31 days)

DERIVATION
Latin, from *decem* (ten), originally the tenth month.

1 Queen Alexandra b. 1844; Beveridge Report 1942
2 Battle of Austerlitz 1805; Monroe Doctrine 1823; First Nuclear Chain Reaction 1942
3 Samuel Crompton b. 1753; Sir Rowland Hill b. 1795
4 Thomas Carlyle b. 1795; Robert Louis Stevenson d. 1894
5 Wolfgang Amadeus Mozart d. 1791; Claude Monet d. 1926
6 Warren Hastings b. 1732
7 Giovanni Lorenzo Bernini b. 1598; Pearl Harbour attacked 1941
8 Jean Sibelius b. 1865
9 John Milton b. 1608
10 Royal Acadamy founded 1768; Edward VIII abdicated 1936
11 Hector Berlioz b. 1803
12 Robert Browning d. 1889; First Transatlantic radio signal 1901
13 Samuel Johnson d. 1784; Heinrich Heine b. 1797
14 Amundsen at South Pole 1911; George Washington d. 1799
15 Sitting Bull d. 1890; Gregory Rasputin d. 1916; BBC incorporated 1922
16 Ludwig van Beethoven b. 1770 [see below, *RTHPL*]; Boston Tea Party 1773; Jane Austen b. 1775
    Sir Humphrey Davy b. 1778; First Aeroplane flight 1903
18 Antonio Stradivari d. 1737; Slavery abolished in USA 1865
19 Carl Wilhelm von Scheele b. 1742; Joseph Mallord William Turner d. 1851
20 Robert Menzies b. 1894
21 Pilgrim Fathers landed 1620; Josef Stalin b. 1879
22 St Francis Xavier d. 1552; Giacomo Puccini b. 1858
23 Sir Richard Arkwright b. 1732
24 St Ignatius Loyola b. 1491; Vasco da Gama d. 1524; Matthew Arnold b. 1822
25 Sir Isaac Newton b. 1642
26 Mao Tse-tung b. 1893; Radium discovered 1898
27 Louis Pasteur b. 1822; Charles Lamb d. 1834
28 Woodrow Wilson b. 1856; Lord Macaulay d. 1859
    Ewart Gladstone b. 1809; Jameson Raid 1895
30 Rudyard Kipling b. 1865; Stephen Leacock b. 1869
31 Charles Edward Stewart (the Young Pretender) b. 1720; John Wycliffe d. 1384

The Animal Kingdom

A Classification (excluding wholly extinct groups)

Subkingdom Protozoa (Greek, *protos* = first; *zōon* = an animal)
The Protozoans are organisms consisting of one cell or of colonies of similar cells, and are the simplest (most primitive) of all animals. They are generally aquatic, and mostly microscopic in size. A single phylum, *Protozoa*, with about 30 000 described species, grouped as follows:

Class Mastigophora (Greek, *mastigos*, genitive of *mastix* = a whip; *phoros* = a bearing) **or Flagellata** (Latin, *flagellum*, diminutive of *flagrum* = a whip). Protozoans with from one to many flagella, i.e. whip-like appendages, in the principal phase of the life history. Two sub-classes, *Phytomastigina* (Greek, *phyton* = a plant) or *Phytoflagellata*, which contains ten orders of plant-like protozoans, and *Zoomastigina*, or *Zooflagellata*, four orders which are unequivocally animals and more complex in structure, including *Protomonadina* (Latin, *monadis*, genitive of *monas* = a unit), containing the family *Trypanosomidae* (Greek, *trypanon* = a borer; *soma* = the body), whose parasite members are responsible for sleeping-sickness.

Class Rhizopoda (Greek, *rhiza* = a root; *podos*, genitive of *pous* = a foot) **or Sarcodina** (Greek, *sarkōdēs* = fleshy). Four orders, including *Amoebina* (Greek, *amoibē* = a change), formerly regarded as the most primitive of all protozoans, and containing the genus *Entamoeba* (Greek, *entos* = within), the cause of amoebic dysentery.

Class Actinopoda (Greek, *aktinos*, genitive of *aktis* = a ray). Two orders, the larger being *Radiolaria* (Latin, *radiolus*, diminutive of *radius* = a ray).

Class Sporozoa (Greek, *spora* = a seed) **or Telosporidia** (Greek, *telos* = the completion; Latin, *sporidium*, diminutive of Greek, *spora* = a seed). Protozoans in whose life history reproduction at some stage is by 'spores'. Multiple fission is followed by gamete formation and finally by sporulation. Two sub-classes, *Gregarinomorpha* (Latin, *gregarius* = belonging to a herd; Greek, *morphē* = shape), the gregarines, three orders, common parasites of invertebrates, and *Coccidiomorpha* (Latin, *coccidium* = a kernel), the coccidians, two orders, intracellular parasites of many invertebrates and vertebrates, generally confined to a single host. The order *Eucoccidia* (Greek *eu* = true) includes the sub-order *Haemosporidia* (Greek, *haima* = blood), whose most important genus is *Plasmodium*, containing the malarial parasites of man carried by anopheline mosquitoes. Other genera of this sub-order are responsible for various forms of cattle-fever.

Class Cnidosporidia (Greek, *knidē* = nettle), **also called Nematocystida** (Greek, *nēmatos*, genitive of *nēma* = thread; *kystis* = a pouch), **Neosporidia** (Greek, *neos* = new), **or Amoebosporidia.** Protozoans characterised by resistant spores with polar capsules, Mostly parasites of fishes. Four orders.

Class Ciliata (Latin, *ciliatus* = furnished with hairs) **also called Ciliophora or Infusoria** (Latin, *infusorium* = a vessel for pouring). The most highly organised protozoans, characterised chiefly by the presence of cilia (hairs or hairlike, processes) and by two types of nuclei. Two sub-classes, *Holotricha* (Greek, *holos* = whole; *trichos*, genitive of *thrix* = the hair) and *Spirotricha* (Greek, *speira* = a coil). The holotrichs have unspecialised cilia and are mostly free-living. They include the Order *Trichostomatida* (Greek, *stomatos*, genitive of *stoma* = mouth), containing the genus *Balantidium* (Greek, *balantion* = a bag), the cause of dysentery; and the Order *Hymenostomatida* (Greek, *hymenos*, genitive of *hymēn* = a parchment or membrane), whose sub-order *Peniculina* includes the genus *Paramecium* (Greek, *paramēkes* = oval), the slipper animalcule.

Subkingdom Metazoa (Greek, *meta* = later in time; *zōon* = an animal).
Multicellular animals composed of unlike cells that may lose their boundaries in the adult state, and with at least two cell layers. Contains 21 phyla, as listed below, with about one million described species.

Phylum Mesozoa (Greek, *mesos* = middle, the half). Minute parasitic animals, composed of a surface layer of epithelial (i.e. non-vascular) cells enclosing reproductive cells. About 50 described species, forming two orders, the *Dicyemida* (Greek, *di* = two; *kyēma* = embryo) or *Rhombozoa* (Greek, *rhombos* = turning), which are found only in the kidneys of cephalopods, and the *Orthonectida* (Greek, *orthos* = straight; *nēktos* = swimming), which infest ophiurids, polychaets, nemertines, turbellarians and possibly other groups. Members of this phylum are often considered to be degenerate members of phylum *Platyhelminthes* (see below).

Phylum Parazoa (Greek, *para* = near), **also called Porifera** (Latin, *porus* = a pore; *fero* = to bear) **or Spongiida** (Latin, *spongia* = a sponge).[1] The sponges. Porous animals whose bodies consist of a rather loose aggregation of several kinds of different cells supported by a framework of spicules or fibres which form intricate skeletal structures. There is an incomplete arrangement into tissues, so there is little co-ordination among the parts of the body. They are fixed objects often of indefinite shape, without organ systems or mouth. Reproduction may be either sexual (sponges are often bisexual) or asexual, by means of gemmules. About 4200 described species, which may be divided into two classes:

Class Nuda (Latin, *nudus* = naked) [N.B. Class *Nuda* also occurs in phylum *Ctenophora* (see below)]. Two orders, the *Calcarea* (Latin, *calx* = lime, or chalk) or *Calcispongiae* (Latin, *calcis*, genitive of *calx*), calcareous sponges, whose skeletons have spicules made of calcite ($CaCO_3$), and the *Hexactinellida* (Greek, *hex* = six; *aktis* = a ray; Latin, *-ell*, suffix added to form diminutives), also called *Triaxonida* (Greek, *treis* = three; *axōn* = an axle) or *Hyalospongiae* (Greek, *hyaleos* = glassy, shining), the glass sponges, whose skeletons consist of siliceous spicules, i.e. made of opal (SiO_2nH_2O). Includes the Venus's flower basket.

Class Gelatinosa (Latin, *gelatina* = a gummy juice) **or Demospongiae** (Greek, *dēmos* = multitude). Two orders, the *Tetraxonida* (Greek, *tetra* = four; *axōn* = an axle), including the loggerhead sponge, and the *Keratosa* (Greek, *keratos*, genitive of *keras* = a horn) or horny sponges, including the genus *Spongia* (or *Euspongia*), the bath sponge.

Phylum Cnidaria (Greek, *knidē* = nettle) **or Coelenterata**[2] (Greek, *koilos* = hollow; *enteron* = bowel). The coelenterates, the first group of the Metazoa whose cells are completely arranged in tissues, and differentiated into nervous and muscular systems, giving efficient co-ordination of parts and powers of locomotion. The body consists of a small sac, with a single opening at one end (the blastopore). The walls of the sac contain two layers of cells (the inner known as the endoderm, the outer the ectoderm), one passing into the other at the margin of the blastopore. It thus contains only one principal internal cavity, the coelenteron, with one opening to the exterior, the mouth. Coelenterates also bear nematocysts, or stinging cells, and

Phylum Parazoa: Bread-Crumb Sponge (Heather Angel)

---

[1] The classification used here is by Bidder.
[2] This name is sometimes applied to a group comprising Phylum *Cnidaria* and Phylum *Ctenophora*.

14

have two types of shape, the polyp (e.g. a sea anemone) and the medusa. Coelenterates have a tendency towards asexual reproduction, either by fission or budding. This phylum contains about 9600 described species, grouped as follows:

Class Hydrozoa (Greek, *hydōr* = water; *zōon* = an animal) **or Hydromedusae** (Latin, *Medusa*, the Gorgon with snaky hair). Six orders, including *Siphonophora* (Greek, *siphon* = a tube; *phoros* = a bearing), which contains the genus *Physalia* (Greek, *physalis* = bubble), or Portuguese man-of-war.

Class Scyphozoa or Scyphomedusae (Greek, *skyphos* = a cup). The jellyfish. Five orders.

Class Anthozoa (Greek, *anthos* = a flower). Three sub-classes:
  Ceriantipatharia (Greek, *keras* = a horn; *anti-* = against; *pathos* = suffering). Two orders, including *Antipatharia* (black corals).
  Octocorallia (Latin, *octo* = eight; Greek, *korallion* = coral) or Alcyonaria. The soft corals. Three orders.
  Zoantharia (Greek, *zōon* = animal; *anthos* = flower). Five orders, including *Actiniaria* (sea anemones) and *Scleractinia* (true corals, stony corals).

Class Scyphozoa: Stinging Jellyfish (Heather Angel)

Phylum Ctenophora (Greek, *ktenos*, genitive of *kteis* = comb; *phoros* = a bearing). The comb jellies. Marine animals with a body structure similar to coelenterates, i.e. a single internal cavity opening by one main aperture, the mouth, but with three layers of tissue, the ectoderm, the endoderm, producing the sex cells, and between these the jellylike mesoderm, containing cells and muscle fibres. The bilaterally symmetrical body has eight strips of modified ectoderm cells, each bearing a comb-like plate whose teeth are made up of large waving cilia (hairs). There are no nematocysts (stinging cells). This phylum contains about 80 described species, grouped as follows:

Class Tentaculata (Latin, *tentaculum* = a feeler). Four orders. Includes sea gooseberry and Venus's girdle.

Class Nuda (Latin, *nudus* = naked). A single order, *Beroida* (Greek, *Beroē* = one of the nymphs, daughter of Oceanus).

Phylum Platyhelminthes (Greek, *platys* = flat; *helminthos*, genitive of *helmins* = a worm) **or Platodaria** (Greek, *platos* = flat; Latin, *-od* = form).[1] The flatworms. Soft-bodied animals with three layers of cells and bilateral symmetry. Mostly hermaphrodites, i.e. each individual is functionally both male and female. Tissues and organs developed from three embryonic layers. Muscles render the body capable of great contraction, elongation and variability in shape. No space between digestive tube and body wall. This phylum contains about 15 000 described species, grouped as follows:

Class Turbellaria (Latin, *turbellae*, diminutive of *turba* = a disturbance). The turbellarians. Five orders.

Class Temnocephaloidea (Greek, *temnō* = to cut; *kephalē* = a head). One order, *Temnocephalidea*, also called *Dactylifera* (Greek, *daktylos* = a finger, or toe; *fero* = to bear) or *Dactyloda*.

Class Monogenea (Greek, *monas* = single; *geneos*, genitive of *genos* = a race, kind) **or Heterocotylea** (Greek, *heteros* = other, different; *kotylē* = cup-shaped). Two sub-classes:
  Monopisthocotylea (Greek, *opisthen* = behind), with five orders.
  Polyopisthocotylea, with four orders.

Class Cestodaria (Greek, *kestos* = a girdle). Two orders.

Class Cestoda (Greek, *kestos* = a girdle). Two sub-classes:
  Didesmida (Greek, *di-* = two; *desma* = a chain, band). One order, *Pseudophyllidea* (or *Bothriocephaloidea*).
  Tetradesmida (Greek, *tetra* = four). Nine orders.

Class Trematoda (Greek, *trēmatōdēs* = perforated). The flukes. Two sub-classes.
  Aspidogastrea (Greek, *aspidos*, genitive of *aspis* = a shield; Greek, *gastēr* = the stomach), also called *Aspidocotylea* (Greek, *kotylē* = cup-shaped) or *Aspidobothria* (Greek, *bothrion*, diminutive of *bothros* = a hole).
  Digenea (Greek, *di-* = two; *genos*, genitive of *genos* = a race, kind) or *Malacocotylea* (Greek, *malakos* = soft, gentle; *kotylē* = cup-shaped).

Phylum Nemertina, or Nemertea (Greek, *Nēmertēs* = the name of a Nereid), **also called Rhynchocoela** (Greek, *rhynchos* = a beak, snout; *koilos* = a hollow). The nemertines, or ribbon worms. These have soft, ciliated bodies without external indication of segmentation and without a distinct body cavity, the internal organs being separated by gelatinous parenchyma (soft tissue). The intestine opens at the posterior end. They have a long, muscular proboscis, used to capture food. Most species are free-living and marine, and the sexes are generally separate. This phylum contains about 550 described species, grouped as follows:

Class Anopla (Greek, *anoplos* = unarmed). The mouth posterior to the brain. Two orders. Includes the bootlace worm.

Class Enopla (Greek, *enoplos* = armed). The mouth anterior to the brain. Two orders, including *Hoplonemertina* (Greek, *hoplon* = a weapon), in which the proboscis is armed with one or more calcareous stylets.

Phylum Aschelminthes (Greek, *askos* = a bag or bladder; *helminthos*, genitive of *helmins* = a worm). Small, worm-like animals with a pseudocoelom between the digestive tract and the body wall. They usually have an anus, and almost all have a mouth and digestive tract. This phylum contains about 12 000 described species, grouped as follows:

Class Rotifera (Latin, *rota* = a wheel; *fero* = to bear) **or Rotatoria**. The rotifers, or wheel animalcules. Microscopic aquatic animals. Three orders. About 1500 described species.

Class Gastrotricha (Greek, *gastros* (*gasteros*), genitive of *gastēr* = stomach; *trichos*, genitive of *thrix* = hair). Tiny aquatic animals. Two orders. About 140 described species.

Class Echinoderida (Greek, *echinōdēs* = like a hedgehog) **or Kinorhyncha** (Greek, *kineō* = to move; *rhynchos* = a beak, snout). Minute wormlike animals, living chiefly in the slime of the ocean floor. Three orders. About 100 described species.

Class Priapulida (Greek, *Priapos* = god of gardens and reproduction). Small marine worms. 5 described species.

[1] The classification given here is by Baer.

Class Nematomorpha (Greek, *nēmatos*, genitive of *nēma* = thread; *morpha* = shape) or **Gordiacea** (Greek, *Gordios* = name of a king of Phrygia; hence the Gordian knot). The horse-hair worms. Two orders. About 250 described species.

Class Nematoda, or Nemata[1] (Greek, *nēmatos*, genitive of *nēma* = thread). The round-worms. About 10 000 described species. Two sub-classes:
Phasmidia. Nematodes with phasmids (lateral caudal pores). Eight orders.
Aphasmidia. Nematodes without phasmids. Nine orders.

Phylum Acanthocephala (Greek, *akantha* = a thorn; *kephalē* = a head). The thorny-headed worms. Parasitic animals with no specialised organs for digestion. They live in the intestines of vertebrates and absorb food through the body wall. The sexes are always separate, and males are usually smaller than females. Their length ranges from less than $\frac{1}{10}$ in to over 20 in. They have a hook-covered proboscis used as an anchor. Three orders. About 600 described species.

Phylum Entoprocta, or Endoprocta (Greek, *entos* or *endon* = within; *proktos* = the anus), **also called Clyassozoa** (Greek, *kalos* = beautiful, *yssos* = a javelin; *zōon* = an animal), **Kamptozoa** (Greek, *kamptos* = flexible, bent), **Polyzoa Endoprocta** (Greek, *poly*, singular of *polys* = much, many), **or Polyzoa Entoprocta**. These aquatic animals are similar to the *Polyzoa* (see below). In this phylum the anterior end bears the lophophore (the ridge bearing the ciliated tentacles) which is circular, and encloses both mouth and anus. Reproductive organs continuous with ducts. They have definite excretory organs. Three families. About 60 described species.

Phylum Polyzoa (Greek, *poly*, singular of *polys* = much, many; *zōon* = an animal), **also called Bryozoa** (Greek, *bryon* = a lichen), **Polyzoa Ectoprocta, or Ectoprocta** (Greek, *ektos* = outside, without; *prōktos* = the anus). In these tiny aquatic animals, the lophophore (see above) is circular or crescentic, enclosing the mouth but not the anus. Specific excretory organs are absent. Reproductive organs not continuous with ducts. They live in the compartments of tubes which they secrete, and capture their food by sweeping the water with tentacles. The individuals bud and remain attached to each other, to form colonies which are generally about an inch across and sometimes plantlike. The colonies are generally encrusting and resemble the growth of lichens. Mostly marine. About 4000 described species, grouped as follows:
Class Phylactolaemata (Greek, *phylaktos*, genitive of *phylax* = a guard; *laimos* = the throat) **or Lophopoda** (Greek, *lophos* = the crest; *podos*, genitive of *pous* = a foot). Lophophore generally horseshoe-shaped, guarded by an epistome, a flap of tissue like a lip.
Class Gymnolaemata (Greek, *gymnos* = naked; *laimos* = the throat) **or Stelmatopoda** (Greek, *stelma* = a crown). Lophophore circular, without epistome. Five orders, including two completely extinct.

Phylum Phoronida (Latin, *Phoronis* = surname of Io, daughter of Inachus, who was changed into a white heifer). The phoronids. Small, marine, wormlike hermaphrodite animals which live as adults in self-secreted tubes embedded in the sea bottom or attached to solid surfaces. The body is roughly elongate (from 0·3 in to 8 in) and bears at one end a crown of from 50 to over 300 tentacles, each one bearing fine hairs (cilia), and arranged in a double row around the usually crescent shaped mouth, which is covered by an epistome. The digestive tract is U-shaped, and the anus is immediately outside the tentacles. The larvae are free-swimming. Only two genera and about 16 described species.

Phylum Brachiopoda (Greek, *brachiōn* = the upper part of the arm; *podos*, genitive of *pous* = a foot). The brachiopods or lamp shells. Marine animals enclosed in a bivalve shell. Inside the valves two coiled, cirrate appendages (brachia), one on each side of the mouth, serve as food-gathering organs. The sexes are usually separate. The valves are bilaterally symmetrical, and the front (ventral) valve is usually larger than the dorsal (or brachial) valve on the back. About 260 described species, grouped as follows:
Class Inarticulata (Latin, *in-* = not; *articulatus* = divided into joints). Two orders.
Class Articulata (Latin, *articulatus* = divided into joints). Originally two orders (now discarded) and four sub-orders.

Phylum Mollusca (Latin, *molluscus* = soft). The molluscs. The viscera (entrails) are enclosed in a soft sheath, whose lower part is modified as a muscular organ of locomotion, the foot, while the upper part (the mantle) is extended on each side and hangs down as a free fold around the body, enclosing the mantle-cavity. The mantle usually secretes an external calcareous shell of one or more pieces. The coelom is much reduced by the extensive vascular system. Except in the *Bivalvia* (see below), the anterior tegumentary region is modified as a more or less mobile head, usually provided with sensory appendages and sense organs, and the alimentary system is characterised by a tongue (radula) beset with chitinous teeth. This phylum contains 128 000 described species, grouped as follows:
Class Polyplacophora[1] (Greek, *poly*, singular of *polys* = much, many; *plakos*, genitive of *plax* = tablet; *phoros* = a bearing), **or Loricata** (Latin, *loricatus* = clad in mail). Marine molluscs, including the chitons, or coat of mail shells, with eight articulated plates. From $\frac{1}{8}$ in to 8 in in length. Two orders.
Class Aplacophora[2] (Greek, *a-* = without) **or Solenogastres** (Greek, *sōlēnos*, genitive of *sōlēn* = a channel; *gastēr* = the stomach). Marine molluscs without shells and with the foot greatly reduced. Two orders.
Class Monoplacophora (Greek, *monas* = single). Deep-sea molluscs with a single cap-shaped shell. One order. Two rare and small species.
Class Gastropoda (Greek, *gastros* (*gasteros*), genitive of *gastēr* = the stomach; *podos*, genitive of *pous* = a foot). Land, fresh-water and marine molluscs with a flattened foot. The shell is generally a spirally coiled single structure, though may be modified, and sometimes covered by a mantle or entirely absent. From 1 mm to 2 ft in length. Three sub-classes:
Prosobranchia (Greek, *pros* = forward, towards, in advance of; *branchia* = fins, or the gills of fishes) or *Streptoneura* (Greek, *streptos* = twisted; *neuron* = tendon). Includes the limpet, periwinkle, cowrie and whelk. Three orders.
Opisthobranchia (Greek, *opisthen* = behind). Includes the sea-hare, sea-butterflies and sea-slugs. Eleven orders.
Pulmonata (Latin, *pulmonatus* = having lungs). Includes the pond snail, fresh-water limpet, land snail and land slugs. Three orders.

[1] The classification given here is by Chitwood & Chitwood (1950) and Thorne (1949).
[2] These two classes are sometimes grouped together as *Amphineura* (Greek, *amphi* = double; *neuron* = tendon).

Class Scaphopoda (Greek, *skaphē* = a bowl; *podos*, genitive of *pous* = a foot). Marine, tubular-shelled, burrowing molluscs, commonly called tusk-shells.

Class Bivalvia (Latin, *bi-* = two; *valva* = a leaf of a folding door), **also called Lamelli-branchia** (Latin, *lamella*, diminutive of *lamina* = a thin plate; Greek, *branchia* = the gills of fishes) **or Pelecypoda** (Greek, *pelekys* = a hatchet; *podos*, genitive of *pous* = a foot). The bivalves. Aquatic headless molluscs, mostly marine, which generally live buried in sand or mud. The shell has two hinged parts, Includes the cockle, mussel, oyster, scallop, gaper and clam. Four orders.

Class Cephalopoda (Greek, *kephalē* = a head; *podos*, genitive of *pous* = a foot) **or Siphonopoda** (Greek, *siphon* = a tube). Marine molluscs, some without shells. The head and foot are approximate, hence the mouth is situated in the middle of the foot, and the edges of the foot are drawn out into arms and tentacles, equipped with suckers. Includes the cuttlefish, squid, octopus, pearly nautilus. Three sub-classes.

Phylum Sipunculoidea (Latin, *sipunculus* = a little tube). These animals are marine worms which inhabit burrows, tubes or borrowed shells. The anus is anterior, situated on the dorsal surface near the base of the proboscis. There is apparently a total lack of segmentation. The body is divided into two regions, a trunk consisting chiefly of the elongated belly of the worm, and a retractile proboscis which bears at its anterior end the mouth, which is partly or completely surrounded by tentacles or tentacle-bearing folds. The proboscis is generally armed with chitinous spines and hooks. About 275 described species.

Phylum Echiuroidea (Greek, *echis* = a serpent; *oura* = the tail; *-oideos* = form of). These marine worm-like animals are similar to the *Annelida* (see below), but there is an apparent lack of segmentation. The bodies are generally sac-shaped, and they inhabit U-shaped tubes on sandy-mud bottoms. Attached to the anterior end of the trunk is a preoral lobe (prostomium), about half as long as the trunk and shaped like a hemispherical fan when fully extended. It is ciliated on its ventral surface and forms a funnel around the mouth. Three orders. About 150 described species, including the spoon-worms.

Phylum Annelida or Annulata (Latin, *annela* or *annulatus* = ringed). The annelids or segmented worms. These animals are generally provided with movable bristles known as setae (or chaetae), each embedded in a setal follicle, the cell which secretes it. The body consists of an outer tube, or body wall, and an inner tube, or alimentary canal, separated by the body cavity (coelom), which is generally divided into compartments by transverse partitions, the septa. This phylum contains about 8000 described species, grouped as follows:

Class Polychaeta (Greek, *poly*, singular or *polys* = much, many; Latin, *chaeta* = a bristle). These are primarily marine and have numerous tufts of setae, borne upon projecting lobes (parapodia) at the sides of the body. Sometimes divided into two sub-classes. *Errantia* (Latin, *errantis*, genitive of *errans* = wandering) and *Sedentaria* (Latin, *sedentarius* = sitting), which includes the lugworm.

Class Myzostomaria (Greek, *myzō* = to suck in; *stoma* = mouth). Usually external or internal parasites.

Class Oligochaeta (Greek, *oligos* = few; Latin, *chaeta* = a bristle). Terrestrial, limicolous or fresh-water worms, sometimes secondarily marine or parasitic. Sometimes divided into two orders. Includes the white worm and earthworms.

Class Hirudinea (Latin, *hirudinis*, genitive of *hirudo* = a leech). The leeches. These are annelids with terminal suckers, 34 body segments or somites, no parapodia nor setae. They are hermaphrodites, and the body cavity is largely obliterated. The length is from about ¼ in to 18 in. Three orders.

Class Archiannelida (Greek, *archi-* = first). Largely marine or brackish water inhabitants.

Phylum Arthropoda (Greek, *arthron* = a joint; *podos*, genitive of *pous* = a foot) The arthropods. Bilaterally symmetrical animals whose bodies are divided into segments, arranged in a chain along a horizontal axis, each segment typically bearing a pair of jointed appendages (legs). The skin is composed of a layer of cells (the hypodermis), a supporting internal basement membrane, and an external layer of chitinous material, which contains hardened or sclerotised areas or plates. This phylum, the largest in the animal kingdom, it grouped as follows:

Class Onychophora (Greek, *onychos*, genitive of *onyx* = claw; *phoros* = a bearing). Tropical worm-like anthropods, apparently allied to primitive *Annelida* (see above). 100 described species.

NB The next four classes form the old group *Myriapoda* (Greek, *myrias* = the number 10 000, hence many; *podos*, genitive of *pous* = a foot), containing about 11 000 described species.

Class Pauropoda (Greek, *pauros* = small; *podos*, genitive of *pous* = a foot). Minute progoneates with nine or ten pairs of legs.

Class Diplopoda (Greek, *diploos* = double). The millipedes. Trunk composed of many double segments, each bearing two pairs of legs. Two sub-classes:

Pselaphognatha (Greek, *psēlaphaō* = to feel about; *gnathos* = the jaw). Small, soft-bodied millipedes bearing bristles (setae) of several kinds arranged in rows and bundles (fascicles). No copulatory organs (gonopods). One order.

Chilognatha (Greek, *cheilos* = a lip). The skin forms a hard shell bearing setae singly. Gonopods well developed. Three super-orders, containing ten orders.

Class Chilopoda (Greek, *cheilos* = a lip; *podos*, genitive of pous = a foot). The centipedes. worm-like body divided into head and trunk. The many segments of the trunk each bear a single pair of legs. Two sub-classes:

Epimorpha (Greek, *epi* = on, upon; *morphē* = form, shape). The young hatch with the full number of body segments and walking legs. Two orders.

Anamorpha (Greek, *ana-* = up, throughout). The young hatch with usually 7 but sometimes 12 pairs of legs. Additional segments and legs appear later. Two orders.

Class Symphyla (Greek, *sym-* = together; *phylē* = a tribe, race). With long antennae. Trunk with 12 or more single segments and 12 pairs of legs.

Class Insecta (Latin, *in-* = into; *sectus* = cut, cleft) **or Hexapoda** (Greek, *hex* = six; *podos*, genitive of *pous* = a foot). The insects, Body divided into head (with mouth parts and sense organs), thorax (usually with wings and three pairs of legs) and abdomen (with the digestive, respiratory, reproductive and excretory organs). About 950 000 described species.

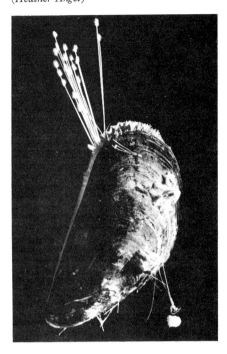

Class Bivalvia: Mussel, showing byssal threads (Heather Angel)

17

Two sub-classes:

Apterygota (Greek, *a-* = without; *pterygotōs* = winged) or *Ametabola* (Greek, *a-* = without; *metabola* = change). Primitive wingless insects with nine pairs of appendages on the abdomen and no true metamorphosis (i.e. change in form). Includes spring-tails and bristle-tails. Four orders.

Pterygota (Greek, *pterygotōs* = winged) or *Metabola* (Greek, *metabola* = change). Insects which have wings, or vestiges of wings, and in which metamorphosis takes place. Two divisions:

Palaeoptera (Greek, *palaios* = ancient; *pteron* = wing). May-flies and dragonflies. Two orders.

Neoptera (Greek, *neos* = new, recent; *pteron* = wing). Three sections:

Polyneoptera (Greek, *poly*, singular of *polys* = much, many). Includes cockroaches, termites, grasshoppers, crickets, locusts and earwigs. Nine orders.

Paraneoptera (Greek, *para* = beside, near). Includes lice, thrips and bugs. Four orders.

Oligoneoptera (Greek, *oligos* = few, small), also called *Endopterygota* (Greek, *endon* = within; *pterygotos* = winged) or *Holometabola* (Greek, *holos* = entire; *metabola* = change). Complete metamorphosis. Includes beetles, caddis flies, butterflies, moths, flies, mosquitoes, fleas, ants, wasps and bees. Ten orders.

Class Insecta: Blowfly feeding (Heather Angel)

Class Crustacea (Latin, *crustaceus* = having a shell or rind). The crustaceans. Generally aquatic, they have two pairs of antenna-like appendages in front of the mouth. They breathe by gills or by the general surface of the body. Head and thorax usually fused. About 25 000 described species. Seven sub-classes:

Branchiopoda (Greek, *branchion* = a fin; *podos*, genitive of *pous* = a foot). The branchiopods. Mostly in fresh water, their limbs are flattened and leaf-like. Includes the water fleas. Five orders.

Ostracoda (Greek, *ostrakōdés* = testaceous, resembling a shell). The ostracods. Minute aquatic clamlike crustaceans, whose body and limbs are completely enclosed in a hinged double shell (bivalve). Four orders.

Copepoda (Greek, *kōpē* = handle, oar; *podos*, genitive of *pous* = a foot). The copepods. Abundant microscopic aquatic crustaceans, an important source of food (as plankton) in the sea. Many are parasitic. Seven orders.

Mystacocarida (Greek, *mystakos*, genitive of *mystax* = upper lip, moustache; Latin, *caridis*, genitive of *caris* = a shrimp). One order.

Branchiura (Greek, *branchia* = the gills of fishes). Fish lice.

Cirripedia (Latin *cirrus* = a curl; *pedis*, genitive of *pes* = a foot). The cirripedes. Completely sedentary aquatic crustaceans. Many are parasitic. Includes the barnacles and acorn shells. Four orders.

Malacostraca (Greek, *malakos* = soft; *ostrakon* = a shell). Crustaceans whose bodies are composed of nineteen somites, all of which generally have appendages. The thorax has eight parts, and the abdomen six pairs of limbs. Six super-orders:

Leptostraca (Greek, *leptos* = thin, small; *ostrakon* = a shell) or *Phyllocarida* (Greek, *phyllon* = a leaf; Latin, *caridis*, genitive of *caris* = a shrimp). Marine and mud-burrowers. The abdomen has seven segments. One order.

Syncarida (Greek, *syn-* = together; Latin, *caridis*, genitive of *caris* = a shrimp). A small fresh-water group. Two orders.

Peracarida (Greek, *Pēra* = a pouch). Includes opossum-shrimps, wood-lice, the fresh-water shrimp, shore hopper and whale louse. One order.

Hoplocarida (Greek, *hoplon* = a tool, weapon). The mantis shrimps. Exclusively marine, One order.

Pancarida (Greek, *pan* = all). Minute, blind, creeping crustaceans. One order.

Eucarida (Greek, *eu-* = true). The eyes are stalked, and the carapace (shell) fused dorsally with all thoracic somites. Includes krill, prawns, shrimps, crayfish, lobsters and crabs. Two orders.

Class Crustacea: Edible crab (Heather Angel)

Class Merostomata (Greek, *mēros* = the thigh; *stomatos*, genitive of *stoma* = mouth). The king crabs. Large marine arthropods whose bodies are composed of a cephalothorax bearing six pairs of appendages and an abdomen terminated by a long, strong spine. Respiration aquatic. One order. Four described species.

Class Arachnida (Greek, *arachnē* = a spider). Arthropods whose bodies are composed of cephalothorax, generally bearing four pairs of legs, and abdomen. There are no antennae. Respiration aerial by means of book-lungs or by tracheae. Includes scorpions, spiders, phalangids, mites and ticks. Ten orders. About 60 000 described species.

Class Pycnogonida (Greek, *pyknos* = solid, strong; *gōnia* = a joint), **or Pantopoda** (Greek, *pantos*, genitive of *pan* = all; *podos*, genitive of *pous* = a foot). Sea spiders. Marine anthropods whose bodies are composed of a five-segmented cephalothorax and a minute abdomen, with 4–9 pairs of very long legs. The genital pores are paired, on the second segment of the last two legs of the male and all legs of female. There are no respiratory or excretory organs. Four orders. About 440 described species.

Class Pentastomida (Greek, *penta-* = five; *stoma* = mouth) **or Linguatulida** (Latin, *linguatus* = with a tongue). The pentastomes. Unsegmented but superficially annulated, worm-like, bloodsucking arthropods which live as internal parasites of vertebrates. Two orders. About 60 described species.

Class Tardigrada (Latin, *tardus* = slow; *gradior* = to walk). The tardigrades, or water-bears (bear animalcules). Minute free-living arthropods whose bodies are divided into a well-developed head region and a trunk of four fused segments, each bearing a pair of short unjointed legs. generally with several claws. Found among aquatic vegetation and other damp places. Two orders. About 280 described species.

Phylum Chaetognatha (Latin, *chaeta* = a bristle; Greek, *gnathos* = the jaw). The arrow worms. Transparent, mostly pelagic, worm-like animals. The body is usually between 0·4 in and 1·2 in, divided into head, trunk and tail, separated from each other by two transverse septa. The head is covered by a retractable hood, and bears upon its side a number of sickle-shaped, chitinous hooks and rows of low spines. They are hermaphrodite and have no gill-slits. About 50 described species.

Phylum Pogonophora (Greek, *pōgōnos*, genitive of *pōgōn* = beard; *phoros* = a bearing) **or Brachiata** (Latin, *brachiatus* = having arms). The beard worms. Worm-like animals which live on the sea-floor. Enclosed in a chitinous tube and may be up to 12 in long. A 'beard' of tentacles at the front end. No mouth or anus. Separate sexes. Two orders. 100 known species.

Phylum Echinodermata (Greek, *echinos* = a hedgehog; *dermatos*, genitive of *derma* = skin). The echinoderms, Marine headless animals in which most of the body structures are divided into five sectors, often giving a radial appearance. The skin contains minute spicules of calcite, which usually grow together into plates, small bones or prickles. There is no definite excretory system. The mouth is originally in a median position but moves to the left as the animal develops. The blood system consists of a number of spaces, and there is no heart or regular circulation. About 5700 described species, grouped as follows:

> **Sub-phylum Pelmatozoa** (Greek, *pelmatos*, genitive of *pelma* = a stalk; *zōon* = an animal). Mostly deep-water echinoderms. The body is normally borne on a stem, with five arms (brachia) containing the organs and systems. One class:
>> **Class Crinoidea** (Latin, *crinis* = hair; *oideus* = form of). Includes feather stars and sea lilies. One order.
>
> **Sub-phylum Eleutherozoa** (Greek, *eleutheros* = free; *zōon* = an animal). Free-moving echinoderms not borne on a stem. Four classes:
>> **Class Holothuroidea** (Greek, *holos* = whole; *thura* (*thyra*) = a door). The holothurians, or sea cucumbers. The surface turned to the sea-floor is always the same. They normally move only in the direction of the mouth. Five orders.
>> **Class Echinoidea** (Greek, *echinos* = a hedgehog). The echinoids. The prickles (radioles) are highly developed, moveable and sometimes poisonous. They live with the mouth downwards and can move sideways in any direction. Two sub-classes:
>>> *Perischoechinoidea* (Greek, *peri* = near; *schoinos* = a reed). One order of sea urchins.
>>> *Euechinoidea* (Greek, *eu-* = true). Four super-orders:
>>>> *Diadematacea* (Greek, *dia* = through; *dema* = a bundle). Two orders of sea urchins.
>>>> *Echinacea* (Greek, *echinos* = a hedgehog). Five orders of sea urchins.
>>>> *Gnathostomata* (Greek, *gnathos* = the jaw; *stoma* = mouth). Includes sand-dollars and cake urchins. Two orders.
>>>> *Atelostomata* (Greek, *atelēs* = imperfect). Includes heart urchins. Four orders.
>> **Class Asteroidea** (Greek, *asteroeidēs* = like a star). The starfishes. Generally live with the mouth downwards. From it radiate five ciliated grooves. They move by crawling. Three orders.
>> **Class Ophiuroidea** (Greek, *ophis* = a snake; *oura* = the tail; *ōideos* = form of). The brittle stars. Similar to *Asteroidea*, but they move by wriggling. Most have no more than five arms. Includes the serpent stars. Two orders.

Phylum Chordata (Latin, *chordata* = having a notochord). The chordates. Sometime during their life these have an elongated skeletal rod, or notochord (Greek, 'Back-string') which stiffens the body, with a single, hollow nerve located on the dorsal side. They possess a pharynx, an enlarged chamber whose sides are perforated by gill-slits, just behind the mouth. The blood is contained within vessels and propelled by a heart located on the ventral side, and they generally have a tail extending beyond the anus. About 45 000 described species, grouped as follows:

> **Sub-phylum Hemichordata** (Greek, *hēmi-* = half), **also called Stomochordata** (Greek, *stoma* = mouth) **or Branchiotremata** (Greek, *branchion* = a fin; *trématos*, genitive of *trēma* = a hole). the hemichordates. Soft-bodied marine worm-like chordates whose notochord is only a tiny tubular rod in the head region, 91 described species, comprising three classes:
>> **Class Enteropneusta** (Greek, *enteron* = bowel, intestine; *pneustikos* = for breathing). The acorn worms. Burrowing hemichordates whose bodies are composed of a proboscis, a mouth, a ringlike collar and a very long trunk with a terminal anus. The nerve cord is partly tubular and there are numerous gill-slits.
>> **Class Pterobranchia** (Greek, *pteron* = fin; *branchia* = the gills of fishes). The pterobranchs. Small (0·04 in to 0·3 in) hemichordates which form colonies of tubes in which they breed by budding as well as by sexual reproduction. The nerve cord is solid and there are few or no gill-slits. They have a pair tentaculated arms. Two orders.
>> **Class Planctosphaeroidea** (Greek, *plankton* = wandering; *sphaira* = a ball, sphere; *ōideos* = form of). A few larvae of unknown parentage.
>
> **Sub-phylum Urochordata** (Greek, *oura* = the tail) **or Tunicata** (Latin, *tunicatus* = clothed with a tunic). The urochordates or tunicates. Exclusively marine chordates, which are mostly fixed growing organisms, roughly resembling a potato, and without a capacity for locomotion. They produce a free-swimming larva with chordate features, but these, except for the gills, are usually lost in the adult state. A rigid tunic is secreted by the skin and helps to anchor them to some solid structure. About 1600 described species, grouped as follows:
>> **Class Ascidiacea** (Greek, *askidion*, diminutive of *askos* = a bag or bladder). The ascidians, or sea squirts. Attached urochordates with a dorsal exhalant siphon. The pharynx had transverse rows of ciliated gill-slits. Two orders.
>> **Class Thaliacea** (Greek, *Thalia* = a muse, patroness of comedy). Pelagic urochordates with inhalant and exhalant siphons at opposite ends of the body. They have long, simple gill-slits. Three orders.
>> **Class Larvacea** (Latin, *larva* = the immature form of a changing animal). Small oceanic urochordates which never bud and have a permanent tail. One order, *Copelata* (Greek, *kōpēlatēs* = a rower).
>
> **Sub-phylum Cephalochordata** (Greek, *kephalē* = a head), **also called Acrania** (Latin, *a-* = without; *cranium* = the skull) **or Leptocardii** (Greek, *leptos* = thin, small; *kardia* = heart). The cephalochordates. Small marine fish-like chordates that burrow in sand. Similar to *Urochordata* (see above), but they retain the notochord and powers of locomotion throughout life. 13 described species, including the lancelet.
>
> **Sub-phylum Vertebrata** (Latin, *vertebratus* = joined) **or Craniata** (Latin, *cranium* = the skull). The vertebrates. Chordates with an internal skeleton, comprising a skull, a vertebral column, or backbone, usually two pairs of limb elements and a central nervous system partly enclosed within the backbone. The muscular system consists primarily of bilaterally paired masses. About 43 000 described species, grouped as follows:
>> The fishes, 23 000 described species of cold-blooded aquatic vertebrates which swim by fins and breathe by gills, comprising four classes:

Class Marsipobranchii (Greek, **marsypos (marsipos)** = a bag; *branchion* = a fin) **or Agnatha** (Greek, *a-* = without; *gnathos* = the jaw). The marsipobranchs. Mostly marine, eel-like fishes without jaws or paired fins. One existing sub-class:

Cyclostomata (Greek, *kyklos* = a circle; *stomatos*, genitive of *stoma* = mouth). The cyclostomes, Blood-sucking fishes, comprising lampreys, hagfishes and slime eels. Two orders.

Class Selachii (Greek, *selachos* = shark), **also called Chondropterygii** (Greek, *chondros* = a grain; *pterygos*, genitive of *pteryx* = the fin), **Chondrichthyes** (Greek, *ichthys* = a fish) **or Elasmobranchii** (Greek, *elasmos* = a thin plate; *branchion* = a fin). The selachians. Fishes with jaws, and branchial arches supporting the gills. They have median and paired fins with horny rays, and the skeleton is a series of cartilaginous rods. The mouth is on the underside of the body. There is no air bladder. Four sub-classes, three of them Palaeozoic, one existing:

Euselachii (Greek, *eu-* = true). Includes sharks, dogfishes, angel-fishes and rays. Two orders.

Class Bradyodonti (Greek, *bradys* = slow; *odontos*, genitive of *odous* = tooth). Fishes with long tapering tails and large paddle-like pectoral fins. One existing sub-class:

Holocephali (Greek, *holos* = whole, entire; *kephalē* = a head). The rabbit-fishes.

Class Pisces (Latin, *piscis* = a fish) **or Osteichthyes** (Greek, *osteon* = bone; *ichthys* = a fish). The bony fishes. The skeleton is bony, and the slimy skin is covered with scales, or bony plates. The mouth is at the front end. Three sub-classes:

Palaeopterygii (Greek, *palaios* = ancient; *pterygos*, genitive of *pteryx* = the fin). Includes the sturgeon, paddle-fish, bichir and reed-fish. Two orders.

Neopterygii (Greek, *neos* = new, recent). The ray-finned fishes. Includes the bow-fins, gar-pikes and all the typical present-day fish, such as the herring, sardine, pilchard, salmon, trout, roach, minnow, carp, cod, whiting, hake, sea-horse, perch, bass, mackerel, tunny, barracuda and eels. 34 orders.

Crossopterygii (Greek, *krossoi* = a fringe, tassels). Includes the coelacanth and lung-fishes. Two orders.

Class Amphibia (Greek, *amphibios* = leading a double life). The amphibians, Cold-blooded vertebrates who breathe air largely through their moist skin. They are mostly four-limbed, live on land, and lay their eggs in water. The larvae pass through a fish-like aquatic phase (e.g. tadpoles) before metamorphosis. About 3000 described species, grouped as follows:

Order Caudata (Latin, *caudatus* = having a tail) **or Urodela** (Greek, *oura* = the tail). Amphibians with four legs, a long body and a tail. Some live permanently in water, breathing with gills. Includes the salamanders, axolotl, newts and siren. Five sub-orders.

Order Salientia (Latin, *salientis*, genitive of *saliens*, present participle of *salio* = to jump) **or Anura** (Greek, *an-* = without; *oura* = the tail). Frogs and toads. Tail-less amphibians with long hind legs adapted for jumping. Five sub-orders.

Order Gymnophiona (Greek, *gymnos* = naked; *ophioneos* = like a serpent) **or Apoda** (Greek, *a-* = without; *podos*, genitive of *pous* = a foot). The caecilians. Small, primitive, limbless, worm-like, burrowing amphibians with a very short tail. Some have scales. Found in tropical climates.

Class Reptilia (Latin, *reptilis* = creeping). The reptiles. Dry-skinned vertebrates whose body temperature is variable, and who breathe air by lungs. The skin is usually covered with horny scales formed by the epidermis. There is a well-developed tongue. Fertilisation is internal. The typical reptile has four five-toed limbs. About 6000 described species, grouped as follows:

Order Rhynchocephalia (Greek, *rhynchos* = a beak, snout; *kephalē* = a head). Primitive lizard-like reptiles with beaked upper jaws. The only living species is the tuatara of New Zealand.

Order Testudines (Latin, *testudinis*, genitive of *testudo* = a tortoise) **or Chelonia** (Greek, *chelōnē* = a tortoise) Tortoises and turtles. Aquatic and land-dwelling reptiles whose trunk is enclosed in a hard shell built up from a series of dermal bones. They all lay their eggs on land. Two sub-orders.

Order Crocodilia (Latin, *crocodilus* = a crocodile) **or Loricata** (Latin, *loricatus* = clad in mail). Crocodiles and aligators. Reptiles with short limbs, adapted to aquatic life. They have elongated, heavily-jawed heads and long, flattened tails.

Order Squamata (Latin, *squamatus* = scaly). Horny-scaled reptiles. Two sub-orders:

Sauria (Greek, **sauros** = lizard) or *Lacertilia* (Latin, *lacerta* = a lizard). The lizards.

Serpentes (Latin, *serpentis*, genitive of *serpens* = a serpent) or *Ophidia* (Greek, *ophidion*, diminutive of *ophis* = a snake). The snakes. The jaws are joined by an elastic ligament, and there is no trace of any limbs, except in boas and pythons.

Class Aves (Latin, *aves*, plural of *avis* = a bird). The birds. Warm-blooded, egg-laying feathered vertebrates whose front limbs are modified into wings. Most are thus able to fly. About 8590 described species, grouped as follows:

Order Struthioniformes (Latin, *struthionis*, genitive of *struthio* = an ostrich; *forma* = shape, nature). The ostriches. One family.

Order Rheiformes (Greek, *Rhea* = mother of Zeus). The rheas. One family.

Order Casuariiformes (Malay, *kasuari* = the cassowary). The emu and cassowary. Two existing families.

Order Apterygiformes (Greek, *apterygos* = without wings). The kiwis. One family.

Order Tinamiformes (from *tinamou*, the native name) **or Crypturi** (Greek, *kryptos* = hidden; *oura* = the tail). The tinamous. One family

Order Gaviiformes[1] (Latin, *gavia*, the name possibly of the sea-mew). The divers. One family.

Order Podicipediformes[1] (Latin, *podicis*, genitive of *podex* = the rump; *pedis*, genitive of *pes* = a foot). The grebes. One family.

Order Sphenisciformes (Greek, *sphēniskos* = a small wedge). The penguins. One existing family.

Order Procellariiformes (Latin, *procella* = a tempest) **or Turbinares** (Latin, *turbinis*, genitive of *turbo* = something which spins). Includes the petrels, shear-

Class Aves: North African Ostrich (Denzil J Reeves)

[1] These two orders are also called *Pygopodes* (Greek, *pygē* = the rump; *podos*, genitive of *pous* = a foot) or *Colymbi-formes* (Greek, *kolymbos* = a diving bird).

water, fulmar and albatross. Four families.

Order Pelecaniformes (Greek, *pelekan* = a pelican) **or Steganopodes** (Greek, *steganos* = covered; *podos* = genitive of *pous* = a foot). Includes the tropic bird, pelican, cormorant, gannet and frigate bird. Six existing families.

Order Ciconiiformes (Latin, *ciconia* = a stork) **also called Ardeiformes** (Latin, *ardea* = a heron) **or Gressores** (Latin, *gressor* = a walker). Includes the herons, bitterns, storks, ibis and spoonbill. Six families.

Order Phoenicopteriformes (Greek, *phoinikos*, genitive of *phoinix* = crimson; *pteron* = wing). The flamingos. One existing family.

Order Anseriformes (Latin, *anser* = a goose). The screamers, ducks, geese and swans. Two existing families.

Order Falconiformes (Latin, *falco* = a falcon) **or Accipitres** (Latin, *accipiter* = a bird of prey). Includes the vultures, eagles, secretary bird, hawks, kestrel, falcon and osprey. Six existing families.

Order Galliformes (Latin, *gallus* (fem. *gallina*) = a fowl). Includes the megapode, curassow, grouse, pheasant, quail, peafowl, turkeys, hoatzin and fowl. Seven existing families.

Order Gruiformes (Latin, *gruis*, genitive of *grus* = the crane). Includes the crane, rail, coot and bustard. Twelve existing families.

Order Charadriiformes (Greek, *charadrios* = a cleft-dwelling bird) **or Larolimicolae** (Greek, *laros* = a ravenous sea-bird (Latin *larus* = a gull); Latin, *limus* = mud; *colo* = to inhabit). Includes the plover, gulls, snipe, skua, tern, razorbill, sandpiper, oyster-catcher, puffin, woodcock and avocet. 16 existing families.

Order Columbiformes (Latin, *columba* = a dove, pigeon). Includes the sand grouse, pigeon and dove. Three families.

Order Psittaciformes (Greek, *psittakē* (*psittakos*) = a parrot). The lories, cockatoos, parrots and macaws. One family.

Order Cuculiformes (Latin, *cuculus* = the cuckoo). Includes the plantain-eater and cuckoo. Two families.

Order Strigiformes (Greek, *strigos*, genitive of *strix* = an owl). The owls. Two existing families.

Order Caprimulgiformes (Latin, *caper* (fem. *capra*) = a goat; *mulgeo* = to milk, to suck). Includes the oil bird, frogmouth and goatsucker (i.e. the nightjar). Five families.

Order Apodiformes (Greek, *a-* = without; *podos*, genitive of *pous* = a foot), **also called Micropodiformes** (Greek, *mikros* = small) **or Macrochires** (Greek, *makros* = long, large; *cheir* = head). The swifts and humming-birds. Three existing families.

Order Coliiformes (Greek, *kolios* = a king of woodpecker). The colies, or mouse birds. One family.

Order Trogoniformes (Greek, *trōgōn* = gnawing). The trogons, including the quetzal. One family.

Order Coraciiformes (Greek, *korakiao* = a kind of raven). Includes the kingfisher, tody, motmot, bee-eater, roller, hoopoe and hornbill. Nine families.

Order Piciformes (Latin, *picus* = a woodpecker). Includes the jacamar, puff-bird, toucan and woodpecker, Six families.

Order Passeriformes (Latin, *passer* = a sparrow). The perching birds. Four suborders:

Eurylaimi (Greek, *eurys* = wide, broad; *laimos* = the throat). The broadbills. One family.

Tyranni (Latin, *tyrannus* = a tyrant). Includes the ovenbird and cotinga. 13 families.

Menurae (Greek, *mēnē* = moon; *oura* = the tail). Includes the lyre-bird. Two families.

Passeres (Latin, *passer* = a sparrow) or *Oscines* (Latin, *oscines*, plural of *oscen* = a singing bird). The songbirds. Includes the larks, swallow, martins, crows, rook, jackdaw, magpie, jay, bird of paradise, tits, nuthatch, dippers, wren, thrush, blackbird, chats, nightingale, robin, warblers, shrikes, starling, finches and sparrow. 57 existing families.

Class Mammalia (Latin, *mammalis*, possessive of *mamma* = breast). The mammals. Warm-blooded, hairy vertebrates whose young are typically born alive and suckled, i.e. nourished with milk from the mother's breasts. About 4500 described species, grouped as follows:

Sub-class Prototheria (Greek, *prōtos* = first; *thērion* = a wild animal). The most primitive mammals. One order:

Order Monotremata (Greek, *monas* = single; *trematos*, genitive of *trema* = a hole). The monotremes. Egg-laying mammals, with a single cloaca, a common outlet for the genital, urinary and digestive organs. They have a beak instead of teeth, no external ears, and milk glands without nipples. Comprises the echidnas, or spiny ant-eaters, and the duck-billed platypus.

Sub-class Theria (Greek, *thērion* = a wild animal). Mammals with teeth, external ears, separate orifices for the intestine, bladder and reproductive organs and mammary glands with nipples.

Infra-class Metatheria (Greek, *meta* = next to). One order:

Order Marsupialia (Latin, *marsupium*, from Greek, *marsypion*, diminutive of *marsypos* = a bag). The marsupials. Mammals in which the female has a pouch on the under side, with the nipples of the mammary glands inside the pouch. The young are born in an immature state and finish their development inside the mother's pouch. Includes the opossums, kangaroo, wallaby, wombats, phalanger, bandicoot and koala.

Infra-class Eutheria (Greek, *eu-* = true). The eutherians, or placental mammals. The developing embryo is fed by the mother's blood indirectly through an organ known as the placenta. 16 orders:

Order Insectivora (Latin, *insecta* = insects; *voro* = to devour). The insectivores. Placental mammals with a dentition adapted to an insect diet. The feet generally

Above: Class Aves: Rosy Flamingo (David Roberts)

Below: Class Aves: Monkey eating eagle (Fox Photos)

have five toes, each with a claw. Mostly nocturnal and terrestrial. Includes the tenrec, hedgehog, shrew, mole and desman.

Order Tupaioidea (*Toepai*, native name). The tree shrews.

Order Dermoptera (Greek, *derma* = skin, leather; *pteron* = wing); Herbivorous, climbing mammals with claws and a gliding membrane. Two species of the colugo, or cobego, commonly called flying lemurs.

Order Chiroptera (Greek, *cheir* = hand; *pteron* = wing). The bats. The forelimbs are modified to form wings, and these are the only truly flying mammals. Two sub-orders:

Megachiroptera (Greek, *megas* = great). The fruit bats, including the flying fox.
Microchiroptera (Greek, *mikros* = small). The insectivorous bats.

Order Primates (Latin, *primus* = first). The primates. Chiefly tree-dwelling mammals with hands and feet adapted for climbing. The fingers and toes are provided with nails. Three sub-orders:

Prosimii (Greek, *pro-* = before; Latin, *simia* = ape) or *Lemuroidea* (Latin, *lemures* = shades, ghosts). The lower primates. Includes the loris, bush baby, common lemur and the tarsiers.
Anthropoidea (Greek, *anthrōpos* = a man). The brain is highly developed. Includes the marmoset, monkey, baboon, chimpanzee, gorilla and man.

Order Edentata (Latin, *e-* (*ex-*) = out, without; *dentatus* = toothed). The edentates. The teeth are either completely absent or undifferentiated, and always absent in the front of the jaws. The edentates have long snouts and long tongues. Includes the sloth, armadillo and anteater.

Order Pholidota (Greek, *pholidōtos* = armed with scales). The pangolins, or scaly anteaters. Similar to the edentates, but the body is covered with overlapping horny scales, composed of cemented hairs.

Order Lagomorpha (Greek, *lagōs* = a hare; *morphē* = form, shape). Similar to **Rodentia** (see below), but the teeth include two pairs of upper incisors. Includes the pika, hares and rabbits.

Order Rodentia (Latin, *rodentis*, genitive of *rodens* = gnawing). The rodents. Gnawing mammals, with one pair of chisel-like incisor teeth, above and below. The feet are generally five-toed. They feed chiefly on plants. Three sub-orders:

Sciuromorpha (Greek, *skiouros* (Latin, *sciurus*) = a squirrel; *morphē* = form, shape). Includes the squirrel, gopher, beaver, marmot, wood-chuck and chipmunk.
Myomorpha (Greek, *myos*, genitive of *mys* = mouse). Includes the mouse, rat, dormouse, vole, hamster, lemming and jerboa.
Hystricomorpha (Greek, *hystrichos*, genitive of *hystrix* = a porcupine). Includes the guinea pig, capybara, chinchilla, coypu and porcupine.

Order Cetacea (Greek, *kētos* = a whale). Mammals adapted for aquatic life, mostly marine. The five-fingered skeletal forelimbs are enclosed as paddle-like flippers. The tail has flukes, and there is generally a dorsal fin. There is a short neck but no external hind limbs or ears. Hair absent except on lips. Two existing sub-orders:

Odontoceti (Greek, *odontos*, genitive of *odous* = tooth). The toothed whales. Includes the sperm whale, porpoises and dolphins.
Mysticeti (Greek, *mystis* = a mystic). The whalebone whales. Includes the rorqual and blue whale.

Order Carnivora (Latin, *carnis*, genitive of *caro* = flesh; *voro* = to devour). The carnivores. Mostly flesh-eating mammals, with the teeth adapted for tearing flesh. There are never less than four toes on each foot, each toe with a compressed claw. Carnivores with paw-like feet divided into toes. The cheek-teeth are of several kinds. Includes the dog, wolf, jackal, fox, bear, raccoon, panda, ferret, weasel, mink, ermine, polecat, stoat, marten, sable, badger, skunk, otter, mongoose, hyaena, civet, cat, lion, tiger, jaguar, panther, leopard and cheetah.

Order Pinnipedia (Latin, *pinna* = a wing). Aquatic with limbs adapted to fins. The upper limbs are short and the feet are swimming paddles. The cheek-teeth are all alike. Includes the seals, sea lion and walrus.

Order Tubulidentata (Latin, *tubulus*, diminutive of *tubus* = a tube; *dentatus* = toothed). The aardvark (Dutch, 'earth-pig'), or African antbear. A nocturnal burrowing anteater, similar to *Edentata* (see above), but with a tubular mouth and long ears.

Order Proboscidea (Latin, *proboscidis*, genitive of *proboscis* = a proboscis, from Greek, *proboskis* = an elephant's trunk). The elephants. Large mammals whose heads bear a proboscis (the trunk), a long flexible muscle organ with one or two finger-like processes at its tip.

Order Hyracoidea (Greek, *hyrakos*, genitive of *hyrax* = a shrew mouse). Small hoofed mammals, with squat, almost tail-less bodies. Includes the hyrax, dassie and coney (or cony).

Order Sirenia (Latin, *siren* = a Siren, a mermaid). Aquatic mammals with torpedo-shaped bodies. The body has a horizontal tail fluke and very mobile lips. Comprises the dugong and manatees.

Order Perissodactyla (Greek, *perisso* = uneven, odd; *daktylos* = a finger, toe). The perissodactyls, or odd-toed ungulates (hoofed mammals). Herbivorous mammals whose hindfeet each have one or three digits. Two sub-orders:

Hippomorpha (Greek, *hippos* = a horse; *morphē* = form, shape). Includes the horse, donkey and zebra.
Ceratomorpha (Greek, *keratos*, genitive of *keras* = a horn). Includes the tapir and rhinoceros.

Order Artiodactyla (Greek, *artios* = even-numbered; *daktylos* = a finger, toe). The artiodactyls, or even-toed ('cloven-hoofed') ungulates. The hindfeet each have two or four digits. Three sub-orders:

Suiformes (Latin, *suis*, genitive of *sus* = the pig; *forma* = appearance). Includes the pig, peccary, warthog and hippopotamus.
Tylopoda (Greek, *tylos* = a knot; *podos*, genitive of *pous* = a foot). Includes the llama, alpaca, vicuna, camel and dromedary.
Ruminantia (Latin, *ruminantis*, genitive of *ruminans* = chewing again). The ruminants, Artiodactyls who 'chew the cud'. Includes the deer, giraffe, buffalo, cattle, bison, antelope, gazelle, goat and sheep.

Class Mammalia: Chimpanzee

Class Mammalia: Zebra

British mammals
The Mammalia are represented in the British Isles by 64 land species (94 if all the dubious sub-species of insular field mice and voles are included) and 25 marine mammals, making a total of 99 (or 129).

This total includes 5 introduced species of deer, the brown rat (1728), the grey squirrel (1889 from North America), and the coypu (1927 from Argentina) which are non-indigenous. The American mink is now becoming established.

Among British mammals which have become extinct in historic times are brown bears (A.D. c. 1075); beavers (c. 1250); wild boar (1683), and wolves (1743 in Scotland and c. 1766 in Ireland).

Order Insectivora (The Insectivores, or insect-eating mammals)
  Family Erinaceidae (The Hedgehogs and Rat-shrews)
    Genus *Erinaceus*
    Erinaceus europaeus — Common Hedgehog
  Family Talpidae (The Moles and Desmans)
    Genus *Talpa*
    Talpa europaea — Common Mole
  Family Soricidae (The Tree Shrews)
    Genus *Sorex*
    Sorex minutus — Pygmy or Lesser Shrew
    Sorex araneus — Common Shrew
    Sorex araneus fretalis — Jersey Red-toothed Shrew
    Sorex araneus granti — Islay Shrew
    Genus *Neomys*
    Neomys fodiens — Water Shrew
    Genus *Crocidura*
    Crocidura suaveolens — Scilly Islands Shrew or Lesser White-toothed Shrew
    Crocidura russula — Guernsey White-toothed Shrew

Order Chiroptera (The Bats)
  Suborder Microchiroptera (Insectivorous Bats)
  Family Rhinolophidae (The Leaf-nosed Bats)
    Genus *Rhinolophus*
    Rhinolophus ferrum-equinum — Greater Horseshoe Bat
    Rhinolophus hipposideros — Lesser Horseshoe Bat
  Family Vespertilionidae (The Typical Bats)
    Genus *Myotis*
    Myotis mystacinus — Whiskered Bat
    Myotis nattereri — Natterer's Bat
    Myotis bechsteini — Bechstein's Bat
    Myotis daubentoni — Daubenton's or Water Bat
    Myotis brandti — Brandt's Bat
    Myotis myotis — Mouse-eared Bat
    Genus *Eptesicus*
    Eptesicus serotinus — Serotine
    Genus *Nyctalus*
    Nyctalus leisleri — Leisler's Bat
    Nyctalus noctula — Noctule Bat
    Genus *Pipistrellus*
    Pipistrellus pipistrellus — Pipistrelle
    Genus *Barbastella*
    Barbastella barbastellus — Barbastelle
    Genus *Plecotus*
    Plecotus auritus — Long-eared Bat
    Plecotus austriacus — Grey Long-eared Bat
    Genus *Vespertilio*
    Vespertilio murinus — Parti-coloured Bat

Order Lagomorpha (The Pikas, Hares and Rabbits)
  Family Leporidae (The Hares and Rabbits)
    Genus *Lepus*
    Lepus capensis — Brown Hare
    Lepus timidus hibernicus — Irish Hare
    Lepus timidus scoticus — Scottish Mountain or Blue Hare
    Genus *Oryctolagus*
    Oryctolagus cuniculus — European Rabbit

Order Rodentia (The Rodents, or gnawing mammals)
  Suborder Sciuromorpha (Squirrels, Marmots, Beavers, Gophers, etc.
  Family Sciuridae (The Typical Squirrels and marmots)
    Genus *Sciurus*
    Sciurus vulgaris leucourus — Red Squirrel
    Sciurus carolinensis[1] — Grey squirrel
  Suborder Myomorpha (Dormice, Rats, Mice, Voles)
  Family Gliridae or Muscardinidae (The Dormice)
    Genus *Glis*
    Glis glis[2] — Fat or Edible Dormouse
    Genus *Muscardinus*
    Muscardinus avellanarius — Dormouse
  Family Muridae (The Rats and Mice)
    Genus *Micromys*
    Micromys minutus — Harvest Mouse
    Genus *Apodemus*
    Apodemus sylvaticus — Field or Wood Mouse

[1] Introduced from North America, beginning in 1889.
[2] Introduced from continental Europe, c. 1910.

Apodemus flavicollis wintoni	Yellow-necked Field Mouse
Genus *Rattus*	
Rattus rattus	Black or Ship Rat
Rattus norvegicus	Brown Rat
Genus *Mus*	
Mus musculus	House Mouse

Family Cricetidae (The Voles)
    Genus *Clethrionomys*

Clethrionomys glareolus britannicus	Bank Vole
Clethrionomys glareolus skomerensis	Skomer Vole
Clethrionomys glareolus alstoni	Mull Vole
Clethrionomys glareolus caesarius	Jersey Vole
Clethrionomys rufocanus erica	Raasay Vole
Genus *Arvicola*	
Arvicola terrestris amphibius	Water Vole
Genus *Microtus*	
Microtus avalis sarnius	Guernsey Vole
Microtus arvalis orcadensis	Orkney Vole

Suborder Hystricomorpha (Porcupines, Guinea Pigs, Chinchillas, etc.)
    Family Capromyidae (The Tuco-tucos, Hutias, etc.)
      Genus *Myocaster*

Myocastor coypus[1]	Nutria or Coypu Rat

Order Carnivora (The Carnivores, or flesh-eating mammals)

Family Canidae (The Dogs, Wolves, Jackals, and Foxes)
    Genus *Vulpes*

Vulpes vulpes	Fox

Family Mustelidae (Martens, Weasels, Badgers, Otters, Skunks, Sables, Ferrets, Minks, Ermines, Wolverines, etc.)
    Genus *Martes*

Martes martes	Pine Marten
Genus *Mustela*	
Mustela erminea hibernica	Irish Stoat
Mustela erminea stabilis	Stoat
Mustela erminea ricinae	Islay Stoat
Mustela nivalis	Weasel
Mustela putorius	Polecat
Genus *Meles*	
Meles meles	Common Badger
Genus *Lutra*	
Lutra lutra	Common Otter

Family Felidae (The Cats)
    Genus *Felis*

Felis silvestris grampia	Scottish Wild Cat

Order Pinnipedia (The fin-footed Carnivores—Seals, Sea-lions and Walruses)

Family Phocidae (The True Seals)
    Genus *Halichoerus*

Halichoerus grypus	Grey, or Atlantic Seal
Genus *Phoca*	
Phoca vitulina	Common seal

Order Artiodactyla (The even-toed Ungulates, or hoofed mammals)

Suborder Ruminantia (The Ruminants—Cattle, Sheep, Goats, Antelopes, Deer, Giraffe, etc.)
    Family Cervidae (The True Deer)
      Genus *Cervus*

Cervus elaphus	Red Deer
Cervus nippon nippon[2]	Japanese Sika
Genus *Dama*	
Dama dama	Fallow Deer
Genus *Capreolus*	
Capreolus capreolus	Common Roe Deer
Genus *Hydropotes*	
Hydropotes inermis[3]	Chinese Water Deer
Genus *Muntiacus*	
Muntiacus reevesi[4]	Chinese Muntjac or Barking Deer

Order Cetacea (The Whales, Dolphins and Porpoises)

Suborder Mysticeti (The Whalebone Whales)
    Family Balaenidae (The Right Whales)
      Genus *Eubalaena*

Eubalaena glacialis	North Atlantic Right Whale

Family Balaenopteridae (The Rorquals or Fin Whales)
    Genus *Megaptera*

Megaptera novaeangliae	Humpback Whale
Genus *Balaenoptera*	
Balaenoptera physalus	Common Rorqual or Fin Whale
Balaenoptera acutorostrata	Lesser Rorqual or Pike Whale
Balaenoptera musculus	Blue Whale
Balaenoptera borealis	Sei Whale

Suborder Odontoceti (The Toothed Whales)
    Family Physeteridae (The Sperm Whales)
      Genus *Physeter*

Physeter catodon	Sperm Whale or Cachalot

Family Ziphiidae (The Bottle-nosed or Beaked Whales)
    Genus *Hyperoödon*

Hyperoödon ampullatus	Bottle-nosed Whale

British Mammals

[1] Introduced from Argentina in 1927.
[2-4] These occur in the wild state as a result of escapes from parks and zoological gardens, for which they have been imported at various times since *c.* 1860.

Young fox at the entrance to the earth (Michael Clark)

Muntjac Buck (Michael Clark)

Noctule bat (*Nyctalus noctula*)

Red deer (*cervus elaphus*)

Wild cat (*Felis silvestris*)

Badger (*Meles meles*)

Harvest mouse (*Micromys minutus*)

Michael Clark

Genus *Ziphius*	
Ziphius cavirostris	Cuvier's Beaked Whale
Genus *Mesoplodon*	
Mesoplodon bidens	Sowerby's Whale
Mesoplodon mirus	True's Whale
Family Monodontidae (The Narwhals)	
Genus *Monodon*	
Monodon monoceros	Narwhal
Genus *Delphinapterus*	
Delphinapterus leucas	White Whale or Beluga
Family Delphinidae (The Dolphins)	
Genus *Globicephala*	
Globicephala melaena	Blackfish, Pilot Whale or Caa'ing Whale
Genus *Grampus*	
Grampus griseus	Risso's Dolphin
Genus *Orcinus*	
Orcinus orca	Killer Whale or Grampus
Genus *Pseudorca*	
Pseudorca crassidens	False Killer
Genus *Tursiops*	
Tursiops truncatus	Bottle-nosed Dolphin
Genus *Lagenorhynchus*	
Lagenorhynchus albirostris	White-beaked Dolphin
Lagenorhynchus acutus	White-sided Dolphin
Genus *Delphinus*	
Delphinus delphis	Common Dolphin
Genus *Stenella*	
Stenella styx	Euphrosyne Dolphin
Family Phocaenidae (The Porpoises)	
Genus *Phocaena*	
Phocaena phocaena	Porpoise

Animal Kingdom—Dimensions by species

Protozoa—30 000 species: generally microscopic down to *Mycoplasma* some of which have a diameter of only 100 millimicrons or 0·000 005 in. The thread-like *Pelomyxa pallustris* may grow up to 0·6 in in length.

Mollusca—128 000 species: ranging in size between the minute marine gastropods *Homalogyra atomus* and *H. rota* of 0·03 in, and a known 57 ft 3 in of the giant squid (*Architeuthis longimanus*), which is the largest of all invertebrates.

Insecta—950 000 (1974) described species of a suspected total of perhaps some 3 million: ranging in size between the Battledore wing fairy fly (*Hymenoptera mymaridae*) 0·0075 in long to the bulky 3½-oz 5¾-in-long African goliath beetle (*Macrodontia cervicornis*).

Crustacea—25 000 species: ranging in size from the extremely primitive trilobite-like *Hutchinsonella* and the water flea *Alonella* species at 0·01 in long to the Giant Japanese Spider crab (*Macrocheira kaempferi*) with a spread of 12½ ft between claws.

Amphibia—3000 species: ranging in size between the thread-like caecilians and the 5½-ft-long giant salamander (*Megalobatrachus maximus*) weighing up to 88 lb.

Reptilia—6000 species: ranging in size between the 1·5-in-long Malagasy chameleon and the South American snake anaconda (*Eunectes murinus*), which has been reported to attain 37½ ft in length.

Aves—c. 8950 species: ranging in size from the 0·07-oz Cuban bee humming bird (*Mellisuga helenae*) up to the 300-lb 8-ft-tall ostrich (*Struthio camelus*).

Mammalia—c. 4500 species: ranging in size, on land, between the 0·1-oz Etruscan shrew (*Suncus etruscus*) and the African elephant (*Loxodonta africana*) which may very rarely attain nearly 11 tons; and, at sea, between the 85-lb sea otter (*Enhydra lutris*) and the 135-ton Blue Whale (*Sibbaldus musculus*).

Animal longevity

Data are still sparse and in many species unreliable or non-existent. Animals in captivity may not reflect the life span of those in their natural habitat.

Maximum life span (yrs)	species
138	Box Tortoise (*Testudo carolina*)
116	Tortoise (*Testudo graeca*)
113	Man (*Homo sapiens*)—highest proven age
>90	Killer Whale (*Orcinus orca*)
82	Sturgeon (*Acipenser transmontanus*)
80	Fresh Water Oyster (*Ostrea edulis*)
73	Cockatoo (*Cacatua galerita*)
c. 70	Indian Elephant (*Elephas maximus*)
57	Aligator Snapping Turtle
55	Giant Salamander (*Megalobatrachus japonicus*)
54	Hippopotamus (*Hippopotamus amphibius*)
52	Horse (*Equus caballus*)
>50	Termites (*Isoptera*)
50	Chimpanzee (*Pan troglodytes*)
c. 49	Carp, mirror (*Cyprinus carpio* var.)
47	Rhinoceros, Indian (*Rhinoceros unicornis*)
43	Ringed Seal (*Pusa hispida*)
38	Common Boa (*Boa constrictor*)
35	Pigeon, domestic (*Columba livia domestica*)
33	Cat (domestic) (*Felis catus*)
33	Polar Bear (*Thalarctos maritimus*)
30	Giant Clam (*Tridacna gigas*)
28	Dog (Labrador) (*Canis familiaris*)
27	Camel, Bactrian (*Camelus bactriarus*)
27	Pig (*Sus scofa*)
24	Bat (*Myotis lucifugus*)
24	Pike (*Esox lucius*)
20	Sheep (*Ovis aries*)
18	Goat (*Capra hircus*)
18	Rabbit (*Oryctolagus cuniculus*)
17	Cicada (*Magicicada septendecim*)
4·5	Snail (both freshwater and land)
4·0	Rat, house (*Rattus rattus*)
0·5	Bedbug (*Cimex lectularius*)
0·2	Fly, house (*Musca domestica*)

Velocity of animal movement

The data on this topic are notoriously unreliable because of the many inherent difficulties of timing the movement of most animals—whether running, flying, or swimming—and because of the absence of any standardisation of the method of timing, of the distance over which the performance is measured, or of allowance for wind conditions.

The most that can be said is that a specimen of the species below has been timed to have attained as a maximum the speed given.

MPH

110·07*	Racing Pigeon (*Columba palumbus*)
106·25	Spine-tailed swift (*Chaetura caudacuta*)
88	Spurwing Goose (*Plectropterus gambensis*)
82*	Peregrine Falcon (*Falco peregrinus*)
68	Sailfish (*Istiophorus* sp.)
65	Mallard (*Anas platyrhyncha*)
61	Pronghorn Antelope (*Antilocapra americana*)
60–63†	Cheetah (*Acinonyx jubatus*)
57	Quail (*Coturnix coturnix*)
57	Swift (*Apus apus*)
56	Red Grouse (*Lagopus scoticus*)
55	Swan (*Cygnus* sp.)
53	Partridge (*Perdix perdix*)
50	House Martin (*Delichon urbica*)
50	Starling (*Sturnus vulgaris*)
45	English Hare (*Lepus timidus*)
45	Red Kangaroo (*Megaleia rufa*)
43·26	Race Horse (*Equus caballus*) (mounted)
43	Saluki (*Canis familiaris*)
42	Red Deer (*Cervus elephus*)
41·72‡	Greyhound (*Canis familiaris*)
40	Emu (*Dromiceus novaehollandiae*)
40	Jackdaw (*Corvus monedula*)
38	Swallow (*Hirundo rustica*)
37	Dolphin (*Delphinus* sp.)
36	Dragonfly (*Austrophlebia*)
35	Flying Fish (*Cypsilurius cyanopterus*) (airborne)
35	Rhinoceros (*Cerathotherium simus*)
35	Wolf (*Canis lupus*)
33	Hawk Moth (*Sphingidae*)
32	Giraffe (*Giraffa camelopardalis*)
32	Guano Bat (*Tadarida mexicana*)
30	Blackbird (*Turdus merula*)
28	Fox (*Vulpes fulva*)
28	Grey Heron (*Ardea cinerea*)
27·89§	Man (*Homo sapiens*)
27	Cuckoo (*Cuculus canorus*)
24	African Elephant (*Loxodonta africana*)
23	Salmon (*Salmo salar*)
22·8	Blue Whale (*Sibbaldus musculus*)
22	Wren (*Troglodytes troglodytes*)
20	Monarch Butterfly (*Danaus plexippus*)
18	Race Runner Lizard (*Cnemidophorus sexlineatus*)
16	Flying Frog (*Hyla venulosa*) (gravity glide)
15‖	Black mamba (*Dendroaspis polylepsis*)
13·3	Hornet (*Vespula maculata*)
12	Wasp (*Vespa vulgaris*)
8·5¶	Penguin (Adélie) (*Pygoscelis adeliae*)
4·5**	Flea (Order *Siphonaptera*)
1·36	Sloth (*Bradypus tridactylus*)
1·2	Spider (*Tegenaria atrica*)
0·17	Giant Tortoise (*Testudo gigantea*) (in Mauritius)
0·03	Snail (*Helix aspera*)

* Strong following wind—60 m.p.h. in still air.
† Unable to sustain a speed of over 44 m.p.h. over 350 yards.
‡ Average over 410 yards.
§ Over 15 yards (flying start).
‖ Unable to sustain a speed of over 7 m.p.h.
¶ Under water.
** Jumping.

The Plant Kingdom

A CLASSIFICATION OF THE PLANT KINGDOM

Green plants lacking any differentiation into stem and leaf and lacking true roots, commonly known as algae, are now grouped in 11 divisions. In most of these, the reproductive organs are one-celled, and where they are multicellular every cell is fertile. There are about 19 000 species, which usually grow immersed in water, fresh or marine, and include plants popularly known as seaweeds, pond scums and the like.

Division Cyanophyta (Greek, *kyanos* = corn-flower (hence a dark blue colour); *phyton* = a plant). Blue-green algae, about 1400 species, all of microscopic size, more than 80 per cent of which are fresh-water and either aquatic or terrestrial. The only algae in which photosynthetic pigments are not localised in definite chromatophores and in which the nuclear substances are not localised in definite nuclei. The photosynthetic pigments are evenly distributed through the cytoplasm (i.e. the general protoplasm of the cell) and are masked by a blue pigment (phyco-cyanin); sometimes there is also a red pigment. These algae have no motile flagellated cells, either vegetative or reproductive, and no members of the phylum reproduce sexually. In some cases many plants may be aggregated to form a macroscopic mass (i.e. visible to the naked eye) of definite shape. The majority are multicellular (i.e. formed of more than one cell).

Division Chlorophyta (Greek, *chlōros* = grass green; *phyton* = a plant). Green algae in which the chromatophores (i.e. plastids, or protoplasmic granules in active cells) are green and with the same pigments as vascular plants, i.e. those composed of vessels, as opposed to cells, but without their conducting system. About 5500 species. The plant body never grows by means of an apical cell (i.e. the single cell which is the origin of all longitudinal growth) and the reproductive organs are always one-celled and without a sheath of vegetative cells.

Division Euglenophyta (Greek, *eu-* = true; *glēnē* = a cavity; *phyton* = a plant). Mostly naked motile (Latin, *motus* = a moving), i.e. movable, unicellular organisms, frequently found in stagnant fresh waters. Algae with grass-green chromatophores. The food reserves are either paramylum (an insoluble carbohydrate related to starch) or fats. Flagella (Latin, *flagellum* = a whip), i.e. whip-like appendages by which the plants are able to progress through the water, differ from those of other major groups in that they are inserted in a small interior chamber at the anterior end of a cell. Reproduction is by cell division but several genera are known to form thick-walled resting stages. Sexual reproduction is not definitely known for any species.

Division Charophyta (Greek, *chairō* = to rejoice)—stoneworts, growing submerged in fresh or brackish waters. The plant body is multicellular, a slender cylindrical axis bearing nodes (Latin, *nodus* = a knot), i.e. whorls of short branches ('leaves'), separated by internodes. The growth is initiated by an apical cell. The sex organs (male and female) are surrounded by envelopes of sterile cells.

Division Phaeophyta (Greek, *phaios* = brown and swarthy; *phyton* = a plant). Brown algae. About 900 species, all but 3 being strictly marine, growing along rocky ocean shores, predominantly in the algal flora of colder seas, and usually where the water is less than 50 ft deep. These are all multicellular and the primary food reserve is laminarin, a carbohydrate dissolved in the cell sap.

Three kinds of life history are found in the Phaeophyta which have been named as under.

Class Isogeneratae (Greek, *isos* = equal to; Latin, *generatio* = a begetting). The life history consists of the alternation of similar generations.

Class Heterogeneratae (Greek, *heteros* = other). The life history consists of the alternation of dissimilar generations. The gametophytes (i.e. the generations bearing the sexual organs) are always irregularly branched filaments.

Class Cyclosporeae (Greek, *kyklos* = a circle). About 350 species, mostly in oceans. In this class there is no gametophytic generation, and the spores function as gametes. The reproductive organs are borne in round cavities (conceptacles) within tips of the sporophytic plant body, and each conceptacle contains many sex organs.

Bladder wrack: Fucus vesiculosus *of the division Phaeophyta. (Heather Angel)*

Division Rhodophyta (Greek, *rhodon* = a rose (hence a red colour); *phyton* = a plant). Red algae. About 2500 species, of which about 50 are fresh-water and the rest marine, predominantly in the algal flora of tropical seas. The Rhodophytes have chromatophores in which the photosynthetic pigments are masked by a red pigment (phycoerythrin; from Greek, *erythros* = red); sometimes there is also a blue pigment (phycocyanin). The chief food reserve is an insoluble carbohydrate, floridean starch. Sexual reproduction is unique in that non-flagellate male gametes (spermatia) are passively transported to female sex organs. The plant body is usually a simple blade, a much-divided blade or more complex and differentiated into stem- and blade-like portions.

Division Chrysophyta (Greek, *chrysos* = gold; *phyton* = a plant). These have golden-brown chromatophores and a storage of reserve foods as leucosin or fats. They form a distinctive type of spore (Greek, *spora* = a seed), the endospore, i.e. a spore formed within.

Division Xanthophyta (Greek, *xanthos* = yellow) or Heterokontae (Greek, *heteros* = other; *kontos* = a pole). Yellowish-green algae, almost exclusively fresh-water. About 200 species. These have yellowish-green chromatophores and store foods as leucosin or as oils, never as starch.

Division Bacillariophyta (Latin, *bacillus* = a staff). Diatoms. Microscopic unicellular or colonial algae. Over 5500 species. These have cell-walls composed of two overlapping halves and a bilateral or radially symmetrical ornamentation of the wall.

Division Pyrrophyta (Greek, *pyrrhos* = flame coloured; *phyton* = a plant). The Pyrrophytes are the only algae with yellowish to brownish chromatophores that store reserve foods as starch or starch-like compounds. Motile cells are biflagellate, usually with the flagella unequal in length and movement.

Class Desmophyceae (Greek, *desmos* = a bond). All rare organisms, mostly marine. These have a cell wall vertically divided into two homogeneous, i.e. uniform, halves (valves). Motile cells have two apically inserted flattened flagella that differ from each other in type of movement.

Class Dinophyceae (Greek, *dinos* = whirling). About 950 species, almost all marine plankton. 90 per cent of the genera are unicellular and motile. The cells of most species have numerous golden-brown to chocolate-brown chromatophores, but the cells of certain species lack chromatophores. Motile cells and zoospores are encircled by a transverse groove—the girdle. The two flagella are inserted in or near the girdle; one of them encircles the girdle, the other extends vertically backward.

Division Cryptophyta (Greek, *cryptos* = hidden). The cryptomonads. The cells have one or two brownish-yellow chromatophores and granules of starch. Motile vegetative cells and zoospores (free-moving spores) are biflagellate, with the two flagella alike, except for slight differences in length.
Non-green plants lacking any differentiation into stem and leaf and without true roots include the groups commonly known as the bacteria and the fungi. There are an estimated 50 000 species.

Division Schizomycota (Greek *schizo* = I split; *mykēs* = a fungus). The bacteria. About 1400 species. Typical bacteria are microscopic and apparently one-celled, but not infrequently multicellular, organisms in which increase is by binary fission (the division of a mother cell into two like daughter cells) or by motile gonidia (i.e. propagative cells). Most bacteria are spherical or rod-like, the last being straight, curved or twisted, but there are also fixed or free filamentous forms, having true or false branching.

Division Myxomycota (Greek, *myxa* = mucus; *mykēs* = a fungus). Fungi with plasmodium (protoplasm showing amoeboid movements) or plasmodium-like structures occurring in the life cycle. In *Myxomycota*, the assimilative phase is a true plasmodium. This division contains about 450 species, mostly slime moulds.

Division Mycota. The true fungi, in which plasmodium is lacking; the thallus is sometimes multinucleate (i.e. having more than one nucleus to a cell) or unicellular (i.e. formed of one cell), but characteristically filamentous, i.e. formed of filaments or fibres. This division contains about 40 000 species.

Six classes are now recognised.

Class I. Chytridiomycetes. The fungi of this group have motile cells with a single posterior whiplash flagellum.

Class II. Oomycetes. In this group the motile cells have one tinsel flagellum. The directed forwards and a whiplash flagellum directed backwards. Coenocytic mycelium bears gametangia; fertilisation of the oospheres is followed by the formation of large oospores.

Class III. Zygomycetes. There are no motile cells. The coenocytic hyphae somewhat or considerably differentiated; serial sporangiophores bearing sporangia with many spores, or in some, conidiophores bear conidia. Multinucleate gametangia equal or differing somewhat in size.

Class IV. Ascomycetes. (Greek, *askos* = a bag or bladder). The sac fungi, such as yeasts and truffles. The mycelium is septate (the segments being 1-, 2-, or few-nucleate), and rarely lacking. In such a case, the cells reproduce by budding or, very rarely, by fission. The members of this class (and the next two classes) are rarely parasitic on algae, but, when they are, they are not symbiotically associated, i.e. they do not live together in the same thallus, as in the case of lichens. The mycelium is immersed in humus, soil, dung, or the tissues of other fungi, green plants, or animals, sometimes largely subaerial, i.e. situated almost on the ground level. In this class, the perfect stage (i.e. the stage of the life-cycle in which spores are formed after nuclear fusion or by parthenogenesis, the apomictic development (of sexual cells into spores, without being fertilised) of haploid cells (with a single chromosome set)), when present, is characterised by spores borne in asci, sac-like cells in which the spores (generally eight), called ascospores, are produced by 'free cell formation'.

Class V. Basidiomycetes (from Latin, *basidium* = a little pedestal). The club fungi, such as mushrooms, toadstools, stinkhorns, earthstars, and puffballs. Similar to Ascomycetes, except that the perfect stage is characterised by spores borne on basidia, i.e. organs which, after karyogamy (the fusion of two sex nuclei after cell fusion) and meiosis (reduction of chromosomes), bear the spores, called basidiospores.

Class VI. Deuteromycetes (Greek, *deuteros* = the second) or **Fungi Imperfecti.** Similar to Ascomycetes and Basidiomycetes, except that neither asci nor basidia are present, and relationships are not otherwise inferable with reasonable assurance. They lack, or rarely produce, the perfect stage, and many are believed to be incomplete forms of Ascomycetes.

Lichens are compound organisms consisting of a fungus and an alga living together. As the fungus appears to be the dominant partner the modern trend is to classify lichens within the fungi where most of them are fitted into the Ascomycetes, a much smaller number falling into the Basidiomycetes.

Division Bryophyta (Greek, *bryon* = a moss) or Atracheata (Greek, *a-* = without; Latin, *trachia* = the wind-pipe). The Bryophytes—mosses and liverworts. The sex cells (gametes) are contained in a single-layered jacket of cells, as opposed to a simple cell-wall (as in Algae).

Class Hepaticae (from Latin, *hepaticus* = pertaining to the liver). The typical liverworts, sometimes called the hepatics. The spore case (capsule) frequently has sterile slender cells (elaters) among the spores, or in some cases no sterile tissue. The elaters, if present, are unicellular. The cells of the sporophyte have several to many small chloroplasts (i.e. green plastids). There are both leafy and thalloid forms. The leafy members of the class often resemble mosses, but usually have two rows of leaves, or two rows of large leaves and a third row of small leaves on the side of the stem towards the substrate. The thalloid forms are flattened ribbons or rosettes without leaflike structures on the stems.

Class Anthocerotae (Greek, *anthos* = a flower; *keras* = a horn). A group of horned liverworts, often called hornworts. Similar to Hepaticae, except for the indeterminate basal growth of the needle-shaped sporophyte, so that mature spores may be falling from the top of the apically split sporophyte while new ones are being initiated at the base. The cells of the sporophyte have two large chloroplasts containing starch-producing bodies called pyrenoids. The sporo-

Parasol mushrooms: Lepiota procera *of the division Mycota. (Heather Angel)*

phyte has a sterile central column (columella) and pores (stomata) in the epidermis (the plant-skin or covering). The members of this class usually have irregular multicellular elaters. This class is sometimes included within the Hepaticae. There are about 9000 liverworts.

Class Musci (Latin, *muscus* = moss). The true mosses. The spore case has a cylinder of sterile tissue (columella) in the centre surrounded by many minute spores and usually has a definite lid (operculum) which opens by splitting loose when the spores are ripe. Under the operculum is a single or double row (peristome) of slender, triangular teeth which ring the mouth and are hygroscopic (i.e. susceptible to extension or shrinkage on the application or removal of water or vapour) and move in response to changes in moisture. When the teeth are dry they curl back exposing the interior of the capsule; when moist, they curve inward, effectively blocking the mouth of the capsule, thus controlling to some extent the dissemination of spores. The mosses are usually classified into three orders: *Sphagnales* (usually known as bog or peat mosses), *Andreaeales* (slit mosses), and *Bryales*. There are about 14 000 mosses.

Division Tracheophyta (or Tracheata) (Latin, *trachia* = the windpipe). The Tracheophytes—plants possessing tracheae, i.e. spiral ducts or water-conducting vessels in the woody tissue of plants, formed from the coalescence of series of cells by the disappearance of the partitions between them. The vascular plants.

Sub-division Psilophyta (Greek, *psilos* = naked, smooth). Grasslike plants with a creeping stem, small, scale-like leaves and no true roots. This class contains two orders, Psilophytales (comprising only fossil types) and Psilotales, which contains the single family Psilotaceae. These plants grow epiphytically (i.e. on other plants, but not parasitically) or in soil rich in humus.

Sub-division Lycopsida (Greek, *lykos* = a wolf). Club-mosses and quillworts. These are in fact vascular plants and quite distinct from the true mosses. The leaves are relatively small and simple in form while the sporangia are seated singly, one in the axil of each leaf of the fertile region, or spreading outwards on its base.

Sub-division Sphenopsida (Greek, *sphen* = a wedge; *opsis* = appearance). Horsetails. These are Pteridophytes which have their appendages disposed in successive whorls, with long internodes between them. The class contains three orders, Hyeniales, Sphenophyllales (both extinct now) and Equisetales (from Latin, *equus* = a horse; *seta* = a bristle), which has two families—Calamitaceae (extinct) and Equisetaceae. This latter family contains a single genus, *Equisetum*, comprising the horse-tails—semi-aquatic plants varying in height from a few inches to 30 ft or more, with erect shoots arising from richly branched, subterranean stems, which are themselves rooted in the soil.

Sub-division Pteropsida (Greek, *pteris* = a fern).

Class Filicinidae (Latin, *filix* = a fern). The ferns—over 9500 living species. The most distinctive feature of this group is that on the relatively large leaves many sporangia are borne, either singly or in groups (sori). Most ferns flourish under moist conditions with a moderate temperature, and the plant varies in size from a minute herb to a tree-like body, rising to a height of 80 ft. The life cycle is split into two distinct bodily phases, or generations—the leafy spore-bearing fern plant and the prothallus, a small green scale-like body which represents the sexual generation. This class contains five orders, the Cladoxylales, Coenopteridales (both extinct), Ophioglossales (adder's tongue ferns), Marattiales (from the genus Marattia) and Filicales (the 'true' ferns).

Class Gymnospermidae (or Gymnospermae) (Greek, *gymnos* = naked; *sperma* = seed). The Gymnosperms form the first of the two groups of living seed plants. The members of this class have naked ovules, exposed to the pollen at the time of pollination, and naked seeds, and the male gametophytes always produce more sterile cells than those of the angiosperms. The female gametophyte is comparatively large and produces large eggs in cellular structures called archegonia. The gymnosperms have several embryos beginning their development, depending upon how many eggs are fertilised, but only one usually survives the intense competition to maturity. The roots are predominantly tap-roots (i.e. straight roots tapering to a point growing directly downwards from the stem). The reproductive unit is the strobilus or cone, which consists of a large axis bearing either megasporophylls (the ovule-containing organs), each subtended, in conifers, by a sterile bract (a modified leaf), or microsporophylls (the pollen-containing organs). Living gymnosperms include only woody perennial plants which are usually evergreen trees, seldom shrubs, or lianas. The gymnosperms may be divided into three groups:

Sub-class Cycadopsida. The cycads and cycad-like plants
Order Cycadofilicales (or Pteridospermales)—the so-called seed ferns (now extinct).
Order Bennettitales (or Cycadeoidales)—cycad-like plants probably of pteridospermous origin (now extinct).
Order Cycadales (Greek, *kykas*, from *kiakos*, plural of *koix* = name of a kind of palm)—the Cycads, of which there are about 100 living species, which all grow very slowly. Those of the columnar type attain their maximum height only after many centuries of growth. They have only a scanty zone of wood surrounding a very large pith and enclosed by a very large cortex (i.e. bark or rind), so the stem is relatively weak.
Order Caytoniales. A small group, probably of pteridospermous origin with the ovules borne in hollow spherical bodies (cupules) They are sometimes included with Pteridospermales.

Sub-class Coniferopsida. The conifers and related plants.
Order Cordaitales (resembling the extinct genus *Cordaites*). These were mostly trees of considerable size, resembling modern conifers.
Order Ginkgoales. This order is almost entirely extinct, being represented by only a single living species, *Ginkgo biloba* (the maidenhair tree), which is native to China. The twigs of this tree are long shoots, bearing many dwarf branches, which continue their growth on the end of long shoots of the previous year, bearing leaves that alternate in a spiral arrangement.
Order Coniferales (Latin, *conus* = a cone; *fero* = I bear). The conifers, of which there are about 550 living species, such as the pine, spruce, cedar, larch and Douglas fir. The conifers are cone-bearing trees, which are usually evergreen and have profusely branched stems, with needlelike leaves that are usually small and simple and normally persist for about three to ten years. There is a lateral growth zone or cambium which gives rise to a large amount of wood surrounded by a thin cortex and enclosing only a small amount of pith. The seed cones may be large and made up of dozens of cone scales, but in some cases the seed-bearing scales are single ovules. All conifers have pollen borne in cones which are usually quite small.

Hen and chicken fern: Asplenium bulbiferum *of the sub-division Pteropsida.* (Heather Angel)

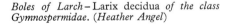

Boles of Larch – Larix decidua *of the class* Gymnospermidae. (Heather Angel)

Order Taxales. The Taxads (formerly included in Coniferales)—yew trees and related plants. The members of this order are, in most respects, similar to conifers, but it has been discovered that they have never had ovulate cones, i.e. the ovules are borne terminally and singly on axes of the plant and are not aggregated into cone-like structures.

Sub-class Gnetopsida

Order Gnetales—contains about 71 species. This order contains perennial, normally dioecious (i.e. unisexual) plants with opposite simple leaves. The cones consist of an axis bearing decussate pairs (i.e. alternately at right angles) of bracts or a number of superposed whorls of bracts, each whorl connate (united) in a cup-like form. The ovulate or staminate structures (called 'flowers') are axillary to these bracts (i.e. growing in an axil), and consist of one or two pairs of free or connate scales, the perianth, enclosing either a single ovule with a long projecting micropylar tube (i.e. from an aperture in the outer coat of the ovule), or from one to six stamens.

Class Angiospermae (from Greek, *angeion* = receptacle; *sperma* = seed). The true flowering plants, of which there are more than 250 000 species. The Angiosperms have ovules enclosed within the ovary of a pistil (gynoccium) and the seeds are enclosed within the ripened ovary, which, when matured, becomes a fruit that may be single-seeded or many-seeded. The angiosperms usually have fibrous roots and soft herbaceous stem tissue. The leaves contain extensive mesophytic tissue (i.e. requiring only an average amount of moisture). The reproductive unit is the flower, which typically consists of a very short central axis bearing one or more apical megasporophylls, commonly called carpels, subtended by microsporophylls (termed stamens) and by two sets of sterile bract-like appendages collectively termed the perianth (composed of petals and sepals). In the simplest form of the flower, the ovules are borne along the inner margin of the megasporophyll—like peas in the pod. In all modern angiosperms the megasporophyll is closed and fused marginally, with the ovules in the loculus (cavity) thus formed. In this form, the carpel is termed the pistil and consists of the ovary (the ovule-containing organ) and its apical stigma (the pollen-receiving part). The microsporophylls are closed until maturity, when they open and their pollen is released. The pollen-producing part is the anther and the supporting stalk the filament. The fertilisation (which follows pollination) takes place entirely within the carpel of the flower. After the pollen grain (microgametophyte) reaches the receptive stigmatic surface of the pistil, a pollen tube is developed within, and into it moves the generative nucleus, which divides to form two male nuclei, each of which is a male gamete. Stimulated by the environment created in the stigma, the pollen tube grows through the wall of the pollen grain and into the tissue of the stigma and its style (i.e. the usually attenuated part of a pistil between the ovary and the stigma). This growth continues down the style until the tube penetrates the ovary. Growth continues and when the tube reaches the ovule it enters the micropyle (a pore at the tip of the ovule) or elsewhere through the integuments (i.e. the two outer layers of the ovule) and finally the female gametophyte (enclosed within the ovule). As pollen-tube growth progresses from stigma to female gametophyte it carries with it both male nuclei. On approach to the egg nucleus, within the female gametophyte, the two haploid male nuclei are released. One unites with the haploid egg nucleus and forms a diploid sporophyte, called the zygote, and the other unites with the polar nuclei to form a triploid endosperm nucleus. The zygote thus formed is a new generation, and becomes the embryo within the seed. The zygote (enclosed by a membrane) undergoes a series of divisions leading to wall formation (either transverse or longitudinal) separating the terminal cell from the basal cell. The terminal cell continues to divide to produce the axis or hypocotyl of the embryo, from which are later produced the cotyledons (Greek, *kotylēdōn* = cup-shaped hollow) or seed leaves (either one or two—see below under sub-classes). The basal cell divides to form a chain of cells that functions as a suspensor, and the lowest is attached to the embryo and ultimately gives rise to the root and root cap of the embryo. The endosperm nucleus, together with the embryo sac, multiplies to form the endosperm tissue of the seed. This tissue multiplies as the embryo developes, but the bulk of it is digested by the embryo. The angiosperms may be divided into two groups:

Sub-class Dicotyledonae (Greek, *di* = two). The dicotyledons—over 200 000 species. This sub-class contains angiosperms in which the embryo has two cotyledons (seed leaves). The stems produce a secondary growth by successive cylinders of xylem tissue (Greek, *xylē* = wood), the wood element which, in angiosperms, contains vessels for water conduction and wood fibres for support. The veins of the leaves are typically arranged in a network, i.e. reticulate venation. Leaves may be simple, with entire or toothed margins, or compound with leaflets arranged on either side of, or radiating from a peticole, or footstalk. The petals and sepals of the flowers number mostly four or five, or multiples of four or five, and the pollen grains are mostly tricolpate (with three furrows). This group may be sub-divided into 40 or more orders, of which the following are among the larger and more important. They are listed in the general sequence of primitive to advanced.

Order Ranales (or Magnoliales)—Buttercup, magnolia, tulip tree, marsh marigold, barberry, lotus, custard apple, nutmeg, etc.

Order Rosales—Rose, strawberry, blackberry, apple, cherry, legumes, saxifrages, witch hazel, plane tree, etc.

Order Papaverales (or Rhoeadales)—Poppy, cabbage and relatives, mignonette, bleeding heart, the mustard family (Cruciferae), etc.

Order Geraniales—geranium, flax, castor bean, the citrus group, rubber, etc.

Order Umbellales—The carrot family, English ivy, the dogwoods, etc.

Order Rubiales—Madder, honeysuckle, coffee, cinchona, teasel, etc.

Order Campanulales—The bellflowers, the aster family (Compositae), etc.

Order Caryophyllales—The pinks, pigweed, spinach, buckwheat, sea lavender, thrift, etc.

Order Ericales—Heath, rhododendron, mountain laurel, blueberry, cranberry, etc.

Order Gentianales—Gentian, buddleia, olive, privet, ash, dogbane, milkweed, etc.

Order Polemoniales—Polemonium, morning-glory, phlox, forget-me-not, potato, tobacco, petunia, etc.

Order Lamiales—The mints, salvia, verbena, teak, lantana, etc.

Order Scrophulariales—Snapdragon, mimulus, trumpet vine, gloxinia, bladderwort, acanthus, etc.

There are several families of dicotyledons which appear to have no direct relationship with any other group. These include the Salicaceae (willows and poplars), Casuarinaceae (the Australian pine, not a true pine), Fagaceae (beeches and oaks) and the Proteaceae.

Sub-class Monocotyledonae (Greek, *monos* = one). The monocotyledons—about 50 000

Two species of the class Angiospermae. Above a beech tree, Fagus sylvatica *of the sub-class Dicotyledonae. Below, wild daffodils,* Narcissus pseudonarcissus *of the sub-class Monocotyledonae. (Heather Angel)*

species. The embryo has one cotyledon. The members of this sub-class have stems without any secondary thickening; the vascular strands are scattered through the stem and no cylinders of secondary xylum tissue are produced. The leaves have entire margins, the blades generally lack a petiole, and the veins are arranged in parallel form. The flower parts are always in multiples of three, and the sepals are often petal-like. The pollen grains are always mono-colpate (i.e. with one furrow). This sub-class contains 15 orders, of which the Liliales (Lily order) is considered the most primitive, and the Orchidales (Orchid order) the most advanced. This sub-class also contains palms, grasses, and bamboos.

Principal trees in Britain
In each case the height given is the maximum recorded living height and the girth is taken at 5 ft *1,52 m* above the ground.
1. **Grand Fir** (*Abies grandis*); height *c.* 185 ft *56,38 m* Leighton Park, Powys, Wales; girth 19¾ ft *6 m* at Lochanhead House, Dumfries and Galloway; intro: 1832 from W North America by David Douglas.
2. **Douglas Fir** (*Pseudotsuga menziesii*); height 181 ft *55,1 m* at Powis Castle, Powys; girth 23¼ ft *7 m* at Eggesford, Devon; intro: 1827 from W North America by David Douglas.
3. **European Silver Fir** (*Abies alba*); height *c.* 180 ft *55 m* at Kilbryde, Inverary, Strathclyde; girth 23 ft *7 m* at Ardkinglas, Strathclyde; intro: 1603 from Central Europe.
4. **Canadian** or **Sitka Spruce** (*Picea sitchensis*); height 174 ft *53 m* at Murthly, Tayside; girth 24 ft 7 in *7,5 m* at Fortescue Estates, Devon; used for aircraft and boat-oars; intro: 1831 from Canada.
5. **Wellingtonia** (*Sequoiadendron giganteum*); height 165 ft *50 m* at Endsleigh, Devon; girth 28½ ft *8,6 m* at Crichel House, Dorset; intro: 1853 from California.
6. **Common Lime** (*Tilia vulgaris*); height 150 ft *45,7 m* at Duncombe Park, North Yorkshire; girth 12½ ft *3,8 m* also at Duncombe Park; indigenous hybrid of *T platyphyllos* and *T cordata*.
7. **Common Ash** (*Fraxinus excelsior*); height 148 ft *45,1 m* at Duncombe Park, North Yorkshire; girth 19½ ft *5,9 m* at Holywell Hall, Lincolnshire; indigenous in Europe and Asia Minor.
8. **Common Larch** (*Larix decidua*); height 146 ft *44,5 m* at Parkhatch, Surrey; girth 18½ ft *5,6 m* at Monzie, Perth; intro: *ante* 1629 from Central Europe.
9. **London Plane** (*Platanus acerifolia*); height 145 ft *44,2 m* at Bryanston School, Blandford, Dorset; girth 26½ ft *8,0 m* at Bishop's Palace, Ely, Cambridgeshire; intro: *ante* 1700, probably hybrid arising at Oxford Botanical Gardens.
10. **Corsican Pine** (*Pinus nigra* var. *maritima*); height 144·3 ft *44 m* at Stanage Park, Powys; girth 14¼ ft *4,4 m* at Arley Castle, Worcestershire; intro: 1759.
=11. **Beech** (*Fatus sylvatica*); height 142 ft *43,2 m* at Yester House, Lothian; girth 26 ft 1 in *7,9 m* at Eridge Park, Sussex; used for indoor furniture; indigenous in Europe.
=11. **Common** (or **Norway**) **Spruce** (*Picea excelsa* or *P abies*); height 142 ft *43,2 m* and girth 14 ft *4,2 m*, both at Inverary, Strathclyde; used as plywood and white deal; intro: *ante* 1548 from N Europe.
13. **Black Italian Poplar** (*Populus nigra serotina*); height 140 ft *42,6 m* at Fairlawne, Kent; girth 20 ft 1 in *6,1 m* at Killagordan Farm, Truro, Cornwall; intro: 1750 from France.
14. **Durmast Oak** (*Quercus petraea*); height 138 ft *42 m* at Whitfield, Hereford; used for ship-building, fencing, flooring, *parquet*, panelling, furniture, charcoal; indigenous.
15. **Cedar of Lebanon** (*Cedrus libani*); height 132 ft *40,2 m* at Petworth House, Sussex; girth 39¾ ft *12,1 m* at Cedar Park, Cheshunt, Hertfordshire; used for aromatic turnery; intro: *c.* 1660 from Lebanon or Syria.
16. **Redwood** (*Sequoia sempervirens*); height 131 ft *40 m*, girth 20⅔ ft *6,2 m* at Taymouth Castle, Tayside; intro: 1843 from California.
17. **Wych** (or **Scotch**) **Elm** (*Ulmus glabra*); height 128 ft *39 m* at Rossie Priory nr. Dundee; indigenous.
18. **Horse Chestnut** (*Aesculus hippocastanum*); height 125 ft *38,1 m* at Petworth House, Sussex; girth 20 ft 10 in *6,3 m* in Hatfield Forest, Essex; almost valueless; intro: 1620 from Greece or Albania.
=19. **Oak** (*Quercus robur*); height 121 ft *37 m*, Fredville, Kent; used for boat-building, flooring, *parquet*, panelling, fencing, furniture, charcoal; indigenous.
=19. **Japanese Larch** (*Larix leptolepis*); height 121 ft *37 m* at Blair Atholl, Tayside; girth 8 ft 11 in *2,7 m* at Dunkeld House, Tayside; intro: 1861 from Japan.
21. **Scots Pine** (*Pinus sylvestris*); height 120 ft *36,6 m* in Oakley Park, Ludlow; girth 18 ft *5,4 m* in Spye Park, Wiltshire, used for yellow deal, boxes and crates; primeval British forest tree.
22. **Lombardy Poplar** (*Populus nigra italica*); height 119 ft *36,5 m* at Marble Hill, Twickenham; girth 14⅔ ft *4,4 m* at Upper Edgebold, Salop; intro: 1758 from Italy.
=23. **Smooth-leaved Elm** (*Ulmus carpinifolia*); height 118 ft *35,9 m* at Kensington Gardens, London; girth 37 ft 10 in *11,5 m* at Cobham Hall, Kent; indigenous.
=23. **English Elm** (*Ulmus procera*); height 118 ft *35,9 m* Holkham Hall, Norfolk; girth 31 ft *9,4 m* at East Bergholt, Suffolk; used for panelling, coffins, farm buildings; indigenous.
=23. **Spanish** or **Sweet Chestnut** (*Castanea sativa*); height 118 ft *35,9 m* at Godington Park, Kent; girth 39½ ft *12,0 m* at Canford, Dorset; used for hop poles and palings; intro: *c.* 50 BC by the Romans.
26. **Sycamore** or **Great Maple** (*Acer Pseudoplatanus*); height 112 ft *34,1 m* at Drumlarig Castle, Dumfries and Galloway, Scotland; girth 22¼ ft *6,7 m* at Birnam, Tayside; used for turnery and veneers.
27. **Hornbeam** (*Carpinus betulus*); height 105 ft *32 m* at Durdans, Epsom, Surrey; girth 17 ft 7 in *5,3 m* in Hatfield Forest, Essex; used for making piano keys; indigenous in Europe and Asia Minor.
28. **Silver** or **Common Birch** (*Betula pendula*); height 97 ft *29,5 m* at Woburn Sands, Bedfordshire; girth 11½ ft *3,5 m*; indigenous in Europe and Siberia.
29. **Oriental Plane** (*Platanus orientalis*); height 90 ft *27,4 m* at Jesus College, Cambridge; girth 25½ ft *7,7 m* in Woodstock Park, Kent; used for lacewood furniture; intro: *c.* 1520 from SE Europe.

=30. **Yew** (*Taxus baccata*); height 85 ft *25,9 m* at Midhurst, Sussex; girth 34 ft 7 in *10,5 m* at Ulcombe, Kent; used for inlay work, bows, topiary; indigenous in Europe and Central Asia.

=30. **White Willow** (*Salix alba*); height 85 ft *25,9 m* at Sandringham Park, Norfolk; girth 20 ft *6,0 m* used for osiers (cricket bats from var. *coelurea*); indigenous in Europe and N Asia.

=30. **Alder** (*Alnus glutinosa*); height 85 ft *25,9 m* at Sandling Park, Kent; used for making clogs; indigenous in Europe, Asia Minor and Africa.

=30. **Monkey Puzzle** (*Araucaria araucana*); height 85 ft *25,9 m* at Endsleigh, Devon; girth 12 ft 1 in *3,6 m* at Bicton, Devon; used for decorative work; intro: 1795 from Chile.

=34. **Field Maple** (*Acer campestre*); height 82 ft *24,9 m* at Kinnettles, Tayside, Scotland; used for turnery small cabinet work; indigenous in Europe.

=34. **Walnut** (*Juglans regia*); height 82 ft *24,9 m* in Laverstock Park, Hampshire; girth 21½ ft *6,5 m* at Pilton Church, Northamptonshire; used for furniture, veneers, gunstocks; introduced in early times.

=34. **White Birch** (*Betula pubescens*); height *c.* 82 ft *24,9 m*; girth 10 ft *3,0 m*; indigenous.

=37. **Aspen** (*Populus tremula*); height *c.* 80 ft *24,3 m*, girth 8½ ft *2,5 m*; indigenous in Europe, N Africa and Asia Minor.

=37. **Crack Willow** (*Salix fragilis*); height 80 ft *24,3 m* at Farnham, Surrey; girth 14½ ft *4,4 m*; indigenous in Europe and N Asia.

39. **Weeping Willow** (*Salix babylonica*); height 76 ft *23,2 m*; girth 10 ft *3,0m*; used for decorative work; intro: 1730 from China *via* Iraq.

40. **Common Holly** (*Ilex aquifolium*); height 74 ft *22,5 m* at Staverton Thicks, Surrey; girth 31¾ ft *9,6 m* at Scaftworth Hall, Doncaster; used for inlays, slide rules, pseudo ebony; indigenous in Europe, N Africa and W Asia.

41. **'Wild Service'** (*Sorbus torminalis*); height 71 ft *21,6 m* at The Grove, Penshurst, Kent; girth 9 ft *2,7 m* at Chiddingstone, Kent; used for furniture and turnery; indigenous in Europe.

=42. **Rowan** or **Mountain Ash** (*Sorbus aucuparia*); height 62 ft *18,9 m* Ramster, Chiddingfold, Surrey; girth 8 ft *2,4 m*; used for making cabinets, small turnery; indigenous in Europe and W Asia.

=42. **Whitebeam** (*Sorbus aria*); height 62 ft *18,9 m* at Tubney Wood, Berkshire; girth 7 ft *2,1 m*; used for furniture and turnery; indigenous in Europe.

44. **Juniper** (*Juniperus communis*); height 52 ft *15,8 m* at Oakley Park, Ludlow, Salop; (bush—no girth); oil of juniper is used in gin-making; indigenous in Europe.

Fruit

Common name	Scientific name	Geographical origin	Date first described or known
Apple	*Malus pumila*	Southwestern Asia	Early times; Claudius 450 BC
Apricot	*Prunus armeniaca*	Central and western China	BC (Piling and Dioscoridês)
Avocado (Pear)	*Persea americana*	Mexico and Central America	Early Spanish explorers, Clusius 1601
Banana	*Musa sapientum*	Southern Asia	Intro: Africa 1st century AD, Canary Isles 15th century
Cherry	*Prunus avium*	Europe (near Dardanelles)	Prehistoric times
Date	*Phoenix dactylifera*	unknown	Prehistoric times
Fig	*Ficus carica*	Syria westward to the Canary islands	*c.* 4000 BC (Egypt)
Grape	*Vitis vinifera*	around Caspian and Black Seas	*c.* 4000 BC
Grapefruit	*Citrus grandis*	Malay Archipelago and neighbouring islands	12th or 13th century
Lemon	*Citrus limon*	S.E. Asia	11th–13th centuries
Lime	*Citrus aurantifolia*	Northern Burma	11th–13th centuries
Mandarin (Orange)	*Citrus reticulata*	China	220 BC in China; Europe 1805
Mango	*Mangifera indica*	Southeastern Asia	*c.* 16th century; Cult. India 4th or 5th century BC
Olive	*Olea europaea*	Syria to Greece	Prehistoric times
Orange	*Citrus sinensis*	China	2200 BC (Europe 15th century)
Papaya	*Carica papaya*	West Indian Islands or Mexican mainland	14th–15th centuries
Peach	*Prunus persica*	China ?	300 BC (Greece)
Pear	*Pyrus communis*	Western Asia	Prehistoric times
Pineapple	*Ananas comosus*	Guadeloupe	*c.* 1493 (Columbus)
Plum	*Prunus domestica*	Western Asia	Possibly 100 AD
Quince	*Cydonia oblonga*	Northern Iran	BC
Rhubarb	*Rheum rhaponticum*	Eastern Mediterranean lands and Asia Minor	2700 BC (China)
Water Melon	*Citrullus laratus*	Central Africa	*c.* 2000 BC (Egypt)

Vegetables

Common name	Scientific name	Geographical origin	Date first described or known
Asparagus	*Asparagus officinalis*	Eastern Mediterranean	*c.* 200 BC
Beetroot	*Beta vulgaris*	Mediterranean Area	2nd century BC
Broad Bean	*Vicia faba*	—	widely cultivated in prehistoric times
Broccoli	*Brassica oleracea* (variety *Italica*)	Eastern Mediterranean	1st century AD
Brussels Sprouts	*Brassica oleracea* (variety *gemmifera*)	Northern Europe	1587 (Northern Europe)
Cabbage	*Brassica oleracea* (variety *capitata*)	Eastern Mediterranean lands and Asia Minor	*c.* 600 BC
Carrot	*Daucus carota*	Afghanistan	*c.* 500 BC
Cauliflower	*Brassica oleracea* (variety *botrytis*)	Eastern Mediterranean	6th century BC
Celery	*Apium graveolens*	Caucasus	*c.* 850 BC
Chive	*Allium schoenoprasum*	Eastern Mediterranean	*c.* 100 BC
Cucumber	*Cucumis sativus*	Northern India	2nd century BC (Egypt 1300 BC)
Endive	*Cichorium endivia*	Eastern Mediterranean lands and Asia Minor	BC

Garden Pea	*Pisum sativum*	Central Asia	3000–2000 BC
Garlic	*Allium sativum*	Middle Asia	*c.* 900 BC (Homer)
Gherkin (W. Indian)	*Cucumis anguria*	Northern India	2nd century BC
Globe Artichoke	*Cynara scolymus*	Western and Central Mediterranean	*c.* 500 BC
Kale	*Brassica oleracea* (variety *acephala*)	Eastern Mediterranean lands and Asia Minor	*c.* 500 BC
Leek	*Allium porrum*	Middle Asia	*c.* 1000 BC
Lettuce	*Lactuca sativa*	Iran	4500 BC (Egyptian tomb)
Marrow	*Cucurbita pepo*	America ?	16th–17th century (Mexican sites 7000–5500 BC)
Muskmelon	*Cucumis melo*	Africa	Roman times
Onion	*Allium cepa*	Middle Asia	*c.* 2400 BC 3200 BC (Egypt)
Parsnip	*Pastinaca sativa*	Caucasus	1st century BC
Pepper	*Capsicum frutescens*	Peru	Early burial sites, Peru; intro: Europe 1492
Potato	*Solanum tuberosum*	Southern Chile	*c.* 1530
Radish	*Raphanus sativus*	Western Asia	*c.* 3000 BC
Runner Bean	*Phaseolus vulgaris*	Central America	*c.* 1500 (known from Mexican sites 7000–5000 BC)
Soybean	*Soja max*	China	*c.* 2850 BC
Spinach	*Spinacia oleracea*	Iran	AD 647
Swede	*Brassica napobrassica*	Europe	1620
Sweet Corn	*Zea mays*	Andes	Cult. early times in America: intro: Europe after 1492
Tomato	*Lycopersicon esculentum*	Bolivia-Ecuador-Peru area	Europe after 1523
Turnip	*Brassica rapa*	Greece	2000 BC

Man and Medicine

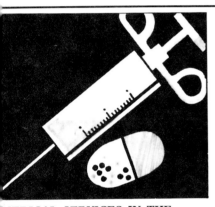

MEDICAL SERVICES IN THE UNITED KINGDOM

1 The National Health Service

The Public Health Act, 1875, was the first comprehensive attempt to control disease in this country by the notification of various illnesses and the improvement of sewerage, drinking water and conditions of work. The National Health Insurance Act, 1911, produced greater involvement of the State in individual health and a statutory obligation to provide hospitals as well as some social benefits.

The Beveridge Report, 1942, was the precursor of the National Health Service Act, 1946, starting the present comprehensive National Health Service on 1 Aug. 1948. This is virtually free to all United Kingdom residents. This Act divided the Health Service into three main parts: hospital practice, public health service, and general practice.

The National Health Service Reorganisation Act, 1973, has radically changed the running of the NHS and abolished the three separate parts in an attempt at unification. All Regional Hospital Boards, Hospital Management Committees, Executive Councils and Joint Pricing Committees are abolished. In their place the Secretary of State for the Department of Health and Social Security delegates his duties to a Regional Health Authority which can further delegate to the smaller Area Health Authorities. These Area Health Authorities, through smaller District Management Teams, administer the local hospitals, including teaching hospitals, community health services, co-ordinated by the District Community Physician, and finally through a Family Practitioner Committee the general practitioner, dental, ophthalmic and pharmaceutical services.

The general public is now involved through Local Advisory Committees and a Community Health Council to keep an eye on the running of the Health Service.

Local Authorities are involved in Joint Consultative Committes in which, amongst other things, dental inspection of local schools can be co-ordinated.

A new feature is a duty to make arrangements for family planning advice and supply of contraceptives.

A Health Service Commissioner, with staff, has been appointed to investigate complaints into the possible failure of any part of the National Health Service, but he cannot investigate complaints against professional competence of doctors.

2 A Patient and the NHS

Everyone should register with a doctor in their area. They should know his address, telephone number, and the times at which he holds his surgery. A list of general practitioners is kept at the local Post Office. Their qualifications etc. can be obtained from the Medical Directory at the local public library. A medical card will tell you how to contact your doctor and before what time in the morning he should be rung if you require a visit because you are sick at home.

If you are taken ill when you are away from home you may go to a local doctor and register as a temporary resident.

In the event of an accident you can go straight to the accident (casualty) department of a local hospital. If it is a serious accident an ambulance can be obtained by dialling 999 on the telephone.

If the doctor requires a second opinion, an appointment will be made to be seen by a specialist at the local hospital. If you are seriously ill, an admission may be made directly into hospital. A diagram of the possible ways of using a hospital is seen below.

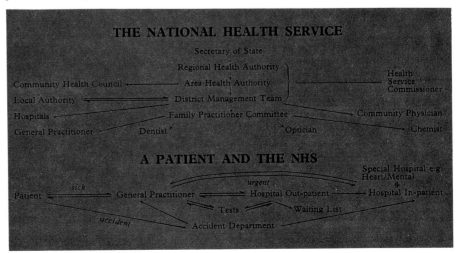

THE NATIONAL HEALTH SERVICE

A PATIENT AND THE NHS

Drugs are prescribed on a special form which can be presented to a qualified pharmacist. They will be dispensed and a fee paid for each item regardless of the cost to the Health Service. Some people receive drugs free, e.g.: those over sixty-five or under fifteen and those holding an exemption certificate for social or chronic medical reasons. Drugs in hospital are free.

Many services are available to the old or disabled through the Community Health Physician.

Dental services: Dental surgeons supply a service for each course of work that is done and a fee is payable to them for this, regardless of the time spent. The dentist may decide whether he is prepared to do the treatment on the National Health Service or not.

Ophthalmic services: If the general practitioner considers an eye test is necessary, a form will be given to the patient which can be presented to a qualified optician and spectacles obtained. A fee must be paid.

Hearing aids: These can be supplied through the Hearing Aid Centre at the local hospital if an appointment is made by the general practitioner.

3 Doctors

Doctors qualify after a six year course of study at a teaching centre, approved by the General Medical Council, having passed examinations of a required standard. They are then allowed provisionally to register their names and work in approved posts under supervision in the hospital service. Normally this would consist of twelve months' residency in surgery and medicine. If a satisfactory standard is achieved they are then allowed full registration and permitted to practise in more senior hospital posts or outside the hospital service.

Hospital service: Doctors gain experience and skill by obtaining posts in the specialty of their choice in increasing seniority from House Officer upwards to Senior Registrar. These posts are all full-time employment. A Consultant is appointed on a sessional basis of a possible eleven sessions a week. This may be split between various posts, e.g. four sessions at one hospital, three at another and perhaps two in a research post, leaving the other two which he may keep for private practice. However, many consultants are employed full-time by the NHS.

Community health physician: This is a new post developed from the old Medical Officer of Health with increased powers in the social medicine field as well as the social services.

General Practitioners: They are independent but under contract to the NHS to supply a service for patients registered with them. The NHS allows each doctor a maximum of 3500 patients. A patient may choose a doctor or leave him and the doctor may refuse to accept the patient, often because he has a full list or because the patient is outside his contracted area of practice, or have him removed from his list if he feels that he is unable to look after him. The Family Practitioner Committee is under an obligation to find a doctor for a patient if he requires one.

General Practitioners may practise alone or in partnership. They must ensure that a doctor is always available to care for their patients when they are absent. Many practices now run appointment systems and have ancillary help with secretaries, practice nurses, midwives and health visitors.

General practitioners may have private fee-paying patients and a few work entirely outside the NHS.

Other medical posts outside the NHS include police surgeons, insurance and factory doctors, as well as those working in University and Research units, e.g. Medical Research Council, although they will often

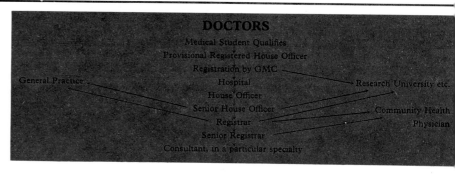

work within the framework of the Health Service and have honorary appointments to look after patients.

Commercial drug firms employ doctors both in research and promotion of new products.

4 The General Medical Council

The Medical Acts of 1956 and 1969 make the functions of the General Medical Council threefold:

1 To keep a Medical Register of all doctors and their recognised qualifications and addresses.

2 To oversee and enforce standards of medical education at Universities and other licensing bodies, e.g. the Royal Colleges of Physicians and Surgeons; and Universities in the Commonwealth.

3 Enforcement of discipline on members of the profession who fall below the expected standards for a doctor. The prime duty is to protect the public and not to punish the doctor. The Council may: (i) warn a doctor, e.g. after conviction for driving under the influence of alcohol; (ii) suspend for a certain period of time, e.g. with drug or alcohol addiction; (iii) remove the doctor's name (erasure) from the Register, e.g. adultery, advertising, fraud, association with unqualified people in medical practice and a variety of other unethical practices. A doctor can appeal from the Disciplinary Committee of the GMC to the Privy Council against his punishment.

5 Nursing Services

1 *Hospital Nursing Service:* The Salmon Report, 1966, has completely reorganised the hospital nursing service into various grades. A three year course as a student nurse ends

	Salmon Grade
Student Nurse	
State Registered Nurse (SRN) (Staff Nurse)	5
Charge Nurse (Sister)	6
Nursing Officer (Matron)	7
Senior Nursing Officer (Senior Matron)	8
Principal Nursing Officer	9
Chief Nursing Officer	10

with state registration (SRN). At this stage the nurse can make her career up the ladder of promotion to Chief Nursing Officer, see diagram, decide to seek further qualifications in midwifery, psychiatric nursing, or teach. It is the Staff and Charge Nurses that are dealing with hospital ward care.

State Enrolled Nurses require no education standard and take two years to qualify (SEN).

2 *Community Health Nursing:* The nursing

services outside the hospital are the responsibility of the Community Health Physician who will help to co-ordinate the District Nurses, Midwives, Child and Geriatric Nursing Services as well as the psychiatric services. Many general practitioners will have a nurse working with them, e.g. midwives at the doctor's ante-natal clinic.

Prediction of Human Stature

The table below shows the average mean percentage of mature height for both boys and girls at each age from birth to 18 years. These percentages, taken from large samples, essentially reflect the proven average expectation of ultimate height.

Age in Years	Boys	Girls
Birth	28·6%	30·9%
$\frac{1}{4}$	33·9%	36·0%
$\frac{1}{2}$	37·7%	39·8%
$\frac{3}{4}$	40·1%	42·2%
1	42·2%	44·7%
1½	45·6%	48·8%
2	49·5%	52·8%
2½	51·6%	54·8%
3	53·8%	57·0%
4	58·0%	61·8%
5	61·8%	66·2%
6	65·2%	70·3%
7	69·0%	74·0%
8	72·0%	77·5%
9	75·0%	80·7%
10	78·0%	84·4%
11	81·1%	88·4%
12	84·2%	92·9%
13	87·3%	96·5%
14	91·5%	98·3%
15	96·1%	99·1%
16	98·3%	99·6%
17	99·3%	100·0%
18	99·8%	100·0%

Thus a boy measuring 4 ft 6 in (54 in) on his ninth birthday could be expected to be

$$54 \times \frac{100}{75·0} = 72 \text{ in or 6 ft 0 in as a man.}$$

In practice because of maternal factors, the prediction of adult stature becomes of value only after the age of 2 or 2½ years. After the age of 9½ prediction is more accurately based on skeletal rather than chronological age. The accuracy tends to be greater throughout for girls than for boys, who, at 14 are subject to a standard deviation of error of 4 per cent, *viz.* the 91·5 per cent figure can be 95·8 per cent for a physically advanced boy, and 87·6 per cent for a retarded one.

Sense of Smell

According to the stereochemical theory of olfaction there are for man seven primary odours each associated with a typical shape of molecule:

1. camphoraceous — spherical molecules
2. ethereal — very small or thin molecules
3. floral — kite shaped molecules
4. musky — disc shaped molecules

5. peppermint   wedged shaped molecules
6. pungent   undetermined
7. putrid   undetermined

Other smells are complexes of the above basic seven, e.g. almonds are a complex of , 3 and 5.

Human Expenditure of Energy

Men

	Rate in calories per hour
Lying at ease	90
Sitting at ease	108
Sitting and writing	114
Standing at ease	118
Driving a car	168
Driving a motor cycle	204
Dressing, washing, shaving	212
Walking 4 mph	492
Climbing 6 in stairs at 1½ mph	620
Tree felling	640
Bicycling at 13 mph	660
Running at 5 mph	850
Running at 7½ mph	975
Rowing at 33 strokes/min	1140
Swimming breaststroke at 56 strokes/min	1212
Nordic skiing (level loose snow) at 9·15 mph	1572

Women

Darning (sitting)	76
Knitting	78
Typing at 60 wpm	80
Ironing	100
Washing up	198
Bed making	420

Inflammatory conditions

The suffix -itis is the feminine form of the Greek -ites, meaning connected with. Originally, for example, carditis was termed carditis nosus, meaning the disease connected with the heart. Soon the nosus was dropped and the -itis suffix was used to indicate, more narrowly, an inflammation of a part of the body.

adenitis—lymphatic glands
appendicitis—vermiform appendix
arthritis—joints
blepharitis—eyelid
bronchitis—bronchial tubes
bursitis—bursa
carditis—heart
cephalitis—brain (not now used)
cerebritis—brain (rare)
cervicitis—neck of the uterus
cheilitis—lip
cholecystitis—gall bladder
chondritis—cartilage
colitis—colon
conjunctivitis—conjunctiva
coxitis—hip joint
cystitis—bladder
dermatitis—skin
diaphragmatitis—diaphragm
diverticulitis—diverticulae of colon
duodenitis—duodenum
encephalitis—brain
encystitis—'an encysted tumour'
endocarditis—endocardium
enteritis—bowels
entero-colitis—colon and small intestine
epididymitis—epididymis
fibrositis—fibrous tissues
gastritis—stomach
gingivitis—gums
glossitis—tongue
gnathitis—upper jaw or cheek
hepatitis—liver
hyalitis—vitreous humour of the eye
hysteritis—uterus
iritis—iris
keratitis—cornea
laminitis—part of a vertebra
laryngitis—larynx
mastitis—the breast (female)

meningitis—meninges
meningomyelitis—meninges and spinal cord
mesenteritis—mesentery
metritis—uterus
mephitis—a noxious emanation (especially from the earth)
myelitis—spinal cord
myelomeningitis—(see meningomyelitis)
myocarditis—myocardium
myositis—muscle
nephritis—kidneys
neuritis—nerves
œsophagitis—œsophagus
omphalitis—navel
oophoritis—ovary
ophthalmitis—whole eye
orchitis—testes
osteitis—bone
otitis—ear
ovaritis—ovaries
pancreatitis—pancreas
parotitis—parotid glands (e.g. mumps)
pericarditis—pericardium
periodontitis—jaw (part around the tooth)
periostitis—periosteum
peritonitis—peritoneum (or of the bowels)
perityphlitis—tissue surrounding the caecum
pharyngitis—pharynx
phlebitis—vein
phrenitis—brain (rare)
pleuritis—pleura
pneumonitis—lungs
poliomyelitis—inflammation of grey matter of spinal cord (or paralysis due to this)
pyelitis—pelvis of the kidney
rachitis—spine
rectitis—rectum
retinitis—retina
rhinitis—nose
salpingitis—salpinx
sclerotitis—sclerotic
scrotitis—scrotum
sinusitis—sinus
sphenoiditis—air cavity in the sphenoid bone
splenitis—spleen
spondylitis—vertebrae
stomatitis—mouth
synovitis—synovial membrane
tonsillitis—tonsils
tracheitis—trachea
tympanitis—ear-drum
typhlitis—caecum
ulitis—gums
ureteritis—ureter
urethritis—urethra
uteritis—womb
vaginitis—vagina
vulvitis—vulva

The Hippocratic Oath

A form of the following oath, attributed to Hippocrates (c. 460–377 BC), the Greek physician called the 'Father of Medicine', is sworn to at some medical schools on the occasion of taking a degree.

'I swear by Apollo the healer, invoking all the gods and goddesses to be my witnesses, that I will fulfil this oath and this written covenant to the best of my ability and judgement.

'I will look upon him who shall have taught me this art even as one of my own parents. I will share my substance with him, and I will supply his necessities if he be in need. I will regard his offspring even as my own brethren, and I will teach them this art, if they would learn it, without fee or covenant. I will impart this art by precept, by lecture and by every mode of teaching, not only to my own sons but to the sons of him who has taught me, and to disciples bound by covenant and oath, according to the law of medicine.

'The regimen I adopt shall be for the benefit of the patients according to my ability and judgement, and not for their hurt or for any wrong. I will give no deadly drug to any, though it be asked of me, nor will I counsel

Hippocrates

such, and especially I will not aid a woman to procure abortion. Whatsoever house I enter, there will I go for the benefit of the sick, refraining from all wrongdoing or corruption,' and especially from any act of seduction, of male or female, of bond or free. Whatsoever things I see or hear concerning the life of men, in my attendance on the sick or even apart therefrom, which ought not to be noised abroad, I will keep silence thereon, counting such things to be as sacred secrets. Pure and holy will I keep my life and my art.'

Human genetics

The normal human has 46 chromosomes. The chromosome is the microscopic thread-like body within cells which carries hereditary factors or genes. These are classified as 22 pairs of non-sex chromosomes or autosomes (one of each pair derived from the father and one from the mother) and two sex chromosomes or gonosomes, making 46. In a female both gonosomes are Xs, one from the father and one from the mother. In a male they are an X from the mother and a Y from the father. The X chromosome is much larger than the Y, thus women possess four per cent more deoxyribonucleic acid than males. This may have a bearing on their greater longevity. The human sometimes exhibits 47 chromosomes.

One such instance is the XXX female in which the supernumerary is an extra X. In some cases of hermaphroditism the supernumerary is a Y.

Chimpanzees, gorillas, and orang-outangs have 48 chromosomes. It has been suggested that man's emergence from the primitive man-ape population may have occurred by a process known as 'reciprocal translocation'. This is a mechanism whereby two dissimilar chromosomes break and two of the four dissimilar parts join with the possible net loss of one chromosome. It is possible that 47 and 46 chromosome hominoids enjoyed a bipedal advantage on forest edges over brachiating apes and thus the evolution of man began from this point.

Skin

The skin is by far the largest single organ of the human body. It weighs about 16 per cent of the total body weight and in an average adult male has a surface area of 2800 in² 18000 cm². The three main groups into which Man is divided by the colour of his skin are *Leukoderms* (white-skinned), *Melanoderms* (black-skinned) and *Xanthoderms* (yellow-skinned). Pigment-producing cells in the basal layers of the epidermis are called melanoblasts (Greek *melas*—black *blastos*—bud).

The number (up to 4000 per sq cm) and the size do not vary significantly in white and negro skin but are more active and productive in the latter so protecting the iris and the retina against the brightness of the sun.

The human brain
It is estimated that a human brain, weighing about 3 lb *1·36 kg*, contains 10 000 000 000 nerve cells. Each of these deploys a potential 25 000 interconnections with other cells. Compared with this the most advanced computers are giant electronic morons.

Sex ratio
In the United Kingdom about 1056 boys are born to every 1000 girls.

Medical and surgical specialties
There are in medicine a great number of specialties. It is possible to have Departments of Neurology, Paediatrics and Paediatric-Neurology in the same hospital. This list provides an explanation of medical departments.

Allergy—reaction of a patient to an outside substance, e.g. pollen or Penicillin, producing symptoms which may vary between being inconvenient e.g. hay fever or rashes to fatal, e.g. asthma.

Anaesthetics—the skill of putting a patient to sleep with drugs.

Anatomy—the study of the structure of the body.

Anthropology—the study of man in his environment.

Apothecary—a pharmacist or, in its old-fashioned sense, a general practitioner was once described as an apothecary.

Audiology—the assessment of hearing.

Aurology—the study of ear disease.

Bacteriology—the study of bacterial infections. This usually includes viruses as well.

Biochemistry—the study of the variation of salts and chemicals on the body.

Bio-engineering—the study of the mechanical workings of the body, particularly with reference to artificial limbs and powered appliances which the body can use.

Biophysics—the study of electrical impulses from the body. This can be seen with assessment of muscle disease etc.

Cardiology—the study of heart disease.

Community medicine—the prevention of the spread of disease and the increase of physical and mental well being within a community.

Cryo-surgery—the use of freezing techniques in surgery.

Cytogenetics—the understanding of the particles within a cell which help to reproduce the same type of being again.

Cytology—the microscopic study of body cells.

Dentistry—the treatment and extraction of teeth.

Dermatology—the treatment of skin diseases.

Diabetics—the treatment of diabetes.

Embryology—the study of the growth of the baby from the moment of conception to about the 20th week.

Endocrinology—the study of the diseases of the glands which produce hormones.

E.N.T. *see* Otorhinolaryngology

Entomology—the study of insects, moths, with particular reference to their transmission of disease.

Epidemiology—the study of epidemics and the way that diseases travel from one person to another.

Forensic medicine—the study of injury and disease caused by criminal activity and the detection of crime by medical knowledge.

Gastro-enterology—the study of stomach and intestinal diseases.

Genetics—the study of inherited characteristics, disease and malformations.

Genito-urinary disease—the study of diseases of the sexual and urine-producing organs.

Geriatrics—the study of diseases and condition of elderly people.

Gerontology—the study of diseases of elderly people and in particular the study of the ageing process.

Gynaecology—the study of diseases of women.

Haematology—the study of blood diseases.

Histochemistry—the study of the chemical environment of the body cells.

Histology—the microscopic study of cells.

Histopathology—the microscopic study of diseased or abnormal cells.

Homeopathy—is a form of treatment by administering minute doses which in larger doses would reproduce the symptoms of the disease that is being treated. The theory is that the body is thereby stimulated into coping with the problem by itself. Standard treatment by antidotes a allopathy.

Immunology—the study of the way the body reacts to outside harmful diseases and influences, e.g. the production of body proteins to overcome such diseases as diphteria or the rejection of foreign substances like transplanted kidneys.

Laryngology—the study of throat diseases.

Metabolic disease—diseases of the interior workings of the body, e.g. disorders of calcium absorption etc., thyroid disease or adrenal gland disease.

Microbiology—the study of the workings of cells.

Nephrology—the study of kidney disease.

Neurology—the study of a wide range of diseases of the brain or nervous system.

Neurosurgery—operations on the brain or nervous system.

Nuclear medicine—treatment of diseases with radio-active substances.

Obstetrics—the care of the pregnant mother and the delivery of the child.

Oncology—study of cancer.

Ophthalmology—the study of diseases of the eye.

Optician—the measurement of disorders of the lens of the eye done by a medically unqualified but trained practitioner so that spectacles can be given to correct the disorder.

Orthodontology—a dental approach to producing teeth that are straight.

Orthopaedics—fractures and bone diseases.

Orthoptics—medically unqualified but trained practitioner treatment of squints of the eye.

Orthotist—an orthopaedic appliance technician.

Otology—the study of diseases of the ear.

Otorhinolaryngology—the study of diseases of the ear, nose and throat often referred to as E.N.T.

Paediatrics—diseases of children.

Parasitology—the study of infections of the body by worms.

Pathology—the study of dead disease by *post mortem* examination either under the microscope or the whole organ.

Pharmacology—the study of the use of drugs in relation to medicine.

Physical Medicine—the treatment of damaged parts of the body with exercises, electrical treatments etc. or the preparation of the body for surgery, e.g. breathing exercises and leg exercises.

Physiology—the study and understanding of the normal workings of the body.

Physiotherapist—a trained person who works in the physical medicine department.

Plastic surgery—the reconstruction and alteration of damaged or normal parts of the body.

Proctology—the study of diseases of the rectum or back passage.

Prosthetics—the making of artificial limbs and appliances.

Psychiatry—the study and treatment of mental disease.

Psycho-analysis—the investigation of the formation of mental illness by long-term repeated discussion.

Psychology—the study of the mind with particular reference to the measurement of intellectual activity.

Psychotherapy—treatment of mental disorder

Radiobiology—the treatment or investigation of disease using radio-active substances.

Radiography—the taking of X-rays.

Radiology—the study of X-rays.

Radiotherapy—the treatment of disease with X-rays.

Renal diseases—the diseases of the kidney or urinary tract.

Rheumatology—the study of diseases of muscles and joints.

Rhinology—the study of diseases of the nose

Therapeutics—curative medicine, the healing of physical and/or mental disorder.

Thoracic surgery—surgery on the chest or heart.

Toxicology—the understanding and analysis of poisons.

Urology—the study of diseases of the kidney or urinary tract.

Vascular disease—diseases of the blood vessels.

Venereology—the study of sexually transmitted disease.

Virology—the study of virus diseases.

PRINCIPAL COMMUNICABLE DISEASES

Chicken pox (or Varicella).
Incubation period: 11–21 days. Communicable one day before to six days after rash develops. About 80 per cent of adults have had the disease. Caused by a virus which is similar, if not identical, to the virus causing shingles (*Herpes zoster*). Symptoms an initial fever of 39–40 °C (102·2–104 °F) followed by a rash of raised red papules on trunk and spreading to limbs, changing to clear vesicles and becoming purulent before forming scabs in 3–4 days. One or two 'waves' of additional vesicles may occur in the following 2–3 days. Treatment: symptomatic with bed rest, isolation and exhortation against or prevention of scratching. First described by G F Ingrassia (Italy) in 1553 but definitively differentiated from Smallpox by W Heberden (GB) (1710–1801).

Cholera
Incubation period: 1–3 days. Transmitted by water which has been contaminated by faeces. Caused by a flagellated bacterium either the classical *Vibrio cholerae* or the recent biotype El Tor, which can survive for nearly 3 weeks in warm, polluted water. Symptoms: vomiting and profuse diarrhoea of fluid, odourless stools leading to extreme dehydration and collapse. Death in 30–50 per cent of untreated cases in a population of poor nutrition. Treatment: intravenous and oral salt-containing fluids with antibiotics furazolidone or tetracycline reduces mortality to less than 3 per cent. Isolation, if this is practicable, until three rectal swabs have proved negative growth. Probably that there are 28 asymptomatic cases to each ill patient. In Britain the first epidemic was October 1831 and the last one, in Cleethorpes, in 1879. John Snow (England) 1849 first suggested it was water borne and in 1854 proved it by stopping an epidemic by removing the pump handle of a suspected well. The bacterium were first isolated by Koch (Germany) in 1883. Still endemic in the Indian subcontinent and travels in dry season to Africa and sometimes Europe. Partial protection can be obtained by immunisation with two injections of the killed Cholera organism.

Common cold (or Coryza)
Incubation period: about 48 hours. Caused by at least 40 different varieties of virus causing similar symptoms of sneezing itching eyes, running nose, headaches, sometimes slight fever and muscle aching. Treat-

Human dentition

Man normally has two sets of teeth during his life span. The primary (milk or deciduous) set of 20 is usually acquired between the ages of 6 and 24 months. The secondary (or permanent) dentition of 32 teeth grows in usually from about the sixth year.

The four principal types of teeth are:—
Incisors (Lat. *incidere*—to cut into) total eight. Two upper central, flanked by two upper lateral with four lower.
Canine (Lat. *canis*—a dog) total four. These are next to the lateral incisors and are thus the third teeth from the mid-line in each quadrant of the mouth. These are also referred to as *cuspids* (Lat. *cuspis*—a point).
Pre-Molars (Lat. *molare*—to grind) total eight. These are next in line back from the incisors, two in each quadrant. Because these have two cusps these are alternatively known as bi-cuspids.
Molars (see above) total twelve. These are the furthest back in the mouth—three in each quadrant. The upper molars often have four cusps and the lower five cusps for grinding. The third (hindermost) molars are known also as 'wisdom teeth' and do not usually appear until the age of 18 to 20.

---

ment: is symptomatic with aspirin, anti-histamines, warm room and isolation. It is probable that the adult population only develop about 1 in 10 of the cold viruses they catch. Children are much more frequently and severely afflicted.

Dengue fever

Incubation period: 5–6 days. Transmitted by the *Aedes aegypti* mosquito which remains infective throughout its life. In an epidemic in susceptible population 70–80 per cent will become infected. Symptoms: sudden onset of high fever, 41–42 °C, (105·8–107·6 °F) with excruciating muscle pain and severe headache behind eyes. Thus known as 'break-bone fever'. Temperature will settle to around 39 °C (102·2 °F) after 2–3 days when a faint rash may develop before rising again with exacerbation of symptoms to last a total of 5–7 days. This gives a typical 'saddle back' temperature chart. Treatment: is symptomatic with Aspirin and pain-killing drugs with plenty of fluid. It is often followed by 2–3 weeks of extreme lassitude and depression. First described by D Bylon (Netherlands) in Java in 1779.

Diphtheria

Incubation period: 1–7 days. Caused by *Corynebacterium diphtheriae*, first isolated by E Klebs (Germany) in 1883. Communicable for up to 4 weeks but rarely a carrier state occurs. Symptoms: sore throat, fever, obstruction of throat by membrane of dead tissue, and a toxin which can cause nerve damage, paralysis and heart weakness. Treatment: with antitoxin and antibiotics. If necessary a tracheotomy, a surgical opening in the trachea, may be done to ensure clear airway. Prevented by a course of three injections of immunising toxoid killed organism. Nationwide immunisation started in UK after 1941 when there were 1622 deaths. There were no deaths in 1972. First described by P Bretonneau (France) in 1826 who also performed the first successful tracheotomy.

Dysentery, Amoebic

Incubation period: variable for weeks or months. Caused by faecal contamination of food by *Entamoeba hystolytica* cysts which change into motile trophozoites in the large intestine. Symptoms: vary from the occasional diarrhoea to severe bloody dysentery and fever with ulceration of the bowel wall. May

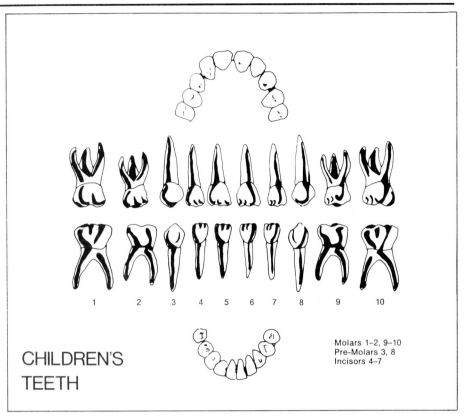

CHILDREN'S TEETH

Molars 1–2, 9–10
Pre-Molars 3, 8
Incisors 4–7

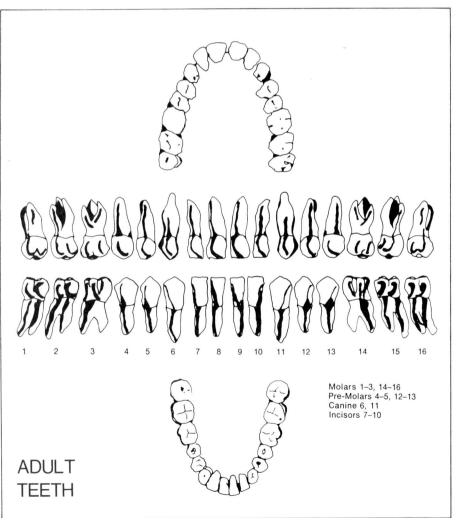

ADULT TEETH

Molars 1–3, 14–16
Pre-Molars 4–5, 12–13
Canine 6, 11
Incisors 7–10

spread to involve liver or cause peritonitis and finally strictures of the bowel. Mainly a warm climate disease and probably 10 per cent of the world are infected. A 95 per cent cure is effected with metronidazole in acute cases. Probably first described by F Lösch (Russia) in 1875.

Dysentery, Bacillary
Incubation period: 1–7 days. Caused by various kinds of *Shigella* with *Sonnei* and *Flexner* the commonest in the UK. Symptoms: the illness is worse in children. Diarrhoea with blood, mucus and abdominal colic, often with fever and vomiting. Transmitted: by food etc. contaminated by faeces and sometimes by flies. Treatment: with intestinal sedatives and in severe cases appropriate antibiotic. Patient is infective as long as organism is excreted, and this may be for months. At least three negative stool cultures should be obtained before allowing normal freedom. Bacillus first discovered by K Shiga (Japan) in 1898.

German measles (Rubella)
Incubation period: 14–21 days. Some 80 per cent of young adults have had it. Symptoms: mild feverish sore throat and then faint rash first appearing on face and spreading downwards over body. Frequently enlargement of lymph glands at back of neck and often infection may occur without a rash. Sometimes produces painful joint-swelling. Quarantine: for 5 days after onset. Congenital damage to eye, ear and heart is at least 50 per cent in first month of pregnancy and by the fourth month this has fallen to about 4 per cent, twice the expected risk. Injections of gamma globulin do not seem to give much protection. In UK injections of modified living virus are recommended to be given to all girls between the ages of 11–13, before fertile phase of life is started. First described by Wagner (Germany) in 1829.

Glandular fever
Incubation period: uncertain but probably between 4–7 weeks. Probably transmitted by saliva, hence known as the 'kissing disease'. Probably caused by Epstein-Barr virus. Symptoms: variable, mainly afflicting 15–25 age group. High fever with or without very sore throat, in large lymph glands, spleen, and often a rash. Less often jaundice and rarely nervous system involvement. Diagnosis made by white blood cells and positive Paul-Bunnell test. Many cases may be much milder. Treatment: is symptomatic with bed rest and Aspirin. Antibiotics and cortisone-type drugs are rarely needed.

Hepatitis, Viral
Two main viruses A and B. Virus A, with incubation period 2–7 weeks. Transmitted in faecal-contaminated food or water and rarely by injection. Virus B, incubation: 2–25 weeks. Transmitted mainly by injection and rarely by mouth. There is no cross-immunity between the two groups and they can be differentiated by the Australia antigen protein found in the blood of virus B infections. The mortality is very low (about 0·1 per cent) in Virus A and variable (0·5–25 per cent) in Virus B infections in patients ill enough to be in hospital. Symptoms: fever, mild indigestion, nausea and sometimes vomiting for several days, followed by an improvement with the onset of jaundice which lasts 1–2 weeks. Treatment: there is no specific treatment. Alcohol should be avoided for about 6 months. Scarring of the liver, cirrhosis, rarely occurs. Gamma globulin injections can give passive protection to contacts or those going into epidemic areas for about 3–4 months. Classical description by G Hayem (France) in 1874.

Influenza
Incubation period: 2–3 days and communicable from just before onset for about 8 days. Main epidemics usually caused by Influenza A or subvarieties A_1 (1947), A_2 (1957, Asian). Lesser epidemics by varieties of Influenza B. Symptoms: sudden onset of rigor, fever and generalised aching, sore throat and cough, lasting 5–6 days. Complication of virus pneumonia may occur and is very serious if secondary infection with *staphylococci*. Treatment: symptomatic with aspirin, bed rest, isolation and plentiful fluids. Antibiotics only given if secondary bacterial infections occur. Immunisation: 70 per cent protection can be given with injections of killed vaccine. Modified living virus nasal insufflation may give better protection. Probably first described by Caius (GB) in 1485. Earliest use of the word was by John Huxham in 1750. Highly fatal pandemics named Russian Flu 1889–92 and one named Spanish Flu April–November 1918 (deaths estimated at 21·6 million) have occurred. Pandemic of Influenza A_2, termed Asian 'Flu, was in 1957–8.

Leprosy
Incubation period: not known, but may be months or years. Mainly infectious to children unless prolonged contact in adults. Symptoms: very variable and may range from minor areas of skin anaesthesia, to muscle paralysis, skin ulceration and nerve nodules. Treatment: isolation of open cases of infectious leprosy and the use of the drug dapsone for at least two years. Plastic surgery to repair defects if necessary. Mainly occurs in tropical countries with low standards of living. Rare cases in Europe from contact in Tropics. Caused by bacillus *Mycobacterium leprae*, identified by G H A Hansen (Norway) in 1868 and first described by Aretaeus (Greece) *c.* AD 120.

Malaria
Caused by protozoa *Plasmodium* and transmitted by Anopheles mosquito. Four main kinds: *P. ovale*, *P. malariae*, *P. vivax* and *P. falciporum*. Incubation period: varies with species and may be prolonged if antimalarial drugs have been taken. Symptoms: sudden rigor and fever with variable delirium. Each species gives different course. *P. falciparum* (malignant tertian malaria) is the most dangerous as the brain (cerebral malaria), kidneys (blackwater fever) etc. may be involved and lead to sudden death. Temperature will suddenly descend to leave a period of a day or two of freedom before rising again. Treatment: with chloroquine is curative for *P. falciparum* but should be combined with primaquine for the other species. Prevention: by taking paludrine, daraprim or chloroquine for a week before and throughout and for one month after return from infectious area. Incidence in an area is reduced by destroying mosquito breeding areas, draining stagnant water etc., oil on surface and DDT sprays. Protozoa isolated by Laveran (France) in 1880 and transmission in mosquito proved by Sir Ronald Ross (GB) in 1895. Common in millions throughout the hot, humid areas of the world. Described by Hippocrates (*c.* 400 BC) and Celsus (*c.* AD 30) gave a good account of the disease.

Measles (Rubeola)
Incubation period: 8–14 days to onset of rash and infectious for 4 days before to 5 days after the onset of the rash. Caused by a virus. Symptoms: fever and catarrhal symptoms for 3–4 days when little white spots, Koplik's spots, may be noticed inside the mouth. Then blotchy red rash develops behind ears, spreads onto face and down across the body with an increase of fever. Rash fades after 3–4

days. The catarrhal cough may lead to infectious complications in ears, sinuses and chest. 1 in 1000 patients develop encephalitis and rarely a progressive brain illness, known as subacute sclerosing panencephalitis, which occurs some years later. Treatment: symptomatic during the virus stage of the illness. Secondary infections may be treated with antibiotics etc. Immunisation: can be given with a modified living virus to give prolonged, probably lifetime, protection with minimal feverish symptoms and no risk of encephalitis. 80 per cent of 20 year-olds have had the illness. Described by Rhazes (Persia) *c.* AD 900. In 1960 the UK annual rate was 300 000–600 000 and since immunisation this has fallen to around 150 000. Mortality rate in England and Wales in 1948 was 327, and in 1972 it was 29.

Meningitis, (a) Bacterial
Five commonest organisms are: *Neisseria meningitidis* (Cerebro-spinal fever), first described by Weichselbaum in 1887; *Streptococcus pneumoniae*; *Haemophilus influenzae*; *Mycobacterium tuberculosis*; *Bacillus coli* (very common in new-born infants). Symptoms: onset of fever, severe headache, neck stiffness, vomiting, alteration of level of consciousness with dislike of bright light and sometimes epileptiform fits. The speed of onset depends on the type of infection. Treatment: depends on accurate diagnosis following lumbar puncture for examination of the spinal fluid and then appropriate antibiotic. Prevention is by examination of others to exclude latent infection in throat or lungs.

Meningitis, (b) Viral
A great variety of viruses can cause meningitis and although it may be of acute onset and associated with another illness, e.g. 'flu or mumps, it is usually not severe and spontaneous recovery can be expected.

Mumps (Infectious Parotitis)
Incubation period: 10–28 days, usually about 21. Caused by a paramyxovirus which may cause a very mild or non-existent illness in 25–40 per cent of those infected. Infectious for 7 days before and for 10 days after the onset or 3 days after the last swelling has gone down, whichever is the longer. Symptoms: 4–5 days of fever and vague malaise followed by painful swelling of the salivary glands on the side of the face. They also infect the testes in up to 20 per cent of men, less commonly the ovaries of women, and rarely the genitalia in children. It may also cause meningitis, pancreatitis, or rarely deafness of one ear. Treatment: symptomatic with pain-killing drugs. Immunisation: a modified living virus vaccine has now been prepared which gives good protection. Earliest modern description by R Hamilton (GB) in 1773. Hippocrates (*c.* 400 BC) gave a good description of it.

Paratyphoid
See Typhoid. It gives a similar but milder illness and usually of shorter incubation. Caused by *Salmonella paratyphi* A, B and C. First isolated by Schottmüller (Germany) in 1900.

Plague
Incubation period: 1–6 days, rarely longer in Bubonic and rather less in Pneumonic plague. Caused by the bacillus *Pasteurella pestis*, which infects the flea, usually *Xenopsylla cheopis*, of the rat, either *Rattus rattus* or *R Norvegicus*. The rats die of the plague and the infected fleas look for new hosts. The flea faeces can infect the human either by inhalation, causing pneumonia, or through the skin when a flea bites, causing swelling

of the local lymph glands, Babos. Symptoms:
a) pneumonic; high fever of sudden onset,
severely ill and rapidly progressing to semi-
comotosed condition with copious, bloody
sputum and death in nearly 100 per cent of
untreated patients. (b) Bubonic; high fever
with extremely tender, swollen lymph glands
in the region of the flea bite which then
suppurate before the infection spreads to
further glands. A 60 per cent death rate in
untreated cases within a week. Treatment:
must be given early in the disease to prevent
death. Chloramphenicol or streptomycin
are the drugs of choice. Historically: Plague
of Justinian (AD 542), spread throughout the
Mediterranean world. Black Death (AD 1348)
which gave an estimated 75 000 000 deaths
in Western Europe. Great Plague of London
AD 1665) in which there were over 68 000
deaths. Identified by Kitasato (Japan) and
Yersin (France) independently of each other,
in 1894. Control of the disease is by killing
the rats and by a higher standard of hygiene
as well as the use of insecticides, e.g. DDT.
Plague vaccination with killed organism is
probably moderately effective.

Poliomyelitis, anterior (Infantile Paralysis)
Incubation period: 3 days to 5 weeks, usually
5–21 days. Caused by 3 similar, but different,
poliomyelitis viruses, types 1, 2 and 3.
Symptoms: in about 95 per cent of those
infected the illness is so mild as to probably
be missed. The rest may have a slight
feverish cold-like illness with muscle aching
and sometimes gastro-intestinal symptoms of
nausea and diarrhoea, lasting 2–3 days. This
may develop into varying degrees of meningitis and finally some cases will develop
paralysis of various muscle groups or be so
severe as to lead to respiratory failure and
death. Treatment: paralytic polymyelitis;
complete rest in bed, pain-killing drugs,
observations of respiration, some use of
artificial respirator if necessary. Splints to
prevent contraction deformity with careful
soft padding of afflicted limbs. After the
acute phase physiotherapy and, if necessary,
appropriate orthopaedic surgery. There is an
increased severity of the illness in muscle
groups that have been recently exerted,
locally injured, following immunising injections and also tonsillectomy. Isolation for
5 weeks as virus is excreted in faeces.
Immunisation with oral Sabin (US) 1957
vaccine containing all 3 viruses) in 3 doses in
infancy and booster later. The killed Salk
vaccine is seldom used. First described by
M Underwood (GB) in 1789. Landsteiner
(Austria) and Popper in 1909 first transmitted
the disease in monkeys. Deaths in England
and Wales in 1948 were 241 and in 1972 nil.
The illness is rare in Western Europe but
still prevalent amongst children in tropical
countries.

Rabies (Hydrophobia)
Incubation period: 10 days to over one year.
Can occur in all warm-blooded animals and is
transmitted in the saliva through broken
skin. Usually transmitted to man by rabid
dog bite but in some areas bats are principal
source of infection. Symptoms: initially fever,
malaise and abnormal sensations around the
bitten area, followed by spasms of throat
muscles, particularly when stimulated (hence
hydrophobia), and later other muscles with
interludes of maniacal behaviour. Finally
increasing paralysis and death in virtually
100 per cent of cases. Treatment: there is no
treatment of the acute case except for
sedation. If a bite is suspected to be infected,
then immediate treatment with anti-rabies
serum and a course of vaccine injections
(first given by Pasteur of France in 1885).
Historically mentioned in Eshuna Code
(2300 BC). Last recorded local infected case

in GB in 1922. Found in infected animals
throughout the world.

Scarlet fever (Scarletina)
Incubation period: 1–7 days. Due to beta-
haemolytic Streptococcus Lancefield Group
A (*Strep pyogenes*). Allied to organism
causing acute nephritis, rheumatic fever and
erysipelas. Communicable for about 10 days
or until negative throat swabs. Carriers often
occur. Symptoms: fever, sore throat, tonsillitis, red 'strawberry' tongue and then red
rash with tiny bright red spots, spreading
from face all over the body. As it fades the
skin peels. It lasts 3–4 days. Treatment:
Penicillin for 10 days. First described by G
F Ingrassia (Italy) in 1553. A hundred years
ago there were 30 000 deaths a year in GB,
now there are none, partly due to anti-biotics,
and partly due to a natural waning in organism virulence.

Shingles (Herpes zoster)
Incubation period: not known but usually
within a week of contact with chicken pox.
Von Bokay (1909) first recorded infection
from another case of shingles. Caused by
chicken pox virus infecting the sensory nerves,
usually in someone who has had chicken pox
when younger, hence occurring in an older
age group. Usually involves 1–2 nerves on one
side of the chest (50 per cent cases), but may
infect any nerve on body. Starts with mild
malaise and sometimes fever, followed by
pain in infected area with clear blisters which
become pus-containing and scab in 3–4 days.
Serious when eye is involved as healing of
scab leaves small area of anaesthesia. Sometimes scarring at nerve ends gives severe
post-herpetic neuralgia for many months.
Treatment: pain-killing drugs and recently
local application of anti-viral agent, idox-
uridine. Illness may be severe or even fatal
if patient is already debilitated with another
disease, e.g. cancer.

Smallpox (Variola)
Two forms caused by the viruses, *Variola
major*, the severer and more virulent, and
Variola minor. Incubation period: 11–13
days. Symptoms: fever, severe headache,
vomiting, severe limb pains and severe illness
with vague pink generalised rash followed by
typical rash 3 days later of red marks which
turn into little papules, turning into clear
blisters before altering into pustules, and
finally scabs, which fall off 2–3 weeks later.
It starts on face and limbs (unlike chicken pox
which is worse on trunk). May be fatal before
onset of rash. Treatment: N-methylisatin
thiosemicarbazone (marboran) reduces incidence in contacts but no specific treatment
during the illness. Rhazes c. 910 (Persia)
first differentiated it from measles. In early
18th Century enforced contact with mild
smallpox (probably *Variola minor*) gave
protection and was introduced from Con-
stantinople. In 1796 Jenner (GB) confirmed
cowpox vaccination gave protection but it
had been done sporadically before this.
Vaccination should be done on all people
going to an endemic area, principally the
Indian sub-continent, and immediately to
any contacts of the disease. Close contacts
should be isolated for 2 weeks. Free vaccination in England from 1840 and made
compulsory in 1853–68 and effectively so
from then until about 1900. In 1871–2 there
were 44 000 deaths in England and Wales.
Major form died out from 1912 and minor
form from 1935. The first year without a case
was 1941. Smallpox is still introduced into
UK by air travel and contact infection may
occur.

Syphilis—see Venereal disease

Toxoplasmosis
Infection with protozoa *Toxoplasma gondii*
by eating uncooked meat of infected animal.
Many people are infected and do not become
ill. Usually illness is a mild fever with lymph
gland swelling. Rarely it infects heart, brain,
lung etc. and can lead to local damage. In a
generalised form it can be fatal. Recovery is
expected and infection detected by special
laboratory tests. In pregnant women can
cross placenta to infect and damage embryo,
most commonly causing visual damage or
hydrocephalus. Treatment with sulphonamides, pyrimethamine (Daraprim) and
spiramycin. First identified in man by Wolf
(USA) in 1939. World-wide distribution.

Tuberculosis
Caused by *Mycobacterium tuberculosis*, either
from human or bovine source. Transmitted
either by inhalation to infect lungs, usually
from another human, or through the mouth
to infect neck or abdominal lymph glands,
usually from milk. Primary infection has
incubation of about 5 weeks and usually heals
leaving small local scar. Sometimes spreads in
blood to cause distant infection, e.g. meningitis, kidney infection or osteomyelitis. This can
lead to rapid death. Healing creates development of immunity and a positive change in
Mantoux or Heaf test skin reaction to a
solution of killed tubercule. Secondary infection, or breakdown of primary healed scar,
may occur later in life with lung damage and.
Detected by chest X-ray, sputum analysis and
Mantoux skin test. Infectious until sputum is
clear of organism. Treatment with drugs,
Isoniazid (INAH), para-amino salicylic acid
(PAS), Thiacetazone, Ethambutol, Rifampi-
cin, injections of Streptomycin in various
combinations. Surgical operation may be
done to remove seriously diseased areas, e.g.
kidney or section of lung. Bacille Calmette-
Guerin, BCG, introduced in 1906, is a very
mild form of TB and given by injection to
produce a mild primary TB infection in
Mantoux negative people to protect them
against virulent organism. Organism first
discovered by Koch (Germany) in 1882. A
disease has been found in an Egyptian
mummy from 10th Century BC. Mortality rate
in England and Wales has dropped from an
annual peak of 60 000 in the 1850s to less than
1000 in the 1970s.

Typhoid
Incubation period: 10–14 days but sometimes longer. Caused by *Salmonella typhi*,
transmitted by contaminated food and water
from an ill patient or healthy carrier of the
disease. Flies rarely transmit it. Symptoms:
usually gradual onset of fever, aching, headache and mental confusion. Then 'rose' spots
on body and increasing illness over 2 weeks
with onset of some diarrhoea and often
haemorrhage. Gradual recovery after about
3 weeks. Treatment with chloramphenicol,
ampicillin or Co-Trimazole. Carrier state in
3 per cent due to gall bladder or kidney
infection. Severity of illness can be reduced
by previously giving 2 immunising injections
with killed organism (TAB = Typhoid,
paratyphoid A and B). Untreated mortality
rate in the region of 10–15 per cent. First
described by T Willis (GB) in 1659 and
organism discovered by Eberth (Germany)
in 1880. Widal (Germany) 1896 made first
blood test to show evidence of previous or
present typhoid infection. British epidemics
in Maidstone 1897–8, Croydon, October
1937 to February 1938 (43 deaths); Aberdeen
1964 (414 cases).

Typhus
Incubation period: 10–14 days. Caused by
Rickettsia prowazeki. Carried in human louse,
Pediculus humanus, from one human to

another. Murine typhus, *R mooseri*, transmitted by rat flea, *Xenopsylla cheopsis*, gives a milder illness. Symptoms: 2–3 days malaise and then sudden onset of high fever, 40 °C (104 °F) for 10–14 days, cough, delirium and then macular rash after 5 days over body. Death in 30 per cent untreated cases. Treatment: tetracyclines or chloramphenicol cause rapid improvement if given early. First described by Fracastorius (Italy) in 1546, organism discovered by H da Rocha-Lima (Brazil) in 1916. Named in honour of two dead contempories (Ricketts and Prowazek).

VENEREAL DISEASES

The term of Venereal Disease is legally restricted to Syphilis, Gonorrhoea and Chancroid (Soft Chancre) by the Public Health (Venereal Diseases) Regulations, 1916, and the Venereal Diseases Act, 1917. In a general sense it also includes: Non-specific urethritis, lymphogranuloma venereum and granuloma inguinale. Trichomoniasis is also frequently sexually transmitted.

Chancroid (Soft Chancre)

Caused by *Haemophilus ducreyi*. First described by Ducrey (Italy) 1889. Incubation period 2–14 days. Symptoms: red papule on genitals or nearby skin which ulcerates, multiplies and spreads to cause abscesses of local lymph glands. Treatment: cured with sulphonamides, tetracyclines or streptomycin. Occurs mainly in tropical climates.

Gonorrhoea

Caused by *Neisseria gonorrhoea*. Incubation period 2–10 days, average 4 days. Symptoms: in men; purulent discharge from penis and sometimes infection of epididymis. Joint infection, septic arthritis, may occur. Later scarring may cause stricture of urethra. In women, about 50 per cent are without symptoms and the rest have vaginal discharge, urinary symptoms and abdominal pain and fever due to infection of Fallopian tubes, salpingitis. Treatment: with single large injection of Penicillin is usually effective unless organism is resistant, when another antibiotic is used. Organism first discovered by A Neisser (Germany) in 1879. Increase in England and Wales, from 17 536 in 1956 to 53 525 in 1970.

Granuloma Inguinale

Caused by *Donovania granulomatis* which forms a slightly tender nodule that ulcerates and spreads locally. Usually cured with tetracycline or streptomycin.

Lymphogranuloma venereum

Caused by a virus of the psittacosis-lymphogranuloma group and most common in tropical climates. Incubation period: 3–30 days. Symptoms: a small slight transient ulcer on genitals and then abscesses of local lymph glands (hence name of tropical or climatic bubo), with fever and gradual healing in weeks. Spread may cause arthritis and eye lesions. Treatment: sulphonamides and tetracyclines.

Non-specific urethritis (NSU)

A group of infections, probably due to viruses, but in 10 per cent due to *Trichomonas vaginalis* or *herpes genitalis*. Incubation period: 1–2 weeks but it may be months. Symptoms: seldom causing any in women but in men they may vary from a slight urethral discharge to a purulent, painful one. It may spread to cause prostatitis and sometimes Reiter's Disease in which the NSU is combined with arthritis and conjunctivitis. Treatment: 10 days of tetracycline will cure 80 per cent but frequent relapses. 10 794 cases in 1951 and 46 075 in 1970.

Syphilis

Caused by the spirochoete *Treponema pallidum*, first isolated by Schaudinn and Hoffmann (Germany) in 1905. Incubation period: 9–90 days but usually 15–30. Symptoms: primary stage is an ulcer (Hard Chancre) on infected place, usually transmitted to genitals or lips, followed by a rash (secondary stage) 6 weeks later. Then a long phase of inactivity, the latent phase, followed by swellings (gumma) of skin, bones, blood vessels etc. (tertiary stage) and in some cases progress to neuro-syphilis causing Tabes dorsalis or General Paralysis of the Insane (GPI). Diagnosis made by initial observation of organisms under microscope and later by blood tests, Wasserman (WR) or Venereal Diseases Research Laboratory (VDRL) tests. Treatment: with adequate doses of Penicillin and careful follow-up to ensure success. Probably virulent strain of syphilis came from America when Columbus returned to Palso, Spain on 15 Mar. 1493 but may have had milder form in Europe before this. In 1530 Fracastoro (Italy) wrote a poem 'Syphilis sive morbus Gallicus', from the hero of which the disease now has its name.

Trichomoniasis

Caused by protozoon *Trichomonas vaginalis*. Incubation period: 1–3 weeks in women. Symptoms: frothy, irritating vaginal discharge but rarely causes symptoms in men when it may be a form of non-specific urethritis. Treatment: first course of Metronidazole will give 90 per cent cure rate. May be associated with other venereal infections or Candida albicans (thrush). Infection may be transmitted by contaminated towels etc.

Whooping cough

Caused by *Bordetella* (Haemophilus) *pertussis*. Incubation period: 7–14 days and infectious from 7 days after the first exposure to 3 weeks after onset of symptoms. Symptoms: mild catarrh and malaise followed by cough which becomes paroxysmal, ending in typical 'whoop' and sometimes vomiting. Highly infectious. Complications of ear infections, bronchitis or pneumonia. Convulsions and coma may rarely occur and lead to permanent brain damage or death. Treatment: symptomatic. Prevention by immunising injections of killed organism has given rise to debate as to whether hazards of immunisation outweigh hazards of natural infection. First described by G de Baillou (France) in 1598 and first isolated by J Bordet and O Gengoa (France) in 1906. In 1948, in England and Wales, 748 (70 per cent under the age of 1) died of whooping cough and in 1972 only 2 children, both under 6 months, died.

Vaccines

Anthrax—a killed vaccine which is recommended for workers at particular risk, e.g. farmers, and butchers. Doses should be given yearly.

Bubonic Plague—killed and live vaccines can be used to limit epidemics. They give about six months' protection.

Cholera—two injections of the killed organism should be given 10 days apart and will give 3–6 months' protection. Thereafter injections should be given six-monthly. It only gives moderate protection.

Diphtheria—the killed organism is given in a course of 3 injections to infants and a booster dose at the age of 5 will give long-lasting immunity. Anti-toxin is used for those who have caught diphtheria. It gives temporary protection.

German Measles (Rubella)—a modified living vaccine is recommended to be given to all girls between the age of 11 and 13, i.e. before the onset of menstruation, and protect against infection of the foetus and thu congenital malformations.

Influenza—killed vaccines will give about 7 per cent protection for 9 months to a year in epidemics of a similar virus. They are particularly useful in those who tend to have respiratory illness, the infirm or elderly. Modified living virus vaccines are at present under assessment.

Measles—a modified living vaccine is given in the second year of life and will give prolonged protection and, in about 50 per cent, will produce a very mild feverish illness. It does not produce encephalitis.

Meningococcal meningitis—killed vaccines of both types A and C have been produced. They help in the prevention of the spread of epidemics.

Mumps—a modified living vaccine gives long-lasting protection. It is often used for adults who have not had the natural infection.

Poliomyelitis—Sabin modified living oral vaccine gives long-term protection. It is usually given in 3 doses to infants and a booster dose at the age of 5, and sometimes in the early teens. It rarely causes cases of clinical poliomyelitis. Salk vaccine is the killed virus and gives short-term protection. It is seldom used nowadays.

Rabies—14 consecutive daily injections of the killed virus are given into the stomach wall of those who may have been infected with the rabies virus. Newer vaccines are at present being evaluated.

Smallpox—a live vaccine gives protection for up to 5 years. The international regulations recognise a certificate lasting 3 years. It is no longer recommended to be used routinely in the United Kingdom. Outbreaks of smallpox are treated by vaccinating all those who have been in contact or close to anybody who has been in contact.

Tetanus—the killed organism is usually given in 3 injections combined with diphtheria and sometimes whooping cough. A booster dose at the age of 5 and then boosters every 5 years.

Tuberculosis—Bacille Calmette-Guerin (BCG) is a modified living organism which is given to those aged between 10 and 13 in the UK by the school health authorities. It gives lifelong immunity.

Typhoid and *Paratyphoid*—Typhoid and paratyphoid A & B (TAB) vaccine is prepared from the killed organisms. Newer vaccines contain the typhoid by itself. There is a cross-protection between typhoid and paratyphoid A & B. Two injections are given at 10 days to a month apart. These will prevent the severity of the disease but may not stop the patient catching it. Booster doses should be given yearly in areas where the infection is prevalent and every 2–3 years for those visiting these areas.

Typhus—highly effective killed vaccines will give protection for about a year.

Whooping Cough—this is usually combined with the 3 injections with diphtheria and tetanus. The present view is that it may occasionally cause damage to infants and some authorities recommend it should not be given.

Yellow Fever—a modified living vaccine will give 10 years' protection and this is recognised on an international vaccination certificate.

Bones in the human body

Skull	Number
Occipital	1
Parietal—1 pair	2
Sphenoid	1
Ethmoid	1
Inferior Nasal Conchae—1 pair	2
Frontal—1 pair, fused	1
Nasal—1 pair	2
Lacrimal—1 pair	2
Temporal—1 pair	2
Maxilla—1 pair	2
Zygomatic—1 pair	2
Vomer	1
Palatine—1 pair	2
Mandible—1 pair, fused	1
	22

The Ears	
Malleus	2
Incus	2
Stapes	2
	6

Vertebrae	
Cervical	7
Thoracic	12
Lumbar	5
Sacral—5, fused to form the Sacrum	1
Coccyx—between 3 and 5, fused	1
	26

Vertebral Ribs	
Ribs, 'true'—7 pairs	14
Ribs, 'false'—5 pairs of which 2 pairs are floating	10
	24

Sternum	
Manubrium	1
'The Body' (Sternebrae)	1
Xiphisternum	1
Hyoid	1
	4

Pectoral Girdle	
Clavicle—1 pair	2
Scapula—(including Coracoid)—1 pair	2
	4

Upper Extremity (each arm)	
Humerus	1
Radius	1
Ulna	1
Carpus:	
Scaphoid	1
Lunate	1
Triquetral	1
Pisiform	1
Trapezium	1
Trapezoid	1
Capitate	1
Hamate	1
Metacarpals	5
Phalanges:	
First Digit	2
Second Digit	3
Third Digit	3
Fourth Digit	3
Fifth Digit	3
	30

Pelvic Girdle	
Ilium, Ischium and Pubis (combined)— 1 pair of hip bones, innominate	2

Lower Extremity (each leg)	
Femur	1
Tibia	1
Fibula	1
Tarsus:	
Talus	1
Calcaneus	1
Navicular	1
Cuneiform medial	1
Cuneiform, intermediate	1
Cuneiform, lateral	1
Cuboid	1
Metatarsals	5
Phalanges:	
First Digit	2
Second Digit	3
Third Digit	3
Fourth Digit	3
Fifth Digit	3
	29

Total	
Skull	22
The Ears	6
Vertebrae	26
Vertebral Ribs	24
Sternum	4
Pectoral Girdle	4
Upper Extremity (arms)—2 × 30	60
Hip Bones	2
Lower Extremity (legs)—2 × 29	58
	206

Normal pulse rates in man

	Beats per minute
Embryo 5 months	156
6 months	154
7 months	150
8 months	142
9 months	145
Newborn (premature)	110–185
Newborn (full term)	135
2 years	110
4 years	105
6 years	95
8 years	90
10 years	87
15 years	83
20 years	71
21–25	74
25–30	72
30–35	70
35–40	72
40–45	72
45–50	72
50–55	72
55–60	75
60–65	73
65–70	75
70–75	75
75–80	72
>80	78
Lying down (adult)	66
Sitting (adult)	73
Standing (adult)	82
Sleeping (adult)	♂59 ♀65
Waking (adult)	♂78 ♀84

PHARMACOLOGY

Below are listed a selection of the most used and important drugs in medical practice. These are listed in order of the date of their introduction so that the weakness or strength of the pharmacological armoury can be seen at a glance at any point in time.

ante

800 BC *Ethyl alcohol* (C_2H_5OH). One of the earliest drugs used to stupify.

c. 1550 *Digitalis*, from the leaf of the Foxglove (*Digitalis purpurea* L.). Myocardial stimulant, used by herbalists since *c.* 1550 and introduced into scientific medicine by William Withering (GB) in 1785.

Principal drugs in order of their discovery

1805 *Morphine* (hydrochloride is $C_{17}H_{19}NO_3HCl.3H_2O$). Narcotic analgesic, an alkaloid of opium which is the dried latex from the unripe capsules of the poppy (*Papaver somniferum*). First recognised by Friedrich Sertürner (Germany) in 1805 but not used in medical practice till 1821. Not totally synthesised until 1952.

1818 *Quinine hydrochloride* ($C_{22}H_{24}N_2O_2HCl.2H_2O$). Obtained from Cinchona tree bark. Separated by P J Pelletier and J B Caventou (France) 1818 to 1820.

1819 *Atropine* ($C_{17}H_{23}NO_3$). A parasympatholytic. First isolated in 1819 by Rudolph Brandes from belladonna (*Atropa belladonna*).

1820 *Colchicine* ($C_{22}H_{25}NO_6$). Analgesic derived from meadow saffron (*Colchicum Autumnale*), used particularly in the treatment of gout. Isolated in 1820 by P J Pelletier and J B Caventou.

1821 *Codeine* or *methylmorphine* (phosphate is $C_{18}HNO_3H_3PO_4.\frac{1}{2}H_2O$). Occurs naturally in opium and is a derivative of morphine (q.v.). Antitussive, weak analgesic.

1842 *Ether* (diethyl, $(C_2H_5)_2O$). General anaesthetic. First administered by Dr C W Long (1815–78) in Jefferson, Georgia, on 30 Mar. 1842 for a cystectomy.

1844 *Nitrous Oxide* (N_2O) (Dinitrogen Monoxide, or Laughing Gas). Anaesthetic in operations of short duration as prolonged inhalation can cause death. Also used as a propellant in food aerosols. Discovered in 1776 by Joseph Priestly. First used as anaesthetic in 1844 by an American dentist, Horace Wells.

1846 *Ether* (Dimethyl ether, $(CH_3)_2O$). Crude anaesthetic known in the 13th century. Earliest reference to the name as a drug was in 1730 by F G Frobenius. First used as anaesthetic 16 Oct. 1846 by W T G Morton (USA) (1819–68) in Boston, Mass.

1846 *Glyceryl Trinitrate* (Nitroglycerin, $C_3H_5N_3O_9$). Known mainly as an explosive. Used as a vasolidator in easing cardiac pains in angina pectoris. First prepared in 1846 by Ascanio Sobrero of Italy.

1847 *Chloroform*. Introduced as an anaesthetic by Sir James Simpson (GB).

1859 *Cocaine* (from the Peruvian coca bean (*Erythroxylon coca*)). First separated by Niemann. Formula established by Wöhler in 1860.

1867 *Phenol* (Carbolic acid C_6H_5OH). Earliest germicidal disinfectant, discovered by Lister in 1867. Antiseptic and antipruritic.

1891 *Thyroid*. First use as injection in

treatment for Myxoedema by George Murray in 1891.

1893 *Aspirin* (a trade name for acetyl-salicylic acid) ($C_9H_8O_4$). An analgesic, and the earliest antiuretic. Introduced in 1893 by Hermann Dresser.

1893 *Paracetamol* (Acetaminophen) ($C_8H_9NO_2$). First used in medicine by Joseph von Mering in 1893, but only gained popularity as an analgesic and antipyretic in 1949.

1901 *Adrenaline* (epinephrine) ($C_9H_{13}NO_3$). A sympathomimetic. The active principles are secreted by the medulla of the adrenal glands of domesticated animals. A vasoconstrictor. First isolated in 1901 by J Takamine (1854–1922) and T B Aldrick and synthesised in 1904 by Friedrich Stolz (1860–1936).

1903 *Phenobarbitone* (Luminal) is 5-ethyl-5-phenylbarbituric acid ($C_{12}H_{12}N_2O_3$). A hypnotic, long-acting sedative, and anticonvulsant.

1905 *Procaine* (Novocaine) (Procain hydrochloride, $C_{13}H_{20}N_2O_2$ HCl). Local anaesthetic, introduced as a substitute for cocaine by Alfred Einhorn. Non-habit forming but low penetrating power.

1907 *Histamine* (β-iminoazolylethylamine). Isolated by Adolf Windus (1876–1959) and Karl Vogt (b. 1880). The earliest anti-histamine was 933 F discovered by G Ungar (France, et al. in 1937.

1912 *Acriflavine*. Introduced as an antiseptic by Paul Ehrlich.

1917 *Oxygen* (O). The most plentiful element in the Earth's crust. Essential to life as we know it. Discovered c. 1772 by the Swede, Carl Wilhelm Scheele and independently in 1774 by John Priestly. First used therapeutically by J S Haldane in 1917.

1921 *Ergotmetrine maleate* ($C_{19}H_{23}N_3O_2$ $C_4H_4O_4$). Used as a uterine stimulant. First isolated by K Spiro and A Stoll (Germany) in 1921. Ergot in rye grain infected with the fungus *Claviceps purpurea*.

1921 *Insulin*, the specific antidiabetic principle from the mammalian pancreas. Isolated by Sir Frederick Banting (1891–1941) and Dr C H Best (b. 1899) at Toronto, Canada, in 1921. First synthesised in 1964.

1929 *Progesterone* ($C_{21}H_{30}O_2$). Hormone secreted by female productive system. Regulates condition of inner lining of the uterus. Isolated by G Corner and W Allen in 1929.

1929 *Testosterone* ($C_{19}H_{28}O_2$). Androgenic, or masculanising, hormone. First obtained in 1929 by C Moore, T Gallagher and F Koch. Anabolic steroid used by participants in sporting activities.

1930 *Pentobarbitone Sodium* (Nembutal) ($C_{11}H_{17}N_2NaO_3$). Hypnotic; sedative.

1930 *Mepacrine* (or *quinacrine* or *atebrin*). Now replaced by Chloroquine. Antimalarial.

1933 *Adrenocorticotropic hormone* (ACTH) First isolated by J B Collip (b. 1892) et al. Active against arthritis.

1935 *Pentothal* (thiopentone sodium, $C_{11}H_{18}N_2O_2S$ + Na). Intravenous anaesthetic.

1935 *Tubocurarine chloride* ($C_{38}H_{44}Cl_2N_2O_6$). Crystalline alkaloid isolated from curare in 1935 by Harold King, used as a skeletal-muscle relaxant.

1936 *Oestradiol* ($C_{25}H_{28}O_3$). Oestrogen

isolated by D MacCorquodale in 1936.

1937 *Dapsone* ($C_{12}H_{12}N_2O_2S$). Effects in treatment of leprosy noted in 1937.

1938 *Sulphanilomide*. The sulpha drug prototype Prontosil Red was discovered in 1935 by G Domagk (1899–1964). The most used early sulpha drug was sulphapyridine (May and Baker 693), $C_{11}H_{14}N_3O_2S$ from 1937 (Dr Arthur Ewins).

1938 *Phenytoin* ($C_{15}H_{12}N_2O_2$). Anticonvulsant introduced in 1938 by Merritt and Pulman as a primary drug for all types of epilepsy except absence seizures.

1939 *DDT* (Dichloro-diphenyl-trichloro-ethane). A powerful insecticide developed by Dr Paul Müller which has vastly lowered the malarial death rate.

1939 *Pethidine hydrochloride* ($C_{15}H_{21}NO_2$, HCl). A narcotic analgesic particularly for childbirth. Introduced 1939 from Hoechst. Synthesised by Eisleb and Schaumann.

1940 *Penicillin* (penicillin G, the benzyl derivative, $C_{16}H_{17}N_2Na$(or K)O_4S). Antibiotic. Discovered in 1928 by Sir Alexander Fleming (1881–1955) by the chance contamination of a petri dish at St Mary's Hospital, London. First concentrated in 1940 by Sir Howard Florey (b. 1898) and E B Chain (b. 1906). Not identified as *Pencillium notatum* until 1930. Penicillin G introduced 1946. Ampicillin ($C_{16}H_{19}N_3O_4S$) derivative introduced later, combats typhoid fever.

1941 *Sulfadiazine* (2-(4-aminobenzene-sulphonamido) pyrimidine, $C_{10}H_{10}N_4O_2S$). A bactericide.

1943 *LSD-25*. Dextro-lysergic acid diethylamide. A hallucinogen, discovered by Albert Hofman (Switzerland) in Apr. 1943.

c. 1943 *Dimercaprol* (*BAL*) (Formerly Brtish Anti-Lewisite) ($C_3H_8OS_2$). Developed during the war by L Stocken and R Thompson, to combat lethal war gas, lewisite. Later uses discovered as antidote to poisoning by arsenic, gold or mercury.

1944 *Amphetamine* (commercial name for the sulphate is Benzedrine). Dextro-amphetamine is marketed as Dexedrine. A fatigue-inhibiting mildly addictive synthetic drug.

1944 *Streptomycin* (sulphate is ($C_{21}H_{39}N_7O_{12}$)$_2$, $3H_2SO_4$). An antibiotic discovered by S A Waksman (Russian born, USA) in 1944.

c. 1944 *Paludrine* (proguanil hydrochloride). An antimalarial drug.

1947 *Chloramphenicol* ($C_{11}H_{12}Cl_2N_2O_5$). An antibiotic from *Streptomyces venezuelae* used for treatment of typhoid. First isolated by Buckholder (USA) in 1947 and first synthesised in 1949.

1948 *Aureomycin* (*Chlortetracycline*) *Hydrochloride* ($C_{22}H_{24}N_2O_2$, HCl). An antibiotic first isolated in 1948 at Pearl River, NY, USA, by Dr Benjamin M Duggar.

1948 *Imipramine* ($C_{11}H_{24}N_2$). A dibenza-zepine derivative, synthesised by Häfliger in 1948. One of the most effective antidepressant drugs.

1949 *Cortisone Acetate* ($C_{23}H_{30}O_6$). A steroid hormone from adrenal cortical extracts so named in 1939. First used in treatment of rheumatoid arthritis in 1949.

1950 *Terramycin* (*oxytetracyline*). Discovered by the Pfizer group and

first described by A C Finlay in January 1950. Isolated from the bacterium *Streptomyces rimosis*. An antibiotic.

1951 *Halothane* ($C_2HBrClF_3$). General anaesthetic first synthesised in 1951 by Suckling. Incorporates most of the attributes of the ideal anaesthetic.

1952 *Chlorpromazine* ($C_{17}H_{19}ClN_2S$). Potent synthetic tranquilliser first synthesised by Charpentier in 1952. Acts selectively upon higher centres in brain as a central nervous system depressant.

1952 *Isoniazide* (Isotonic Acid Hydrazide-INH) ($C_6H_7N_3O$). Use in the treatment of tuberculosis reported on by Edward Robitzek in 1952.

1954 *Methyldopa* ($C_{10}H_{13}NO_4$, $1\frac{1}{2}H_2O$). Used in treatment of hypertension. Effects first noted in 1954 by Sourkes.

1954 *Reserpine* ($C_{33}H_{40}N_2O_9$). Tranquilliser from Ravwolfia, a genus of plant in the dogbane family, used in treatment of high blood pressure and hypertension. Effects noted in modern times by Kline in 1954.

1955 *Oral Contraceptives*. The first reported field studies of a pill containing synthetic hormones that prevent ovulation were those by Pincus using Enovid in 1955, in Puerto Rico.

1955 *Metronidazole* ($C_6H_9N_3O_3$). Based on discovery of Azomycin in 1955 by Nakamura. Used in treatment of trichomoniasis, and intestinal and hepatic amoebiasis.

1956 *Amphotericin B*. An antifungal antibiotic used typically. Elucidated in 1956 by Vandeputte *et al*.

c. 1958 *Chlorothiazide* ($C_7H_6ClN_3O_4S_2$). A diuretic.

1958 *P-silocybin*, a hallucinogen, synthesised in 1958 by Albert Hofman (Switzerland) from a Mexican mushroom.

c. 1960 *Tolbutamide* ($C_{12}H_{18}N_2O_3S$). Reduces blood sugar level in diabetics.

1960 *Chlordiazepoxide* ($C_{16}H_{14}ClN_3O$). Tranquilliser for treatment of anxiety and tension states, convulsive states and neuromuscular and cardiovascular disorders. Effects first noted in 1960 by Randall *et al*.

c. 1960 *Frusemide* ($C_{12}H_{11}ClN_2O_5S$). A diuretic.

1961 *Thiabendazole* ($C_{10}H_7N_3S$). Efficacy in dealing with intestinal tract infestations noted by Brown *et al* in 1961. Administered orally to rid an organism of roundworms.

1962 *6-Aminopenicillanic Acid*. Antimicrobial agent reported on by Ernst Chain in 1962.

1962–3 *Clofibrate* ($C_{12}H_{15}ClO_3$). Lowers the fatty acid and cholesetrol levels in the blood. Effects noted in 1962–3 by Thorp and Waring.

1963 *BW 33T57* (1-methylisatin-beta-thiosemicarbazone). First effective antiviral drug (smallpox) developed since 1953 by, *inter alia*, Dr D J Dauer of the Wellcome Laboratories and Dr R L Thompson.

1963 *Allopurinol* ($C_5H_4N_4O$). Used in treatment of gout, it slows rate at which body forms uric acid. Reported on by Hitchings, Elion *et al* in 1963.

1963 *Cephalosporin*, antibiotic discovered in 1945 in Sardinia by Prof Brotzu. First utilised in 1963. Developed by Sir Howard (now Lord) Florey and Glaxo Laboratories.

1963 *Ag 246* (Chlorhydrate of morpholino-ethyl-2 methyl 4 phenyl-6 pyridazone 3) an analgesic discovered by Dr Henri Laborit (France).

1963 *Diazepam* ($C_{16}H_{13}ClN_2O$). Compounds of this type initially synthesised in 1933. Introduced into USA in 1963 as tranquilliser for anxiety and tension states, and as aid in preoperative and postoperative sedation.

1964 *Tolnaftate*, an anti-fungal agent announced October 1964. Highly effective against epidermiphytosis (athlete's foot) which infected some 40 per cent of adult males in USA.

1965 *Ambilhar* 1(5-nitro-2-thiazolyl)-2-imidazolidinone. Discovered 1961 (announced December 1965) by Dr Paul Schmidt of CIBA, Basle. Treatment of debilitating liver-infestation disease Bilharzia (250 million world incidence).

1966 *Protopam* (Proprietory name for Pralidoxime Chloride)($C_7H_9ClN_2O$). Antidote for pesticide poisoning by the phosphate esters.

1966 *Tromethamine* ($C_4H_{11}NO_3$). A diuretic. Counteracts systemic acidosis which sometimes complicates surgery. Introduced in USA in 1966.

1967 *Nitrazepam* (Trade name—Mogadon) ($C_{15}H_{11}N_3O_3$). Tranquilliser and hypnotic.

1967 *Levodopa* (L-Dopa) ($C_9H_{11}NO_4$). Reported on by Cotzias and others in 1967. Used in treatment of Parkinson's Disease.

1968 *Propranolol* (A β-adrenergic blocking drug ($C_{16}H_{21}NO_2$). Affects rate and rhythm of the heart and may be helpful in angina pectoris.

Average height and weight at birth

	Boys			Girls		
	Length	Weight		Length	Weight	
Nationality	in ins	lb	oz	in ins	lb	oz
British	20·1	7	6·4	20·0	7	4·8
German	20·0	7	11·2	19·8	7	4·8
Swiss	20·0	7	4·8	19·7	6	12·8
USA (White)	19·9	7	12·8	19·7	7	9·6
Japanese	19·7	6	11·5	19·4	6	8·6
French	19·6	6	12·8	19·3	6	12·8
USA (Negro)	19·5	7	1·6	19·1	6	12·8
Russia	19·1	7	8	19·1	7	4·8
China	18·9	6	12·8	18·9	6	9·6
Africa (Pygmy)	18·0	7	14·4	18·2	8	3·2

In humans the musclature normally accounts for some 40 per cent of the total bodyweight. There are 639 named muscles in the human anatomy.

Vitamins

Vitamins		Deficiency Symptoms	Natural Sources	Requisite Adult Daily Dosage mg = milligram
A	axerophthol	nyctalopia (night blindness), xerophthalmia, cornification of the epithelial tissue, stunting of growth	dairy produce, fish-liver oils, carotene	1500 mg mixed carotene and Vitamin A alcohol, or 2250 mg carotene
B_1	aneurin or thiamine	beriberi, impaired metabolism of carbohydrate	meat, yeast, eggs, cereal germ, pulses	1 mg
B_2	riboflavin	ariboflavinosis, cheilitis, glossitis, angular stomatitis	yeast, eggs, cereal germ, pulses, milk cheese	1·8 mg
B_6	pyridoxal, pyridoxamine and pyridoxine	severe reddening and erosion of the skin convulsions in infants	rice, maize and yeast	
B_{12}	cyanocobalamin	inability to absorb causes pernicious anaemia (found in vegans)	meat, liver, kidney	Total requirement <3 mg
C	ascorbic acid	scurvy	fruit and vegetables	30 mg
D	calciferol	rickets in infants, osteomalacia in adults	fish-liver oils, egg yolk, milk, butter, cheese	150 mg (unless synthesised from sunshine)
K	phylloquinone	blood fails to clot in bleeding	normally synthesised in the intestine	
M	folacin (folic acid or pteroyglutamic acid)	inability to absorb causes macrocytic anaemia	yeast, liver, cheese, fruit, vegetables	c. 100 mg
PP	(pellagra preventive) nicotinic acid (niacin)	pellagra, intestinal disorders, dermatitis, mental disturbance	yeast, meat, liver, cereal germ	10 mg

Notes:
The term vitamin A_2 has been used for axerophthol from fresh-water fish-liver oils.
Vitamin B_3 is a name given to pantothenic acid; B_4 to a mixture of arginine, glycine and cystine; B_5 is now presumed to be indentical to B_6 ($C_8H_{11}O_3N$), B_7, B_8 and B_9 never existed; B_{10} and B_{11} (variously known as Vitamin T or torulitine) now known to be a mixture of Vitamins B_{12} and M.
Vitamin B_{12} was first isolated by Glaxo Laboratories in May 1948. Its ultra complex structure ($C_{53}H_{86}O_{13}N_{14}PCo$) has defied synthesis.
Vitamin D commercially synthesised by ultra-violet irradiation of ergosterol is sometimes termed Vitamin D_2, and was first manufactured at Evansville Indiana, USA in 1927.
Vitamin D naturally formed subcutaneously by sunlight is sometimes termed Vitamin D_3. Formula is $C_{28}H_{44}O$.
A deficiency of a substance termed Vitamin E was believed to contribute to human infertility. First reported in 1922, first isolated (as .α Tocopherol) in 1935.
Vitamin F is an obsolete name for unsaturated fatty acids (linoleic, linolenic and arachidonic), a deficiency of which causes no known symptoms.
Vitamin H or biotin is not now regarded as a human vitamin.
Vitamin L was once regarded as essential to proper human lactation.
Vitamin P (citrin or rutin) is no longer considered a dietary essential.
Vitamin T or torulitine, see Vitamin B_{12} above.

PHOBIAS

Acerophobia	Sourness
Acrophobia	Sharpness (pinnacles)
Agoraphobia	Open spaces
Aichurophobia	Points
Ailourophobia	Cats
Akousticophobia	Sound
Algophobia	Pain
Altophobia	Heights
Amathophobia	Dust
Ancraophobia	Wind
Androphobia	Men
Anginophobia	Narrowness
Anglophobia	England or things English
Anthropophobia	Human beings
Antlophobia	Flood
Apeirophobia	Infinity
Apiphobia	Bees
Arachnophobia	Spiders
Asthenophobia	Weakness
Astraphobia	Lightning
Atephobia	Ruin
Atelophobia	Imperfection
Aulophobia	Flute
Auroraphobia	Auroral lights
Bacilliphobia	Microbes
Barophobia	Gravity
Bathophobia	Depth
Batophobia	Walking
Batrachophobia	Reptiles
Belonephobia	Needles
Bibliophobia	Books
Blennophobia	Slime
Brontophobia	Thunder
Carcinophobia	Cancer
Cardiophobia	Heart condition
Chaetophobia	Hair
Cheimatophobia	Cold
Chionophobia	Snow
Chrometophobia	Money
Chromophobia	Colour
Chronophobia	Duration
Claustrophobia	Enclosed spaces
Clinophobia	Going to bed
Cnidophobia	Stings
Coprophobia	Faeces
Cryophobia	Ice, frost
Crystallophobia	Crystals
Cymophobia	Sea swell
Cynophobia	Dogs
Demophobia	Crowds
Demonophobia	Demons
Dendrophobia	Trees
Dermatophobia	Skin
Dikephobia	Justice
Doraphobia	Fur
Eisoptrophobia	Mirrors
Elektrophobia	Electricity
Eleutherophobia	Freedom
Enetephobia	Pins
Entomophobia	Insects
Eosophobia	Dawn
Eremitophobia	Solitude
Ergophobia	Work
Erythrophobia	Blushing
Gallophobia	France or things French
Gametophobia	Marriage
Genophobia	Sex
Germanophobia	Germany or things German
Geumatophobia	Taste
Graphophobia	Writing
Gymnophobia	Nudity
Gynophobia	Women
Haematophobia	Blood
Haptophobia	Touch
Harpaxophobia	Robbers
Hedonophobia	Pleasure
Hippophobia	Horses
Hodophobia	Travel
Homichlophobia	Fog

Hormephobia	Shock
Hydrophobia	Water (see also Rabies p. 39)
Hygrophobia	Dampness
Hypegiaphobia	Responsibility
Hypnophobia	Sleep
Hypsophobia	High place
Ideophobia	Ideas
Kakorraphiaphobia	Failure
Katagelophobia	Ridicule
Kenophobia	Void
Kinesophobia (Kinetophobia)	Motion
Kleptophobia	Stealing
Koniphobia	Dust
Kopophobia	Fatigue
Kyphophobia	Stooping
Lalophobia	Speech
Limnophobia	Lakes
Linonophobia	String
Logophobia	Words
Lyssophobia	Insanity
Maniaphobia	Insanity
Mastigophobia	Flogging
Mechanophobia	Machinery
Mettallophobia	Metals
Meteorophobia	Meteors
Monophobia	One thing
Musophobia	Mice
Musicophobia	Music
Mysophobia	Dirt
Myxophobia	Slime
Necrophobia	Corpses
Negrophobia	Negroes
Nelophobia	Glass
Neophobia	New
Nephophobia	Clouds
Nosophobia	Disease
Nyctophobia	Darkness
Ochophobia	Vehicles
Odontophobia	Teeth
Oikophobia	Home
Olfactophobia	Smell
Ommetaphobia	Eyes
Oneirophobia	Dreams
Ophiophobia	Snakes
Ornithophobia	Birds
Ouranophobia	Heaven
Panphobia (Pantophobia)	Everything
Parthenophobia	Young girls
Pathophobia	Disease
Patroiophobia	Heredity
Peccatophobia	Sinning
Pediculophobia	Lice
Peniaphobia	Poverty
Phagophobia	Swallowing
Phasmophobia	Ghosts
Pharmacophobia	Drugs
Phobophobia	Fears
Phonophobia	Speaking aloud
Photophobia	Strong light
Pnigerophobia	Smothering
Pogonophobia	Beards
Poinephobia	Punishment
Polyphobia	Many things
Potophobia	Drink
Pteronophobia	Feathers
Pyrophobia	Fire
Russophobia	Russia or things Russian
Rypophobia	Soiling
Satanophobia	Satan
Sciophobia	Shadows
Selaphobia	Flashes
Siderophobia	Stars
Sinophobia	China or things Chinese
Sitophobia	Food
Spermophobia (Spermatophobia)	Germs
Stasophobia	Standing
Stygiophobia (Hadephobia)	Hell
Syphilophobia	Syphilis
Tachophobia	Speed
Taphophobia	Burial alive

Teratophobia	Monsters
Terdekaphobia	Number thirteen
Thaasophobia	Sitting idle
Thalassophobia	Sea
Thanatophobia	Death
Theophobia	God
Thermophobia	Heat
Thixophobia	Touching
Tocophobia	Childbirth
Toxiphobia	Poison
Traumatophobia	Wounds, injury
Tremophobia	Trembling
Trypanophobia	Inoculations, injections
Xenophobia (Zenophobia)	Foreigners
Zelophobia	Jealousy
Zoophobia	Animals

Art

Painting

Painting is the visual and aesthetic expression of ideas and emotions in two dimensions, using colour, line, shapes, texture and tones.

Palaeolithic art	24 000–1500 BC	Cave painting of the Perigordian (Aurignacian period) and the later Solutrean and Magdalenian periods (18 000–11 000 BC) first discovered at Chaffaud, Vienne, France in 1834. Lascoux examples discovered 1940. Cave painting also discovered in Czechoslovakia. the Urals, USSR, India, Australia (Mootwingie dates from c. 1500 BC) and North Africa (earliest is from the Bubulus period in the Sahara *post* 5400 BC).
Ancient near east	6000–3200 BC	Catal Hüyük, Analolin wall paintings.
Egyptian art	3100–341 BC	Covering the Protodynastic period of the 1st Dynasty (3100–2890 BC) to that of the 30th Dynasty (378–391 BC). Neither primitive nor Western.
Greek art	2000 BC	Minoan frescoes and Kamares painted pottery till 1700 BC. Mycenaean period ended c. 1100 BC. Black figure painting in Athens. Zenith c. 550 BC. Hellenistic period 320–150 BC.
Roman art	750 BC–400 AD	Inherited Hellenistic or late Greek influence and the realistic Etruscan form. Pompeian painting c. 150 BC–70 AD.
Early Christian	200 AD	Funerary fresco painting in the Roman catacombs ended with Constantine.
Byzantine art		The Zenith occurred in the 9th–12th centuries.
Migration period	150–1000	A general term covering the art of the Huns with strong Asian influence and the Revised post-Roman Celtic art in Ireland and Britain, the pre-Carolingian Frankish art and the art of the Vikings.
Romanesque art	1000–1125	A period of childish exaggeration of expressive detail and general naivety in Europe.
Gothic art	1125–1450	Originally confined to a style of architecture but now applied to the contemporary decorative arts.
The Renaissance period	1435–1545	Literally meaning a rebirth of forms centred in former classical styles and nurtured in Northern Italy. The High Renaissance faded with the emergence of Mannerism.
The Baroque	1600–1720	The word is seemingly derived from the word for 'strange', *barocco*. Noted for ceiling paintings and landscapes of illusionism with mythological figures.
The Rococo	1699–1750	The genre of elegance yet theatricality.
Neo-classical period	1750–1850	A period of great variation but conscious visual awareness of antique classical forms particularly illustrative of moral rectitude.
Romantic period	1785–1835	An artist-based school of visual literacy less concerned with craftsmanship than with intellectualism.
Realism	1845–1870	The period of representation of the real and existing things and persons including the belief in the validity of what is ugly.
Pre-Raphaelite	1848–1856	A brotherhood of 8 London artists formed to make a 'child-like reversion' to the careful pre-Renaissance Italian forms as a protest against the frivolity of the prevailing English School of the day.
Impressionism	1875–1886	The term was inadvertently introduced by Monet in seeking a description for his unrecognisable view of Le Havre (1873). Stress on speed and painting *plein air*.
20th century forms		
Expressionism	1900	A style occupying the narrow fiery no mans land between the banal and the alienated.
Cubism	1907	Invented by Picasso (1881–1973) and Braque (1882–1963) a style in which the subject is dislocated by being conceived from several aspects.
Abstract art	1909	A rejection of any recognisable form of reality and a reliance on form, colour, texture and line.
Constructivist	1920	A term coined in Moscow by Tatlin and used, after the Revolution, of the school contending that art must be 'useful' rather than solely aesthetic. Lenin supported a 'Realism' idealising 'The Worker'.
Surrealist	1924	Painting in the exploration of the sub-conscious.

Media

Tempera	Dry pigment *tempered* with an emulsion of oil, water and egg-yolk dating from early Egyptian art.
Fresco	From the Italian *freco*, fresh, i.e. painting directly onto a wall or ceiling. The oldest of methods used in Palaeolithic art reached its Zenith in 16th Century Italy.
Oil	Mixing dry powdered pigment with refined linseed oil. First used as a fine-art medium by Hubert Van Eyck (d. 1426), who was significantly formerly a book-illustrator. Applied with hog-bristle brushes.
Water colour	Pigments are ground with gall and gum arabic and thinned in use with water. The technique was used as early as 1503 by Albrecht Dürer but did not achieve widespread use until the emergence of the English School of water-colourists in the first half of the 19th century. Applied with squirrel or sable brushes on white

	or tinted paper.
Gouache	Quick-drying poster paint with a mat finish and the elimination, if desired, of brush strokes.
Acrylic resin	A quick-drying waterproof colour-fast emulsion, which can be built up by a spatula to opaque impastos or thinned to a translucent glaze. Available in intense and fluorescent colours suitable for op art.
Ink	The return of Oriental art. Ground gum-bound carbon applied with badger, goat or wolf hair usually on silk or paper.

The world's most renowned painters with famous examples of their Masterpieces

AUSTRIA
KOKOSCHKA, Oskar (1886–) 'View of the Thames'

BELGIUM
BREUGEL, Pierre 'The Elder' (c. 1525–69) 'Massacre of the Innocents', 'Children's Games'.
BREUGEL, Pierre 'The Younger' (c. 1564–1638) 'Visit to the Farm'.
BREUGEL, Jan 'de Velours' (1568–1625) 'The Garden of Eden'.
JORDAENS, Jacob (1593–1678) 'The Bean-King'.
RUBENS, Pierre-Paul (1577–1640) 'Venus and Adonis'.
TENIERS, David 'The Younger' (1610–90) 'Peasants Playing Bowls'.
VAN DER WEYDEN, Rogier (c. 1400–64) 'Deposition', 'The Magdalen'.
VAN DYCK, Antoine (1599–1641) 'Charles I of England'.
VAN EYCK, Hubert (c. 1370–c. 1426) 'Ghent Altarpiece'.
VAN EYCK, Jan (c. 1390–1441) 'Madonna with Chancellor Rollin'.

FRANCE
ARP, Hans (Jean) (1887–1966) 'Flower Hammer'.
BONNARD, Pierre (1867–1947) 'The Window'.
BOUCHER, François (1703–70) 'Diana Bathing'.
BRAQUE, Georges (1882–1963) 'Head of a Woman'.
CÉZANNE, Paul (1839–1906) 'Mont Sainte-Victoire', 'Bathers'.
CHAGALL, Marc (1887–) 'I and the Village', 'Calvary'.
CHARDIN, Jean-Baptiste Siméon (1699–1779) 'The Skate'.
COROT, Jean-Baptiste Camille (1796–1875) 'Le Lac de Terni', 'The Dell'.
DAUMIER, Honoré (1808–79) 'The Third-Class Carriage'.
DAVID, Louis (1748–1825) 'The Rape of the Sabines'.
DEGAS, Edgar (1834–1917) 'La Danseuse au Bouquet'.
DELACROIX, Eugène (1798–1863) 'The Massacre of Chios'.
DUCHAMP, Marcel (1887–1968) 'Nude Descending a Staircase'.
FOUQUET, Jehan (Jean) (c. 1420–c. 80) 'Étienne Chevalier with St. Stephen'.
FRAGONARD, Jean-Honoré (1732–1806) 'The Love Letter', 'Baigneuses'.
FROMENT, Nicolas (c. 1435–84) 'The Rising of Lazarus', 'Virgin of the Burning Bush'.
GAUGUIN, Paul (1848–1903) 'Ia Orana Marie (Hail Mary)'.
INGRES, Jean-Auguste Dominique (1780–1867) 'Odalesque'.
MANET, Édouard (1823–83) 'In a Boat', 'Déjeuner sur l'Herbe'.
MATISSE, Henri (1869–1954) 'Odalesque', 'La Luxe'.
MILLET, Jean-François (1814–75) 'Man with the Hoe'.
MONET, Claude (1840–1926) 'Rouen Cathedral', 'Water-lilies'.
RENOIR, Pierre Auguste (1841–1919) 'Luncheon of the Boating Party'.
ROUSSEAU, Henri (1844–1910) 'The Dream', 'Flowers'.
SEURAT, Georges (1859–91) 'Sunday Afternoon on the Grande Jatte'.
TOULOUSE-LAUTREC, Henri de (1864–1901) 'At the Moulin Rouge'.
UTRILLO, Maurice (1883–1955) 'Sacred-Heart and Montmartre Square'.
WATTEAU, Antoine (1684–1721) 'The Embarkation for Cythera'.

GERMANY
CRANACH, Lucas 'The Elder' (1472–1553) 'Venus', 'Rest on Flight into Egypt'.
DÜRER, Albrecht (1471–1528) 'The Four Apostles', 'Apocalypse'.
HOLBEIN, Hans 'The Elder' (c. 1465–1524) 'Weingarten Altarpiece'.
HOLBEIN, Hans 'The Younger' (1497–1543) 'Henry VIII', 'The Ambassadors'.
MENGS, Anton Raphael (1728–79) 'Parnassus with Apollo and the Muses'.
OVERBECK, Johann Friedrich (1789–1869) 'The Rose Miracle of Mary'.

GREAT BRITAIN
BURNE-JONES, Sir Edward (1833–98) 'The Golden Stairs'.
CONSTABLE, John (1776–1837) 'The Hay Wain'.
GAINSBOROUGH, Thomas (1727–88) 'Blue Boy'.
HOGARTH, William (1697–1764) 'The Orgy (Rake's Progress)', 'Marriage à la Mode'.
HUNT, William Holman (1827–1910) 'The Lady of Shallot'.
JOHN, Augustus Edwin (1878–1961) 'Decorative Group'.
KNELLER, Sir Godfrey (c. 1646–1723) 'John Dryden'.
LANDSEER, Sir Edwin (1802–73) 'The Old Shepherd's chief Mourner', 'Shoeing'.
LELY, Sir Peter (1618–80). 'Comtesse de Gramont'.
MILLAIS, Sir John Everett (1829–96) 'The Sower'.
RAEBURN, Sir Henry (1756–1823) 'Sir John Sinclair'.
REYNOLDS, Sir Joshua (1723–92) 'Mrs Siddons as the Tragic Muse', 'The Three Graces'.
ROSSETTI, Dante Gabriel (1828–82) 'Death of Lady Macbeth'.
SISLEY, Alfred (1839–99) 'Flood at Port Marly'.
TURNER, John Mallord William (1775–1851) 'The Grand Canal, Venice'.

ITALY
BELLINI, Giovanni (c. 1429–1516) 'Pieta', 'Coronation of the Virgin', 'Feast of the Gods'
BOTTICELLI, Saidro (Alessandro di Mariano Filipepi) (1444–1510) 'Birth of Venus', 'Mystic Nativity'.

The Gravenor Family as painted by Gainsborough

CANALETTO, Giovanni Antonio (Canale) (1697–1768) 'Venice: A Regatta on the Grand Canal'.
CARAVAGGIO, Michelangelo Merisi (1573–1610) 'David with Goliath's Head', 'St Matthew'.
CORRÈGGO, Antonio (Allegri) (c. 1489–1534). 'Antiope', 'Jupiter and Io'.
FRANCESCA, Piero della (c. 1410–92) 'Duke of Urbino'.
FRA ANGELICO, Giovanni da Fiesole (1387–1455) 'Annunciation'.
FRA FILIPPO LIPPI (c. 1406–69) 'Adoration of the Child'.
GIOTTO DI BONDONE (c. 1266–1337) 'Pieta'.
GIORGIONE, Giorgio da Castelfranco (c. 1477–1510) 'Sleeping Venus'.
LEONARDO DA VINCI (1452–1519) 'Mona Lisa (La Gioconda)'.
MICHELANGELO, Buonarroti (1475–1564) 'Creation of Adam'.
MODIGLIANI, Amadeo (1884–1920) 'Portrait of Madame Zboroski',
RAPHAËL, Sanzio (Raffaello Santi) (1483–1520) 'Sistine Madonna'.
TIEPOLO, Giovanni Battista (Giambattista) (1690–1770) 'The Finding of Moses'.
TINTORETTO, Jacopo (Robusti) (c. 1518–94) 'Last Supper'.
TITIAN (Tiziano Vecelli) (c. 1490–1576) 'The Tribute Money', 'Assunta'.
VÉRONÈSE, Paulo (Calliari) (1528–88) 'Marriage at Cana'.

NETHERLANDS
BOSCH, Jérôme (Heronymus van Allen) (c. 1450–1516) 'Christ Crowned with Thorns', 'Garden of Earthly Delights'.
HALS, Frans (c. 1580–1666) 'Laughing Cavalier'.
HEEMSKERCK, Maerten van (1498–1574) 'St Luke Painting the Virgin'.
HOOCH, Pieter de (1629–84) 'An Interior'.
MONDRIAN, Piet (1872–1944) 'Composition'
REMBRANDT, Harmensz van Rijn (1606–69) 'The Night Watch', 'The Anatomy Lesson'.
RUISDAEL, Jacob van (c. 1628–c. 82) 'View of Haarlem',
VAN GOGH, Vincent (1853–90) 'Wheat Field and Cypress Trees'.
VERMEER, Jan (1632–75) 'Young Woman with a Water Jug'.

NORWAY
MUNCH, Edvard (1863–1944) 'Dance of Death'.

SPAIN
DALI, Salvador (1904–) 'Crucifixion'.
EL GRECO (Domenikos Theotokopoulos) (c. 1540–1614) 'The Burial of Count Orgaz', 'View of Toledo'.
GOYA, Francisco de (1746–1828) 'The Naked Maja'.
MURILLO, Bartolomé Esteban (1618–82) 'Virgin and Child'.
PICASSO, Pablo Ruiz Blasco (1881–1973) 'Guernica', 'Les Demoiselles d'Avignon'.
RIBERA, Josede (c. 1588–1652). 'The Martyrdom of St Bartholomew'.
VELÁZQUEZ, Diego (1599–1660). 'Maids of Honour'.

SWITZERLAND
KLEE, Paul (1879–1940) 'Twittering Machine'.

UNITED STATES OF AMERICA
AUDUBON, John James (1785–1851) 'Birds of America'.
MOSES, Grandma (Anna Mary Robertson) (1860–1961), 'The Thanksgiving Turkey'.
POLLOCK, Jackson (1912–56) 'Autumn Rhythm'.
ROTHKO, Mark (1903–70) 'Green on Blue'.
WHISTLER, James Abbott McNeil (1834–1903) 'Arrangement in Grey and Black—The Artist's Mother'.

Raphael's Madonna and Child enthroned with Saints Catherine, Peter, Cecilia, Paul and the Infant St John the Baptist. (Metropolitan Museum of Art)

The Dance

Dancing is the art of rhythmic body movement, usually to music, to express an emotion or an idea or to narrate a theme or for the delight in movement and the exercise it provides.

A chronology of modern western and African dance forms.

Ballet comique	1581	Queen Catherine of France's promotion from Italy.
Ballet systématique	c. 1660	Five classic positions; first history published 1682. Ballets Russes by Diaghilev, Paris 1909
Waltz	c. 1770	Of southern German and Austrian origin as the *Dveher* or landler; Viennese operatic debut 1787; arrived in England 1812.
Cancan	c. 1835	High kicking exhibitionist female dance of Parisian origin originally in $\frac{4}{4}$ time to quadrille music.
Polka	1843	Bohemian folk courtship dance (3 quick steps and a hop in $\frac{2}{4}$ time) introduced to Paris.
Cakewalk	1872	American negro satire dance adapted in ballrooms c. 1900. Named from contest prizes of decorated cakes.
Eightsome Reel	1875	Eightsome minuets where recorded in 1795.
Samba	1885	Brazilian negro dance.
Quickstep	1900	Earliest reference.
Tango	1907	Earliest contest in Nice, France; first English use 1913.
Foxtrot	1915	Mixed quick and slow steps, walking and chasses in sincopatist $\frac{9}{4}$ allegedly named after Harry Fox (US).

Rumba (or Rhumba)	1923	Cuban negro dance.
Charleston	1923	Side kick from the knee named after Mack and Johnson song 'Charleston' after the South Carolina town.
Black Bottom	1926	First recorded in New York Times on 19 Dec. of this year.
Conga	1935	Latin American form of an African single file dance of three steps forward followed by a kick.
Mambo	1948	An off-beat rumba also of Cuban origin.
Modern Discothèque style	1951	Word coined for clubs with solely recorded music in Paris.
Rock n' Roll	1953	Heavy beat with simple melody entered mainstream of popular music and dance.
Cha cha cha	1954	Latin American variation on the Mambo.
Go Go	1965	Repetitious dance of verve often exhibitionist.
Reggae	1969	Strong accentuations off-beat.

Music

ORCHESTRAL INSTRUMENTS

(Woodwinds 1–10; Brass 11–14; Percussion 15–23; Strings 24–29; Keyboard 30–33)

Name (earliest concerto)	Earliest orchestral use	History
1 Piccolo or Octave Flute (Vivaldi, c. 1735)	1717 (Handel's Water Music)	Name 'piccolo' dates from 1856, but the origin goes back to prehistory via flute and sopranino recorder.
2 Recorder or Flûte-a-bec (c. 1690)	c. 1690	Earliest written mention 1388.
3 Flute—transverse or cross-blown (Vivaldi, c. 1729)	1672 (Lully)	Prehistoric; the modern Boehm flute dates from 1832.
4 Oboe (Marcheselli, 1708)	1657 (Lully's L'amour malade)	Originated Middle Ages in the schalmey family. The name comes from Fr. hautbois (1511) = loud wood.
5 Clarinet (Vivaldi, c. 1740?)	1726 (Faber: Mass)	Developed by J C Denner (1655–1707) from the recorder and schalmey families.
6 Cor anglais (J M Haydn, c. 1775?)	1760 (in Vienna)	Purcell wrote for 'tenor oboe' c. 1690: this may have originated the name English Horn.
7 Bass Clarinet	1838 (Meyerbeer's Les Huguenots)	Prototype made in 1772 by Gilles Lot of Paris. Modern Boehm form from 1838.
8 Bassoon (Vivaldi, c. 1730?)	c. 1619	Introduced in Italy c. 1540 as the lowest of the double-reed group.
9 Double Bassoon	c. 1730 (Handel)	'Borrowed' from military bands for elemental effects in opera.
10 Saxophone (Debussy's Rhapsody, 1903)	1844 (Kastner's Last King of Judah)	Invented by Adolphe Sax, c. 1840.
11 Trumpet (Torelli, before 1700)	c. 1800 (keyed) 1835 (valved, in Halévy's La Juive)	The natural trumpet is of pre-historic origin; it formed the basis of the earliest orchestras.
12 Trombone (Wagenseil, c. 1760)	c. 1600 (as part of bass-line)	From Roman buccina or slide-trumpet, via the mediaeval sack-but to its modern form c. 1500.
13 Horn (Bach, 1717–23, or Vivaldi)	1639 (Cavalli)	Prehistoric. The earliest music horns were the German helical horns of the mid-16th century. Rotary valve horn patented in 1832.
14 Tuba (Vaughan Williams, 1954)	1830 (Berlioz' Symphonie Fantastique)	Patented by W Wieprecht and Moritz, Berlin, 1835.

15 Timpani/Kettle drum (Milhaud, 1929)	1607 (Monteverdi's *Orfeo*)	Originated in the ancient Orient.
16 Bass Drum	1748 (Rameau's *Zaïs*)	As timpani.
17 Side or Snare drum	1749 (Handel's *Fireworks Music*)	Derived from the small drums of prehistory, via the Mediaeval tabor. Achieved its modern form in the 18th century.
18 Tenor Drum	1842	
19 Tambourine	1820	Dates back to the mediaeval Arabs; prototype used by Assyrians and Egyptians. Earliest use of the word 1579.
20 Cymbals	1680 (Strungk's *Esther*)	From Turkish military bands of antiquity.
21 Triangle	1777 (J M Haydn's *Zaïre*)	As cymbals.
22 Xylophone	1873 (Lumbye's *Traumbilder*)	Primitive; earliest 'art' mention 1511.
23 Gong or Tam tam	1791 (Gossec's *Funeral March*)	Originating in the ancient Far East.
24 Glockenspiel	1739 (Handel's *Saul*)	Today strictly a keyboard instrument, in the 19th century the metal plates were struck by hand-held hammers. The original instrument dates from 4th century Rome.
25 Violin Torelli, 1709)	*c.* 1600	Descended from the Lyre via the 6th century crwth, rebec and fiddle. Modern instrument of Lombardic origin *c.* 1545. The words violin and fiddle derive ultimately from Roman *vitulari*.
26 Viola (Giranek or Telemann, 'before 1762')	*c.* 1600	As violin.
27 Violoncello (Jacchini, 1701)	*c.* 1600	As violin.
28 Double bass (Vaňhal, *c.* 1770)	*c.* 1600	Developed alongside the violin family, but is a closer relative to the bass viol or Violone.
29 Harp (Handel, 1738)	*c.* 1600	Possibly prehistoric: attained its modern form by 1792.
30 Vibraphone	1934	First used in dance bands in the 1920s.
31 Celesta	1880 (Widor's *Der Korrigane*)	Invented by Mustel in 1880.
32 Pianoforte (J C Bach, 1776)	1776	Descended from the dulcimer. Invented by Cristofori *c.* 1709. First concert use 1767 in London.
33 Organ (Handel, *c.* 1730)	1886 (Saint-Saëns' Symphony No. 3)	Ultimate origin lies in the antique panpipes.

HISTORY OF MUSIC

Dates (approx.)	Name of era	Musical developments	Principal composers
	Prehistoric	Improvisatory music-making. Music and magic virtually synonymous	
8th century BC to 4th century AD to 6th century AD	Primitive (Ancient Greece and Rome; Byzantium)	Improvisatory music-making in domestic surroundings. Competitive music-making in the arena.	
4th century AD	Ambrosian	The beginnings of plainsong and the establishment of order in liturgical music.	Bishop Ambrose of Milan (*c.* 333–97) established four scales.
6th to 10th century	Gregorian	Church music subjected to strict rules, e.g.: melodies sung only in unison.	Pope Gregory I, 'The Great' (540–604) extended the number of established scales to eight.

1100–1300	Mediaeval	Guido d'Arezzo (c. 980–1050) was called the inventor of music: his teaching methods and invention of a method of writing music transformed the art. Beginning of organised instrumental music; start of polyphony in church music.	Minstrels (10th–13th centuries). Goliards (travelling singers of Latin songs: 11th–12th centuries). Troubadours (c. 1100–1210) Trouvères (from 1100). Bernart de Ventadorn (c. 1150–95) encouraged singing in the vernacular.
1300–1600	Renaissance	The great age of polyphonic church music. Gradual emergence of instrumental music. Appearance of Madrigals, chansons, etc. The beginnings of true organisation in music and instruments.	Guillaume de Machut (c. 1300–77) John Dunstable (d. 1453) Guillaume Dufay (c. 1400–74) Johannes Ockeghem (1430–95) Josquin des Pres (1450–1521) John Taverner (c. 1495–1545) Giovanni da Palestrina (c. 1525–94) Orlando de Lasso (c. 1530–94) Thomas Morley (1557–1603) John Dowland (1563–1626) Michael Praetorius (1571–1621)
1600–1750	Baroque	Beginnings of opera and oratorio. Rise of instrumental music; the first orchestras, used at first in the opera house but gradually attaining separate existence. Beginnings of sonata, concerto, suite, and symphony. The peak of polyphonic writing.	Giovanni Gabrieli (1557–1612) Claudio Monteverdi (1567–1633) Orlando Gibbons (1583–1625) Pietro Cavalli (1602–76) Jean-Baptiste Lully (1632–87) Arcangelo Corelli (1653–1713) Henry Purcell (1658–95) Alessandro Scarlatti (1660–1725) Reinhard Keiser (1674–1739) Georg Philipp Telemann (1681–1767) Jean Philippe Rameau (1683–1764) Domenico Scarlatti (1685–1757) Johann Sebastian Bach (1685–1750) George Frideric Handel (1685–1759)
1750–1800+	Classical	The age of the concert symphony and concerto. Beginning of the string quartet and sinfonia concertante. Decline of church music. Important developments in opera.	Giovanni Battista Sammartini (c. 1700–75) Christoph Willibald von Gluck (1714–87) Carl Philipp Emanuel Bach (1714–88) Franz Joseph Haydn (1732–1809) Wolfgang Amadeus Mozart (1756–91) Luigi Cherubini (1760–1842)
1800–50	Early Romantic	High maturity of the symphony and concerto, etc. in classical style. Romantic opera. The age of the piano virtuosi. Invention of the Nocturne. Beginnings of the symphonic poem. Lieder. Beginnings of nationalism.	Ludwig van Beethoven (1770–1827) Nicolo Paganini (1782–1840) Carl Maria von Weber (1786–1826) Gioacchino Rossini (1792–1868) Franz Schubert (1797–1828) Hector Berlioz (1803–69) Jakob Ludwig Felix Mendelssohn (1809–47) Frederic François Chopin (1810–49) Robert Schumann (1810–56)
1850–1900	High Romanticism	The development of nationalism. Maturity of the symphonic and tone poems Emergence of music drama.	Mikhail Glinka (1804–57) Franz Liszt (1811–86) Richard Wagner (1813–83) Bedřich Smetana (1824–84) Johannes Brahms (1833–97) Pyotr Il'ich Tchaikovsky (1840–93) Antonín Dvořák (1841–1904) Edvard Hagerup Grieg (1843–1907)
1900–	Modern	Impressionism and post-romanticism. Neo-classicism and other reactionary movements. Atonalism.	Claude Debussy (1862–1918) Richard Strauss (1864–1949) Carl Nielsen (1865–1931) Jean Sibelius (1865–1957) Alexander Skryabin (1872–1915) Ralph Vaughan Williams (1872–1958) Sergei Rakhmaninoff (1873–1943) Arnold Schoenberg (1874–1951) Charles Ives (1874–1954) Béla Bartók (1881–1945) Igor Stravinsky (1882–1971) Anton Webern (1883–1945) Alban Berg (1885–1934) Samuel Barber (b. 1910) Benjamin Britten (b. 1913)
Today	Avant-garde	Avant-Garde is history in the making and any list of composers would be arbitrary since one cannot tell which of the many directions taken by modern music will prove most influential. There have always been avant-garde composers, without which the art of music would never have developed: we would take many names from the above chart as good examples. Here are some names of avant-gardistes of prominence.	Luigi Dallapiccola (b. 1904) John Cage (b. 1912) Luigi Nono (b. 1924) Hans Werner Henze (b. 1926) Karlheinz Stockhausen (b. 1928) Iannis Xenakis (b. 1922)

THE GREAT COMPOSERS

Abbreviations

arr	arranged
clt	clarinet
cor	horn
fag	bassoon
fl	flute
hps	harpsichord
instr	instruments
keyb'd	keyboard
misc	miscellaneous
ob	oboe
orch	orchestra(l)
pf	pianoforte
pf4	piano quartet*
Rhap	Rhapsody
Sinf Conc	Sinfonia Concertante
str	strings
str4	string quartet*
str5	string quintet*
tpt	trumpet
v d'a	viola d'amor
vl	violin
vla	viola
w	wind (woodwind and/or brass)
w5	wind quintet*

* and similar combinations of abbreviations.

Introduction

A chart of the main works by history's major composers, their music listed in generic columns. Lost and disputed works are ignored, as are those in sketch form, but important works which were not completed by the composer have been included (e.g.: Schubert's Symphony No. 8, *Unfinished*) where performances are possible.

Each of the categories should be regarded as covering its respective field in a wide sense. For example, Tchaikovsky's *Manfred*, although not numbered as a symphony, is included as one of his seven, and Berg's *Lyric Suite* for string quartet, even though not called a string quartet as such by the composer, is included in that column. Where totals are unknown or obscure, only the general outline of a corpus of works has been indicated using asterisks: one for a handful of such pieces, two for a significant contribution, and three indicating 'very many'. In some cases where the information might be useful, these vague symbols are amplified by details in the extreme right-hand column.

In all cases the figures in the 'Concertos' columns include other major works (concertinos, rhapsodies, etc.) for the given instrument and orchestra.

Dates	Composer	symphonies	orchestral	Concertos keyb'd	violin	other	Chamber str4	trios	vl sons	other	Keyb'd sonatas	solos	organ	Vocal operas	choral	lieder song, &c	other	Other important works
c. 1240–86	Hal(l)e, Adam de la French														*	**		Pastoral drama: Le Jeu de Robin et Marion. Motets
c. 1400–53	Dunstable, John English														**			
c. 1450–1521	Des Pres, Josquin Flemish														**			Masses: ** Motets: **
c. 1505–85	Tallis, Thomas English											**	*		** *	*		
c. 1525–94	Palestrina, Giovanni Pierluigi Italian												**		**	*		Masses: 98 Motets: 265
1532–94	Lassus, Orlando de Flemish														** *	**		Madrigals: *** Motets: ***
1543–1623	Byrd, William English									music for viols *		** *			** *	**	Anthems ** Madrigals **	Motets: 63 Masses: ** Canciones Sacrae and Gradualia: 170
c. 1548–1611	Victoria, Thomás Luis de Spanish														**	**	hymns ***	Masses: 21 Motets: 46
1557–1612	Gabrieli, Giovanni Italian									**			*		**			Madrigals ** Motets ** Vocal concerti **
c. 1563–1626	Dowland, John English									**						**		
1567–1643	Monteverdi, Claudio Italian													19	** *	**		Ballets ** Madrigals etc. **
1571–1621	Praetorius, Michael (alias of Michael Schul(t)z(e) German									*					*			Theoretical works
1583–1623	Gibbons, Orlando English									***		**			*	**	Psalms ** Anthems ** Madrigals **	Masks: 4
1632–87	Lully, Jean-Baptiste (b. Giovanni Battista Lulli) Italian/French		*											15	*	*		Ballets: 49
1637–1707	Buxtehude, Dietrich Danish									**			**		**	**		
1653–1713	Corelli, Arcangelo Italian					2 vl, cello: 12	48	12										

Dates	Composer	symphonies	orchestral	Concertos			Chamber				Keyb'd			Vocal works				Other important works
				keyb'd	violin	other	str4	trios	vl sons	other	sonatas	solos	organ	operas	choral	lieder song,&c	other	
1658/9–1695	Purcell, Henry English		*				24	12		misc. *			**		6	*	** *		Incidental music: 44 Anthems: 62
c. 1660–1725	Scarlatti, Pietro Alessandro Gasparo Italian	12				str: 12 fl: 7				*		*		70	**	**		Oratorios: 24 Cantatas, Motets, etc.: c. 800 Masses: 11
1668–1733	Couperin, François French					misc: 14		6		*		222			**	*		
1678–1741	Vivaldi, Antonio Lucio Italian	52		238		fl: 17 ob: 20 fag: 39 2 tpt: 1 2 cor: 2 cello: 27 misc str: 19 misc: 53	2	18	31	2 vl: 20 cello: 9				45	**	**		Cantatas: 36 Oratorios: 3
1681–1767	Telemann, Georg Philipp German			20		fl: 14 ob: 10 cor: 1 tpt: 1 vla: 1 misc: 53	*	**		***		** *		40	** *			Orchestral Suites: c. 600 Passions: 40 Cantatas: 100
1683–1764	Rameau, Jean-Philippe French					*				6 tets: 6		56		20	*			Music for ballets: 18 Cantatas: 8
1685–1750	Bach, Johann Sebastian German		**	7	2	2 vl: 1 fl; vl; hps: 1 2 hps: 3 3 hps: 2 4 hps: 1 Orch: 6		7		cello: ** vl: **		** *	** *		** *	*		Orchestral Suites: 4 Art of Fugue Musical Offering Magnificat: 1 Masses: 5 Contatas: 212 Oratorios: 3 Passions: 3
1685–1759	Handel, George Frideric German, nat. English		**	1		ob: 3 organ: 20 2 organs: 1 conc grossi 20 misc: *		6		**		**	*	58	** *	**		Water Music Fireworks Music Oratorios, etc: 32 Cantatas: 99
1685–1757	Scarlatti, Domenico Italian	7									555			13	*	*		Stabat Mater: 1 Oratorios: 5
1714–88	Bach, Carl Philipp Emanuel German	18		63		2 keyb'd: 2 fl: 4 ob: 2 } arr cello: 3 }		31	10	fl: 17 misc: ***	154	183	7		**	*		Passions: 2 Oratorios: 2 Magnificat: 1 Cantatas: 16
1714–87	Gluck, Christoph Willibald von German	9						7		*				52	*	*		Pantomimes (Ballets): 4
1732–1809	Haydn, Franz Joseph Austrian	108		11	4	tpt: 1 2 lyre: 5 vl, hps: 1 cello: 2 cor: 1 sinf conc: 1	65	40 ** *	5		55	*	*	13	**	*	*	Overtures: 19 Divertimenti: c. 60 Marches: 7 Dances: *** Baryton trios: 125 Oratorios: 4 Masses: 12 Te Deums: 2 Cantatas: *
1756–91	Mozart, Wolfgang Amadeus (Johannes Chrysostomus Wolfgangus Theophilus) Austrian	49	***	27	8	fl: 2 clt: 1 fag: 1 cor: 4 fl, harp: 1 2 pf: 1 3 pf: 1 Sinf conc: 2	23	**	37	str5: 6 clt5: 1 pf, w5: 1 cor5: 1 pf4: 2 fl4: 4 ob4: 1 misc: ***	18	** *	*	19	**	*		Masses: 17
1770–1827	Beethoven, Ludwig van German	10	**	6	1	pf, vl, cello: 1	16	**	10	cello: 5 misc: **	35	**	*	1	**	80		Stage works: ** Arias with orch: ** Masses: 2 Cantatas: 2 Oratorio: 1
1786–1826	Weber, Carl Maria Friedrich Ernst von German	2		3		clt: 3 fag: 1 cello: 1			6	pf4: 1 clt4: 1 misc: *	4	**		8				Stage works: ** Concert overtures: * Masses: 2 Cantatas: 8 Offertoria: 2
1792–1868	Rossini, Gioacchino Italian						6			w5: 5 misc: *		*		38	*	*		
1797–1828	Schubert, Franz Peter Austrian	9	**		1		15	**	4	pf5: 1 Octet: 1 str5: 1	21	** *		17	** *	** *	***	Dramatic music: ** Masses: 7
1803–69	Berlioz, Louis Hector French	4	**							*				5	** *	**		
1804–57	Glinka, Mikhail Russian	1	*				2	*		str, w6: 1 vla: 1 misc: *		**		2	*	**		Prince Khomsky incidental music

Dates	Composer	symphonies	orchestral	Concertos			Chamber				Keyb'd			Vocal works				Other important works
				keyb'd	violin	other	str4	trios	vl sons	other	sonatas	solos	organ	operas	choral	lieder song, &c	other	
1809–47	Mendelssohn-Bartholdy, Jacob Ludwig Felix German	17	★★	3	2	vl, pf: 1 2pf: 1	8	2	1	str8: 1 pf4: 3 str5: 2 pf6: 1 misc: ★★		★★	6	2	★★ ★	★★ ★		Stage music: 4 Songs Without Words: 48 Elijah
1810–49	Chopin, Frédéric François Polish			6				1		cello: 1 pf duets ★ 2pf ★	3	★★ ★				18			
1810–56	Schumann, Robert, Alexander German	5	★★	2	1	cello: 1 4 cor: 1	3	3	2	pf4: 1 pf5:1	3	★★ ★	★	1	★	★★ ★		Manfred incidental music
1811–86	Liszt, Ferencz Hungarian	2	23	2					1	pf duets: ★★ 2pf: ★★ misc: ★	1	72 +	22	1	93	★★ ★		Symphonic poems: 12
1813–1901	Verdi, Giuseppe Italian						1			★				32	★★ ★			Requiem Four Sacred Pieces
1813–83	Wagner, Richard Wilhelm German	1	★★				1			★	2	★		15	★	★		
1824–96	Bruckner, Anton Austrian	11	★				1			str5: 1 misc: ★					★★			Te Deum Overture in G minor
1824–84	Smetana, Bedřich Bohemian	1	★★				2	1				★		9	10	★		
1825–99	Strauss, Johann II Austrian		★★ ★											16				Waltzes, Marches, Polkas, etc. ★★★
1833–97	Brahms, Johannes German	4	★★	2	1	vl, cello: 1	3	6	3	str6: 2 str5: 2 clt5: 1 pf4: 3 cello (clt): 2	3	★★ ★	★		★★	★★ ★		St Anthony Variations Overtures: 2 Serenades: 2 Hungarian Dances: 21 German Requiem
1835–1921	Saint-Saëns, Camille French	5	★★	5	4	cello: 2	4	2	2	6tet: 1 pf5: 1 pf4: 1 cello: 2 ob: 1 clt: 1 fag: 1 misc: ★		★★	★	13	★★	★★		Carnival of the Animals Incidental music
1839–81	Mussorgsky, Modest Petrovitch Russian		★									★★		4	★	★★		
1840–93	Tchaikovsky, Pyotr Il'ich Russian	7	★★	3	1	cello: 1	3	1		str6: 1		★★		11	★★	★★ ★		Ballet music: ★★ 1812 Overture and other concert overtures Orchestral Suites: 4
1841–1904	Dvořák, Antonin Czech	9	★★	1	1	cello: 2	14	5	2	str5: 3 pf5: 2 str6: 1 pf4: 2 pf duets: ★★ misc: ★		★★		10	★★	★★		Overtures: 5 Slavonic Dances: 16 Slavonic Rhapsodies: 3 str Serenade: 1 w Serenade: 1 Scherzo Capriccio
1843–1907	Grieg, Edvard Hagerup Norwegian	1	★	1			1		3	cello: 1 pf duets: ★ 2pf: ★		★★			★	★★ ★		Peer Gynt incidental music Symphonic Dances: 4
1844–1908	Rimsky-Korsakov, Nikolai Russian	3	★	1		trombone: 1 ob: 1★ clt: 1	3	1		str6: 1 pf, w5: 1		★		16	16	★★ ★		Scheherazade Capriccio Espagnole Incidental music: 1
1857–1934	Elgar, Sir Edward William English	2	★★		1	cello: 1 fag: 1	1		1	pf5: 1 w5: 1	1	★	★		★★ ★	★		Dream of Gerontius Enigma Variations incidental music: ★★ Pomp & Circumstance Marches: 5
1858–1924	Puccini, Giacomo Italian									★				12	★			
1860–1911	Mahler, Gustav Austrian	10												3	★★	★★ ★		Song of the Earth Lieder Eines Farenden Gesellen
1860–1903	Wolf, Hugo Austrian						1			★		★		2	21	★★ ★		Italian Serenade Incidental music: 2
1862–1934	Delius, Frederick English		★	1	3	vl, cello: 1	2		4	cello: 1		★		6	★★	★★		Mass of Life

Dates	Composer	symphonies	orchestral	Concertos keyb'd	violin	other	Chamber str4	trios	vl sons	other	Keyb'd sonatas	solos	organ	Vocal operas	choral	lieder song, &c	other	Other important works
1864–1949	Strauss, Richard Georg German	3	**		2	horn: 2 ob: 1	1		1	w13: 2 w16: 1 pf4: 1 cello: 1		*		15	21	** *		Ballets: 2
1865–1931	Nielsen, Carl August Danish	6	**		1	fl: 1 clt: 1	4		2	w5: 1 misc: *		**	2	2	*	**		Helios Overture Little Suite for str.
1865–1957	Sibelius, Jan Julian Christian Finnish	8	** *		1		3	2	3	pf5: 1 pf4: 2 misc: *		**	*	1	** *	**		Tapiola En Saga
1872–1958	Vaughan Williams, Sir Ralph English	9	**		1	2pf: 1 tuba: 1 ob: 1	4			str5: 1		*	*	6	**	**		Ballets: 4 Incidental music: The Wasps Film music: **
1873–1943	Rakhmaninoff, Sergei Russian	3	*	5					1	cello: 1 pf duet: *	2	**		3	7	**		
1874–1951	Schoenberg, Arnold Austrian	2	*	1	1		5	1		str6: 1 misc: *		*	*	4	**	*		Gurre-Lieder
1875–1937	Ravel, Maurice French		**		2		1	1	3	vl, cello: 1		*		2	*	**		Ballets: 4 Bolero
1881–1845	Bartók, Béla Hungarian		**	4	4	2 pf: 1 vla: 1	6	1	3	pf5: 1	2			1	*	*		Concerto for orch Ballets: 2 Suites for orch: 2 Divertimento for str
1882–1971	Stravinsky, Igor Russian, nat. French, then American	4	**	1	1	str: 1 orch: *				2 pf: 1 misc: **	2	*		4	*	*		Stage works
1883–1945	Webern, Anton Austrian	1	*			9 instr: 1	3	1		pf5: 1 pf, sax, vl, clt: 1		*			5	*		
1885–1935	Berg, Alban Austrian		*		1		2				1			2	*	*		
1890–1959	Martinů, Bohuslav Jan Czech	6	**	5	2	fl, vl: 1 cello: 2 vl; pf: 1 str4: 1 misc: **	7	2	5	str6: 1 str5: 1 w5: 1 pf4: 1 misc: ***		**		10	*	*		Ballets: 10
1891–1953	Prokofiev, Sergei Russian	7	**	5	2	cello: 1	2		2	w, str5: 1 2 vl: 1	9	**		7	10	*		Ballets: 6 Peter and the Wolf Incidental and film music **
1897–1963	Hindemith, Paul German	3	**	3	1	vla: 1 cello: 1 cor: 1 misc: *	7		7	vla: 1 v d'a: 1 cello: 1 misc: *** 2pf: *	4	*	3 +	7	*	*		Symphonic Metamorphosis on Themes of Weber Stage works: **
1906–75	Shostakovitch, Dmitri Russian	15	*	2	2	cello: 2 misc: *	15	2	1	2pf: 1 cello: 2 str8: 1 pf5: 1	2	*		2	**	**		Film music: 21 Incidental music: 10 Ballets: 3
1913	Britten, Edward Benjamin English	3	**	2	1		2			misc: *		*		12	**	** *	*	Young Person's Guide to the Orchestra Stage and film music: ** War Requiem

Language and Literature

WORLD'S PRINCIPAL LANGUAGES

The world's total of languages and dialects is now estimated to be about 5500. The most widely spoken, together with the countries in which they are used are as follows:

1. GUOYU (standardised Northern Chinese or Běifanghirà). Alphabetised into *Zhuyin Zimu* (39 letters) in 1918 and converted to the *Pinyin* Latin alphabetic system in 1958. Spoken in China (Mainland). Language family: Sino-Tibetan. 575 000 000.

2. ENGLISH. Evolved from an Anglo-Saxon, Norman-French and Latin amalgam *c.* 1350. Spoken in Australia, Bahamas, Canada, Sri Lanka (3rd), Cyprus (3rd), The Gambia, Ghana, Guyana, India (non-constitutional), Ireland, Jamaica, Kenya (official with Swahili), Malaysia, Malta (official with Maltese), New Zealand, Nigeria (official), Pakistan (now only 1 per cent), Rhodesia, Sierra Leone (official), Singapore (2nd at 24 per cent), South Africa (38 per cent of white population), Tanzania (official with swahili), Trinidad and Tobago, Uganda (official), UK, USA and also widely as the second language of educated Europeans and of citizens of the USSR. Language family: Indo-European. 360 000 000.

3. GREAT RUSSIAN. The foremost of the official languages used in the USSR and spoken as the first language of 60 per cent of the population. Language family: Indo-European. 230 000 000.

4. HINDUSTANI (a combination of Hindi and Urdu) foremost of the 845 languages of India of which 14 are 'constitutional'. Hindi (official) is spoken by more than 25 per cent, Urdu by nearly 4 per cent and Hindustani, as such, by 10 per cent. In Pakistan, Hindustani is the third most prevalent language (7½ per cent). Language family: Indo-European. 200 000 000.

5. SPANISH. Dates from the 10th

century AD; spoken in Argentina, Bolivia, Canary Islands, Chile, Colombia, Costa Rica, Cuba, Dominican Republic, Guatemala, Honduras, Mexico, Nicaragua, Panama, Paraguay, Peru, Philippines, Puerto Rico, Rio de Oro, Salvador, Spain, Uruguay, Venezuela. Language family: Indo-European. 200 000 000.

6. GERMAN. Known in written form since the 8th century AD. Spoken in the Federal Republic of Germany (West) and the German Democratic Republic (East) and Austria and Switzerland. Also among minorities in the USA, USSR, Hungary, Poland, Romania and in formerly colonised German territories in eastern and southern Africa and the Pacific. Language family: Indo-European 125 000 000.

7. BENGALI. Widely spoken in the Ganges delta area of India and Bangladesh. Language family: Indo - European. 120 000 000.

8. ARABIC. Dates from the early 6th century. Spoken in Algeria, Bahrain, Iraq (80 per cent), Israel (16 per cent), Jordan, Kuwait, Lebanon, Libya, Maldive Is., Morocco (65 per cent), Oman, Qatar, Saudi Arabia, Sudan (52 per cent), Syria, Tunisia, United Arab Republic and both Yemens. Language family: Hamito - Semitic. 120 000 000.

9. PORTUGUESE. Distinct from Spanish by 14th century and, unlike it, was more influenced by French than by Arabic. Spoken in Angola, Brazil, Goa, Macao, Mozambique, Portugal, Portuguese Guinea, Portuguese Timor. Language family: Indo-European. 120 000 000.

10. JAPANESE. Earliest inscription (in Chinese characters) dates from the 5th century. Spoken in Japan, Formosa (Taiwan) Hawaii and some formerly colonised Pacific Islands. Unrelated to any other language. 110 000 000.

11. MALAY-INDONESIAN. Originated in Northern Sumatra, spoken in Indonesia (form called Bahasa is official), Malaysia, Sabah, Sarawak, Thailand (southernmost parts). Language family: Malayo-Polynesian. 95 000 000.

12. FRENCH. Developed in 9th century as a result of Frankish influence on Gaulish sub-stratum. Fixed by Academic Francaise from 17th century. Spoken in France, French Pacific Is., Belgium, Guadeloupe, Haiti, Louisiana, Luxembourg, Martinique, Monaco, Switzerland, the Italian region of Aosta, Canada, and widely in former French colonies in Africa. Language family: Indo-European. 90 000 000.

13. ITALIAN. Became very distinct from Latin by 10th century. Spoken in Eritrea, Italy, Libya, Switzerland and widely retained in USA among Italian population. Language family: Indo-European. 60 000 000.

14. CANTONESE. A distinctive dialect of Chinese spoken in the Kwang-tung area. Language family: Sino-Tibetan. 50 000 000.

14. TELUGU. Used in south India. Known in a written, grammatic form from the 11th century. Language family: Dravidian. 50 000 000.

14. KOREAN. Not known to be related to any other tongue. 50 000 000.

14. TAMIL. The second oldest written Indian language. Cave graffiti date from the 3rd century BC. Spoken in Sri Lanka, southern India, and among Tamils in Malaysia. Language family: Dravidian. 50 000 000.

14. MARATHI. A language spoken in west and central India, including Goa and part of Hyderabad and Poona with written origins dating from about AD 500. Language family: Indo-European. 50 000 000.

14. PUNJABI. One of the 14 constitutional languages of India spoken by the region of that name. Also spoken in parts of Pakistan. 50 000 000.

20. JAVANESE. Closely related to Malay. Serves as the language of 50 per cent of Indonesian population. Language family: Malayo-Polynesian. 45 000 000

21. UKRAINIAN (Little Russian). Distinction from Great Russian discernible by 11th century, literary zenith late 18th and early 19th century. Banned as written language in Russia 1876–1905. Discouraged since 1931 in USSR. Spoken in Ukrainian SSR, parts of Russian SFSR and Romania. Language family: Indo - European. 40 000 000.

21. WU. A dialect in China spoken, but not officially encouraged, in the Yang-tse delta area. Language family: Sino-Tibetan. 40 000 000.

21. MIN (Fukien). A dialect in China which includes the now discouraged Amoy and Fuchow dialects and Hainanese. Language family: Sino-Tibetan. 40 000 000.

21. TURKISH. Spoken in European and Asian Turkey—a member of the Oghuz division of the Turkic group of languages. 40 000 000.

25. VIETNAMESE. Used in the whole of eastern Indo-China. Classified as a Mon-Khmer by some and as a Tai language by other philologists. 35 000 000.

26. POLISH. A western Slavonic language with written records back to the 13th century, 300 years before its emergence as a modern literary language. Spoken in Poland, and western USSR and among émigré populations notably in the USA. Language family: Indo-European. 35 000 000.

ORIGINS OF THE ENGLISH LANGUAGE

The three Germanic dialects on which English is based are descended from the Indo-Germanic or Aryan family of languages, spoken since *c.* 3000 BC by the nomads of the Great Lowland Plain of Europe, which stretches from the Aral Sea in the Soviet Union to the Rhine in West Germany. Now only fragments of Old Lithuanian contain what is left of this ancestral tongue.

Of the three inherited Germanic dialects, the first was Jutish, brought into England in AD 449 from Jutland. This was followed 40 years later by Saxon, brought from Holstein, and Anglican, which came with the still later incursions from the area of Schleswig-Holstein.

These three dialects were superimposed on the 1000-year-old indigenous Celtic tongue, along with what Latin had survived in the towns from nearly 15 generations of Roman occupation (AD 43–410). The next major event in the history of the English language was the first of many Viking invasions, beginning in 793, from Denmark and Norway. Norse and Danish left permanent influences on the Anglo-Frisian Old English, though Norse never survived as a separate tongue in England beyond 1035, the year of the death of King Canute (Cnut), who had then reigned for 19 years over England, 16 years over Denmark and 7 years over Norway.

The Scandinavian influence now receded before Norman French, though Norse still struggled on in remote parts of Scotland until about 1630 and in the Shetland Islands until *c.* 1750. The Normans were, however, themselves really Vikings, who in five generations had become converts to the Latin culture and language of northern France.

For three centuries after the Norman conquest of 1066 by William I, descendant of Rollo the Viking, England lived under a trilingual system. The mother tongue of all the first 12 Kings and Queens, from William I (1066–1087) until as late as Richard II (1377–99), was Norman. English became the language of court proceedings only during the reign of Edward III, in October, 1362, and the language for teaching in the Universities of Oxford and Cambridge in *c.* 1380.

English did not really crystallise as an amalgam of Anglo-Saxon and Latin root forms until the 14th century, when William Langland (*c.* 1332–*c.* 1400), and Geoffrey Chaucer (?1340–1400) were the pioneers of a literary tradition, which culminated in William Shakespeare, who died in 1616, just four years before the sailing of the *Mayflower*.

The suffix-cide

The suffix -cide derives from the Latin *caedo*, to kill. The following list of 41 words with this suffix is believed to be complete.

avicide—birds
deicide—god
episcopicide—bishop
felicide—cat
femicide—women
filicide—son or daughter
foeticide—foetus
fratricide—brother (or sister)
fungicide—fungi
genocide—a race
germicide—germs
giganticide—giant
gynaecide—women
hereticide—heretic
homicide—human being
infanticide—infant
insecticide—insects
larvicide—larvae
leporicide—hares
liberticide—liberty
matricide—mother
menticide—the mind
nematocide—nematodes
ovicide—sheep
parasiticide—parasites
parenticide—parent
parricide—father or mother
patricide—father
pesticide—pest
prolicide—one's own child (before or immediately after birth)
regicide—king
senicide—old men
sororicide—sister
suicide—oneself
taenicide—tapeworms
tauricide—bull
tyrannicide—tyrants
uxoricide—wife
vaticide—prophet
vermicide—worms
vulpicide—fox (other than by hunting)

ENGLISH LITERATURE

Nothing definite has survived of the stories or songs possessed by the ancient Britons who were invaded by Caesar on 26 Aug. 55 BC. Barely anything has survived from the 367-year-long Roman occupation until AD 410. English literature thus begins at least by being English.

The earliest known British born author was Pelagius (fl. 400–18) from whom survive some remains of theological disputations written in Rome.

The earliest English poem known to us is Widseth, about a wandering minstrel of the 6th century. In the Exeter Book 150 lines of this poem survive.

The oldest surviving record of a named English poet who composed on British soil is from the paraphrase by Bede (673–735) of a hymn attributed to Caedmon of Streaneshalch (Whitby, Yorkshire), who was living in 670. This survives in the Cambridge manuscript of Bede (or Baeda) in a hand possibly of the 18th century.

The first great book in English prose is the Old English Chronicle supervised by King Aelfred until 892. Aelfred himself translated some of the writings of Baeda and of Gregory the Great's *Pastoral Care* into West Saxon.

The Lindisfarne Gospels, a beautiful vellum quarto Latin manuscript now in the British Museum, London, was written *c.* 700. In *c.* 950 Aldred added an interlinear gloss in Northumbrian dialect.

The leading authors of the Old English Period are:

Aelfric	*c.* 955–*c.* 1020
King Aelfred	849–99
Venerable Bede	*c.* 672–735
Caedmon	fl. 670
Cynewulf	? 9th century
Wulfstan	d. 1023

BIBLIOGRAPHY. Below are brief notes and a list of the major works of the 12 British writers who have the longest entries in the *Oxford Dictionary of Quotations*. They are listed in order of length of their entry.

Shakespeare, William (1564–1616)

The greatest contribution to the world's store of poetry and drama has been made by William Shakespeare (1564–1616). Born at Stratford-on-Avon, this third child of a local Alderman and trader produced in the space of the seventeen years between 1594 (*Titus Andronicus*) and 1611 (*The Tempest*) probably thirty-seven plays which total 814 780 words.

Shakespeare's golden outpourings of sheer genius have excited and amazed the critics of every age since. His contemporary Ben Jonson called him 'The applause! delight! the wonder of our stage!' Milton refers to him as 'Sweetest Shakespeare, Fancy's child'. To Thomas Carlyle, looking at his massive brow, he was 'The greatest of intellects'. Matthew Arnold refers to him as 'out-topping knowledge'.

Venus and Adonis	1593
The Rape of Lucrece	1594
Titus Andronicus	1594
*Henry VI Part 2	1594
The Taming of the Shrew (see also 1623, First Folio)	1594
*Henry VI Part 3	1595
*Romeo and Juliet	1597
Richard II	1597
Richard III	1597
Henry IV Part 1	1598
Love's Labour's Lost (Revised version, original (? 1596) probably lost)	1598
Romeo and Juliet	1599
Henry IV Part 2	1600
A Midsummer Night's Dream	1600
The Merchant of Venice	1600
Much Ado About Nothing	1600
Henry V (First 'true' text published 1623 in First Folio)	1600
Sir John Falstaff and the Merry Wives of Windsor (First 'true text published in 1623 in First Folio)	1602
*Hamlet	1603
Hamlet ('according to the true and perfect copy')	1604
King Lear	1608
Pericles, Prince of Tyre	1609
Troilus and Cressida	1609
Sonnets (1640 in 'Poems')	1609

*Bad quartos or unauthorised editions.

Posthumously Published

Othello	1622
First Folio—36 plays in all including the first publication of *The Taming of the Shrew* (Shakespeare's revised version of the 1594 version)	1623

Henry VI Part 1	*Macbeth*
The Two Gentlemen of Verona	*Timon of Athens*
	Antony and Cleopatra
The Comedy of Errors	*Coriolanus*
King John	*Cymbeline*
As You Like It	*A Winter's Tale*
Julius Caesar	*The Tempest*
Twelfth Night	*Henry VIII*
Measure for Measure	
All's Well That Ends Well	

The Second Folio (1632), the Third Folio (1663 1st issue, 1664 2nd issue) and the Fourth Folio (1685) added nothing of authority to Heming and Condell's monumental First Folio.

Scientific study of Shakespeare began with Edward Capell (1713–81) and his researches published from 1768. The eminently honest and painstaking work of Alexander Dyce's edition of 1857 led to the publication in 1863–66 of what is regarded as the standard text, *The Cambridge Shakespeare*, edited by W C Clark and J Glover.

Tennyson, Alfred, First Baron (1809–92)

b. Somersby, Lincolnshire; the son of the rector; his first published work (with his brother, Charles) was *Poems by Two Brothers* in 1827; educated at home, Louth Grammar School and Trinity College, Cambridge, where he won the Chancellor's Medal for English verse with *Timbuctoo*, 1829; became engaged to Emily Selwood about 1833, but did not marry her until 1850; left his family home in 1837 and then lived in turn in Epping, Tunbridge Wells and Boxley; appointed Poet Laureate in 1850 on the death of Wordsworth; lived at Twickenham after his marriage, then in the Isle of Wight in 1853; his *Idylls of the King*, published in 1859, made him famous and popular; built a home near Haslemere in 1868 and was created a peer in 1884; buried in Westminster Abbey in 1892

Poems (including *The Lotus Eaters* and *The Lady of Shallot* (dated 1833)	1832
Poems (two volumes) (including *Ulysses*, *Sir Galahad*, *Morte d'Arthur*, *Locksley Hall*)	1842
In Memoriam A.H.H. (Arthur Henry Hallam)	1850
Ode on the Death of the Duke of Wellington	1852
Charge of the Light Brigade	1854
Maud and Other Poems	1859
Idylls of the King	1857–85
	(completed edition 1889)
Enoch Arden (including *Old Style*)	1864
Holy Grail	1869
The Revenge: A Ballad of the Fleet	1878
Becket	1884
Locksley Hall 60 Years After	1886
Demeter and Other Poems (including *Crossing the Bar*)	1889

Milton, John (1608–74)

b. in London; the son of John Milton, a lawyer; educated St Paul's School and Christ's College, Cambridge; lived at Horton near Windsor and toured Italy in 1638-9; on return lived in London and about 1643 married Mary Powell, aged 17, who soon left him to return in 1645; she bore three daughters and died in 1652 on the birth of a fourth; went blind in 1652 but continued to write with assistants; he married a second time (1656) Katherine Woodcock, who died in childbirth in 1658; in 1662 he married a third time, Elizabeth Minsehull, who survived him for over 50 years; the Great Fire of 1666 destroyed his home and the plague drove him out to Chalfont St Giles. He returned to London for his last peaceful years, and died of gout in 1674, and was buried in an unidentified grave at St

Giles', Cripplegate.

On the Death of Fair Infant Dying of a Cough	1625
L'Allegro and Il Penseroso	1632
Arcades	1633
Comus (2 Masques)	1634
Lycidas	1638
Areopagitica (a Tract)	1644
Tenure of Kings and Magistrates (a Pamphlet)	1649
Paradise Lost	finished 1657
Paradise Regained	1671
Samson Agonistes	1671

Kipling, Joseph Rudyard (1865–1936)

Rudyard Kipling (The Mansell Collection)

b. in Bombay; the son of the curator of the Lahore Museum and cousin of Stanley Baldwin, the Prime Minister; ed. at the United Services College at Westward Ho!; became a journalist in Lahore in 1882 and moved to London in 1889; finally settled in Burwash (1902); awarded the Nobel Prize for Literature 1907, and three times asked to be excused from accepting the Order of Merit.

Departmental Ditties	1886
Plain Tales from The Hills	1888
Soldiers Three	1888
Wee Willie Winkie	1888
The Light That Failed	1891
Barrack Room Ballads	1892
Many Inventions	1893
Jungle Books (Two volumes)	1894–95
The Seven Seas (including *Mandalay*)	1896
Captains Courageous	1897
Recessional	1897
Stalky & Co.	1899
Kim	1901
Just So Stories for Little Children	1902
Puck of Pook's Hill	1906
Rewards and Fairies	1910
A School History of England	1911

Wordsworth, William (1770–1850)

b. at Cockermouth, Cumberland; a double orphan before he was 14; after an unhappy childhood dominated by intolerant grandparents, he went in 1787 to St John's College, Cambridge; after a tour of France on foot he settled in London, only to return to France during part of the Revolution; he had an illegitimate daughter by Marie-Anne Vallon ('Annette'); returned to England in 1792–93 and was prevented by the war from returning to France until 1802; on inheriting a legacy in 1795, he set up home with his sister, Dorothy, at Racedown, Dorset; in 1797 they moved to Somerset to be near their friend Coleridge who was living at Nether Stowey; after visiting Germany 1798–99 Wordsworth settled permanently at Grasmere in the Lake District and later married Mary Hutchinson; the rest of his life he travelled extensively to Scotland (met Sir Walter Scott) and Ireland, he became Poet Laureate in 1843 and was buried at Grasmere in 1850.

Lyrical Ballads (with Coleridge)	1798 & 1800
Prelude	1805
Poems in Two Volumes (including *Ode to Duty* and *Ode on Intimations of Immortality*)	1807
Excursion: a portion of the Recluse	1814
Poems, including the *Borderers*	1842

Shelley, Percy Bysshe (1792–1822)

b. at Field Place, near Horsham, Sussex; the grandson of a first baronet; ed. at Eton where he was interested in both the classics and science; went to University College, Oxford, but was sent down; was irregularly married in Scotland (1811) when 19 to 16-year-old Harriet Westbrook; after an unsuccessful visit to Ireland he became ensnared in a romance with Elizabeth Hitchener, a school-mistress ten years his senior; in 1813 he remarried in England his first wife, who bore him two children; the next year he eloped with Mary Wollstonecraft Godwin to Switzerland, and she bore him a son in 1816; in October of that year Mary's half sister, Fanny Imlay, committed suicide, it is said because of infatuation for Shelley, and two months later his first wife, Harriet, also committed suicide; Shelley at once married Mary; in 1818 Shelley left England for ever; his first two children by Mary both died young, but in 1819 a son named Percy Florence was born who succeeded as the 3rd baronet and lived until 1889; in 1822 on a sea trip from Leghorn to Spezzia Shelly was lost; his body was washed up later at Viareggio and cremated on the spot in the presence of Lord Byron and Leigh Hunt; some remains were buried in the Protestant cemetery in Rome.

Alastor	1816
Ode to The West Wind	1819
The Cenci	1819
Prometheus Unbound	1820
The Witch of Atlas	1820
To a Skylark	1820
The Cloud	1820
Epipsychidion	1821
Adonais	1821
Queen Mab	1821
Hellas	1822
Defence of Poetry (uncompleted)	

Johnson, Dr Samuel (1709–84)

b. at Lichfield; son of a bookseller; educated at Lichfield and at Pembroke College, Oxford, left without a degree, but made MA in 1755 and Doctor of Law 1775; briefly a schoolmaster; employed by *The Gentleman's Magazine* from March 1738; bibliographer; lexicographer; pamphleteer; conversationalist; arrested for debt 1756; met Boswell 1763; LL.D (Dublin) 1765; buried in Westminster Abbey.

A Voyage to Abyssinia by Father Jerome Lobo (Translation)	1735
London: a Poem, in Imitation of the Third Satire of Juvenal (anon.)	1738
Parliamentary Reports disguised as Debates in the Senate of Magna Lilliputia July 1741–Mar.	1744
Life of Savage	1744
Plan of a Dictionary of the English Language	1747
Irene (Theatrical tragedy produced by Garrick at Drury Lane)	1748
The Vanity of Human Wishes	1749
The Rambler (essays in 208 bi-weekly issues) Mar. 1750–Mar.	1752
A Dictionary of the English Language (8 years' work, 1747–55)	1755
The Prince of Abyssinia, A Tale	1759
The Idler (essays in the *Universal Chronicle* or the *Weekly Gazette*) Apr. 1758–Apr.	1760
Rasselas	1759
Shakespeare, a new Edition	1765
A Journey to the Western Highlands	1775
The Lives of the Poets vols. i–iv 1779, vols. v–x	1781
Dr Johnson's Diary, posthumously published	1816

Browning, Robert (1812–89)

b. in Camberwell, London; the son of a Bank of England clerk; received a liberal education, but was barred from attending Oxford or Cambridge because of his non-conformity; lived in London until 1846 except for one brief visit to Russia and two to Italy; in 1846 he married Elizabeth Barrett secretly to avoid the wrath of her domineering father; the Brownings established their home at Florence; in 1861 the frail Mrs Browning died and the poet returned grief-stricken to England with his infant son; he died in Venice in 1889 and was buried in Westminster Abbey.

Paracelsus	1835
Sordello	1840
Christmas-Eve and Easter-Day	1850
Men and Women (including *One Word More* and *Bishop Blougram's Apology*)	1855
Dramatis Personae (including *Rabi ben Ezera* and *Caliban upon Setebos*)	1864
The Ring and The Book	1868–69
A Grammarian's Funeral	
Soliloquy of the Spanish Cloister	
The Pied Piper of Hamelin	
Asolando posthumously	1890
New Poems (with Elizabeth Barrett Browning) posthumously	1914

Byron, George Gordon, sixth baron (1788–1824) (adjective Byronic)

b. London; spent childhood with a hysterical mother in Aberdeen after his father's death when he was 3; lame in both feet; succeeded to title in 1798 aged 10; wrote lampoons at 11 and love verses at 12; educated Harrow (1801–5) and Trinity College, Cambridge (1805–8); toured Spain, Portugal, Malta, Albania, Greece and Turkey 1809–11; swam the Hellespont 3 May 1810; married 1815 Anne Isabella Milbanke, breach of marriage 1816; spent self-imposed exile until death in Belgium, Rhine country, Geneva and Italy; settled in Venice, later Ravenna, Pisa and Genoa; sailed to Greek War of Independence (against Turkey) July 1823, died of marsh fever at Missolonghi, Greece, 19 Apr. 1824; burial in Westminster refused, buried Hucknall Torkard, Newstead Abbey, Nottinghamshire.

Fugitive Pieces (privately printed)	1806
Hours of Idleness (reprint of the above with amendments)	1807
English Bards and Scotch Reviewers	1809
Childe Harold (began at Janina, 1809), Cantos i and ii	1812
The Giaour	1813
The Corsair	1814
Lora	1814
The Siege of Corinth	1816
The Prisoner of Chillon	1816
Childe Harold (written in Switzerland), Canto iii	1816
Childe Harold (written in Venice), Canto iv	1817
Manfred	1817
Don Juan (first five cantos)	1818–20
Autobiography	(burnt 1824)
Cain	1821
Don Juan (later cantos)	1821–22
Contribution to *The Liberal* newspaper, 'Vision of Judgement'	1822
The Island	1823
Heaven and Earth	1824

Dickens, Charles John Huffam (1812–70) (adjective Dickensian)

Charles Dickens (Radio Times Hulton Picture Library)

b. Portsmouth; son of a dockyard clerk who later became an inmate of the Marshalsea Debtors' Prison; after a childhood of dire poverty Dickens in 1824 was put to work aged 12 potting and labelling blacking in a small factory; on his father's release he was, against his mother's will, sent to school; he got a job as a boy clerk in a solicitor's office, taught himself shorthand and became a parliamentary reporter to *True Sun* and *Morning Chronicle* (1835); in 1847 Dickens became also a theatrical manager and in 1858 began to give public readings of his works in England, and in America in 1867–68, buried in Westminster Abbey on 14 June 1870.

Sketches of Young Gentlemen, Sketches of Young Couples, The Mudfog Papers	unpublished
A Dinner at Poplar Walk (re-entitled *Mr. Minns and his Cousin*)	Dec. 1833
Sketches by Boz. Illustrative of Every Day Life and Every Day People published in *Monthly Magazine* (1833–35) and *Evening Chronicle*	1835
The Pickwick Papers	from Apr. 1836
Oliver Twist (in Bentley's *Miscellany*)	1837–39
Nicholas Nickleby (in monthly numbers)	1838–39
Master Humphrey's Clock (*Barnaby Rudge* and *The Old Curiosity Shop*)	1840–41
Pic-Nic Papers (Editor)	1841
The Old Curiosity Shop (as a book)	1841
Barnaby Rudge (as a book)	1841
American Notes	1842

Martin Chuzzlewit (parts)	1843–44
A Christmas Carol	1843
The Chimes (written in Italy)	1844
The Cricket on the Hearth	1845
Pictures from Italy	1846
Daily News (later the *News Chronicle*) Editor	Jan.–Feb. 1846
The Battle of Life	1846
The Haunted Man	1847
Dombey and Son (parts) (written in Switzerland)	1847–48
Household Word (weekly periodical) Editor (included *Holly-Tree*)	1848–59
David Copperfield	1849–50
Bleak House (in parts)	1852–53
A Child's History of England (in three volumes)	1852-3-4
Hard Times. For These Times (book form)	1854
Little Dorrit	1857-8
All the Year Round (Periodical) Editor	1859–70
Great Expectations	1860–61
The Uncommercial Traveller (collected parts of *A Tale of Two Cities*)	1861
Our Mutual Friend	1864–65
The Mystery of Edwin Drood (unfinished)	1870

Keats, John (1795–1821)

b. London; educated at Enfield; son of a London livery-stableman; became surgeon apprentice and dresser at St Thomas's Hospital, 1816; lived his whole life in lodgings; when only 24 was attacked by consumption and died in Rome aged 25 years 4 months.

Imitation of Spenser	1813
First Looking into Chapman's Homer	1816
Poems by John Keats	1817
Sleep and Poetry	
Endymion	1818
The Eve of St Agnes	1819
Hyperion (unfinished)	begun 1818
Ode to a Nightingale	1819
Ode on a Grecian Urn	1819
Ode to Psyche	1819
Ode to Autumn	1819
Ode on Melancholy	1819
La Belle Dame sans Merci	1820
Lamia and other Poems	1820
Isabella	1820
Bright Star	1820
The Fall of Hyperion (posthumously published)	1856–57

Pope, Alexander (1688–1744)

b. in London; the son of a linen draper who retired about 1700 to Windsor; poor health and the fact that he was a Roman Catholic denied him formal classic education; in 1719 he leased a house at Twickenham which was his home for the rest of his life; he never married but was greatly enamoured by Martha Blount to whom he willed a life interest in his property; he died in 1744 and is buried in Twickenham church.

An Essay on Criticism	1711
The Rape of the Lock	1712
The Dunciad	1712
Iliad (a translation)	1715–20
An Essay on Man	1733
Epistle to Dr Arbuthnot	1735
Odyssey (a translation) (12 of the 24 books completed by 1725)	

Other classic British writers (14th to 19th centuries)

The writers below are listed in chronological order of year of birth, together with their best-known work or works.

14th century

LANGLAND, William (c. 1332–c. 1400). *Vision of Piers Plowman.*

CHAUCER, Geoffrey (?1340–1400). *Canterbury Tales.*

15th century

MALORY, Sir Thomas (d. 1471?). *Morte D'Arthur.*
MORE, Sir Thomas (1478–1535). *Utopia.*

16th century

SPENSER, Edmund (?1552–99). *The Faerie Queene.*
SIDNEY, Sir Philip (1554–86). *The Countesse of Pembrokes Arcadia; Astrophel and Stella; The Defence of Poesie.*
BACON, Francis (Baron Verulam, Viscount St Albans) (1561–1626). *Essayes.*
MARLOWE, Christopher (1564–1593). *Tamburlaine The Great; Dr Faustus.*
DONNE, John (?1571–1631). *Poems*
JONSON, Benjamin (1572–1637). *Every Man in his humour* (produced 1598, published 1601); *Every Man out of his humour* (1600); *Volpone: or the foxe* (1607); *The Alchemist* (1610, published 1612); *Bartholomew Fayre* (1614, published 1631).
HERRICK, Robert (1591–1674). *Hesperides.*

17th century

BUNYAN, John (1628–88). *The Pilgrim's Progress.*
DRYDEN, John (1631–1700). *All For Love.*
PEPYS, Samuel (1633–1703). *Memoirs* (Diary)
NEWTON, Sir Isaac (1642–1727). *Philosophiae Naturalis Principia Mathematica; Opticks.*
DEFOE, Daniel (1660–1731). *The Life and Adventures of Robinson Crusoe.*
SWIFT, Jonathan (1667–1745). *Travels* (by Lemuel Gulliver).
CONGREVE, William (1670–1729). *The Way of the World.*
ADDISON, Joseph (1672–1719). *The Spectator.*

18th century

FIELDING, Henry (1707–54). *Tom Thumb; The History of Tom Jones.*
STERNE, Laurence (1713–68). *Life and Opinions of Tristram Shandy.*
GRAY, Thomas (1716–71). *An Elegy Wrote in a Country Churchyard.*
SMOLLETT, Tobias George (1721–71). *The Adventures of Peregrine Pickle.*
GOLDSMITH, Oliver (1728–74). *The Vicar of Wakefield; She Stoops to Conquer.*
BURKE, Edmund (1729–97). *Reflections on the Revolution; The Annual Register.*
COWPER, William (1731–1800). *Poems.*
GIBBON, Edward (1737–94). *A History of the Decline and Fall of the Roman Empire.*
PAINE, Thomas (1737–1809). *Rights of Man.*
SHERIDAN, Richard Brinsley (1751–1816). *The Rivals; The School For Scandal.*
BLAKE, William (1757–1827). *Songs of Innocence; Songs of Experience.*
BURNS, Robert (1759–96). *Poems chiefly in the Scottish dialect* (1786); *Tam O' Shanter* (1795); *The Cotters Saturday Night* (1795); *The Jolly Beggars* (1799).
SMITH, Rev Sydney (1771–1845). *The Letters of Peter Plymley; Edinburgh Review.*
SCOTT, Sir Walter (1771–1832). *Waverley; Rob Roy; Ivanhoe; Kenilworth; Quentin Durward; Redgauntlet.*
COLERIDGE, Samuel Taylor (1772–1834). *Lyrical Ballads* (Ancient Mariner).
SOUTHEY, Robert (1774–1843). *Quarterly Review* (contributions); *Life of Nelson.*
AUSTEN, Jane (1775–1817). *Sense and Sensibility* (1811); *Pride and Prejudice* (1813); *Mansfield Park* (1814); *Emma* (1816); *Northanger Abbey and Persuasion* (1818).
LAMB, Charles (1775–1834). *Tales from Shakespeare* [largely by his sister, Mary Lamb (1764–1847)]; *Essays of Elia.*
HAZLITT, William (1778–1830). *My First Acquaintance with Poets; Table Talk; The Plain Speaker.*

Sir Walter Scott (Radio Times Hulton Picture Library)

HUNT, James Henry Leigh (1784–1859). *The Story of Rimini; Autobiography.*
DE QUINCEY, Thomas (1785–1859). *Confessions of an English Opium Eater.*
CARLYLE, Thomas (1795–1881). *The French Revolution.*
HOOD, Thomas (1799–1845). *The Song of the Shirt; The Bridge of Sighs; To The Great Unknown.*
MACAULAY, Thomas Babington (Lord) (1800–59). *Lays of Ancient Rome.*

19th century

DISRAELI, Benjamin (Earl of Beaconsfield) (1804–81). *Coningsby; Sybil; Tancred.*
FITZGERALD, Edward (1809–83). *Rubáiyát of Omar Khayyám.*
THACKERAY, William Makepeace (1811–63). *Vanity Fair.*
LEAR, Edward (1812–88). *A Book of Nonsense; Nonsense Songs.*
DARWIN, Charles Robert (1809–82). *On the Origin of Species; The Descent of Man.*
TROLLOPE, Anthony (1815–82). *The Five Barsetshire Novels.*
BRONTË (later Nicholls), Charlotte (1816–55). *Jane Eyre.*
BRONTË, Emily Jane (1818–48). *Wuthering Heights.*
RUSKIN, John (1819–1900). *Praeterita.*
'ELIOT, George' (Mary Ann [or Marian] Evans, later Mrs J W Cross) (1819–80). *Scenes of Clerical Life* (1858); *Adam Bede* (1859); *The Mill on the Floss* (1860); *Silas Marner* (1861); *Middlemarch* (1871–72).
KINGSLEY, Charles (1819–75). *Westward Ho!; The Water Babies.*
ARNOLD, Matthew (1822–88). *The Strayed Reveller* ('Sohrab and Rustum' and 'Scholar Gypsy').
MEREDITH, George (1828–1909). *Modern Love.*
ROSSETTI, Dante Gabriel (1828–82). *Poems; Ballads and Sonnets.*
'CARROLL, Lewis' (Charles Lutwidge Dodgson) (1832–98). *Alice's Adventures in Wonderland; Through The Looking Glass.*
GILBERT, Sir William Schwenck (1836–1911). *The Mikado; The Gondoliers; HMS Pinafore.*
SWINBURNE, Algernon Charles (1837–1909). *Rosamund.*
HARDY, Thomas (1840–1928). *Under The Greenwood Tree; Tess of the D'Urbervilles.*

JAMES, Henry (1843–1916). *Daisy Miller* (1879); *The Portrait of a Lady* (1881); *Washington Square* (1881); *The Turn of the Screw* (1898); *The Golden Bowl* (1904).

BRIDGES, Robert Seymour (1844–1930). *The Testament of Beauty*.

HOPKINS, Gerard Manley (1844–89). *The Notebooks and Papers of Gerard Manley Hopkins*.

STEVENSON, Robert Louis (1850–94). *Travels with a Donkey in the Cévennes* (1879); *New Arabian Nights* (1882); *Treasure Island* (1883); *Strange Case of Dr Jekyll and Mr Hyde* (1886); *Kidnapped* (1886); *The Black Arrow* (1888); *The Master of Ballantrae* (1889); *Weir of Hermiston* (unfinished) (1896).

WILDE, Oscar Fingal O'Flahertie Wills (1854–1900). *The Picture of Dorion Gray* (1891); *Lady Windermere's Fan* (1893); *The Importance of Being Ernest* (1899).

SHAW, George Bernard (1856–1950) (adjective Shavian). *Plays Pleasant and Unpleasant* (1893) (including *Mrs Warren's Profession*, *Arms and the Man* and *Candida*); *Three Plays for Puritans* (1901) (*The Devil's Disciple*, *Caesar and Cleopatra* and *Captain Brassbound's Conversion*); *Man and Superman* (1903); *John Bull's Other Island* and *Major Barbara* (1907); *Androcles and the Lion*, *Overruled* and *Pygmalion* (1916); *Saint Joan* (1924); *Essays in Fabian Socialism* (1932).

CONRAD, Joseph (*né* Józef Teodor Konrad Nalecz Korzeniowski) (1857–1924). *Almayer's Folly; An Outcast of the Islands; The Nigger of the 'Narcissus'; Lord Jim; Youth; Typhoon; Nostromo; The Secret Agent.*

DOYLE, Sir Arthur Conan (1859–1930). *The White Company; The Adventures of Sherlock Holmes; The Hound of the Baskervilles.*

THOMPSON, Francis (1859–1907). *The Hound of Heaven.*

HOUSMAN, Alfred Edward (1859–1936). *A Shropshire Lad.*

QUILLER-COUCH, Sir Arthur ('Q') (1865–1944). *On the Art of Writing; Studies in Literature.*

YEATS, William Butler (1865–1939). *Collected Poems.*

WELLS, Herbert George (1866–1946). *The Invisible Man; The History of Mr Polly.*

MURRAY, Gilbert Amié (1866–1957). *Hippolytus; The Trojan Womèn*

BENNETT, Enoch Arnold (1867–1931). *Anna of the Five Towns; The Old Wives' Tale; Clayhanger; The Card; Riceyman Steps.*

GALSWORTHY, John (1867–1933). *The Forsyte Saga; The White Monkey.*

BELLOC, Joseph Hilaire Pierre (1870–1953). *The Path to Rome.*

BEERBOHM, Sir Max (1872–1956). *Zuleika Dobson.*

DE LA MARE, Walter (1873–1956). *Poems; Desert Islands and Robinson Crusoe.*

CHESTERTON, Gilbert Keith (1874–1936). *The Innocence of Father Brown; The Ballad of The White Horse.*

CHURCHILL, Sir Winston Spencer (1874–1965). *Marlborough; The Second World War; A History of The English-Speaking Peoples.*

MASEFIELD, John (1878–1967). *Barrack-Room Ballads; Ballads and Poems.*

MAUGHAM, William Somerset (1874–1965). *Of Human Bondage; The Moon and Sixpence; The Razor's Edge.*

TREVELYAN, George Macaulay (1876–1962). *History of England; English Social History.*

FORSTER, Edward Morgan (1879–1970). *Where Angels Fear to Tread; A Room with a View; Howards End; A Passage to India.*

JOYCE, James (1882–1941). *Ulysses; Finnegans Wake.*

WOOLF (*née* Stephen), Virginia (1882–1941). *The Voyage Out; Night and Day; Jacob's Room; The Years.*

KEYNES, John Maynard (Baron) (1883–1946). *The Economic Consequences of the Peace; The General Theory of Employment.*

FLECKER, James Elroy (1884–1915). *Thirty-Six Poems; Hassan.*

LAWRENCE, David Herbert (1885–1930). *Sons and Lovers; Love Poems and Others.*

SASSOON, Siegfried (1886–1967). *Memoirs of a Fox-Hunting Man.*

SITWELL, Dame Edith, DBE (1887–1964). *Collected Poems; Aspects of Modern Poetry.*

BROOKE, Rupert Chawner (1887–1915). *1914 and Other Poems; Letters from America.*

ELIOT, Thomas Stearns, OM (1888–1965). *Murder in the Cathedral.*

LAWRENCE, Thomas Edward (later Shaw) (1888–1935). *Seven Pillars of Wisdom.*

OWEN, Wilfred (1893–1918). *Poems.*

PRIESTLY, John Boynton (b. 1894). *The Good Companions.*

HUXLEY, Aldous Leonard (1894–1963). *Brave New World; Stories, Essays and Poems.*

GRAVES, Robert Ranke (b. 1895). *Poems and Satires.*

THE GREEK ALPHABET

The Greek alphabet consists of 24 letters—seven vowels and seventeen consonants. The seven vowels are alpha (short a), epsilon (short e), eta (long e), iota (short i), omicron (long o), upsilon (short u, usually transcribed y), and omega (short o).

Name	Capital	Lower case	English equivalent	Name	capital	Lower case	English equivalent
Alpha	A	α	a	Nu	N	ν	n
Beta	B	β	b	Xi	Ξ	ξ	x
Gamma	Γ	γ	g	Omicron	O	o	ŏ
Delta	Δ	δ	d	Pi	Π	π	p
Epsilon	E	ε	ĕ	Rho	P	ρ	r
Zeta	Z	ζ	z	Sigma	Σ	$\sigma\varsigma$	s
Eta	H	η	ē	Tau	T	τ	t
Theta	Θ	θ	th	Upsilon	Y	υ	ŭ or y
Iota	I	ι	i	Phi	Φ	φ	ph
Kappa	K	κ	k	Chi	X	χ	ch
Lambda	Λ	λ	l	Psi	Ψ	ψ	ps
Mu	M	μ	m	Omega	Ω	ω	ō

Greek has no direct equivalent to our c, f, h, j, q, u, v, or w.

THE RUSSIAN ALPHABET

The Russian alphabet is written in Cyrillic script, so called after St Cyril, the 9th century monk who is reputed to have devised it. It contains 31 characters, including 5 hard and 5 soft vowels.

Capital	Lower case	Name	English equivalent	Capital	Lower case	Name	English equivalent
А	а	ah	ā	Т	т	teh	t
Б	б	beh	b	У	у	oo	oo
В	в	veh	v	Ф	ф	eff	f
Г	г	gheh	g	Х	х	hah	h
Д	д	deh	d	Ц	ц	tseh	ts
Е	е	yeh	ye	Ч	ч	cheh	ch
Ж	ж	zheh	j	Ш	ш	shah	sh
З	з	zeh	z	Щ	щ	shchah	shch
И	и	ee	ee	Ъ	ъ	(hard sign)	—
К	к	kah	k	Ы	ы	yerih	I
Л	л	ell	l	Ь	ь	(soft sign)	—
М	м	em	m	Э	э	eh	e
Н	н	en	n	Ю	ю	you	yu
О	о	aw	aw	Я	я	ya	yā
П	п	peh	p	Ё	ё	yaw	yo
Р	р	err	r	Й	й	short и	elided 'y'
С	с	ess	s				

LANGUAGE AND LITERATURE

ENGLISH LANGUAGE: PUNCTUATION

In the English language there are nine principal varieties of punctuation marks:

(1) . A period, full stop or full point marks the end of a sentence.
(2) : A colon marks an abrupt pause before a new but connected statement within the same sentence.
(3) ; A semicolon separates different statements within a sentence.
(4) , A comma separates clauses, phrases, participles and adjectives qualifying the same noun.
(5) ! An exclamation mark indicates surprise.
(6) ? An interrogation mark poses a question.
(7) " " Quotation marks, or inverted commas, define quoted or direct speech.
(8) ' An apostrophe indicates an elision or the possessive case.
(9) (), [], — — Marks of parenthesis, brackets, dashes or em rules enclose clarification, interpolations or irregularities within a sentence.

Parts of speech

There are generally agreed to be eight parts of speech in the English Language:

1. Nouns or Substantives—these denote persons or things.
2. Adjectives—denoting qualities such as colour, size, etc.
3. Pronouns—these are used instead of nouns or adjectives to denote a word already used. The sub-divisions of pronouns are personal (I or We), demonstrative (there or that), relative (his or hers), interrogative (where, whose), indefinite (one). The definite and indefinite articles 'the' and 'a' or 'an', and numerals are best treated as pronouns.
4. Verbs—denote actions, happenings, or states (e.g. to run, to stage, to loathe).
5. Adverbs—serve to modify or qualify either verbs, adjectives or other adverbs (e.g. finely drawn, or beautifully clear).
6. Prepositions—mark the relations between words (e.g. 'to', 'for' or 'by').
7. Conjunctions—used to connect either words within a clause or clauses themselves.
8. Interjections—ejaculations that stand outside the form of any ordinary sentence, for example 'Bravo!' or 'Hear, Hear', etc.

In English there are only 13 irregular plurals which survive:

1. brother   brothers or brethren
2. child   children
3. cow   cows or kine
4. die   dice
5. foot   feet
6. goose   geese
7. louse   lice
8. man   men
9. mouse   mice
10. ox   oxen
11. penny   pennies or pence
12. tooth   teeth
13. woman   women

LATIN AND MODERN LANGUAGES

	Latin	French	German	Italian	Spanish
Days of the Week					
Sunday	dies Solis	dimanche	Sonntag	domenica	domingo
Monday	dies Lunae	lundi	Montag	lunedì	lunes
Tuesday	dies Martis	mardi	Dienstag	martedì	martes
Wednesday	dies Mercurii	mercredi	Mittwoch	mercoledì	miércoles
Thursday	dies Jovis	jeudi	Donnestag	giovedì	jueves
Friday	dies Veneris	vendredi	Freitag	venerdì	viernes
Saturday	dies Saturni	samedi	Samstag (Sonnabend)	sabato	sábado
Months of the Year					
January	Ianuarius	janvier	Januar	gennaio	enero
February	Februarius	février	Februar	febbraio	febrero
March	Martius	mars	März	marzo	marzo
April	Aprilis	avril	April	aprile	abril
May	Maius	mai	Mai	maggio	mayo
June	Iunius	juin	Juni	giugno	junio
July	Quinctilis (later Iulius)	juillet	Juli	luglio	julio
August	Sextilis (later August)	août	August	agosto	agosto
September	Semptember	septembre	September	settembre	septiembre
October	October	octobre	Oktober	ottobre	octubre
November	November	novembre	November	novembre	noviembre
December	December	décembre	Dezember	decembre	diciembre
Seasons of the Year					
Spring	ver	le printemps	der Frühling	la primavera	la primavera
Summer	aestas	l'été	der Sommer	l'estate	el verano
Autumn	auctumnus	l'automne	der Herbst	l'autunno	el ontoño
Winter	heims	l'hiver	der Winter	l'inverno	el invierno

Sport

OLYMPIC GAMES

The earliest celebration of the ancient Olympic Games of which there is a certain record is that of July 776 BC, though their origin probably dates from *c.* 1370 BC. A cessation in hostilities for some Games are recorded in 884 BC. The ancient Games were terminated by an order issued in Milan in AD 393 by Theodosius I, 'the Great' (*c.* 346–395), Emperor of Rome. At the instigation of Pierre de Fredi, Baron de Coubertin (1863–1937), the Olympic Games of the modern era were inaugurated in Athens on 6 Apr. 1896.

Celebrations have been allocated as follows:

I	Athens	6–15 Apr. 1896	XII	*Tōkyō, then Helsinki	1940
II	Paris	20 May–28 Oct. 1900	XIII	*London	1944
III	St. Louis	1 July–23 Nov. 1904	XIV	London	29 July–14 Aug. 1948
†	Athens	22 Apr.–2 May 1906	XV	Helsinki	19 July–3 Aug. 1952
IV	London	27 Apr.–31 Oct. 1908	XVI	Melbourne	22 Nov.–8 Dec. 1956
V	Stockholm	5 May–22 Jul. 1912	XVII	Rome	25 Aug.–11 Sept. 1960
VI	*Berlin	1916	XVIII	Tōkyō	10–24 Oct. 1964
VII	Antwerp	20 Apr.–12 Sept. 1920	XIX	Mexico City	12–27 Oct. 1968
VIII	Paris	4 May–27 Jul. 1924	XX	Munich	26 Aug.–10 Sept. 1972
IX	Amsterdam	17 May–12 Aug. 1928	XXI	Montreal	17 July–1 Aug. 1976
X	Los Angeles	30 July–14 Aug. 1932	XXII	Moscow	19 July–3 Aug. 1980
XI	Berlin	1–16 Aug. 1936	XXIII	Not yet allocated	1984

* Cancelled due to World Wars   † Intercalated Celebration not numbered but officially organised by the IOC (International Olympic Committee)

The Winter Olympics were inaugurated in 1924 and have been allocated as follows:

I	Chamonix, France	25 Jan.–4 Feb. 1924	VII	Cortina d'Ampezzo, Italy	26 Jan.–5 Feb. 1956
II	St Moritz, Switzerland	11–19 Feb. 1928	VIII	Squaw Valley, California	18–28 Feb. 1960
III	Lake Placid, USA	4–15 Feb. 1932	IX	Innsbruck, Austria	29 Jan.–9 Feb. 1964
IV	Garmisch-Partenkirchen, Germany	6–16 Feb. 1936	X	Grenoble, France	6–18 Feb. 1968
			XI	Sapporo, Japan	3–13 Feb. 1972
V	St Moritz, Switzerland	30 Jan.–8 Feb. 1948	XII	Innsbruck, Austria	4–15 Feb. 1976
VI	Oslo, Norway	14–25 Feb. 1952	XIII	Lake Placid, USA	1980

Table of medal winners by nations 1896–1976

Note: These totals include all first, second and third places including those events no longer on the current (1976) schedule. Also included are medals for the *official* Olympic art competitions of 1912 to 1948. The 1906 Games which were *officially* staged by the International Olympic Committee have accordingly been included.

Olympic games (Summer) 1896–1972

		Gold	Silver	Bronze	Total
1.	United States of America	594	438½	385½	1418
2.	USSR	211	182	174	567
3.	Great Britain	157½	193½	163	514
4.	France	138	150	152	440
5.	Germany (1896 to 1964: West Germany from 1968)	125½	169	161	455½
6.	Sweden	123½	121	152	396½
7.	Italy	122	108	102	332
8.	Hungary	103	94	103	300
9.	Finland	88	70	98	256
10.	Japan	64	58	53	175
11.	Australia	62	50	61	173
12.	Switzerland	39	62	51	152
12.	Norway	39	29	31	99
14.	Czechoslovakia	38	41	35½	114½
14.	Netherlands	38	40	50	128
16.	Belgium	35	45	40	120
17.	Poland	31	33	61	125
18.	East Germany (from 1968)	29	32	30	91
19.	Denmark	27½	58	49	134½
20.	Canada	26	38	47	111

Winter olympic games (1924–76)
(and including ice events held in 1908 and 1920)

		Gold	Silver	Bronze	Total
1.	USSR	51	32	35	118
2.	Norway	50	52	43	145
3.	United States of America	30	38	27	95
4.	Sweden	25	23	26	74
5.	Finland	24	34	23	81
6.	Austria	22	31	27	80
6.	Germany (1908–64: West Germany from 1968)	22	20	17	59
8.	Switzerland	15	17	16	48
9.	East Germany (from 1968)	12	10	16	38
9.	France	12	9	12	33
9.	Canada	12	7	14	33
12.	Italy	10	7	7	24
13.	Netherlands	9	13	9	31
14.	Great Britain	5	4	10	19

Note: Results of demonstration events are not included.

Development of the summer Olympic Games
These figures relate to the Summer Games and exclude Demonstration Sports.

	Countries Represented	Number of Sports	Number of Competitors Male	Female
1896	13	9	311	0
1900	22	17	1319	11
1904	12	14	617	8
1906	20	11	877	7
1908	22	21	1999	36
1912	28	14	2490	57
1920	29	22	2543	64
1924	44	18	2956	136
1928	46	15	2724	290
1932	47	15	1281	127
1936	49	20	3738	328
1948	59	18	3714	385
1952	69	17	4407	518
1956	71	17	2958	384
1960	83	17	4738	610
1964	93	19	4457	683
1968	112	18	4750	781
1972	122	21	6077	1070

Development of the winter Olympic Games
These figures relate to the winter games, and ice events in 1908 and 1920.

Games	Number of Countries	Number of Sports	Number of Competitors Male	Female
London (IVth Summer)	6	1	14	7
Antwerp (VIIth Summer)	10	2	73	12
I Chamonix	16	5	281	13
II St Moritz	25	6	468	27
III Lake Placid	17	5	274	32
IV Garmisch	28	6	675	80
V St Moritz	28	7	636	77
VI Oslo	22	6	623	109
VII Cortina	24	6	687	132
VIII Squaw Valley	27	5	521	144
IX Innsbruck	36	7	986	200
X Grenoble	37	7	1065	228
XI Sapporo	35	7	1128	217
XII Innsbruck	36	7	788	248

Olympic sports (current schedule)
21 Summer events

1. Archery
2. Athletics (Track and Field)
3. Basketball
4. Boxing
5. Canoeing
6. Cycling
7. Equestrian Sports
8. Fencing
   Field Hockey, see Hockey (Field)
9. Football (Association)
10. Gymnastics
11. Handball
12. Hockey (Field)
13. Judo
14. Modern Pentathlon
15. Rowing
    Soccer, see Football (Association)
16. Shooting
17. Swimming, including Diving and Water Polo
    Track and Field Athletics, see Athletics
18. Volleyball
    Water Polo, see Swimming
19. Weightlifting
20. Wrestling
21. Yachting

These can be divided into three Stadium sports (Athletics, Equestrianism (Grand Prix and Dressage), Football); eight Indoor hall sports (Basketball, Boxing, Gymnastics, Handball, Judo, Volleyball, Weightlifting and Wrestling); four Aquatic Sports (Canoeing, Rowing, Swimming (including Diving and Water Polo) and Yachting); and other Field Sports (Archery, other Equestrian events, Hockey). Cycling events are staged partly on the roads and partly in a Velodrome.

7 Winter events

1. Nordic Skiing (including Ski-Jumping and Biathlon)
2. Alpine Skiing
3. Figure Skating
4. Speed Skating
5. Bobsleigh
6. Tobogganing (Lugeing)
7. Ice Hockey

ORIGINS AND ANTIQUITY OF SPORTS

Date BC	Sport	Location and Notes
c. 3000	Coursing	Egypt. Saluki dogs. Greyhounds used in England AD 1067, Waterloo Cup 1836.
c. 2350	Wrestling	Tomb of Ptahhotap, Egypt; ancient Olympic games c. 704 BC, Greco-Roman style, France c. AD 1860; Internationalised 1912.
c. 2050	Hockey	Beni Hasan tomb, Egypt. Lincolnshire AD 1277. Modern forms c. 1875. Some claims to be of Persian origin in 2nd millennium BC.
c. 1600	Falconry	China-Shang dynasty. Earliest manuscript evidence points to Persian origin.
c. 1520	Boxing	Thera fresco, Greece. First ring rules 1743 England. Queensberry Rules 1867.
c. 1360	Fencing	Egyptians used masks and blunted swords. Established as a sport in Germany c. AD 1450. Hand guard invented in Spain c. 1510. Foil 17th century, épée mid-19th century, and sabre in Italy, late 19th century.
c. 1300	Athletics	Ancient Olympic Games. Modern revival c. AD 1810, Sandhurst, England.
c. 800	Ice Skating	Bone skates superseded by metal blades c. AD 1600.
c. 776	Gymnastics	Ancient Olympic Games, modern revival c. AD 1780.
c. 624	Horse Racing	Twenty-third ancient Olympic Games. Roman diversion c. AD 210 Netherby, Yorkshire. Chester course 1540.
c. 600	Equestrianism	Riding of horses dates from c. 1400 BC Anatolia. Show jumping Paris AD 1886.
c. 525	Polo	As Pula, Persia. Possibly of Tibetan origin.

c.	10	Fly Fishing	Earliest reference by the Roman Martial.
ante	1	Jiu Jitsu	Pre-Christian Chinese origin, developed as a martial art by Japan.

AD

c.	300	Archery	Known as a neolithic skill (as opposed to a sport). Natal, South Africa *ante* 46 000 BC. Practised by the Genoese. Internationalised 1931.
c.	1050	Tennis (Royal)	Earliest surviving court, Paris, France, 1496. First 'world' champion *c.* 1740.
ante	1300	Bowls	On grass in Britain, descended from the Roman game of boccie.
	1429	Billiards	First treatise by Marot (France) *c.* 1550. Rubber cushions 1835, slate beds 1836.
c.	1450	Golf	Earliest reference: parliamentary prohibition in March 1457, Scotland. Rubber core balls 1902, steel shafts 1929.
	1474	Shooting	Target shooting recorded in Geneva, Switzerland.
ante	1492	Lacrosse	Originally American Indian *baggataway*. First non-Indian club, *Montreal*, 1839.
c.	1530	Football (Association)	26-a-side, Florence, Italy. Rules codified, Cambridge University, 1846. Eleven-a-side standardised 1870. Chinese ball-kicking game *Tsu-chin* known *c.* 350 BC.
c.	1550	Cricket	Earliest recorded match, Guildford, Surrey, England 1598. Earliest depictment *c.* 1250. Eleven-a-side Sussex 1697.
	1557	Fox hunting	Earliest reference in England (28 Feb.). Previously deer or hare hunted.
c.	1560	Curling	Netherlands, Scotland 1716.
	1600	Ice Yachting	Earliest patent in low countries. Sand yacht reported Belgian beach 1595.
	1603	Swimming	Inter-school contests in Japan by Imperial edict; sea-bathing at Scarborough by 1660; earliest bath, Liverpool in 1828.
c.	1660	Ice Hockey	Netherlands. Kingston, Ontario, Canada 1860. Rules devised in Montreal 1879.
	1661	Yachting	First contest Thames (1 Sept.). Earliest club in Cork, Ireland, 1720.
c.	1676	Caving	Pioneer explorer, John Beaumont, Somerset, England.
	1698	Mountaineering	Rock climbing in St Kilda; first major ascent (Mont Blanc) 1786; continuous history since only 1854.
c.	1700	Bull fighting	Francisco Romero of Ronda, Andalusia, Spain.
	1716	Rowing	Earliest contest sculling race on Thames (1 Aug.). First English regatta, 1775, Henley Regatta 1839.
	1744	Baseball	Of English provenance, Cartwright, Rules codified 1845.
c.	1750	Trotting	Harness racing sulky introduced 1829.
	1760	Roller Skating	Developed by Joseph Merlin (Belgium). Modern type devised by J L Plympton (USA) in 1866.
	1765	Fives (Eton type)	Buttress hand-ball, Babcary, Somerset. New Courts at Eton, 1840; rules codified 1877.
	1771	Surfing	First recording by Capt. James Cook in the Hawaiian Islands. Sport revived by 1900 at Waikiki, Honolulu.
	1787	Beagling	Newcastle Harriers, England.
c.	1790	Shinty	Inter-village or clan game West and Central Highlands of Scotland as gaelic *lomain* (driving forward).
	1793	Lawn Tennis	Field tennis, as opposed to Court tennis, first recorded in England (29 Sept.). Leamington Club founded 1872; patent as *sphairistike* by Major W C Wingfield Feb. 1874.
	1798	Rackets	Earliest covered court, recorded, Exeter.
	1823	Rugby	Traditional inventor Rev William Webb Ellis (*c.* 1807–72) at Rugby School (Nov.). Game formulated at Cambridge, 1839. The Rugby Union founded in 1871.
c.	1835	Croquet	Ireland as 'Crockey'. Country house lawn game in England, *c.* 1856. First rules 1857. The word dated back to 1478.
	1843	Skiing (Alpine)	Tromsö, Norway. Kiandra Club, New South Wales 1855. California 1860. Alps 1883.
	1845	Bowling (ten-pin)	Connecticut State, USA, to evade ban on nine-pin bowling. *Kegel*—a German cloister sport known since 12th century.
	1847	Rodeo	Sante Fe, New Mexico, USA. Steer wrestling, 1903.
c.	1850	Fives (Rugby type)	Earliest inter-school matches *c.* 1872.
c.	1850	Squash rackets	Evolved at Harrow School, England. First US championship 1906.
	1853	Gliding	Earliest flight by John Appleby, coachman to Sir George Cayley, Brompton Hall, Yorkshire. World championships 1948.
	1853	Australian Rules Football	Ballarrat goldfields, Australia.
c.	1863	Badminton	Made famous at Badminton Hall, Avon, England.
	1865	Canoeing	Pioneered by John Macgregor (Scotland).
	1868	Cycling	First International Race 31 May, Parc de St Cloud, Paris.
	1869	Water Polo	Developed in England from 'Water Soccer'; an Olympic event since 1900.
	1875	Snooker	Devised by Col Sir Neville Chamberlain, Ootacamund Club, India as a variant of 'blackpool'.
	1876	Greyhound Racing	Railed 'hare' and windlass, Hendon, North London (Sept.). Emeryville, California, USA, 1919. First race in UK, Manchester 24 July 1926.
	1879	Ski jumping	Huseby, near Oslo, Norway.
	1882	Judo	Devised (February) by Dr Jigora Kano (Japan) from Jiu Jitsu (see above).
	1884	Bobsledding	First contests, St Moritz, Switzerland. Skeleton (one-man), 1892.
	1886	Equestrianism (Show Jumping)	Paris. Pignatelli's academy, Naples *c.* 1580.
	1889	Table Tennis	Devised by James Gibb as 'Gossima' from a game known in 1881. Ping Pong Association formed in London, 1902. Sport resuscitated, 1921.
	1891	Weightlifting	First international contest, Cafe Monico, London (28 Mar.).
	1891	Netball	Invented in USA. Introduced to England 1895.
	1892	Basketball	Invented (20 Jan.) Springfield, Mass, USA, by Dr James A Naismith. Mayan Indian game *Pok-ta-Pok* dated BC.
	1895	Motor Racing	Earliest race Paris–Bordeaux, France, (11–13 June).
	1895	Rugby League	Professional breakaway, 1895 (29 Aug.). Team reduced from 15 to 13 in 1906, (12 June).
	1895	Volleyball	Invented by William G Morgan at Holyoake, Mass, USA as *Minnonette;* Internationalised 1947.
	1896	Marathon running	Marathon to Athens, 1896 Olympics. Standardised at 26 miles 385 yds, *42,195 km* in 1924. Named from the run from the Marathon battlefield, Greece by Phidippides in 490 BC.
	1897	Motorcycling	Earliest race Paris–Dieppe, France.
	1901	Small Bore Shooting	·22 calibre introduced as a Civilian Army training device.
	1912	Modern Pentathlon	First formal contest, Stockholm Olympic Games.
	1914	Water Skiing	Plank-riding behind motor boat, Scarborough, England; shaped skis by Ralph Samuelson, Lake Pepin, Minnesota, USA, 1922; devised ramp jump at Miami, Florida, 1928; sport internationalised 1946.
	1922	Skiing (Slalom)	Devised by Sir Arnold Lunn, Müven, Switzerland (21 Jan.).
	1923	Speedway	West Maitland, NSW, Australia (Nov.); first World Championships Sept. 1936.
	1936	Trampoline	Developed by George Nissen (US). First championships 1948. Used in show-business since 1910.
	1951	Sky Diving	First world championships in Yugoslavia.
	1960	Aerobatics	First world championships instituted.

SPEED IN SPORT

mph	km/h	Record	Name	Place	Date
2070·102	3 331,506	Official air speed record (para military)	Col R L Stephens & Lt Col D Andre (USA)	over Edwards Air Base California, USA	1 May 1965
631·367	1 016,086	Highest land speed (four wheeled rocket powered)	Gary Gabelich (US) in The Blue Flame	Bonneville Salt Flats, Utah USA	23 Oct. 1970
614	988	Parachuting free-fall in mesosphere (military research)	Capt J W Kittinger (USA)	Tularosa, New Mex, USA	16 Aug. 1960
429·311	690,909	Highest land speed (wheel driven)	Donald Campbell (GB) in Bluebird (gas turbined)	Lake Eyrie, South Australia	17 Jul. 1964
418·504	673,516	Highest land speed (four wheel direct drive)	R Summers (USA) in Goldenrod	Bonneville Salt Flats, Utah, USA	12 Nov. 1965
328	527,8	Highest water borne speed	Donald Campbell (GB) in Bluebird K7	Coniston Water, Cumbria England	4 Jan. 1967
307·692	495,169	Highest speed motor cycle	Don Vesco (US)	Bonneville Salt Flats, Utah	28 Sept. 1975
285·213	459,065	Official water speed record	Lee Taylor (US) in Hustler	Lake Guntersville, Alabama, USA	30 Jun. 1967
221·027	355,699	Motor racing—closed circuit	Mark Donohue Jr (US)	Talladega, Alabama, USA	9 Aug. 1975
203·19	327,37	Model aircraft (jet model)	E Zanin (Italy)	Rome, Italy	26 Apr. 1964
202·46	325,83	Hydroplane record (propeller driven)	Larry Hill (USA)	Long Beach, California	1973
199·071	320,373	Lap record 500 miles *804 km* Motor racing	Johnny Rutherford (US) (Electrically timed)	Indianapolis (USA)	12 May 1973
170	270	Golf ball		USA	1960
c.160	255	Pelota		USA	
155·627	250,457	Lap record (practice) 24 hr Endurance Motor racing	Jackie Oliver	Le Mans, France	18 Apr. 1971
140·5	226,1	Cycling, motor paced	Dr Allan V Abbott (US)	Bonneville Salt Flats, Utah	25 Aug. 1973
125·69	202,27	Water Skiing	Danny Churchill (US)	Oakland Marine Stadium, California, USA	1971
117–185	188–297	Sky-Diving—lower atmosphere	Terminal velocity (varies with attitude)		post 1950
120·784	194,384	Downhill Schuss (Alpine Skiing)	Pino Meynet (Italy)	Cervinia, Italy	July 1975
118	189	Ice hockey—puck	Bobby Hull (Canada)	Chicago, Illinois, USA	1965
102·73	165,34	Gliding (*100 km* triangular course)	K Briegleb (US) in a Kestrel 17	over USA	18 Jul. 1974
83·8	134,8	Tobogganing—Cresta Run	Fl Lt Colin Mitchell (UK)	St Moritz, Switzerland	Feb. 1960
76·342	122,862	Cycling behind pacemaker—1 hr	Leon Vanderstuyft (Belgium)	Montlhery Motor Circuit, France	30 Sept. 1928
66·538	107,084	Downhill Alpine Skiing (Olympic course) (average)	Franz Klammer (Austria)	Innsbruck, Austria	5 Feb. 1976
52·46	84,42	Speedway (4 laps of 430 yd *393 m*)	Dave Morton (GB)	Crewe, England	12 Aug. 1974
43·26	69,62	Horse racing (440 yd *402 m* in 20·8 s)	Big Racket	Mexico City, Mexico	5 Feb. 1945
42·20	67,92	Track cycling (*200 m* 219 yd) unpaced in 10·6 s	Antonio Maspes (Italy)	Milan, Italy	28 Aug. 1962
41·72	67,14	Greyhound racing (410 yd *374 m* straight 26·13 s)	The Shoe (Australia)	Richmond, NSW, Australia	25 Apr. 1968
35·80	57,61	Sailing—55 ft *16,76 m* proa *Crossbow* 31·09 knots)	T J Coleman (UK) *et al.*	Portland, Dorset, England	30 Sept. 1975
35·06	56,42	Horse racing—The Derby (1 mil 885 yd *2,41 km*)	Mahmoud	Epsom, Surrey, England	June 1936
35	56	Boxing—speed of punch	Sugar Ray Robinson (USA)	USA	Jan. 1957
30·397	49,432	Cycling—1 hr, unpaced	Eddie Merckx (Belgium)	Mexico City, Mexico	25 Oct. 1972
29·80	47,96	Steeplechasing—The Grand National (4 miles 856 yd *7,220 km*) in 9 min 1·9 s	Red Rum ridden by Brian Fletcher	Aintree, Liverpool, England	31 Mar. 1973
29·43	47,36	Ice speed skating (500 m *546 yd* in 37·00 s on 400 m *437 yd* rink)	Yevgeniy Kulikov (USSR)	Medeo, USSR	29 Mar. 1975
27·89	44,88	Sprinting (during 100 yd *91 m*)	Robert Hayes (USA)	St Louis, Missouri, USA	21 June 1963
21·49	34,58	Cycling—average maintained over 24 hr	Tearo Louhivuori (Finland)	Tampere-Kolari, Finland	10 Sept. 1974
13·45	21,65	Rowing (2000 m *2187 yd*)	East German Eight	Copenhagen, Denmark	21 Aug. 1971
12.24	19,69	Marathon run (26 miles 385 yd *42,195 km*)	Derek Clayton (Australia)	Antwerp, Belgium	30 May 1969
8·84	14,24	Walking—1 hr	Bernd Kannenberg (WG)	Hamburg, W. Germany	25 May 1974
4·42	7,11	Swimming (100 m)—Long Course in 50·59 s	James Montgomery (US)	Kansas City, USA	28 Aug. 1975
2·2	3,5	Channel swimming (effective speed)	Barry Watson (UK)	France to England	15–16 Aug. 1964
0·00084	0,00135	Tug 'o War (2 hr 41 min pull—12 ft *3,6 m*)	2nd Derbyshire Regt (UK)	Jubbulpore, India	12 Aug. 1889

WEIGHTS AND DIMENSIONS IN SPORT

Association Football
Ball circum: 27–28 in *68–71 cm*
Ball wt: 14–16 oz *396–453 g*
Pitch length: 100–130 yd *91–120 m*
Pitch width: 50–100 yd *45–91 m*

Basketball
Ball circum: 29½–31½ in *74,9–80 cm*

Cricket
Ball circum: 8 3/16–9 in *20,79–22,8 cm*
Ball wt: 5½–5¾ oz *155–163 g*
Pitch: 22 yd *20,11 m* from stump to stump, creases 4 ft *1,21 m* apart each end.

Croquet
Ball diam: 3⅝ in *9,2 cm*

Golf (UK)
Ball min diam: 1·620 in *4,1 cm*
Ball max wt: 1·62 oz *45 g*
In USA min diam: 1·680 in *4,2 cm*

Hockey
Ball circum: 8 13/16–9¼ in *22,3–23,4 cm*
Ball wt: 5½–5¾ oz *155–163 g*

Lawn Bowls
Ball circum: max 16½ in *41,9 cm*

Lawn Tennis
Ball diam: 2½–2⅝ in *6,35–6,66 cm*
Ball wt: 2–2 1/16 oz *56–58 g*
Court: outside dimensions 78 ft *23,77 m* long 27 ft *8,22 m* wide (singles) 36 ft *10,97 m* (doubles)

Rugby League
Ball length: 10¾–11½ in *27,3–29,2 cm*
End on diam: 28¾–29¾ *73,0–75,5 cm*
Diam in width: 23–24 in *58,4–60,9 cm*
Ball wt: 13½–15½ oz *382–439 g*
Pitch (max): 75 yd *68,58 m* wide, 110yd *100,58 m* between goal lines.

Rugby Union
Ball length: 11–11¼ in *27,9–28,5 cm*
End on diam: 28¾–29¾ in *73,0–75,5 cm*
Diam in width: 23–24 in *58,4–60,9 cm*
Ball wt: 13½–15 oz *382–439 g*
Pitch (max): 68·58 m *75 yd* width, 91·44 m *100 yd* between goal lines.

Squash
Ball diam: 1 9/16–1⅝ in *3,9–4,12 cm*
Ball wt: 360–380 grains *23–24 g*

Table Tennis
Ball circum: 4½–4¾ in *11,4–12,0 cm*
Ball wt: 37–39 grains *2,4–2,5 g*

The Earth

GEOLOGY

Rocks of the Earth's crust are grouped in three principal classes:

(1) Igneous rocks have been solidified from molten *Magma*. These are divided into extrusive rock, viz. larva and pumice, or intrusive rock, such as some granites or gabbro which is high in calcium and magnesium and low in silicon. It should be noted that extreme metamorphism can also produce granitic rocks from sediment.

(2) Sedimentary rocks are classically formed by the deposition of sediment in water, viz. conglomerates (e.g. gravel, shingle, pebbles), sandstones and shales (layered clay and claystone). Peat, lignite, bituminous coal and anthracite are the result of the deposition of organic matter. Gypsum, chalk and limestone are examples of chemical sedimentation.

(3) Metamorphic rocks were originally igneous or sedimentary but have been metamorphosed (transformed) by the agency of intense heat, pressure or the action of water. Gneiss is metamorphosed granite; marble is metamorphosed limestone; and slate is highly pressurised shale. Metamorphic rocks made cleavable by intense heat and pressure are known generically as schist. Their foliate characteristics are shared by both gneiss and slate.

Gemstones

Gemstones are minerals possessing a rarity and usually a hardness, colour or translucency which gives them strong aesthetic appeal. Diamond, emerald, ruby and sapphire used to be classed as 'precious stones' and all others as 'semi-precious'. This distinction is no longer generally applied. The principal gemstones in order of hardness are listed below with data in the following order:— name; birthstone (if any); chemical formula; classic colour; degree of hardness on Mohs' Scale 10–1; principal localities where found and brief notes on outstanding specimens. A metric carat is $\frac{1}{5}$th of a gram. It should be noted that most gems are found in many colours and that only the classic colour is here described. In 1937 the National Association of Goldsmiths unified the various national lists of birthstones; their list, which completely agrees with the earlier US version, is followed here.

Diamond: (birthstone for April); C (pure crystalline isotope); fiery bluish-white; Mohs 10·0; S, SW and E Africa and India with alluvial deposits in Australia, Brazil, Congo, India, Indonesia, Liberia, Sierra Leone and USSR (Urals). Largest uncut: *Cullinan* 3106 carats (over 20 oz) by Capt M F Wells, Premier Mine, Pretoria, S Africa on 26 Jan. 1905. Cut by Jacob Asscher in Amsterdam 1909. Largest cut: *Cullinan I* or *Star of Africa* from the above in British Royal Sceptre at 530·2 carats. *Koh-i-nor* originally 186 now re-cut to 106 carats; also in British Crown Jewels. The largest coloured diamond is the 44·4 carat vivid blue *Hope Diamond* from Killur, Golconda, India (ante 1642) in the Smithsonian Institution, Washington DC since November 1958.

Ruby: (birthstone for July); Al_2O_3 (corundum with reddening trace of chromic oxide); dark red; 9·0; Brazil, Burma, Sri Lanka, Thailand. Largest recorded gem 1184 carat stone from Burma; broken red corundum originally of 3421 carats (not gem quality) July 1961, USA.

Sapphire: (birthstone for September); Al_2O_3 (corundum with bluish trace of iron or titanium); dark blue; 9·0; Australia, Burma, Sri Lanka, Kashmir, USA (Montana). Largest

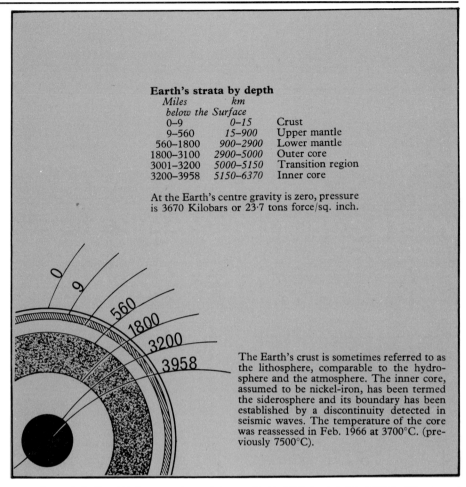

Earth's strata by depth

Miles	km	
below the Surface		
0–9	*0–15*	Crust
9–560	*15–900*	Upper mantle
560–1800	*900–2900*	Lower mantle
1800–3100	*2900–5000*	Outer core
3001–3200	*5000–5150*	Transition region
3200–3958	*5150–6370*	Inner core

At the Earth's centre gravity is zero, pressure is 3670 Kilobars or 23·7 tons force/sq. inch.

The Earth's crust is sometimes referred to as the lithosphere, comparable to the hydrosphere and the atmosphere. The inner core, assumed to be nickel-iron, has been termed the siderosphere and its boundary has been established by a discontinuity detected in seismic waves. The temperature of the core was reassessed in Feb. 1966 at 3700°C. (previously 7500°C).

cut: *Star of India*, 563·5 carats from Sri Lanka now in American Museum of Natural History, New York City. Largest uncut: 1200 carats (white stone) from Anakie, Queensland, May 1956.

Alexandrite: $Al_2[BeO_4]$ (chrysoberyl); dull green (daylight) but blood red (artificial light); 8·5; Brazil, Moravia, USA (Connecticut), USSR (Urals).

Cat's Eye: $Al_2[BeO_4]$ (chrysoberyl, variety cymophane); yellowish to brownish-green with narrow silken ray; 8·5.

Topaz: (birthstone for November); $Al_2 SiO_4F_2$; tea coloured; 8·0; Australia, Brazil, Sri Lanka, Germany, Nam i bia, USSR. The largest recorded is one of 596 lb from Brazil.

Spinel: $MgAl_2O_4$ with reddening trace of Fe_2O_3; red; 8·0 mainly Sri Lanka and India.

Emerald: (birthstone for May); $Al_2Be_3 Si_6O_{18}$ (beryl); vivid green; 7·5–8·0; Austria, Colombia, Norway, USA (N Carolina), USSR (Urals); largest recorded beryl prism (non-gem quality) 135 lb from Urals; largest gem: Devonshire stone of 1350 carats from Muso, Colombia.

Aquamarine: (birthstone for March); $Al_2Be_3Si_6O_{18}$ (beryl), pale limpid blue; 7·5–8·0; found in emerald localities and elsewhere, including Brazil; largest recorded 229 lb near Marambaia, Brazil, 1910.

Garnet: (birthstone for January); silicates of Al, Ca, Cr, Fe, Mg, Ti; purplish-red (Almandine, $Fe_3Al_2[SiO_4]_3$; 7·5–8·0; India, Ceylon, USA (Arizona)); green (Demantoid, $Ca_3Fe_2[SiO_4]_3$; 6·5–7·0; USSR (Siberia and Urals); black (Malanite, $TiCa_3$) (Fe, Ti, Al)$_2[SiO_4]_3$, 6·5.

Zircon: $Zr(SiO_4)$; colourless but also blue and red-brown (hyacinth); 7·0–7·5; Australia (NSW), Burma, Sri Lanka, India, North America, Thailand, USSR (Siberia).

Tourmaline: complex boro-silicate of Al, Fe, Mg alkalis; notably deep green, bluish green, deep red; 7·0–7·25; Brazil, Sri Lanka, USSR (Siberia).

Rock Crystal: (birthstone for April, alternative to diamond); SiO_2; Colourless; 7·0; Brazil, Burma, France, Madagascar, Switzerland, USA (Arkansas). The largest recorded crystal ball is one of 106 lb from Burma now in the US National Museum, Washington DC.

Rose quartz: SiO_2; coarsely granular pale pink; 7·0; Bavaria, Brazil, Finland, Nam i bia, USA (Maine); USSR (Urals).

Cairngorm: (Smoky quartz); SiO_2; smoky yellow to brownish; 7·0; Brazil, Madagascar, Manchuria, Scotland (Cairngorm Mountains), Switzerland, USA (Colorado), USSR (Urals).

Amethyst: (birthstone for February); SiO_2; purple 7·0; Brazil, Sri Lanka, Germany, Madagascar, Uruguay, USSR (Urals).

Chrysoprase (Chalcedony form): (birthstone for May, alternative to emerald); SiO_2 with nickel hydroxide impurity; apple green (opaque); 6·5–7·0; Germany, USA.

Jade: $NaAlSi_2O_6$; dark to leek green; 6·5–7·0; Burma, China, Tibet (pale green and less valuable form is nephrite, Na_2Ca_4 $(Mg, Fe)_{10}[(OH)_2O_2Si_{16}O_{44}]$).

Cornelian (Chalcedony form); often (wrongly) spelt carnelian: (birthstone for July, alternative to ruby); SiO_2 with ferric oxide impurity; blood red to yellowish-brown; 6·5–7·0; widespread, including Great Britain.

Agate (Striped chalcedony); SiO_2; opaque white to pale grey, blue; 6·5–7·0; a variety is moss agate (milky white with moss-like inclusions, often green); Brazil, Germany, India, Madagascar, Scotland.

Onyx: a black and white banded agate (see Agate).

Sardonyx: (birthstone for August, alternative to Peridot); a reddish-brown and white-banded agate (see Agate).

Jasper (Chalcedony): SiO_2 with impurities; brown (manganese oxide), red (ferric oxide), yellow (hydrated ferric oxide); opaque; 6·5–7·0; Egypt, India.

Peridot (Green Olivine): (birthstone for August); $(Mg, Fe)_2[SiO_4]$ green; 6·0–7·0; Australia (Queensland); Brazil, Burma, Norway, St John's Island (Red Sea).

Bloodstone or Blood Jasper (Chalcedony): (birthstone for March, alternative to aquamarine); SiO_2; dark green with red spots (oxide of iron); 6·0–7·0.

Moonstone (Feldspar): (birthstone for June, alternative to pearl); $K[AlSi_3O_6]$; white to bluish, irridescent; 6·0–6·5; Brazil, Burma, Sri Lanka.

Opal: (birthstone for October); $SiO_2.nH_2O$: rainbow colours on white background; other varieties include fire opal, water opal, black opal; 5·0–6·5; Australia, Mexico and formerly Hungary. The largest recorded is one of 143 oz named *Olympic Australis* near Coober Pedy, S Australia in August 1956.

Turquoise: (birthstone for December); $CuAl_6[(OH)_8(PO_4)_4]5H_2O$; sky blue; 5·5–6·0; UAR (Sinai Peninsula), Iran, Turkey, USA (California, Nevada, New Mexico, Texas).

Lapis Lazuli: (birthstone for September, alternative to sapphire); $(Na, Ca)_8[(S, Cl, SO_4)_2(AlSiO_4)_6]$; deep azure blue, opaque; 5·5–5·75; Afghanistan, Chile, Tibet, USSR (Lake Baikal area).

Obsidian: (glassy lava); green or yellowish-brown; 5·0–5·5; volcanic areas.

Non-mineral gem material

Amber (organic): about $C_{40}H_{64}O_4$; honey yellow; clear; or paler yellow, cloudy; 2·0–2·5; Mainly Baltic and Sicily coasts. A variety is fly amber in which the body of an insect is encased.

Coral (polyps of *Coelenterata*): varied colourations including Blood or Red Coral; Australasia, Pacific and Indian Oceans.

Pearl: (birthstone for June); (secretions of molluscs, notably of the sea-water mussel genus *Pinctada* and the fresh-water mussel *Quadrula*); Western Pacific; largest recorded is the *Hope Pearl* weighing nearly 3 oz, circumference $4\frac{1}{2}$ in. Anacreous mass of 14 lb 2oz from a giant clam (*Tridacna gigas*) was recovered in the Philippines in 1934 and is known as the 'Pearl of Allah'.

Geo-chronology

Christian teaching as enunciated by Archbishop Ussher in the 17th century dated the creation of the Earth as occurring in the year 4004 BC. Lord Kelvin (1824–1907) calculated in 1899 that the earth was of the order of possibly some hundreds of millions of years old. In 1905 Lord Rutherford suggested radioactive decay could be used as a measurement and in 1907 Boltwood showed that a sample of pre-Cambrian rock dated from 1640 million years before the present (BP) measured by the uranium-lead method.

Modern dating methods using the duration of radioisotopic half-lives include also the contrasts obtained from thorium-lead, potassium-argon, rubidium-strontium, rhenium-osmium, helium-uranium and in the recent range of up to 40 000 years BP carbon-14. Other methods include thermoluminesence since 1968 and racemisation of amino acids since 1972 which latter is dependant upon the change from optically active to inactive forms which decline varies with the elapse of time.

The table below is based on the Fitch, Forster and Miller revised Potassium-Argon time scale published in 1974 and the Geological Society Phanerozoic Time Scale, 1964 as amended by Lambert (1971).

The geological past is divided into four principal eras. Going backwards in time these are the Cenozoic, the Mesozoic, the Palaeozoic and the Pre-Cambrian, which last stretches back to the formation of the Earth. This is now generally believed to be at least 4700 million years ago except by a few recent authorities who prefer a date of *c.* 6500 million years ago.

---

(1) Cenozoic Era (the present to 64 million years ago). The name is derived from the Gk. *kainos*, new or recent; *zo-os*, life, indicating that life-forms are all recent. The era is divided into the Quaternary Period (the Age of Man, and animals and plants of modern type) back to two million years (formerly only one million years) ago and the Tertiary Period from 2–64 million years ago. This was the age of mammals and the rise and development of the highest orders of plants such as orchids. The Cenozoic is sub-divided thus:

Present to 50 000 BC
Holocene—Gk. *holos*, entirely; *kainos*, recent (all forms recent)

50 000 BC to *c.* 1 750 000 BC
Pleistocene—Gk. *pleisto*, very many (great majority of forms recent)

2 to *c.* 7 million years BP
Pliocene—Gk. *pleion*, more (majority of forms recent)

c. 7 to 26 million years BP
Miocene—Gk. *meios*, less (minority of forms recent)

26 to 38 million years BP
Oligocene—Gk. *oligos*, few (few forms recent)

38 to 54 million years BP
Eocene—Gk. *eos*, dawn (dawn of recent forms)

54 to 64 million years BP
Palaeocene—Gk. *palaious*, ancient (earliest recent forms)

---

(2) Mesozoic Era (65 to 225 million years ago). The name is derived from the Gk. *mesos*, middle; *zo-os*, life, indicating that life-forms are intermediate between the recent evolutions and the ancient forms. The era is divided into three periods thus:

64 to ?135 million years BP
Cretaceous (Latin *creta*, chalk; period of deposition and chalk formation). This was the age of reptiles and the fall of the dinosaurs (*c.* 120 million BP). First abundance of hardwood trees (*c.* 130 million BP) also the palms and seed-bearing plants.

?135 to *c.* 210 million years BP
Jurassic (after the Jura Mountains). This period saw the earliest gliders (*Archaeopteryx*, *c.* 150 million BP) and the earliest mammals (*Morganucodon*, *c.* 160 million BP).

c. 210 to 235 million years BP
Triassic (adj. of trias, the old three-fold German division). First appearance of dinosaurs (*c.* 210 million BP).

---

(3) Palaeozoic Era (*c.* 235 to <597 million years ago). The name is derived from the Gk. *palaios*, ancient; *zo-os*, life, indicating that fossilised life-forms are of ancient forms. The era is broadly divided into the Upper Palaeozoic (225–395 million BP) and the Lower Palaeozoic from 395–570 million years BP. The sub-divisions are as follows:

c. 235 to 280 million years BP
Permian (named in 1841 after the Russian province Perm). Earliest land reptile (*Seymouria*) date from *c.* 250 million BP.

c. 280 to 360 million years BP
Carboniferous (carbon-bearing, so named in 1822). Earliest spider (*Palaeotenizo crassipes*) and earliest quadruped, the amphibian *Ichthyostega*, both date from *c.* 300 million BP. The earliest conifers great coal forests, tree ferns and huge mosses date from *c.* 340 million BP. In North America the late Carboniferous is called the Pennsylvanian and the early carboniferous the Mississippian period.

c. 360 to *c.* 405 million years BP
Devonian (named after the English county). The earliest insects (*Collembola*) date from *c.* 360 million BP. Molluscs abundant.

c. 405 to ?435–460 million years BP
Silurian (named after the ancient British tribe, *Silures*). The earliest land plants date from the late Silurian. Reef-building corals active.

?435–460 to *c.* 510 million years BP
Ordovician (named after the Welsh border tribe, *Ordovices*). Earliest known fish (*Ostracoderms*) and molluscs (the still living *Neopilina*) both date from *c.* 500 million BP.

>510 to <597 million years BP
Cambrian (from the Latin, *Cambria*, Wales, scene of pioneer rock investigations). Marine invertebrates were abundant *c.* 550 million BP.

---

(4) Pre-Cambrian Era (earlier than 597 million years before the present). The name indicates merely all time pre (from Latin, *prae*, before) the Cambrian period (see above). This era includes such events as the earliest dated algal remains (*c.* 2100 million BP), problematica of the Oscillatorioid class (*c.* 2600 million BP) and the earliest certainly dated rock formations of 3980 ±170 million BP.

The Pre-Cambrian is divided into the Late Precambrian (<597 to 2400 million BP); the Middle Precambrian (2400–3500 million BP) and Early Precambrian (3500–*c.* 4600 million BP).

Ice Ages

Climatic variations occur in many time scales ranging from day to day weather changes in the shortest term and seasonal cycles up to major meteorological variations known as 'fourth order climatological changes.

Weather is the present state of the climate in which temperature has been known to change 49 °F *27,2 °C* in 2 minutes. Second order temperature changes are those trends which now show that the mean temperature in the Northern Hemisphere which peaked in the period 1940–45 has dropped sharply by 2.7 °F *1,5 °C* to a point lower than the 1900 average when the world was emerging from the so called 'Little Ice Age' of the period 1595–1898.

Third order climatological changes are now being measured by the ratio of oxygen isotopes found in seashells. These reveal 8 Ice Ages in the last 700 000 years thus:

Ice Age	Duration BC	Nadirs BC
Last Ice Age	75 000–9000	60 000 & 18 000
Penultimate	130 000–105 000	115 000
Pre-penultimate	285 000–240 000	250 000
Fourth	355 000–325 000	330 000
Fifth	425 000–400 000	410 000
Sixth	520 000–500 000	510 000
Seventh	620 000–580 000	605 000
Eighth	685 000–645 000	670 000

Many theories have been advanced on the causes of Ice Ages which most profoundly affect human, animal and plant life. The most recent is that the Solar System which is revolving round the centre of the Milky Way at 480 000 mph *772 500 km/h* passes through dust belts which dim the Sun's heating and lighting powers.

Fourth order climatological change will be determined by the Sun's conversion from a yellow dwarf to a red giant as it burns 4 million tons of hydrogen per second. Thus in 5000 million years the oceans will boil and evaporate.

Earthquakes

It was not until as recently as 1874 that subterranean slippage along overstressed faults became generally accepted as the cause of tectonic earthquakes. The collapse of caverns, volcanic action, and also possibly the very rare event of a major meteoric impact can also cause tremors. The study of earthquakes is called seismology.

The two great seismic systems are the Alps-Himalaya great circle and the circum-Pacific belt. The foci below the epicentres are classified as shallow (<50 km deep), intermediate (50–200 km) and deep (200–700 km).

Earthquakes are classified on the modified Mercalli Intensity Scale based on impression rather than measurement thus:

I Just detectable by experienced observers when prone. Microseisms.

II Felt by few. Delicately poised objects may sway.

III Vibration but still unrecognised by many. Feeble.

IV Felt by many indoors but by few outdoors. Moderate.

V Felt by almost all. Many awakened. Unstable objects moved.

VI Felt by all. Heavy objects moved. Alarm. Strong.

VII General alarm. Weak buildings considerably damaged. Very strong.

VIII Damage general except in proofed buildings. Heavy objects overturned.

IX Buildings shifted from foundations, collapse, ground cracks. Highly destructive.

X Masonry buildings destroyed, rails bent, serious ground fissures. Devastating.

XI Few if any structures left standing. Bridges down. Rails twisted. Catastrophic.

XII Damage total. Vibrations distort vision. Objects thrown in air. Major catastrophe.

Instrumental measurements are made on seismographs on the Gutenberg-Richter scale. Cataclysmic earthquakes have an energy of the order of 3×10^{19} ergs. The greatest measured readings are 8·6 for the Colombian shock of 31 Jan. 1906 and the Assam earthquake shock of 15 Aug. 1950. The Lisbon 'quake of 1 Nov. 1755 was probably of even greater violence but was not instrumentally measured.

Seismographs can denote P (primary) waves, S (secondary) waves with their reflections, L (long) and M (maximum) waves. It was from a double P wave that A Mohorovičić (Croatia) in 1909 first deduced a discontinuity in the Earth's crustal structure.

On the comparative scale of the Mantle Wave magnitudes (defined in 1968) the most cataclysmic earthquakes since 1930 have been

Mag. 8.9	Prince William Sound, Alaska	28 Mar. 1964
Mag. 8.8	Kamchatka, USSR	4 Nov. 1952
Mag. 8.8	Concepción, Chile	22 May 1960

The Great Lisbon Earthquake of 1 Nov. 1755, 98 years before the invention of the seismograph killed 60 000: it would have rated a magnitude of 8¾ to 9. Attendant phenomena include:
(i) *Tsunami* (wrongly called tidal waves) or gravity waves which radiate in long, low oscillations from submarine disturbances at speeds of 450–490 mph *725–790 km/h*. The 1883 Krakatoa *tsunami* reached a height of 135 ft *41 m* and that off Valolez, Alaska in 1964 attained a height of 220 ft *67 m*.
(ii) *Seiches* (a Swiss-French term of doubtful origin, pronounced sāsh). Seismic oscillations in landlocked water. Loch Lomond had a 2 ft *60 cm* seiche for 1 hr from the 1755 Lisbon 'quake.
(iii) *Fore and After Shocks*. These often occur before major 'quakes and may persist after these for months or years.

Historic Earthquakes
The four earthquakes in which the known loss of life has exceeded 100 000 have been:

830 000	Shensi Province, China	24 Jan. 1556
300 000	Calcutta, India	11 Oct. 1737
180 000	Kansu Province, China	16 Dec. 1920
142 807	Kwanto Plain, Honshū, Japan	1 Sept. 1923

The material damage done in the Kwanto Plain, which includes Tōkyō, was estimated at £1 000 000 000.
Other notable earthquakes during this century, with loss of life in brackets, have been:

1906	San Francisco, USA (18 Apr.) (452)
1908	Messina, Italy (28 Dec.) (75 000)
1915	Avezzano, Italy (13 Jan.) (29 970)
1932	Kansu Province, China (26 Dec.) (70 000)
1935	Quetta, India (31 May) (60 000)
1939	Erzingan, Turkey (27 Dec.) (23 000)
1960	Agadir, Morocco (29 Feb.) (12 000)
1964	Anchorage, Alaska (28 Mar.) (131)
1970	Northern Peru (31 May) (66 800)
1972	Nicaragua (23 Dec.) (10 000)

Other major natural disasters

Landslides caused by earthquakes in the Kansu Province of China on 16 Dec. 1920 killed 200 000 people.

The Peruvian snow avalanches at Huaras (13 Dec. 1941) and from Huascarán (10 Jan. 1962) killed 5000 and 3000 people respectively. The Huascarán aluvian flood triggered by the earthquake of 31 May 1970 wiped out 25 000.
1976 Guatamala (4 Feb.) (22 000 prov.)

Both floods and famines have wrecked a greater toll of human life than have earthquakes. The greatest river floods on record are those of the Hwang-ho, China. From September into October in 1887 some 900 000 people were drowned. The flood of August 1931 killed some 3 700 000. A typhoon flood at Haiphong in North Vietnam (formerly Indo-China) on 8 Oct. 1881 killed an estimated 300 000 people. The cyclone of 12–13 Nov. 1970 which struck the Ganges Delta islands, Bangladesh drowned an estimated 1 000 000.

History's worst famines have occurred in Asia. In 1770 nearly one third of India's total population died with ten million dead in Bengal alone. From February 1877 to September 1878 an estimated 9 500 000 people died of famine in northern China.

British Earthquakes

The earliest British earthquake of which there is indisputable evidence was that of AD 974 felt over England. The earliest precisely recorded was that of 1 May 1048, in Worcester. British earthquakes of an intensity sufficient to have raised or moved the chair of the observer (Davison's Scale 8) have been recorded thus:

25 Apr.	1180	Nottinghamshire
15 Apr.	1185	Lincoln
1 June	1246	Canterbury, Kent
21 Dec.	1246	Wells
19 Feb.	1249	South Wales
11 Sept.	1275	Somerset
21 May	1382	Canterbury, Kent
28 Dec.	1480	Norfolk
26 Feb.	1575	York to Bristol
6 Apr.	1580*	London
30 Apr.	1736	Menstrie, Clackmannan
1 May	1736	Menstrie, Clackmannan
14 Nov.	1769†	Inverness
18 Nov.	1795	Derbyshire
13 Aug.	1816‡	Inverness
23 Oct.	1839	Comrie, Perth
30 July	1841	Comrie, Perth
6 Oct.	1863	Hereford
22 Apr.	1884§	Colchester
17 Dec.	1896	Hereford
18 Sept.	1901	Inverness
27 June	1906‖	Swansea
30 July	1926	Jersey
15 Aug.	1926	Hereford
7 June	1931	Dogger Bank
11 Feb.	1957	Midlands

* About 6 p.m. First recorded fatality—an apprentice killed by masonry falling from Christ Church.
† 'Several people' reported killed. Parish register indicates not more than one. Date believed to be 14th.
‡ At 10.45 p.m. Heard in Aberdeen (83 miles *133 km*), felt in Glasgow (115 miles *185 km*). Strongest ever in Scotland.
§ At 9.18 a.m. Heard in Oxford (108 miles *174 km*), felt in Exeter and Ostend, Belgium (95 miles *152 km*). One child and probably at least 3 others killed. Strongest ever in British Isles.
‖ At 9.45 a.m. Strongest in Wales. Felt over 37 800 miles² *98 000 km²*.

Petroleum

Most deposits of petroleum are found in sedimentary rocks representing deposition in shallow new seas which once supported flora and fauna. The assumption that oil is a downward migration of such organic decay is now modified by the abiogenic theory which maintains that some of the heavy hydrocarbons may have sprung, already polymerised, from deep layers of hot magma.

Exploration in the North Sea began on 26 Dec. 1964 from the drilling rig 'Mr Cap'. The first show of methane (CH_4) gas came of 20 Sept. 1965 from the drill of British Petroleum's 'Sea Gem' 42 miles east of the Humber estuary. This gas-field is expected to yield 50 000 000 ft³ of gas per day which will reach the consumer by 1967. The boundary of the Permian and Carboniferous geological layers of about 270 million years antiquity is at a depth of about 9500 ft *2895 m* in the North Sea.

In 1965 the daily average production of the Middle East (7 610 000 bbl in 1964) surpassed that of the USA (7 665 000 bbl in 1964). By 1990 a world consumption of oil and natural gas of 100 million bbl per day is forecast.

Geochemical abundances of the elements

	Lithosphere* (Parts per Mill. %)	Hydrosphere (Parts per Mill. %)
Oxygen	466·0	857
Silicon	277·2	0·003 to 0·00002
Aluminium	81·3	0·00001
Iron	50·0	0·00001
Calcium	36·3	0·40
Sodium	28·3	10·50
Potassium	25·9	0·38
Magnesium	20·9	1·35
Titanium	4·4	—
Phosphorus	1·2	0·00007
Manganese	1·0	0·000002
Fluorine	0·8	0·0013
Sulfur	0·52	0·88
Chlorine	0·48	19
Carbon	0·32	0·028
Rubidium	0·31	0·0001
Zirconium	0·22	—
Chromium	0·2	0·00000005
Hydrogen	—	103
Nitrogen	0·046	0·0005

*Assessment based on igneous rock.

Beaufort Scale

A scale of numbers, designated Force 0 to Force 12, was originally devised by Commander Francis Beaufort (1774–1857) (later Rear-Admiral Sir Francis Beaufort, KCB, FRS) in 1805. Force numbers 13 to 17 were added in 1955 by the US Weather Bureau.

Force No.	Descriptive term	Wind speed mph	knots
0	Calm	0–1	0–1
1	Light air	1–3	1–3
2	Light breeze	4–7	4–6
3	Gentle breeze	8–12	7–10
4	Moderate breeze	13–18	11–16
5	Fresh breeze	19–24	17–21
6	Strong breeze	25–31	22–27
7	Moderate gale	32–38	28–33
8	Fresh gale	39–46	34–40
9	Strong gale	47–54	41–47
10	Whole gale	55–63	48–55
11	Storm	64–75	56–65
12	Hurricane	76–82	66–71
13	Hurricane	83–92	72–80
14	Hurricane	93–103	81–89
15	Hurricane	104–114	90–99
16	Hurricane	115–125	100–108
17	Hurricane	126–136	109–118

Dense fog envelops both Forth bridges which connect the Scottish counties of Lothian and Fife. (Aerofilms)

METEOROLOGY

Phenomena and Terms

'Blue Moon'
The defraction of light through very high clouds of dust or smoke, as might be caused by volcanic eruptions (notably Krakatoa, 27 Aug. 1883) or major forest fires (notably in British Columbia, 26 Sept. 1950), can change the colour of the Sun (normally white overhead and yellow or reddish at sunrise or sunset) and the Moon (normally whitish) on such rare occasions to other colours, notably green and even blue.

Ball Lightning
A very rare phenomenon. A spheroid glowing mass of energised air, usually about one ft *30 cm* in diameter. On striking an earthed object it seems to disappear, hence giving the impression that it has passed through it. Only one photograph exists of the phenomenon taken in August 1961.

Brocken Spectre
A person standing with his (or her) back to the Sun and looking down from higher ground onto a lower bank of fog or cloud, casts a shadow known by this name.

Coronae
When the Sun's or Moon's light is diffracted by water droplets in some types of cloud, a ring of light (sometimes two or more) may be seen closely and concentrically around the Sun or Moon.

Cyclone
The local name given to a tropical depression that results in a violent circular storm in the northern part of the Indian Ocean (see also Hurricane and Typhoon). The term can also be used for a low-pressure system, in contrast to the Anticyclone or high-pressure system. The cyclone of 12–13 Nov. 1970 in the Ganges Delta area, Bangladesh, resulted in about 1 000 000 deaths mainly from drowning. Cyclone Tracy which struck the Darwin area of N. Australia in 24–25 Dec. 1974 produced measured wind speeds of 134·8 mph *216,9 km/h*.

Fogbow
In rainbow conditions, when the refracting droplets of water are very small, as in fog or clouds, the colours of the rainbow may overlap and so the bow appears white. Alternative names for this phenomenon are a *Cloudbow*, or *Ulloa's Ring*.

Flachenblitz
A rare form of lightning which strikes upwards from the top of Cumulonimbus clouds and ends in clear air.

Glory
At the anti-solar point, from an observer in the situation that gives a *Brocken spectre* (see left) a corona is seen round the head of the observer. When several people are standing side by side, each can see a *glory* round the shadow of his own head.

Haloes
When the Sun's light is refracted by ice crystals in Cirrus or Cirrostratus clouds, a bright ring of light, usually reddish on the inside and white on the outside, may be seen round the Sun with a 22° radius. Much more rarely a 46° *halo* may appear, and, very rarely indeed, haloes of other sizes with radii of 7° upwards. Halo phenomena may also be seen round the Moon.

Hurricanes
The local name given to a tropical depression that results in a violent circular storm in the southern part of the North Atlantic, notably the Caribbean Sea (see also Cyclone and

Lightning illuminates the skyline at Jacksonville, Florida, USA (Aerofilms)

adoes in the south central states of the USA killed 689. At Wichita Falls, Texas on 2 Apr. 1958 a wind speed of 280 mph *450 km/h* was recorded.

Typhoon
The local name given to a tropical depression that results in a violent circular storm in the south-western part of the North Pacific and especially the China Sea (see also Cyclone and Hurricane). A barometer pressure as low as 877 millibars (25·90 in) was recorded 600 miles *965 km* north west of Guam in the Pacific on 24 Sept. 1958.

Waterspout
The same phenomenon as a tornado, except that it occurs over the sea, or inland water. These may reach an extreme height of 5000 feet *1524 m*.

Whiteout
When land is totally covered by snow, the intensity of the light refracted off it may be the same as that refracted off overhead cloud. This results in the obliteration of the horizon, and makes land and sky indistinguishable.

Fog
A convenient meteorological definition of fog is a 'cloud touching the ground and reducing visibility to less than one kilometre (1100 yd)'.

Fog requires the coincidence of three conditions:
(i) Minute hygroscopic particles to act as nuclei. The most usual source over land is from factory or domestic chimneys, whereas at sea salt particles serve the same purpose. Such particles exist everywhere, but where they are plentiful the fog is thickest.
(ii) Condensation of water vapour by saturation.
(iii) The temperature at or below dew point. The latter condition may arise in two ways. The air temperature may simply drop to dew point, or the dew point may rise because of increased amounts of water vapour.

Sea fog persists for up to 120 days in a year on the Grand Banks, off Newfoundland. London has twice been beset by 114 hours continuous fog recently—26 Nov. to 1 Dec. 1948 and 5–9 Dec. 1952.

Thunder and Lightning
At any given moment there are some 2200 thunderstorms on the Earth's surface which are audible at ranges of up to 18 miles *29 km*. The world's most thundery location is Bogor (formerly Buitenzorg), Java, Indonesia, which in 1916–19 averaged 322 days per year with thunder. The extreme in the United Kingdom is 38 days at Stonyhurst, Lancashire in 1912, and in Huddersfield, West Yorkshire in 1967.

Thunder arises after the separation of electrical charges in cumulonimbus (q.v.) clouds. In the bipolar thundercloud the positive charge is in the upper layer. Thunder is an audible compression wave, the source of which is the rapid heating of the air by a return lightning stroke.
Lightning: The speed of lightning varies greatly. The downward leader strokes vary between 100 and 1000 miles per second *150 to 1500 km/s*. In the case of the powerful return stroke a speed of 87 000 miles per second *140 000 km/s*, nearly half the speed of light) is attained. The length of stroke varies with cloud height and thus between 300 ft *90 m* and 4 miles *6 km* though lateral strokes as long as 20 miles *32 km* have been recorded. The central core of a lightning channel is extremely narrow—perhaps as little as a half-inch *1,27 cm*. In the case of

Typhoon). Hurricane Betsy in 1965 caused damage estimated at more than $1000 million on which $750 million was paid out in insurance.

Iridescence (or Irisation)
When conditions giving rise to coronae illuminate clouds, the phenomena is so described.

Mirages
Mirages are caused by the refraction of light when layers of the atmosphere have sharply differing densities (due to contrasting temperature). There are two types of mirages: with the *inferior mirage*—the more common of the two—an object near the horizon appears to be refracted as in a pool of water; with the *superior mirage* the object near—or even beyond—the horizon appears to float above its true position.

Mock Suns
In halo conditions the ice crystals when orientated in a particular way can refract light so as to produce one or more *mock suns* or *parhelia* on either or both sides of the Sun and usually 22° away from it.

Nacreous Clouds and Noctilucent 'Clouds'
Nacreous, or mother-of-pearl, clouds occasionally appear after sunset over mountainous areas, at a height of from 60 000 to 80 000 ft. These are lit by sunlight from below the horizon, so may be seen hundreds of miles away, for example in Scotland over Scandinavia.

Noctilucent 'clouds' are a phenomena, possibly formed by cosmic dust, that appear bluish in colour at a very great height of 300 000 ft, say 60 miles or *100 km*. This phenomenon was reported from the Shetlands 33 times in 1967 and 15 in 1970.

Rainbows
If an observer stands with his back to the Sun and looks out on a mass of falling raindrops lit by the Sun, he will see a *rainbow*. A *primary bow* is vividly coloured with violet on the inside, followed by blue, green, yellow, orange, and red. A *secondary bow*, which, if visible, is only about a tenth of the intensity of its primary, has its colour sequence reversed. Further bows, even more feeble, can on very rare occasions be seen.

Saint Elmo's Fire (or Corposants)
A luminous electrical discharge in the atmosphere which emanates from protruding objects, such as ships' mastheads, lightning conductors and windvanes.

Sun Pillars
In halo conditions, when the ice crystals are orientated in a particular way, a *sun pillar*, which is a bright image of the Sun extending both above and below it, may appear.

Thunderbolts
These do not in fact exist, but the effect of the intense heating of a lightning strike may fuse various materials and so give the false impression that a solid object in fact hit the ground. A lightning strike may boil water almost instantaneously and so, for example, shatter damp masonry, so giving the appearance that it has been struck by a solid object.

Tornado
A *tornado* is the result of intense convection which produces a violent whirlwind extending downwards from a storm cloud base, often reaching the ground. The width varies between about 50 metres and 400 metres and it moves across country at speeds varying from 10 to 30 mph *15–50 km/h* causing great damage. The British frequency is about 12 per annum, one in 1638 causing 60 casualties at Widecombe, Devon. On 18 Mar. 1925 torn-

the more 'positive giant' stroke the temperature reaches *c.* 30 000 °C or over five times that of the sun's surface. In Britain the frequency of strikes is only 6 per mile² per annum. British fatalities have averaged 11·8 per annum this century with 31 in 1914 but nil in 1937.

Constituents of Air

Gas	Formula	% By volume
Invariable component gases of dry carbon dioxide-free air		
Nitrogen	N_2	78·110
Oxygen	O_2	20·953
Argon	A	0·934
Neon	Ne	0·001818
Helium	He	0·000524
Methane	CH_4	0·0002
Krypton	Kr	0·000114
Hydrogen	H_2	0·00005
Nitrous Oxide	N_2O	0·00005
Xenon	Xe	0·0000087
		99·9997647 %

Variable components		
Water Vapour	H_2O	0 to 7·0*
Carbon dioxide	CO_2	0·01 to 0·10 average 0·034
Ozone	O_3	0 to 0·000007
Contaminants		
Sulphur dioxide	SO_2	up to 0·0001
Nitrogen dioxide	NO_2	up to 0·000002
Ammonia	NH_3	trace
Carbon monoxide	CO	trace

* This percentage can be reached at a relative humidity of 100 per cent at a shade temperature of 40 °C (104 °F).

World and UK Meteorological Absolutes and Averages

Temperature: The world's overall average annual day side temperature is 59 °F (15° C). Highest shade (**world**): 136·4°F (*57,7 °C*) Al'Aziziyah, Libya, 13 Sept. 1922. **UK**: 100·5 °F (*38,0 °C*) Tonbridge, Kent, 22 July 1868. The hottest place (**world**) on annual average is Dallol Ethiopia with 94 °F *34,4 °C* (1960–66) and in **UK** Penzance, Cornwall, 52·7 °F (*11,5 °C*). Annual Means: England 50·3 °F; Scotland 47·6 °F.
Lowest Screen (**world**): −126·9 °F (−*88,3 °C*) Vostock, Antarctica, 25 Aug. 1960. **UK**: −17 °F (−*27,2 °C*) Braemar, 11 Feb. 1895 (N.B.—Temperature of −23 °F at Blackadder, Borders, in 1879 and of −20 °F at Grantown-on-Spey, in 1955 were not standard exposures.) The coldest place (**world**) on annual average is the Pole of Cold, 150 miles *240 km* west of Vostok, Antarctica at −72 °F (−*57,8 °C*) and in the **UK** at Braemar, Grampian 43·7 °F (*6,5 °C*).

Barometric Pressure: The world's average barometric pressure is 1013 mb. Highest (**world**): 1083·8 mb. (*32·00 in*), Agata, Siberia, USSR, 31 Dec. 1968 and **UK**: 1054·7 mb (*31·11 in*) at Aberdeen, 31 Jan. 1902.
Lowest (**world**): 877 mb (*25·90 in*), recorded at sea 600 miles *965 km* NW of Guam, Pacific Ocean, 24 Sept. 1958 and **UK**: 925·5 mb (*27·33 in*), Ochtertyre, near Crieff, Tayside, 26 Jan. 1884

Wind Strength: Highest sustained surface speed (**world**) 231 mph *371 km/h*, Mt Washington (6288 ft *1916 m*), New Hampshire, USA, 24 Apr. 1934. **UK**: 144 mph *231 km/h* (125 knots). Coire Cas ski lift (3525 ft *1074 m*) Cairngorm, Highland 6 Mar. 1967. (NB—The 177·2 mph reading widely reported from Saxa Vord, Unst, Shetland Islands, on 16 Feb. 1962 was unofficially recorded with non-standard equipment.) Windiest place (**world**): Commonwealth Bay, George V coast, Antarctica, several

200 mph *320 km/h* gales each year. **UK**: Tyree, Strathclyde annual average 17·4 mph *28 km/h*.

Rainfall: Highest (**world**) **Minute**: 1·23 in *31,2 mm* Unionville, Maryland, USA, 4 July 1956; **Day**: 73·62 in *1870 mm* Cilaos, La Réunion Island, on 15–16 March 1952. S. Indian Ocean; **12 months**: 1041·78 in *26 461 mm* Cherrapunji, Assam, 1 Aug. 1860 to 31 July 1961. Highest (**UK**) **Day**: 11·00 in *279 mm* Martinstown, Dorset, 18 July 1955; **Year**: 257·0 in *6527 mm* Sprinkling Tarn, Cumbria, in 1954. Wettest Place (**world**) Mt Wai-'ale-'ale (5080 ft *1548 m*), Kauai I, Hawaiian Islands, annual average 451 in *11 455 mm* (1920–72). Most rainy Days in a Year (**world**) up to 350 on Mt. Wai-'ale-'ale; **British Isles**: 309 at Ballynahinch, Galway, Ireland, in 1923.
Lowest (**world**) at places in the Desierto de Atacama of Chile, including Calama, where no rain has ever been recorded in the *c.* 400 years to 1971. Lowest (**UK**) Year: 9·29 in *236 mm* Margate, Kent, in 1921. Longest Drought: 73 days from 4 March to 15 May 1893 at Mile End, Greater London.

Snowfall: Greatest (**world**) **Single Storm**: 175·4 in *4455 mm* Thompson Pass, Alaska, USA, 26–31 Dec. 1955; **Day**: 76 in *1870 mm* Silver Lake, Colorado, 14–15 Apr. 1921; **Year**: 1224·5 in *31 102 mm* Paradise Ranger Station, Mt Rainer, Washington, USA, in 1971–2. **UK**: Annual days of snowfall vary between extremes of 40 in the Shetland Islands and 5 in Penzance, Cornwall. The gulleys on Ben Nevis (4406 ft *1342 m*) were snowless only 7 times in the 31 years 1933–64. An accumulated level of 60 in was recorded in February 1947 in both Upper Teesdale and the Clwyd Hills of North Wales.

Sunshine: Maximum (**world**): in parts of the eastern Sahara the sun shines strongly enough to cast a shadow for 4300 hours in a year or 97 per cent of possible. **UK**: The highest percentage for a month is 78·3 per cent (382 hours) at Pendennis Castle, Falmouth, Cornwall, June 1925.
Minimum (**world**): the longest periods of total darkness occur at the North Pole (over 9000 ft less altitude than South Pole) with 186 days. **UK**: the lowest monthly reading has been 6 min at Bunhill Row, London, in Dec. 1890. All 6 mins occurred on 7 December.

Earth's Atmosphere—Layers

Troposphere	—the realm of clouds, rain and snow in contact with the lithosphere (land) and hydrosphere (sea). The upper limit is 17 km *11 miles* (58 000 ft) at the equator or 6–8 km *3·7–4·9 miles* (19 700–25 000 ft) at the Poles. In middle latitudes in high pressure conditions the limits may be extended between 13 km *8 miles* to 7 km *4 miles* in low pressure conditions.
Stratosphere	—the second region of the atmosphere marked by a constant increase in temperature with altitude up to a maximum of 270°K at about 50 km *30 miles* (160 000 ft)
Mesosphere	—the third region of the atmosphere about 50 km *30 miles* (160 000 ft) marked by a rapid decrease in temperature with altitude to a minimum value even below 160 °K at about 85 km *55 miles* (290 000 ft) known as the mesopause.
Thermosphere	—the fourth region of the atmosphere above the mesosphere characterised by an unremitting rise in temperature up to a night maximum during minimum solar activity of 500 °K at about 230 km *140 miles* to above 1750 °K in a day of maximum solar activity at 500 km *310 miles* This region is sometimes termed the heterosphere because of the widely differing conditions in night and day and during solar calm and solar flare.
Exosphere	—this is the fifth and final stage above the exobase at 500 km *310 miles* in which the upper atmosphere becomes space and in which temperature no longer has the customary terrestrial meaning.

Northern and Southern Lights

Polar lights are known as Aurora Borealis in the northern hemisphere and Aurora Australis in the southern hemisphere. These luminous phenomena are caused by electrical solar discharges in the upper atmosphere between altitudes of 620 miles *1000 km* and 45 miles *72,5 km* and are usually visible only in the higher latitudes.
It is believed that in an auroral display some 100 million protons (hydrogen nuclei) strike each square centimetre of the upper atmosphere each second. Colours vary from yellow-green (attenuated oxygen), reddish (very low pressure oxygen), red below green (molecular nitrogen below ionised oxygen) or bluish (ionised nitrogen). Displays, which occur on every dark night in the year above 70° N or below 70° S (eg Northern Canada or Antarctica), vary in frequency with the 11-year sunspot cycle. Edinburgh may expect perhaps 25 displays a year against 7 in London, and Malta once a decade. The most striking recent displays over Britain occurred on 25 Jan. 1938 and 4–5 Sept. 1958. On 1 Sept. 1909, a display was reported from just above the equator at Singapore (1° 12′ N). In 1957 203 displays were recorded in the Shetland Islands (geometric Lat. 63° N).

CLOUDS-Classification

Genus (with abbreviation)	Ht of base (ft)	(m)	Temp at base level (°C)	Official description
Cirrus (Ci)	16 500 to 45 000	5000 to 13 700	−20 to −60	Detached clouds in the form of white, delicate filaments, or white or mostly white patches or narrow bands. They have a fibrous (hair-like) appearance or a silky sheen, or both.
Cirrocumulus (Cc)	16 500 to 45 000	5000 to 13 700	−20 to −60	Thin, white patch, sheet or layer of cloud without shading, composed of very small elements in the form of grains, ripples, etc., merged or separate, and more or less regularly arranged.
Cirrostratus (Cs)	16 500 to 45 000	5000 to 13 700	−20 to −60	Transparent, whitish cloud veil of fibrous or smooth appearance, totally or partly covering the sky, and generally producing halo phenomena.
Altocumulus (Ac)	6500 to 23 000	2000 to 7000	+10 to −30	White or grey, or both white and grey, patch, sheet or layer of cloud, generally with shading, composed of laminae, rounded masses, rolls, etc. which are sometimes partly fibrous or diffuse, and which may or may not be merged.
Altostratus (As)	6500 to 23 000	2000 to 7000	+10 to −30	Greyish or bluish cloud sheet or layer of striated, fibrous or uniform appearance, totally or partly covering the sky, and having parts thin enough to reveal the sun at least vaguely.
Nimbostratus (Ns)	3000 to 10 000	900 to 3000	+10 to −15	Grey cloud layer, often dark, the appearance of which is rendered diffuse by more or less continually falling rain or snow which in most cases reaches the ground. It is thick enough throughout to blot out the sun. Low, ragged clouds frequently occur below the layer with which they may or may not merge.
Stratocumulus (Sc)	1500 to 6500	460 to 2000	+15 to −5	Grey or whitish, or both grey and whitish, patch, sheet or layer of cloud which almost always has dark parts, composed of tessellations, rounded masses, rolls, etc., which are non-fibrous (except for virga) and which may or may not be merged.
Stratus (St)	surface to 1500	surface to 460	+20 to −5	Generally grey cloud layer with a fairly uniform base, which may give drizzle, ice prisms or snow grains. When the sun is visible through the cloud its outline is clearly discernible. Stratus does not produce halo phenomena (except possibly at very low temperatures). Sometimes stratus appears in the form of ragged patches.
Cumulus (Cu)	1500 to 6500	460 to 2000	+15 to −5	Detached clouds, generally dense and with sharp outlines, developing vertically in the form of rising mounds, domes or towers, of which the bulging upper part often resembles a cauliflower. The sunlit parts of these clouds are mostly brilliant white; their bases are relatively dark and nearly horizontal.
Cumulonimbus (Cb)	1500 to 6500	460 to 2000	+15 to −5	Heavy and dense cloud, with a considerable vertical extent, In the form of a mountain or huge towers. At least part of its upper portion is usually smooth, or fibrous or striated, and nearly always flattened; this part often spreads out in the shape of an anvil or vast plume. Under the base of this cloud, which is often very dark, there are frequently low ragged clouds either merged with it or not, and precipitation, sometimes in the form of virga.

THE EARTH'S STRUCTURE

Mass, density and volume

The Earth has a mass estimated to be 5 882 000 000 000 000 000 000 tons *5·976 × 10²¹ tonnes* and has a density 5·517 times that of water. The volume of the Earth has been estimated at 259 875 620 000 miles³ *1 083 208 840 000 km³*.

Dimensions

Its equatorial circumference is 24 901·47 miles *40 075,03 km* with a polar or meridianal circumference of 24 859·75 miles *40 007,89 km* indicating that the Earth is not a true sphere but flattened at the poles and hence an ellipsoid. The Earth also has a slight ellipticity at the equator since its long axis (about longitude 0°) is 174 yd *159 m* greater than the short axis. Artificial satellite measurements have also revealed further departures from this biaxial ellipsoid form in minor protuberances and depressions varying between extremes of 244 ft *74 m* in the area of Papua New Guinea and a depression of 354 ft *108 m* south of Sri Lanka (formerly Ceylon) in the Indian Ocean. The equatorial diameter of the Earth is 7 926·385 miles *12 756,280 km* and the polar diameter 7 899·809 miles *12 713,510 km*.

Land and sea surfaces

The estimated total surface area of the Earth is 196 937 600 miles² *510 066 100 km²* of which the sea or hydrosphere covers five sevenths or more accurately 71·43 per cent and the land or lithosphere two sevenths or 28·57 per cent. The mean depth of the hydrosphere is 11 660 ft *3554 m*. The total volume of the oceans is 308 400 000 miles³ or *1 285 600 000 km³*, or 0·021 per cent by weight of the whole earth, viz. 1·2 × 10¹⁸ tons.

The oceans and seas

The strictest interpretations permit only three oceans—The Pacific, Atlantic and Indian. The so-called Seven Seas would require the three undisputed oceans to be divided by the equator into North and South and the addition of the Arctic Sea. The term Antarctic Ocean is not recognised by the International Hydrographic Bureau.

Ocean with adjacent seas	Area in millions miles²	Area in millions km²	Percentage of world area	Greatest depth (ft)	Greatest depth (m)	Location
Pacific	69·3	*179,4*	35·25	35 760	*10 900*	Mariana Trench
Atlantic	41·0	*106,1*	20·9	27 498	*8381*	Puerto Rico Trench
Indian	28·9	*74,8*	14·65	26 400	*8046*	Diamantina Trench
Total	139·67	*361,7*	70·92			

If the adjacent seas are detached and the Arctic Sea regarded as an ocean, the oceanic areas may be listed thus:

	Area (miles²)	Area (km²)	Percentage of sea area
Pacific	63 800 000	165 240 000	45·7
Atlantic	31 800 000	82 360 000	22·8
Indian	28 400 000	73 550 000	20·3
Arctic	5 400 000	13 980 000	3·9
Other Seas	10 270 000	26 600 000	7·3
	139 670 000	361 730 000	100·0

Ocean depths are zoned by oceanographers as bathyl (down to 6561 ft or *2000 m*); abyssal (between 6561 ft and 19 685 ft *2000 m and 6000 m*) and hadal (below 19 685 ft *6000 m*).

Principal seas	Area (miles²)	Area (km²)	Average depth (ft)	Average depth (m)
Malay Sea (inc. South China Sea and Malacca Straits)	3 144 000	*8 142 000*	4000	*1200*
Caribbean Sea	1 063 000	*2 753 000*	8000	*2400*
Mediterranean Sea	966 750	*2 503 000*	4875	*1485*
Bering Sea	875 750	*2 268 180*	4700	*1400*
Gulf of Mexico	595 750	*1 542 985*	5000	*1500*
Sea of Okhotsk	589 800	*1 527 570*	2750	*840*
East China Sea	482 300	*1 249 150*	600	*180*
Hudson Bay	475 800	*1 232 300*	400	*120*
Sea of Japan	389 000	*1 007 500*	4500	*1370*
Andaman Sea	308 000	*797 700*	2850	*865*
North Sea	222 125	*575 300*	300	*90*
Black Sea	178 375	*461 980*	3600	*1100*
Red Sea	169 000	*437 700*	1610	*490*
Baltic Sea	163 000	*422 160*	190	*55*
Persian Gulf	92 200	*238 790*	80	*24*
Gulf of St Lawrence	91 800	*237 760*	400	*120*
English Channel with Irish Sea	68 900	*178 450*	190	*55*

Deep sea trenches

Length (miles)	Length (km)	Name	Deepest point	Depth (ft)	Depth (m)
1400	2250	Mariana Trench,* W Pacific	Challenger† Deep	35 760	10 900
1600	2575	Tonga-Kermadec Trench, S Pacific	Vityaz 11 (Tonga)	35 598	10 850
1400	2250	Kuril-Kamchatka Trench,* W Pacific		34 587	10 542
825	1325	Philippine Trench, W Pacific	Galathea Deep	34 578	10 539
400	640	Solomon or New Britain Trench, S Pacific		29 988	9140
500	800	Puerto Rico Trench, W Atlantic	Milwaukee Deep	28 374	8648
350	560	Yap Trench,* W Pacific		27 976	8527
1000	1600	Japan Trench,* W Pacific		27 591	8412
600	965	South Sandwich Trench, S Atlantic	Meteor Deep	27 112	8263
2000	3200	Aleutian Trench, N Pacific		26 574	8100
2200	3540	Pepu-Chile (Atacama) Trench, E Pacific	Bartholomew Deep	26 454	8064
600	965	Romanche Trench, N-S Atlantic		25 800	7864
1400	2250	Java (Sunda) Trench, Indian Ocean	Planet Deep	25 344	7725
600	965	Cayman Trench, Caribbean		24 720	7535
650	1040	Nansei Shotó (Ryukyu) Trench, W Pacific		24 630	7505
200	320	Diamantina Trench, Indian Ocean	Diamantina Deep	19 890	6062

* These four trenches are sometimes regarded as a single 4600 mile *7400 km* long system.
† Subsequent visits to the Challenger Deep since 1951 have produced claims for greater depths in this same longitude and latitude. In Mar. 1959 the USSR research ship Vityaz claimed 36 198 ft *11 033 m*, using echo-sounding only.

The continents

There is ever increasing evidence that the Earth's land surface once comprised a single primeaval land mass, now called Pangaea, and that this split during the Upper Cretaceous period (65 000 000 to 100 000 000 years ago) into two super-continents, called Laurasia in the North and Gondwanaland in the South. The Earth's land surface embraces seven continents, each with their attendant islands. Europe, Africa and Asia, though politically distinct, physically form one land mass known as Afro-Eurasia. Central America is often included in North America (Canada, the USA and Greenland). Europe includes all the USSR territory west of the Ural Mountains. Oceania embraces Australasia (Australia and New Zealand) and the non-Asian Pacific Islands.

Continent	Area in miles²	Area in km²	Greatest overland distance between extremities of land masses			
			North to South (miles)	North to South (km)	East to West (miles)	East to West (km)
Asia	16 993 000	44 011 000	4000	6435	4700	7560
America	16 233 000	42 043 000				
North America	8 301 000	21 500 000	2900	4665	2900	4665
Central America	1 062 000	2 750 000	820	1320	950	1530
South America	6 870 000	17 793 000	4500	7240	3200	5150
Africa	11 673 000	30 232 000	4400	7080	3750	6035
Antarctica	c. 5 250 000	c. 13 600 000	—	—	2700*	4340
Europe†	4 063 000	10 523 000	1800	2900	2500	4000
Oceania§	3 450 000	8 935 000	1870‡	3000	2300‡	3700
		57 270 000				

* Greatest transit from coast to coast.
† Includes 2 151 000 miles² *5 571 000 km²* of USSR territory west of the Urals.
‡ Figures applicable only to Australian mainland (2 944 800 miles² *7 627 000 km²*).
§ Includes 159 376 miles² *412 781 km²* in West Irian (West New Guinea), politically part of Indonesia, which is largely in Asia.

World's largest islands

Name	Area in miles²	Area in km²	Location
* Australia	2 948 300	7 636 000	—
1. Greenland	840 000	2 175 000	Arctic Ocean
2. New Guinea	305 500	791 250	W Pacific
3. Borneo	280 100	725 545	Indian Ocean
4. Madagascar (Malagasy Republic)	227 800	590 000	Indian Ocean
5. Baffin Island	183 810	476 065	Arctic Ocean
6. Sumatra	182 860	473 600	Indian Ocean
7. Honshū	88 031	228 000	NW Pacific
8. Great Britain	84 186	218 041	North Atlantic
9. Ellesmere Island	82 119	212 687	Arctic Ocean
10. Victoria Island	81 930	212 197	Arctic Ocean
11. Celebes	72 987	189 035	Indian Ocean

Table continued over page

World's largest islands—continued

12. South Island, New Zealand	58 093	*150 460*	SW Pacific
13. Java	48 763	*126 295*	Indian Ocean
14. North Island, New Zealand	44 281	*114 687*	SW Pacific
15. Cuba	44 217	*114 522*	Caribbean Sea
16. Newfoundland	43 359	*112 300*	North Atlantic
17. Luzon	41 845	*108 378*	W Pacific
18. Iceland	39 768	*103 000*	North Atlantic
19. Mindanao	36 381	*94 226*	W Pacific
20. Ireland (Northern Ireland and the Republic of Ireland)	31 839	*82 460*	North Atlantic
21. Hokkaido	30 077	*77 900*	NW Pacific
22. Hispaniola (Dominican Republic and Haiti)	29 530	*76 480*	Caribbean Sea
23. Sakhalin	28 597	*74 060*	NW Pacific
24. Tasmania	26 215	*67 900*	SW Pacific
25. Sri Lanka	25 332	*65 600*	Indian Ocean

* Geographically regarded as a continental land mass, as are Antarctica, Afro-Eurasia, and America.

World's largest peninsulas

	miles²	km²
Arabia	1 250 000	*3 250 000*
Southern India	800 000	*2 072 000*
Alaska	580 000	*1 500 000*
Labrador	500 000	*1 300 000*
Scandinavia	309 000	*800 300*
Iberian Peninsula	225 500	*584 000*

Principal deserts of the world

Name	Approx. area in miles²	Approx. area in km²	Territories
Sahara	3 250 000	*8 400 000*	Algeria, Chad, Libya, Mali, Mauritania, Niger, Spanish Sahara, Sudan, Tunisia, Egypt, Morocco. Embraces the Libyan Desert (600 000 miles² *1 560 000 km²*) and the Nubian Desert (100 000 miles² *260 000 km²*)
Australian Desert	600 000	*1 550 000*	Australia. Embraces the Great Sandy (or Warburton) (160 000 miles² *420 000 km²*), Great Victoria (125 000 miles² *325 000 km²*), Simpson (Arunta) (120 000 miles² *310 000 km²*), Gibson (85 000 miles² *220 000 km²*) and Sturt Deserts
Arabian Desert	500 000	*1 300 000*	Southern Arabia, Saudi Arabia, Yemen. Includes the Ar Rab'al Khali or Empty Quarter (250 000 miles² *64 750 km²*), Syrian (125 000 miles² *323 750 km²*) and An Nafud (50 000 miles² *129 500 km²*) Deserts
Gobi	400 000	*1 040 000*	Mongolia and China (Inner Mongolia)
Kalahari Desert	200 000	*520 000*	Botswana
Takla Makan	125 000	*320 000*	Sinkiang, China
Kara Kum	105 000	*270 000*	Turkmenistan, USSR
Thar Desert	100 000	*260 000*	North-western India and Pakistan
Atacama Desert	70 000	*180 000*	Northern Chile
Kyzyl Kum	70 000	*180 000*	Uzbekistan-Kazakhstan, USSR
Dasht-e-Lut	20 000	*52 000*	Eastern Iran
Mojave Desert	13 500	*35 000*	Southern California, USA
Desierto de Sechura	10 000	*26 000*	North-west Peru

THE WORLD'S HIGHEST MOUNTAINS

Mountain	Height (ft)	Height (m)	Range	Date of First Ascent (if any)
1. Mount Everest	29 028	8848	Himalaya	29 May 1953
2. K 2 (Chogori)	28 250	8610	Karakoram	31 July 1954
3. Kangchenjunga I	28 208	8597	Himalaya	25 May 1955
4. Lhotse I	27 923	8511	Himalaya	18 May 1956
Yalung Kang	*27 894*	*8502*	*Himalaya*	*14 May 1973*
Kangchenjunga S Peak	*27 848*	*8488*		
5. Makalu I	27 824	8481	Himalaya	15 May 1955
Kangchenjunga Middle Peak	*27 806*	*8475*	*Himalaya*	*Unclimbed*
Lhotse Shar (Lhotse II)	*27 504*	*8383*	*Himalaya*	*12 May 1970*
6. Dhaulagiri I	26 795	8167	Himalaya	13 May 1960
7. Manaslu I (Kutang I)	26 760	8156	Himalaya	9 May 1956
8. Cho Uyo	26 750	8153	Himalaya	19 Oct. 1954
9. Nanga Parbat (Diamir)	26 660	8125	Himalaya	3 July 1953
10. Annapurna I	26 546	8091	Himalaya	3 June 1950
11. Gasherbrum I (Hidden Peak)	26 470	8068	Karakoram	5 July 1958
12. Broad Peak I	26 400	8047	Karakoram	9 June 1957
13. Gasherbrum II	26 360	8034	Karakoram	7 July 1956

World's highest
mountain—
continued

Mountain	Height (ft)	Height (m)	Range	Date of First Ascent (if any)
14. Shisha Pangma (Gosainthan)	26 291	8013	Himalaya	2 May 1964
15. Gasherbrum III	26 090	7952	Karakoram	11 Aug. 1975
16. Annapurna II	26 041	7937	Himalaya	17 May 1960
17. Gasherbrum IV	26 000	7924	Karakoram	6 Aug. 1958
18. Gyachung Kang	25 990	7921	Himalaya	10 Apr. 1964
19. Kangbachen	25 925	7902	Himalaya	26 May 1974
20. Disteghil Sar I	25 868	7884	Karakoram	9 June 1960
21. Himal Chuli	25 801	7864	Himalaya	24 May 1960
22. Khinyang Chhish	25 762	7852	Karakoram	26 Aug. 1971
23. Nuptse	25 726	7841	Himalaya	16 May 1961
24. Peak 29 (Manaslu II)	25 705	7835	Himalaya	Oct. 1970
25. Masherbrum East	25 660	7821	Karakoram	6 July 1960
26. Nanda Devi	25 645	7816	Himalaya	29 Aug. 1936
27. Chomo Lönzo	25 640	7815	Himalaya	30 Oct. 1954
28. Ngojumba Ri (Cho Uyo II)	25 610	7805	Himalaya	5 May 1965
29. Rakaposhi	25 550	7788	Karakoram	25 June 1958
30. Batura Muztagh I (Hunza Kunji I)	25 542	7785	Karakoram	Unclimbed
31. Zemu Peak	25 526	7780	Himalaya	Unclimbed
32. Kanjut Sar	25 460	7760	Karakoram	19 July 1959
33. Kamet	25 447	7756	Himalaya	21 June 1931
34. Namcha Barwa	25 445	7755	Himalaya	Unclimbed
35. Dhaulagiri II	25 429	7751	Himalaya	18 May 1971
36. Saltoro Kangri I	25 400	7741	Karakoram	24 July 1962
37. Batura Muztagh II (Hunza Kunji II)	25 361	7730	Karakoram	Unclimbed
38. Gurla Mandhata	25 355	7728	Himalaya	Unclimbed
39. Ulugh Muztagh	25 340	7725	Kunlun Shan	Unclimbed
40. Qungur II	25 326	7719	Pamir	Unclimbed
41. Dhaulagiri III	25 318	7715	Himalaya	23 Oct. 1973
42. Jannu	25 294	7709	Himalaya	27 Apr. 1962
43. Tirich Mir	25 282	7706	Hindu Kush	21 July 1950
44. Saltoro Kangri II	25 280	7705	Karakoram	Unclimbed
45. Disteghil Sar E	25 262	7710		Unclimbed
Tirich Mir, East Peak	*25 236*	*7691*	*Hindu Kush*	*25 July 1963*
46. Saser Kangri I	25 170	7672	Karakoram	Unclimbed
47. Chogolisa II	25 164	7669	Karakoram	Unclimbed
48. Phola Gangchhen	25 135	7661	Himalaya	Unclimbed
49. Dhaulagiri IV	25 134	7661	Himalaya	9 May 1975
50. Shahkang Sham	25 131	7660		Unclimbed
51. Makalu II (Kangshungtse)	25 120	7656	Himalaya	22 Oct. 1954
52. Chogolisa I ('Bride Peak')	25 110	7654	Karakoram	4 Aug. 1958
53. Trivor	25 098	7650	Karakoram	17 Aug. 1960
54. Ngojumba Ri II	25 085	7646		Unclimbed
55. Khinyang Chhish S	25 000	7620		Unclimbed
56. Shispare	21 997	7619	Karakoram	21 July 1974
57. Dhaulagiri V	24 993	7618	Himalaya	1 May 1975
58. Qungur I	24 918	7595	Pamir	16 Aug. 1956
59. Peak 38 (Lhotse II)	24 898	7589	Himalaya	Unclimbed
60. Minya Konka	24 891	7587	(Sikiang, China)	28 Oct. 1932
61. Annapurna III	24 787	7555	Himalaya	6 May 1961
62. Khula Kangri I	24 784	7554	Himalaya	Unclimbed
63. Changtse (North Peak)	24 780	7552	Himalaya	Unclimbed
64. Huztagh Ata	24 757	7546		Unclimbed
65. Skyang Kangri	24 751	7544	Karakoram	Unclimbed
66. Khula Kangri II	24 740	7541	Himalaya	Unclimbed
67. Khulu Kangri III	24 710	7532	Himalaya	Unclimbed
68. Yalung Peak	24 710	7532		Unclimbed
69. Yukshin Gardas Sar	24 705	7530		Unclimbed
70. Mamostong Kangri	24 692	7526	Karakoram	Unclimbed
71. Annapurna IV	24 688	7525	Himalaya	30 May 1955
72. Khulu Kangri IV	24 659	7516	Himalaya	Unclimbed
73. Saser Kangri II	24 649	7513	Karakoram	Unclimbed

South America

The mountains of the Cordillera de los Andes are headed by Aconcagua at 22 834 ft *6959 m* (first climbed on 14 Jan. 1897), which has the distinction of being the highest mountain in the world outside the great ranges of Central Asia. The following list contains the 19 Andean summit peaks in excess of 21 000 ft *6400 m* above sea-level, as given in the *American Alpine Journal*, 1963.

Name	Height (ft)	Height (m)	Country
1. Cerro Aconcagua	22 834	6960	Argentina
2. Ojos del Salado	22 598	6888	Argentina–Chile
3. Nevado de Pissis	22 241	6779	Argentina–Chile
4. Huascarán, South Peak	22 205	6768	Peru
5. Llullaillaco volcén	22 057	6723	Argentina–Chile
6. Mercedario	21 884	6670	Argentina–Chile

Continued over page

MOUNTAINS
Continued

Name	Height (ft)	Height (m)	Country
7. Huascarán N	21 834	6655	Peru
8. Yerupaja	21 758	6632	Peru
9. Nevados de Tres Cruces C	21 720	6620	Argentina–Chile
10. Coropuna	21 705	6616	Peru
11. Nevado Incahuasi	21 657	6601	Argentina–Chile
12. Tupungato	21 490	6550	Argentina–Chile
13. Sajama	21 427	6531	Bolivia
14. Nevado González	21 326	6500	Argentina
15. Cerro del Nacimiento	21 302	6493	Argentina
16. Illimani	21 260	6480	Bolivia
17. El Muerto	21 253	6478	Argentina–Chile
18. Illimani S	21 201	6462	Bolivia
19. Anto Falla	21 162	6450	Argentina
20. Ancohuma (Sorata N)	21 086	6427	Bolivia
21. Nevado Bonete	21 031	6410	Argentina
22. Cerro de Ramada	21 031	6410	Argentina

North America
Mt McKinley (first ascent 1913) is the only peak in excess of 20 000 ft *6100 m* in the entire North American continent.

Name	Height (ft)	Height (m)	Country
1. McKinley, South Peak	20 320	6193	Alaska
2. Logan	19 850	6050	Canada
3. Citlaltépetl or Orizaba	18 700	5700	Mexico
4. St Elias	18 008	5489	Alaska–Canada
5. Popocatépetl	17 887	5451	Mexico
6. Foraker	17 400	5304	Alaska
7. Lucania	17 150	5227	Alaska
8. King Peak	17 130	5221	Alaska
9. Iztaccihuatl	17 000	5182	Mexico
10. Steele	16 625	5073	Alaska
11. Bona	16 500	5029	Alaska
12. Blackburn	16 390	4996	Alaska
13. Sanford	16 237	4949	Alaska

Note: Mt McKinley, North Peak, is 19 470 ft *5934 m.*

Africa
All the peaks listed in the Congo (Kinshasa) and Uganda are in the Ruwenzori group.

Name	Height (ft)	Height (m)	Location
1. Kilimanjaro			
(Uhuru Point,* Kibo)	19 340	5894	Tanganyika
Hans Meyer Peak, Mawenzi	*16 890*	*5148*	
2. Mount Kenya (Batian)	17 058	5199	Kenya
Nelion	*17 022*	*5188*	
Point Piggott	*16 265*	*4957*	
Point John	*16 020*	*4882*	
3. Mount Stanley			
(Margherita Peak)	16 763	5109	Congo–Uganda
Albert Peak	*16 735*	*5100*	*Congo (Kinshasa)*
Alexandra Peak	*16 726*	*5098*	*Congo–Uganda*
Elena Peak	*16 388*	*4995*	*Uganda*
Great Tooth	*16 290*	*4965*	*Uganda*
Savoia Peak	*16 269*	*4958*	*Uganda*
Philip Peak	*16 239*	*4949*	*Uganda*
Elizabeth Peak	*16 236*	*4948*	*Uganda*
Moebius	*16 134*	*4917*	*Uganda*
Unnamed peak	*c. 15 500*	*4725*	*Uganda*
Unnamed peak	*c. 15 100*	*c. 4600*	*Uganda*
4. Duwoni or Mt Speke			
(Victorio Emanuele Peak)	16 042	4889	Uganda
Ensonga Peak	*15 961*	*4864*	*Congo–Uganda*
Johnston Peak	*15 906*	*4848*	*Uganda*
5. Mount Baker (Edward Peak)	15 889	4842	Uganda
Semper Peak	*15 843*	*4828*	*Uganda*
Wollaston Peak	*15 286*	*4659*	*Uganda*
Moore Peak	*15 269*	*4653*	*Uganda*
6. Mount Emin			
(Umberto Peak)	15 797	4814	Congo (Kinshasa)
Kraepelin Peak	*15 720*	*4791*	*Congo (Kinshasa)*
7. Mount Gessi (Iolanda Peak)	15 470	4715	Uganda
Bottego Peak	*15 418*	*4699*	*Uganda*
8. Mount Luigi di Savoia			
(Sella Peak)	15 179	4626	Uganda
Weismann Peak	*15 157*	*4619*	*Uganda*
9. Ras Dashan (Dejen)	15 158	4620	Simien Mts, Ethiopia
10. Humphreys Peak	15 021	4578	Uganda

* Formerly called Kaiser Wilhelm Spitze.

Europe

The Caucasus range, along the spine of which runs the traditional geographical boundary between Asia and Europe, includes the following peaks which are higher than Mont Blanc (15 771 ft [*4807 m*]).

	Name	Height (ft)	Height (m)		Name	Height (ft)	Height (m)
1.	El'brus, West Peak	18 481	*5633*	8.	Dzhangi Tau	16 565	*5049*
	El'brus, East Peak	18 356	*5594*	9.	Kazbek	16 558	*5046*
2.	Shkara	17 060	*5199*	10.	Katuintau (Adish)	16 355	*4985*
3.	Dych Tau	17 054	*5198*	11.	Mishirgitau,		
4.	Pik Shota				West Peak	16 148	*4921*
	Rustaveli	17 028	*5190*		*Mishirgitau,*		
5.	Koshtantau	16 880	*5145*		*East Peak*	*16 135*	4917
6.	Pik Pushkin	16 732	*5100*	12.	Kunjum Mishikgi	16 011	*4880*
7.	Janga, West Peak	16 572	*5051*	13.	Gestola	15 940	*4858*
	Janga, East Peak	*16 529*	5038	14.	Tetnuld	15 938	*4857*

Highest Alps

The highest point in Italian territory is a shoulder of the main summit of Mont Blanc (Monte Bianco) through which a 4760-m *15 616–ft* contour passes. The highest top exclusively in Italian territory is Picco Luigi Amedeo (4460 m *14 632 ft*) to the south of the main Mont Blanc peak, which is itself exclusively in French territory.

Subsidiary peaks or tops on the same massif have been omitted except in the case of Mont Blanc and Monte Rosa, where they have been indented in italic type.

		Height (m)	Height (ft)	Country	First Ascent
1.	Mont Blanc	4807	*15 771*	France	1786
	Monte Bianco di Courmayeur	4748	*15 577*	France	1877
2.	Monte Rosa				
	Dufourspitze	4634·0	*15 203*	Switzerland	1855
	Nordend	4609	*15 121*	Swiss–Italian border	1861
	Ostpitze	4596	*15 078*	Swiss–Italian border	1854
	Zumstein Spitze	4563	*14 970*	Swiss–Italian border	1820
	Signal Kuppe	4556	*14 947*	Swiss–Italian border	1842
3.	Dom	4545·4	*14 911*	Switzerland	1858
4.	Lyskamm (Liskamm)	4527·2	*14 853*	Swiss–Italian border	1861
	Silberstattel Nord (Monte Rosa)	4517	*14 819*	Swiss–Italian border	
5.	Weisshorn	4505·5	*14 780*	Switzerland	1861
6.	Taschhorn	4490·7	*14 733*	Switzerland	1862
7.	Matterhorn	4475·5	*14 683*	Swiss–Italian border	1865
	Le Mont Maudit (Mont Blanc)	4465	*14 649*	Italy–France	1878
	Picco Luigi Amedeo (Mont Blanc)	4460	*14 632*	Italy	
8.	La Dent Blanche	4356·6	*14 293*	Switzerland	1862
9.	Nadelhorn	4327·0	*14 196*	Switzerland	1858
10.	Le Grand Combin de Grafaneire	4314	*14 153*	Switzerland	1859
	Dome du Gouter (Mont Blanc)	4304	*14 120*	France	
11.	Lenzspitze	4294	*14 087*	Switzerland	1871
12.	Finsteraarhorn	4273·8	*14 021*	Switzerland	1829★

Note: In the *Dunlop Book* (1st Edition) this list was extended to include the 24 additional Alps over (13 123 ft) *4000 m*.
★ Also reported climbed in 1812 but evidence lacking.

Antarctica

Large areas of Eastern Antarctica remain unsurveyed. Immense areas of the ice cap around the Pole of Inaccessibility lie over 12 000 ft *3650 m* above sea-level rising to 14 000 ft *4265 m* in 82° 25′ S 65° 30′ E.

	Name	Height (ft)	Height (m)	Location
1.	Vinson Massif	16 863	*5140*	Sentinel range, Ellsworth Mts
2.	Mt Tyree	16 289	*4965*	Sentinel range, Ellsworth Mts
3.	Mt Shinn	15 750★	*4800★*	Sentinel range, Ellsworth Mts
4.	Mt Gardner	15 354	*4688*	Sentinel range, Ellsworth Mts
5.	Mt Kirkpatrick	14 860	*4529*	Queen Alexandra Range
6.	Mt Elizabeth	14 698	*4480*	Queen Elizabeth Range
7.	Mt Markham	14 250	*4343*	Queen Elizabeth Range
8.	Mt MacKellar	14 082	*4292*	Queen Alexandra Range
9.	Mt Kaplan	13 960	*4255*	Queen Maud Range
10.	Mt Sidley	13 850	*4221*	Executive Committee Range
11.	Mt Ostenso	13 711	*4179*	Sentinel range, Ellsworth Mts
12.	Mt Minto	13 648	*4160*	Queen Elizabeth Range
13.	Mt Long Gables	13 622	*4152*	Sentinel range, Ellsworth Mts
14.	Mt Miller	13 600	*4145*	Queen Elizabeth Range
15.	Mt Falla	13 500	*4115*	Queen Alexandra Range
16.	Mt Fridtjof Nansen	13 350	*4069*	Queen Maud Range
17.	Mt Fisher	13 340	*4066*	Queen Maud Range
18.	Mt Wade	13 330	*4063*	Queen Maud Range
19.	Mt Lister	13 205	*4025*	Royal Society Range
20.	Mt Huggins	12 870	*3923*	Royal Society Range

★ The world's most southerly known active volcano, and the only known one in Antarctica.

Oceania

Name	Height (ft)	Height (m)	Location
1. Ngga Pulu (formerly Mt Sakarno)	c. 16 500	c. 5029	Irian Jaya (W New Guinea)
2. Idenburg Peak	15 748	4800	W Irian
3. *Mt Mohammed Yamin (Wilhelmina Top)	15 525	4732	Irian Jaya (W New Guinea)
4. *Mt Trikora (Juliana Top)	15 420	4700	Irian Jaya (W New Guinea)
5. Mt Wilhelm	15 400	4694	NE New Guinea
6. Mt Kubur	14 300	4359	NE New Guinea
7. Mt Herbert	14 000	4267	NE New Guinea
8. Mt Leonard Darwin	13 887	4233	W Irian
9. †Mauna Kea	13 796	4205	Hawaii, Hawaiian Is
10. †Mauna Loa	13 680	4170	Hawaii, Hawaiian Is
11. Mt Giluwe	13 660	4164	Papua (SE New Guinea)
12. Mt Bangeta	13 473	4107	NE New Guinea
13. Mt Kinabalu	13 455	4101	Borneo
14. Mt Victoria	13 363	4073	Papua (SE New Guinea)
15. *Sneeuw Gebergte Peak	13 125	4000	Irian Jaya (W New Guinea)
16. Mt Albert Edward	13 100	3993	Papua (SE New Guinea)
17. †Mokuaweoweo	13 018	3968	Hawaii, Hawaiian Is
18. Burgess Mt	13 000	3962	NE New Guinea
19. †Lua Hohonu	12 805	3903	Hawaii, Hawaiian Is
20. Mt Auriga	12 728	3878	NE New Guinea
21. Mt Sirius	12 631	3850	NE New Guinea

* Politically regarded as in Asian territory.
† Since 21 Aug. 1959 politically part of the USA.

Volcanoes

It is estimated that there are about 535 active volcanoes of which 80 are submarine. Vulcanologists classify volcanoes as extinct, dormant or active (which includes rumbling, steaming or erupting). Areas of volcanoes and seismic activity are well defined, notably around the shores of the N Pacific and the eastern shores of the S Pacific, down the Mid-Atlantic range, the Africa Rift Valley and across from Greece and Turkey into Central Asia, the Himalayas and Meghalaya (Assam).

Cerro Aconcagua (22 834 ft) *6960 m* the highest Andean peak is an extinct volcano, while Kilimanjaro (19 340 ft *5895 m*) in Africa and Volcán Llullaillaco in Chile (22 057 ft *6725 m*) are classified as dormant. Among the principal volcanoes active in recent times are:

Name	Height (ft)	Height (m)	Range or Location	Country	Date of Last Notified Eruption
Guallatiri	19 882	6060	Andes	Chile	1959
Lascar	19 652	5990	Andes	Chile	1951
Cotopaxi	19 347	5897	Andes	Ecuador	1942–Steams
Volcán Misti	19 167	5842	Andes	Peru	
Tupungatito	18 504	5640	Andes	Chile	1959
Popocatépetl	17 887	5452	Altiplano de Mexico	Mexico	1932–Steams
Sangay	17 159	5230	Andes	Ecuador	1946
Cotacachi	16 192	4935	Andes	Ecuador	1955
Puracé	15 604	4756	Andes	Colombia	1950
Klyuchevskaya sopta	15 913	4850	Sredinnyy Khrebet (Kamchatka Peninsula)	USSR	1962
Tajumulco	13 812	4210		Guatemala	Rumbles
Mauna Loa	13 680	4170	Hawaii	USA	1950
Cameroon Mt	13 350	4069	(monarch)	Cameroon	1959
Tacama	13 333	4064	Sierra Madre	Guatemala	
Fuego	12 582	3835	Sierra Madre	Guatemala	1973
Erebus	12 450	3795	Ross Is	Antarctica	Steams
Rindjani	12 224	3726	Lombok	Indonesia	1964
Pico de Tiede	12 198	3718		Teneriffe	
Tolbachik	12 080	3682		USSR	1941
Semeru	12 060	3676	Java	Indonesia	1963
Nyiragongo	11 385	3470	Virunga	Zaire (Kinshasa)	1972
Koryakskaya	11 339	3456	Kamchatka Peninsula	USSR	1957
Irasu	11 268	3432	Cordillera Central	Costa Rica	1963
Chiriqui	11 253	3430	Cadelia de Talamanca	Panama	
Slamat	11 247	3428	Java	Indonesia	1953
Mt Spurr	11 070	3374	Alaska Range	USA	1953
Mt Etna	10 705	3363	Sicily	Italy	1974

Other Notable Active Volcanoes

Name	Height (ft)	Height (m)	Range or Location	Country	Date of Last Notified Eruption
Tambora	9351	2850	Sumbawa	Indonesia	
The Peak	6760	2060	Tristan da Cunha	S Atlantic	1961
Mt Lamington	5535	1687		Papua New Guinea	1951
La Soufrière	4813	1467	Basselerre Island	Guadaloupe	
Mt Pelée	4800	1463		Martinique	1902
Hekla	4747	1447		Iceland	1948
Vesuvius	4198	1280	Bay of Naples	Italy	1944
Kilauea	4077	1240	Hawaii	USA	1973
Stromboli	3038	926	Island	Mediterranean	1971
Santorin	1960	584	Thera	Greece	
Surtsey	568	173	off SE Iceland	Iceland	1965
Anak Krakatau	510	155	Island	Indonesia	1960

DEPRESSIONS, GLACIERS AND CAVES

World's deepest depressions

	Maximum depth below sea level	
	(ft)	(m)
Dead Sea, Jordan–Israel	1296	395
Turfan Depression, Sinkiang, China	505	153
Munkhafad el Qattâra (Qattâra Depression), UAR	436	132
Poluostrov Mangyshlak, Kazakh SSR, USSR	433	131
Danakil Depression, Ethiopia	383	116
Death Valley, California, USA	282	86
Salton Sink, California, USA	235	71
Zapadnyy Chink Ustyurta, Kazakh SSR	230	70
Prikaspiyskaya Nizmennost', Russian SFSR and Kazakh SSR	220	67
Ozera Sarykamysh, Uzbek and Turkmen SSR	148	45
El Faiyûm, UAR	147	44
Península Valdiés Lago Enriquillo, Dominican Republic	131	40

Note: Immense areas of West Antarctica would be below sea level if stripped of their ice sheet. The deepest estimated crypto-depression is the bed rock on the Hollick–Kenyon plateau beneath the Marie Byrd Land ice cap (84° 37′ S 110° W) at −8100 ft (*2468 m*). The bed of Lake Baykal (USSR) is 4872 ft (*1484 m*) below sea level and the bed of the Dead Sea is 2600 ft (*792 m*) below sea-level. The ground surface of large areas of Central Greenland under the overburden of ice up to 11 190 ft *341 m* thick are depressed to 1200 ft *365 m* below sea-level. The world's largest exposed depression is the Prikaspiyskaya Nizmennost' stretching the whole northern third of the Caspian Sea (which is itself 92 ft *28 m* below sea level) up to 250 miles *400 km* inland. The Qattara Depression extends for 340 miles *547 km* and is up to 80 miles *128 km* wide.

World's longest glaciers

miles	km	
c. 320	515	Lambert-Fisher Ice Passage, Antarctica (disc. 1956–7)
260	418	Novaya Zemlya, North Island, USSR (1160 miles² 3004 km²)
225	362	Arctic Institute Ice Passage, Victoria Land, E Antarctica
180	289	Nimrod–Lennox–King Ice Passage, E Antarctica
150	241	Denman Glacier, E Antarctica
140	225	Beardmore Glacier, E Antarctica (disc. 1908)
140	225	Recovery Glacier, W Antarctica
124	200	Petermanns Gletscher, Knud Rasmussen Land, Greenland
120	193	Unnamed Glacier, SW Ross Ice Shelf, W Antarctica
115	185	Slessor Glacier, W Antarctica

Glaciated areas of the world

It is estimated that 6 050 000 miles² *15 670 000 km²* or about 10·5 per cent of the world's land surface is permanently covered with ice, thus:

	miles²	km²		miles²	km²
South Polar Regions	5 250 000	13 597 000	Asia	14 600	37 800
North Polar Regions			South America	4600	11 900
(inc Greenland with			Europe	4128	10 700
695 500)	758 500	1 965 000	New Zealand	380	984
Alaska–Canada	22 700	58 800	Africa	92	238

Notable Glaciers in other areas include:

		Length (miles)	Length (km)	Area (miles²)	Area (km²)
Iceland	Vatnajökull	88	141	3400	8800
Alaska	Malaspina Glacier	26	41	1480	3830
Alaska	Nabesna Glacier	43½	70	770	1990
Pamirs	Fedtschenko	47	75	520	1346
Karakoram	Siachen Glacier	47	75	444	1150
Norway	Jostedalsbre	62	100	415	1075
Karakoram	Hispar-Biafo Ice Passage	76	122	125 240	323 620
Himalaya	Kanchenjunga	12	19	177	458
New Zealand	Tasman Glacier	18	29	53	137
Alps	Aletschgletscher	16½	26,5	44	114

World's deepest caves

Cave	ft	m
Gouffre de la Pierre Saint Martin, Basses-Pyrénées, France	4363	1330
Gouffre Jean Bernard, Savoie Alps, France	4133	1260
Gouffre Berger, Sornin Plateau, Vercors, France	3743	1141
Chourun des Aguilles, Dauphine Alps, France	3214	980
Gouffre André Touya, Western Pyrénées, France	3116	950
Grotta di Monte Cuco, Perugia, Italy	3024	922
Abisso Michele Gortani, Julian Alps, Italy	3018	920
Gouffre de Cambou de Liard, Central Pyrénées, France	2979	908
Réseau Félix Trombe, Eastern Pyrénées, France	2952	900
Spluga Della Preta, Dolomites, Italy	2870	875

Note: The most extensive cave system is the Mammoth Cave system in Kentucky, USA, discovered in 1799 and now with an explored length of 150 miles *240 km* of passages. The largest known cavern is the Big Room in the Carlsbad Caverns, New Mexico, USA, which has maximum measurements of 4720 ft *1438 m* in length, 328 ft *100 m* high and 656 ft *200 m* across.

WORLD'S GREATEST MOUNTAIN RANGES

World's greatest mountain ranges

The greatest mountain system is the Himalaya-Karakoram-Hindu Kush-Pamir range with 104 peaks over 24 000 ft *7315 m*. The second greatest range is the Andes with 54 peaks over 20 000 ft *6096 m*.

Length (miles)	Length (km)	Name	Location	Culminating Peak	Height (ft)	Height (m)
4500	*7200*	Cordillera de Los Andes	W South America	Aconcagua	22 834	*6960*
3750	*6000*	Rocky Mountains	W North America	Mt Robson	12 972	*3954*
2400	*3800*	Himalaya–Karakoram–Hindu Kush	S Central Asia	Mt Everest	29 028	*8847*
2250	*3600*	Great Dividing Range	E Australia	Kosciusko	7310	*2228*
2200	*3500*	Trans-Antarctic Mts	Antarctica	Mt Kirkpatrick	14 860	*4529*
1900	*3000*	Brazilian Atlantic Coast Range	E Brazil	Pico da Bandeira	9482	*2890*
1800	*2900*	West Sumatran–Javan Range	W Sumatra and Java	Kerintji	12 484	*3805*
1650★	*2650*	Aleutian Range	Alaska and NW Pacific	Shishaldin	9387	*2861*
1400	*2250*	Tien Shan	S Central Asia	Pik Pobeda	24 406	*7439*
1300	*2100*	Eastern Ghats	E India	—	5 340	*1627*
1250	*2000*	Central New Guinea Range	Irian Jaya–Papua/ N Guinea	Ngga Pulu (formerly Mt Sukarno)	c. 16 500	*c. 5030*
1250	*2000*	Altai Mountains	Central Asia	Gora Belukha	14 783	*4505*
1250	*2010*	Uralskiy Khrebet	Russian SFSR	Gora Narodnaya	6214	*1894*
1200	*1930*	†Range in Kamchatka	E Russian SFSR	Klyuchevskaya Sopka	15 584	*4750*
1200	*1930*	Atlas Mountains	NW Africa	Jebel Toubkal	13 665	*4165*
1000	*1610*	Verkhoyanskiy Khrebet	E Russian SFSR	Gora Mas Khaya	9708	*2959*
1000	*1610*	Western Ghats	W India	Anai Madi	8841	*2694*
950	*1530*	Sierra Madre Oriental	Mexico	Citlaltepec (Orizaba)	18 865	*5750*
950	*1530*	Kūhhā-ye-Zāgros	Iran	Zard Kūh	14 921	*4547*
950	*1530*	Scandinavian Range	W Norway	Galdhopiggen	8104	*2470*
900	*1450*	Ethiopian Highlands	Ethiopia	Ras Dashan	c. 15 100	*c. 4600*
900	*1450*	Sierra Madre Occidental	Mexico	Nevado de Colima	13 993	*4265*
850	*1370*	Malagasy Range	Madagascar	Maromokotro	9436	*2876*
800	*1290*	Drakensberg (edge of plateau)	SE Africa	Thabana Ntlenyana	11 425	*3482*
800	*1290*	Khrebet Cherskogo	E Russian SFSR	Gora Pobeda	10 325	*3147*
750	*1200*	Caucasus	Georgia, USSR	El'brus	18 481	*5633*
700	*1130*	Alaska Range	Alaska, USA	Mt McKinley	20 320	*6193*
700	*1130*	Assam–Burma Range	Assam–W Burma	Hkakado Razi	19 296	*5881*
700	*1130*	Cascade Range	Northwest USA–Canada	Mt Rainier	14 410	*4392*
700	*1130*	Central Borneo Range	Central Borneo	Kinabulu	13 455	*4101*
700	*1130*	Tihāmat ash Shām	SW Arabia	Jebel Hadhar	12 336	*3760*
700	*1130*	Appennini	Italy	Corno Grande	9617	*2931*
700	*1130*	Appalachians	Eastern USA	Mt Mitchell	6684	*2037*
650	*1050*	Alps	Central Europe	Mt Blanc	15 771	*4807*
600	*965*	Sierra Madre del Sur	Mexico	Teotepec	12 149	*3703*
600	*965*	Khrebet Kolymskiy (Gydan)	E Russian SFSR	—	7290	*2221*

★ Continuous mainland length (excluding islands) 450 miles *720 km*.   † Comprises the Sredinnyy and Koryaskiy Khrebets.

WORLD'S GREATEST RIVERS

THE WORLD'S GREATEST RIVERS

The importance of rivers still tends to be judged on their length rather than by the more significant factors—their basin areas and volume of flow. In this compilation all the world's river systems with a watercourse of a length of 1500 miles *2400 km* or more are listed with all three criteria where ascertainable.

Length (miles)	(km)	Name of Watercourse	Source	Course and Outflow	Basin Area (miles²)	(km²)	Mean Discharge Rate (ft³/s)	(m³/s)	Notes
1 4145	6670	Nile (Bahr-el-Nil)–White Nile (Bahr el Jabel)–Albert Nile–Victoria Nile–Victoria Nyanza–Kagera–Luvironza	Rwanda: Luvironza branch of the Kagera, a feeder of the Victoria Nyanza	Through Tanganyika (Kagera), Uganda (Victoria Nile and Albert Nile), Sudan (White Nile), U.A.R. (Egypt) to eastern Mediterranean	1 293 000	*3 350 000*	110 000	*3120*	Navigable length to first cataract (Aswan) 960 miles *1545 km* U.A.R. Irrigation Dept. states length as 4164 miles *6700 km*. Discharge 93 200 ft³/s *2600m³/s* near Aswan. Delta is 9250 miles² *23 960 km²*
2 4007	6648	Amazon (Amazonas)	Peru: Lago Villafro, head of the Apurimac branch of the Ucayali, which joins the Marañon to form the Amazonas	Through Colombia to Equatorial Brazil (Solimões) to South Atlantic (Canal do Sul)	2 722 000	*7 050 000*	6 350 000	*180 000*	Total of 15 000 tributaries, ten over 1000 miles *1600 km* including Madeira (2100 miles *3380 km*). Navigable 2300 miles *3700 km* up stream. Delta extends 250 miles *400 km* inland
3 3710	5970	Mississippi–Missouri–Jefferson–Beaver-head–Red Rock	Beaverhead County, southern Montana, U.S.A.	Through N. Dakota, S. Dakota, Nebraska–Iowa, Missouri–Kansas, Illinois, Kentucky, Tennessee, Arkansas, Mississippi, Louisiana, South West Pass into Gulf of Mexico	1 245 000	*3 224 000*	650 000	*18 400*	Missouri is 2315 miles *3725 km* the Jefferson-Beaverhead–Red Rock is 217 miles *349 km*. Lower Mississippi is 1171 miles *1884 km*. Total Mississippi from Lake Itasca, Minn., is 2348 miles *3778 km*. Longest river in one country. Delta is 13 900 miles² *36 000 km²*
4 3442	5540	Yenisey-Algara-Selenga	Mongolia: Ideriin branch of Selenga (Selenge)	Through Buryat A.S.S.R. (Selenga feeder) into Ozero Baykal, thence *via* Angara to Yenisey confluence at Strelka to Kara Sea, northern U.S.S.R.	996 000	*2 580 000*	670 000	*19 000*	Estuary 240 miles *386 km* long. Yenisey is 2200 miles *3540 km* long and has a basin of 792 000 miles² *2 050 000 km²*. The length of the Angara is 1150 miles *1850 km*

Length (miles) (km)	Name of Watercourse	Source	Course and outflow	Basin area (mile²) (km²)	Mean Discharge Rate (ft³/s) m(³/s)	Notes
5 3436 5530	Yangtze Kiang (Ch'ang Chiang)	Western China, Kunlun ShanMts. (as Dre Che and T'ungt'ien)	Begins at T'ungt'ien, then Chinsha, through Yünnan Szechwan, Hupeh, Anhwei, to Yellow Sea	756 000 *1 960 000*	770 000 *21 800*	Flood rate (1931) of 3 000 000 ft³/s *85 000 m³/s.* Estuary 120 miles *190 km* long
6 3362 5410	Ob'-Irtysh	Mongolia: Kara (Black) Irtysh *via* northern China (Sin Kiang) feeder of Ozero Zaysan	Through Kazakhstan into Russian S.F.S.R. to Ob' confluence at Khanty Mansiysk, thence Ob' to Kara Sea, northern U.S.S.R.	1 150 000 *2 978 000*	550 000 *15 600*	Estuary (Obskaya Guba) is 450 miles *725 km* long. Ob' is 2286 miles *3679 km* long, Irtysh 1840 miles *2960 km* long
7 3000 4830	Hwang Ho (Yellow River)	China: Tsaring-nor, Tsinghai Province	Through Kansu, Inner Mongolia, Hunan, Shantung to Po Hai (Gulf of Chili), Yellow Sea, North Pacific	378 000 *979 000*	100 000 *2800* to to 800 000 *22 650*	Changed mouth by 250 miles *400 km* in 1852. Only last 25 miles *40 km* navigable. Longest river in one country in Asia.
8 2920 4700	Congo	Zambia-Congo (Kinshasa) border, as Lualaba	Through Congo (Kinshasa) as Lualaba along to Congo (Brazzaville) border to N.W. Angola mouth into the South Atlantic	1 314 000 *3 400 000*	1 450 000 *41 000*	Navigable for 1075 miles *1730 km* from Stanleyville to Kinshasa (formerly Léopoldville). Estuary 60 miles *96 km* long
9 2734 4400	Lena-Kirenga	U.S.S.R. Hinterland of west central shores of Ozero Baykal as Kirenga	Northwards through Eastern Russia to Laptu Sea, Arctic Ocean	960 000 *2 490 000*	575 000 *16 300*	Lena Delta (17 375 miles² *45 000 km²*) extends 110 miles *177 km* inland, frozen 15 Oct. to 10 July Second longest solely Russian river
10 2700 4345	Amur–Argun'	Northern China in Khingan Ranges (as Argun')	North along Inner Mongolian–U.S.S.R. and Manchuria–U.S.S.R. border for 2326 miles *3743 km* to Tarter Strait, Sea of Okhotsk, North Pacific	787 000 *2 038 000*	438 000 *12 400*	Amur is 1771 miles *2850 km* long (711 600 basin and 388 000 flow). *China Handbook* claims total length to be 2903 miles *4670 km* of which only 575 miles *925 km* is exclusively in U.S.S.R. territory
11 2635 4240	Mackenzie-Peace	Tatlatui Lake, Skeena Mts., Rockies, British Columbia, Canada (as River Findlay)	Flows as Findlay for 250 miles *400 km* to confluence with Peace. Thence 1050 miles *1690 km* to join Slave (258 miles *415 km*) which feeds Great Slave Lake whence flows Mackenzie (1077 miles *1733 km*) to Beaufort Sea	711 000 *1 841 000*	400 000 *11 300*	Peace 1195 miles *1923 km*
12 2600 4180	Mekong (Me Nam Kong)	Central Tibet (as Lants'ang), slopes of Dza-Nag-Lung-Mong, 16 700 ft *5000 m*	Flows into China, thence south to form Burma–Laotian and most of Thai-Laotian frontiers, thence through Cambodia to S. Vietnam into South China Sea	381 000 *987 000*	388 000 *11 000*	Max flood discharge 1 700 000 ft³/s *48 000 m³/s*
13 2600 4180	Niger	Guinea: Loma Mts. near Sierra Leone border	Flows through Mali, Niger and along Dahomey border into Nigeria and Atlantic	730 000 *1 890 000*	415 000 *11 750*	Delta extends 80 miles *128 km* inland and 130 miles *200 km* in coastal length
14 2485 4000	Rió de la Plata–Paraná	Brazil: as Paranáiba. Flows south to eastern Paraguay border and into eastern Argentina	Emerges in confluence with River Uruguay to form Rio de la Plata, South Atlantic	1 600 000 *4 145 000*	970 000 *27 500*	After the 75-mile- *120-km*-long Delta estuary, the river shares the 210-mile- *340 km*-long estuary of the Uruguay called Rio de la Plata (River Plate)
15 2330 3750	Murray-Darling	Queensland, Australia: as the Culgoa continuation of the Condamine, which is an extension of the Balonne-branch of the Darling	Balome (intermittent flow) crosses into New South Wales to join Darling, which itself joins the Murray on the New South Wales–Victoria border and flows west into Lake Alexandria, in South Australia	408 000 *1 059 000*	14 000 *400*	Darling c. 1700 miles *2740 km* Murray 1609 miles *2590 km* or 1160 miles *1870 km*
16 2293 3690	Volga	USSR	Flows south and east in a great curve and empties in a delta into the north of the Caspian Sea	525 000 *1 360 000*	287 000 *8200*	Delta exceeds 175 miles *280 km* inland and arguably 280 miles *450 km*
2100 3380	Madeira–Mamoré–Grande (Guapay)	Bolivia rises on the Beni near Illimani	Flows north and east into Brazil to join Amazon at the Ilha Tupinambarama	Tributary of No. 2	530 000 *15 000*	World's longest tributary, navigable for 663 miles *1070 km*
2000 3200	Purus	Peru: as the Alto Purus	Flows north and east into Brazil to join Amazon below Beruri	Tributary of No. 2	— —	World's second longest tributary. Navigable for 1600 miles *2575 km*
17 2200 3540	Zambezi (Zambeze)	Rhodesia: north-west extremity, as Zambesi	Flows after 45 miles *72 km* across eastern Angola for 220 miles *354 km* and back into Rhodesia (as Zambesi), later forming border with eastern end of Caprivi strip of South-West Africa, thence over Victoria Falls into Kariba Lake. Thereafter into Mozambique and out into southern Indian Ocean	514 000 *1 330 000*	250 000 *7 000*	Navigable 380 miles *610 km* up to Quebrabasa Rapids and thereafter in stretches totalling another 1200 miles *1930 km*
18 1979 3185	Yukon-Teslin	North-west British Columbia, Canada, as the Teslin	Flows north into Yukon Territory and into west Alaska, USA, and thence into Bering Sea	330,000 *855 000*	— —	Delta 85 miles *136 km* inland, navigable (shallow draft) for 1775 miles *2855 km*
19 1945 3130	St Lawrence	Head of St Louis River, Minn., USA	Flows into Lake Superior, thence Lakes Huron, Erie, Ontario to Gulf of St Lawrence and North Atlantic	532 000 *1 378 000*	360 000 *10 200*	Estuary 253 miles *407 km* long or 383 miles *616 km* to Anticosti Island. Discovered 1535 by Jacques Cartier
20 1885 3033	Rio Grande (Rio Bravo del Norte)	South-western Colorado, USA: San Juan Mts.	Flows south through New Mexico, USA, and along Texas–Mexico border into Gulf of Mexico, Atlantic Ocean	172 000 *445 000*	3000 *85*	

Length (miles) (km)	Name of Watercourse	Source	Course and outflow	Basin area (mile²) (km²)	Mean Discharge Rate (ft³/s) m(³/s)	Notes
21 1800 2900	Ganges–Brahmaputra	South-western Tibet as Matsung (Tsangpo)	Flows east 770 miles *1240 km* south, then west through Assam, north-eastern India, joins Ganges (as Jamuna) to flow into Bay of Bengal, Indian Ocean	626 000 *1 620 000*	1 360 000 *38 500*	Joint delta with Ganges extends 225 miles *360 km* across and 205 miles *330 km* inland. Area 30 800 mile² *80 000 km²* the world's largest. Navigable 800 miles *1290 km*
22 1800 2900	São Francisco	Brazil: Serra da Canastra	Flows north and east into South Atlantic	270 000 *700 000*	— —	Navigable 148 miles *238 km*
23 1790 2880	Indus	Tibet: as Sengge	Flows east through Kashmir, into West Pakistan and out into northern Arabian Sea	450 000 *1 166 000*	195 000 *5 500*	Delta (area 3100 miles² *8000 km²* extends 75 miles *120 km* inland
24 1770 2850	Danube	South-western Germany: Black Forest as Breg or Brigach	Flows (as Donau) east into Austria, along Czech-Hungarian border as Dunai into Hungary (273 miles *440 km*) as Duna, to Yugoslavia as Dunav along Romania–Bulgaria border and through Romania as Dunărea to Romania–USSR border as Dunay, into the Black Sea	315 000 *815 000*	250 000 *7 000*	Delta extends 60 miles *96 km* inland, Flows in territory of 8 countries
25 1750 2810	Salween	Tibet	Flows (as Nu) east and south into western China, into eastern Burma and along Thailand border and out into Gulf of Martaban, Andaman Sea	125 000 *325 000*	— —	
26 1700 2740 =	Tigris–Euphrates (Shatt al-Arab)	Eastern Turkey as Murat	Flows west becoming the Firat, thence into Syria as Al Furāt and south and east into Iraq joining Tigris as Shatt al Arab flowing into Persian Gulf at Iran–Iraq border	430 000 *1 115 000*	50 000 *400 low 2 700 high*	
27 1700 2700	Tocantins	Brazil: near Brazilia as Parans	Flows north to join Pará in the Estuary Bára de Marajó and the South Atlantic	350 000 *905 000*	360 000 *10 000*	Not properly regarded as an Amazon tributary. Estuary 275 miles *440 km* in length
28 1700 2740	Orinoco	South-eastern Venezuela	Flows north and west to Columbia border, thence north and east to north-eastern Venezuela and the Atlantic	400 000 *1 036 000*	— —	
29 1650 2650	Si Kiang (Hsi-Chiang)	China: in Yünnan plateau as Nanp'an	Flows east as the Hungshai and later as the Hsün to emerge as the Hsi in the South China Sea, west of Hong Kong	232 300 *602 000*	— —	Delta exceeds 90 miles *145 km* inland and includes the Pearl River or Chu
30 1616 2600	Kolyma	USSR: in Khrebet Kolymskiy	Flows north across Arctic Circle into eastern Siberian Sea	206 000 *534 000*	134 000 *3 800*	
31 1600 2575	Amu-Dar'ya (Oxus)	Wakhan, Afghanistan, on the border with Sinkiang China, as Oxus	Flows west to form Tadzhik SSR–Afghan border as Pyandzh for 680 km *420 miles* and into Turkmen SSR as Amu-Dar'ya. Flows north and west into Aral'skoye More (Aral Sea)	179 500 *465 000*	— —	
32 1600 2575	Nelson–Saskatchewan	Canada: eastern Alberta as South Saskatchewan	Flows north and east through Saskatchewan and into Manitoba through Cedar Lake into Lake Winnipeg and out through northern feeder as Nelson to Hudson Bay	414 000 *1 072 000*	80 000 *2250*	Saskatchewan is 1205 miles *1940 km* in length
33 1575 2540	Ural	USSR: South-central Urals	Flows south and west into the Caspian Sea	84 900 *220 000*	— —	
=34 1500 2410	Japurá	South-west Colombia in Cordillera Oriental as the Caquetá	Flows east into Brazil as Japurá, thence forms a left bank tributary of the Amazon opposite Tefé	Tributary of No. 2	— —	
=34 1500 2410	Paraguay	Brazil: in the Mato Grosso as Paraguai	Flows south to touch first Bolivian then Paraguayan border, then across Paraguay and then on to form border with Argentina. Joins the Paraná south of Humaitá	444 000 *1 150 000* Tributary of No. 14	— —	

Other Rivers of 1000 miles *1600 km* or Longer

Miles	km	Name and Location	Area of Basin (miles²) (km²)	Miles	km	Name and Location	Area of Basin (miles²) (km²)
1450	2335	Arkansas, USA	Tributary of No. 3	1180	1900	Indigirka-Khastakh, USSR	139 000 *360 000*
1450	2335	Colorado, USA	228 000 *590 000*	1150	1850	Sungari (or Sunghua), China	Tributary of No. 9
1420	2285	Dnepr (Dnieper), USSR	194 200 *503 000*	1150	1850	Tigris, Turkey–Iraq	Included in No. 25
1400	2255	Rio Negro, Colombia-Brazil	Tributary of No. 2	1112	1790	Pechora, USSR	126 000 *326 000*
1360	2188	Orange (Oranje), South Africa	394 000 *1 020 000*	1018	1638	Red River, USA	Tributary of No. 3
1343	2160	Olenek, USSR	95 000 *246 000*	1000	1600	Churchill (or Missinipi), Canada	150 000 *390 000*
1330	2140	Syr-Dar'ya, USSR	175 000 *453 000*	1000	1600	Uruguay, Brazil–Uruguay–Argentina	Included in No. 14
1306	2100	Ohio-Allegheny, USA	Tributary of No. 3				
1250	2010	Irrawaddy, China-Burma	166 000 *430 000*	1000	1600	Pilcomayo, Bolivia–Argentina–Paraguay	Tributary of Paraguay and sub-tributary of Paraná
1224	1969	Don, USSR	163 000 *422 000*				
1210	1950	Columbia-Snake, Canada-USA	258 000 *668 000*				

Note: Some sources state that the Amazon tributary the Juruá is over 1133 miles *1823 km* and the Lena tributary the Vitim, is 1200 miles *1931 km* long.

Worlds Greatest Waterfalls
By Height

	Name	Total Drop (ft)	(m)	River	Location
1.	Angel (highest fall—2648 ft *807 m*)	3212	*979*	Carrao, an upper tributary of the Caroni	Venezuela
2.	Tugela (5 falls) (highest fall—1350 ft *410 m*)	3110	*947*	Tugela	Natal, S. Africa
3.	Utigård (highest fall—1970 ft *600 m*)	2625	*800*	Jostedal Glacier	Nesdale, Norway
4.	Mongefossen	2540	*774*	Monge	Mongebekk, Norway
5.	Yosemite	2425	*739*	Yosemite Creek, a tributary of the Merced	Yosemite Valley, Yosemite National Park, Cal., USA
	(Upper Yosemite—1430 ft *435 m*; Cascades in middle section—675 ft *205 m*; Lower Yosemite —320 ft *97 m*)				
6.	Østre Mardøla Foss (highest fall—974 ft *296 m*)	2154	*656*	Mardals	Eikisdal, W. Norway
7.	Tyssestrengane (highest fall—948 ft *289 m*)	2120	*646*	Tysso	Hardanger, Norway
8.	Kukenaom (or Cuquenán)	2000	*610*	Arabopó, upper tributary of the Caroni	Venezuela
9.	Sutherland (highest fall—815 ft *248 m*)	1904	*580*	Arthur	nr. Milford Sound, Otago, S. Island, New Zealand
10.	Kile* (or Kjellfossen) (highest fall—490 ft *149 m*)	1841	*561*	Naero fjord feeder	nr. Gudvangen, Norway
11.	Ribbon	1612	*491*	Ribbon Fall Stream	3 miles west of Yosemite Falls, Yosemite National Park, Cal., USA
12.	King George VI	1600	*487*	Utshi, upper tributary of the Mazaruni	Guyana
13.	Wollombi (highest fall—1100 ft *335 m*)	1580	*481*	Wollombi Rivers, tributary of the Macleay	New South Wales, Australia
14.	Roraima	1500	*457*	an upper tributary of the Mazaruni	Guyana
15.	Cleve-Garth	1476	*449*	—	New Zealand
16.	Kalambo	1400	*426*	S.E. feeder of Lake Tanganyika	Tanzania–Zambia
17.	Gavarnie	1384	*421*	Gave de Pau	Pyrenees Glaciers, France
18.	Glass	1325	*403*	Iguazú	Brazil
19.	Krimmler fälle (4 falls, upper fall 460 ft *140 m*)	1280	*390*	Krimml Glacier	Salzburg, Austria
20.	Lofoi	1259	*383*	—	Congo (Kinshasa)
21.	Takkakaw (highest fall—1000 ft *300 m*)	1248	*380*	A tributary of the Yoho	Daly Glacier, British Columbia, Canada
22.	Silver Strand (Widow's Tears)	1170	*356*	Merced tributary	Yosemite National Park, Cal., USA

*Some authorities would regard this as no more than a 'Bridal Veil' waterfall, *i.e.*, of such low volume that the fall atomizes.

By Volume of Water

Name	Maximum Height (ft)	(m)	Width (ft)	Width (m)	Mean Annual Flow (ft³/s)	(m³/s)	Location
Stanley (7 cataracts)	200 (total)	*60*	2 400 (7th)	*730*	c. 600 000	*17 000*	Congo River, nr. Stanleyville
Guaíra (or Salto das Sete Quedas) ('Seven Fall's)	374	*114*	15 900	*4846*	470 000*	*13 000*	Alto Paraná, River Brazil–Paraguay
Khône	70	*21*	35 000	*10 670*	400 000 to 420 000	*11 000 to 12 000*	Mekong River, Laos
Niagara:					212 000	*6 000*	
Horseshoe (Canadian)	160	*48*	2500	*760*	(Horseshoe—94%)		Niagara River, Lake Erie to Lake Ontario
American	167	*50*	1000	*300*			Niagara River, Lake Erie to Lake Ontario
Paulo Afonso	192	*58*	—	—	100 000	*2 800*	São Francisco River, Brazil
Urubu-punga	40	*12*	—	—	97 000	*2700*	Alto Paraná River, Brazil
Cataratas del Iguazú (or Iguacu)	308	*93*	c. 13 000	c. *4000*	61 660	*1700*	Iguazú (or Iguacu) River, Brazil–Argentina
Patos–Maribondo	115	*35*	—	—	53 000	*1500*	Rio Grande, Brazil
Victoria (Mosi-oa-tunya):							
Leaping Water	355	*108*	108	*33*	} 38 430	*1100*	Zambezi River, nr. Livingstone, N. Rhodesia–S. Rhodesia
Main Fall	} (maximum)		{ 2694	*821*			
Rainbow Falls			1800	*550*			
Grand	245	*75*			30 000 to 40 000	*850 to 1100*	Hamilton River, Labrador, Canada
Kaieteur (Köituök)	741	*225*	300 to 350	*90 to 105*	23 400	*660*	Potaro River, Guyana

*The peak flow has reached, 1,750,000 ft³/s.

Lakes of the World

	Name	Country	Area (miles²)	(km²)	Length (miles)	(km)	Maximum Depth (ft)	(m)	Average Depth (ft)	(m)	Height of Surface above Sea-level (ft)	(m)
1.	Caspian Sea	USSR and Iran	143 550	*371 800*	760	*1220*	3215	*980*	675	*205*	—92	*—28*
2.	Superior	Canada and USA	31 820	*82 400*	350	*560*	1333	*406*	485	*147*	602	*183*
3.	Victoria Nyanza	Uganda, Tanzania, and Kenya	26 828	*69 500*	225	*360*	265	*80*	130	*39*	3720	*1134*
4.	Aral'skoye More (Aral Sea)	USSR	25 300	*65 500*	280	*450*	223	*68*	52	*15,8*	174	*53*
5.	Huron	Canada and USA	23 010	*59 600*	206	*330*	750	*228*	196	*59*	579	*176*
6.	Michigan	USA	22 400	*58 000*	307	*494*	923	*281*	275	*83*	579	*176*
7.	Tanganyika	Congo (Kinshasa), Tanzania, and Zambia	12 700	*32 900*	450	*725*	4708	*1435*	—	—	2534	*772*
8.	Great Bear	Canada	12 275	*31 800*	232	*373*	270	*82*	—	—	390	*118*
9.	Ozero Baykal	USSR	11 780	*30 500*	385	*620*	5315	*1620*	2300	*700*	1493	*455*
10.	Malawi (formerly Nyasa)	Tanzania, Malawi, and Mozambique	11 430	*29 600*	360	*580*	2226	*678*	895	*272*	1550	*472*
11.	Great Slave	Canada	10 980	*28 500*	298	*480*	535	*163*	—	—	512	*156*
12.	Erie	Canada and USA	9930	*25 700*	241	*387*	210	*64*	60	*18,2*	572	*174*
13.	Winnipeg	Canada	9464	*24 500*	266	*428*	120	*36*	—	—	713	*217*
14.	Ontario	Canada and USA	7520	*19 500*	193	*310*	780	*237*	260	*79*	246	*75*
15.	Ozero Ladozhskoye (Lake Ladoga)	USSR	6835	*17 700*	120	*193*	738	*225*	170	*51*	13	*3,9*
16.	Ozero Balkhash	USSR	6720	*17 400*	300	*482*	85	*26*	—	—	1112	*339*
17.	Lac Tchad (Chad)	Niger, Nigeria, Chad and Cameroon	6300*	*16 300*	130	*209*	13–24	*3,9–7,3*	5	*1,5*	787	*240*
18.	Ozero Onezhskoye (Onega)	USSR	3710	*9600*	145	*233*	361	*110*	105	*32*	108	*33*
19.	Eyre	Australia	3700†	*9580*	115	*185*	65	*19,8*	—	—	—39	*—11,8*
20.	Lago Titicaca	Peru and Bolivia	3200	*8300*	130	*209*	1000	*304*	338	*103*	12 506	*3811*
21.	Athabasca	Canada	3120	*8100*	208	*334*	407	*124*	—	—	699	*213*
22.	Saimaa complex‡	Finland	c. 3100	c. *8030*	203	*326*	—	—	—	—	249	*75*
23.	Lago de Nicaragua	Nicaragua	3089	*8000*	100	*160*	200	*60*	—	—	110	*33*

* Highly variable area between 4250 and 8500 miles² *11 000 and 22 000 km²*
† Highly variable area between 3100 and 5800 miles² *8030 and 15 000 km²*.
‡ The Saimaa proper (The Lake of a Thousand Isles), is, excluding the islands, c. 500 miles² *1300 km²*

Sea Level
Mean Sea Level has long been regarded as an equipotential geodetic surface and a fool-proof basis for measuring land altitudes. The British Ordnance Survey datum level is based on levels at Newlyn, Cornwall, in the period 1915–20. In fact average sea levels vary with time (century by century) and from place to place over the Earth. The cross-channel slope Ramsgate to Dunkerque was some 8 cm *3 in.* in 1957–8.

Factors affecting sea levels are: (1) Surf beat (long waves superimposed on wind generated waves); (2) Tsunami (from submarine earthquakes); (3) Seiches (resonant wave oscillations across bays and bights); (4) Atmospheric pressures; (5) Storm surges; (6) Thermal effects (1 °C over all oceans would raise the level by 60 mm *2·3 in*; (7) Perihelion-Aphelion (sun distance).

Since 1900 a rise in the world's temperature and the melting of polar ice has raised sea levels by 6 cm. This has increased the Earth's radius of gyration and hence slowed down our rate of rotation. Tidal friction would be expected to lengthen the day by 2·3 milliseconds per century, thus indicating some as yet unidentified compensatory accelerating force.

Tides
Tides are caused by the gravitational attraction of the Moon and the Sun. The Sun's power, because its greater mass is not fully outweighed by its greater distance, is only 46 per cent that of the Moon.

Normally the interval between high waters is 12 hrs 25 min of half that of the Moon's apparent revolution around the Earth. There are wide variations in the intervals, e.g. at Southampton, England, high waters are often doubled while at places in the China Sea the interval oftens extends to over 24 hr.

The range also varies very widely being 53½ft *16,3 m* in the Minas Basin of the Bay of Fundy, Nova Scotia and a matter of inches in the Mediterranean.

United Kingdom

PHYSICAL AND POLITICAL GEOGRAPHY

The various names used for the islands and parts of islands off the north-west coast of Europe geographically known as the British Isles are confusing. Geographical, political, legal and popular usages unfortunately differ, thus making definition necessary.

British Isles
A convenient but purely *geographical* term to describe that group of islands lying off the north-west coast of Europe, comprising principally the island of Great Britain and the island of Ireland. There are four political units: the United Kingdom of Great Britain and Northern Ireland; the Republic of Ireland; the Crown dependencies of the Isle of Man and, conveniently, also the Channel Islands.
Area: 121 651 miles². *Population (mid-1975 estimate):* 59 125 000.

The United Kingdom (UK) (of Great Britain and Northern Ireland)
The political style of the island of Great Britain, with its offshore islands and, since the partition of Ireland (see below), the six counties of Northern Ireland. The term United Kingdom, referring to Great Britain and (the whole island of) Ireland first came into use officially on 1 Jan. 1801 on the Union of the two islands. With the coming into force of the Constitution of the Irish Free State as a Dominion on 6 Dec. 1922, the term 'United Kingdom of Great Britain and Ireland' had obviously become inappropriate. It was dropped by Statute from the Royal style on 13 May 1927 in favour of 'King of Great Britain, Ireland and of, etc.'. On the same date Parliament at Westminster adopted as its style 'Parliament of the United Kingdom of Great Britain and Northern Ireland'. On 29 May 1953 by Proclamation the Royal style conformed to the Parliamentary style—Ireland having ceased to be a Dominion within the Commonwealth on 18 Apr. 1949.
Area: 94 214 miles². *Population (mid-1975):* 55 972 000.

Great Britain (GB) is the geographical and political name of the main or principal island of the solely geographically named British Isles group. In a strict geographical sense, off-shore islands, for example the Isle of Wight, Anglesey, or Shetland, are not part of Great Britain. In the political sense Great Britain was the political name used unofficially from 24 Mar. 1603, when James VI of Scotland succeeded his third cousin twice removed upwards, Queen Elizabeth of England, so bringing about a Union of the Crowns, until on 1 May 1707 the style was formally adopted with the Union of the Parliaments of England and Scotland and was used until 1 Jan. 1801. The government of Great Britain is unitary, but in 1975 plans for separate Scottish and Welsh assemblies were first published.
Area: 88 755 miles². *Population (mid-1975):* 54 425 000.

England
Geographically the southern and greater part of the island of Great Britain. The islands off the English coast, such as the Isle of Wight and the Isles of Scilly, are administratively part of England. Politically and geographically England (historically a separate Kingdom until 1707) is that part of Great Britain governed by English law which also pertains in Wales and, since 1746, in Berwick-upon-Tweed.

The term 'England' is widely (but wrongly) used abroad to mean the United Kingdom or Great Britain.
Area: 50 869 miles². *Population (mid-1975):* 46 454 000.

Wales (The principality of) now comprises eight instead of twelve counties. The area was incorporated into England by Act of Parliament in 1536. The county of Monmouthshire, though for all administrative intents and purposes part of Wales, only became an integral part of Wales on 1 Apr. 1974. The boundary between England and Wales (excluding, however, the boundary between Wales and Monmouthshire) expressly could not be altered by the ordinary processes of local government reorganisation.

Wales may not, by Statute, be represented by less than 35 MPs at Westminster.
Wales
Area: 8017 miles². *Population (mid-1975):* 2 765 000.

Scotland consists of the northern and smaller part of the island of Great Britain. The Kingdom of Scotland was united with England on 24 March 1603 when King James VI of Scotland (ascended 1567) became also King James I of England. Both countries continued, however, to have their separate Parliaments until the Union of the Parliaments at Westminster, London, on 1 May 1707. Scotland continues to have its own distinctive legal system. By Statute Scotland may not be represented by less than 71 MPs at Westminster. Proposals for a separate Scottish Assembly of some 140 seats were published in 1975. On 16 May 1975 the 33 traditional counties were reduced to 12 Geographical regions.
Area: 30 411 miles². *Population (mid-1975):* 5 206 000.

Ireland
The geographical name of the second largest island in the British Isles. Henry VIII assumed the style 'King of Ireland' in 1542, although Governors of Ireland (the exact title varied) ruled on behalf of the Kings of England from 1172. The viceroyalty did not disappear until 1937. The Union of the Parliaments of Great Britain and Ireland occurred on 1 Jan. 1801.
Area: 32 594 miles². *Population (mid-1975 estimate):* 3 140 000

Northern Ireland consists of six counties in the north-eastern corner of the island. They are all within the larger ancient province of Ulster which originally consisted of nine counties. The government's relationship to the Imperial Parliament in England was federal in nature. Certain major powers were reserved by the Imperial Parliament, the sovereignty of which was unimpaired. There is a provision in the Ireland Act of 1949 that Northern Ireland cannot cease to be part of the United Kingdom, or part of the Queen's Dominions without the express consent of her Parliament. This Parliament, known as Stormont and established in 1921, was however abolished by the Northern Ireland Constitution Act, 1973. Devolved government came into effect on 1 Jan. 1974, but the Northern Ireland Assembly was prorogued on 29 May 1974 after the Executive collapsed. Arrangements for a Constitutional Convention, under the Northern Ireland Constitution Act 1974, which came into force in July 1974, collapsed in February 1976. Northern Ireland is represented by the fixed number of twelve Members of the Imperial Parliament at Westminster.
Area: 5459 miles². *Population (mid-1975):* 1 597 000.

The Republic of Ireland
This State came into being on 15 Jan. 1922 and consists of 26 of the pre-partition total of 32 Irish counties. The original name was 'The Irish Free State' (or in Irish Gaelic 'Saorstát Éireànn') and the country had Dominion status within the British Commonwealth. A revised Constitution, which became operative on 29 Dec. 1937, abolished the former name and substituted the title 'Éire', which is the Gaelic word for 'Ireland'. On 18 Apr. 1949 the official description of the State became 'The Republic of Ireland' (Poblacht na h-Éireann), but the name of the State remains 'Ireland' in the English and 'Éire' in the Irish Gaelic language. On the same date the Republic of Ireland ceased to be a member of the British Commonwealth.
Area: 27 135 miles². *Population (mid-1975 estimate):* 3 140 000.

BRITISH ISLES EXTREMITIES

Island of Great Britain

Great Britain, the eighth largest island in the world, has extreme dimensions thus:

Most Northerly Point	Easter Head, Dunnet Head, Highland	Lat 58° 40′ 25″ N
Most Westerly Point	Garbhlach Mhor, Ardnamurchan, Strathclyde	Long 6° 14′ 12″ W
Most Southerly Point	Lizard Point, Cornwall	Lat 49° 57′ 33″ N
Most Easterly Point	Lowestoft Ness, Lowestoft, Suffolk	Long 1° 46′ 20″ E

Other extreme points in its 3 constituent countries are:

Most Southerly Point in Scotland	Gallie Craig, Mull of Galloway, Dumfries & Galloway	Lat 54° 38′ 27″ N
Most Easterly Point in Scotland	Keith Inch, Peterhead, Grampian	Long 1° 45′ 49″ W
Most Northerly Point in England	Meg's Dub, Northumberland	Lat 55° 48′ 37″ N
Most Westerly Point in England	Dr Syntax's Head, Land's End, Cornwall	Long 5° 42′ 15″ W
Most Northerly Point in Wales	Point of Air, Clwyd	Lat 53° 21′ 08″ N
Most Westerly Point in Wales	Porthtaflod, Dyfed	Long 5° 19′ 43″ W
Most Southerly Point in Wales	Rhoose Point, South Glamorgan	Lat 51° 22′ 40″ N
Most Easterly Point in Wales	Pinfold Farm, Redbrook, Clwyd	Long 2° 43′ 26″ W

Island of Ireland (20th largest island in the world)

Most Northerly Point in Ireland	Malin Head, Donegal	Lat 55° 22′ 30″ N
Most Northerly Point in Northern Ireland	Benbane Head, Antrim	Lat 55° 15′ 0″ N

Island of Ireland continued

Most Westerly Point in Ireland	Dunmore Head, Kerry	Long 10° 28′ 55″ W
Most Westerly Point in Northern Ireland	Cornaglah, Fermanagh	Long 8° 10′ 30″ W
Most Southerly Point in Ireland	Brow Head, Cork	Lat 51° 26′ 30″ N
Most Southerly Point in Northern Ireland	Cranfield Point, Down	Lat 54° 01′ 20″ N
Most Easterly Point in Ireland (Northern)	Townhead, Ards Peninsula, Down	Long 5° 25′ 52″ W
Most Easterly Point in Republic of Ireland	Wicklow Head, Wicklow	Long 5° 59′ 40″ W

Isles of Scilly
Area: 4,041 acres.
Population: 1,950 (mid 1965). There are five populated islands—Bryher (pop. 80, 1964), St Agnes (pop. 65), St Martin's (pop. 125), St Mary's (pop. 1,355) and Tresco (pop. 205).

The islands are administered by a Council, consisting of a Chairman, 4 aldermen and 21 councillors; which is a unique type of local government unit set up by an Order made under Section 292 of the Local Government Act, 1933. For some purposes the Isles are administered in Company with the Cornwall County Council. The islands form part of the St Ives electoral division.

United Kingdom mountain and hill ranges

Scotland

Range	Length (miles)	Length (km)	Culminating peak	Height (ft)	Height (m)
Grampian Mountains	155	250	Ben Macdhui, Grampian	4300	1310
North West Highlands	140	225	Càrn Eige, Highland	3877	1181
*Southern Uplands (Scottish Lowlands)	125	200	Merrick Mountain, Galloway & Dumfries	2764	842
Monadh Liadth Mountains	35	55	Càrn Dearg Highland	3093	942

England

Range	Length (miles)	Length (km)	Culminating peak	Height (ft)	Height (m)
Pennines	120	195	Cross Fell, Cumbria	2930	893
North Downs	85	135	Leith Hill, Surrey	965	294
Cotswold Hills	60	95	Cleve Hill, Gloucestershire	1083	330
South Downs	55	85	Blackdown Hill, West Sussex	918	279
Cheviot Hills	45	70	The Cheviot, Northumbria	2676	815
Chiltern Hills	45	70	Coombe Hill, Buckinghamshire	852	259
Berkshire Downs (White Horse Hills)	35	55	Walbury Hill, Berkshire	974	296
Cumbrian Mountains	30	50	Scafell Pike, Cumbria	3210	978
Exmoor	30	50	Dunkery Beacon, Somerset	1706	519
North Yorkshire Moors (Cleveland and Hambleton Hills)	30	50	Cringle Moor, North Yorkshire	1427	434
Hampshire Downs	25	40	Pilot Hill, Hampshire	938	285
Yorkshire Wolds	22	35	Garrowby Hill, Humberside	808	296

Wales

Range	Length (miles)	Length (km)	Culminating peak	Height (ft)	Height (m)
Cambrian Mountains	110	175	Snowdon (Yr Wyddfa), Gwynedd	3560	1085
Berwyn Mountains	40	65	Aran Fawddwy, Gwynedd	2972	905

Northern Ireland

Range	Length (miles)	Length (km)	Culminating peak	Height (ft)	Height (m)
Sperrin Mountains	40	65	Sawel Mt, Londonderry-Tyrone	2240	682
Mountains of Mourne	30	50	Slieve Donard, County Down	2796	852
Antrim Hills	25	40	Trostan, Antrim	1817	553

* Includes: Lammermuir Hills (Lammer Law, Lothian 1733 ft *528 m*); Lowther Hills (Green Lowther, Strathclyde, 2403 ft *732 m*); Pentland Hills (Scald Law, Lowthian 1898 ft *578 m*) and the Tweedsmuir Hills (Broad Law, Borders, 2723 ft *829 m*).

Highest peaks in the British Isles

Though the eighth largest island in the world, Great Britain does not possess any mountains of great height.

In only two Scottish regions, those of Grampian and Highland, does the terrain surpass a height of 4000 ft *1219 m*. In Great Britain there are seven mountains and five subsidiary points (tops) above 4000 ft *1219 m* all in Scotland, and a further 283 mountains and 271 tops between 3000 ft and 4000 ft *914–1219 m* of which only 21 (see below) are in England or Wales. South of the border, 3000 ft *914 m* is only surpassed in Gwynedd and Cambria. Scotland possesses 54 mountains higher than Snowdon and 165 higher than the Scafell Pike. Ben Nevis was probably first climbed about 1720 and Ben Macdhui was thought to be Great Britain's highest mountain until as late as 1870.

Scotland's ten highest peaks

		ft	m
1.	Ben Nevis, Highland	4406	1392
2.	Ben Macdhui, Grampian	4300	1310
3.	Braeriach, Grampian-Highland border	4248	1294
	North top (Ben Macdhui)	4244	1293
4.	Cairn Toul, Grampian	4241	1292
	South Plateau (Braeriach) (also c. 4160 ft)	4149	1264
	Sgòr an Lochan Uaine (Cairn Toul)	4116	1254
	Coire Sputan Dearg (Ben Macdhui)	4095	1248
5.	Cairngorm, Grampian-Highland border	4084	1244
6.	Aonach Beag,	4060	1237
	Coire an Lochain (Braeriach)	4036	1230
7.	Càrn Mòr Dearg, Highland	4012	1222
8.	Aonach Mor, Highland	3999	1218
	Carn Dearg (Ben Nevis)	3990	1216
	Coire an t-Saighdeir (Cairn Toul)	3989	1215
9.	Ben Lawers, Tayside	3984	1214
	Cairn Lochan (Cairngorm)	3983	1214
10.	Beinn a' Bhùird (North Top), Grampian	3924	1196

Wales' ten highest peaks
(all in Gwynedd)

		ft	m
1.	Snowdon (Yr Wyddfa)	3560	1085
	Garnedd Ugain or Crib Y Ddisg (Yr Wyddfa)	3493	1065
2.	Carnedd Llewelyn	3484	1062
3.	Carnedd Dafydd	3426	1044
4.	Glyder Fawr	3279	999

Continued from page 85.

		ft	m
5.	Glyder Fâch	3262	*994*
	Pen Yr Oleu-wen (Carnedd Dafydd)	3210	*978*
	Foel Grâch (Carnedd Llewelyn)	3195	*974*
	Yr Elen (Carnedd Llewelyn)	3151	*960*
6.	Y Garn	3104	*946*
7.	Foel Fras	3091	*942*
8.	Elidir Fawr	3029	*923*
	Crib Goch (Yr Wyddfa)	3023	*921*
9.	Tryfan	3010	*917*
10.	Aran Fawddwy	2970	*905*

Ireland's ten highest peaks

		ft	m
1.	Carrauntual (or Carrauntoohil), Kerry	3414	*1041*
2.	Beenkeragh, Kerry	3314	*1010*
3.	Caher, Kerry	3200	*975*
4.	Ridge of the Reeks (*two other tops of the same height, a third* of 3141, and a *fourth* of *c.* 3050), Kerry	3200	*c. 975*
5.	Brandon, Kerry	3127	*953*
	Knocknapeasta (Ridge of the Reeks)	3062	*933*
6.	Lugnaquillia, Wicklow	3039	*926*
7.	Galtymore, Tipperary	3018	*920*
8.	Slieve Donard, County Down	*2796	*852*
9.	Baurtregaum, Kerry	2796	*852*
10.	Mullaghcleevaun, Wicklow	2788	*849*

* Highest peak in Northern Ireland.

England's ten highest peaks
(all in Cumbria)

		ft	m
1.	Scafell Pike	3210	*978*
2.	Sca Fell	3162	*963*
3.	Helvellyn, border	3118	*950*
	Broad Crag (Scafell Pikes)	3054	*930*
4.	Skiddaw	3053	*930*
	Little Man (Helvellyn)	3033	*922*
	Ill Crags (Scafell Pikes)	c. 3025	*c. 922*
	Great End (Scafell Pikes)	2984	*909*
5.	Bow Fell, border	2960	*902*
6.	Great Gable	2949	*898*
7.	Cross Fell	2930	*893*
8.	Pillar Fell	2927	*992*
	Catstye Cam (Helvellyn)	2917	*889*
9.	Esk Pike	2903	*884*
	Raise (Helvellyn)	2889	*880*
10.	Fairfield	2863	*872*

Longest Rivers in the United Kingdom

Specially compiled maps issued by the Ordnance Survey in the second half of the last century are still the authority for the length of the rivers of the United Kingdom. It should, however, be noted that these measurements are strictly for the course of a river bearing the one name, thus for example where the principal head stream has a different name its additional length is ignored—unless otherwise indicated.

Length (miles)	Length km	Names	Remotest source	Mouth	Area of Basin (miles²)*	Area of Basin km²	Extreme Discharge (cusecs)†
220	*355*	Severn (for 158 miles)	Lake on E side of Plinlimmon, Powys	Bristol Channel	4409·7	*11 421*	23 100 (1937)
210	*338*	Thames (111 miles)—Isis (43 miles)	Trewsbury Mead	North Sea	3841·6	*9950*	27 900 (1894)
185	*300*	Trent (147)—Humber (38)	Biddulph Moor, Staffs.	North Sea (as Humber)	4029·2	*10 436*	5 510
161	*260*	Aire (78)—(Yorkshire) Ouse (45) and Humber (38)	NW of North Yorks.	North Sea (as Humber)	4388·4	*11 366*	4580 (Aire only)
143	*230*	Ouse (Great or Bedford)	nr Brackley, Oxfordshire	The Wash	3 313·6	*8582*	11 000
135	*215*	Wye (or Gwy)	Plinlimmon, Powys	Into Severn 2½ miles S of Chepstow Mon.	1 615·3	*4184*	32 000
117	*188*	Tay (93·2)—Tummel	(Tay) Beinn Oss' Tayside	North Sea	1961·6	*5080*	49 000
100	*161*	Nene (formerly Nen)	nr Naseby, Northants.	The Wash	914·5	*2369*	13 500
98·5	*158*	Clyde (inc. Daer Water)	nr Earncraig Hill, extreme S Strathclyde	Atlantic Ocean (measured to Port Glasgow)	1173·8	*3040*	20 200
98·0	*157,5*	Spey	Loch Spey, Highland	North Sea	1153·5	*2988*	34 200
96·5	*155,3*	Tweed	Tweed's Well, Borders	North Sea	1992·3	*5160*	21 400
85·2	*137,1*	Dee (Aberdeenshire)	W of Cairn Toul, Grampian	North Sea	817·2	*2116*	40 000
85	*136,7*	Avon (Warwickshire or Upper)	nr Naseby, Northants.	Into Severn at Tewkesbury	(part of Severn Basin)		8560
80·5	*129,5*	Don (Aberdeenshire)	Carn Cuilchathaidh, Grampian	North Sea	515·7	*1336*	Not available
79	*127*	Tees	Cross Fell, Cumbria	North Sea	863·6	*2237*	13 600
76	*122*	Bann (Upper Bann—Lough Neagh—Lower Bann)	Mountains of Mourne, SW Down	Atlantic Ocean	—	*—*	—
73	*117,5*	Tyne (34)—North Tyne (39)	Cheviots between Pell Fell and Carter Fell	North Sea	1126·4	*2917*	42 000
70	*112,5*	Dee (Cheshire)	Bala Lake, Gwynedd	Irish Sea	818·1	*2119*	16 000
69	*111*	Eden (Cumberland)	Pennines, SE of Kirby Stephen	Solway Firth, Irish Sea	926·7	*2400*	—
65	*104,5*	Usk	Talsarn Mt, Brecknock	Bristol Channel	672·0	*1740*	23 700
65	*104,5*	Wear	W of Wearhead, Northumberland	North Sea	462·6	*1198*	6130
65	*104,5*	Wharfe	7½ miles S of Hawes, North Yorks.	Into York Ouse, nr Cawood	(part of Yorks Ouse Basin)		15 300
64·5	*103,5*	Forth	Dichray Water (13½ miles), Ben Lomond	Firth of Forth, North Sea	627·9	*1626*	—

* This column gives the hydrometric area of the whole river system as per *The Surface Water Survey* (Min of Housing and Local Govt).
† This column gives the highest recorded discharge in cubic feet per second (*note:* 1 cusec = 0·0283168 m³/sec 538,170 gallons per day) taken at the lowest sited gauging on the name river.

Waterfalls

The principal waterfalls of the British Isles are:

Height (ft)	Height (m)	Name
658	200	Eas-Coul-Aulin, Highland
370	112	Falls of Glomach, Highland
350	106	Powerscourt Falls, County Wicklow
240	73	Pistyll Rhaiadr, Clwyd
205	62	Foyers, Highland
204 (total)	62	Falls of Clyde, Strathclyde (comprises Bonnington Linn (30 ft 9 m). Corra Linn (84 ft 25 m), Dundaff Linn (10 ft 3 m) and Stonebyres Linn (80 ft 24 m) cataracts
200	60	Falls of Bruar, Tayside (upper fall)
200	60	Cauldron (or Caldron Snout), Cumbria
200	60	Grey Mare's Tail, Dumfries & Galloway

Area (miles²)	Area km²	Name and County	Max. Length (miles)	Max Length km	Max Breadth (miles)	Max Breadth km	Max Depth (ft)	Max Depth m
Northern Ireland								
147·39	381,7	Lough Neagh, Antrim, Down, Armagh, Tyrone, Londonderry	18	28	11	17	102	31
40·57	105,0	Lower Lough Erne, Fermanagh	18	28	5·5	8,8	226	68
12·25	31,7	Upper Lough Erne, Cavan	10	16	3·5	5,6	89	27

Area (miles²)	Area km²	Name and County	Max. Length (miles)	Max Length km	Max Breadth (miles)	Max Breadth km	Max Depth (ft)	Max Depth m
Scotland (Fresh-water (inland) lochs, in order of size of surface area)								
27·5	71,2	Loch Lomond, Strathclyde-Central	22·64	36,4	5	8	623	189
21·87	56,6	Loch Ness, Highland	22·75	36,6	2	3,2	751	228
14·95	38,7	Loch Awe, Strathclyde	25·5	41,0	2	3,2	307	93
11·0	28,4	Loch Maree, Highland	13·5	21,7	2	3,2	367	111
10·3	26,6	Loch Morar, Highland	11·5	18,5	1·5	2,4	1017	309
10·19	26,3	Loch Tay, Tayside	14·55	23,4	1·07	1,7	508	154
8·70	22,5	Loch Shin, Highland	17·25	27,7	1	1,6	162	49
7·56	19,5	Loch Shiel, Highland	17·5	28,1	0·9	1,4	420	128
7·34	19,0	Loch Rannoch, Tayside	9·75	15,6	1·1	1,7	440	134
7·18	18,5	Loch Ericht, Highland-Tayside	14·6	23,4	1·1	1,7	512	156
6·25	16,1	Loch Arkaig, Highland	12·0	19,3	0·9	1,4	359	109
5·9	15,2	Loch Lochy, Highland	9·9	15,9	1·25	2,0	531	161

England (Lake District lakes in order of size of surface area)
(all in Cumbria)

Area (miles²)	Area km²	Name	Max. Length (miles)	Max Length km	Max Breadth (Yd)	Max Breadth km	Max Depth (ft)	Max Depth m
5·69	14,7	Windermere	10·50	16,8	1,610	1,47	219	66
3·44	8,9	Ullswater	7·35	11,8	1,100	1,0	205	62
2·06	5,3	Bassenthwaite Water	3·83	6,1	1,300	1,18	70	21
2·06	5,3	Derwentwater	2·87	4,6	2,130	1,94	72	21
1·89	4,8	Coniston Water	5·41	8,7	870	0,79	184	56
1·12	2,9	Ennerdale Water	2·40	3,8	1,000	0,9	148	45
1·12	2,9	Wastwater	3·00	4,8	880	0,8	258	78
0·97	2,5	Crummock Water	2·50	4,0	1,000	0,9	144	43
0·54★	1,3	Haweswater	2·33	3,7	600	0,54	103	31
0·36	0,9	Buttermere	1·26	2,0	670	0,61	94	28

Wales

Area (miles²)	Area km²	Name	Max. Length (miles)	Max Length km	Max Breadth (Yd)	Max Breadth km	Max Depth (ft)	Max Depth m
1·69	4,3	Bala Lake (Llyn Tegid)	3·8	6,1	·850	0,77	125	38
3·18	8,2	Lake Vyrnwy (dammed)	4·7	7,5	·1000	0,9	120	36

Depressions

A very small area of Great Britain is below sea-level. The largest such area is in the Fenland of East Anglia, and even here a level of 9 ft 2,7 m below sea-level is not exceeded in the Holme Fen near Ely, Cambridgeshire. The beds of three Lake District lakes are below sea-level with the deepest being part of the bed of Windermere, Cumbria at —90 ft —27 m.

Caves

Large or deep caves are few in Great Britain. Great Britain's deepest cave is Ogof Fynnon Ddu (1010 ft, 307 m) in Powys, Wales. It is also the largest system with 23·92 miles 38,5 km of surveyed passages. England's deepest cave is Oxlow Cavern, Giant's Hole, Derbyshire which descends 642 ft 196 m. Scotland's largest cave is Great Smoo, Highland. Ireland's deepest is Carrowmore, County Sligo being460 ft 140 m deep.

United Kingdom's largest islands

A unique check list of more than 1000 islands of Great Britain will appear in the forthcoming *Guinness Book of British Islands*

England (12 largest)	mile²	km²	*Scotland* (12 largest)	mile²	km²	*Wales* (12 largest)	mile²	km²
Isle of Wight	147·09	380,99	Lewis with Harris	844·68	2187,72	*Anglesey (Yenys Mon)	275·60	713,80
*Sheppey	36·31	94,04	Skye	643·28	1666,08	Holy Is	15·22	39,44
*Hayling	10·36	26,84	Mainland, Shetland	373·36	967,00	Skomer	1·12	2,90
*Foulness	10·09	26,14	Mull	347·21	899,25	Ramsey	0·99	2,58
*Portsea	9·36	24,25	Islay	246·64	614,52	Caldey	0·84	2,79
*Canvey	7·12	18,45	Mainland, Orkney	206·99	536,10	Bardsey	0·76	1,99
*Mersea	6·96	18,04	Arran	168·08	435,32	Skokholm	0·41	1,06
*Walney	5·01	12,99	Jura	142·99	370,35	Flat Holm	0·13	0,33
*Isle of Grain	4·96	12,85	North Uist	135·71	351,49	*Llanddwyn Is	0·12	0,31
*Wallosea	4·11	10,65	South Uist	128·36	332,45	Puffin Island	0·11	0,28
St Mary's, Isles of			Yell	82·69	214,16	The Skerries	0·06	0,15
Scilly	2·84	7,37	Hoy, Orkney	52·84	136,85	Cardigan Island	0·06	0,15
Thorney	1·91	4,96						

*Bridged to the mainland

Northern Ireland's principal off-shore island is Rathlin Island (5·56 mile² *14,41 km²*)

The principal Channel Isles comprise	mile²	km²		Crown Dependency:	mile²	km²
Jersey	44·87	116,21		Isle of Man	220·72	571,66
Guernsey	24·46	63,34		Calf of Man	0·96	2,49
Alderney	3·07	7,94				
Sark	1·99	5,15				
Herm	0·50	1,29				

The 55 cities of the United Kingdom

The term City as used in the United Kingdom is a title of dignity applied to 55 towns of varying local Government status by virtue of their importance as either archiepiscopal or episcopal sees or former sees, or as commercial or industrial centres. The right has been acquired in the past by (1) traditional usage—for example, the Doomsday Book describes Coventry, Exeter and Norwich as *civitas*; by (2) statute; or by (3) royal prerogative, and in more recent times solely by royal charter and letters patent—the most recent examples are Lancaster (1937), Cambridge (1951) Southampton (1964), Swansea (1969) and the extension of the City of Westminster to include the former Metropolitan Boroughs of Paddington and St Marylebone in 1965. *Is styled 'Rt Hon'.

Name of City with Geographical County	First Recorded Charter	Title of Civic Head
Aberdeen, Grampian, S.	1179	Lord Provost
Bangor, Gwynedd, W	1883	Mayor
Bath, Avon	1590	Mayor
Belfast, Antrim, N I	1613	Lord Mayor*
Birmingham, West Midlands	1838	Lord Mayor
Bradford, West Yorkshire	1847	Lord Mayor
Bristol, Gloucestershire	1188	Lord Mayor
Cambridge, Cambridgeshire	1207	Mayor
Canterbury, Kent	1448	Mayor
Cardiff, South Glamorgan, W	1608	Lord Mayor
Carlisle, Cumbria	1158	Mayor
Chester, Cheshire	1506	Mayor
Chichester, West Sussex	1135–54	Mayor
Coventry, West Midlands	1345	Lord Mayor
Dundee, Tayside, S	c. 1179	Lord Provost
Durham, Durham	1602	Mayor
Edinburgh, Lothian, S	c. 1124	Lord Provost*
Ely, Cambridgeshire	no charter	Chairman
Exeter, Devon	1156	Mayor
Glasgow, Strathclyde, S	1690	Lord Provost*
Gloucester, Gloucestershire	1483	Mayor
Hereford, Herefordshire	1189	Mayor
Kingston upon Hull, Humberside	1440	Lord Mayor
Lancaster, Lancashire	1193	Mayor
Leeds, West Yorkshire	1626	Lord Mayor
Leicester, Leicestershire	1589	Lord Mayor
Lichfield, Staffordshire	1549	Mayor
Lincoln, Lincolnshire	1154	Mayor
Liverpool, Merseyside	1207	Lord Mayor
London, Greater London	1066–87	Lord Mayor*
Londonderry, Londonderry, N I	1604	Mayor
Manchester, Greater Manchester	1838	Lord Mayor
Newcastle upon Tyne, Tyne and Wear	1157	Lord Mayor
Norwich, Norfolk	1194	Lord Mayor
Nottingham, Nottinghamshire	1155	Lord Mayor
Oxford, Oxfordshire	1154–87	Lord Mayor
Peterborough, Cambridgeshire	1874	Mayor
Plymouth, Devon	1439	Lord Mayor
Portsmouth, Hampshire	1194	Lord Mayor
Ripon, North Yorkshire	886	Mayor
Rochester, Kent	1189	Mayor

New Towns

There are 19 New Towns ('*Development Corporations*') in England (15) and Scotland (4). When a New Town in England or Wales has substantially fulfilled its purpose it becomes vested in the *Commission for the New Towns*. On 1 Apr. 1962 Crawley (Sussex) and Hemel Hempstead (Herts.) were so vested, so can be regarded as ex-New Towns.

Stevenage, Herts. (1946)
Harlow, Essex. (May 1947)
Aycliffe, Durham. (July 1947)
East Kilbride, Strathclyde. (Aug. 1947).
Peterlee, Durham. (Mar. 1948)
Welwyn Garden City, Herts. (June 1948)
Hatfield, Herts. (June 1948)
Glenrothes, Fife. (Oct. 1948)
Basildon, Essex. (Feb. 1949)
Bracknell, Berks. (Oct. 1949)
Cwmbran, Gwent. (Nov. 1949)
Corby, Northants. (1950)
Cumbernauld, Strathclyde. (1956)
Skelmersdale, Lancashire. (1962)
Livingston, Lothian. (1962)
Telford, Salop. (1963).
Runcorn, Cheshire. (1964)
Redditch, Worcester. (1964)
Washington, Tyne & Wear. (1964)
Irvine, Strathclyde (1966)
Milton Keynes, Buckinghamshire (1967)
Newtown, Powys (1967)
Northampton, (1968)
Peterborough (1968)
Warrington, Cheshire (1968)
Central Lancashire New Town (1970)
Stonehouse, Strathclyde (1973)

Name of City with Geographical County	First Recorded Charter	Title of Civic Head
St Albans, Hertfordshire	1553	Mayor
Salford, Greater Manchester	1835	Mayor
Salisbury, Wiltshire	1227	Mayor
Sheffield, South Yorkshire	1843	Lord Mayor
Southampton, Hampshire	1447	Mayor
Stoke-on-Trent, Staffordshire	1910	Lord Mayor
Swansea, West Glamorgan, W	1969	Mayor
Truro, Cornwall	1589	Mayor
Wakefield, West Yorkshire	1848	Mayor
Wells, Somerset	1201	Mayor
Westminster, Greater London	1965	Lord Mayor
Winchester, Hampshire	1155	Mayor
Worcester, Worcestershire	1189	Mayor
York, North Yorkshire	1396	Lord Mayor★

The 157 most populous cities, towns and districts (i.e. over 100 000) in the United Kingdom

The figures are those officially estimated by the Registrar-General.

1. Greater London — 7 281 800
2. Birmingham, West Midlands — 1 084 000
3. Glasgow city — 905 000
4. Leeds, West Yorkshire — 748 300
5. Liverpool, Merseyside — 610 135
6. Sheffield, South Yorkshire — 561 500
7. Manchester, Greater Manchester — 530 580
8. Edinburgh, City — 472 000
9. Bradford, West Yorkshire — 461 000
10. Bristol, Avon — 418 600
11. Kirkless, West Yorkshire — 375 200
12. Belfast, City — 374 300
13. Wirral, Merseyside — 349 200
14. Coventry, West Midlands — 335 000
15. Sandwell, West Midlands — 320 100
16. Sefton, Merseyside — 307 200
17. Wigan, Greater Manchester — 306 600
18. Wakefield, West Yorkshire — 305 300
19. Dudley, West Midlands — 298 700
20. Newcastle upon Tyne, Tyne & Wear — 297 000
21. Stockport, Greater Manchester — 294 400
22. Sunderland, Tyne & Wear — 292 600
23. Leicester — 287 300
24. Nottingham — 287 000
25. Cardiff, South Glamorgan — 284 700
26. Doncaster, South Yorkshire — 280 830
27. Kingston-upon-Hull, Humberside — 278 800
28. Salford, Greater Manchester — 273 600
29. Walsall, West Midlands — 271 000
30. Stoke-on-Trent, Staffs — 258 300
31. Wolverhampton, West Midlands — 268 200
32. Bolton, Greater Manchester — 261 800
33. Plymouth, Devon — 251 200
34. Rotherham, South Yorkshire — 248 100
35. Trafford, Greater Manchester — 227 400
36. Oldham, Greater Manchester — 224 700
37. Barnsley, South Yorkshire — 224 100
38. Tameside, Greater Manchester — 222 600
39. Ipswich, Suffolk — 222 500
40. Gateshead, Tyne & Wear — 222 300
41. Derby, Derbyshire — 217 800
42. Southampton, Hampshire — 213 000
43. Rochdale, Lancashire — 210 600
44. Dundee, Scotland — 207 000
45. North Tyneside, Tyne & Wear — 206 700
46. Renfrew, Strathclyde — 204 000
47. Solihull, West Midlands — 199 800
48. Portsmouth, Hampshire — 195 130
49. Calderdale, West Yorkshire — 192 400
50. St Helens, Merseyside — 192 140
51. Knowsley, Merseyside — 191 700
52. Swansea, West Glamorgan — 189 800
53. Aberdeen, Scotland — 181 840
54. Bury, Lancashire — 181 290
55. South Tyneside, Tyne & Wear — 175 540
56. Luton, Bedfordshire — 165 900
57. Stockton-on-Tees, Cleveland — 162 500
58. Warrington, Cheshire — 161 000
59. Motherwell, Strathclyde — 160 860
60. Brighton, East Sussex — 160 290
61. Southend-on-Sea, Essex — 160 200
62. Middlesborough, Cleveland — 153 900
63. Langbaurgh, Cleveland — 150 750
64. Blackpool, Lancashire — 150 100
65. Wycombe, Buckinghamshire — 149 700
66. Kirkcaldy, Fife — 148 020
67. Woodspring, Avon — 147 800
68. Bournemouth, Dorset — 146 400
69. Macclesfield, Cheshire — 145 620
70. Meadway, Kent — 143 080
71. Blackburn, Lancashire — 141 700
72. Falkirk, Central — 141 170
73. Thamesdown, Wiltshire — 141 110
74. South Oxfordshire — 138 900
75. Basildon, Essex — 137 600
76. Northampton — 137 300
77. New Forest, Hampshire — 137 100
78. Newport, Gwent — 134 700
79. Harrogate, North Yorkshire — 134 300
80. Reading, Berkshire — 133 280
81. Preston, Lancashire — 132 000
82. Charnwood, Leicestershire — 131 000
83. Cunninghame, Strathclyde — 129 810
84. Bedford — 129 700
85. Chelmsford, Essex — 128 700
86. Ogwr, Mid Glamorgan — 128 100
87. Windsor & Maidenhead, Berkshire — 128 000
88. Colchester, Essex — 127 500
89. Thurrock, Essex — 126 800
90. Lancaster, Lancashire — 125 500
91. Maidstone, Kent — 124 700
92. Guildford, Surrey — 124 210
93. Dacorum, Hertfordshire — 122 600
94. St Albans, Hertfordshire — 122 580
95. Newcastle under Lyme, Staffordshire — 121 900
96. Yeovil, Somerset — 121 700
97. Norwich, Norfolk — 121 680
98. West Lothian — 121 170
99. Dunfermline, Fife — 121 000
100. Perth & Kinross, Tayside — 117 910
101. Aylesbury Vale, Buckingham — 117 600
102. Thanet, Kent — 117 600
103. Chester, Cheshire — 117 000
104. Basingstoke, Hampshire — 116 800
105. Canterbury, Kent — 116 780
106. Reigate & Banstead, Surrey — 115 600
107. Oxford — 115 100
108. Epping Forest, Essex — 114 800
109. Havant, Hampshire — 114 800
110. West Norfolk — 114 400
111. Stafford — 114 300
112. Wealden, East Sussex — 113 000
113. North Avon — 112 800
114. Elmbridge, Surrey — 112 800
115. Poole, Dorset — 112 800
116. Wrekin, Salop — 112 500
117. Newbury, Berkshire — 111 400
118. Huntingdon, Cambridgeshire — 111 300
119. Warwick — 111 100
120. Nuneaton, Warwickshire — 110 810
121. Kyle & Carrick, Strathclyde — 110 000
122. Inverclyde, Strathclyde — 109 610
123. Vale Royal, Cheshire — 109 500
124. Wokingham, Berkshire — 108 600
125. Easington, Durham — 108 300
126. Tendring, Essex — 107 700
127. Wrexham Maelor, Clwyd — 107 200
128. Amber Valley, Derbyshire — 107 100
129. Beverley, Humberside — 106 700
130. Vale of Glamorgan, South Glamorgan — 106 490
131. Torbay, Devon — 106 400
132. Waverley, Surrey — 106 290
133. Halton, Cheshire — 106 200
134. Arun, West Sussex — 106 000
135. Mid Sussex — 105 900
136. Swale, Kent — 105 600
137. Hamilton, Strathclyde — 105 000
138. East Hertfordshire — 104 400
139. York, North Yorkshire — 103 800
140. North Hertfordshire — 103 700
141. Cherwell, Oxfordshire — 103 400
142. West Lancashire — 103 400
143. Dover, Kent — 102 810
144. Broxtowe, Nottinghamshire — 102 500
145. Newark, Nottinghamshire — 102 100
146. Rhymney Valley, Mid Glamorgan — 102 000
147. Slough, Berkshire — 101 805
148. Ashfield, Nottinghamshire — 101 700
149. Sevenoaks, Kent — 101 420
150. Salisbury, Wiltshire — 101 105
151. Braintree, Essex — 101 100
152. North Wiltshire — 100 800
153. Carlisle, Cumbria — 100 740
154. East Devon — 100 300
155. Cambridge — 100 250
156. Gedling, Nottinghamshire — 100 200
157. Erewash, Derbyshire — 100 000

The Crown Dependencies

The Isle of Man

The Isle of Man (Manx-Gaelic, *Ellan Vannin*) is a Crown dependency.

Area: 145 325 acres *58 811 ha* (227·07 miles²) (*588,1 km²*), including Calf of Man (5·4 acres *2,18 ha*) and Chicken Rock.
Population: 56 289 (Census 1971).
Administrative headquarters: Douglas 20 389. The ancient capital was Castletown (2 820).
History: Continually inhabited since Mesolithic times, *c.* 6000 BC. By about AD 450 the island was occupied by Gaelic-speaking people. Christian missionaries came, probably from Iona, before AD 600. Invasions from Scandinavia *c.* 800, and Norsemen settled during the 9th century. The most notable Norse chieftain was Godred (Crovan) I, who conquered Man in 1079 and ruled until 1095. Norse kings reigned until the Treaty of Perth on 2 July 1266, when the

title was sold to Alexander III of Scotland, succeeded by Margaret, the Maid of Norway. The Island was taken in 1290 by Edward I of England. Edward II lost it to Bruce, but Scotland later lost it to Edward III, who gave the kingship of the island to the 1st Earl of Salisbury. The 2nd Earl sold it to Sir William le Scrope, later executed by the order of Henry IV, who in 1406 granted the island to the Stanley family. The Stanleys (Earls of Derby after 1485) ruled as 'lords of Mann' until 1594, when Elizabeth I took over the island. James I gave it to the Earls of Salisbury in 1607, but it was returned to the Derbys in 1609. The tenth Earl died in 1736, and his daughter, the Duchess of Atholl, succeeded. The manorial rights of the Atholls were bought by Parliament in 1828. After agitation, a modified form of home rule was restored in 1866.

Administration: For administrative purposes, the island is divided into six 'sheadings'. The monarch, as lord of Man, appoints the Lieutenant Governor. The island's legislature, called the Tynwald, consists of two houses—the Legislative Council and the House of Keys. The Council president is the Lieutenant-Governor and the other members are: the Bishop of Sodor and Man, the two Deemsters (judges of the high court), the Attorney-General, two members appointed by the Lieutenant-Governor and four members appointed by the House of Keys. The 24 members of the House of Keys are made up as follows: 13 from the six sheadings, seven from Douglas, two from Ramsey, one from Castletown and one from Peel. After Bills have been passed by both houses, they are signed by the members and then sent for Royal Assent.

Highest point above sea-level: Snaefell (2034 ft *619 m*).

Leading Industries: Tourism; conferences; agriculture, chiefly oats, hay, and sheepgrazing; kippered herrings; Manx tweed; flour milling.

Places of Interest: Tynwald Hill at St Johns, where the annual reading of the laws takes place on 5 July (old midsummer day); Meayl (or Mull) circle, near Cregnish. The Laxey waterwheel (1854) of 288 ft *69 m* circumference.

The Channel Islands

The Channel Islands (French, *Iles Normandes*) are a Crown dependency. There is a Channel Isle department in the Home Office, Whitehall, London.

Area: 48 083 acres *19 458 ha* (75·13 miles² *194,6 km²*).
Guernsey—15 654 acres *6334 ha* (24·46 miles² *63,3 km²*)
Jersey—28 717 acres *11 621 ha* ' (44·87 miles² *116,2 km²*).
Dependencies of Guernsey:
Alderney—1962 acres *794 ha* (3·07 miles² *7,9 km²*).
Sark (Sercq)—1274 acres *515 ha* (1·99 miles² *5,1 km²*).
(Great Sark, 1035 acres *419 ha 4,2 km²*; Little Sark 239 acres *96 ha 0,9 km²*).
Herm—320 acres *129 ha 1,29 km²*.
Brechou (Brecqham)—74 acres *30 ha 0,3 km²*.
Jethou—44 acres *18 ha.*
Lihou (Libon)—38 acres *15 ha.*
Other islands include Ortach, Burhou, the Casquets, Les Minquiers (including Maîtresse Ile) and the Ecrehou Islands (including Marmaoutier, Blanche Ile, and Maître Ile).

Population: 110 748.
Jersey—72 532　　Alderney—1686
Guernsey—51 458　　Sark—590

Administrative headquarters: Jersey—St Helier, Guernsey and dependencies—St Peter Port.

History: The islands are known to have been inhabited by Acheulian man (before the last Ice Age) and by Neanderthal man. Continuously inhabited since Iberian settlers, who used flint implements, arrived in the 2nd millenium BC. The islands were later settled by the Gauls, and after them the Romans; Christian missionaries came from Cornwall and Brittany in the 6th century AD. The Vikings began raiding the islands in the 9th century. Rollo, the Viking nobleman, established the duchy of Normandy in AD 911. His son, the second duke, William I 'Longsword' annexed the Channel Islands in 933. Jethou was ceded to England in 1091. The other islands were annexed by the crown in 1106. Normandy was conquered by France, and the King (John) was declared to have forfeited all his titles to the duchy. The islanders, however, remained loyal to John. Administration has since been under the control of his successors, while maintaining a considerable degree of home rule and, until 1689, neutrality. Before the Reformation the islands formed part of the diocese of Coutances, but were later placed under the bishops of Winchester. From the 9th century everyone in the islands spoke Norman French, but English became dominant by the mid-19th century. The islands were occupied by Nazi Germany on 30 June–1 July 1940, and fortified for defence. They were relieved by British forces on 9 May 1945.

Administration: The islands are divided into two Bailiwicks, the States of Jersey and the States of Guernsey. The two Bailiwicks each have a Lieutenant-Governor and Commander-in-Chief, who is the personal representative of the Monarch and the channel of communication between HM Government and the Insular Governments. The Crown appoints Bailiffs, who are both Presidents of the Assembly of the States (the Legislature) and of the Royal Court. In Jersey the States consists of elected senators, *connétables* (constables) and deputies; in Guernsey, *conseillers* (councillors), elected by an intermediate body called the States of election, people's deputies, representatives of the *douzaines* (parish councils) and representatives of Alderney.

Highest points above sea-level:
Jersey—453 ft *138 m*
Guernsey—349 ft *106 m*
Alderney—281 ft *85,5 m*
Sark—375 ft *114 m*, near the centre of Great Sark
Herm—235 ft *71,5 m*
Jethou—267 ft *81 m*
Lihou—68 ft *21 m*

Leading Industries: Agriculture, chiefly cattle, potatoes, tomatoes, grapes, and flowers; tourism; granite quarrying.

Places of Interest: The Museum of the Société Jersiaise; the church of St Peter Port.

The 46 United Kingdom universities

There are 46 institutions of university or degree-giving status in the United Kingdom. The list below is given in order of seniority of date of foundation.

	Name	*Year of Foundation*	*Location*	*(Population Full Time)*
1.	The University of Oxford	1249★	Oxford OX1 2JD	8011 (1974)

Men's Colleges, Halls and Societies: University (1249), Balliol (1263), Merton (1264), Exeter (1314), Oriel (1326), Queen's (1340), New College (1379), Lincoln (1427), All Souls (1438), Magdalen (1458), Brasenose (1509), Corpus Christi (1517), Christ Church (1546), Trinity (1554), St John's (1555), Jesus (1571), Wadham (1612), Pembroke (1614), Worcester (1714), Hertford (1874), St Edmund Hall (1270), Keble (1868), St Catherine's (1962), Campion Hall (1962), St Benet's Hall (1947), St Peter's (1929), St Antony's (1950), Nuffield (1937), Linacre House (1962), Mansfield (1886), Regent's Park, Greyfriars Hall.
Women's Colleges and Hall: Lady Margaret Hall (1878), Somerville (1879), St Hugh's (1886), St Hilda's (1893), St Anne's (1952).

2.	The University of Cambridge	1284★	Cambridge	8892 (1974–5)

Men's Colleges: Peterhouse (1284), Clare (1326), Pembroke (1347), Gonville and Caius (1348), Trinity Hall (1350), Corpus Christi (1352), King's (1441), Queen's (1448), St Catharine's (1473), Jesus (1496), Christ's (1505), St John's (1511), Magdalene (1542), Trinity (1546), Emmanuel (1584), Sidney Sussex (1596), Downing (1800), Selwyn (1882), Churchill (1960), Fitzwilliam House (1869).
Women's Colleges and Halls: Girton (1869), Newnham (1871), Hughes Hall (1885), New Hall (1954).

3.	The University of St Andrews	1411	St Andrews and Dundee	3284 (1974–5)

Colleges: United College of St Salvator and St Leonard; College of St Mary; Queen's College, Dundee.

4.	The University of Glasgow	1451	Gilmorehill, Glasgow G12 8QQ	10 007 (1974–5)
5.	The University of Aberdeen	1494	Aberdeen AB9 1FX	4883 (1975)
6.	The University of Edinburgh	1582	South Bridge Edinburgh EH8 9YL	11 204 (1974–5)
7.	The University of Durham	1832	Old Shire Hall, Durham DH1 3HP	3962 (1974–5)

Colleges: University, Hatfield, Grey, St Chad's, St John's, St Mary's, St Aidan's, Bede, St Hild's, Neville's Cross, St Cuthbert's Society, Van Mildert, Trevelyan.

8.	The University of London	1836	Greater London	40 198 (1973–4)

Schools: Bedford College, Birkbeck College, Imperial College of Science and Technology, King's College, London School of Economics and Political Science, Queen Elizabeth College, Queen Mary College, Royal Holloway College, School of Oriental and African Studies, School of Pharmacy, University College, Westfield College, Wye College, King's College Theological Department, New College, Richmond College, Lister Institute of Preventive Medicine.
Medical Schools: Charing Cross Hospital, Guy's Hospital, King's College Hospital, The London Hospital, The Middlesex Hospital, Royal Dental Hospital of London, Royal Free Hospital, St Bartholomew's Hospital, St George's Hospital, St Mary's Hospital, St Thomas's Hospital, University College Hospital, Westminster Hospital, and numerous post-graduate teaching hospitals; and various training colleges.

University of London—continued

Institutes: Courtauld Institute of Art, Institute of Advanced Legal Studies, Institute of Archaeology, Institute of Classical Studies, Institute of Commonwealth Studies, Institute of Education, Institute of Germanic Languages and Literature, Institute of Historical Research, School of Slavonic and East European Studies, Warburg Institute.

9. The University of Manchester	1851	Oxford Road, Manchester M13 9PL	13 252 (1974–5)
10. The University of Newcastle upon Tyne	1852	Newcastle upon Tyne NE1 7RU	6316 (1974–5)
11. The University of Wales	1893	*see* colleges	

Colleges: Aberystwyth, Bangor, Cardiff, Swansea, National School of Medicine (Cardiff), Institute of Science and Technology (Cardiff), St. David's College, Lampeter

12. The University of Birmingham	1900	Edgbaston, Birmingham B15 2TT	7633 (1974–5)
13. The University of Liverpool	1903	Brownlow Hill, Liverpool L69 3BX	7826 (1975)
14. The University of Leeds	1904	Leeds LS2 9JT	9536 (1975)
15. The University of Sheffield	1905	Sheffield S10 2TN	6647 (1974–5)
16. The Queen's University of Belfast	1908	Belfast and Londonderry	6647 (1974–5)
			5471 (1974–5)

College: Magee University College (1865), Londonderry.

17. The University of Bristol	1909	Bristol BS8 1TH	6329 (1974)
18. The University of Reading	1926	London Road, Reading RG6 2AH	5137 (1974)
19. The University of Nottingham	1938	University Park, Nottingham NG7 2RD	5797 (1974–5)
20. The University of Southampton	1952	Southampton SO9 5NH	5051 (1974–5)
21. The University of Hull	1954	Kingston upon Hull HU6 7RX	3968 (1974–5)
22. The University of Exeter	1955	Exeter EX4 4QJ	3750 (1974–5)
23. The University of Leicester	1957	Leicester	3775 (1974–5)
24. The University of Sussex	1961	Falmer, Brighton BN1 9QX	3979 (1974–5)
25. The University of Keele	1962	Keele, Staffordshire ST5 5BG	2316 (1974–5)
26. The University of Strathclyde†	1963	George Street, Glasgow G1 1XW	5875 (1974–5)
27. The University of East Anglia	1963	Earlham Hall, Norwich NOR 88C	3400 (1974–5)
28. The University of York	1963	Heslington, York YO1 5DD	2300 (1974)
29. The University of Lancaster	1964	Bailrigg, Lancaster	3250 (1975–6)
30. The University of Essex	1964	Wivenhoe Park, Colchester CO4 35Q	2200 (1975–6)
31. The University of Warwick	1965	Coventry CV4 7AL	3375 (1974–5)
32. The University of Kent	1965	Canterbury CT2 7N2	2800 (1975–6)
33. Heriot-Watt University	1966	Chambers Street, Edinburgh EH1 1HX	2607 (1974–5)
34. Loughborough University of Technology	1966	Loughborough, Leicester	3735 (1974–5)
35. The University of Aston in Birmingham	1966	Gosta Green, Birmingham 4	4054 (1974–5)
36. The City University	1966	St John's Street, London, EC 1V 4PB	2400 (1974–5)
37. Brunel University	1966	Uxbridge UB8 3PH	3700 (1974–5)
38. New University of Ulster	1965	Coleraine, Co. Londonderry	1467 (1974–5)
39. University of Bath	1966	Claverton Down, Bath BA7 7AY	2824 (1974–5)
40. University of Bradford	1966	Bradford BD7 1DP	2253 (1974–5)
41. University of Surrey	1966	Guildford GU2 5XH	2247 (1974–5)
42. University of Salford	1967	Salford M5 4WT	3261 (1974–5)
43. University of Dundee	1967	Dundee DD1 4HN	2711 (1974–5)
44. University of Stirling	1967	Stirling FK9 4LA	1919 (1974–5)
45. The Open University	1969	Walton Hall, Milton Keynes MK7 6AA	50 000 (1975)‡
46. The University College at Buckingham§	1976	Buckingham MK18 1EG	68 (1976)

*Year of foundation of oldest constituent college
‡Tuition mainly be correspondence

†Formerly the Royal College of Science and Technology, founded 1796
§Independently financed from the University Grants Committee and H M Treasury

Note: The Royal College of Art (1837) Kensington Gore, London (568 post graduates) and The Cranfield Institute of Technology (1969), Cranfield, Bedford (575 post graduates, 2500 short course students) grant degrees.

*Cambridge
University's oldest College—
Peterhouse, founded in 1284*

UNITED KINGDOM COUNTIES

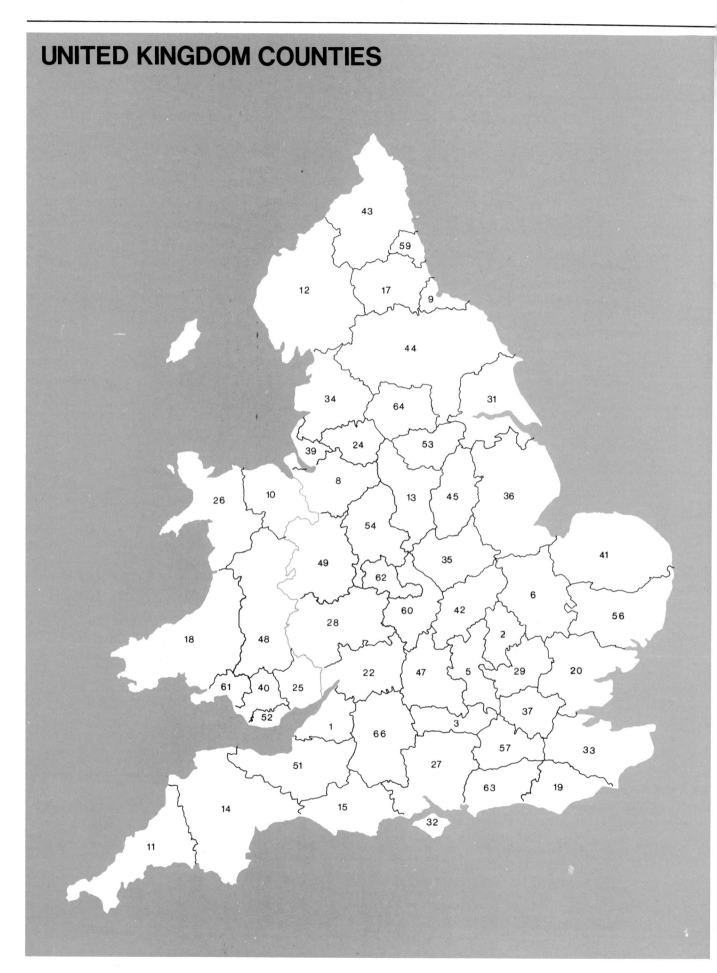

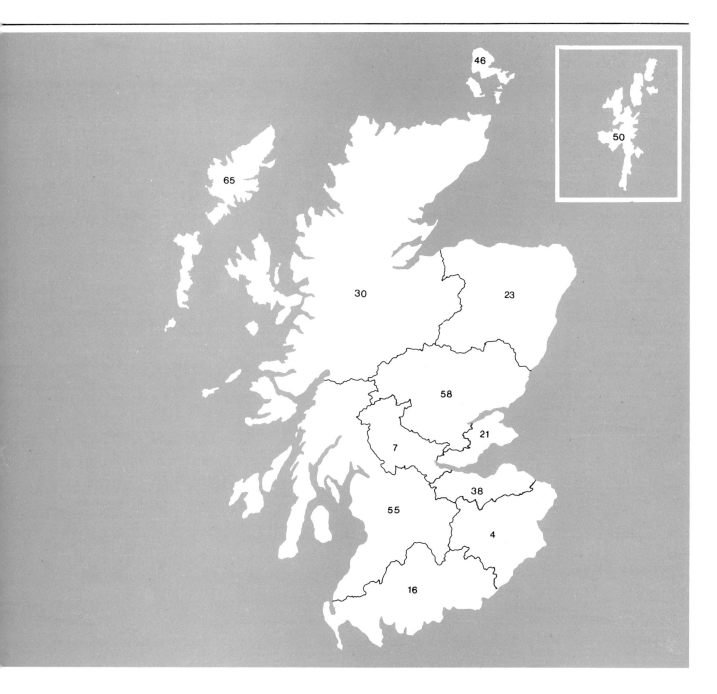

1. Avon	23. Grampian	45. Nottinghamshire
2. Bedfordshire	24. Greater Manchester	46. Orkney
3. Berkshire	25. Gwent	47. Oxfordshire
4. Borders	26. Gwynedd	48. Powys
5. Buckinghamshire	27. Hampshire	49. Salop
6. Cambridgeshire	28. Hereford and Worcester	50. Shetland
7. Central	29. Hertfordshire	51. Somerset
8. Cheshire	30. Highland	52. South Glamorgan
9. Cleveland	31. Humberside	53. South Yorkshire
10. Clwyd	32. Isle of Wight	54. Staffordshire
11. Cornwall	33. Kent	55. Strathclyde
12. Cumbria	34. Lancashire	56. Suffolk
13. Derbyshire	35. Leicestershire	57. Surrey
14. Devon	36. Lincolnshire	58. Tayside
15. Dorset	37. London, Greater	59. Tyne & Wear
16. Dumfries and Galloway	38. Lothian	60. Warwickshire
17. Durham	39. Merseyside	61. West Glamorgan
18. Dyfed	40. Mid Glamorgan	62. West Midlands
19. East Sussex	41. Norfolk	63. West Sussex
20. Essex	42. Northamptonshire	64. West Yorkshire
21. Fife	43. Northumberland	65. Western Isles
22. Gloucestershire	44. North Yorkshire	66. Wiltshire

The United Kingdom of Great Britain and Northern Ireland's traditional 91 counties were in 1974 and 1975 reduced to 66 in Great Britain and six in Northern Ireland.

England has 46 *geographical* counties (formerly 40)

Scotland has 12 *geographical* regions (formerly 33 counties)

Wales has 8 *geographical* counties (formerly 12)

Northern Ireland has 6 *geographical* counties (divided into 26 districts)

Names of the counties: For some counties there are alternatives such as Devon and Devonshire. We however have generally only added the suffix 'shire' where there is a town of the same name as its county. This occurs in 17 cases but to these must be added four others which traditionally (but not statutorily) use 'shire': Berkshire, Cheshire, Lancashire, and Wiltshire. 'Hampshire was adopted in 1959 in favour of the County of Southampton.

Abbreviations are frequently used for counties, but we have only given the 23 that are officially listed as 'Postally acceptable' in the Post Office Guide.

County worthies by birth: The term 'worthy' is used in its sense of famous man or woman and some cases fame includes notoriety. As an extreme example Pontius Pilate, son of a Roman legionary (traditionally said to have been born in the former county of Perthshire, now Tayside) is included.

AVON

First recorded name and derivation: 1973. From the river of that name.
Area: 332 596 acres *134 597 ha.*
Population: 915 300
Density: 2·75 per acre *6·80 per ha*
Administrative HQ: Avon House, The Haymarket, Bristol.
Highest point above sea-level: Southern Duxbury (on southern boundary) 870 ft *265 m*

Road lengths:	miles	km
motorway and trunk	108	174
principal	213	343
other	2410	3878

Schools: Nursery 17; Primary 395; Secondary 61; Special 29.
Colleges: Further Education 13.
Places of interest: Bath (Roman remains); Clevedon Court; Bristol Cathedral; Stanton Drew (standing stones); Clifton Suspension Bridge.
County worthies by birth: Sebastian Cabot (1474–1557); John Locke (1632–1704); Thomas Chatterton (1752–70); Robert Southey (1774–1843); Samuel Plimsoll (1824–98); W G Grace (1848–1915).

BEDFORDSHIRE

First recorded use of name and derivation: 1011 (Bedanfordscir), Beda's ford, or river crossing.
Area: 305 026 acres *123 440 ha*
Population: 501 500
Density: 1·64 per acre *4·06 per ha*
Administrative HQ: County Hall, Cauldwell St, Bedford.

Highest point above sea-level: Dunstable Downs 798 ft *243 m.*

Road lengths:	miles	km
motorway	15	25
trunk	69	112
principal	132	213
other	1098	1967

Schools: Nursery 9; Primary/Lower 230; Middle 18; Secondary High 28; Upper 12; Special 13; Sixth form college 1.
Colleges: Further Education 3; Technology 1; Agriculture 1; Education 3.
Places of interest: Woburn Abbey; Whipsnade Park (Zoo); Luton Hoo; Elstow Moot Hall; Dunstable Priory Church.
County worthies by birth: John Bunyan (1628–88); Sir Joseph Paxton (1801–65); Thomas Tompion (1638–1713).

BERKSHIRE

First recorded use of name and derivation: AD 860, wooded hill district named after Bearruc hill.
Area: 310 179 acres *125 525 ha.*
Population: 653 400.
Density: 2·11 per acre *5·21 per ha.*
Administrative HQ: Shire Hall, Reading.
Highest point above sea-level: Walbury Hill, 974 ft *296 m.*

Road lengths:	miles	km
motorway	61	98
trunk	65	104
principal	169	291
other	1540	2478

Schools: Nursery 19; Primary 282; Secondary 67; Special 21.
Colleges: Further Education 5; Agriculture 1; Art 1; Education 1.
Places of interest: Windsor Castle (St George's Chapel); Reading Abbey (ruin); Royal Military Academy, Sandhurst; Eton College.
County worthies by birth: Edward III (1312–77); Henry VI (1421–71); Archbishop William Land (1628–88); Sir John Herschel (1792–1871).

BORDERS

First recorded use of name and derivation: 1975, from the district bordering on the boundary between England and Scotland from the Middle English word *bordure*; Term 'border' used in Act of the English Parliament, 1580.
Area: 1 154 288 acres *467 124 ha.*
Population: 99 105.
Density: 0·09 per acre *0,21 per ha.*
Administrative HQ: Newtown St Boswells
Highest point above sea-level: Broad Law, 2756 ft *840 m.*
Districts (with population): Berwickshire pop. 17 163; Ettrick and Lauderdale pop. 32 335; Roxburgh pop. 35 767; Tweeddale pop. 13 517.

Road lengths:	miles	km
trunk	113	182
principal	274	441
classified	835	1343
unclassified	614	988

Schools: Nursery 2; Primary 86; Grammar, Secondary Modern and Comprehensive 9; Special 4.
Colleges: Further Education 3; Agriculture 1.
Places of interest: Edin's Hall, nr. Duns; Dryburgh Abbey; Condingham Priory.
County worthies by birth: Johannus Duns Scotus (1265–1308); James Thomson (1700–48); James Hogg (1770–1835); Mungo Park (1771–1806); Dr John Leyden (1775–1811);

Sir David Brewster (1781–1865); Henry Lyte (1793–1847); Sir James Murray (1837–1915).

BUCKINGHAMSHIRE

First recorded use of name and derivation: 1016 (Buccingahamscir) the hamm (water-meadow) of Bucca's people.
Area: 464 000 acres *187 920 ha.*
Population: 497 800
Density: 1·07 per acre *2,64 per ha.*
Administrative HQ: County Hall, Aylesbury.
Highest point above sea-level: Nr. Aston Hill 857 ft *261 m.*

Road lengths:	miles	km
motorway	33	53
trunk	57	91
principal	220	354
others	1823	2933

Schools: Nursery 5; First 137; Middle 63; Combined 91; Grammar 14; Special 14; Secondary Modern 30; Comprehensive 6.
Colleges: Further Education 5; Education 2.
Places of interest: Claydon House; Cliveden; Hughenden Manor; Stowe House; Chequers; Hellfire Caves (West Wycombe).
County worthies by birth: James Brudenell, 7th Earl of Cardigan (1797–1868); William Grenfell, Baron Desborough (1855–1945); William Malcolm, Baron Hailey (1872–1969).

CAMBRIDGESHIRE

First recorded use of name and derivation: 1010 (Grantabrycgscir), a Norman corruption of Grantabrice (bridge over River Granta).
Area: 842 433 acres *340 921 ha.*
Population: 540 300.
Density: 0·64 per acre *1,58 per ha.*
Administrative HQ: Shire Hall, Castle Hill, Cambridge.
Highest point above sea-level: 300 yd *275 m* south of the Hall, Great Chishill. 478 ft *145 m.*

Road lengths:	miles	km
trunk	198	319
principal	228	367
classified	1058	1702
unclassified	1119	1800

Schools: Nursery 290; Primary 80; Secondary 52; Special 14.
Colleges: Further Education 4; Agriculture and horticulture 3; Art 1.
Places of interest: Cambridge University; The Backs, Cambridge; Ely Cathedral; Peterborough Cathedral; Sawston Hall; Peckover House.
County worthies by birth: Orlando Gibbons (1583–1625); Oliver Cromwell (1599–1658); Jeremy Taylor (1613–67); Octavio Hill (1838–1912); Lord Keynes (1883–1946).

CENTRAL

First recorded use of name and derivation: self-explanatory, pertaining to the centre, the word *central*, first recorded in this sense, 1647.
Area: 622 080 acres *251 747 ha.*
Population: 263 000.
Density 0·42 per acre *1,04 per ha.*
Administrative HQ: Stirling.
Highest point above sea-level: Ben More, 3852 ft *1174 m.*
Districts (with population): Clackmannan pop. 46 092; Falkirk pop. 141 001; Stirling pop. 76 091.

Road lengths:	miles	km
trunk	111	178
principal	186	299
classified	371	597
unclassified	436	701

Schools: Nursery 11; Primary 123; Comprehensive 22; Special 12.
Colleges: Further Education 2; Education 1.
Places of interest: Stirling Castle; Old Stirling Bridge; Cambuskenneth Abbey; Field of Bannockburn; Loch Lomond (east side); Doune Castle.

CHESHIRE

First recorded use of name and derivation: AD 980 (Legeceasterseir), corrupted from the camp (*castra*) of the legions (*legiones*).
Area: 573 835 acres *232 223 ha.*
Population: 904 600.
Density: 1·58 per acre *3,90 per ha.*
Administrative HQ: County Hall, Chester.
Highest point above sea-level: Shining Tor 1834 ft *559 m.*

Road lengths:	miles	km
motorway	64	102
trunk	192	309
principal	359	578
classified	864	1390
unclassified	1742	2802

Schools: Primary 513; Secondary 87; Independent/Direct Grant Grammar 15; Special 36.
Colleges: Further Education 6; Agriculture 1; Art 1; Education 3.
Places of interest: Roman remains within walled city of Chester; Gawsworth Hall; Jodrell Bank.
County worthies by birth: John Bradshaw (1602–59); Emma, Lady Hamilton (*c.* 1765–1815); Rev Charles Dodgson (Lewis Carroll) (1832–98).

CLEVELAND

First recorded use of name and derivation: 1110, *Clivelanda*, 'the hilly district'.
Area: 144 030 acres *582 87 ha.*
Population: 565 600.
Density: 3·93 per acre *9,70 per ha.*
Administrative HQ: Municipal Building, Middlesbrough.
Highest point above sea-level: Hob on the Hill 1078 ft *328 m.*

Road lengths:	miles	km
trunk	24	39
principal	146	236
other	990	1594

Schools: Nursery 10; Primary 275; Grammar 1; Sixth Form Colleges 8; Comprehensive 52; Special 19.
Colleges: Further Education 5; Agriculture 1; Art 2; Education 1; Polytechnic 1.
Places of interest: Church of St Hilda (Hartlepool).
County worthies by birth: Capt James Cook (1728–79); Thomas Sheraton (1751–1806); Sir Compton Mackenzie (1823–1972).

CLWYD

First recorded use of name and derivation: 1973 from the river of that name.
Area: 599 481 acres *242 602 ha.*
Population: 373 300.
Density: 0·61 per acre *1,54 per ha.*
Administrative HQ: Shire Hall, Mold.
Highest point above sea-level: Moel Sych 2713 ft *826 m.*

Road lengths:	miles	km
trunk	121	195
principal	262	422
other	2339	3763

Schools: Nursery 1; Primary 254; Comprehensive 35; Special 11.
Colleges: Further Education 3; Horticulture 1; Agriculture 1; Education 1.
Places of interest: Denbigh Castle; Valle Crucis (Cistercian Abbey); Rhuddlan Castle (ruins); Bodrhyddan Hall; Wrexham Church
County worthies by birth: William Salisbury (*c.* 1520–84); Sir Hugh Myddleton (1560–1631); Sir Henry M Stanley (1841–1904).

CORNWALL

First recorded use of name and derivation: 884 (Cornubia) and 981 (Cornwalum), possible the territory of the Welsh tribe Cornovii.
Area: 876 296 acres *354 625 ha.*
Population: 399 000.
Density: 0·46 per acre *1,13 per ha.*
Administrative HQ: County Hall, Truro.
Highest point above sea-level: Brown Willy 1377 ft *419 m.*

Road lengths:	miles	km
trunk	147	237
principal	284	457
classified	1892	3044
unclassified	1710	2951

Schools: Nursery 1; Primary 263; Grammar 6; Secondary Modern 15; Comprehensive 19; Special 3.
Colleges: Further Education 5; Art 1.
Places of interest: Chun Castle (ring-fort); Chysauster (Iron Age village); Cotehele House (Tudor house); Land's End; Lanhydrock House (17th century house); Lanyon Quoit; The Lizard; Rame Head; Restormel (moated castle); St Buryan (Bronze Age stone and 15th century church); St Cleer (holy well); St Michael's Mount; St Neot church (stained glass); Tintagel (ruins); Kynance Cove.
County worthies by birth: Samuel Foote (1720–77); John Opie (1761–1807); Richard Trevithick (1771–1883); Sir Humphrey Davy (1778–1829); Richard (1804–34) and John (1807–39) Lander; Sir Arthur Quiller-Couch (1863–1944); Robert Fitzsimons (1862–1917).

CUMBRIA

First recorded use of name and derivation: AD 935 Cumbra land, land of the Cumbrians from the Welsh *Cymry*.
Area: 1 701 455 acres. *688 555 ha.*
Population: 475 700.
Density: 0.28 per acre *0,69 per ha.*
Administrative HQ: The Courts, Carlisle.
Highest point above sea-level: Scafell Pike 3 210 ft *978 m.*

Road lengths:	miles	km
motorways	60	96
trunk	270	434
principal	350	563
other	4100	6597

Schools: Nursery 6; Primary 373; Grammar 8; Secondary Modern 11; Secondary Technical 1; Special 15; Comprehensive 42.
Colleges: Further Education 4; Agriculture 1; Art 1; Education 1.
Places of interest: Hadrian's Wall; Lake District; Grasmere (Wordsworth monuments—museum, cottage, grave); Levens Hall.
County worthies by birth: John Dalton (1766–1844); William Wordsworth (1770–1850); John Peel (1776–1854); Sir William H Bragg (1862–1942).

DERBYSHIRE

First recorded use of name and derivation: 1049 (Deorbyscir), village with a deer park.
Area: 650 092 acres *263 083 ha.*
Population: 902 820
Density: 1·38 per acre *3,43 per ha.*
Administrative HQ: County Offices, Matlock.
Highest point above sea-level: Kinder Scout 2088 ft *636 m.*

Road lengths:	miles	km
motorway	24	39
trunk	146	235
principal	333	536
classified	1090	1954
unclassified	1541	2479

Schools: Nursery 8; Primary 494; Secondary 99; Special 29.
Colleges: Further Education 8; Agriculture 1; Art 1; Education 1.
Places of interest: Peak District; Chatsworth House; Repton School; Haddon Hall; Hardwick Hall; Melbourne Hall.
County worthies by birth: Samuel Richardson (1689–1761); Marquess Curzon of Kedleston (1859–1925); James Brindley (1716–72); Thomas Cook (1808–92).

DEVON

First recorded use of name and derivation: AD 851 (Defenascir), territory of the Dumonii (An aboriginal Celtic tribal name adopted by the Saxons).
Area: 1 658 278 acres *671 082 ha.*
Population: 928 800.
Density: 0·56 per acre *1,38 per ha.*
Administrative HQ: County Hall, Exeter.
Highest point above sea-level: High Willhays 2038 ft *621 m.*

Road lengths:	miles	km
trunk	201	323
principal	596	959
classified	3166	5094
unclassified	4221	6791

Schools: Nursery 5; Primary 455; Grammar, Secondary Modern and Comprehensive 84; Special 22.
Colleges: Further Education 13; Agriculture 1; Education 2.
Places of interest: Exeter Castle (ruins); Exeter Cathedral; Devonport dockyard; Dartmoor.
County worthies by birth: Sir John Hawkins (1532–95); Sir Francis Drake (c. 1540–96); Sir Walter Raleigh (?1552–1618); 1st Duke of Albermarle (George Monk)

(1608–70); 1st Duke of Marlborough (1650–1722); Thomas Newcomen (1663–1729); Sir Joshua Reynolds (1723–92); Samuel Taylor Coleridge (1772–1834); Sir Charles Kingsley (1819–75); William Temple (1881–1944); Dame Agatha Christie (1891–1976).

DORSET

First recorded use of name and derivation: AD 940 (Dorseteschire), dwellers (*saete*) of the place of fist-play (*Dorn-gweir*).
Area: 664 116 acres *268 758 ha.*
Population: 570 500.
Density: 0·86 per acre. *2,12 per ha.*
Administrative HQ: County Hall, Dorchester.
Highest point above sea-level: Pilsdon Pen 908 ft *276 m.*

Road lengths:	miles	km
all-purpose	58	93
principal	264	425
classified	934	1504
unclassified	1351	2175

Schools: Primary 221; Middle 13; Grammar 12; Secondary Modern 21; Special 15; Comprehensive 12; Bi-lateral 10.
Colleges: Further Education 3; Agriculture 1; Art 1; Education 1.
Places of interest: Corfe Castle; Sherborne Abbey; Wimborne Minster; Maiden Castle; Clouds Hill (Nat. Trust); Cerne Giant; Forde Abbey; Milton Abbey; Poole Harbour.
County worthies by birth: 1st Earl of Shaftesbury (1621–83); William Barnes (1801–86); Thomas Hardy (1840–1928); Sir Frederick Treves (1853–1923).

DUMFRIES and GALLOWAY

First recorded use of name and derivation: Dumfries *c.* 1183, Fort *Dum*, of the Welsh *prys* (copse). Galloway: *c.* 990, Gall-Gaidheal, the foreign Gael.
Area: 1 574 400 acres *637 138 ha.*
Population: 143 711
Density: 0·09 per acre *0,23 per ha.*
Administrative HQ: Dumfries.
Highest point above sea-level: Merrick, 2770 ft *844 m.*
Districts (with population): Annandale and Eskdale pop: 34 808; Nirthsdale pop: 56 266; Stewartry pop: 22 367; Wigtown pop: 30 089.

Road lengths:	miles	km
trunk	415	668
principal	352	566
classified	1077	1733
unclassified	1000	1609

Schools: Nursery 2; Primary 137; Secondary Modern 8; Comprehensive 13; Special 13.
Colleges: Further Education 2; Agricultural.
Places of Interest: Stranraer Castle; Dunskey Castle; St Ninian's Cave; Glenluce Abbey; Threave Castle (ruins); Glentrool National Park; The Ruthwell Cross; Caerlaverock Castle; Drumlamrig Castle; Burn's House and Mausoleum (Dumfries).
County worthies by birth: John Dalrymple, 1st Earl of Stair (1646–95); Thomas Telford (1757–1834); Sir John Ross (1777–1856); Thomas Carlyle (1795–1881).

DURHAM

First recorded use of name and derivation: *c.* 1000 (Dunholme), the hill (old English, *dun*) crowning a holm or island.
Area: 601 939 acres. *243 596 ha.*
Population: 610 900
Density: 1·01 per acre *2,51 per ha.*
Administrative HQ: County Hall, Durham.
Highest point above sea-level: Mickle Fell 2591 ft *798 m.*

Road lengths:	miles	km
motorway	28	45
trunk	53	85
principal	237	381
classified	703	1131
unclassified	1235	1987

Schools: Nursery 19; Primary 347; Grammar, Secondary Modern and Comprehensive 83; Special 21.
Colleges: Further Education 5; Agriculture 1; Education 2.
Places of interest: Durham Cathedral, Raby Castle.
County worthies by birth: Earl of Avon (Anthony Eden) (b. 1897); Elizabeth Barrett Browning (1806–61).

DYFED

First recorded use of name and derivation: 1973. The name of an ancient province.
Area: 1 424 668 acres *576 543 ha.*
Population: 320 100.
Density: 0·22 per acre *0,56 per ha.*
Administrative HQ: County Hall, Carmarthen.
Highest point above sea-level: Carmarthen Fan Foel 2500+ ft *762+ m.*

Road lengths:	miles	km
trunk	382	615
principal	548	882
other	6952	11 185

Schools: Nursery 2; Primary 339; Grammar, Secondary Modern and Comprehensive 40; Special 6.
Colleges: Further Education 7; Agriculture 1; Art 1.
Places of interest: Cardigan Castle (ruins); Aberystwyth Castle (ruins); Strata Florida Abbey; Nanteos Mansion; Kidwelly Castle; Carreg-Cennon Castle, Talley Abbey; Pendine Sands, Laugharne, St David's Cathedral and Bishop's Palace; Pentre Cfae (burial chamber), near Newport; Pembroke Castle; Carew Castle; Bishop's Palace (Lamphey) Manorbier Castle; Cilgerran Castle.
County worthies by birth: Griffith Jones of Llanddowror (1684–1761); Henry VII (1457–1509); Cambrensis (Giraddus) (1146–1220); John Dyer (1700–1758); Sir Lewis Morris (1833–1907); Dafydd ap Gwilym (14th century); Sir John Rhys (1840–1915); St David (d. 601 ?); Bishop Asser (d. 909 ?); Augustus John (1878–1961); Robert Ricorde (1510 ?–1558).

EAST SUSSEX

First recorded use of name and derivation: 1973 AD 722 (Suth Seaxe), the territory of the southern Saxons or suthseaxa.
Area: 443 627 acres *179 530 ha.*
Population: 661 000.
Density: 1·49 per acre. *3,68 per ha.*
Administrative HQ: County Hall, St Andrew's Lane, Lewes.
Highest point above sea-level: Ditchling Beacon 813 ft *247 m.*

Road lengths:	miles	km
trunk	62	100
principal	294	473
classified	786	1264
unclassified	1318	2120

Schools: Nursery 2; Primary 167; Grammar 11; Secondary Modern 26; Secondary Technical 1; Comprehensive 11; Special 17.
Colleges: Further Education 2; Agriculture 1; Art 1; Education 4; Technical 2; Polytechnic 1.
Places of interest: Pevensey Castle; Bodiam Castle; Brighton Pavilion; Lewes Castle; Herstmonceux (Royal Observatory).
County worthies by birth: John Fletcher (1579–1625).

ESSEX

First recorded use of name and derivation: AD 604 (East Seaxe), territory of the eastern Saxons.
Area: 907 849 acres *367 394 ha.*
Population: 1 397 840.
Density: 1·53 per acre *3,80 per ha.*
Administrative HQ: County Hall, Chelmsford.
Highest point above sea-level: In High Wood, Langley 480 ft *146 m.*

Road lengths:	miles	km
trunk	97	156
principal	370	595
classified	1396	2246
unclassified	2333	3754

Schools: Nursery 4; Primary 586; Grammar 19; Secondary Modern 31; Comprehensive 71; Special 39.
Colleges: Further Education 9; Agriculture 1; Art 3; Education 2.
Places of interest: Waltham Abbey; Colchester Castle; Epping Forest (part of); Thaxted Church and Guildhall; Hadleigh Castle; Castle Hedingham Keep; St Osyth Priory.
County worthies by birth: Sir Rowland Hill (1795–1879); Lord Lister (1827–1912).

FIFE

First recorded use of name and derivation: AD *c.* 590, from Fibh (disputed), possibly one of the seven sons of Criuthne, British patriot.
Area: 322 560 acres *130 536 ha*
Population: 337 690
Density: 1·05 per acre *2,59 per ha.*
Administrative HQ: Cupar
Highest point above sea-level: West Lomond 1713 ft *522 m.*
Districts (with population): Dunfermline pop: 120 999; Kirkcaldy pop: 145 983; North East Fife pop: 61 046.

Road lengths:	miles	km
motorway	13	21
trunk	83	133
principal	189	304
classified	341	549
unclassified	594	956

Schools: Nursery 5; Primary 150; Comprehensive 24; Special 5.
Colleges: Further Education 3; Agriculture 1.
Places of interest: St Andrew's; Dunfermline: Falkland Palace; Isle of May; Culross; Inchcolm; Dysart; East Neuk Villages; Aberdour Castle.
County worthies by birth: Sir David Lyndsay (*c.* 1486–1555); Charles 1 (1600–49) Alexander Selkirk (1676–1721); Adam Smith (1723–90); Robert (1728–92) and James (1730–94) Adams; Dr Thomas Chalmers (1780–1847); Sir David Wilkie (1785–1841); Sir Joseph Noel Paton (1821–1901); Andrew Carnegie (1835–1918).

GLOUCESTERSHIRE

First recorded use of name and derivation: AD 1016 (Gleawcestrescir), the shire

around the foot (*ceaster*) at the splendid place (Old Welsh, *gloiu*).
Area: 652 229 acres *263 948 ha.*
Population: 485 400.
Density: 0·74 per acre *1,84 per ha.*
Administrative HQ: Shire Hall, Gloucester.
Highest point above sea-level: Cleeve Cloud 1083 ft *330 m.*

Road lengths:	miles	km
motorway	32	*51*
trunk	156	*251*
principal	254	*409*
classified	1130	*1818*
unclassified	1560	*2510*

Schools: Nursery 1; Primary 296; Grammar, Secondary Modern and Comprehensive 54; Special 15.
Colleges: Further Education 4; Agriculture 1; Art 1; Education 1.
Places of interest: Tewkesbury Abbey; Gloucester Cathedral; Roman remains at Chedworth and Cirencester; Berkeley Castle; Sudeley Castle.
County worthies by birth: Edward Jenner (1749–1823); Gustav Theodore Holst (1874–1934).

GRAMPIAN

First recorded use of name and derivation: 1526 possibly derived from Old Welsh crwb, a haunch or hump or more probably the Gaelic *greannich*, gloomy or rugged.
Area: 2 150 798 acres *870 398 ha.*
Population: 447 435
Density: 0·21 per acre *0,51 per ha.*
Administrative HQ: Aberdeen.
Highest point above sea-level: Ben Macdhui, 4296 ft *1309 m.*
Districts (with population): Aberdeen (city) pop: 208 356; Banff and Buchan pop: 73 556; Gordon pop: 45 388; Kincardine and Deeside pop: 33 450; Moray pop: 76 481

Road lengths:	miles	km
trunk	222	*357*
principal	528	*849*
classified	1950	*3137*
unclassified	1857	*2988*

Schools: Nursery 7; Primary 262; Secondary 16; Comprehensive 30; Special 12.
Colleges: Further Education 4; Agriculture 1; Art 1; Education 1.
Places of interest: Balmoral Castle (near Crathie); Kildrummy Castle (ruins); Aberdeen University; Braemar (annual Highland games); Findlater Castle; Duff House (Banff); Marden Stone; Haddo House; Leith Hall; Huntly Castle.
County worthies by birth: John Barbour (1316–95); James Sharp (1618–79); Alexander Cruden (1689–1770); James Ferguson (1710–76); Sir James Clark (1788–1870); James Gordon Bennett (1795–1872); James Ramsay Macdonald (1866–1937); John Charles Walsham Reith, 1st Baron (1889–1971).

GREATER LONDON

First recorded use of name and derivation: AD 115 (*Londinium*), possibly from the Old Irish *Londo*, a wild or bold man.
Area: 390 302 acres *157 950 ha.*
Population: 7 167 600.
Density: 18·36 per acre *45,38 per ha.*
Administrative HQ: County Hall, London SE1.
Highest point above sea-level: 809 ft *246 m* 33 yd *30 m* South-east of Westerham Heights (a house) on the Kent-GLC boundary.

London boroughs in order of population
1.	Croydon	332 880
2.	Bromley	305 530
3.	Barnet	302 140
4.	Lambeth	299 380
5.	Wandsworth	294 000
6.	Ealing	292 510
7.	Brent	275 150
8.	Enfield	264 790
9.	Lewisham	258 710
10.	Southwark	248 230
11.	Havering	245 610
12.	Redbridge	237 180
13.	Hillingdon	235 030
14.	Haringey	234 690
15.	Waltham Forest	232 580
16.	Newham	231 100
17.	Westminster	226 240
18.	Bexley	217 210
19.	Greenwich	215 040
20.	Hackney	213 020
21.	Hounslow	207 380
22.	Harrow	204 660
23.	Camden	194 440
24.	Islington	188 160
25.	Hammersmith	177 560
26.	Kensington and Chelsea	176 900
27.	Merton	176 640
28.	Richmond upon Thames	170 940
29.	Sutton	168 210
30.	Barking	157 800
31.	Tower Hamlets	153 360
32.	Kingston upon Thames	138 620

Places of interest: Buckingham Palace; Houses of Parliament; St Paul's Cathedral; Tower of London; Westminster Abbey; British Museum; National Gallery; Trafalgar Square; Port of London; Hampton Court Palace; Syon House, Isleworth; Chiswick House, W.4; Osterley Park, Osterley; Harrow School; London Airport (Heathrow).
County worthies by birth:
The following 17 Kings and Queens (see separate section for details): Edward I, Edward V, Henry VIII, Edward VI, Mary I, Elizabeth I, Charles II, James II, Mary II, Anne, George III, George IV, William IV, Victoria, Edward VII, George V, Elizabeth II.

The following 15 Prime Ministers (see separate section for details): Earl of Chatham, Duke of Grafton, Lord North, William Pitt, Henry Addington, Spencer Perceval, George Canning, Viscount Goderich, Viscount Melbourne, Lord John Russell, Benjamin Disraeli, Earl of Rosebery, Earl Attlee, Harold Macmillan, Lord Home of the Hirsel.

Thomas à Becket (1118–70); Sir Thomas More (1478–1535); Edmund Spenser (1552–99); Ben Jonson (1572–1637); Inigo Jones (1573–1652); Earl of Stafford, Thomas Wentworth (1593–1641).

Sir Thomas Browne (1605–82); John Milton 1608–74); Edmond Halley (1656–1742); Daniel Defoe (1660–1737); Viscount Bolingbroke (1678–1751); Alexander Pope (1688–1744); Earl of Chesterfield (1694–1773).

Thomas Gray (1716–71); Richard Howe (1726–99); Edward Gibbon (1737–94); John Nash (1752–1835); Joseph Turner (1775–1851); Sir Charles Napier (1782–1853); Viscount Stratford de Redcliffe (1786–1880); Michael Faraday (1791–1867); Thomas Hood (1799–1855).

John Stuart Mill (1806–73); Robert Browning (1812–83); Anthony Trollope (1815–82); George F. Watts (1817–1904); John Ruskin (1819–1900); Lord Lister (1827–1912); Dante Gabriel Rossetti (1828–82); Sir William Gilbert (1836–1911); Algernon Charles Swinburne (1837–1909); Sir Arthur Sullivan (1842–1900); Lord Baden-Powell (1857–1941); Marquess of Reading (1860–1935); H G Wells (1866–1946); Sir Max Beerbohm (1873–1956); G K Chesterton (1874–1936); Sir Charles Chaplin (1889–   ).

GREATER MANCHESTER

First recorded use of name and derivation: AD 923 *Mameceaster*, first element reduced from the Old British *Mamucion* to which was added the Old English *ceaster*, a camp.
Area: 318 560 acres *128 917 ha.*
Population: 2 730 000.
Density: 8·57 per acre *21,18 per ha.*
Administrative HQ: Piccadilly Gardens, Manchester.
Highest point above sea-level: Featherbed Moss 1774 ft *540 m.*

Road lengths:	miles	km
motorway	77	*125*
trunk	75	*121*
principal	441	*710*
other	3878	*6240*

Places of interest: Foxdenton Hall; Chethams Hospital School and Library; Manchester: Cathedral, City Art Gallery; Haigh Hall and Zoo; Peel Tower; Holcombe Village; Manchester Ship Canal.
County worthies by birth: Samuel Crompton (1753–1827); Sir Robert Peel (1788–1850); John Bright (1811–89); James Prescott Jowle (1818–89); Emmeline Pankhurst (1858–1928); 1st Earl Lloyd-George of Dwyfor (1863–1945); L. S Lowry (1887–1976); Gracie Fields (1898–   ); Sir William Walton (1902–   ).

GWENT

First recorded use of name and derivation: 1973. The name of an ancient province.
Area: 339 933 acres *137 566 ha.*
Population: 440 500.
Density: 1·29 per acre *3,20 per ha.*
Administrative HQ: County Hall, Cwmbran.
Highest point above sea-level: Chwarel-y-Fan. 2228 ft *679 m.*

Road lengths:	miles	km
motorway	19	*30*
trunk	86	*138*
principal and classified	688	*1107*

Schools: Nursery 16; Primary 302; Grammar, Secondary Modern and Comprehensive 47; Special 9.
Colleges: Further Education 5; Agriculture 1; Art 1; Education 1.
Places of interest: Tintern Abbey; Caldicot Priory; Caerleon (Roman remains); Raglan Castle.
County worthies by birth: Henry V (1387–1422).

GWYNEDD

First recorded use of name and derivation: 1973. The name of an ancient province.
Area: 955 244 acres *386 574 ha.*
Population: 223 500.
Density: 0·22 per acre *0,58 per ha.*
Administrative HQ: County Offices, Caernarvon.
Highest point above sea-level: Snowdon. 3560 ft *1085 m.*

Road lengths:	miles	km
trunk	209	336
principal	257	413
classified	1141	1836
unclassified	2855	4594

Schools: Primary 207; Comprehensive 24; Special 10.
Colleges: Further Education 4.
Places of interest: Harlech Castle; Beaumaris Castle; Caernarvon Castle; Conway Castle; Snowdonia National Park; Bryn Celli Dhu; Portmeirion; Lloyd George Memorial and Museum, Llanystumdwy.
County worthies by birth: Edward I (1284–1327); Lewis Morris (1700–65); Goronwy Owen (1723–69); Sir Hugh Owen (1804–81); T E Lawrence (1888–1935).

HAMPSHIRE

First recorded use of name and derivation: AD 755 (Hamtunscir), the shire around Hamtun (*ham*, a meadow; *tun* a homestead).
Area: 934 474 acres *378 169 ha.*
Population: 1 434 700.
Density: 1.54 per acre *3,79 per ha.*
Administrative HQ: The Castle, Winchester.
Highest point above sea-level: Pilot Hill 937 ft *285 m.*

Road lengths:	miles	km
motorway	25	40
trunk	151	243
principal	474	763
classified	1558	2507
unclassified	2842	4573

Schools: Nursery 5; Primary 595; Grammar 13; Secondary Modern 47; Special 35; Comprehensive 60; Partly Selective 5.
Colleges: Further Education 10; Agriculture 1; Art 3; Education 1.
Places of interest: Winchester Cathedral; New Forest; Ocean Terminal, Southampton, Portsmouth dockyard (with HMS Victory).
County worthies by birth: Henry III (1207–72); William of Wykeham (1324–1404); Gilbert White (1720–93); Jane Austen 1775–1817); Viscount Palmerston (1784–1865); Isambard Kingdom Brunel (1806–59); 1st Earl Wavell (1883–1950); James Brudenell, 1st Earl of Cardigan (1797–1868).

HEREFORD and WORCESTER

First recorded use of name and derivation: AD *c.* 1038 Hereford, *herepaeth,*

military road, meaning ford, a river crossing and AD 889 *Uuegorna ceastre,* the fort (Latin caester) of the Weogoran tribe, probably named from the Wyre Forest.
Area: 970 203 acres *392 628 ha.*
Population: 585 000.
Density: 0·60 per acre *1,49 per ha.*
Administrative HQ: Shire Hall, Worcester
Highest point above sea-level: In Black Mountains 2306 ft *702 m.*

Road lengths:	miles	km
motorway	60	96
trunk	148	238
principal	452	727
other	3415	5495

Schools: Nursery 1; Primary 348; Grammar 9; Secondary Modern 18; Comprehensive 38; Special 16;
Colleges: Further Education 6; Agriculture 2; Horticulture 1; Art 1; Education 3.
Places of interest: Offa's Dyke; Hereford Cathedral; Worcester Cathedral; Weobley; Malvern Priory; Pershore Abbey; Dinmore Manor.
County worthies by birth: Richard Hakluyt (1552–1616); Samuel Butler (1612–80); David Garrick (1717–79); Sir Rowland Hill (1795–1879); Sir Edward Elgar (1857–1934); A E Housman (1859–1936); Stanley Baldwin (1867–1947).

HERTFORDSHIRE

First recorded use of name and derivation: AD 866 (Heortfordscir), the river crossing (ford) of the stags (harts).
Area: 403 797 acres *163 411 ha.*
Population: 941 700.
Density: 2·33 per acre *5,76 per ha.*
Administrative HQ: County Hall, Hertford.
Highest point above sea-level: Hastoe 802 ft *244 m.*

Road lengths:	miles	km
motorway	35	56
trunk	106	170
principal	202	325
other	2206	3549

Schools: Nursery 17; Primary 475; Secondary 110; Middle 10; Special 30.
Colleges: Further Education 10; Polytechnic 1; Technology 2; Agriculture 1; Art 1; Education 2; Building 1.
Places of interest: St Albans Cathedral, Roman remains of Verulamium (now at St Albans); Hatfield House; Knebworth House; Salisbury Hall.
County worthies by birth: Nicholas Breakspear (Pope Adrian IV) (1100–1159); Sir Henry Bessemer (1813–1898); Henry Manning (1808–1892); Queen Elizabeth, the Queen Mother (b. 1900–); Third Marquess of Salisbury (1830–1903); William Cowper (1731–1800); Cecil Rhodes (1853–1902); Sir Richard Fanshawe (1608–1666).

HIGHLAND

First recorded use of name and derivation: *c.* 1425 (implied in *hielandman*) from adjective *high,* noun *land.*
Area: 6 280 320 acres *2 541 558 ha.*
Population: 176 000.
Density: 0·03 per acre *0,07 per ha.*
Administrative HQ: Inverness.
Highest point above sea-level: Ben Nevis 4406 ft *1342 m.*
Districts (with population): Badenoch and Strathspey, pop: 9122; Caithness pop: 29 809; Inverness pop: 49 445; Lochaber pop: 19 237; Nairn pop: 11 054; Ross and Cromarty pop: 35 089; Sky and Lochaish pop: 9761; Sutherland pop: 11 932.

Road lengths:	miles	km
trunk	504	811
principal	973	1565
other	2794	4495

Places of interest: St Mary's Chapel (Forse Thurso); Dunbeath Castle; Site of John O'Groat's House (Portland Firth); Girnigoe Castle; Castle of Mey; Glencoe; Callanish Stones; Reay Forest; Cape Wrath; Dunrobin Castle; Dun Dornadilla; Culloden Battlefield; Glenfinnan Monument (raising of Prince Charles Stewart's standard).
County worthies by birth: Hugh Mackay (1640–92); Duncan Forbes (1685–1746); Gen Arthur St Clair (1734–1818); Sir Alexander Mackenzie (1755–1820); Hugh Miller (1802–56); Alexander Bain (1810–77); Sir Hector MacDonald (1853–1903).

HUMBERSIDE

First recorded use of name and derivation: AD *c.* 730 *humbri,* the British river name, side.
Area: 867 784 acres *351 180 ha.*
Population: 848 800.
Density: 0·98 per acre *2,42 per ha.*
Administrative HQ: Kingston House, Bond St, Kingston-upon-Hull.
Highest point above sea-level: Cot Nab 807 ft *246 m.*

Road lengths:	miles	km
trunk	94	151
principal	294	473
classified	1131	1820
unclassified	1879	3023

Schools: Nursery 8; Primary 385; Grammar, Secondary Modern and Comprehensive 124; Special 18.
Colleges: Further Education 9; Agriculture 1; Art 1; Education 1.
Places of interest: Kingston upon Hull: Trinity House, Wilberforce House, Trinity Church, Mortimer Museum. Beverley Minster; Thornton Abbey.
County worthies by birth: Andrew Marvell (1621–78); William Wilberforce (1759–1833); Amy Johnson (1903–41); John Fisher (*c.* 1459–1535).

ISLE OF WIGHT

First recorded use of name and derivation: AD 730 Wiht (cognate with Latin *vectis,* a lever) that which rises (from the sea) (disputed).
Area: 94 146 acres *38 100 ha.*
Population: 112 000.
Density: 1·19 per acre *2,94 per ha.*
Administrative HQ: County Hall, Newport
Highest point above sea-level: St Boniface Down 785 ft *239 m.*

Road lengths:	miles	km
principal	76	122
classified	166	267
unclassified	203	327

Schools: Primary 47; Middle 16; Comprehensive High 4; Special 2.
Colleges: Further Education 1;
Places of interest: Osborne House; Carisbrooke Castle; Brading (Roman Villa); Royal Yacht Squadron at Cowes.
County worthies by birth: Sir Thomas Fleming (1544–1613); Dr Thomas James (1580–1629); Robert Hooke (1635–1702); Dr Thomas Arnold (1795–1842).

KENT

First recorded use of name and derivation: c. 308 BC Celtic canto, a rim or coastal area.
Area: 921 665 acres 372 985 ha.
Population: 1 440 800.
Density: 1·56 per acre 3,86 per ha.
Administrative HQ: County Hall, Maidstone.
Highest point above sea-level: Westerham 824 ft 251 m.

Road lengths:	miles	km
trunk	139	224
principal	439	706
other	4245	6830

Schools: Nursery & Primary 617; Grammar 20; Secondary Modern 57; Comprehensive 4; Special 35.
Colleges: Further Education 11; Technical 6; Agriculture 1; Art 3; Education 2.
Places of interest: Canterbury Cathedral; Dover Cliffs; Pilgrim's Way; North Downs: Knole; Oenshurst Place; Deal Castle.
County worthies by birth: Christopher Marlow (1564–93); Sir William Jenner (1815–98); Sir William Harvey (1578–1657); Robert Bridges (1844–1930); General James Wolfe (1727–59); William Caxton (c. 1422–91); Edward Richard George Heath (1916–   ).

LANCASHIRE

First recorded use of name and derivation: the shire around Lancastre AD 1087; camp, (castrum) on the River Lune.
Area: 753 689 acres 305 007 ha.
Population: 1 362 800.
Density: 1·81 per acre 4,47 per ha.
Administrative HQ: County Hall, Preston.
Highest point above sea-level: Gragareth 2057 ft 626 m.

Road lengths:	miles	km
motorway	61	98
trunk	165	265
principal	315	507
classified	1093	1759
unclassified	2560	4119

Schools: Nursery 38; Primary 691; Grammar 17; Secondary Modern 48; Comprehensive 58; Special 48.
Colleges: Further Education 13; Polytechnic 1; Agriculture 1; Art 2; Education 3.
Places of interest: Blackpool Tower; Gawthorpe Hall; Lancaster Castle; Browsholme Hall.
County worthies by birth: Sir Richard Arkwright (1732–92); James Hargreaves (?1745–78); Sir Ambrose Fleming (1849–1945).

LEICESTERSHIRE

First recorded use of name and derivation: 1087 (Laegreceastrescir) from the camp (castra) of the Ligore, dwellers on the River Legra (now the R Soar).
Area: 641 460 acres 259 590 ha.
Population: 829 800.
Density: 1·29 per acre 3,20 per ha.
Administrative HQ: County Hall, Glenfield, Leicester.
Highest point above sea-level: Bardon Hill 912 ft 277 m.

Road lengths:	miles	km
motorway	42	67
trunk	128	206
principal	250	402
classified	902	1451
unclassified	1722	2771

Schools: Nursery 1; Primary 381; Secondary Modern 25; High 34; Grammar 9; Upper 16; Comprehensive 1; Special 27.
Colleges: Further Education 7; Agriculture 1; Art 1; Education 2; Polytechnic 1.
Places of interest: Belvoir Castle; Ashby-de-la-Zouche Castle; Kirby Muxloe Castle; Stanford Hall.
County worthies by birth: Queen Jane (1537–54); George Fox (1624–91); Thomas Babbington Macauley (1800–59); Hugh Latimer (?1485–1555); Titus Oates (1649–1705).

LINCOLNSHIRE

First recorded use of name and derivation: 1016 (Lincolnescire), a colony (colonia) by the lindum (a widening in the river, i.e. River Witham).
Area: 1 454 273 acres 588 524 ha.
Population: 519 500.
Density: 0·36 per acre 0,88 per ha.
Administrative HQ: County Offices, Lincoln.
Highest point above sea-level: Normanby-le-Wold 550 ft 167 m.

Road lengths:	miles	km
trunk	212	342
principal	518	834
other	4697	7588

Schools: Nursery 7; Primary 351; Grammar, Secondary Modern and Comprehensive 74; Special 20.
Colleges: Further Education 7; Agriculture 2; Art 1; Education 1.
Places of interest: Lincoln Cathedral; Tattershall Castle; Church of St Botolph, Boston; Lincoln Castle; Burghley House.
County worthies by birth: Henry IV (1366–1413); John Foxe (1516–87); Sir Isaac Newton (1642–1727); John (1703–91) and Charles Wesley (1707–38); Sir John Franklin (1786–1847); Alfred, Lord Tennyson (1809–92).

LOTHIAN

First recorded use of name and derivation: c. AD 970 from personal name, possibly a Welsh derivative of Laudinus.
Area: 433 920 acres 175 601 ha.
Population: 758 500.
Density: 1·75 per acre 4,32 per ha.
Administrative HQ: Edinburgh.
Highest point above sea-level: Blackhope Scar 2137 ft 651 m.
Length of coastline: 63 miles 101 km.
Districts (with population): East Lothian pop: 77 535; Edinburgh (city) pop: 472 224; Midlothian pop: 80 178; West Lothian pop: 112 320.

Road lengths:	miles	km
motorway	30	48
trunk	64	103
principal	258	416

Schools: Nursery 76; Primary 232; Secondary 45; Special 24.
Colleges: Further Education 6.
Places of interest: Dunbar Castle; Tantallon Castle (ruins); Muirfield Golf Centre (Gullane); Aberlady (bird sanctuary); Rosslyn chapel; Borthwick Castle; Newbattle Abbey; Dalkeith Palace; Edinburgh Castle; St Giles Cathedral; Cricktown Castle; Palace of Holyrood House; Craigmillar Castle; Linlithgow Palace; Dundas Castle; The Binns (near Queensferry); Torpichen Church; Hopetown House.
County worthies by birth: John Knox (1505–72); John Napier (1550–1617); Sir Walter Scott (1771–1832); James Nasmyth (1808–90); Alexander Melville Bell (1819–1905); Sir Herbert Maxwell (1845–1937); Arthur James Balfour (1848–1930); Robert Louis Stevenson (1850–94); Alexander Graham Bell (1847–1922); Sir Arthur Conan Doyle (1859–1930).

MERSEYSIDE

First recorded use of name and derivation: AD 1002 Maerse from Old English Maeres-ea boundary river (between Mercia and Northumbria).
Area: 160 000 acres 64 750 ha.
Population: 1 602 700.
Density: 10·02 per acre 24,75 per ha.
Administrative HQ: Metropolitan House, Old Hall St, Liverpool.
Highest point above sea-level: Billinge Hill 588 ft 179 m.
Length of coastline: 56 miles 93 km.

Road lengths:	miles	km
motorway	29	47
trunk	63	101
principal	264	425
classified	304	489
unclassified	1824	2935

Schools: Nursery 14; Primary 669; Secondary 189; Special 80.
Colleges: Further Education 21; Polytechnic 1; Education 6; Adult Education 4.
Places of interest: Liverpool: Roman Catholic Cathedral, Speke Hall, Walker Art Gallery.
Knowsley Safari Park; Ainsdale Nature Reserve.
County worthies by birth: George Stubbs (1724–1806); William Ewart Gladstone (1809–98); 1st Earl of Birkenhead (1872–1930).

MID GLAMORGAN

First recorded use of name and derivation: 1242 (Gwlad Morgan) the terrain of Morgan, a 10th century Welsh Prince.
Area: 251 732 acres 101 872 ha.
Population: 536 080.
Density: 2·13 per acre 5,26 per ha.
Main town: Rhondda (?).
Highest point above sea-level: On boundary c. 1920 ft 585 m.

Road lengths:	miles	km
trunk & classified	505	812
unclassified	1014	1631

Schools: Nursery 18; Primary 317; Grammar 4; Secondary Modern 9; Comprehensive 34; Special 11.
Colleges: Further Education 6; Polytechnic 1; Agriculture 1.
Places of interest: Ewenny Priory; Caerphilly Castle.

NORFOLK

First recorded use of name and derivation: AD 1043 (Norfolk), the territory of the *nor* (northern) *folk* (people) of East Anglia.
Area: 2 362 900 acres *956 233 ha.*
Population: 650 300.
Density: 0·28 per acre *0,68 per ha.*
Administrative HQ: County Hall, Martineau Lane, Norwich.
Highest point above sea-level: Sandy Lane, east of Sheringham 335 ft *102 m.*
Places of interest: The Broads; Sandringham House, Blickling Hall; Holkham Hall; Breckland; Scolt Head; Norwich Cathedral; The Castle, Norwich; Maddermarket Theatre, Norwich; Castle Acre; Grimes Graves.
County worthies by birth: Sir Edward Coke (1552–1634); 2nd Viscount Townshend (1674–1738); Sir Robert Walpole (1676–1745); Thomas Paine (1737–1809); 1st Viscount Nelson (1758–1805); Elizabeth Fry (1780–1845); George Borrow (1803–81); 1st Earl of Cromer (1841–1917); Edith Cavell (1865–1915); George VI (1895–1952).

NORTHAMPTONSHIRE

First recorded use of name and derivation: *c.* AD 1011 (Hamtunscir) [see Hampshire], the northern homestead.
Area: 585 009 acres *236 745 ha.*
Population: 496 400.
Density: 0·85 per acre *2,10 per ha.*
Administrative HQ: County Hall, Northampton.
Highest point above sea-level: Arbury Hill, 734 ft *223 m.*

Road lengths:	miles	km
motorway	28	45
trunk	133	214
principal	193	310
classified	687	1105
unclassified	850	1368

Schools: Nursery 10; Primary 261; Grammar 7; Secondary Modern 15; Upper 5; Special 19. Middle and High 12; Comprehensive 19; Lower 12.
Colleges: Further Education 5; Agriculture 1; Art 1; Education 1.
Places of interest: Earls Barton Church; Sulgrave Manor; Fotheringay; Brixworth Church.
County worthies by birth: Richard III 1452–85); John Dryden (1631–1700); Christopher Hatton (1540–91).

NORTHUMBERLAND

First recorded use of name and derivation: AD 895 (Norohymbraland), the land to the north of the Humber.
Area: 1 243 466 acres *503 213 ha.*
Population: 285 700.
Density: 0·23 per acre *0,57 per ha.*
Administrative HQ: County Hall, Newcastle-upon-Tyne.
Highest point above sea-level: The Cheviot 2676 ft *815 m.*

Road lengths:	miles	km
trunk	134	216
principal	221	355
classified	1295	2084
unclassified	1318	2121

Schools: Nursery 2; Primary 146; Grammar 7; Secondary Modern 32; Comprehensive 50; Special 11.
Colleges: Further Education 1; Agriculture 1; Education 3.
Places of interest: Hadrian's Wall, Lindis-farne Priory; Alnwick Castle; Warkworth Castle; Hexham Abbey; Tynemouth Priory; Bamburgh Castle.
County worthies by birth: Lancelot ('Capability') Brown (1715–83); 2nd Earl Grey (1764–1845); Grace Darling (1815–42); Robert ('Bobbie') Charlton (1937–   ).

NORTH YORKSHIRE

First recorded use of name and derivation: AD 150 Ebórakon (Ptolemy); AD 1050 *Eoferwiscir*, land possessed by Eburos.
Area: 2 055 000 acres *831 630 ha.*
Population: 648 600.
Density: 0·32 per acre *0,78 per ha.*
Administrative HQ: County Hall, Northallerton.
Highest point above sea-level: Whernside 2419 ft *737 m.*

Road lengths:	miles	km
motorway	6	10
trunk	236	380
principal	432	695
classified	2169	3490
unclassified	2952	4750

Schools: Nursery 4; Primary 458; Grammar 8; Secondary Modern 19; Comprehensive 40; Special 17.
Colleges: Further Education 8; Agriculture 1; Art 1; Education 1.
Places of interest: Richmond Castle; Scarborough Castle; City of York (the Minster and the Five Sisters Windows); Byland Abbey; Castle Howard; Rievaulx Abbey; Fountains Abbey; Bolton Priory (ruins).
County worthies by birth: Alcuin (735–804); John Wycliffe (*c.* 1320–84); Guy Fawkes (1570–1606); John Flaxman (1755–1826); William Etty (1787–1849); William Stubbs (1825–1901); Sir William Harcourt (1827–1904); Frederick, Lord Leighton (1830–78); Edith Sitwell (1887–1964); Wyston Hugh Amden (1907–73).

NOTTINGHAMSHIRE

First recorded use of name and derivation: 1016 (Snotingahamscir), the shire around the dwelling (ham) of the followers of Snot, a Norseman.
Area: 546 637 acres *221 216 ha.*
Population: 981 000.
Density: 1·79 per acre *4,43 per ha.*
Administrative HQ: County Hall, West Bridgford, Nottingham.
Highest point above sea-level: Herrod's Hill, 652 ft *198 m.*

Road lengths:	miles	km
motorway	9	15
trunk	134	216
principal	293	472
other	2164	3482

Schools: Nursery 6; Primary 462; Secondary Modern, Comprehensive and Grammar 110; Special 23.
Colleges: Further Education 10; Agriculture 1; Art 1; Education 3.
Places of interest: Southwell Cathedral; Sherwood Forest; The Dukeries; Wollaton Hall; Newstead Abbey.
County worthies by birth: Thomas Cranmer (1489–1556); Edmund Cartwright (1743–1823); Gen William Booth (1829–1912); Samuel Butler (1835–1902); D H Lawrence (1885–1930).

ORKNEY

First recorded use of name and deriva-tion: *c.* 308 BC as Orkas (Pytheas) from Norse ork, a whale; old Norse-*ay*, island.
Area: 240 848 acres *97 468 ha.*
Population: 17 462
Density: 0·07 per acre *0,18 per ha.*
Administrative HQ: Kirkwall.
Highest point above sea level: Ward Hill, Hoy 1570 ft *478 m.*

Road lengths:	miles	km
principal	100	161
classified	225	362
unclassified	228	367

Schools: Primary 24; Comprehensive 7.
Colleges: Agriculture 1.
Places of interest: Noltlandcastle (ruins); the underground village of Skara Brae; the stone circle at Brogar; Old Man of Hoy.

OXFORDSHIRE

First recorded use of name and derivation: AD 1010 (Oxnfordscir), the shire around Oxford (a river ford for oxen). The town (city) was first recorded (as Osnafoxda) in AD 912.
Area: 645 314 acres *261 150 ha.*
Population: 535 300.
Density: 0·82 per acre *2,05 per ha.*
Administrative HQ: County Hall, New Road, Oxford.
Highest point above sea-level: White Horse Hill, 856 ft *260 m.*

Road lengths:	miles	km
motorway	9	14
trunk	154	248
principal	237	381
classified	909	1462
unclassified	1088	1750

Schools: Nursery 14; Primary 273; Grammar, Secondary Modern and Comprehensive 57; Special 15.
Colleges: Further Education 6; Polytechnic 1.
Places of interest: Oxford University; Blenheim Palace, nr Woodstock; Rollright Stones; Broughton Castle; Radcliffe Camera Bodleian Library, Oxford.
County worthies by birth: Alfred (849–99); Richard I (1157–99); John (1167–1216); Sir William D'Avenant (1606–68); Warren Hastings (1732–1818); Lord Randolph Churchill (1849–95); Sir Winston Churchill (1874–1965); William Morris, 1st Viscount Nuffield (1877–1963).

POWYS

First recorded use of name and derivation: The name of an ancient province.
Area: 1 254 656 acres *507 742 ha.*
Population: 100 200.
Density: 0·08 per acre *0,20 per ha.*
Administrative HQ: County Hall, Llandrindod Wells.
Highest point above sea-level: Pen-y-Fan (Cadet Arthur) 2907 ft *885 m.*

Road lengths:	miles	km
trunk	268	431
principal	153	246
classified	1600	2574
unclassified	1490	2397

Schools: Nursery; Primary 140; Comprehensive 12; Special 4.
Colleges: Further Education 3.
Places of interest: Brecon Beacons; Priory of St John (or Brecon Cathedral); Powis Castle and gardens; Lake Vyrnwy; Montgomery Castle; Gregynog Hall.
County worthies by birth: Owen Glen-

dower (c. 1359–1416); George Herbert (1593–1633); Robert Owen 1771–1858).

SALOP

First recorded use of name and derivation: AD 1094 *Salopesberia*, a Norman-French version of Scrobbesbyrig or Shrewsbury.
Area: 862 479 acres *349 033 ha*.
Population: 354 400.
Density: 0·41 per acre *1,02 per ha*.
Administrative HQ: Abbey Foregate, Shrewsbury.
Highest point above sea-level: Brown Clee Hill 1772 ft *540 m*.

Road lengths:	miles	km
trunk	158	254
principal	253	407
classified	1508	2426
unclassified	1500	2413

Schools: Nursery 3; Primary 233; Grammar 12; Secondary Modern 21; Comprehensive 10; Special 9.
Colleges: Further Education 2.
Places of interest: Offa's Dyke; Ludlow Castle; Shrewsbury Abbey and Castle; Stokesay Castle; Coalbrookdale and Cronbridge; The Wrekin; Candover Hall; Hodnet Hall.
County worthies by birth: Lord Clive of Plassey (1725–74); Charles Darwin (1809–82); Capt Matthew Webb (1848–83); Mary Webb (1881–1927).

SHETLAND

First recorded use of name and derivation: 1289, land of Hjalto (Old Norse personal name c.f. Scots, Sholto) or hilt-shaped land.
Area: 352 337 acres *142 586 ha*.
Population: 18 445.
Density: 0·05 per acre *0,13 per ha*.
Administrative HQ: Lerwick.
Highest point above sea-level: Ronas Hill, Mainland, 1486 ft *452 m*.
Districts (with population):

Road lengths:	miles	km
principal	124	199
classified	217	349
unclassified	171	275

Schools: Nursery; Primary 26; Comprehensive 1; Junior High School 7; Special.
Places of interest: Scalloway Castle; Jarishof; Broch of Mousa; Broch of Clickimin; St Ninian's Isle.
County worthies by birth: Arthur Anderson (1792–1868); Sir Robert Stout (1844–1930).

SOMERSET

First recorded use of name and derivation: AD 1015 *Sumaersaeton*, the land of the dwellers (Saete) dependent on Sumerton (a summer-only settlement).
Area: 854 488 acres *345 799 ha*.
Population: 400 400.
Density: 0·47 per acre *0,16 per ha*.
Administrative HQ: County Hall, Taunton.
Highest point above sea-level: Dunkery Beacon 1705 ft *519 m*.

Road lengths:	miles	km
motorway	8	13
trunk	95	153
principal	363	584
classified	1579	2541
unclassified	1550	2494

Schools: Nursery 2; Primary 255; Grammar

3; Secondary Modern 16; Comprehensive 26; Special 8.
Colleges: Further Education 7; Agriculture 1; Art 1.
Places of interest: Cheddar Gorge; Wookey Hole; Wells Cathedral; Exmoor National Park; Glastonbury Abbey (ruins).
County worthies by birth: St Dunstan (925–988); Roger Bacon (1214–94); John Pym (1584–1643); Robert Blake (1599–1657); Henry Fielding (1707–54).

SOUTH GLAMORGAN

First recorded use of name and derivation: 1242 (Gwlad Morgan) the terrain of Morgan, a 10th century Welsh Prince.
Area: 102 807 acres *41 605 ha*.
Population: 391 100.
Density: 3·8 per acre *9,40 per ha*.
Administrative HQ: Newport Road, Cardiff.
Highest point above sea-level: Nr St Hilary 451 ft *137 m*.

Road lengths:	miles	km
motorway and trunk	22	35
principal	67	108
classified	246	396
unclassified	585	941

Schools: Nursery 12; Primary 170; Secondary 31; Special 13.
Colleges: Further Education 6.
Places of interest: Cardiff Castle; St Fagan's Castle (Welsh Folk Museum); St Donat's Castle.

SOUTH YORKSHIRE

First recorded use of name and derivation: c. AD 150 Ebórakon (Ptolemy). 1050 (Eoferwiscir), land possessed by Eburos.
Area: 385 610 acres *156 051 ha*.
Population: 1 317 200.
Density: 3·42 per acre *8,44 per ha*.
Administrative HQ: County Hall, Barnsley.
Highest point above sea-level: Margery Hill, 1791 ft *545 m*.

Road lengths:	miles	km
motorway	53	85
trunk	85	137
principal	232	373
classified	560	901
unclassified	2020	3250

Places of interest: Sheffield: Cathedral Church of ss Peter and Paul; Cutler's Hall; Conisbrough Castle; Roche Abbey (ruins).
County worthies by birth: Gordon Banks (1938–   ).

STAFFORDSHIRE

First recorded use of name and derivation: 1016 (Staeffordscir), the shire around a ford by a *staeth* or landing place.
Area: 671 184 acres *271 618 ha*
Population: 991 100.
Density: 1·48 per acre *3,65 per ha*.
Administrative HQ: County Buildings, Stafford.
Highest point above sea-level: Oliver Hill, 1684 ft *513 m*.

Road lengths:	miles	km
motorway	51	82
trunk	133	214
principal	291	468
classified	1043	1678
unclassified	1082	1741

Schools: Nursery 12; Primary 42; Grammar 13; Secondary Modern 37; Comprehensive 33; Special 22.
Colleges: Further Education 5; Agriculture 1; Art 1; Education 2.
Places of interest: Lichfield Cathedral; Croxden Abbey; Cannock Chase; Alton Towers; Blithfield Hall; Tamworth Castle; Sandon Hall.
County worthies by birth: Isaak Walton (1593–1683); Dr Samuel Johnson (1709–84); Josiah Wedgwood (1730–95); Admiral Earl of St Vincent (1735–1823); Arnold Bennett (1867–1931); Havergal Brian (1876–1972).

STRATHCLYDE

First recorded use of name and derivation: c. AD 85 Clota, the river (per Tacitus) AD 875 Straecled Wenla cyning.
Area: 3 422 520 acres *1 385 046 ha*.
Population: 527 129.
Density: 0·74 per acre *1,82 per ha*.
Administrative HQ: Melrose House, Cadogan St, Glasgow.
Highest point above sea-level: Bidean nam Bian 3766 ft *1147 m*.
Districts (with population): Argyll and Bute pop: 64 361; Bearsden Milngavie pop: 35 728; Clydebank pop: 59 189; Cumbernauld pop: 45 823; Cumnock and Doon Valley pop: 49 110; Cunninghame pop: 126 736; Dumbarton pop: 78 486; East Kilbride pop: 74 117; Eastwood pop: 49 947; Glasgow (city) pop: 983 548; Hamilton pop: 104 629; Enverclyde pop: 109 615; Kilmarnock and Loudoun pop: 81 468; Kyle and Carrick pop: 110 359; Lanark 53 109; Monklands pop: 109 850. Motherwell pop: 162 286; Renfrew pop: 203 568; Strathkelvin pop: 77 385.

Road lengths:	miles	km
motorway	47	76
trunk	532	856
principal	1034	1664
other	5852	9416
private	187	301

Schools: Nursery 90; Primary 917; Comprehensive/Secondary 199; Special 67.
Colleges: Further Education 23; Agriculture 2; Art 1; Education 4.
Places of interest: Fingal's Cove (off the island of Staffe); Iona: Loch Lomond; Dumbarton Rock and Castle; Newark Castle; Pollock House (Pollockshaws); Glasgow Cathedral; St Kentigern's Church (Lanark); Bothwell Castle (ruins); Culzean Castle (National Trust of Scotland); Burn's Cottage and Museum (Alloway).
County worthies by birth: Colin MacLaurin (1698–1746); James Watt (1736–1819); John Boyd Dunlop (1840–1921); James Chalmers (1841–1901); John Logie Baird (1888–1946).

SUFFOLK

First recorded use of name and derivation: AD 895 (Suthfolchi), the territory of the southern folk (of East Anglia).
Area: 940 800 acres *380 729 ha.*
Population: 567 300.
Density: 0·60 per acre *1,49 per ha.*
Administrative HQ: County Hall, Ipswich.
Highest point above sea-level: Rede, 420 ft *128 m.*

Road lengths:	miles	km
trunk	114	183
principal	320	515
classified	1519	2444
unclassified	1786	2874

Schools: Nursery 2; Primary 283; Grammar 3; Secondary Modern 17; Secondary Comprehensive 1; Middle 36; Upper and High Comprehensive 17.
Colleges: Further Education 3; Agriculture 1.
Places of interest: Flatford Mill and Willy Lott's Cottage; Framlingham Castle; Kyson Hill; Saxstead Green Windmill; Gainsborough's House; Lavenham (Guild Hall, Wool Hall); Long Melford Church; Newmarket; Bury St Edmunds (Abbey ruins); Ickworth Mansion; The Maltings, Snape.
County worthies by birth: Sir Joseph Hooker (1817–1911); John Constable (1776–1837); Cardinal Thomas Wolsey (c. 1475–1530); Edward Fitzgerald (1809–83); Thomas Gainsborough (1727–88); Robert Bloomfield (1766–1823).

SURREY

First recorded use of name and derivation: AD 722 (Suthrige), from the Old English, *suther-gé* or southern district.
Area: 414 922 acres *167 913 ha.*
Population: 1 005 900.
Density: 2·42 per acre *5,99 per ha.*
Administrative HQ: County Hall, Kingston upon Thames.
Highest point above sea-level: Leith Hill 965 ft *294 m.*

Road lengths:	miles	km
motorway	17	27
trunk	58	93
principal	325	523
classified	590	949
unclassified	1559	2508

Schools: Nursery 6; Primary 382; Grammar

16; Secondary Modern 53; Comprehensive 16; Special 33.
Colleges: Further Education 4; Agriculture 1; Art 3; Education 1; Inst of Further Education 13.
Places of interest: Guildford Cathedral; Waverley Abbey; Royal Horticultural Soc Gardens, Wisley; Box Hill.
County worthies by birth: William of Ockham (d. 1349?); Thomas Malthus (1766–1834); John Galsworthy (1867–1933); Duke of Windsor (King Edward VIII) (1894–); Aldous Huxley (1894–1936); Sir Lawrence Olivier (1907–); John Evelyn (1620–1706).

TAYSIDE

First recorded use of name and derivation: c. AD 85 *Taus* or *Tanaus* (Tacitus).
Area: 1 894 080 acres *766 507 ha.*
Population: 401 183
Density: 0·21 per acre *0,52 per ha.*
Administrative HQ: Dundee
Highest point above sea-level: Ben Lawers 3984 ft *1214 m.*
Length of coastline: 76 miles *122 km.*
Districts (with population): Angus pop: 84 481; Dundee pop: 197 537; Perth and Kinross pop: 114 578.

Road lengths:	miles	km
motorway	13	21
trunk	149	239
principal	406	653
others	2220	3571

Schools: Nursery 14; Primary 226; Secondary 33; Special 15.
Colleges: Further Education 4.
Places of interest: Glamis Castle; Arbroath Abbey (ruins); Brechin Cathedral and Round Tower; Scone Palace; Bridge of Dun (near Montrose); Guthrie Castle; Blair Castle; Edzell Castle; Pitlochry Lodder and Fish Dam.
County worthies by birth: Pontius Pilate fl AD 36 Sir William Wallace (1274–1305); Sir James Barrie (1860–1937); John Buchan 1st Baron Tweedsmuir (1875–1940); HM Queen Elizabeth the Queen Mother (1900–); HRH The Princess Margaret, Countess of Snowdon (1930–).

TYNE and WEAR

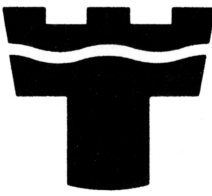

First recorded use of name and derivation: c. AD 150 Tina (river) (Ptolomy) and c. AD 720 Wirus (river) (Bede).
Population: 1 189 500.
Area: 133 390 acres *53 981 ha.*
Density: 8·92 per acre *22,04 per ha.*
Administrative HQ: Sandyford House, Newcastle-upon-Tyne.
Highest point above sea-level: Nr Chopwell 851 ft *259 m.*

Places of interest: Church of St Andrew Roker; Monkwearmouth (ruins); Tynemouth Castle.
County worthies by birth: The Venerable Bede (673–735); Admiral (1st) Lord Collingwood (1750–1810); Owen Brannigan (1908–1973).

WARWICKSHIRE

First recorded use of name and derivation: 1016 (Waerincwicsir) possibly Old English (*wering*, a weir; *wick*, cattle farm).
Area: 489 405 acres *198 055 ha.*
Population: 469 500.
Density: 0·96 per acre *2,37 per ha.*
Administrative HQ: Shire Hall, Warwick.
Highest point above sea-level: Ilmington Downs 854 ft *260 m.*

Road lengths:	miles	km
motorway	53	85
trunk	258	415
principal	300	483
classified	1169	1881
unclassified	1625	2615

Schools: Nursery 5; Primary 26; Grammar 12; High 35; Comprehensive 2; Bilateral 3; Special 24.
Colleges: Further Education 4; Agriculture 1; Education 1.
Places of interest: Coventry Cathedral; Warwick Castle; Kenilworth Castle; Stratford-upon-Avon (Shakespeare's birthplace); Compton Wyngates; Charlecote; Coughton Court; Ragley Hall; Arbury Hall.
County worthies by birth: William Shakespeare (1564–1616); Earl of Wilmington (1673–1743); Walter Landor (1775–1864); Richard Cosgrove (1818–99); Marion Evans (George Eliot) (1819–80); Rupert Brooke (1887–1915).

WEST GLAMORGAN

First recorded use of name and derivation: 1242 (Gwlad Morgan) the terrain of Morgan, a 10th century Welsh Prince.
Area: 201 476 acres *81 535 ha.*
Population: 371 400.
Density: 1·84 per acre *4,56 per ha.*
Administrative HQ: Guildhall, Swansea.
Highest point above sea-level: Cefnffordd 1969 ft *600 m.*

Road lengths:	miles	km
motorway	8	13
trunk	48	77
principal	110	177
classified	186	299
unclassified	617	993

Schools: Nursery 12; Primary 205; Comprehensive 4; Senior 6; Junior 28; Special 7.
Colleges: Further Education 3; Technology 1; Art 1; Education 1.
Places of interest: Neath Abbey (ruins); Penrice Castle.
County worthies by birth: Dylan Thomas (1914–1953).

WEST MIDLANDS

First recorded use of name and derivation: 1555 mydlande, mid lands (applied to the middle counties of England).
Area: 222 250 acres *89 941 ha.*
Population: 2 779 800.
Density: 12·51 per acre *30,91 per ha.*
Administrative HQ: County Hall, Queensway, Birmingham.

Highest point above sea-level: Turner's Hill 876 ft *267 m.*

Road lengths:	miles	km
motorway	30	*48*
trunk	60	*96*
principal	350	*563*
Class II	270	*435*
Class III	250	*402*
unclassified	2960	*4763*

Places of interest: Dudley Castle; Birmingham: Aston Hall, City Museum and Art Gallery, Museum of Science and Industry.
County worthies by birth: George Cadbury (1839–1922); Sir Henry Newbolt (1862–1938); Neville Chamberlain (1869–1940).

WEST SUSSEX

First recorded use of name and derivation: 1973, AD 722 (*Suth, Seaxe*), the territory of the southern Saxons or *suthseaxa.*
Area: 498 321 acres *201 664 ha.*
Population: 615 400.
Density: 1·23 per acre *3,05 per ha.*
Administrative HQ: County Hall, West St, Chichester.
Highest point above sea-level: Blackdown Hill 919 ft *280 m.*

Road lengths:	miles	km
trunk	45	*72*
principal	248	*399*
classified	538	*866*
unclassified	480	*772*

Schools: Nursery 4; Primary 218; Middle 14; Grammar 3; Secondary Modern 9; Special 11; Comprehensive 25.
Colleges: Further Education 3; Agriculture 1; Art 1; Education 1; Sixth Form College 1.
Places of interest: Chichester Cathedral; Arundel Castle; Goodwood House; Petworth House; Uppark.
County worthies by birth: John Selden (1584–1654); William Collins (1721–59); Percy Bysshe Shelley (1792–1822); Richard Cobden (1804–65).

WEST YORKSHIRE

First recorded use of name and derivation: *c.* AD 150 Ebórakon (Ptolemy), 1050 (Eoferwiscir), land possessed by Eburos.
Area: 503 863 acres *203 906 ha.*
Population: 2 082 200.
Density: 4·13 per acre *10,21 per ha.*
Administrative HQ: County Hall, Wakefield.
Highest point above sea-level: Black Hill 1908 ft *581 m.*

Road lengths:	miles	km
motorway	70	*113*
trunk	144	*233*
principal	459	*739*
classified	604	*973*
unclassified	3173	*5106*

Places of interest: Bronte Museum (Haworth); Kirkstall Abbey; Ilkley Moor; Temple Newsom House; Harewood House.
County worthies by birth: Sir Martin Frobisher (*c.* 1535–94); Thomas Fairfax (1612–1671); Thomas Chippendale (1718–79); Joseph Priestley (1733–1804); Charlotte Bronte (1816–55); Anne Bronte (1820–49); Emily Bronte (1818–48); Frederick Delius (1862–1934); Barbara Hepworth (1903–75); John Boynton Priestley (1894–   ); Wilfred Rhodes (1877–1973); James Harold Wilson (1916–   ).

WESTERN ISLES

Area: 716 800 acres *290 079 ha.*
Population: 31 000
Density: 0·04 per acre *0,11 per ha.*
Main town: Stornoway, Isle of Lewis.
Highest point above sea-level: Clisham, Harris 2622 ft *799 m.*
Main Islands: The largest islands in the Long Island archipelago.

	miles²	km²
Lewis with Harris	859·19	*2225*
North Uist	135·71	*351*
South Uist	128·36	*332*

Places of interest: Kisimul Castle (Isle of Barra); Kilpheder (south west); Callahish—stone circle and cairn (Isle of Lewis).
County worthies by birth: Flora Macdonald (1720–90).

WILTSHIRE

First recorded use of name and derivation: AD 878 (Wiltunschir), the shire around *Wiltun* (tun, town) on the flooding river (Wiley).
Area: 860 099 acres *348 070 ha.*
Population: 506 700.
Density: 0·59 per acre *1,46 per ha.*
Administrative HQ: County Hall, Trowbridge.
Highest point above sea-level: Milk Hill and Tan Hill 964 ft *293 m.*

Road lengths:	miles	km
motorway	29	*47*
trunk	130	*210*
principal	356	*573*
non-principal	1209	*1946*
unclassified	1109	*1785*

Schools: Primary 310; Secondary 56; Middle 1; Special 13.
Colleges: Further Education 4; Agriculture 1; Art 1.
Places of interest: Salisbury Cathedral; Longleat; Stonehenge; Avebury; Wilton House; Stourhead.
County worthies by birth: 1st Duke of Somerset (*c.* 1500–52); Edward (Hyde) 1st Earl of Clarendon (1609–74); Sir Christopher Wren (1632–1723); Joseph Addison (1672–1719); William H F Talbot (1800–77); Sir Isaac Pitman (1813–97).

HISTORY & CONSTITUTION

Britain's pre-history
British history starts with the earliest written references dating from *c.* 525 BC by Himilco of the Tunisian city of Carthage. All events prior to that belong to pre-history—a term invented by Daniel Wilson in 1851.

Pre-historic events are subject to continuous reassessment as new dating methods are advanced. Most notable among these has been radiocarbon dating invented by Dr Willard F Libby (US) in 1949. This is based upon the decay rate of the radio-active carbon isotope C14, whose half-life is 5730 years (formerly thought to be 5568 years). Other modern methods include dendrochronology calibration by study of tree-rings developed by Professor C W Ferguson since 1969 and thermoluminescence, pollen analysis and amino-acid testing.

BC	
	Beestonian glaciation, possibly equivalent to the alpine Günz glaciation.
—	Cromercan interglacial.
? 350 000–250 000	Anglian glaciation possibly contemporary with the alpine Mindel glaciation with ice sheets reaching the Thames valley. Human occupation (known as pre-Hoxnian) may have occurred during a warmer interstadial phase of this glaciation, e.g. course hand-axe culture at Fordwich, Kent (published 1968) and Kents Cavern, near Torquay, Devon (reassessed 1971).
? 250 000–200 000	Hoxnian interglacial (so named after Hoxne site, Suffolk, disc. 1797). Clactonian flake assemblages followed by Acheulian hand-axe industry, which latter yielded earliest British human remains at Swanscombe, Kent found by Marston in 1935–6. Sea level 30–35 m *98–114 ft* above present datum.
200 000–125 000	Wolstonian glaciation, probably contemporary with the alpine Riss glaciation.
125 000–70 000	Ipswichian interglacial—sea level 8 m *26 ft* above present datum.
70 000–14 000	Last or Devensian glaciation, contemporary with the alpine Würm glaciation, reaching to the latitude of York. Britain probably discontinuously unpopulated. Probably populated during the warmer Chelford interstadial of 59 000 BC and during a further interstadial of 40 000 to 36 000 BC.
26 770 ± 450	Earliest upper palaeolithic radio-carbon dating from Kent's Cavern.
18 000–14 000	Maximum extension of ice-sheets. Sea-level fall of 100–150 m *328–492 ft.*
10 500–8000	Mesolithic Creswellian period and the close of the late Upper Paleolithic era.
c. 9050	Irish Sea land-bridge breached.
8400	Start of the present Flandrian post-glacial period. Earliest (Maglemosian) to latest (Lussa, Jura) datings of Mesolithic finds. Mesolithic man may have had herds by 4300 BC.
c. 6850	The North Sea land bridge between East Yorkshire and the Netherlands breached by the rising sea-level.
c. 6450	The English Channel attained its current width under the impact of the Flandrian transgression.
6100	Earliest dated habitation in Scotland, microlithic industry at Morton in Fife.
4580	Earliest dated habitation in Ireland—neolithic site at Ballynagilly, Tyrone two centuries earlier than England's earliest neolithic sites at Broome Heath, Norfolk; Findon, Sussex and Lambourn, Berkshire.
4210–3990	Earliest dated British farming site at Hemberg, Devon (first excavated 1934–5).
3795	Earliest dated pottery at Ballynagilly (see above).
3650–3400	Dating of Avebury Stone Circle building, Wiltshire.
2930–2560	Dating of giant Silbery Hill round barrow, Wiltshire.

2940–2590	Dating of Phase I at Stonehenge.
2760	Earliest Bronze Age dating with Beaker pottery from Ballynagilly (see above) four centuries before earliest English datings at Chippenham, Cambridge and Mildenhall, Suffolk.
1260	Earliest dated hill-fort, Ivinghoe, Buckinghamshire.
c. 750	Introduction of iron into Britain from Hallstatt by the Celts. Hill-forts proliferate.
c. 308	First circumnavigation of Great Britain by Pytheas, the Greek sea-captain from Massilia (Marseille).
c. 125	Introduction of Gallo-Belgic gold coinage via Kent from the Beauvais region of France.
c. 90	Earliest British coinage—Westerham gold staters so named after the hoard find in Kent in 1927.
55 (26 Aug.)	Julius Caesar's exploratory expedition with 7th and 10th legions and 98 ships from Boulogne and Ambleteuse.
54 (18 or 21 July)	Second Julian invasion with five legions and 2000 cavalry.
AD 43	Claudian invasion and the start of the Roman Occupation.

Roman era (55 BC–AD 410)

Caesar arrived off Dover from Boulogne with 98 transports and two legions in the early hours of 26 Aug. 55 BC. He landed against beach opposition between Deal and Walmer. Repeated skirmishing prevented the reconnaisance being a success and Caesar withdrew. He returned in 54 BC (variously on 18 or 21 July) with five legions and 800 vessels, and encamped on the Kentish shore and crossed the Thames near Brentford. He was much harried by the British leader, Cassivellaunus, based on the old Belgic capital of St Albans (*Verulamium*). The occupation was not sustained.

It was nearly a century later in AD 43 when the third Roman landing was made with some 20 000 men in three waves under the command of Plautius. This invasion is referred to as the Claudian Invasion, after the Roman emperor of that time. The British leader, Cunobelinus, was aged but resistance remained bitter. Roman cruelties against the king of the Iceni tribe and his family in East Anglia fired a native 'death or liberty' revolt under his widow, Queen Bodicca (Boadicea) in AD 61. Colchester (*Camulodunum*), London (*Londinium*) and St Albans were in turn sacked. The total death roll was put at 70 000 by Tacitus. Boadicea's horde of some 80 000 was met by Suetonius' 14th and 20th Legions of 10 000 men on a battlefield perhaps near Hampstead Heath, North London. For the loss of only about 400 of the fully-armed Romans, 70 000 Britons were claimed to have been killed. Subjugation, however, was not achieved until AD 83, when Agricola, the Roman Governor, won the Battle of Mons Graupius, suggested by some to be the Pass of Killiecrankie, Tayside.

For nearly 300 years the Roman régime brought law, order, peace, food, and even unknown warmth and cleanliness for the few who aspired to villas. The legions recruited locally to maintain 40 000 troops, garrisoned at Chester, Caerleon-on-Usk, York, and Hadrian's Wall. Hadrian arrived in Britain in 122 after the annihilation of the 9th Legion by the Picts. The 74½-mile-long *120 km* wall across the Tyne–Solway isthmus was built between AD 122 and 129. The 37-mile-long *59,5 km* Forth–Clyde or Antonine Wall was built c. 150, but was abandoned within 40 years. Emperor Severus re-established military order in the period 208–11, but by the time of Carasius, who ruled in 287–93, raids by the Saxons (*Seax*, short, one-handed sword) from the Schleswig–Holstein area were becoming increasingly troublesome. Demands were made by the Saxons, Scots and Picts that Emperor Valentinian sent his General Theodosius in 367 to restore order in the Province. In 400 Theodosius in turn sent his general, Stilicho, to deliver the Province from the ever-increasing pressure of the barbarians, but by 402 he was forced to recall the Roman garrison to help resist the incursions in Northern Italy of the Visigoths under Alaric. In 405 there was mutiny in the remaining garrison in Britain, who elected Gratinius, a Briton, as rival emperor in 410. Emperor Honorius told the Britons from Rome that they must 'defend themselves' against the Saxons, Picts, and Scots. By 449 a Jutish Kingdom had been set up in Kent by Hengist and Horsa. The 5th and 6th centuries were a period of utter confusion and misery with conflict between the English and the remaining Britons, whose last champion was reputedly King Arthur. Some time between 493 and 503 Arthur fought the Battle of Mountbadon on an uncertain site, now ascribed to Liddington Camp, Badbury, near Swindon, Wiltshire.

British rulers between the end of the Roman occupation (AD 410) and the Norman conquest (1066)

England (excluding Cumbria) did not again become a unified state before AD 954. Some earlier kings exercised direct rule over all England for intermittent periods during their reigns. Edward the Elder (899–924 or 925), son of Alfred (871–99) the most famous of the Kings of the West Saxons, had suzerainty over the whole of England though he did not directly rule the Danish kingdom of York, which was not finally extinguished until 954.

The following nine kingdoms existed in England before it became a unified kingdom. All existed contemporaneously during the first half of the 7th century (c. AD 604 to 654), but became absorbed in each other until the Kings of Wessex established overall authority.

1. Kings of Kent	c. 455 to 825, conquered by West Saxons.
2. Kings of the South Saxons	477–c. 786, absorbed by Wessex.
3. Kings of West Saxons	519–954, established authority over all England.
4. Kings of Bernicia	547–670, annexed by Northumbria.
5. Kings of Northumbria	c. 588–?878, reduced by the Danish Kingdom of York.
6. Kings of Mercia	c. 595–*ante* 883, first acknowledged overlordship of West Saxons 829.
7. Kings of Deira	599 or 560 to 654, annexed by Bernicia.
8. Kings of the East Angles	c. 600–870, conquest by Danes.
9. Kings of the East Saxons	*ante* 604–825, submitted to West Saxons.
Danish Kingdom of York	875 or 876–954, expulsion by Eldred, the King of West Saxons.

The West Saxon King Egbert (802–39), grandfather of King Alfred, is often quoted as the first King of All England from AD 829, but in fact he never reduced the Kingdom of Northumbria ruled by Eanred (808 or 810 to 840 or 841).

Kings of All England

Athelstan, eldest son of the eldest son of King Alfred of the West Saxons, acceded 924 or 925. The first to establish rule over all England (excluding Cumbria) in 927. d. 27 Oct. 939 aged over 40 years.

Edmund, younger half-brother of Athelstan; acceded 939 but did not regain control of all England until 944–45. Murdered, 26 May 946 by Leofa at Pucklechurch, Gloucestershire.

Edred, younger brother of Edmund; acceded May 946. Effectively King of All England 946–48, and from 954 to his death, on 23 Nov. 955. Also intermittently during the intervening period.

Edwy, son of Edmund, b. c. 941; acceded November 955 (crowned at Kingston, Surrey); lost control of Mercians and Northumbrians in 957. d. 1 Oct. 959 aged about 18.

Edgar, son of Edmund, b. 943; acceded October 959 as King of All England (crowned at Bath, 11 May 973). d. 8 July 975, aged c. 32.

Edward the Martyr, son of Edgar by Aethelflaed, b. c. 962; acceded 975. d. 18 Mar. 978 or 979, aged 16 or 17.

Ethelred (Unraed, i.e. ill-counselled), second son of Edgar by Aelfthryth, b. ?968–69; acceded 978 or 979 (crowned at Kingston, 14 Apr. 978 or 4 May 979); dispossessed by the Danish king, Swegn Forkbeard, 1013–14. d. 23 Apr. 1016, aged c. 47 or 48.

Swegn Forkbeard, King of Denmark 987–1014, acknowleged King of All England from about September 1013 to his death, 3 Feb. 1014.

Edmund Ironside, prob. 3rd son of Ethelred, b. c. 992; chosen King in London, April 1016. In summer of 1016 made agreement with Cnut whereby he retained dominion only over Wessex. d. 30 Nov. 1016.

Cnut, younger son of King Swegn Forkbeard of Denmark, b. c. 995. Secured Mercia and Danelaw, summer 1016; assumed dominion over all England December 1016; King of Denmark 1019–35; King of Norway 1028–1035; overlord of the King of the Scots and probably ruler of the Norse–Irish kingdom of Dublin. d. 12 Nov. 1035, aged c. 40 years.

Harold Harefoot, natural son of Cnut by Aelfgifu of Northampton, b. ?c. 1016–17; chosen regent for half-brother, Harthacnut, late 1035 or early 1036; sole King 1037. d. 17 Mar. 1040, aged c. 23 or 24 years.

Harthacnut, son of Cnut by Emma, widow of King Ethelred (d. 1016), b. ?c. 1018; titular King of Denmark from 1028; effectively King of England from June 1040. d. 8 June 1042, aged *c.* 24 years.

Edward the Confessor, senior half-brother of Harthacnut and son of King Ethelred and Emma, b. 1002–05; resided with Harthacnut from 1041, acceded 1042 crowned 3 Apr. 1043. d. 5 Jan. 1066, aged between 60 and 64. Sanctified.

Harold Godwinson, brother-in-law of Edward the Confessor and brother of his Queen Edith, son of Godwin, Earl of Wessex, b. ?*c.* 1020; acceded 6 Jan. 1066, d. or k. 14 Oct. 1066.

Edgar Etheling, chosen by Londoners as king after the Battle of Hastings, Oct. 1066; not apparently crowned, submitted to William I before 25 Dec. 1066; believed still livng *c.* 1125.

Rulers in Wales (844–1289)
Province of Gwynedd (North Wales) (844–1283), last prince executed for treason by Edward I.

Province of Deheubarth (South Central and South West Wales) (844–1231), last of line imprisoned in Norwich.

Province of Powys (North Central Wales) (1063–1160), split into Southern and Northern Powys.

Southern Powys (1160–1277), dispossessed.

Northern Powys (1160–*ante* 1289), became marcher lordship.

Kings of Scotland (1005–1603)
The chronology of the early kings of Alba (north of the Clyde and the Forth) before the 10th century is highly obscure.

Malcolm II (1005–34), b. *c.* 954. d. 25 Nov. 1034, aged *c.* 80 years. Formed the Kingdom of Scotland by annexing Strathclyde, *c.* 1016.

Duncan I (1034–40), son of Malcolm II's daughter, Bethoc.

Macbeth (1040–57), ?son of Malcolm II's daughter, Donada. d. aged *c.* 52 years.

Lulach (1057–8), stepson of Macbeth and son of his wife Gruoch. d. aged *c.* 26.

Malcolm III (Canmore) (1058–93), son of Duncan I. d. aged *c.* 62.

Donald Bane (1093–94 and 1094–97), son of Duncan I, twice deposed.

Duncan II (May to October 1904), son of Malcolm III. d. aged *c.* 34.

Edgar (1097–1107), son of Malcolm III, half-brother of Duncan II. d. aged *c.* 33.

Alexander I (1107–24), son of Malcolm III, brother of Edgar. d. aged *c.* 62.

David I (1124–53), son of Malcolm III and brother of Edgar. d. aged *c.* 68.

Malcolm IV (1153–65), son of Henry, Earl of Northumberland. d. aged *c.* 24.

William I (*The Lion*) (1165–1214), brother of Malcolm IV. d. aged *c.* 72 (from 1174 to 1189 King of England acknowledged as overlord of Scotland).

Alexander II (1214–49), son of William I. d. aged 48.

Alexander III (1249–1286), son of Alexander II. d. aged 44.

Margaret (*Maid of Norway*) (1286–90), daughter of Margaret, daughter of Alexander III by King Eric II of Norway. Never visited her realm. d. aged 7.

First Interregnum 1290–92.

John (*Balliol*) (1292–96), son of Dervorguilla, a great-great-granddaughter of David I, awarded throne from 13 contestants by adjudication of Edward I who declared after four years that John would have to forfeit his throne for contumacy.

Second Interregnum 1296–1306.

Robert I (1306–29), son of Robert Bruce and grandson of a 1291 competitor. d. aged *c.* 55.

David II (1329–71), son of Robert I. d. aged 46.

Note: Edward Balliol, son of John, was crowned King in 1332, acknowledged Edward III of England as overlord in 1333 and surrendered all claims to Scottish crown to him in 1356.

Robert II (1371–90), founder of the Stewart dynasty, son of Walter the Steward and Marjorie Bruce. d. aged 74.

Robert III (1390–1406), legitimated natural son of Robert II. d. aged *c.* 69.

James I (1406–37), son of Robert III, captured by English 13 days before accession and kept prisoner in England till March 1424. d. aged 42.

James II (1437–60), son of James I. d. aged 29.

James III (1466–88), son of James II. d. aged 36.

James IV (1488–1513), son of James III and Margaret of Denmark, married Margaret Tudor. d. aged 40.

James V (1513–42), son of James IV and Margaret Tudor. d. aged 30.

Mary (*Queen of Scots*) (1542–67), daughter of James V and Mary of Lorraine, acceded aged 6 or 7 days, abdicated 24 July 1567 and was succeeded by her son (James IV) by her second husband, Henry Stuart, Lord Darnley. She was executed, 8 Feb. 1587, aged 44.

James VI (1567–1625), son of Mary and Lord Darnley (see above), succeeded to the English throne as James I on 24 Mar. 1603, so effecting a personal union of the two realms. d. aged 58.

The eleven royal houses of England since 1066
A royal dynasty normally takes its house name from the family's patronymic. It does not change by reason of a Queen Regnant's marriage—for example, Queen Victoria, a member of the House of Hanover and Brunswick, did not become a member of the House of Saxe-Coburg and Gotha (her husband's family) but her son, Edward VII, and her grandson, George V (until 1917), were members of the house of their respective fathers.

The House of Normandy (by right of conquest) (69 years)
The house name derives from the fact that William I was the 7th Duke of Normandy with the style William II. This was despite the fact that he was illegitimate because his father, Duke Robert II, had him formally instituted as his legal heir.

William I (1066–87); William II (1087–1100); Henry I (1100–35).

The House of Blois (19 years)
The house name derives from the fact that the father of King Stephen was Stephen (sometimes called Henry), Count of Blois.

Stephen (1135–54).

The House of Anjou (331 years)
The house name derives from the fact that the father of King Henry II was Geoffrey V, 10th Count of Anjou and Maine. This family was alternatively referred to as the Angevins, the name deriving from Angers, the town and diocese within the boundaries of Anjou.

Henry II (1154–87) and the next thirteen kings down to and including Richard III (1483–5).

Note: (1) This house, but only since the mid-15th century, and in fact less than 50 years before its male line became extinct, has been referred to as THE HOUSE OF PLANTAGENET. This name originated from Count Geoffrey's nickname 'Plantagenet', which in turn derived, it is said, from his habit of wearing a sprig of broom (*Planta genista*) in his cap during a crusade.

(2) The House of Anjou (or Plantagenet) may be sub-divided after the deposing of

Richard II in 1399 into THE HOUSE OF LANCASTER with Henry IV (1399–1413); Henry V (1413–22); Henry VI (1422–61 and 1470–1) and THE HOUSE OF YORK with Edward IV (1461–83—except 1470–1); Edward V (1483); Richard III (1483–5).

(3) The names Lancaster and York derived respectively from the titles of the 4th and 5th sons of Edward III; John of Gaunt (1340–99) was 1st Duke of Lancaster (of the second creation), and the father of Henry IV; and Edmund of Langley (1341–1402) was 1st Duke of York and a great-grandfather of Edward IV.

The House of Tudor (118 years)
This house name derives from the surname of Henry VII's father, Edmund Tudor, Earl of Richmond, and son of Sir Owen Tudor, by Catherine, widow of King Henry V.

Henry VII (1485–1509); Henry VIII (1509–47); Edward VI (1547–53); after the reign of Queen Jane, Mary I (1553–8); Elizabeth I (1558–1603).

The House of Grey (14 days)
This house name derives from the family and surname of the 3rd Marquess of Dorset, the father of Lady Guil(d)ford Dudley, who reigned as Queen Jane from 6 July, 1553 for 14 days until 19 July when the House of Tudor regained the throne.

The House of Stuart and the House of Stuart and Orange (98 years and 5 years)
This house name is derived from the family and surname of Henry Stuart, Lord Darnley and Duke of Albany, the eldest son of Matthew, 4th Earl of Lennox. Lord Darnley was the second of the three husbands and cousin of Mary Queen of Scots and the father of James VI of Scotland and I of England.

James I (1603–25); Charles I (1625–49); Charles II (*de jure* 1649 but *de facto* 1660–85); James II (1685–8).

The house name became THE HOUSE OF STUART AND ORANGE when in 1689 William III, son of William II, Prince of Orange, became the sovereign conjointly with his wife, Mary II, the 5th Stuart monarch.

The House of Stuart resumed from 1702 to 1714 during the reign of Queen Anne.

The House of Orange
William III reigned alone during his widowerhood from 1694 to 1702. William in fact possessed the sole regal power during his entire reign from 1689.

The House of Hanover and Brunswick-Lüneberg (187 years)
This house name derives from the fact that George I's father, Ernest Augustus, was the Elector of Hanover and a duke of the House of Brunswick-Lüneberg.

George I (1714–27); George II (1727–60); George III (1760–1820); George IV (1820–1830); William IV (1830–7); Queen Victoria (1837–1901).

The House of Saxe-Coburg and Gotha (16 years)
This house name derives from the princely title of Queen Victoria's husband, Prince Albert, later Prince Consort.

Edward VII (1901–10); George V (1910–1917); on 17 July 1917 King George V declared by Royal Proclamation that he had changed the name of the royal house to the House of Windsor.

The House of Windsor (59 years to date)
George V (1917–36); Edward VIII (1936); George VI (1936–52); Elizabeth II (from 1952).

In the normal course of events Prince Charles, Prince of Wales, on inheriting the throne would become the first monarch of the House of Mountbatten but by further Proclamations the Queen first declared in 1952 that her children and descendants will belong to the House of Windsor, and later in 1960 that this Declaration would only affect her descendants in the male line who will bear a royal style and title. Descendants outside this class will bear the surname 'Mountbatten-Windsor'.

Titles of the Royal House
Husbands of Queens Regnant
The husband of a queen regnant derives no title from his marriage. Philip II of Spain, husband of Queen Mary I, was termed 'King Consort'. Prince George of Denmark, husband of Queen Anne, was created Duke of Cumberland. Prince Albert of Saxe-Coburg-Gotha was created 'Royal Highness' and seventeen years after his marriage 'Prince Consort'. The Duke of Edinburgh, husband of Queen Elizabeth II, is HRH and a prince of the United Kingdom of Great Britain and Northern Ireland.

Queens Consort
A queen consort ranks with and shares the king's titles. In the event of her being widowed she cannot continue to use the title 'The Queen'. She must add to it her christian name or use the style additionally, or by itself, of 'Queen Mother' (if she has children), or, as in the case of the widow of King William IV, 'Queen Dowager'.

In the event of her re-marriage, which can only be with the consent of the Sovereign, she does not forfeit her royal status. The last such example was when Queen Catherine (Parr) married, as her fourth husband, Lord Seymour of Sudeley, KG, in 1547.

The Heir to the Throne
The Heir Apparent to the throne can only be the son or grandson (as in the case of the Prince of Wales from 1751 to 1760) of the reigning Sovereign. Should the first person in the order of succession bear any relationship other than in the direct male line, they are the Heir (or Heiress) Presumptive. The last Heiress Presumptive to the Throne was HRH The Princess Elizabeth (1936–52). A female could be an Heiress Apparent if she were the only or eldest daughter of a deceased Heir Apparent who had no male issue.

The eldest surviving son of a reigning Sovereign is born The Duke of Cornwall, The Duke of Rothesay, The Earl of Carrick and The Baron Renfrew, together with the styles of Lord of the Isles, Prince and Great Steward (or Seneschel) of Scotland. The titles Prince of Wales and Earl of Chester are a matter of creation and not of birthright. The Prince of Wales is a part of the establishment of The Order of the Garter. If, however, a Prince of Wales died, as in 1751, his eldest son would automatically succeed to that title and the Earldom of Chester but not to the Dukedom of Cornwall and the other honours because they are expressly reserved for the son (and not the grandson) of a Sovereign.

Princes, Princesses and Royal Highnesses
Since 1917 the style HRH Prince or Princess has been limited to the children of the Monarch and the children of the sons of the Monarch and their wives. Grand-children of a Prince of Wales also would enjoy this style. In practice the sons of a Sovereign have a dukedom bestowed upon them after they become of age. Such 'Royal Dukedoms' only enjoy their special precedence (i.e. senior to the two Archbishops and other dukes) for the next generation. A third duke would take his seniority among the non-royal dukes accord-

ing to the date of the original creation.

The title 'Princess Royal' is conferred (if vacant) for life on the eldest daughter of the Sovereign.

The order of Succession to the Crown
The order of succession is determined according to ancient Common Law rules but these may be upset by an enactment of the Crown in Parliament under powers taken in the Succession to the Crown Act of 1707, provided always (since 1931) that the parliaments of all the Members of the Commonwealth assent. At Common Law the Crown descends lineally to the legitimate issue of the sovereign, males being preferred to females, in their respective orders of age. In the event of failure of such issue (e.g. King Edward VIII in 1936) the Crown passes to the nearest collateral being an heir at law. The common law of descent of the Crown specifically departs from the normal feudal rules of land descent at two points. First, in the event of two or more sisters being next in succession the eldest alone (e.g. the Princess Elizabeth from 1936 to 1952) shall be the heiress and shall not be merely a coparcener with her sister or sisters. Secondly, male issue by a second or subsequent marriage takes precedence over half sisters (e.g. King Edward VI, son of King Henry VIII's third wife, took precedence over Queen Mary I, daughter of his first marriage, and Queen Elizabeth I, daughter of his second marriage).

Below is set out the Order of Succession to the Crown.
1. The heir apparent is HRH The Prince CHARLES Philip Arthur George, KG, The Prince of Wales, The Duke of Cornwall, The Duke of Rothesay, The Earl of Carrick, and the Baron Renfrew, Lord of the Isles and Great Steward of Scotland, born 14 Nov. 1948, then follows his brother:
2. HRH The Prince ANDREW Albert Christian Edward, born 19 Feb. 1960, then his brother:
3. HRH The Prince EDWARD Antony Richard Louis, born 10 Mar. 1964, then his sister:
4. HRH The Princess ANNE Elizabeth Alice Louise, born 15 Aug. 1950, then her aunt:
5. HRH The Princess MARGARET Rose, CI, GCVO, The Countess of Snowdon, born 21 Aug. 1930, then her son:
6. DAVID Albert Charles Armstrong-Jones, commonly called Viscount Linley, born 3 Nov. 1961, then his sister:
7. The Lady SARAH Frances Elizabeth Armstrong-Jones, born 1 May 1964, then her cousin, once removed:
8. HRH Prince RICHARD Alexander Walter George, Duke of Gloucester, born 26 Aug. 1944, then his son:
9. Lord Alexander Patrick George Richard, Earl of Ulster, born 24 Oct. 1974, then his cousin, once removed:
10. HRH Prince EDWARD George Nicholas Paul Patrick, GCVO, the (2nd) Duke of Kent, the Earl of St Andrews and the Baron Downpatrick, born 9 Oct. 1935, then his son:
11. Lord GEORGE Philip Nicholas WINDSOR, commonly called Earl of St Andrews, born 26 June 1962, then his brother:
12. Lord Nicholas Charles Edward Jonathan Windsor, b. 25 July 1970, then his sister:
13. The Lady HELEN Marian Lucy WINDSOR, born 28 Apr. 1964, then her cousin:
14. HRH Prince MICHAEL George Charles Franklin of Kent, born 4 July 1942, then his sister:
15. HRH Princess ALEXANDRA Helen

Elizabeth Olga Christabel of Kent, GCVO, the Hon Mrs Angus J B Ogilvy, born 25 Dec. 1936, then her son:
16. JAMES Robert Bruce Ogilvy, Esq, born 29 Feb. 1964, then his sister:
17. Miss Marina Victoria Alexandra, born 31 July 1966 then her second cousin, once removed upwards:
18. The Rt Hon GEORGE Henry Hubert Lascelles, the (7th) Earl of Harewood, the Viscount Lascelles, the Baron Harewood, born 7 Feb. 1923, then his son:
19. The Hon DAVID Henry George Lascelles, commonly called Viscount Lascelles, born 21 Oct. 1950, then his brother:
20. The Hon JAMES Edward Lascelles, born 5 Oct. 1953, then his brother:
21. The Hon ROBERT Jeremy Hugh Lascelles, born 14 Feb. 1955, then his uncle:
22. The Hon GERALD David Lascelles, born 21 Aug. 1924, then his son:
23. HENRY Ulick Lascelles, Esq, born 19 May 1953, then his third cousin once removed upwards:
24. The Most Noble JAMES George Alexander Bannerman Carnegie, the (3rd) Duke of Fife, and the Earl of Macduff, born 23 Sept. 1929, then his son:
25. DAVID Charles Carnegie, commonly called Earl of Macduff, born 3 Mar. 1961, then his sister:
26. The Lady ALEXANDRA Clare Carnegie, born 20 Jun. 1959, then her third cousin twice removed upwards:
27. HM King OLAV V of Norway (Alexander Edward Christian Frederik), KG, KT, GCB, GCVO, born 2 July 1903, then his son:
28. HRH the Crown Prince HARALD, GCVO, born 21 Feb. 1937, then his son:
29. HRH Prince HAAKON Magnus, born 20 July 1973 then his sister:
30. HRH Princess MARTHA Louise, born 22 Sept. 1971 then her aunt:
31. HRH the Princess RAGNHILD Alexandra, Fru. Erling S Lorentzen, born 9 June 1930, then her son:
32. Hr HAAKON Lorentzen, born 23 Aug. 1954, then his sister:
33. Frk INGEBORG Lorentzen, born 27 Feb. 1957, then her aunt:
34. HRH the Princess ASTRID Maud Ingeborg, Fru Johan M Ferner, born 12 Feb. 1932, then her son:
35. Hr Alexander Ferner, born 15 Mar. 1965, then his sister:
36. Frk CATHRINE Ferner, born 22 July 1962, then her sister:
37. Frk BENEDIKTE Ferner, born 28 Sept. 1963.

This exhausts the line of Queen Victoria's eldest son (Edward VII) and it is then necessary to move to such issue of the late Queen Marie of Rumania, CI, RRC, eldest daughter of her second son, HRH the Duke of Edinburgh, KG, KT, KP, GCB, GCSI, GCMG, GCIE, GCVO, as may not be Roman Catholics nor are, nor have been married to Roman Catholics.

Factors affecting the order
Two further factors should be borne in mind in determining the order of succession. First, no person may unilaterally renounce their right to succeed. Only an Act of Parliament can undo what another Act of Parliament (the Act of Settlement, 1701) has done. Secondly, some marriages among the descendants of George II are null and void and hence the descendants are not heirs at law, by failure to obtain the consent to marry as required by the Royal Marriage Act of 1772. In some cases this failure, prior to 1956, may have been in-

advertent because it was only then confirmed by the House of Lords that every such descendant, born before 1948, is by a statute of 1705 deemed a British subject. So the escape from the requirements of the Royal Marriage Act accorded to all female descendants of George II who apparently married into *foreign* families is not so readily available as was once thought.

The Act of Settlement
On 6 Feb. 1701 the Act of Settlement came into force. It laid down that failing issue from HRH The Princess (later Queen Anne) George (of Denmark) and/or secondly from any subsequent marriage by her first cousin and brother-in-law, the widower King William III, the crown would vest in Princess Sophia, Dowager Electress of Hanover (1630–1714), the granddaughter of King James I, and the heirs of her body with the proviso that all Roman Catholics, or persons marrying Roman Catholics, were for ever to be excluded, as if they 'were naturally dead'.

The Duke of Windsor
The only subsequent change in statute law was on 11 Dec. 1936 by His Majesty's Declaration of Abdication Act, 1936, by which the late HRH The Prince Edward, MC (later HRH The Duke of Windsor), and any issue he might subsequently have had were expressly excluded from the succession.

Conditions of tenure
On succeeding to the Crown the Sovereign must (1) join in Communion with the established Church of England; (2) declare that he or she is a Protestant; (3) swear the oaths for the preservation of both the Established Church of England and the Presbyterian Church of Scotland, and (4), and most importantly, take the coronation oath, which may be said to form the basis of the contract between Sovereign and subject, last considered to have been broken, on the Royal side, by King James II in 1688.

'The King never dies'
The Sovereign can never be legally a minor, but in fact a regency is provided until he or she attains the age of 18.

There is never an interregnum on the death of a Sovereign. In pursuance of the common law maxim 'the King never dies' the new Sovereign succeeds to full prerogative rights instantly on the death of the predecessor.

Notes on the British peerage
There are five ranks in the British temporal peerage—in ascending order they are: 1. Barons or Baronesses; 2. Viscounts or Viscountesses; 3. Earls or Countesses; 4. Marquesses or Marchionesses (or less favoured, Marquises); 5. Dukes or Duchesses.

The British spiritual peerage is of two ranks, Archbishops (of Canterbury and of York) who rank between Royal Dukes and dukes, and twenty-four of the bishops (but always including the Bishops of London, Durham, and Winchester with the Bishop of Sodor and Man always excluded), based on their seniority, who rank between Viscounts and Barons.

A few women hold peerages in their own right and since The Peerage Act, 1963, have become peers of Parliament. The remaining category of membership of the House of Lords is life peers. These are of two sorts: (a) The Lords of Appeal in Ordinary, who are appointed by virtue of the Appellate Jurisdiction Act, 1876. Their number has been increased from the original four to six in 1913, to seven in 1929 and to nine since

1947; (b) by virtue of The Life Peerages Act, 1958, both men and women may be appointed for life membership of the House of Lords. Such creations so far have been confined to the fifth and junior temporal rank of baron or baroness.

1. Peerages of England, i.e. those created prior to the union with Scotland on 1 May 1707.
2. Peerages of Scotland, i.e. those created before the union with England.
3. Peerages of Ireland (the last creation was in 1898 and no further ones are at present likely).
4. Peerages of Great Britain, i.e. those created between the union with Scotland (1707) and the union with Ireland (2 July 1800).
5. Peerages of the United Kingdom of Great Britain and (Northern) Ireland, i.e. those created since 2 July 1800.

All holders of peerages of England, Great Britain and the United Kingdom and (only since The Peerage Act, 1963) also of Scotland, are also peers of Parliament provided they are over 21 and are not unpardoned major felons, bankrupts, lunatics or of alien nationality. Peers who are civil servants may sit but neither speak nor vote.

The single exception to the rule concerning minors is that the Duke of Cornwall (HRH The Prince of Wales) has been technically entitled to a seat from the moment of his mother's accession, when he was only three years of age.

The peers (and peeresses in their own right) of Ireland are not peers of Parliament but they are entitled to stand for election to the House of Commons for any seat in the United Kingdom. The previous system by which this category of peer could elect 28 of its number to sit in the House of Lords has now fallen into disuse because since the Partition of Ireland in 1922 there has been no machinery available to carry out that election and all the representative peers elected prior to that date have since died.

Only the holder of a substantive peerage can be described as noble. In the eyes of the law the holder of a courtesy title is a commoner. For example, the Duke of Marlborough's son is known by courtesy as Marquess of Blandford. Note the omission of the definite article 'the'. The reason is that the Duke of Marlborough is also *the* Marquess of Blandford and his secondary peerage style is merely lent to this son.

The use of 'of' in Peerage Titles
All dukes are The Duke *of* Somewhere. All marquesses except three (the Lords Camden, Conyngham, Townshend) are also 'of'. Most, but by no means all, earls are Earls of Somewhere. No Viscount or Baron is 'Viscount of' or 'Lord of'.

A number of peers, however, attach a territorial designation 'of Somewhere' at the end of their title. For example, The Lord Balfour of Burleigh or The Lord Brabazon of Tara. But this practice should never be used unless the peer, in his patent creating the peerage, has this territorial designation repeated. For example, 'The Baron Nonesuch of Xtown' is correctly called The Lord Nonesuch. If, however, he is to be known as the Lord Nonesuch of Xtown, then his peerage patent must clearly set out that he is 'The Baron Nonesuch of Xtown, of Xtown', i.e. the designation is repeated.

The Signature of Peers
A peer's signature, whether on a formal or informal document, is simply his title without any qualification of rank or the use of a christian name. This also applies to peeresses in their own right. Members of the Royal Family who hold peerages, however, sign with their principal Christian name.

The Descent of Peerages
Usually a peerage descends in the male line. Illegitimate offspring are, of course, excluded. If the direct male line fails, then the succession may go back to the male line in an earlier cadet branch of the family. The ancient category of English baronies by writ provides its own rules of descent. These peerages date back to the time when the original holder was deemed to be a peer solely by virtue of receiving a Writ of Summons to attend Parliament. The invariable practice since those days has been to grant a peerage specifically by Letters Patent.

Abeyant Peerages
The ancient baronies of England are heritable and through females as well as males. So when two or more female heirs inherit as co-parceners the law will not distinguish between them, so the peerage 'falls into abeyance'. In such cases the peerage goes, as it were, into cold storage until either the claim concentrates in a single surviving heiress (and this may take several generations) or the Crown accelerates the process by vesting the peerage in one of the co-heirs.

Scottish Law
In Scottish peerage law an elder or eldest daughter or other family heir can succeed in her own right unless the descent is specifically restricted to male heirs.

Special Remainders
The Crown has power to create what are termed 'special remainders' so that a peerage can, for example, pass to an elder brother or some other relative. An example is that the earldom of Mountbatten of Burma can pass to the present earl's elder daughter and her male issue.

The Extinction of a Peerage
From 1707, when Scottish peerages ceased, every peerage was, until The Peerage Act, 1963, deemed inalienable. Prior to this Act the only means of extinction was for the holder to die without an heir, to be attainted or, in the one special case, to succeed to the Crown. Any hereditary peerage, except Irish peerages, can now be the subject of an irrevocable disclaimer for life within twelve months of succession or, in the case of a minor, within twelve months of his or her twenty-first birthday. This time limit is reduced to one month for such persons who are either Members of Parliament or successful parliamentary candidates. Provided his father has two or more peerages, an heir apparent to a peerage may be 'called up' to the House of Lords by the Crown during his father's lifetime. This practice of acceleration is expressly forbidden under the 1963 Act in the case of the father's having disclaimed his title.

A few peerages were suspended under the Titles Deprivation Act, 1917.

Dormant Peerages
A peerage is deemed dormant when there is no discoverable heir but there is a reasonable presumption that there may be an heir if he or she could be found. The Crown will not permit the use of a name of a peerage for a subsequent creation unless there is absolute certainty that the former creation is truly extinguished.

Life Peers
The Crown in the past used on occasions to grant life peerages, both to men and women. The Wensleydale peerage case of 1856 acknowledged the Crown's right to do this but denied the consequent right of a seat in the House of Lords to such a peer. The two

current categories of life peers are treated above. It should be noted that there is no provision for these non-hereditary peers or peeresses to disclaim their peerages.

Widows of Peers
The only correct style for the widow of a peer is 'The Dowager' prefixed to her peerage title of duchess, marchioness, countess, viscountess, or lady (*note:* 'baroness' is only normally used by a peeress in her own right). But in fact most widowed peeresses dislike this title because of its association with advanced age, so they prefix their Christian name to their title. In the event of a widow remarrying, she should forfeit her previous title but some, quite unjustifiably, retain it.

The Effect of Divorce
Some peeresses who divorce their husbands or have been divorced by them continue to bear their former husband's style though in strict English law they are probably no longer peeresses. If a new wife appears they adopt the practice of most widows and prefix their christian name to their title. With Scottish peerages, however, the position of a divorced peeress is exactly the same as if her husband were dead and hence she takes her legal rights as a widow.

Courtesy Titles
According to the preamble of The Peerage Act, 1963, 'Courtesy titles are, by definition, not matters of law'. They are governed by custom and fall into two categories—those borne by all the children of a peer and those reserved for the heir. The children (except the eldest son) of a duke or marquess take the title 'Lord' or 'Lady' before their christian name and the family name (e.g. Lord Charles Cavendish). The same applies to the daughters of an earl but not, oddly enough, to the younger sons who take the style 'Honourable' which is borne by *all* the children of a viscount, a baron and a temporal life peer. When male holders of this title marry, their wives also become 'The Honourable'. The heir to a dukedom is given the courtesy style 'Marquis', provided, of course, his father has a marquessate, which failing he takes the title 'Earl' but enjoys the precedence of a duke's eldest son. Likewise, the heir to a marquessate takes the courtesy style of 'Earl' (if available) and similarly the heir of an earldom takes the title of his father's viscountcy (if any) or barony.

In the Scottish peerage the term 'Master of' is used by the male heir to many peerages as of right. If he is married, his wife is styled 'The Hon Mrs'.

Courtesy titles in the second generation extend only to the grandchildren who are the children of an elder son.

The Prefix 'Lady'
This title causes more confusion than any other, simply because of the wide range of its use. It can be used as a less formal alternative by marchionesses, countesses, viscountesses and the wives of barons. It is never used by duchesses. It is used, but only with the addition of their christian names, by the daughters of dukes, marquesses and earls. It is also used by the wives of the younger sons of dukes and marquesses, e.g. Lady Charles Cavendish. It is used, but never with the definite article, by the wives of baronets and knights.

THE KINGS & QUEENS OF ENGLAND FROM 1066

William I, the conqueror of England, who, after defeating the English at Hastings, ordered the first extensive written survey of England, in the Domesday Book compiled in 1085. (Radio Times Hulton Picture Library)

The Kings and Queens of England from 1066

The precise dates of all the main events in the lives of the earlier monarchs are not known, and probably now never will be. Where recognised authorities are in dispute, as quite frequently occurs in the first twenty or so reigns, we have adhered to the dates given by the Royal Historical Society's *Handbook of British Chronology* (second edition, 1961) because this work includes the fruits of recent researches based on only acceptable evidence.

Although many of these monarchs had limited personal influence in the course of events in British history, the dates of their reigns still provide an irreplaceable skeleton to the chronology of British history.

King or Queen Regnant, Date of Accession and Final Year of Reign; Style	Date and Place of Birth and Parentage	Marriages and No. of Children	Date, Cause and Place of Death, and Place of Burial	Notes and Succession
1. WILLIAM I 25 Dec. 1066–87 'The Bastard' 'The Conqueror' *Style:* Willielmus Rex Anglorum	1027 or 1038 at Falaise, north France; illegitimate son of Robert I, 6th Duke of Normandy, and Arlette, dau. of Fulbert the Tanner	m. at Eu in 1050 or 1051 MATILDA (d. 1083), d of Baldwin V, Count of Flanders. 4s 5d	d., aged 59 or 60, 9 Sept. 1087 of an abdominal injury from his saddle pommel at the Priory of St Gervais, nr. Rouen. The Abbey of St Stephen at Caen	William I succeeded by right of conquest by winning the 'Battle of Hastings,' 14 Oct. 1066, from Harold II, the nominated heir of Edward III ('The Confessor'). Succeeded as King of England by his third*, but second surviving, son, William
2. WILLIAM II 26 Sept. 1087–1100 'Rufus' *Style:* 'Dei Gratia Rex Anglorum'	between 1056 and 1060 in Normandy; third son of William I and Matilda	unmarried. Had illegitimate issue	d., aged between 40 and 44, 2 Aug. 1100 (according to tradition) of impalement by a stray arrow while hunting in the New Forest nr. Brockenhurst, Hants. Winchester Cathedral	Succeeded by his younger brother, Henry
3. HENRY I 5 Aug. 1100–35 'Beauclerc' *Style:* As No. 2 but also Duke of Normandy from 1106	in the latter half of 1068 at Selby, Yorks; fourth son of William I and Matilda	m. (1) at Westminster Abbey, 11 Nov. 1100, EADGYTH (Edith), known as MATILDA (d. 1118), d of Malcolm III, King of the Scots, and Margaret (grand-d of Edmund 'Ironside') 1s, 1d and a child who died young. m. (2) 29 Jan. 1121 ADELA (d. 1151), d of Godfrey VII, Count of Louvain. No issue	d., aged 67, 1 Dec. 1135, from a feverish illness at St Denis-le-Ferment, nr. Grisors. Reading Abbey	Succeeded by his nephew, Stephen (the third, but second surviving, son of Adela, the fifth d of William I) who usurped the throne from Henry's only surviving legitimate child and d, Matilda (1102–67)
4. STEPHEN 22 Dec. 1135–54 *Style:* As No. 2. *Note* Matilda (see footnote below) was styled 'Imperatrix Henrici Regis filia et Anglorum domina'	between 1096 and 1100 at Blois, France; third son of Stephen (sometimes called Henry), Count of Blois, and Adela	m. 1125, MATILDA (d. 1151), d of Eustace III, Count of Boulogne, and Mary, sister of Queen Matilda, wife of Henry I. 3s 2d	d., aged between 54 and 58, 25 Oct. 1154, from a heart attack at St Martin's Priory, Dover. Faversham Abbey	Succeeded by his first cousin once removed downwards, Henry
5. HENRY II 19 Dec. 1154–1189 *Style:* 'Rex Angliae, Dux Normaniae et Aquitaniae et Comes Andigaviae'	5 Mar. 1133 at Le Mans, France; eldest son of Geoffrey V, Count of Anjou (surnamed Plantagenet), and Matilda (only d of Henry I)	m. at Bordeaux, 18 May, 1152, ELEANOR (c. 1122–1204), d of William X, Duke of Aquitaine, and divorced wife of Louis, later Louis VII, King of France, 5s 3d.	d., aged 56, 6 July 1189, of a fever at the Castle of Chinon, nr. Tours, France. Fontevraud abbey church in Anjou	Succeeded by his third and elder surviving son, Richard. On 14 June 1170, Henry II's second and eldest surviving son Henry was crowned and three years later recrowned with his wife at Winchester as King of England. Contemporaneously he was called King Henry III. He predeceased his father, 11 June 1183
6. RICHARD I 3 Sept. 1189–99 'Coeur de Lion' *Style:* As No. 5	8 Sept. 1157 at Oxford; third son of Henry II and Eleanor	m. at Limassol, Cyprus, 12 May 1191, BERENGARIA (d. soon after 1230), d of Sancho VI of Navarre. No legitimate issue	d., aged 41, 6 Apr. 1199, from a mortal arrow wound while besieging the Castle of Châlus in the Limousine, France. Fontevraud abbey church in Anjou.	Succeeded by his younger brother, John, who usurped the throne from his nephew Arthur, the only son of Geoffrey, Duke of Brittany (1158–86); and from his niece, Eleanor (1184–1241). Arthur (b, post-humously 1187) was murdered (unmarried) 3 Apr. 1203 in his 17th year
7. JOHN 27 May 1199–1216 'Lackland' *Style:* 'Joannes Rex Angliae et Dominus Hiberniae' etc.	24 Dec. 1167 at Beaumont Palace, Oxford; fifth son of Henry II and Eleanor	m. (1) at Marlborough, Wilts, 29 Aug. 1189, ISABEL* (d. 1217). No issue. m. (2) at Angoulême, 24 Aug. 1200, ISABELLA (d. 1246), d of Aimir, Count of Angoulême. 2s 3d	d., aged 48, 18–19 Oct. 1216, of dysentery at Newark Castle, Notts. Worcester Cathedral	In late 1215 the Crown was offered to Louis, son of Philip II of France but despite a visit in 1216 the claim was abandoned in Sept. 1217. Succeeded by his elder son, Henry

King or Queen Regnant, Date of Accession and Final Year of Reign; Style	Date and Place of Birth and Parentage	Marriages and No. of Children	Date, Cause and Place of Death, and Place of Burial	Notes and Succession
8. **HENRY III** 28 Oct. 1216–72 *Style:* Rex Angliae, Dominus Hiberniae et Dux Aquitaniae	1 Oct. 1207 at Winchester; elder son of John and Isabella	m. at Canterbury, 20 Jan. 1236, ELEANOR (d. 1291), d of Raymond Berengar IV, Count of Provence. 2s 3d at least 4 other children who died in infancy	d., aged 65, 16 Nov. 1272, at Westminster. Westminster abbey church	The style 'Dux Normaniae' and Count of Anjou was omitted from 1259. Succeeded by Edward, his first son to survive infancy (probably his third son)
9. **EDWARD I** 20 Nov. 1272–1307 'Longshanks' *Style:* As the final style of No. 8	17/18 June 1239 at Westminster; eldest son to survive infancy (probably third son) of Henry III and Eleanor	m. (1) at the monastery of Las Huelgas, Spain, 13–31 Oct. 1254 ELEANOR (d. 1290), d of Ferdinand III, King of Castile. 4s 7d m. (2) at Canterbury, 10 Sept. 1299 MARGARET (1282–1317), d of Philip III, King of France. 2s 1d	d., aged 68, 7 July 1307, at Burgh-upon-the-Sands, nr. Carlisle. Westminster Abbey	Succeeded by the fourth, and only surviving, son of his first marriage, Edward (created Prince of Wales 7 Feb. 1301)
10. **EDWARD II** 8 July 1307 (deposed 20 Jan. 1327) 'of Caernarvon' *Style:* As the final style of No. 8	25 Apr. 1284 at Caernarvon Castle; fourth and only surviving son of Edward I and Eleanor	m. at Boulogne, c. 25 Jan. 1308, ISABELLA (1292–1358), d of Philip IV, King of France, 2s 2d	murdered, aged 43, 21 Sept. 1327 (traditionally by disembowelling with red-hot iron) at Berkeley Castle. The abbey of St Peter (now the cathedral), Gloucester	Succeeded by his elder son, Edward of Windsor. Edward II was deposed by Parliament on 20 Jan. 1327, having been imprisoned on 16 Nov. 1326
11. **EDWARD III** 25 Jan. 1327–1377 *Style:* As No. 10, until 13th year when 'Dei Gratiã, Rex Angliae, et Franciae et Dominus Hiberniae'	13 Nov. 1312 at Windsor Castle; elder son of Edward II and Isabella	m. at York, 24 June 1328, PHILIPPA (c. 1314–69), d of William I, Count of Holland and Hainault. 7s 5d	d. peacefully, aged 64, 21 June 1377 at Sheen (now Richmond), Surrey. Westminster Abbey	Succeeded by his grandson Richard, the second and only surviving son of his eldest son Edward, the Black Prince
12. **RICHARD II** 22 June 1377–99 *Style:* As final style of No. 11	6 Jan. 1367 at Bordeaux; second, but only surviving, son of Edward, the Black Prince, and Joane, commonly called The Fair Maid of Kent (grand-d of Edward I	m. (1) at St Stephen's Chapel, Westminster, 20 Jan. 1382, ANNE of Bohemia (1366–94), d of Emperor Charles IV. No issue. m. (2) at St Nicholas' Church, Calais, probably 4 Nov. 1396, ISABELLE (1389–1409), d of Charles VI of France. No issue	d., aged 33, probably 14 Feb. 1400, a sufferer from neurasthenia at Pontefract Castle, Yorks. Westminster Abbey	He was a prisoner of Henry, Duke of Lancaster, later Henry IV, from 19 Aug. 1399 until death. He was deposed 30 Sept. 1399. Henry usurped the throne from the prior claims of the issue of his father John of Gaunt's deceased elder brother, Lionel of Antwerp
13. **HENRY IV** 30 Sept. 1399–1413 *Style:* As No. 12	probably Apr. 1366 at Bolingbroke Castle, nr. Spilsby, Lincs.; eldest son of John of Gaunt, 4th son of Edward III, and Blanche, great-great-great-grand-d of Henry III	m. (1) at Rochford, Essex, between July 1380 and Mar. 1381, Lady Mary de Bohun (?1368/70–94), younger d of Humphrey, Earl of Hereford. 5s 2d m. (2) at Winchester 7 Feb. 1403, JOAN (c. 1370–1437), second d of Charles II, King of Navarre. No issue	d., aged probably 46, 20 Mar. 1413, of pustulated eczema and gout in the Jerusalem Chamber, Westminster. Canterbury Cathedral	Succeeded by his second, but eldest surviving, son, Henry of Monmouth
14. **HENRY V** 21 Mar. 1413–1422 *Style:* As No. 13, until 8th year when 'Rex Angliae, Haeres, et Regens Franciae, et Dominus Hiberniae'	probably 16 Sept. 1387 at Monmouth; second and eldest surviving son of Henry IV and the Lady Mary de Bohun	m. at the church of St. John, Troyes, 2 June 1420, CATHERINE of Valois (1401–37), youngest d of Charles VI of France. 1s	d., aged probably 34, 31 Aug./Sept. 1422, of dysentery at Bois de Vincennes, France. Chapel of the Confessor, Westminster Abbey	Succeeded by his only child Henry

King or Queen Regnant, Date of Accession and Final Year of Reign; Style	Date and Place of Birth and Parentage	Marriages and No. of Children	Date, Cause and Place of Death, and Place of Burial	Notes and Succession
15. **HENRY VI** 1 Sept. 1422–1461 and 1470–71 *Style:* 'Dei Gratiâ Rex Angliae et Franciae et Dominus Hiberniae'	6 Dec. 1421 at Windsor; only son of Henry V and Catherine	m. at Tichfield Abbey, 23 Apr. 1445, MARGARET (1430–82), d of René, Duke of Anjou. 1s	murdered by stabbing, aged 49, 21 May 1471 at Tower of London. Windsor	Succeeded by the usurpation of this third cousin, Edward IV
16. **EDWARD IV** 4 Mar. 1461–1483 (except for a period during 1470–71) *Style:* As No. 15	28 Apr. 1442 at Rouen; eldest son of Richard, 3rd Duke of York ('The Protector') and the Lady Cecily Nevill	m. at Grafton, Northants, 1 May 1464, ELIZABETH (c. 1437–92), eldest d of Sir Richard Woodville 3s 7d	d., aged 40, 9 Apr. 1483, of pneumonia at Westminster. Windsor	Edward IV was a prisoner of the Earl of Warwick in Aug. and Sept. of 1469; he fled to the Netherlands 3 Oct. 1470; returned to England 14 Mar. 1471, and was restored to kingship 11 Apr. 1471. Succeeded by his eldest son, Edward
17. **EDWARD V** 9 Apr.–25 June 1483 *Style:* As No. 15	2 Nov. 1470 in the Sanctuary at Westminster; eldest son of Edward IV and Elizabeth Woodville	unmarried	d. (traditionally murdered), aged 12, probably July–Sept. 1483, at the Tower of London. A body of the stature and dentition of a 12 year old male discovered at the Tower on 6 July 1933	Edward V was deposed 25 June 1483, when the throne was usurped by his uncle, Richard III (the only surviving brother of his father)
18. **RICHARD III** 26 June 1483–5 *Style:* As No. 15	2 Oct. 1452 at Fotheringay Castle, Northants; fourth and only surviving, son of Richard, 3rd Duke of York ('The Protector'), and the Lady Cecily Nevill	m. 12 July 1472 the Lady ANNE (1456–85), younger d of Richard Nevill, Earl of Warwick ('The King Maker') and widow of Edward, Prince of Wales, only child of Henry VI. 1s	killed aged 32, 22 Aug. 1485, at the Battle of Bosworth Field. The Abbey of the Grey Friars, Leicester	Richard III was succeeded by his third cousin once removed downwards, Henry Tudor, 2nd Earl of Richmond
19. **HENRY VII** 22 Aug. 1485–1509 *Style:* As No. 15	27 Jan. 1457 at Pembroke Castle; only child of Edmund Tudor, 1st Earl of Richmond, and Margaret Beaufort, great-great-grand-d of Edward III	m. at Westminster, 18 Jan. 1486, ELIZABETH (1466–1503) d of Edward IV. 3s and 4d, of whom 2 died in infancy	d., aged 52, 21 Apr. 1509 of rheumatoid arthritis and gout at Richmond. In his own chapel at Westminster	Succeeded by his second and only surviving son, Henry
20. **HENRY VIII** 22 Apr. 1509–47 *Style:* (from 35th year) 'Henry the eighth, by the Grace of God, King of England, France, and Ireland, Defender of the Faith and of the Church of England, and also of Ireland, on earth the Supreme Head'	28 June 1491 at Greenwich; second and only surviving son of Henry VII and Elizabeth	m. (1) secretly at the chapel of the Observant Friars, 11 June 1509, CATHERINE of Aragon (1485–1536), d of Ferninand II, King of Spain and widow of Arthur, Prince of Wales. 2s 2d and a child who died young.	d., aged 55, 28 Jan. 1547, of chronic sinusitis and periostitis of the leg at the Palace of Westminster. Windsor	Henry was the first King to be formally styled with a post nominal number i.e. VIII. Succeeded by his only surviving son, Edward
Subsequent marriages of HENRY VIII:	m. (2) secretly 25 Jan. 1533, ANNE Marchioness of Pembroke (b. 1507, beheaded 1536), d of Sir Thomas Boleyn, the Viscount Rochford. A daughter and possibly another child	m. (3) in the Queen's Closet, York Place, London, 30 May 1536, JANE (d. 1537), eldest d of Sir John Seymour. 1s	m. (4) at Greenwich, 6 Jan. 1540, ANNE (1515–57), second d of John, Duke of Cleves. No issue. m. (5) at Oatlands, 28 July 1540, CATHERINE (beheaded 1542), d of Lord Edmund Howard. No issue	m. (6) at Hampton Court, 12 July 1543, CATHERINE (c. 1512–48), d of Sir Thomas Parr and widow of 1. Sir Edward Borough and 2. John Neville, 3rd Lord Latimer. No issue
21. **EDWARD VI** 28 Jan. 1547–53 *Style:* As No 20	12 Oct. 1537 at Hampton Court; only surviving son of Henry VIII, by Jane Seymour	unmarried	d., aged 15, 6 July 1553, of pulmonary tuberculosis at Greenwich. Henry VII's Chapel, Westminster Abbey	Succeeded briefly by Lady Guil(d)ford Dudley (Lady Jane Grey), his first cousin once removed
22 **JANE** 6 July (proclaimed 10 July) 1553 (deposed 19 July)	Oct. 1537 at Bradgate Park, Leics.; eldest d of Henry Grey, 3rd Marquess of Dorset, and Frances (d of Mary Tudor, sister of Henry VIII)	m. at Durham House, London, 21 May 1553, Lord GUIL(D)FORD DUDLEY (beheaded 1554), 4th son of John Dudley, Duke of Northumberland. No issue	beheaded, aged 16, 12 Feb. 1554, in the Tower of London. St Peter ad Vincula, within the Tower	Succeeded by her second cousin once removed upwards, Mary

King or Queen Regnant, Date of Accession and Final Year of Reign; Style	Date and Place of Birth and Parentage	Marriages and No. of Children	Date, Cause and Place of Death, and Place of Burial	Notes and Succession
23. **MARY I** 19 July 1553–8 *Style:* As No. 20 (but supremacy title was dropped) until marriage then as footnote:	18 Feb. 1516 at Greenwich Palace; only surviving child of Henry VIII and Catherine of Aragon	m. at Winchester Cathedral, 25 July 1554, PHILIP (1527–98), King of Naples and Jerusalem, son of Emperor Charles V and widower of Maria, d of John III of Portugal. No issue	d., aged 42, 17 Nov. 1558, of endemic influenza at London. Westminster Abbey.	Philip was styled, but not crowned, king. Mary was succeeded by her half sister, Elizabeth, the only surviving child of Henry VIII
24. **ELIZABETH I** 17 Nov. 1558–1603 *Style:* 'Queen of England, France and Ireland, Defender of the Faith' etc.	7 Sept. 1533 at Greenwich; d of Henry VIII and Anne Boleyn	unmarried	d., aged 69, 24 Mar. 1603, of sepsis from tonsillar abscess at Richmond. Westminster Abbey	Succeeded by her first cousin twice removed, James
25. **JAMES I** 24 Mar. 1603–25 and VI of Scotland from 24 July 1567 *Style:* King of England, Scotland, France and Ireland, Defender of the Faith' etc.	19 June 1566 at Edinburgh Castle; only son of Henry Stuart, Lord Darnley, and Mary, Queen of Scots (d of James V of Scotland, son of Margaret Tudor, sister of Henry VIII)	m. 20 Aug. 1589 (by proxy) ANNE (1574–1619), d of Frederick II, King of Denmark and Norway. 3s 4d	d., aged 58, 27 Mar. 1625, of Bright's disease at Theobalds Park, Herts. Westminster Abbey	Succeeded by his second and only surviving son, Charles
26. **CHARLES I** 27 Mar. 1625–49 *Style:* As No. 25	19 Nov. 1600 at Dunfermline, Fife; second and only surviving son of James I and Anne	m. in Paris 1 May 1625 (by proxy) HENRIETTA MARIA (1609–69) d of Henry IV of France. 4s 5d	beheaded, aged 48, 30 Jan. 1649, in Whitehall. Windsor	The Kingship was *de facto* declared abolished 16 Mar. 1649
27. **CHARLES II** 29 May 1660 (but *de jure* 30 Jan. 1649) to 1685 *Style:* As No. 25	29 May 1630 at St James's Palace, London; eldest surviving son of Charles I and Henrietta Maria	m. at Portsmouth, 21 May 1662, CATHERINE (1638–1705), d of John, Duke of Braganza. No legitimate issue	d., aged 54, 6 Feb. 1685, of uraemia and mercurial poisoning at Whitehall. Henry VII's Chapel, Westminster Abbey	Succeeded by his younger and only surviving brother, James
28. **JAMES II** 6 Feb. 1685–8 *Style:* As No. 25	14 Oct. 1633 at St James's Palace, London; only surviving son of Charles I and Henrietta Maria	m. (1) at Worcester House, The Strand, London, 3 Sept. 1660, Anne (1637–71), eldest d of Edward Hyde. 4s 4d m. (2) at Modena (by proxy), 30 Sept. 1673, MARY D'ESTE (1658–1718), only d of Alfonso IV, Duke of Modena. 2s 5d	d., aged 67, 6 Sept. 1701, of a cerebral haemorrhage at St Germains, France. His remains were divided and interred at five different venues in France. All are now lost except for those at the parish church of St Germains	James II was deemed by legal fiction to have ended his reign 11 Dec. 1688 by flight. A Convention Parliament offered the Crown of England and Ireland 13 Feb. 1689 to Mary, his eldest surviving d, and her husband, his nephew, William Henry of Orange
29. **WILLIAM III** 13 Feb. 1689–1702 and **MARY II** 13 Feb. 1689–94 *Style:* 'King and Queen of England, Scotland, France and Ireland, Defenders of the Faith etc.'	4 Nov. 1650 at The Hague; only son of William II, Prince of Orange, and Mary (Stuart), d of Charles I 30 Apr. 1662 at St James's Palace, London; elder surviving d of James II and Anne Hyde	T M were married at St James's Palace, London, 4 Nov. 1677. No issue	d., aged 51, 8 Mar. 1702, of pleuro-pneumonia following fracture of right collarbone, in Kensington d., aged 32, 28 Dec. 1694, of confluent haemorrhagic smallpox with pneumonia, at Kensington. T M were buried in Henry VII's Chapel, Westminster Abbey	The widower, King William III, was succeeded by his sister-in-law, Anne, who was also his first cousin

King or Queen Regnant, Date of Accession and Final Year of Reign; Style	Date and Place of Birth and Parentage	Marriages and No. of Children	Date, Cause and Place of Death, and Place of Burial	Notes and Succession
30. **ANNE** 8 Mar. 1702–14 *Style:* Firstly as No. 25; secondly (after Union with Scotland 6 Mar. 1707) 'Queen of Great Britain, France and Ireland, Defender of the Faith etc.'	6 Feb. 1665 at St James's Palace, London; only surviving d of James II and Anne Hyde	m. at the Chapel Royal, St James's Palace, 28 July 1683, GEORGE (1653–1708), second son of Frederick III, King of Denmark. 2s 3d from 17 confinements	d., aged 49, 1 Aug. 1714, of a cerebral haemorrhage and possibly chronic Bright's disease at Kensington. Henry VII's Chapel, Westminster Abbey	Succeeded in the terms of the Act of Settlement (which excluded all Roman Catholics and their spouses) by her second cousin, George Lewis, Elector of Hanover
31. **GEORGE I** 1 Aug. 1714–27 *Style:* 'King of Great Britain, France and Ireland, Duke of Brunswick-Lüneburg, etc., Defender of the Faith'	28 May 1660 at Osnabrück; eldest son of Ernest Augustus, Duke of Brunswick-Lüneburg and Elector of Hanover, and Princess Sophia, 5th and youngest d and 10th child of Elizabeth, Queen of Bohemia, the eldest d of James I	m. 21 Nov. 1682 (div. 1694), Sophia Dorothea (1666–1726), only d of George William, Duke of Lüneburg-Celle. 1s 1d	d., aged 67, 11 June 1727, of coronary thrombosis, at Ibbenbüren or Osnabrück. Hanover	The Kings of England were Electors of Hanover from 1714 to 1814. Succeeded by his only son, George Augustus
32. **GEORGE II** 11 June 1727–60 *Style:* As No. 31	30 Oct. 1683 at Hanover; only son of George I and Sophia Dorothea	m. 22 Aug. (O.S.), 2 Sept. (N.S.), 1705, Wilhelmina Charlotte CAROLINE (1683–1437), d of John Frederick, Margrave of Brandenburg-Auspach, 3s 5d	d. aged 76, 25 Oct. 1760, of coronary thrombosis at the Palace of Westminster. Henry VII's Chapel. Westminster Abbey	Succeeded by his elder son's eldest son, George William Frederick
33. **GEORGE III** 25 Oct. 1760–1820 *Style:* As No. 31 (until Union of Great Britain and Ireland, 1 Jan. 1801), whereafter 'By the Grace of God, of the United Kingdom of Great Britain and Ireland, King, Defender of the Faith'	24 May (O.S.) 1738 at Norfolk House, St James's Square, London; eldest son of Frederick Lewis, Prince of Wales (d. 20 Mar. 1751) and Princess Augusta of Saxe-Gotha	m. at St James's Palace, London, 8 Sept. 1761, CHARLOTTE Sophia (1744–1818), youngest d of Charles Louis Frederick, Duke of Mecklenburg-Strelitz. 9s 6d	d., aged 81 years 239 days, 29 Jan. 1820, of senility at Windsor. St George's Chapel, Windsor	His eldest son became Regent owing to his insanity 5 Feb. 1811. Hanover was made a kingdom in 1814. Succeeded by his eldest son, George Augustus Frederick
34. **GEORGE IV** 29 Jan. 1820–30 *Style:* As later style of No. 33	12 Aug. 1762 at St James's Palace, London; eldest son of George III and Charlotte	m. (2)* at the Chapel Royal, St James's's Palace, 8 Apr. 1795, CAROLINE Amelia Elizabeth (1768–1821), his first cousin, second d of Charles, Duke of Brunswick-Wolfenbüttel. 1d	d., aged 67, 26 June 1830, of rupture of the stomach blood vessels; alcoholic cirrhosis; and dropsy at Windsor. St George's Chapel, Windsor	Succeeded by his elder surviving brother, William Henry (George's only child, Princess Charlotte, having died in child-birth 6 Nov. 1817)
35. **WILLIAM IV** 26 June 1830–7 *Style:* As No. 34	21 Aug. 1765 at Buckingham Palace; third and oldest surviving son of George III and Charlotte	m. at Kew, 11 July 1818, ADELAIDE Louisa Theresa Caroline Amelia (1792–1849), eldest d of George, Duke of Saxe-Meiningen. 2d	d., aged 71, 20 June 1837, of pleuro-pneumonia and alcoholic cirrhosis at Windsor. Windsor	On William's death the crown of Hanover passed by Salic law to his brother, Ernest, Duke of Cumberland. Succeeded by his niece, Alexandrina Victoria
36. **VICTORIA** 20 June 1837–1901 *Style:* As (except for 'Queen') No. 34 until 1 May 1876, whereafter 'Empress of India' was added	24 May 1819 at Kensington Palace, London; only child of Edward, Duke of Kent and Strathearn, 4th son of George III, and Victoria, widow of Emich Charles, Prince of Leiningen and d of Francis, Duke of Saxe-Coburg-Saafeld	m. at St James's Palace, London, 10 Feb. 1840 her first cousin Francis ALBERT Augustus Charles Emmanuel (1819–61), second son of Ernest I, Duke of Saxe-Coburg-Gotha. 4s 5d	d., aged 81 years 243 days, 22 Jan. 1901 of senility at Osborne, I.o.W. Frogmore	Assumed title Empress of India 1 May 1876. Succeeded by her elder surviving son, Albert Edward

King or Queen Regnant, Date of Accession and Final Year of Reign; Style	Date and Place of Birth and Parentage	Marriages and No. of Children	Date, Cause and Place of Death, and Place of Burial	Notes and Succession
37. **EDWARD VII** 22 Jan. 1901–10 *Style:* 'By the Grace of God, of the United Kingdom of Great Britain and Ireland and of the British Dominions beyond the Seas, King, Defender of the Faith, Emperor of India'	9 Nov. 1841 at Buckingham Palace, London; elder surviving son of Victoria and Albert	m. at St George's Chapel, Windsor, 10 Mar. 1863, ALEXANDRA Caroline Maria Charlotte Louisa Julia (1844–1925), d of Christian IX of Denmark. 3s 3d	d., aged 68, 6 May, 1910, of bronchitis at Buckingham Palace. St George's Chapel, Windsor	Succeeded by his only surviving son, George Frederick Ernest Albert
38. **GEORGE V** 6 May 1910–36 *Style:* As for No. 37 until 12 May 1927, whereafter 'By the Grace of God, of Great Britain, Ireland, and of the British Dominions beyond the Seas, King, Defender of the Faith, Emperor of India'	3 June 1865 at Marlborough House, London; second and only surviving son/of Edward VII and Alexandra	m. at St James's Palace, London, 6 July 1893, Victoria MARY Augusta Louise Olga Pauline Claudine Agnes (1867–1953), eldest child and only d of Francis, Duke of Teck. 5s 1d	d., aged 70, 20 Jan. 1936, of bronchitis at Sandringham House, Norfolk. St George's Chapel, Windsor	Succeeded by his eldest son, Edward Albert Christian George Andrew Patrick David
39. **EDWARD VIII** 20 Jan. 1936–11 Dec. 1936 *Style:* As for No. 38	23 June 1894 at the White Lodge, Richmond Park; eldest son of George V and Mary	m. at the Château de Candé, Monts, France, 3 June 1937, Bessie Wallis Warfield (b. 1896), previous wife of Lt. Earl Winfield Spencer, USN (div. 1927) and Ernest Simpson (div. 1936). No issue	d., aged 77, 28 May, 1972, of cancer of the throat at 4, Route du Champ, D'Entrainement, Paris XVIᵉ, France	Edward VIII abdicated for himself and his heirs and was succeeded by his eldest brother, Albert Frederick Arthur George
40. **GEORGE VI** 11 Dec. 1936–52 *Style:* As for No. 38 until the Indian title was dropped 22 June 1947	14 Dec. 1895 at York Cottage, Sandringham; second son of George V and Mary	m. at Westminster Abbey, 26 Apr. 1923, Lady ELIZABETH Angela Marguerite Bowes-Lyon (b. 1900), youngest d of 14th Earl of Strathmore and Kinghorne. 2d	d., aged 56, 6 Feb. 1952, of lung cancer at Sandringham House, Norfolk. St George's Chapel, Windsor	Succeeded by his elder d, Elizabeth Alexandra Mary
41. **ELIZABETH II** Since 6 Feb. 1952 *Style:* (from 29 May 1953) 'By the grace of God, of the United Kingdom of Great Britain and Northern Ireland and of Her other Realms and Territories, Queen, Head of the Commonwealth, Defender of the Faith'.	21 Apr. 1926 at 17 Bruton Street, London, W 1; elder d of George VI and Elizabeth	m. at Westminster Abbey, 20 Nov. 1947, her third cousin PHILIP (b. Corfu, Greece 10 June 1921), only son of Prince Andrea (Andrew) of Greece and Princess Alice (great-grand-d of Queen Victoria). 3s 1d	—	The Heir Apparent is Charles Philip Arthur George, Prince of Wales, b. 14 Nov. 1948

Right: 37. Edward VII eldest surviving son of Queen Victoria who reigned for 9 years as her successor (Radio Times Hulton Picture Library)
Far right: 38. George V who followed Edward VII to the throne in 1910 (Radio Times Hulton Picture Library)

Queen Victoria, the longest reigning
British Monarch, who remained on
the throne for 63 years 216 days as
Queen until her death, 22 days
into the new century (see p. 113)
(Radio Times Hulton Picture
Library).

THE COMPOSITION OF THE TWO HOUSES OF PARLIAMENT

House of Lords

Peers of the Blood Royal	4
Archbishops	2
Dukes	26
Marquesses	37
Earls	175
Countesses in their own right	6
Viscounts	116
Bishops (by seniority)	24
Barons (hereditary)	465
Baronesses in their own right (hereditary)	13
Life Peers (Barons)	226
Life Peeresses (Baronesses)	36
	1130

House of Commons

The size of the House of Commons has frequently been altered:

1885 By a Representation to the People Act (RPA) membership was increased by 12 to total 670.

1918 By an RPA membership was increased by 37 to an all-time high point of 707.

1922 By two Acts of Parliament (the Partition of Ireland) membership was reduced by 92 to 615. (*Note:* Irish representation was reduced from 105 to 13 members representing Northern Ireland.)

1945 By an RPA membership was increased by 25 to 640.

1948 By an RPA membership was decreased by 15 to 625. (*Note:* This took effect in 1950 and involved the abolition of the 12 university seats and 12 double-member constituencies.)

1955 By an Order in Council under the House of Commons (Redistribution of seats) Act membership was increased by five to a total of 630.

1974 By an Order in Council membership was increased by 5 to the present total of 635.

The 21 General Elections of the Twentieth Century

1900 Lord Salisbury's Conservative Government exercised its undoubted constitutional right to cash in on the apparently victorious (Mafeking and Pretoria) outcome of the Boer War two years before its 7 years of life was expired. The Liberal opposition called these tactics immoral and dubbed the election the 'Khaki Election'. The Government were given the most triumphant encore seen since the Reform Act of 1832 with an overall majority of 134 compared with the Dissolution figure of 128. The Liberal opposition was divided into the 'pro-Boers', comprising Gladstonians with the young Lloyd George, and the followers of Asquith, Haldane and Grey, who were Empire men.

1906 By December 1905 A J Balfour, who had succeeded his uncle as Prime Minister in 1902, had his majority reduced to 68 because of losses in by-elections. Feeling out of tune with the objects of the Tariff Reform League, he resigned. The King asked Campbell-Bannerman to form a government which he did and then immediately went to the country. The result was a landslide victory for the Liberals, who won an overall majority of 84. The Conservatives lost support mainly because of alarm over Chamberlain's Tariff Reform campaign and State support for Church of England schools, which offended nonconformist opinion. Liberal policy was the trinity of Free Trade, Home Rule for Ireland, and Humanitarianism.

1910 (Jan./Feb.) Asquith took over the premiership in 1908 shortly before the death of Campbell-Bannerman. The stock of the Tories rose because of Liberal pacifism in the face of the 'German Menace' and the Government lost 10 by-elections. The Liberal hopes of securing a second term rested on their taking advantage of the Conservative peers' inevitable rejection of Lloyd George's deliberately provocative budget. The government were thus handed on a plate the priceless slogan 'Lords versus the People'. The Liberals, however, only ended up with 125 seats fewer than their 1906 highwater mark. More seriously, they were now at the mercy of the jubilant 82 Irish Nationalists and 40 Labourites.

1910 (Dec.) The Government's House of Lords policy was: (1) abolition of Lords power to veto over certified Money Bills; (2) a delaying power only of three sessions for other Bills, and (3) the life of a Parliament to be reduced from seven to five years. The ostensible reason for another General Election was that the country should vote on these policies. But the real reason was that secretly King George V, who had succeeded his father that May, had insisted on a second appeal to the nation before giving his promise to create if necessary the required number of Liberal peers to vote the Parliament Bill through. The result of the election was almost a carbon copy of that eleven months previously.

1918 The victorious wartime premier, Lloyd George, at the head of the Coalition which had superseded Asquith's Liberal administration in 1916, went to the country in December 1918. The election was called by the opposition the 'coupon election'. This was because Lloyd George (Lib.) and Bonar Law (Con.) jointly signed letters (nicknamed 'coupons') giving support to those they regarded as loyal supporters of the Coalition. The Government's election policy in terms of slogans was 'Hang the Kaiser'; make the Germans pay for the war 'until the lemon pips squeak'; and make the country 'fit for heroes to live in'. Women over 30 were first given the vote. The Coalition won a crushing victory on a very low (58.9 per cent) poll.

1922 The Coalition Government under Lloyd George progressively lost the confidence of its predominant Conservative wing. The Conservatives disliked the Liberal Prime Minister's vacillating and extravagant domestic policies, especially in regard to agriculture and what they regarded as naive foreign policies. Left-wing opinion was displeased with the rate of social progress on the home front. Many major strikes were organised. In Oct. 1922 the Conservatives resolved to fight the next election as an independent party. Lloyd George promptly resigned. Bonar Law formed a Government and went to the country. The Conservatives, with Bonar Law's policy of 'Tranquillity', won a majority of 75 over all other parties. The Labour Party overtook the divided Liberals by nearly doubling their representation to 142 and became the official Opposition.

1923 Bonar Law, who had started his premiership a sick man, retired in May 1923, and died shortly afterwards. His successor, in preference to Lord Curzon, was Stanley Baldwin. The main domestic problem was unemployment. Baldwin took the view that protective tariffs would alleviate it: but he was bound by Bonar Law's promise not to introduce such a measure. The only way out was to appeal to the country. The election saw a tiny change from the 1922 percentages but a dramatic loss of 87 seats by the Conservatives. Baldwin, although now in a

minority of 99, waited to face the new Parliament and was inevitably defeated by a Labour-Liberal alliance and then resigned in favour of Ramsay MacDonald (Labour).

1924 MacDonald found himself embarrassingly short of talented Ministers and under intense pressure and scrutiny from the National Executive of the Labour Party. His greatest success was to sort out the Franco-German squabble over war reparation payments. The Government were brought down when their often unwilling allies, the Liberals, voted with the Tories for a motion for enquiry into the circumstances under which a journalist, J R Campbell, was to have his prosecution by the Attorney General for sedition (he advocated British soldiers disobeying orders if confronted with strikers) withdrawn. The Labour Party lost 40 seats and the Conservatives, profiting from there being fewer Liberal candidates, won an overall majority of 225 seats under Baldwin.

1929 Despite Baldwin's Government's surviving overall majority of 185 seats, Labour won this election with 288 seats, but could not command an absolute majority (Conservatives 260, Liberals 59, Others 8 = 327). Over 5 million women between the ages of 21 and 30 were eligible to vote for the first time. The Conservatives had adopted the uninspiring slogan 'Safety First'. The Labour Party, with the slogan 'Socialism In Our Time', had a three-pronged policy of world peace, disarmament, and a desire to deal more energetically with unemployment. The Liberals also based their appeal on unemployment remedies. The Liberal leader, Mr Lloyd George, decided to support Labour in office.

1931 The Labour Government committed themselves to increased expenditure and the unemployment figures rose alarmingly. A crisis of loss of confidence in sterling caused a summer crisis and Ramsay MacDonald suggested to his Cabinet an economy scheme which included the reduction of unemployment insurance benefits. The National Executive of the Labour Party and the TUC characteristically flatly refused to support any such measure. On 24 Aug. the Labour Government resigned and MacDonald formed a National Government which went to the polls on 27 Oct. The extent of their victory amazed contemporary opinion as the National Government won 554 seats, including 13 by National Labour candidates, while the opposition was reduced to 52 Labour and 4 Liberal Members.

1935 Ramsay MacDonald (National Labour) resigned his premiership in June 1935 and was logically succeeded by Stanley Baldwin (Conservative), who held a snap November General Election by dissolving Parliament two days short of the fourth anniversary of the 1931 election. The main issue was simply, did the nation approve of the work of the National Government in restoring the economy after the slump and want it to continue, or did the Nation want to revert to a Labour Government? The result was a massive vote of confidence in the National (predominantly Conservative) Government which won an overall majority of 249 seats. The Labour Party's main attack was over the 'Means Test' for unemployment assistance ('the dole'), although their own 1929 Government had accepted the principle of it, and the National Government had quickly withdrawn the new unsatisfactory regulations introduced earlier that year. Broadcasting for the first time played a significant rôle in the campaign with the public listening to a series of speeches made by the various Party

Leaders every night during the first part of the election campaign.

1945 During the ten years since the previous election the country underwent the traumatic total war of 1939–45. Baldwin resigned in 1937 and was succeeded by Neville Chamberlain who resigned in 1940 at the nadir of our wartime fortunes. For the remaining five years Winston Churchill gave dynamic leadership which secured victory over Nazi Germany in May 1945. In that month the wartime Coalition broke up and was replaced by a predetermined Conservative administration. This Government, despite Churchill's premiership, was defeated by a Labour landslide. The new Government had Labour's first overall majority—146 seats.

1950 Mr Attlee's administration launched the 'Welfare State' along the lines set out by various wartime White Papers, but his nationalisation measures, especially as regards steel, met fierce resistance. A balance of payments crisis in the autumn of 1949 compelled the Government to devalue the pound against the dollar and make drastic economies. The result of the February election was a narrow Labour victory with an overall majority of only 5.

1951 After 20 months of precarious administration, during which time the Conservatives ceaselessly harried the Government ranks, especially over the nationalisation of steel, Mr Attlee resigned. The last straw was another balance of payments crisis in September following the earlier resignation of Aneurin Bevan (Minister of Labour) and Harold Wilson (Pres., Board of Trade). The nation's reply to Mr Attlee's appeal over the radio for a larger majority was to elect the Conservatives with an overall majority of 17. Winston Churchill returned as Prime Minister.

1955 In April 1955, after 4½ years of government with a small majority, Sir Winston Churchill resigned as Prime Minister in favour of Sir Anthony Eden, who seven weeks later went to the country for a vote of confidence. The Conservatives had succeeded in restoring the nation's finances, had denationalised steel and road haulage, and twice reduced the standard rate of income tax by 6d. The Government's majority rose to 58

and the five years of near deadlock in the House was broken.

1959 In Jan. 1957, following the strain of the Suez crisis, Eden resigned and Harold Macmillan became Prime Minister. The Government had been losing support, largely owing to some unpopularity over the Rent Act. The new Prime Minister, despite a number of difficulties, managed to repair Conservative fortunes. His 1959 visit to the USSR and the further reduction of income tax in April added to general contentment. The election was fought on the Conservative theme 'life is better with us' while Labour got into difficulties with Mr Gaitskell's promises of no higher taxes, yet very expensive projects. The result was that the Government again increased their overall majority to 100 seats.

1964 The Conservative Government, after 13 consecutive years of rule, went to the country in October, as required every five years by the Parliament Act of 1911. After the post-war high-water mark of 1959 (majority 100) Conservative fortunes declined owing notably to the Profumo scandal and a public wrangle over the successorship to Mr Macmillan who resigned in Oct. 1963 owing to ill health. The nation wanted a change: the Conservatives were however defeated by a rise in the Liberal vote from 5·9 per cent to 11·2 per cent rather than the Labour vote which was less than their 1959 total. Labour won by an overall majority of only 4.

1966 After 20 months in power, Mr Wilson became convinced (on the death of the Member for Falmouth in February) of the danger of continuing with his hairline majority. Labour fought the campaign on the slogan 'You Know Labour Government Works'. The Conservatives fought on a policy of entering the Common Market, reforming the 'over-mighty' Trade Unions and making the Welfare State less indiscriminate. Mr Wilson increased his overall majority from 3 to 97 and declared his intention to govern for five years to achieve 'a juster society'.

1970 Having completed four of the five years of his second term in power, Mr Wilson called the Labour Party to action in a bid for his hat-trick in May 1970. Remembered as the General Election most dominated by

the pollsters, their findings consistently showed strong leads for Labour. Wages rates had risen in an unrestrained way in the five-month run-up but prices levels were also just beginning to erode the reality of these monetary gains. Within six days of polling NOP showed a massive Labour lead of 12·4 per cent. In reality, however, the voters gave the Conservatives a 3·4 per cent lead, thus an overall majority of 30 seats.

1974 (Feb.) This was the first 'crisis' election since 1931. It was called to settle 'Who governs Britain?' under the duress of the National Union of Mineworkers' coal strike against the restraints of Stage III of the Incomes Policy. The situation was exacerbated by the Arab decision the previous November to raise the price of oil fourfold. A three-day week for most industries was decreed under Emergency Powers to start on 1 Jan. A ballot inviting the miners to give the NUM authority to call a strike was announced on 4 Feb., an election was called on 7 Feb., and a strike began on 10 Feb. after 81 per cent of the miners had voted in favour of giving the NUM Executive the authority they sought. Mr Wilson spoke of conciliation in place of confrontation and the alternative possibilities under a 'Social Contract' agreed between the Labour Party and the TUC on 18 Feb. 1973. The electorate, largely due to the impact of a successful Liberal campaign, spoke equivocally, giving Labour a majority of four over the Conservatives but 10 less than the combined Conservatives and Liberals. The Liberals rejected a coalition and appealed for a government of National Unity. Two hours after Mr Heath's resignation on 4 Mar., the Queen sent for Mr Wilson for a third time.

1974 (Oct.) For the first time since 1910 there were two elections within the same year. On 11 Mar. the miners returned to full working accepting a National Coal Board offer to raise their wage bill by 29 per cent. In June and July HM Opposition, with Liberal support, defeated Mr Wilson's precarious lobby strength 29 times, notably on the Trade Union and Labour Relation Bill. An election was called by Mr Wilson on 18 Sept. The campaign was fought mainly on the issue of inflation statistics, unemployment prospects and the promise by Labour to hold an EEC ballot. Though less that 29 out

The Results of the 21 General Elections 1900–74						
No. Election and Date			Result (and % share of Total Poll)			% Turn-out of Electorate
		Total Seats	Conservatives	Liberals	Labour	Irish Nationalists and Others	
1	1900 (28 Sept.–24 Oct.)	670	**402** (51·1)	184 (44·6)	2 (1·8)	82 (2·5)	74·6% of 6 730 935
2	1906 (12 Jan.–7 Feb.)	670	157 (43·6)	**400** (49·0)	30 (5·9)	83 (1·5)	82·6% of 7 264 608
3	1910 (14 Jan.–9 Feb.)	670	273 (46·9)	**275** (43·2)	40 (7·7)	82 (2·2)	86·6% of 7 694 741
4	1910 (2–19 Dec.)	670	272 (46·3)	272 (43·8)	42 (7·2)	84 (2·7)	81·1% of 7 709 981
5	1918 (14 Dec.)	707	**383** (38·7)	161 (25·6)	73 (23·7)	90 (12·0)	58·9% of 21 392 322
6	1922 (15 Nov.)	615	**345** (38·2)	116 (29·1)	142 (29·5)	12 (3·2)	71·3% of 21 127 663
7	1923 (6 Dec.)	615	258 (38·1)	159 (29·6)	191 (30·5)	7 (1·8)	70·8% of 21 281 232
8	1924 (29 Oct.)	615	**419** (48·3)	40 (17·6)	151 (33·0)	5 (1·1)	76·6% of 21 731 320
9	1929 (30 May)	615	260 (38·2)	59 (23·4)	**288** (37·1)	8 (1·3)	76·1% of 28 850 870
10	1931 (27 Oct.)	615	**521** (60·5)	37 (7·0)	52 (30·6)	5 (1·7)	76·3% of 29 960 071
11	1935 (14 Nov.)	615	**432** (53·7)	20 (6·4)	154 (37·9)	9 (2·0)	71·2% of 31 379 050
12	1945 (5 July)	640	213 (39·8)	12 (9·0)	**393** (47·8)	22 (2·8)	72·7% of 33 240 391
13	1950 (23 Feb.)	625	298 (43·5)	9 (9·1)	**315** (46·4)	3 (1·3)	84·0% of 33 269 770
14	1951 (25 Oct.)	625	**321** (48·0)	6 (2·5)	295 (48·7)	3 (0·7)	82·5% of 34 465 573
15	1955 (25 May)	630	**344** (49·8)	6 (2·7)	277 (46·3)	3 (1·2)	76·7% of 34 858 263
16	1959 (8 Oct.)	630	**365** (49·4)	6 (5·9)	258 (43·8)	1 (0·9)	78·8% of 35 397 080
17	1964 (15 Oct.)	630	303 (43·4)	9 (11·1)	**317** (44·2)	1 (1·3)	77·1% of 35 894 307
18	1966 (31 Mar.)	630	253 (41·9)	12 (8·5)	**363** (47·9)	2 (1·7)	75·9% of 35 965 127
19	1970 (18 June)	630	**330** (46·4)	6 (7·5)	288 (43·0)	6 (3·1)	72·0% of 39 247 683
20	1974 (28 Feb.)	635	297 (38·2)	14 (19·3)	**301** (37·2)	23 (5·3)	78·8% of 39 752 317
21	1974 (10 Oct.)	635	277 (35·8)	13 (18·3)	**319** (39·3)	26 (6·6)	72·8% of 40 083 286

of each 100 persons eligible to vote cast votes for Labour candidates, only 27 such voters supported Conservative candidates. Thus Mr Wilson won his fourth General Election, with an overall majority of three seats, but with a very secure working majority of 42 over the Conservatives, who were by far the largest party in a fragmented Opposition.

PRIME MINISTERS OF GREAT BRITAIN AND THE UNITED KINGDOM

Below is a complete compilation of the 50 Prime Ministers of Great Britain and the United Kingdom. The data run in the following order: final style as Prime Minister (with earlier of later styles); date or dates as Prime Minister with party affiliation; date and place of birth and death and place of burial; marriage or marriages with number of children; education and membership of Parliament with constituency and dates.

1. The Rt Hon, Sir Robert **WALPOLE**, KG (1726) KB (1725, resigned 1726), (PC 1714), cr. 1st Earl of Orford (of the 2nd creation) in the week of his retirement; ministry, 3 April 1721 to 8 Feb. 1742, (i) re-appointed on the accession of George II on 11 June 1727, (ii) Walpole's absolute control of the Cabinet can only be said to have dated from 15 May 1730; Whig; b. 26 Aug. 1676 at Houghton, Norfolk; d. 18 Mar. 1745 at No. 5 Arlington St, Piccadilly, London; bur. Houghton, Norfolk; m. 1 (1700) Catherine Shorter (d. 1717), m. 2ndly (1738) Maria Skerrett (d. 1738); children, 1st, 3s and 2d; 2nd, 2d (born prior to the marriage); ed. Eton and King's, Camb. (scholar); MP (Whig) for Castle Rising (1701–2); King's Lynn (1702–42) (expelled from the House for a short period 1712–13).

2. The Rt Hon, the Hon Sir Spencer Compton, 1st and last Earl of **WILMINGTON**, KG (1733), KB (1725, resigned 1733), (PC 1716), cr. Baron Wilmington 1728; cr. Earl 1730; ministry, 16 Feb. 1742 to 2 July 1743; Whig; b. 1673 or 1674; d. 2 July 1743; bur. Compton Wynyates, Warwickshire; unmarried; no legitimate issue; ed. St Paul's School, London, and Trinity, Oxford; MP (originally Tory until about 1704) for Eye (1698–1710); East Grinstead (1713–15); Sussex (Whig) (1715–28); Speaker 1715–27.

3. The Rt Hon, the Hon Henry **PELHAM** (PC 1725); prior to 1706 was Henry Pelham, Esq.; ministry 27 Aug. 1743 to 6 Mar. 1754 (with an interregnum 10–12 Feb. 1746); Whig; b. c. 1695; d. 6 Mar. 1754 at Arlington St, Piccadilly, London; bur. Laughton Church, nr. Lewes, Sussex; m. (1726) Lady Catherine Manners; children, 2s and 6d; ed. Westminster School and Hart Hall, Oxford; MP Seaford (1717–22); Sussex (1722–54).

4. The Rt Hon Sir William Pulteney, 1st and last Earl of **BATH** (cr. 1742) PC (1716) (struck off 1731); kissed hands 12 Feb. 1746 but unable to form a ministry; Whig; b. 22 Mar. 1684 in London; d. 7 July 1764; bur. Westminster Abbey; m. Anna Maria Gumley; ed. Westminster School and Christ Church, Oxford; MP Hedon (or Heydon) 1705–34; Middlesex 1734–42.

5. His Grace the 1st Duke of **NEWCASTLE** upon Tyne and 1st Duke of Newcastle under Lyme (The Rt Hon, the Hon Sir Thomas Pelham-Holles, Bt, KG (1718). (PC 1717)); added the surname Holles in July 1711; known as Lord Pelham of Laughton (1711–14); Earl of Claire (1714–15); cr. Duke of Newcastle upon Tyne 1715 and cr. Duke of Newcastle under Lyme 1756; ministry, (a) 16 Mar. 1754 to 26 Oct. 1756, (b) 2 July 1757 to 25 Oct. 1760, (c) 25 Oct. 1760 to 25 May 1762; Whig; b. 21 July 1693; d. 17 Nov. 1768 at Lincoln's Inn Field, London; bur. Laughton Church, nr. Lewes, Sussex; m. (1717) Lady Henrietta Godolphin (d. 1776); no issue; ed. Westminster School and Claire Hall, Camb.

6. His Grace the 4th Duke of **DEVONSHIRE** (Sir William Cavendish, KG (1756), (PC 1751, but struck off roll 1762)); known as Lord Cavendish of Hardwick until 1729 and Marquess of Hartington until 1755; ministry, 16 Nov. 1756 to May 1757; Whig; b. 1720; d. 2 Oct. 1764 at Spa, Germany; bur. All Saints', Derby; m. (1748) Charlotte Elizabeth, Baroness Clifford (d. 1754); children, 3s and 1d; ed. privately; MP (Whig) for Co. Derby (1741–51). Summoned to Lords (1751) in father's Barony Cavendish of Hardwick.

7. The Rt Hon James **WALDEGRAVE**, 2nd Earl of Waldegrave (pronounced Wallgrave) from 1741, PC (1752), KG (1757); kissed hands 8 June 1757 but returned seals 12 June being unable to form Ministry; b. 14 Mar. 1715; d. 28 Apr. 1763; m. Marion Walpole (niece of No. 1); children 3d; ed. Eton; took seat in House of Lords, 1741.

8. The 3rd Earl of **BUTE** (The Rt Hon, the Hon Sir John Stuart, KG (1762), KT (1738, resigned 1762), (PC 1760)); until 1723 was The Hon John Stuart; ministry, 26 May 1762 to 8 April 1763; Tory; b. 25 May 1713 at Parliament Square, Edinburgh; d. 10 Mar. 1792 at South Audley St, Grosvenor Square, London; bur. Rothesay, Bute; m. (1736) Mary Wortley-Montagu later (1761) Baroness Mount Stuart (d. 1794); children, 4s and 4d (with other issue); ed. Eton.

9. The Rt Hon, the Hon George **GRENVILLE** (PC 1754); prior to 1749 was G. Grenville Esq.; ministry, 16 Apr. 1763 to 10 July 1765; Whig; b. 14 Oct. 1712 at ? Wotton, Bucks; d. 13 Nov. 1770 at Bolton St, Piccadilly, London; bur. Wotton, Bucks; m. (1749) Elizabeth Wyndham (d. 1769); children, 4s and 5d; ed. Eton and Christ Church, Oxford; MP for Buckingham (1741–70).

10. The Most Hon The 2nd Marquess of **ROCKINGHAM** (The Rt Hon Lord Charles Watson-Wentworth), KG (1760), (PC 1765); known as Hon Charles Watson-Wentworth until 1739; Viscount Higham (1739–46); Earl of Malton (1746–50); succeeded to Marquessate 14 Dec. 1750; ministry, (a) 13 July 1765 to July 1766, (b) 27 March 1782 to his death on 1 July 1782; Whig; b. 13 May 1730; d. 1 July 1782; bur. York Minster; m. (1752) Mary Bright (her father was formerly called Liddell) (d. 1804); no issue; ed. Westminster School (and possibly St John's Camb.). Took his seat in House of Lords 21 May 1751.

11. The 1st Earl of **CHATHAM** (The Rt Hon William Pitt (PC 1746)); cr. Earl 4 Aug. 1766; ministry, 30 July 1766 to 14 Oct. 1768; Whig; his health in 1767 prevented his being PM in other than name; b. 15 Nov. 1708 at St James's, Westminster, London; d. 11 May 1788 at Hayes, Kent; bur. Westminster Abbey; m. (1754) Hon. Hester Grenville*, later (1761) cr. Baroness Chatham in her own right (d. 1803); children, 3s and 2d; ed. Eton, Trinity, Oxford (took no degree owing to gout), and Utrecht; MP (Whig) Old Sarum (1735–47); Seaford (1747–54); Aldborough (1754–6); Okehampton (1756–7) (also Buckingham (1756)), Bath (1757–66).

12. His Grace the 3rd Duke of **GRAFTON** (The Rt Hon Sir Augustus Henry FitzRoy), KG (1769), (PC 1765); prior to 1747 known as the Hon. Augustus H. FitzRoy; 1747–57 as Earl of Euston; succeeded to dukedom in 1757; ministry, 14 Oct. 1768 to 28 Jan. 1770; Whig; he was virtually PM in 1767 when Lord Chatham's ministry broke down; b. 28 Sept. 1735 at St Marylebone, London; d. 14 Mar. 1811 at Euston Hall, Suffolk; bur. Euston, Suffolk; m. 1st (1756) Hon. Anne Liddell (sep. 1765, mar. dis. by Act of Parl. 1769) (d. 1804), m. 2ndly (1769) Elizabeth Wrottesley (d. 1822); children, 1st, 1s and 1d; 2nd, 6s and 6d (possibly also another d. who died young); ed. private school at Hackney, Westminster School, and Peterhouse, Camb; MP (Whig) Bury St Edmunds (1756–7).

His Grace the 3rd Duke of Grafton (R.T.H.P.L.)

13. Lord **NORTH** (The Rt Hon, the Hon Sir Frederick North), KG (1772), (PC 1766); succ. (Aug. 1790) as 2nd Earl of Guildford; ministry, 28 Jan. 1770 to 20 Mar. 1782; Tory; b. 13 Apr. 1732 at Albemarle St, Piccadilly, London; d. 5 Aug. 1792 at Lower Grosvenor Street, Middlesex; bur. All Saints' Church, Wroxton, Oxfordshire; m. (1756) Anne Speke (d. 1797); children, 4s and 3d; ed. Eton; Trinity, Oxford, and Leipzig; MP (Tory) for Banbury (1754–90) (can be regarded as a Whig from 1783). Took his seat in the House of Lords 25 Nov. 1790.

14. The 2nd Earl of **SHELBURNE** (Rt Hon, the Hon Sir William Petty, KG (1782) (PC 1763)); formerly, until 1751, William Fitz-Maurice; Viscount Fitz-Maurice (1753–61); succeeded to Earldom 10 May 1761; cr. The 1st Marquess of Lansdowne (6 Dec. 1784); Col. 1760; Maj. Gen. 1765; Lt. Gen. 1772, and Gen. 1783; ministry, 4 July 1782 to 24 Feb. 1783; Whig; b. 20 May 1737 at Dublin, Ireland; d. 7 May 1805 at Berkeley Square, London; bur. High Wycombe, Bucks; m. 1st (1765) Lady Sophia Carteret (d. 1771), 2ndly (1779) Lady Louisa Fitz-Patrick (d. 1789); children, 1st, 2s, 2nd, 1s and 1d; ed. local school in S. Ireland, private tutor, and Christ Church, Oxford; MP Chipping Wycombe (1760–1); Took seat in House of Lords (as Baron Wycombe) 3 Nov. 1761.

---

* This lady had the extraordinary distinction of being the wife, the mother, the sister and the aunt of four British Prime Ministers. They were Nos. 11, 16, 9, and 18 respectively.

15. His Grace the 3rd Duke of **PORT-LAND** (The Most Noble Sir William Henry Cavendish Bentinck, KG (1794) (PC 1765)); assumed additional name of Bentinck in 1755; assumed by Royal Licence surname of Cavendish-Bentinck in 1801; Marquess of Titchfield from birth until he succeeded to the dukedom on 1 May 1762; ministry, (a) 2 April 1783 to Dec. 1783, (b) 31 Mar. 1807 to Oct. 1809; (a) coalition and (b) Tory; b. 14th Apr. 1738; d. 30 Oct. 1809 at Bulstrode, Bucks; bur. St Marylebone, London; m. 1766) Lady Dorothy Cavendish (d. 1794); children, 4s and 1d; ed. Westminster or Eton and Christ Church, Oxford; MP (Whig) Weobley, Herefordshire (1761–2).

16. The Rt Hon, the Hon William **PITT** (PC 1782); prior Aug. 1766 was William Pitt, Esq.; ministry, (a) 19 Dec. 1783 to 14 Mar. 1801, (b) 10 May 1804 to his death on 23 Jan. 1806; Tory; b. 28 May 1759 at Hayes, nr. Bromley, Kent; d. 23 Jan. 1806 at Bowling Green House, Putney, Surrey; bur. Westminster Abbey; unmarried. ed. privately and Pembroke Hall, Cambridge, MP (Tory) Appleby.

17. The Rt Hon Henry **ADDINGTON** (PC 1789); cr. 1st Viscount Sidmouth 1805; ministry, 17 Mar. 1801 to 30 April 1804; Tory; b. 30 May 1757 at Bedford Row, London; d. 15 Feb. 1844 at White Lodge, Richmond Park, Surrey; bur. Mortlake; m. 1st (1781) Ursula Mary Hammond (d. 1811), 2ndly (1823) Hon. Mrs Marianne Townshend (née Scott) (d. 1842); children, 1st, 3s and 4d, 2nd, no issue; ed. Cheam, Winchester Col., Lincoln's Inn, and Brasenose, Oxford (Chancellor's Medal for English Essay); MP (Tory) Devizes (1783–1805). Speaker 1789–1801. As a peer he supported the Whigs in 1807 and 1812 administrations

18. The Rt Hon the 1st Baron **GRENVILLE** of Wotton-under-Bernewood (William Wyndham Grenville (PC (I) 1782; PC 1783)); cr. Baron 25 Nov. 1790; ministry, 10 Feb. 1806 to Mar. 1807; b. (the son of No. 9) 25 Oct. 1759; d. 12 Jan. 1834 at Dropmore Lodge, Bucks; bur. Burnham, Bucks; m. (1792) Hon Anne Pitt (d. 1864 aged 91); no issue; ed. Eton, Christ Church, Oxford (Chancellor's prize for Latin Verse), and Lincoln's Inn; MP Buckingham (1782–4), Buckinghamshire (1784–90). Speaker Jan.–June 1789.

19. The Rt Hon, the Hon Spencer **PERCEVAL** (PC 1807), KC (1796); ministry, 4 Oct. 1809 to 11 May 1812; b. 1 Nov. 1762 at Audley Sq., London; murdered 11 May 1812 in lobby of the House; bur. at Charlton; m. (1790) Jane Spencer-Wilson (later Lady Carr) (d. 1844); children, 6s and 6d; ed. Harrow; Trinity, Camb., and Lincoln's Inn; MP (Tory) Northampton (1796 and 1797).

20. The Rt Hon the 2nd Earl of **LIVERPOOL** (Sir Robert Banks Jenkinson, KG (1814) (PC 1799)); from birth to 1786 R B Jenkinson, Esq.; from 1786–96 The Hon R B Jenkinson; from 1796–1808 (when he succeeded to the earldom) Lord Hawkesbury; ministry, (a) 8 June 1812 to 29 Jan. 1820, (b) 29 Jan. 1820 to 17 Feb. 1827; Tory; b. 7 June 1770; d. 4 Dec. 1828 at Coombe Wood, near Kingston-on-Thames; bur. at Hawkesbury; m. 1st (1795) Lady Louisa Theodosia Hervey (d. 1821), 2ndly (1822) Mary Chester (d. 1846); no issue; ed. Charterhouse and Christ Church, Oxford; summoned to House of Lords in his father's barony of Hawkesbury 15 Nov. 1803 (elected MP (Tory) for Appleby (1790) but did not sit as he was under age); Rye (1796–1803).

21. The Rt Hon George **CANNING** (PC 1800); ministry, 10 Apr. 1827 to his death; Tory; b. 11 Apr. 1770 in London; d. 8 Aug. 1827 at Chiswick Villa, Middx.; m. (1800) Joan Scott (later, 1828, cr. Viscountess) (d. 1837); children, 3s and 1d; ed. in London; Hyde Abbey (nr. Winchester); Eton; Christ Church, Oxford (Chancellor's prize, Latin Verse), and Lincoln's Inn; MP (Tory) Newton, I. o. W. (1793–6); Wendover (1796–1802); Tralee (1802–6); Newton (1806–7); Hastings (1807–12); Liverpool (1812–23); Harwich (1823–6); Newport (1826–7), and Seaford (1827).

The Rt Hon George Canning (R.T.H.P.L.)

22. The Viscount **GODERICH** (Rt Hon, the Hon Frederick John Robinson (PC 1812, PC (I) c. 1833)); cr. Earl of Ripon 1833; ministry 31 Aug. 1827 to 8 Jan. 1828; Tory; b. 1 Nov. 1782 in London; d. 28 Jan. 1859 at Putney Heath, Surrey; bur. Nocton, Lincs; m. (1814) Lady Sarah Albinia Louisa Hobart (d. 1867); children, 2s and 1d; ed. Harrow; St John's Col., Camb., and Lincoln's Inn; MP Carlow (1806–7); Ripon (1807–27).

23. His Grace The 1st Duke of **WELLINGTON** (The Most Noble, The Hon Sir Arthur Wellesley, KG (1813), GCB (1815), GCH (1816), (PC 1807, PC (I) 1807)); known as The Hon Arthur Wesley until 1804; then as The Hon Sir Arthur Wellesley, KB, until 1809 when cr. The Viscount Wellington; cr. Earl of Wellington Feb. 1812; Marquess of Wellington Oct. 1812 and Duke May 1814. Ensign (1787); Lieut. (1787); Capt. (1791); Major (1793); Lt-Col (1793); Col (1796); Maj. Gen. (1802); Lt. Gen. (1808); Gen. (1811); Field Marshal (1813); ministry, (a) 22 Jan. 1828 to 26 June 1830, (b) 26 June 1830 to 21 Nov. 1830, (c) 17 Nov. to 9 Dec. 1834; Tory; b. 1 May 1769 at Mornington House, Upper Merrion St., Dublin; d. 14 Sept. 1852 at Walmer Castle, Kent; bur. St Paul's Cathedral; m. (1806) the Hon Catherine Sarah Dorothea Pakenham (d. 1831); children, 2s; ed. Browns Seminary, King's Rd., Chelsea, London; Eton; Brussels, and The Academy at Angiers; MP Rye (1806); St Michael (1807); Newport, Isle of Wight (1807–9). Took his seat in House of Lords as Viscount, Earl, Marquess, and Duke 28 June 1814.

24. The 2nd Earl **GREY** (The Rt Hon, the Hon Sir Charles Grey, Bt (1808), KG (1831), (PC 1806)); styled Viscount Howick 1806–7 and previously The Hon Charles Grey; ministry, 22 Nov. 1830 to July 1834; Whig; b. 13 Mar. 1764 at Fallodon, Northumberland; d. 17 July 1845 and bur. at Howick House, Northumberland; m. (1794) Hon Mary Elizabeth Ponsonby (d. 1861); children, 8s and 5d; ed. at a private school in Marylebone, London; Eton; Trinity, Camb., and Middle Temple; MP (Whig) Northumberland (1786–1807); Appleby (1807); Tavistock (1807).

25. The 3rd Viscount **MELBOURNE** (The Rt Hon, The Hon Sir William Lamb, Bt (PC (UK & I) 1827)); ministry, (a) 16 July 1834 to Nov. 1834, (b) 18 April 1835 to 20 June 1837, (c) 20 June 1837 to Aug. 1841; Whig; b. (of disputed paternity) 15 March 1779 Melbourne House, Piccadilly, London; d. 24 Nov. 1848 at Brocket; bur. at Hatfield; m. (1805) Lady Caroline Ponsonby, separated 1824 (d. 1828); only 1s survived infancy; ed. Eton; Trinity, Cambridge; Glasgow University, and Lincoln's Inn; MP (Whig) Leominster (1806); Haddington Borough (1806–7); Portarlington (1807–12); Peterborough (1816–19); Herts (1819–26); Newport, Isle of Wight (1827); Bletchingley (1827–8). Took his seat in House of Lords 1 Feb. 1829.

26. The Rt Hon Sir Robert **PEEL**, Bt (PC 1812); prior to May 1830 he was Robert Peel, Esq., MP, when he succeeded as 2nd Baronet; ministry, (a) 10 Dec. 1834 to 8 Apr. 1835, (b) 30 Aug. 1841 to 29 June 1846; Conservative; b. 5 Feb. 1788 prob. at Chamber Hall, nr. Bury, Lancashire; d. 2 July 1850 after fall from horse; bur. at Drayton-Bassett; m. (1820) Julia Floyd (d. 1859); children, 5s and 2d; ed. Harrow; Christ Church, Oxford (Double First in Classics and Mathematics), and Lincoln's Inn; MP (Tory) Cashel (Tipperary) (1809–12); Chippenham (1812–17); Univ. of Oxford (1817–29); Westbury (1829–30); Tamworth (1830–50).

27. The Rt Hon Lord John **RUSSELL** (PC 1830), and after 30 July 1861 1st Earl **RUSSELL**, KG (1862), GCMG (1869); ministry, (a) 30 June 1846 to Feb. 1852, (b) 29 Oct. 1865 to June 1866; (a) Whig and (b) Liberal; b. 18 Aug. 1792 in Hertford St, Mayfair; d. 28 May 1878 at Pembroke Lodge, Richmond Park, Surrey; bur. Chenies, Bucks; m. 1st (1835) Adelaide (née Lister), Dowager Baroness Ribblesdale (d. 1838), 2ndly (1841) Lady Frances Anna Maria Elliot-Murray-Kynynmound (d. 1898); children, 1st, 2d, 2nd 3s and 3d; ed. Westminster School and Edinburgh University; MP (Whig) Tavistock (1813–17, 1818–20 & 1830–1); Hunts (1820–6); Bandon (1826–30); Devon (1831–2); S. Devon (1832–5); Stroud (1835–41); City of London (1841–61). Took seat in the House of Lords on 30 July 1861.

28. The 14th Earl of **DERBY**, Rt Hon Sir Edward Geoffry Smith-Stanley, Bt, KG (1859), GCMG (1869), PC 1830, PC (I) 1831); prior to 1834 known as the Hon E G Stanley, MP; then known as Lord Stanley MP until 1844; ministry, (a) 23 Feb. 1852 to 18 Dec. 1852, (b) 20 Feb. 1858 to 11 June 1859, (c) 28 June 1866 to 26 Feb. 1868; Tory and Conservative; b. 19 March 1799 at Knowsley, Lancs; d. 23 Oct. 1869; and bur. at Knowsley, Lancs; m. (1825) Hon Emma Caroline Wilbraham-Bootle (d. 1876); 2s, 1d; ed. Eton; Christ Church Oxford (Chancellor's prize for Latin Verse); MP (Whig) Stockbridge (1822–6); Preston (1826–30); Windsor (1831–2); North Lancs (1832–44). Summoned 1844 to House of Lords as Lord Stanley (of Bickerstaffe); succeeded to Earldom 1851; became a Tory in 1835.

29. The Rt Hon Sir George Hamilton Gordon, Bt, 4th Earl of **ABERDEEN**, KG (1855), KT (1808), (PC 1814); prior to Oct. 1791 known as the Hon G Gordon; from 1791 to Aug. 1801 known as Lord Haddo; assumed additional name of Hamilton Nov. 1818; ministry, 19 Dec. 1852 to 5 Feb. 1855; Peelite; b. 28 Jan. 1784 in Edinburgh; d. 14 Dec. 1860 at Argyll House, St James's, London; bur. at Stanmore, Middlesex; m. 1st (1805) Lady Catherine Elizabeth Hamilton (d. 1812), 2ndly (1815) to her sister-in-law Harriet (née Douglas), Dowager Viscoun-

tess Hamilton (d. 1833); children, 1st, 1s and 3d, 2nd 4s and 1d; ed. Harrow and St John's, Camb.; House of Lords 1814.

30. The Rt Hon Sir Henry John Temple, 3rd and last Viscount **PALMERSTON** (a non-representative peer of Ireland), KG (1856), GCB (1832), (PC 1809); known (1784–1802) as the Hon H J Temple; ministry, (a) 6 Feb. 1855 to 19 Feb. 1858, (b) 12 June 1859 to 18 Oct. 1865; Liberal; b. 20 Oct. 1784 at Broadlands, nr. Romsey, Hants (or possibly in Park St, London); d. 18 Oct. 1865 at Brocket Hall, Herts; bur. Westminster Abbey; m. (1839) Hon. Emily Mary (née Lamb), the Dowager Countess Cowper (d. 1869); no issue; ed. Harrow; Univ. of Edinburgh, and St John's Camb.; MP (Tory) Newport, Isle of Wight (1807–11); Camb. Univ. (1811–31); Bletchingley (1831–2); S. Hants. (1832–4); Tiverton (1835–65); from 1829 a Whig and latterly a liberal.

31. The Rt Hon Benjamin **DISRAELI**, 1st and last Earl of **BEACONSFIELD**, KG (1878), (PC 1852); prior to 12 Aug. 1876 Benjamin Disraeli (except that until 1838 he was known as Benjamin D'Israeli); ministry, (a) 27 Feb. 1868 to November 1868, (b) 20 Feb. 1874 to Apr. 1880; Conservative; b. 21 Dec. 1804 at either the Adelphi, Westminster, or at 22 Theobald's Rd, or St Mary Axe; d. 19 Apr. 1881 at 19 Curzon St, Mayfair, London; bur. Hughenden Manor, Bucks (monument in Westminster Abbey); m. (1839) Mrs Mary Anne Lewis (née Evans) later (1868) Viscountess (in her own right) Beaconsfield; no issue; ed. Lincoln's Inn; MP (Con.) Maidstone (1837–41); Shrewsbury (1841–7); Buckinghamshire (1847–76), when he became a peer.

32. The Rt Hon William Ewart **GLADSTONE** (PC 1841); ministry, (a) 3 Dec. 1868 to February 1874, (b) 23 April 1880 to 12 June 1885, (c) 1 Feb. 1886 to 20 July 1886, (d) 15 Aug. 1892 to 3 March 1894; Liberal; b. 29 Dec. 1809 at 62 Rodney St, Liverpool; d. 19 May 1898 (aged 88 yr 142 days) at Hawarden Castle, Wales; bur. Westminster Abbey; m. (1839) Catherine Glynne (d. 1900); children, 4s and 4d; ed. Seaforth Vicarage; Eton and Christ Church, Oxford (Double First in Classics and Mathematics); MP Tory, Newark (1832–45); Univ. of Oxford (1847–65) (Peelite to 1859, thereafter a Liberal); S. Lancs. (1865–8); Greenwich (1868–80); Midlothian (1880–95).

33. The Rt Hon Robert Arthur Talbot Gascoyne-Cecil, the 3rd Marquess of **SALISBURY**, KG (1878), GCVO (1902), (PC 1866); known as Lord Robert Cecil till 1865, and as Viscount Cranbourne, MP, from 1865 to 1868; ministry, (a) 23 June 1885 to 28 Jan. 1886, (b) 25 July 1886 to Aug. 1892, (c) 25 June 1895 to 22 Jan. 1901, (d) 23 Jan. 1901 to 11 July 1902; Conservative; b. 3 Feb. 1830 at Hatfield House, Herts; d. 22 Aug. 1903 at Hatfield House; bur. at Hatfield; m. (1857) Georgiana Charlotte (née Alderson), Lady of the Royal Order of Victoria and Albert and C.I. (1899) (d. 1899); Children, 4s and 3d; ed. Eton and Christ Church, Oxford (Hon. 4th Cl. Maths.); MP (Con.) for Stamford (1853–68).

34. The Rt Hon Sir Archibald Philip Primrose, Bt, 5th Earl of **ROSEBERY**, KG (1892), KT (1895), VD (PC 1881); b. the Hon A P Primrose; known as Lord Dalmeny (1851–68); Earl of Midlothian from 1911 but style not adopted by him; ministry, 5 Mar. 1894 to 21 June 1895; Liberal; b. 7 May 1847 at Charles St, Berkeley Square, London; d. 21 May 1929 at 'The Durdans', Epsom, Surrey; bur. at Dalmeny; m. (1878) Hannah de Rothschild (d. 1890); children, 2s and 2d; ed. Eton and Christ Church, Oxford.

35. The Rt Hon Arthur James **BAL-FOUR** (PC 1885, PC (I) 1887); KG (1922),

later (1922) the 1st Earl of Balfour, OM (1916); ministry, 12 July 1902 to 4 Dec. 1905; Conservative; b. 25 July 1848 at Whittinge-hame, E. Lothian, Scotland; d. 19 Mar. 1930 at Fisher's Hill, Woking, Surrey; bur. at Whittingehame; unmarried; ed. Eton and Trinity, Camb.; MP (Con.) Hertford (1874–85); E. Manchester (1885–1906); City of London (1906–22).

36. The Rt Hon Sir Henry **CAMP-BELL-BANNERMAN**, GCB (1895), (PC 1884); known as Henry Campbell until 1872; ministry, 5 Dec. 1905 to 5 Apr. 1908; Liberal; b. 7 Sept. 1836 at Kelvinside House, Glasgow; d. 22 Apr. 1908 at 10 Downing Street, London; bur. Meigle, Scotland; m. (1860) Sarah Charlotte Bruce (d. 1906); no issue; ed. Glasgow High School; Glasgow Univ. (Gold Medal for Greek); Trinity, Camb. (22nd Sen. Optime in Maths Tripos; 3rd Cl. in Classical Tripos); MP (Lib.) Stirling District (1868–1908).

37. The Rt Hon Herbert Henry **ASQUITH** (PC 1892, PC (I) 1916); later (1925) 1st Earl of **OXFORD AND AS-QUITH**, KG (1925); ministry, (a) 7 Apr. 1908 to 7 May 1910, (b) 8 May 1910 to 5 Dec. 1916 (coalition from 25 May 1915); Liberal; b. 12 Sept. 1852 at Morley, Yorks; d. 15 Feb. 1928 at 'The Wharf', Sutton Courtney, Berks; bur. Sutton Courtney Church; m. 1st (1877) Helen Kelsall Melland (d. 1891), 2ndly (1894) Emma Alice Margaret Tennant; children, 1st, 4s and 1d, 2nd 1s and 1d; ed. City of London School; Balliol, Oxford (Scholar 1st Class Lit. Hum.); MP (Lib.) East Fife (1886–1918); Paisley (1920–4).

38. The Rt Hon (David) Lloyd **GEORGE**, OM (1919), (PC 1905); later (1945) 1st Earl **LLOYD-GEORGE** of Dwyfor; ministry, 7 Dec. 1916 to 19 Oct. 1922; Coalition; b. 17 Jan. 1863 in Manchester; d. 26 Mar. 1945 at Ty Newydd, nr. Llanystumdwy; bur. on the bank of the river Dwyfor; m. 1st (1888) Margaret Owen, GBE (1920) (d. 1941), 2ndly (1943) Frances Louise Stevenson, CBE; children, 1st 2s and 2d, 2nd no issue; ed. Llanystumdwy Church School and privately; MP Caernarvon Boroughs (1890–1945) (Lib. 1890–1931 and 1935–45; Ind. Lib. 1931–5).

The Rt Hon David Lloyd George
(Radio Times Hulton Picture Library)

39. The Rt Hon (Andrew) Bonar **LAW** (PC 1911); ministry, 23 Oct. 1922 to 20 May 1923; Conservative; b. 16 Sept. 1858 a Kingston, nr. Richibucto, new Brunswick Canada; d. 30 Oct. 1923 at 24 Onslow Grdns., London; bur. Westminster Abbey m. (1891) Annie Pitcairn (d. 1909); children 4s and 2d; ed. Gilbertfield School, Hamilton Glasgow High School; MP (Con.) Blackfriars Div. of Glasgow (1900–6); Dulwich Div. of Camberwell (1906–10); MP Bootle Div. of Lancs (1911–18); Central Div. of Glasgow (1918–23).

40. The Rt Hon Stanley **BALDWIN** (PC 1920, PC (Can.) 1927); later (1937) 1st Earl Baldwin of Bewdley, KG (1937) ministry, (a) 22 May 1923 to 22 Jan. 1924 (Con.), (b) 4 Nov. 1924 to 4 June 1929 (Con.), (c) 7 June 1935 to 20 Jan. 1936 (Nat.), (d) 21 Jan. 1936 to 11 Dec. 1936 (Nat), (e) 12 Dec. 1936 to 28 May 1937 (Nat.); b. 3 Aug. 1867 at Bewdley; d. 14 Dec. 1947; bur. Worcester Cathedral; m (1892) Lucy Ridsdale, GBE (1937) (d. 1945) children, 2s and 4d; ed. Harrow and Trinity Camb.; MP (Con.) Bewdley Div. of Worcestershire (1908–37).

41. The Rt Hon (James) Ramsay **MACDONALD** (PC 1924, PC (Canada) 1929); ministry, (a) 22 Jan. 1924 to 4 Nov 1924 (Labour), (b) 5 June 1929 to 7 June 1935 (Labour and from 1931 National Coalition); b. 12 Oct. 1866 at Lossiemouth Morayshire; d. 9 Nov. 1937 at sea, mid-Atlantic; bur. Spynie Churchyard, nr Lossiemouth, Scotland; m. (1896) Margaret Ethel Gladstone (d. 1911); children, 3s and 3d; ed. Drainie Parish Board School; MP (Lab.) Leicester (1906–18); (Lab.) Aberavon (1922–9); (Lab.) Seaham Div. Co. Durham (1929–31); (Nat. Lab.) (1931–5); MP for Scottish Univs. (1936–7).

42. The Rt Hon (Arthur) Neville **CHAMBERLAIN** (PC 1922); ministry, 28 May 1937 to 10 May 1940; National; b. 18 Mar. 1869 at Edgbaston, Birmingham; d. 9 Nov. 1940 at High Field Park, Hickfield, nr. Reading; ashes interred Westminster Abbey; m. (1911) Annie Vere Cole (d. 12 Feb. 1967); children, 1s and 1d; ed. Rugby School; Mason College (later Birmingham Univ.) (Metallurgy & Engineering Design); MP (Con.) Ladywood Div. of Birmingham (1918–29); Edgbaston Div. of Birmingham (1929–40).

43. The Rt Hon Sir Winston (Leonard **SPENCER-)CHURCHILL**, KG (1953) OM (1946), CH (1922), TD (PC 1907); ministry, (a) 10 May 1940 to 26 July 1945 (Coalition but from 23 May 1945 Conservative), (b) 26 Oct. 1951 to 6 Feb. 1952 (Conservative), (c) 7 Feb. 1952 to 5 Apr. 1955 (Conservative); b. 30 Nov. 1874 at Blenheim Palace, Woodstock, Oxon; d. 24 Jan. 1965 Hyde Park Gate, London; bur. Bladen, Oxfordshire; m. (1908) Clementine Ogilvy Hozier, GBE (1946 cr. 1965 (Life) Baroness Spencer-Churchill; children, 1s and 4d; ed. Harrow School and Royal Military College; MP (Con. until 1904, then Lib.) Oldham (1900–6); (Lib.) N.-W. Manchester (1906–8); (Lib.) Dundee (1908–18 and (Coalition Lib.) until 1922; Epping Div. of Essex (1924–45); Woodford Div. of Essex (1945–64).

44. The Rt Hon Clement (Richard) **ATTLEE** CH (1945), (PC 1935); created 1955 1st Earl Attlee, KG (1956), OM (1951); ministry, 26 July 1945 to 26 Oct. 1951; Labour; b. 3 Jan. 1883 at Putney, London; d. 8 Oct. 1967; m. (1922) Violet Helen Millar; children, 1s and 3d; ed. Haileybury College and Univ. College, Oxford (2nd Cl. Hons. (Mod. Hist.)); MP Limehouse Div. of Stepney (1922–50); West Walthamstow (1950–5).

45. The Rt. Hon Sir (Robert) Anthony **EDEN**, KG (1954), MC (1917), (PC 1934);

r. 1961 1st Earl of Avon; ministry, 6 Apr. 955 to 9 Jan. 1957; Conservative; b. 12 June 897 Windlestone, Durham; m. 1st (1923) eatrice Helen Beckett (m. dis. 1950) (d. 957), 2ndly (1952) Anne Clarissa Spencer-churchill; children, 1st, 2s 2nd, no issue; ed. ton and Christ Church, Oxford (1st Cl. Ions (Oriental Langs)); MP Warwick and eamington (1923–57).

46. The Rt Hon (Maurice) Harold **1ACMILLAN** (PC 1942); ministry, 10 an. 1957 to 18 Oct. 1963; Conservative; b. 0 Feb. 1894, 52 Cadogan Place, London; n. (1920) Lady Dorothy Evelyn Cavendish, BE, 1s and 3d; ed. Eton (Scholar); Balliol, Xford ((Exhibitioner) 1st Class Hon Aods.); MP Stockton-on-Tees (1924–9 and 931–45); Bromley (1945–64).

47. The Rt Hon Sir Alexander (Freder-ck) **DOUGLAS-HOME**, KT (1962) (PC 951); known until 30 April 1918 as the Hon F Douglas-Home; thence until 11 July 951 as Lord Dunglass; thence until his isclaimer of 23 Oct. 1963 as the (14th) Earl f Home; ministry, 19 Oct. 1963 to 16 Oct. 964, Conservative; b. 2 July 1903, 28 South t, London; m. (1936) Elizabeth Hester lington; children, 1s and 3d; ed. Eton; christ Church, Oxford; MP South Lanark 1931–45); Lanark (1950–1); Kinross and Vest Perthshire (1963 to date).

48. The Rt Hon Sir (James) Harold VILSON, KG (1976) OBE(Civ.) (1945) (PC 947); ministry, (a) 16 Oct. 1964 to 30 Mar. 966, (b) 31 Mar. 1966 to 17 June 1970, (c) 4 Aar. 1974 to 10 Oct. 1974, (d) 10 Oct. 1974 o 5 Apr. 1976; Labour; b. 11 Mar. 1916; m. 1940) Gladys Mary Baldwin; children, 2s; d. Milnsbridge C.S.; Royds Hall S.; Wirral i.S.; Jesus College, Oxford (1st Cl. Philo-ophy, Politics and Economics); MP Orms-irk (1945–50); Huyton (1950 to date).

49. The Rt Hon Edward Richard George HEATH, MBE(mil.) (1946), (PC 1955); ninistry, 18 June 1970 to 3 Mar. 1974; conservative; b. 7 July 1916 at Broadstairs, Kent; unmarried; ed. Chatham House chool, Ramsgate and Balliol College,)xford; MP Bexley (1950–74); Bexley-idcup from 1974.

50. The Rt Hon (Leonard) James CALLAGHAN (PC 1964); ministry 5 Apr. 976 to date; Labour; b. 27 Mar. 1912 at 'ortsmouth, Hampshire; m. (1938) Audrey Elizabeth Moulton, children 1s and 2d; ed. 'ortsmouth Northern Secondary Sch.; M.P. ;outh Cardiff 1945–50; South-east Cardiff 950 to date. Other major offices: Chancellor f the Exchequer 1964–67; Home Secretary 967–70; Foreign Secretary 1974–76. Elected eader of Labour Party over Rt Hon Michael 'oot by 176–136 votes on 5 Apr. 1976.

Leader of H.M. Opposition Rt Hon Mrs Margaret (Hilda) Thatcher *née* Roberts (PC 1970) elected leader of Conservative Party over Rt Hon William (Stephen Ian) Whitelaw CH, MC, MP by 136–79 votes on 11 Feb. 1975—Mr Heath (see 49 above) having withdrawn after losing to her on first ballot of 130–119 on 4 Feb. b. 22 Oct. 1926, Grantham, Lincolnshire; m. (1951) Denis Thatcher 1s 1d (twins) ed. Kesteven & Grantham Girls' Sch.; Somerville Coll., Oxford (MA, BSc): MP Finchley 1959–74; Barnet, Finchley 1974 to date.

Authorised post nominal letters in their correct order
There are 70 Orders, Decorations, and Medals which have been bestowed by the Sovereign that carry the entitlement to a group of letters after the name. Of these, 54 are currently awardable. The order (*vide London Gazette*, supplement 27 Oct. 1964) is as follows:

1. V.C.   Victoria Cross.
2. G.C.   George Cross.
3. KG   (but *not* for Ladies of the Order), Knight of the Most Noble Order of the Garter.
4. KT   (but *not* for Ladies of the Order), Knight of the Most Ancient and Most Noble Order of the Thistle.
5. GCB   Knight Grand Cross of the Most Honourable Order of the Bath.
6. OM   Member of the Order of Merit.
†7. GCSI   Knight Grand Commander of the Most Excellent Order of the Star of India.
8. GCMG   Knight (or Dame) Grand Cross of the Most Distinguished Order of St Michael and St George.
†9. GCIE   Knight Grand Commander of the Most Eminent Order of the Indian Empire.
†10. CI   Lady of The Imperial Order of the Crown of India.
11. GCVO   Knight (or Dame) Grand Cross of the Royal Victorian Order.
12. GBE   Knight (or Dame) Grand Cross of the Most Excellent Order of the British Empire.
13. CH   Member of the Order of Companions of Honour.
14. KCB   (but *not* if also a GCB), Knight Commander of the Most Honourable Order of the Bath.
15. DCB   (but *not* if also a GCB) Dame Commander of the Most Honourable Order of the Bath.
†16. KCSI   (but *not* if also a GCSI), Knight Commander of the Most Excellent Order of the Star of India.
17. KCMG   (but *not* if also a GCMG), Knight Commander of the Most Distinguished Order of St Michael and St George.
18. DCMG   (but *not* if also a GCMG) Dame Commander of the Most Distinguished Order of St Michael and St George.
†19. KCIE   (but *not* if also a GCIE), Knight Commander of the Most Eminent Order of the Indian Empire.
20. KCVO   (but *not* if also a GCVO), Knight Commander of the Royal Victorian Order.
21. DCVO   (but *not* if also a GCVO), Dame Commander of the Royal Victorian Order.
22. KBE   (but *not* if also a GBE), Knight Commander of the Most Excellent Order of the British Empire.
22. DBE   (but *not* if also a GBE), Dame Commander of the Most Excellent Order of the British Empire.
24. CB   (but *not* if also a GCB and/or a KCB), Companion of the Most Honourable Order of the Bath.
†25. CSI   (but *not* if also a GCSI and/or a KCSI), Companion of the Most Excellent Order of the Star of India.
26. CMG   (but *not* if also a GCMG and/or a KCMG or DCMG), Companion of the Most Distinguished Order of St Michael and St George.
†27. CIE   (but *not* if also a GCIE and/or a KCIE), Companion of the Most Eminent Order of the Indian Empire.
28. CVO   (but *not* if also a GCVO and/or a KCVO or DCVO), Commander of the Royal Victorian Order.
29. CBE   (but *not* if also a GBE and/or a KBE or DBE), Commander of the Most Excellent Order of the British Empire.
30. DSO   Companion of the Distinguished Service Order.
31. MVO   (if 4th Class, but *not* if also either a GCVO and/or a KCVO or a DCVO, and/or a CVO), Member of the Royal Victorian Order.
32. OBE   (but *not* if also either a GBE and/or a KBE or DBE and/or a CBE), Officer of the Most Excellent Order of the British Empire.
33. ISO   Companion of the Imperial Service Order.
MVO   (if 5th Class, but *not* if also either a GCVO and/or a KCVO or a DCVO, and/or a CVO or a MVO (4th Class), Member of the Royal Victorian Order.
34. MBE   (but *not* if also either a GBE and/or a KBE or DBE and/or a CBE and/or an OBE), Member of the Most Excellent Order of the British Empire.
†35. IOM   (if in Military Division), Indian Order of Merit.
†36. OB   Order of Burma (when* for gallantry).
37. RRC   Member of the Royal Red Cross.
38. DSC   Distinguished Service Cross.
39. MC   Military Cross.
40. DFC   Distinguished Flying Cross.
41. AFC   Air Force Cross.
42. ARRC   (but *not* if also an RRC), Associate of the Royal Red Cross.
†43. OBI   Order of British India.
— OB   Order of Burma (when for distinguished service).
44. DCM   Distinguished Conduct Medal.
45. CGM   (both the Naval and the Flying decorations), Conspicuous Gallantry Medal.
46. GM   George Medal.
†47. KPM   King's or Queen's Police Medal
†48. KPFSM   or Police & Fire Services Medal for Gallantry.
49. QPM
50. QFSM
DCM   (if for Royal West African Frontier Force), Distinguished Conduct Medal.
DCM   (if for the King's African Rifles), Distinguished Conduct Medal.
51. IDSM   Indian Distinguished Service Medal.
†52. BGM   Burma Gallantry Medal.
53. DSM   Distinguished Service Medal.
54. MM   Military Medal.
55. DFM   Distinguished Flying Medal.
55. AFM   Air Force Medal.
57. SGM   Medal for Saving Life at Sea (Sea Gallantry Medal).
† IOM   (if in Civil Division), Indian Order of Merit.
†58. EGM   Empire Gallantry Meda (usable only in reference to pre 1940 honorary awards unexchangeable for the G.C.
59. QGM   Queen's Gallantry Medal.
60. BEM   British Empire Medal, for Gallantry, or the British Empire Medal.
61. CM   (or for French speakers M du C, Medaille du Canada), Canada Medal.

†— KPM
†— KPFSM
— QPM
— QFSM
  See 47–50 above, but for distinguished or good service.

121

62. MSM (but only if awarded for Naval service prior to 20 July 1928), Medal for Meritorious Service.

63. ERD Emergency Reserve Decoration (Army) (for either the obsolescent Volunteer Officers' Decoration (1892–1908) or Volunteer Officers' Decoration (for India and the Colonies) (1894–1930)).

†65. ED (if for the obsolescent Colonial Auxiliary Forces Officers' Decoration (1899–1930)).

66. TD (for either the obsolescent Territorial Decoration (1908–30) or for the current Efficiency Decoration (inst. 1930) when awarded to an officer of the (*Home*) Auxiliary Military Forces).

67. ED (if for the current Efficiency Decoration (inst. 1930) when awarded to an officer of *Commonwealth* or Colonial Auxiliary Military Forces).

68. RD Decoration for Officers of the Royal Naval Reserve.

69. VRD Decoration for Officers of the Royal Naval Volunteer Reserve.

70. CD Canadian Forces Decoration.

Any of the above post nominal letters precede any others which may relate to academic honours or professional qualifications. The unique exception is that the abbreviation 'Bt.' (or less favoured 'Bart.'), indicating a Baronetcy, should be put before *all* other letters, e.g. The Rt Hon Sir John Smyth, Bt., VC, MC.

The abbreviation PC (indicating membership of the Privy Council), which used to be placed after KG, is now not to be used, except possibly with peers, because in their case the style 'Rt Hon' cannot be used to indicate membership of the Privy Council, since Barons, Viscounts and Earls already enjoy this style *ipso facto* and Marquesses and Dukes have the superior styles 'Most Hon' and 'Most Noble' respectively.

There are other British honours which carry no entitlement to post nominal letters. These include The Royal Victorian Chain; the Royal Order of Victoria and Albert; the Kaisar-i-Hind Medal; King's or Queen's Medal for Bravery; the Royal Victorian Medal, and the Imperial Service Medal.

The following previously authorised British post nominal letters are now obsolete but are still encountered in old reference sources:

KB indicated Knightship of the Order of the Bath prior to its division into three classes in 1815.

GCH indicated membership of one of the three classes—Knights Grand Cross, Knights Commander, Knights—of 'The Order of the Guelphs' conferred from 1815 to 1837 during the Union of the Crowns of Hanover and the United Kingdom.

KCH
KH Kingdom.

KSI Knights of the Most Excellent Order of the Star of India. This designation was used between 1861 and 1866 before the Order was enlarged into three classes.

CSC Conspicuous Service Cross (inst. in 1901) was replaced by the DSC in 1914.

† This distinction is no longer awarded, but there are surviving recipients.

UNITED KINGDOM COINAGE

	Standard Weight in grammes	Standard Weight in oz avoirdupois	DIAMETER cms	ins
GOLD (22 carats or 91·66%) Legal tender to any amount				
£5 quintuple sovereign	39,94028	1.40885	3,601	1.418
£2 double sovereign	15,97611	0.56354	2,839	1.118
£1 sovereign	7,98805	0.28177	2,204	0.868
50p half sovereign	3,99402	0.14089	1,9304	0.760

SILVER Silver coinage is now confined to Maundy money in 4 pence, 3 pence, 2 pence and 1 penny pieces in 92·5% silver. These do not circulate.

CUPRO-NICKEL					
50p 50 pence	Legal tender to £10	13,5	0.4761	3,0	1.1811
10p 10 pence	Legal tender to £5	11,31036	0.3989	2,8500	1.122
5p 5 pence	Legal tender to £5	5,65518	0.1994	2,3595	0.9289

BRONZE (Copper 97 parts, zinc 2½ parts, tin ½ part)					
2p 2 pence	Legal tender to 20p	7,12800	0.2514	2,5910	1.0200
1p 1 penny	Legal tender to 20p	3,56400	0.1257	2,0320	0.7999
½p ½ penny	Legal tender to 20p	1,78200	0.0628	1,7145	0.6749

Modern Imperial Coinage (Post 1816)

Imperial coinage struck by or for the Royal Mint, has existed in the following denominations and dates (hyphens indicate consecutive and inclusive dates).

Quarter-Farthing ¹⁄₁₆d	1839, 1851–3, 1868
Third-Farthing ¹⁄₁₂d	1827, 1835, 1844, 1866, 1868, 1876, 1879, 1881, 1884–5, 1902, 1913
Half-Farthing ⅛d	1828, 1830, 1837, 1839, 1842–4, 1847, 1851–4, 1856, 1868
Farthings ¼d	1821–3, 1825–31, 1834–60, 1860–9, 1872–88, 1890–1956
Old Halfpenny ½d	1825–7, 1831, 1834, 1837–9, 1841, 1843–8, 1851–60, 1860–1960, 1902–67
Old Penny 1d	1825–7, 1831, 1834, 1837, 1839, 1841, 1843–9, 1851, 1853–60, 1860–1922, 1926–40, 1944–51, 1953–4, 1961–7
Half New Pence ½p	1971, 1973–5
Three-halfpence 1½d	1834–43, 1860, 1862
One New Penny 1p	1971, 1973–5
Three-Pence (Nickel Brass) 3d	1937–46, 1948–67
Three-Pence (Silver) 3d	1834–7, 1838–51, 1853–1922, 1925–8, 1930–44
Groat 4d	1836–49, 1851–5, 1888
Two New Pence 2p	1971, 1975
Sixpence 6d	1816–21, 1824–9, 1831, 1839–46, 1848–1967
One Shilling 1s	1816–21, 1823–7, 1829, 1834–46, 1848–1966
Five New Pence 5p	1968–71, 1975
Two Shillings (Florin) 2s	1849, 1851–60, 1862–1967
Ten New Pence 10p	1968–71, 1973–5
Half Crown 2s 6d	1816–17, 1820–21, 1823–6, 1828–9, 1834–7, 1839–46, 1848–50, 1874–1967
Double Florin 4s	1887–90
Crown 5s	1818–20, 1821–2, 1831 (proof only), 1844–5, 1847, 1887–1900, 1902, 1927–37, 1951, 1953, 1960, 1965
25 New Pence 25p	1972
50 New Pence 50p	1969–70, 1973
Half Sovereign £½	1817–18, 1820, 1841–61, 1863–7, 1869–80, 1883–1915, 1937, 1953★
Sovereign £1	1838–9, 1841–66, 1868–74, 1876, 1878–80, 1884–5, 1887–96, 1898–1917, 1925, 1937★ (Edward VIII), 1937, 1957–9, 1962–8, 1974
Two Pound Piece £2	1887, 1893, 1902, 1911, 1937★ (Edward VIII), 1937, 1953★
Five Pound Piece £5	1839★, 1887, 1893, 1902, 1911, 1937★ (Edward VIII), 1937, 1953★

★ Pattern or proof only.

Sovereigns:
Melbourne (small M, mintmark on reverse side) 1872–4, 1881–5, 1887–1931.
Sydney (small S) 1871–5, 1877–1926. Ottawa (small C) 1908–11, 1913–14, 1916–19. Perth (small P) 1893–1931. Bombay (small I) 1918. Pretoria (small SA) 1925–32.

Half-Sovereigns:

Sydney	1871–2, 1874–6, 1878–83, 1886–7, 1891–3, 1898–1903, 1906, 1908, 1910–12, 1914–16.
Melbourne	1873, 1877, 1881–2, 1884–7, 1893, 1896, 1896, 1899–1900, 1906, 1908–09, 1915.
Perth	1900, 1904, 1908–9, 1911, 1915, 1919–20.
Pretoria	1925–6.

Bank Notes
In Britain by 1677 there were as many as 44 goldsmiths operating 'running cashes' with deposit receipts which had virtually become promissory notes. The Bank of England's earliest notes in 1694 were mostly manuscript. The first notes with printed denominations were ordered on 5 June 1695 and were of £5, £10, £20, £30, £40, £50 denominations. The oldest surviving note to bearer is a watermarked specimen dated 19 Oct. 1699 for £555. Notes of fixed denomination had again been suspended until 1725.

Bank of England Fixed Denomination Notes (Dates of circulation)

10s.	1928	Legal tender	£50	1725	1943
£1 (first issue)	1797	1821	£60	1745	c. 1802
£1 (reissue)	1928	Legal tender	£70	1745	c. 1802
£2	1797	1821	£80	1745	c. 1802
£5	1793	Legal tender	£90	1745	c. 1802
£10	1759	1943	£100	1725	1943
£10 (reissue)	1964	Legal tender	£200	1745	1928
£15	1759	1822	£300	1745	1885
£20	1725	1943	£400	1745	c. 1802
£20 (reissue)	1970	Legal tender			
£25	1765	1822	£500	1745	1943
£30	1725	1852	£1 000	1745	1943
£40	1725	1851			

The Treasury issued 10s. and £1 currency notes on 6 Aug. 1914 until the issue of the Bank of England 10s. note and the reissue of the £1 on 22 Nov. 1928.

Bank of England notes bore the manuscript signatures of various cashiers of the Bank from 1694–1853, when the signatures of the cashiers were first printed. The office of Chief Cashier has been held as follows:

6 Dec. 1866–2 July 1873,	George Forbes
3 July 1873–8 Nov. 1893,	Frank May
9 Nov. 1893–12 Jan. 1902,	Horace George Bowen
13 Jan. 1902–8 May 1918,	John Gordon Nairne
9 May 1918–8 Apr. 1925,	Ernest Musgrave Harvey
9 Apr. 1925–26 Mar. 1929,	Cyril Patrick Mahon
27 Mar. 1929–18 Apr. 1934,	Basil Gage Catterns
19 Apr. 1934–28 Feb. 1949	Kenneth Oswald Peppiatt
1 Mar. 1949–15 Jan. 1955,	Percy Spencer Beale
16 Jan. 1955–28 Feb. 1962,	Leslie Kenneth O'Brien
1 Mar. 1962–30 June 1966,	Jasper Quintus Hollom
1 July 1966–28 Feb. 1970,	John Standish Fforde
1 Mar. 1970 to date	John Brangwgn Page

ECONOMICS

The United Kingdom's National Debt

The National Debt is the nominal amount of outstanding debt chargeable on the Consolidated Fund of the United Kingdom Exchequer only, i.e. the debt created by the separate Northern Ireland Exchequer is excluded.

The National Debt became a permanent feature of the country's economy as early as 1692. The table below shows how the net total Debt has increased over the years (data being for 31 March of year shown):

Year	National Debt (£ million)	Year	National Debt (£ million)	Year	National Debt (£ million)
1697	14	1917	4 011·4	1952	25 890·5
1727	52	1918	5 871·9	1953	26 051·2
1756	75	1919	7 434·9	1954	26 538·0
1763	133	1920*	7 828·8	1955	26 933·7
1775	127	1921	7 574·4	1956	27 038·9
1781	187	1923	7 742·2	1957	27 007·5
1784	243	1931	7 413·3	1958	27 232·0
1793	245	1934	7 822·3	1959	27 376·3
1802	523	1935†	6 763·9	1960	27 732·6
1815	834	1936	6 759·3	1961	28 251·7
1828	800	1937	6 764·7	1962	28 674·4
1836	832	1938	6 993·7	1963	29 847·6
1840	827	1939	7 130·8	1964	30 226·3
1854	802	1940	7 899·2	1965	30 440·6
1855	789	1941	10 366·4	1966	31 340·2
1857	837	1942	13 041·1	1967	31 985·6
1860	799	1943	15 822·6	1968	34 193·9
1899	635	1944	18 562·2	1969	33 984·2
1900	628·9	1945	21 365·9	1970	33 079·4
1903	770·8	1946	23 636·5	1971	33 441·9
1909	702·7	1947	25 630·6	1972	35 839·9
1910	713·2	1948	25 620·8	1973	36 884·6
1914	649·8	1949	25 167·6	1974	40 124·5
1915	1 105·0	1950	25 802·3	1975	45 886·0
1916	2 133·1	1951	25 921·6	1976	56 577·0

* Beginning 1920, total excludes bonds tendered for death duties and held by the National Debt Commissioner-
† Beginning 1935, total excludes external debt, then £1036·5 million, arising out of the 1914–18 war.

Sterling—US Dollar Exchange Rates

$4·50–$5·00	Post War of Independence	1776
$12·00	All-time Peak (Civil War)	1864
$4·86 21/32	Fixed parity	1880–1914
$4·76 7/16	Pegged rate World War I	Dec. 1916
$3·40	Low point after £ floated, 19 May 1919	Feb. 1920
$4·86 21/32	Britain's return to gold standard	28 Apr. 1925
$3·14½	Low point after Britain forced off Gold Standard (21 Sept. 1931 ($3·43))	Nov. 1932

The economic power of a nation is reflected in its Gross National Product (GNP) and its National Income.

Gross National Product is derived from Gross Domestic Product at factor cost plus net property income from overseas. National Income is GNP less capital consumption.

Gross Domestic Product at factor cost can be determined in two ways, (A) by the expenditure generating it, or (B) the incomes, rent and profits which enable the expenditure. The components in any year are thus:

A	B
Consumers' expenditure	Income from employment
Public authority current spending	Income from self-employment
Gross fixed capital formation	Gross trading profits of companies
Value of work in progress	Gross profits and surpluses of public corporations
Value of physical increase in stocks	Rent *less* stock appreciation
Exports *less* imports	
Income from abroad *less* payments abroad	
Subsidies *less* taxes on expenditure	
= Gross Domestic Product	= Gross Domestic Product

Minimum lending rate

The Bank Rate was maintained at its record low level of 2 per cent for 12 years 13 days from 26 Oct. 1939 to 7 Nov. 1951, throughout World War II and the post-war period of the Cheap Money Policy under the Atlee government. The only previous occasion that such a low rate had been available was in 1852.

On 13 Oct. 1972 the Bank Rate was more descriptively named Bank of England Minimum Lending Rate when standing at 7¼ per cent. On 13 Nov. 1973 the MLR attained its all-time peak of 13 per cent with the Arab Oil Price crisis. It was lowered by

$5.20	High point during floating period	Mar. 1934
$4.03	Fixed rate World War II	4 Sept. 1939
$2.80	First post-war devaluation	18 Sept. 1949
$2.40	Second post-war devaluation	20 Nov. 1967
$2.58	£ Refloated	22 June 1972
$1.99	£ broke $2 barrier	5 Mar. 1976
$1.7125	£ At new all-time low	20 Sept. 1976

20 Top External Trade Markets—1974

		£ million			£ million
1	United States	1757★	11	Italy	510
2	West Germany	1011	12	Canada	488
3	Netherlands	982	13	Denmark	427
4	France	914	14	Norway	332
5	Benelux	837	15	Japan	319
6	Ireland	820	16	Spain	296
7	Sweden	723	17	Iran	278
8	Switzerland	600	18	New Zealand	255
9	Australia	549	19	Finland	228
10	South Africa	526	20	Nigeria	222

★ 10·7% of the total. In 1945 Australia ranked No. 1 with £279 million.

Distribution of Trade by Market Areas—1974

	(Balance in £ millions) Balance	(Imports and Exports as % of total) Imports	Exports
USA	−484	9·7%	10·7%
Canada	−494	9·3%	3·0%
Latin America	−159	2·8%	3·0%
EEC	−2214	33·4%	33·4%
Other non Eastern European	−755	13·0%	13·6%
Commonwealth (excl. Canada)	−86	10·0%	13·5%
Communist Bloc	−2180	2·9%	2·6%

Birth and Death Rates—
Rates for 1000 of population

	1871	1901	1911	1921	1931	1951	1961	1971	1975
Birth Rate	35·0	28·6	24·6	23·1	16·3	15·8	17·8	16·2	12·4
Death Rate	22·1	17·3	14·1	12·7	12·2	12·6	12·0	11·6	11·8
Rate of Natural Increase	12·9	11·3	10·5	10·4	4·1	3·2	5·8	4·6	0·6
Illegitimacy	60	43	45	48	48	48	55	82	88

National Employment and Unemployment

	Working Population (Thousands)	Unemployment Excluding School Leavers and Students	Percentage Rate
1965	25 504	338 200	1·4%
1970	25 293	602 000	2·6%
1971	25 124	775 800	3·4%
1972	25 234	855 000	3·7%
1973	25 578	611 000	2·6%
1974	25 655	600 100	2·6%
1975 Mar.		754 100	3·2%
June		853 500	3·9%
Sept.		1 008 000	4·5%
Dec.		1 163 200	5·0%
1976 Aug.		1 256 500	5·5%

Wage Rates and Earnings (Jan. 1970 = 100)

	Index	Percentage Increase on Previous Year
1965	74·1	7·1%
1970	106·7	12·1%
1971	118·7	11·3%
1972	134·1	15·8%★
1973	152·1	12·7%★
1974	178·8	17·5%

★ Final quarter of the year only.

In the first quarter of 1975 the percentage increase was a peak 31·7% compared with 24·7% for Oct. 1975.

Expectation of life
(Average expectation at birth)

	Male	Female		Male	Female
1900	46	50	1938	61	66
1910	52	55	1950	66	72
1920	56	60	1958	68	74
1930	59	63	1961–3 ★	69·2	75·2

★ Latest available data.

stages to 9¾ per cent until 2 May 1975 aft which it rose to 12 per cent on 14 Nov. 19 but it was again reduced to 9 per cent by Mar. 1976.

Exports
Exports from the UK (1974)

	£ Millio f.o.b.★
Machinery non electric	3081·3
Transport equipment	1839·2
Machinery electric	1131·7
Mineral manufacturers	1060·4
Textile, yarn, fabric	745·8
Chemical elements and compounds	733·6
Petroleum and petroleum products	696·1
Non-ferrous metal	689·4
Iron and steel	553·5
Metal manufacturers	470·6
Scientific, photographic and optical instruments	424·2
Beverages	384·1
Plastics and resins	366·8
Medical and pharmaceutical products	301·6
Clothing	230·0
Dyeing, tanning and colouring materials	213·8
Textile fibres	201·8
Paper, paper board	199·3
Postal packages	174·2
Rubber manufacturers	166·7

★ f.o.b., fee on board

Imports
Imports into the UK (1974)

	£ Millio c.i.f★
Machinery non-electric	1959·2
Machinery electric	1010·2
Non-ferrous metal	1008·6
Non-metallic minerals	982·6
Transport equipment	932·5
Paper and paper board	725·6
Iron and steel	717·0
Chemical elements and compounds	716·8
Textile yarn	688·2
Meat	681·4
Fruit and vegetables	660·7
Cereals	593·0
Wood, lumber and cork	589·6
Metals and scrap	533·5
Clothing	402·4
Scientific, photographic and optical equipment	377·7
Sugar and honey	368·9
Plastics and resins	361·1
Dairy products and eggs	338·7
Pulp and waste paper	329·9
Coffee, tea and cocoa	322·4
Textile fibres	310·5
Metal manufacturers	286·7
Wood and cork manufacturers (excluding furniture)	232·2
Beverages	221·6
Tobacco	185·4
Oil, seeds, nuts and kernels	142·5
Fertilisers and minerals	141·3
Animal feeding stuff	126·8
Foreign caught fish	122·1
Animal and vegetable materials	110·0
Footwear	109·3
Hide, skins and fur	106·4
Crude rubber	100·4

★c.i.f., carriage, insurance and freight

Average weekly household expenditure
The average household weekly income i 1974 was £73.21 of which £15.88 went i income tax and national insurance payments The breakdown of the average expenditur was as follows:

Food	£9.7
Transport and vehicles	£6.3
Housing	£6.8
Clothing and footwear	£4.3
Durable household goods	£2.1
Fuel, light and power	£2.1

British Isles—Progressive population

Date	Estimate	Date	Estimate
c 500 000 BC	200	1348†	4 000 000
c 250 000 BC	1000	1355	2 500 000
12 000 BC	3000	1500	<3 000 000
2000 BC	20 000	1570‡	4 160 000
600 BC	80 000	1600‡	4 811 000
100 BC	250 000	1630‡	5 600 000
AD 43	450 000	1670‡	5 773 000
350	1 250 000	1700‡	6 045 000
1086*	1 250 000	1750‡	6 517 000

* On the evidence of the Domesday Book.
† Prior to onset of the Black Death.
‡ Figures in respect of England only based on the evidence of Parish registration.

Decennial Censuses*

Date	Total	Date	Total
1801	11 944 000	1891	34 264 000
1811	13 368 000	1901	38 237 000
1821	15 472 000	1911	42 082 000
1831	17 835 000	1921	44 027 000
1841	20 183 000	1931	46 038 000
1851	22 259 000	1951	50 225 000
1861	24 525 000	1961	52 676 000
1871	27 431 000	1971	55 515 000
1881	31 015 000	1975	est 55 962 000

* These figures are in respect of the United Kingdom (i.e. the figures for the present area of the Republic of Ireland are excluded). The 1921 and 1931 figures for Northern Ireland are estimates only but were based on censuses subsequently held in 1926 and 1937 respectively.

Strikes

	Working Days Lost	Workers Involved
1960	3 024 000	814 000
1965	2 933 000	867 800
1970	10 980 000	1 793 000
1973	7 197 000	1 513 000
1974	14 750 000	1 622 000
1975	5 957 000	785 000

Tobacco	£2.15
Alcoholic drink	£4.01
Reading matter	£0.71

Distribution of work force as at June 1974

Professional and scientific services	3 374 000
Distributive trades	2 761 000
Transport and communication	1 506 000
Construction	1 328 000
Miscellaneous services	1 320 000
Insurance, banking, finance and business services	1 116 000
Local government services	986 000
Catering, hotels etc.	805 000
National government service	610 000
Agriculture, forestry and fishing	417 000
Mining and quarrying	349 000
Gas, electricity and water	347 000
Mechanical engineering	976 200
Electrical engineering	843 000
Vehicle manufacturing	792 000
Food, drink and tobacco manufacturing	765 900
Paper, printing and publishing	588 800
Textile manufacturing	585 300
Metal good manufacturing	581 700
Metal manufacturing	507 000
Chemicals and allied industries	434 600
Clothing and footwear manufacturing	426 500
Other manufacturing industries	358 200
Bricks, pottery, glass, cement etc. manufacturing	300 800
Timber, furniture etc. manufacturing	283 100
Shipbuilding and marine engineering	185 300
Instrument engineering	160 500
Leather, leather goods and fur manufacturing	42 800
Coal and petroleum products	39 500
Employers and self-employed	1 977 000
HM Forces	345 000
Wholly unemployed	543 000
Total working population	25 655 000

Standard of living—in 19½ million households

	1974
Use of TV set	94%
Refrigerator	80%
Washing machine	68%
Car	55%
Telephone	45%
Central heating	40%
Average disposable income after tax and NHI	£2 979

Internal purchasing power of the £

The worth of the £ at various periods compared with its worth in December 1975 may be regarded thus:

1870	£1	worth	£11
1886	£1	worth	£15
1896	£1	worth	£14.50
1909	£1	worth	£13
1925	£1	worth	£7
1931	£1	worth	£8.40
1949	£1	worth	£4.40
1957	£1	worth	£3
1967	£1	worth	£2.60
1970	£1	worth	£2
1975 (Dec.)	£1	worth	£1

Income, Expenditure and Savings

Year	Population Mid-Year (Thousands)	Gross National Product GNP (£ millions)	Total Personal Income (£ millions)	Consumer Expenditure at prices current (£ millions)	Consumer Expenditure Revalued at 1970 Prices	Personal Saving (£ million)	Personal Saving as % of Disposable Income
1955	51 199	£16 945	£15 622	£13 111		£543	
1960	52 508	£22 756	£21 178	£16 971		£1203	
1965	54 218	£31 588	£30 055	£22 856		£2179	8.7%
1970	55 421	£43 809	£43 163	£31 472		£3150	9.1%
1971	55 610	£49 298	£47 785	£35 075		£3416	8.9%
1972	55 793	£55 259	£54 124	£39 636	£32 397	£4436	10.1%
1973	55 933	£64 321	£62 720	£45 141	£34 318	£5727	11.3%
1974	55 974	£73 977	£75 208	£51 670	£35 962	£8133	13.6%
1975	55 962	£92 841	£94 935	£62 649	£35 741	£10 089	13.9%

Balance of Payments

	Exports	Visible Imports	Balance	Invisible Balance	Current Balance (− Deficit + Surplus)	Current Balance Excluding Petroleum i.e. non-oil balance
1965	4848	5071	−223	+198	−27	—
1970	7907	7919	−12	+747	+735	+1219
1971	8810	8526	+282	+766	+1048	
1972	9140	9830	−690	+818	+128	+786
1973	11 771	14 066	−2295	+1460	−835	+1106
1974	15 886	21 120	−5234	+1566	−3668	−245
1975 (est.)	18 775	22 006	−3230	+1524	−1706	+1416

Public expenditure: 1970–1 to 1975–76 and Projected to 1979–80

£ million at 1975 Survey price

	1970–1	1971–2	1972–3	1973–4	1974–5	1975–6	1976–7	1977–8	1978–9	1979–8
1. Social security	7200	7646	8078	8080	8582	9463	10 002	10 014	9964	996
2. Education and libraries, science and arts	5073	5434	5799	6081	6104	6164	6234	6141	6024	599
3. Defence	4531	4593	4494	4426	4331	4538	4586	4573	4541	454
4. Health and personal social services	4235	4405	4701	4934	5056	5285	5317	5384	5465	554
5. Housing	2827	2492	2555	3330	4429	4018	4097	4064	4014	409
6. Nationalised industries' capital expenditure	2669	2554	2519	2281	2822	3358	3050	2647	2789	290
7. Other environmental services	1855	1888	2014	2156	2088	2217	2045	2062	1991	198
8. Trade, industry and employment: Investment grants	808	635	384	233	102	63	23	5	2	
Other	1080	1234	1755	2538	2763	2618	2249	2085	2121	211
9. Roads and transport	1790	1727	1848	1964	2181	2316	2193	2032	1860	185
10. Law, order and protective services	1093	1175	1189	1260	1339	1444	1470	1462	1439	143
11. Agriculture, fisheries and forestry	632	718	635	751	1468	1438	987	840	641	61
12. Overseas aid and other overseas services	598	646	788	825	798	734	882	953	1027	108
13. Northern Ireland	767	802	896	1015	1200	1321	1336	1306	1263	125
Civil Service staff costs								−50	−140	−13
14. Common services	545	582	599	606	606	713	678	697	716	73
15. Other public services	520	560	757	587	628	682	686	686	675	67
Total programmes	36 223	37 091	39 011	41 067	44 497	46 372	45 835	44 901	44 392	44 67
Debt interest	4142	4031	4048	4764	4757	5000	6200	7000	7500	7500
Contingency reserve							700	900	1200	140
Shortfall						−200	−250	−250	−250	−25
Total	40 365	41 122	43 059	45 831	49 254	51 172	52 485	52 551	52 842	53 32

JUDICIAL SYSTEM IN THE UNITED KINGDOM

England and Wales

In English Law actions are conveniently divided into criminal and civil. The object of the former is to secure the conviction and punishment of an offender, whereas the object of the latter is to seek redress, usually financial, for damage suffered.

Criminal Jurisdiction

The courts in England and Wales with the least jurisdiction are *Magistrates' Courts* or *Petty Sessions*. These are presided over by Justices of the Peace (JPs) who are unpaid laymen appointed by the Lord Chancellor. They have the power to try all non-indictable offences and, if the accused person so desires, many of the less serious indictable offences.

The trial of major offences usually starts in Magistrates' Courts, where the Justice determines whether there is sufficient evidence for the accused to be remitted to the *Quarter Sessions* or, in the most serious offences, the *Assizes*.

In major centres of population there are professional salaried magistrates, known in London as metropolitan magistrates and in the provinces as stipendiary magistrates. Persons under 17 are tried by *Juvenile Courts*.

Quarter Sessions are composed of Justices of the Peace for the county, under the chairmanship of a legally qualified person, usually with a jury. In the larger towns a salaried barrister, called a Recorder, sits alone with a jury.

The Assizes, which deal with major offences are, as it were, a travelling section of the Queen's Bench Division. Sessions are held in county towns and larger cities three, four or five times a year, and are presided over by a judge of the Queen's Bench or a Commissioner of Assize, who is a barrister commissioned to act as a judge. In London the Central Criminal Court (the Old Bailey) serves as the Assize Court for Greater London. Similarly, the Crown Courts of Liverpool and Manchester exercise assize jurisdiction.

Appeals lie from the quarter sessions or assizes to the *Court of Criminal Appeal*, which consists of the Lord Chief Justice and any of the Queen's Bench judges, usually a total of three. The final court of appeal is the *High Court of the Queen in Parliament*, i.e. the House of Lords. Appeals are only accepted with the leave of the lower court, i.e. the Queen's Bench, or the Court of Criminal Appeal, when on a point of law, and only then when it is of general public importance, and when both the lower court and the House of Lords itself have given leave.

Civil Jurisdiction

The great majority of civil actions are tried in *County Courts* which are presided over by a salaried judge. Jurisdiction includes all cases where the sum in dispute does not exceed £400 but this may be extended by the consent of both parties.

The next senior is the *High Court of Justice* which is subdivided into three divisions: Chancery; Queen's Bench; and Probate, Divorce and Admiralty. Chancery deals with equity matters such as the enforcement of trusts, mortgages, company law, bankruptcy and patent proceedings. Queen's Bench tries actions for damages for tort or breach of contract. The third division deals with wills, matrimonial cases and shipping cases, e.g. salvage and collision disputes.

Appeal lies from both County Courts and the High Court to the *Court of Appeal*, which is staffed by the Master of the Rolls and eleven Lord Justices of Appeal. The final court of appeal is the House of Lords.

The judicial committee of the Privy Council is the final court of appeal for Australia, New Zealand, Sri Lanka, the United Kingdom dependent territories, and, in a very few specialised matters, cases arising in the United Kingdom.

SCOTLAND

Criminal Jurisdiction

Minor offences are dealt with by *Magistrate's Courts* as in England. More serious criminal actions start in a *Sheriff Court* of which there are twelve. The highest criminal court and final court of appeal is the *High Court of Justiciary*.

Civil Jurisdiction

The sheriff courts have almost unlimited civil jurisdiction. Appeal lies to the *Court of Session*, which is sub-divided into an Inner House, which has two divisions and acts as an appeal court from the decisions on which further and final appeal may be made to the House of Lords, and an Outer House which deals with all divorce actions and major civil cases.

Northern Ireland

The system in Northern Ireland is basically a miniature of the English system, but there is an important difference in that a Northern Ireland county court judge and a Recorder of a borough are also Chairmen of quarter sessions; and secondly, most of the JPs' powers have been transferred to salaried officers who are known as resident magistrates.

Prison population (daily average)
England and Wales, including Borstals)

1900	14 739	1970	39 028
1910	20 904	1971	39 708
1920	11 000	1972	38 328
1930	11 346	1973	36 774
1940	9377	1974	36 867
1950	20 175	1975	40 075
1960	26 824		

The total United Kingdom figure for 1964 was 34 089.

Police force (1974 figures)
The strength of the police on 1 Jan. 1975 was as follows.

England and Wales

Police	Men	97 319	
	Women	4767	102 086
Civilians			32 971
Cadets		5130	5130
Special Constables			24 178

Scotland

Police	Men	11 187	
	Women	532	11 719

Northern Ireland

Police	Men		4726
	Women		293

United Kingdom Police 118 824

The total strength of the Metropolitan Police was 20 119 men and 637 women and the City of London Police 769 men and 25 women.

The ranks in the police are Police Constable; Sergeant; Station Sergeant;* Inspector; Chief Inspector; Superintendent; Chief Superintendent; Commander; Deputy Assistant Commissioner; Deputy Commissioner; Commissioner.

In the 42 locally administered and independently operated police forces outside the Metropolitan area an Assistant Chief Constable is equivalent to a Commander and above him are Deputy Chief Constables and the Chief Constable.

In the Criminal Investigation Department (CID) the ranks are Police Constable, Detective Constable, Detective Sergeant (2nd Class); Detective Sergeant (1st Class)* and thereafter as in the main force.

* Rank is now obsolescent

CRIMINAL STATISTICS

Offences known to the Police, England and Wales—Year 1974

OFFENCES	*Number of Offences 1974*
VIOLENCE AGAINST THE PERSON	
Murder ⎫	
Manslaughter ⎬ homicide	600
Infanticide ⎭	
Attempted murder	371
Threat or conspiracy to murder	131
Child destruction	2
Causing death by dangerous driving	654
Wounding or other act endangering life	4240
Endangering railway passenger	40
Endangering life at sea	1
Other wounding, etc.	56 500
Assault	1138
Abandoning child under two years	9
Child stealing	53
Procuring illegal abortion	21
Concealment of birth	21
SEXUAL OFFENCES:	
Buggery	587
Attempt to commit buggery, etc.	3096
Indecency between males	1796
Rape	1052
Indecent assault on a female	12 417
Unlawful sexual intercourse with girl under 13	304
Unlawful sexual intercourse with girl under 16	4746
Incest	337
Procuration	67
Abduction	97
Bigamy	199
BURGLARY:	
Burglary in a dwelling	213 819
Aggravated burglary in a dwelling	337
Burglary in a building other than a dwelling	259 138
Aggravated burglary in a building other than a dwelling	113
Going equipped for stealing etc.	10 425
ROBBERY:	
Robbery	8666

OFFENCES	1974
THEFT AND HANDLING STOLEN GOODS:	
Theft from the person of another	16 092
Theft in a dwelling other than from automatic machine or meter	46 816
Theft by an employee	30 980
Theft or unauthorised taking from mail	1718
Theft of pedal cycle	66 097
Theft from vehicle	219 453
Shoplifting	164 063
Theft from automatic machine or meter	29 186
Theft or unauthorised taking of motor vehicle	251 382
Other theft or unauthorised taking	318 622
Handling stolen goods	45 454
FRAUD AND FORGERY:	
Fraud by company director, etc.	63
False accounting	3773
Other fraud	95 911
Forgery or uttering drug prescription	1111
Other forgery or uttering	16 385
CRIMINAL DAMAGE:	
Arson	7094
Criminal damage endangering life	144
Other criminal damage	59 198
Threat, etc. to commit criminal damage	650
OTHER OFFENCES:	
Blackmail	752
High treason	Nil
Treason felony	Nil
Riot	6
Unlawful assembly	16
Other offence against the State or public order	322
Perjury	330
Libel	16
Aiding suicide	4
Other indictable offence	6745
NON-INDICTABLE TRAFFIC OFFENCES	
Reckless or dangerous driving	7898
Driving while unfit through drink or drugs	55 344
In charge of motor vehicle while unfit through drink or drugs	2736
Driving while disqualified	10 826
Other motoring offences	1 150 157

POLICE BADGES OF RANK

CADET · CONSTABLE · SERGEANT · INSPECTOR · CHIEF INSPECTOR · SUPERINTENDENT · CHIEF SUPERINTENDENT · COMMANDER · DEPUTY ASSISTANT COMMISSIONER · ASSISTANT COMMISSIONER · COMMISSIONER

OTHER SELECTED NON-INDICTABLE OFFENCES

Cruelty to animals	790
Cruelty to children	284
Night poaching	142
Day poaching	1314
Indecent exposure	2726
Drunkenness, simple	50 772
Drunkenness with aggravation	49 471
Drug offences	11 883
Offences by pawnbrokers	1
Prostitution	3090
Sunday trading	499
Begging	1184
Sleeping out	336

CRIMINAL STATISTICS
Crimes and Offences known to the Police, Scotland—Year 1974

CRIMES AGAINST THE PERSON

Murder	38
Attempts to murder	121
Culpable homicide	40
Assaults	2442
Threats	182
Cruel and unnatural treatment of children	410
Procuring abortion	Nil
Concealment of pregnancy	1
Incest	32
Unnatural crimes, including attempts	5
Rape	120

Assault with intent to ravish	121
Indecent assault	701
Lewd and libidinous Practices	794
Procuration and Criminal Law Amendment Act, etc., offences	557
Bigamy	26
Other	2491

CRIMES AGAINST PROPERTY WITH VIOLENCE

Housebreaking	74 917
Robbery, and Assaults with intent, etc.	2561
Other	21

CRIMES AGAINST PROPERTY WITHOUT VIOLENCE

Theft	83 032
Reset	1363
Breach of trust and embezzlement	463
Falsehood, fraud, and wilful imposition	7391
Offences in connection with bankruptcy	9
Post Office offences	287
Other	78

MALICIOUS INJURIES TO PROPERTY

Fire-raising	1225
Other	7307

FORGERY AND CRIMES AGAINST CURRENCY

Forgery and uttering	1461
Coining and Other	17

OTHER CRIMES

High treason and treason felony	N
Mobbing and rioting	1
Other crimes against the State and Public order	1
Crimes against public justice (perjury, bribery, etc.)	172
Indecent exposure	143
Other	83

OFFENCES AGAINST INTOXICATING LIQUOR LAWS

Drunk and incapable	18 89
Drunk and disorderly	11

SELECTED MISCELLANEOUS OFFENCES

Breach of the peace, etc.	70 05
Brothel keeping	1
Prostitution	33
Contempt of court	29
Cruelty to animals	14
Offences against Education Acts	2094
Furious and reckless driving	4
Offences relating to motor vehicles (excluding drunk in charge)	151 56
Drunk in charge, etc.	2804
Driving, or in charge of a motor vehicle with blood-alcohol concentration above the prescribed limit	11 22
Taking motor vehicle without consent of owner	18 19

British causes Célèbres of the 20th Century

Year	Accused	Offence alleged	Alleged victim or defendant	Location	Decision
1901	Louise Masset, 36	Murder	Illegitimate son, 3½	Dalston, London E	Executed, 29 Jan.
1903	Amelia Sachs, 29, and Annie Walters, 54	Baby Farming		East Finchley, London	Both executed, 3 Feb.
1903	John Gallagher and Emily Swan	Murder	William Swan (husband)	Wombwell, Yorkshire	Executed, 29 Dec.
1907	Mrs Leslie James	Murder	Child over 1 year	Cardiff	Executed, 14 Aug.
1909	Oscar Slater (né Leschziner)	Murder	Marion Gilchrist, 83	Glasgow	Arraigned 6 May, compensated 1929, £6000
1910	Dr H H Crippen	Murder	Mrs Crippen	Hilldrop Crescent, London N	Executed, 23 Nov.
1910	Cadet Archer-Shee	Larceny of a Postal Order	—	Royal Naval College, Dartmouth	Quashed by Petition of Right
1912	Frederick Seddon	Murder (poison)	Eliza Barrow	Tollington Park, London N	Executed, 12 Apr.
1915	George Joseph Smith	Murder	3 Brides in the bath	Herne Bay, Blackpool, Highgate	Executed, 13 Aug.
1916	Sir Roger Casement, CMG	Treason	The State	Ireland	Executed, 3 Aug.
1922	Herbert Armstrong	Murder (arsenic)	Mrs Armstrong	Cusop Dingle, Breconshire	Executed, 31 May
1922	Horatio Bottomley, MP	Fraud	Victory Bond Club	London	7 years, 29 May
1923	Mrs Edith J Thompson and Frederick Bywaters	Murder	Percy Thompson	Ilford, Essex	Both executed, 29 Jan.
1924	Patrick Mahon	Murder	Emily Kaye	Crumbles, Sussex	Executed, 3 Sept.
1928	Frederick Browne and William Kennedy	Murder	P C Gutteridge	Epping Forest, Essex	Both executed, 31 May
1931	A A Rouse	Murder and arson	A still unknown tramp	Hardingstone, Northamptonshire	Executed, 10 Mar.
1933	Leopold Harris with 13 others	Arson	Insurance Companies	London area	Harris 14 years penal servitude
1935	Mrs A Rattenbury and George P Stoner	Murder	Francis M Rattenbury	Bournemouth, Hampshire	Stoner reprieved, 25 June; Mrs Rattenbury, suicide
1936	Dr Buck Ruxton	Murder	Mrs E Ruxton and Mary Rogerson	Lancaster	Executed, 12 May
1936	Nurse Dorothea Waddington	Murder	Ada Louise Baguely		Executed, 16 Apr.
1936	Charlotte Bryant	Murder	Mr Bryant	Coombe, Dorset	Executed, 15 July
1936	George McMahon	Intent to alarm His Majesty	King Edward VIII	Outside Buckingham Palace	12 months hard labour, 16 July
1937	Frederick Nodder, 44	Murder	Mona Tinsley, 10	Newark, Nottinghamshire	Executed, 30 Dec.
1938	Robert Harley and David Wilmer	Aggravated assault and robbery	Mr Bellenger		Harley 7 years, 20 strokes, 19 Feb.; Wilmer 5 years, 15 strokes, 19 Feb.
1939	John Connell and William Browne	Attempted IRA bombing	(averted by Frederick Child, GC)	Hammersmith Bridge	Connell 20 years, 19 Mar.; Browne 10 years, 29 Mar.
1940	Mahomed Singh Azad	Murder (assassination)	Sir Michael O'Dwyer	Caxton Hall, London	Sentenced 5 June
1940	Anna Walkoff and Tyler Kent	Espionage—Treachery	The State	—	Walkoff 10 years, 7 Nov. Kent 7 years, 7 Nov.
1941	Josef Jacobs (German)	Espionage	The State	—	Executed by shooting at Tower of London, 15 Sept.
1942	Gordon Frederick Cummins, 28	Murder	Six women	London	Executed, 25 June
1943	Pte Lee A Davies (US Army)	Murder and rape	Cynthia Jane Lay	Marlborough	Military execution, 14 Dec.
1945	Pte Karl G Hulton (US Army) and Elizabeth Jones, 18	Murder (cleft chin), 7 Oct. 1944	George Heath	Staines, Middlesex	Hulton executed, 18 Mar.

Year	Accused	Offence alleged	Alleged victim or defendant	Location	Decision
1945	Ronald Hedley, 26, and Thomas James Jenkins, 25	Murder (12 Mar.)	Capt R D Binney, RN	City of London	Hedley executed; Jenkins 8 years
1945	John Amery	Treachery	The State	Germany	Executed, 19 Dec.
1946	Dr Alan Nunn May	Offences under the Official Secrets Act	The State	An atomic research centre	10 years, 1 May
1946	Neville George Clevely Heath, 29	Murder	Mrs Margery Gardner and Doreen Marshall	Notting Hill, London, and Bournemouth, Hants	Executed, 16 Oct.
1947	Hon Thomas John Ley	Murder	John Mudie	Chalk pit, Woldingham	Sentenced 24 Mar., certified insane 5 May
1947	Christopher James Geraghty, 20, and Charles Henry Jenkins, 23	Murder (29 Apr.)	Alec de Antiquis	Charlotte Street, London	Both executed, 19 Sept.
1948	(Steward) James Camb, 30	Murder (18 Oct. 1947)	'Gay' Gibson, 21	Cabin 126, Durban Castle	Found guilty 18 Mar. (capital punishment suspended at time)
1949	John George Haigh	Acid murders (possibly nine)	Mrs Olive Durand-Deacon, 69, et al	Crawley, Sussex	Executed, 10 Aug.
1949	Brian Donald Hume	Accessory to murder	Stanley Setty	Dengie Marshes, Essex	12 years
1950	Klaus Emil Julius Fuchs	Passing Official (atomic) secrets to Soviet Union	The State (1943–7)	Harwell, Berkshire	14 years, 1 Mar.
1950	Thomas Sitwell	Murder (private warrant)	Joan Woodhouse (10 Aug. 1948)	Arundel Castle	Acquitted, Sept.
1950	Scottish Nationalists	Sacrilegious Theft (25 Dec.)	Coronation Stone of Scone	Westminster Abbey	No proceedings
1951	Alfredo Messina, 50	Immoral earnings	—	London	Appeal dismissed. 2 years and £500, 9 July
1953	Alfred George Hinds, 35	Robbery (£38 000)	Maple & Co Ltd	London	Preventive detention 12 years
1954	Donald Merrett, 46, alias Ronald John Chesney	Murder (11 Feb.)	Mrs Isobel Chesney and Miss Mary Menzies	Ealing, Middlesex	Found shot near Cologne, 16 Feb.
1954	Gaston Dominici, 77	Murder (Aug. 1952)	Sir Jack and Lady Drummond and Elizabeth Drummond, 11	Digne, France	Sentenced to death, 28 Nov.; reprieved 4 Aug. 1957
1955	Jack Comer, alias Jack Spot	Unlawful wounding (11 Aug.)	Albert George Dimes	Soho, London	Acquitted, 24 Sept.
1955	Ruth Ellis, 28	Murder	David Blakely, 25	Hampstead, London	Executed, (13 July)
1955	Lt-Col A D Wintle, 57	Assault	Frederick Harry Nye		6 months, 26 July
1956	Eugenio Messina	Living on immoral earnings	—	London	Sentenced to 7 years in Belgium, 6 July
1956	36 Defendants	Cock fighting	—	Christelton, near Chester	Fines totalling £605
1957	Dr John Bodkin Adams	Murder (13 Nov. 1950)	Mrs Edith Morrell	Eastbourne, Sussex	Acquitted after 17-day trial, 9 Apr.
1958	Nine youths, 17–20	Wounding and assaulting	Coloured men	Notting Hill area, London	Each 4 years, 24 Aug.
1958	Peter Thomas Anthony Manuel, 32	Capital murder of 5 females, 2 males	Arraigned on 9 charges, later admitted 3 further murders	Mainly Lanarkshire	Executed, 11 July
1959	Günther Fritz Podola, 30	Capital murder (13 July)	PC Raymond Purdy	S Kensington, London	Executed, Nov. 5
1959	Brian Donald Hume (see 1949)	Murder	Taxi-driver	Zürich, Switzerland	Hard labour for life. Admitted 1949 murder (see above)
1959	Attillio Messina	Procuring	Edna Kallman	Mayfair, London	4 years (9 Apr.)
1960	Herbert Hugh Murray, 64, and Friedrich Grunwald, 34	Fraudulent conversion	Lintang Investments Ltd	City of London	Both 5 years (trial 15 June)
1961	Arthur Albert Jones, 44	(1) Rape (9 Sept. 1960)	girl named Barbara, 11	—	Sentenced 14 years, 15 Mar.
		(2) Murder (11 Dec. 1960)	Brenda Nash, 12	—	Sentenced to life imprisonment, 20 June. Appeal dismissed 6 Feb., 1962
1961	Col Konon Trofimovich Molody, 40, alias Gordon Arnold Lonsdale; Lorna Teresa Cohen (née Petra), alias Helen Joyce Kroger, 47; Maurice Cohen, alias Peter John Kroger, 50; Henry Frederick Houghton, 55; Ethel Elizabeth Gee, 46	Conspiring to commit breaches of Section I of the Official Secrets Act, 1911	The State, radio transmission of Naval secrets to the USSR	Ruislip, Middlesex	Sentenced 22 Mar. In order, 25 years, 20 years, 20 years, 15 years, 15 years. Appeals dismissed, 8 May. Krogers unlawfully released on 24 July 1969
1961	George Blake, 38	Offences under Official Secrets Act, 1911	Unofficially estimated betrayals cost lives of 42 British agents	Berlin, Middle East	3 consecutive 14-year terms (42 years), 3 May. 'Sprung' from Wormwood Scrubs 22 Oct. 1966
1962	James Hanratty, 25	Murder (night 22–3 Aug. 1961)	Michael John Gregsten, 36	Lay-by on the A6	Sentenced to death 17 Feb. Appeal dismissed. Executed 4 Apr.
1962	Kan Ping-kwok, Ah Lee-wong, Yang Hai-lou (crew HMS Belfast)	Trafficking in opium and heroin (illicit value £325 000)	—	—	In order, 5 years, 4 years, 1 year (all sentenced 25 July)
1962	William John Christopher Vassal, 38	Offences under Official Secrets Act, 1911	The State, conveying secrets to the USSR	Moscow 1955, London 1956–62	18 years (22 Oct.)
1963	Dr Stephen Ward, 50	Procuring, living off immoral earnings	—	London W 1	31 July found guilty on two vice charges. Suicide (3 Aug.) before sentence was passed
1963	Ronald Arthur Biggs, Douglas Gordon Goody, Thomas William Wisbey, Charles Frederick Wilson,* James Hussey, Roy John James, Robert Welch and others	Larceny of £2 595 998 worth of used banknotes (8 Aug. 1963)	The Post Office (Mr Frank Dewhurst), the National Provincial, Midland, Barclays, National Commercial and four other Banks and their insurers, principally Lloyds	Sears Crossing and Bridego Bridge, nr Cheddington, Buckinghamshire	These seven were sentenced for 30 years each. Appeals dismissed *Wilson escaped 12 Aug. 1964. Biggs escaped 8 July 1965

continued over page

Torts

In English Law the following torts (i.e. actionable civil wrongs) are well established:
(1) trespass; (2) nuisance; (3) conversion; (4) detinue; (5) trespass to goods; (6) trespass to the person, (a) assault, (b) battery, (c) false imprisonment; (7) defamation; (8) negligence; (9) fraud, (a) deceit (b) injurious falsehood; (10) intimidation; (11) conspiracy; (12) malicious prosecution.

Year	Accused	Offence alleged	Alleged victim or defendant	Location	Decision
1965	Frank Clifton Bossard	Selling secrets to USSR	The State	—	21 years (10 May)
1966	Ian Brady	Murder	John Kilbride Lesley-Ann Downey Edward Evans	Bodies exhumed from Pennine Moors	Life (6 May)
	Myra Hindley	Murder	Lesley-Ann Downey Edward Evans	as above	Life
1966	John Edward Witney	Murder (12 Aug.)	3 Plain Clothes Policemen	Nr Wormwood Scrubs, Shepherds Bush, West London	30 years (16 Aug.)
	Harry Roberts John Duddy	Murder Murder	as above as above	as above as above	30 years (15 Nov.) 30 years (17 Aug.)
1968	Emil Savundra	Conspiring to defraud policy holders	Policy Holders	Fire, Auto and Marine Insurance Co	8 years + £50 000 fine (7 Mar. 1968)
	Stuart De Quincy Walker	as above	as above	as above	5 years + £30 000 fine (7 Mar. 1968)
1969	Raymond Morris	Murder	Christine Darby, 6	Cannock Chase	Life (18 Feb. 1969)
1969	Ronald Kray	Murder	George Cornell Jack 'The Hat' McVitie	East End, London	Life Minimum of 30 years (5 Mar. 1969)
	Reginald Kray	Murder	Jack 'The Hat' McVitie		as above
1970	Nizamodeen and Arthur Hosein	Murder, kidnapping and demanding ransom.	Mrs Muriel McKay	Hertfordshire	Life (6 Oct.)
1971	Angry Brigade	Conspiring to cause explosions	Explosions including bombing of home of Lord Carr of Hadley	London Area	10 years (Jan.)
1971	Frederick Joseph Sewell	Murder (23 Aug.)	Superintendent Gerald Richardson (GC posthumous)	Blackpool	Life—not less than 30 years (7 Oct. 1971)
1972	Dr Ahmed Alami	Murder	Three children	Victoria Hospital, Blackpool	Charged, but was found unfit to plead. (17 Feb.)
1972	Noel Jenkinson (IRA)	Murder (22 Feb.)	5 Women, 1 Chaplain, 1 Gardener	Officers' Mess of Aldershot (16th Paratroopers)	Life, at least 30 years (14 Oct. 1972)
1972	Sub-Lieut David Bungham RN	Selling secrets to USSR	The State	—	21 years (13 March)
1972	Graham Frederick Young	1. Murder by Thalium poisoning 2. Two attempted murders.	2 workmates	Hatfield, Herts	Life (29 June 1972)
1972	John Brook	Murder (4 Nov.)	Mrs Muriel Patience	Barn Restaurant, Braintree, Essex	Life (14 Feb. 1974)
1973	James Tibbs (Leader of East End Gang)	Protection Racket	—	—	15 years (19 Jan.)
1974	John Poulsen	7 charges with William Pottinger of corruption in Architect's Practice. Further charge (15 Mar.) 7 years	—	—	5 years (11 Feb.)
1974	Ian Ball	1. Kidnap attempt	HRH Princess Anne (20 Mar.)	The Mall, London	To be detained under Mental Health Act without limit of time at a special hospital (22 May)
		2. Attempted murder. 3. Attempting to imprison 4. Attempted murder.	Insp Jones Beaton GC HRH Princess Anne 1. Mr A Callender 2. Mr M Hills 3. Mr B McConnell		
1974	Janie Jones	1. Controlling 6 prostitutes. 2. Attempting to pervert the course of justice by threatening violence to 'call girls' witnesses.		London	5 years (18 Apr.) 2 years (18 Apr.)
1974	Carole Richardson Gerard Conlon Patrick Armstrong Paul Hill	Murder (5 Oct.)	5 killed 65 injured	2 Public Houses, Guildford	Life (4 Nov. 1975)
1974	Judith Theresa Ward	Murder (4 Feb. 1974) Causing an explosion Causing an explosion	12 killed National Defence College, Euston Station	M62 coach blast Latimer, Bucks London	20 years⎫to run 10 years⎬consecutively ⎫to run con- 5 years⎬currently with ⎭20 year term
1974	Gerard Conlon Carole Richardson Patrick Armstrong Paul Hill	—	2 killed 34 injured	Kings Arms PH, Woolwich	Life (7 Nov. 1975) Armstrong (Minimum of 35 years)
1974	Earl of Lucan	Charged with alleged murder (8 Nov.)	His children's nanny Mrs Sandra Rivett	His wife's house in Belgravia, London	(Accused still missing) Aug 1976
1974	John Walker, Patrick Hill, Robert Hunter, Noel McIlkenny, William Power, Hugh Callaghan,	Murder (21 Nov. 1974)	21 killed 84 injured	Mulberry Bush The Tavern in the Town Birmingham	Life (6 June 1975)
1975	Donald Neilson	Murder (14 Jan.)	Lesley Whittle	Highley, Nr Kidderminster	Charged 16 Dec. 1975 pending other charges connection with PO offences. 19 Dec. 3 other murder charges
27 Aug. 1975		Bombing	33 injured	Discotheque in Caterham Arms PH, Caterham, Surrey	
5 Sept. 1975		Bombing	2 killed, 60 injured	London Hilton Hotel, Park Lane	
*28 Sept. 1975	Wesley Dick, Anthony Munroe, Frank Davis	1. Attempted Robbery. 2. Kidnapping	7 Italians	Spaghetti House Restaurant, Knightsbridge, London SW 1	
3 Oct. 1975	Peter Cook	6 Rape, 1 Buggery		Cambridge	Life
23 Oct. 1975		Bomb	Prof G Hamilton Fairley	Under car of Hugh Fraser, M.P., London	
6 Dec. 1975		Taking hostages	Mr and Mrs B Matthews	Flat 22, Balcombe St, London	
5 Jan. 1976	10 to 12 Terrorists	Murder	10 Ulster Protestants in a bus	Whitecross, Armagh, Northern Ireland	

Transport

Shipping tonnages

There are four tonnage systems in use, viz. gross tonnage (GRT), net tonnage (NRT), deadweight tonnage (DWT) and displacement tonnage.

(1) *Gross Registered Tonnage*, used for merchantmen, is the sum in cubic ft of all the enclosed spaces divided by 100, such that 1 grt = 100 ft³ of enclosed space.

(2) *Net Registered Tonnage*, also used for merchantmen, is the gross tonnage (above) less deductions for crew spaces, engine rooms and ballast which cannot be utilised for paying passengers or cargo.

(3) *Deadweight Tonnage*, mainly used for tramp ships and oil tankers, is the number of UK long tons (of 2240 lb) of cargo, stores, bunkers and, where necessary, passengers which is required to bring down a ship from her light line to her load-water line, i.e. the carrying capacity of a ship.

(4) *Displacement Tonnage*, used for warships and US merchantmen, is the number of tons (each 35 ft³) of sea water displaced by a vessel charged to its load-water line, i.e. the weight of the vessel and its contents in tons.

Petrol tax

Rate per gallon		Great Britain
30 Apr.	1909	3d
22 Sept.	1915	6d
1 Jan.	1921	repealed
25 Apr.	1928	4d
28 Apr.	1931	6d
11 Sept.	1931	8d
27 Apr.	1938	9d
19 Apr.	1950	1s 6d
4 Apr.	1951	1s 10½d
11 Mar.	1952	2s 6d
4 Dec.	1956	3s 6d
9 Apr.	1957	2s 6d
28 July	1961	2s 9d
11 Nov.	1964	3s 3d
1 Jan.	1970	4s 6d
15 Feb.	1971	22.5p
1 Apr.	1974*	27.5p
18 Nov.	1974*	35p
20 Dec.	1974*	37p

*incl. VAT

The average estimated mileage for a car fell from 8900 miles in 1972 to 8500 miles in 1974. Car ownership rose in the same period from 692 per 1000 families to 730 while 4 star petrol rose from 34½p to 42p per gallon. In 1975 it rose to 72½p and in 1976 to 79p.

Purchase tax on cars

		%
Oct.	1940	33⅓
June	1947	33⅓*
Apr.	1950	33⅓
Apr.	1951	66⅔
Apr.	1953	50
Oct.	1955	60

Apr.	1959	50
July	1961	55
Apr.	1962	45
Nov.	1962	25
July	1966	27½
Apr. 1973 abolished. VAT replaces		
Apr.	1973	10
Apr.	1974	Nil
July	1974	8

*66⅔% if retail value exceeded £1280.

Accidents

The cumulative total of fatalities since the first in the United Kingdom on 17 Aug. 1896 surpassed 250 000 in 1959 and by the end of 1975 reached about *350 000*. There are only

WORLD'S LARGEST SHIPS
Oil tankers in deadweight tons over 350 000

Name	Flag	Dwt (tons)	Length (ft)	Length (m)
Nissei Maru	Japan	484 337	1242	378
Globtik London	UK	483 939	1243	378
Globtik Tokyo	UK	483 664	1243	378
Ioannis Coloctronis	Greece	386 612	1213	369
Hemland	Sweden	372 201	1193	363
Nisseki Maru	Japan	366 813	1138	346
Al Andalus	Kuwait	362 946	1188	362
Sea Scape	Sweden	356 400	1148	350
Sea Saint	Sweden	356 400	1148	350
Sea Stratus	Sweden	356 400	1148	350

Bulk, Ore, Bulk Oil and Ore Oil Carriers (over 250,000 tons dwt)

Name	Flag	Dwt (tons)	Length (ft)	Length (m)
Svealand	Sweden	282 450	1109	338
Docecargon	Liberia	271 235	1113	339
Jose Bonifacio	Brazil	270 358	1106	337
Tarfala	Sweden	265 000	1099	334
Mary R Koch	Liberia	265 000	1090	334
Torne	Sweden	265 000	1090	334
Usa Maru	Japan	264 523	1105	336
Nordic Conqueror	UK	264 485	1101	335
Lauderdale	UK	260 424	1101	335
Licorne Atlantique	France	258 268	1101	335

The largest surviving liner is the *Queen Elizabeth 2* (UK) 66 852 gross tons and 963 ft *293 m* in length. The largest liner of all-time was *Queen Elizabeth* (UK) of 82 998 gross tons and 1031 ft *314 m* completed in 1940 and destroyed by fire in Hong Kong as *Seawise University* on 9 Jan. 1972. The longest liner is *France* of 66 348 gross tons and 1035 ft *315,52 m* completed in 1961 and put out of service in 1975.

United Kingdom motor vehicles and roads

Year	No of Vehicles (Sept.)	Miles of Road (31 Mar.)	No of Yards of Road per Vehicle	Fatalities
1904	c. 18 000	—	—	—
1914	388 860	c. 176 000	796	—
1920	c. 652 000	c. 176 000	475	—
1925	1 538 235	c. 178 000	203	—
1930	2 309 515	179 286	136·7	c. 7400
1935	2 612 093	178 507	120·3	6625
1939	3 208 410	180 527	99·0	8419
1945	1 654 364	c. 183 000	194·7	5380
1950	4 511 626	197 076	77·1	5156
1955	6 567 393	201 724	54·1	5686
1960	9 610 432	207 939	38·1	7142
1961	10 148 714	208 986	36·3	7077
1962	10 763 502	209 937	34·3	6866
1963	11 729 765	212 275	31·8	7098
1964	12 671 817	213 602	29·7	8039
1965	13 263 537	214 958	28·5	8143
1970	15 322 533	222 000	25·5	7771
1974	17 626 273	221 009	22·1	7192

Notes:

Vehicles
Vehicles surpassed 1 million early in 1923.
Cars surpassed 1 million early in 1930, 5 million early in 1949.
Motor cycles (including mopeds, scooters and three-wheelers) surpassed 1 million in 1953.
Trams reached their peak in 1927 with 14 413 and sank by 1965 to 110.
Diesel vehicles surpassed 25% of all goods vehicles in 1961 (2·1% in 1935) and 35% in 1965.

Roads
The mileage includes Trunk roads, Class I, Class II and Unclassified. Statistics prior to 1925 apply to Great Britain only. The earliest dual carriageway was the Southend arterial in 1937 though parts of both the Great West Road and the Kingston by-pass were converted to separate carriageways in 1936.

estimated figures for Northern Ireland in the period 1923–30. The peak reached was 1941 with 9444 killed or 26 per day in Great Britain only. L plates were introduced in May 1935.

Traffic signals: dates of introduction

1868	Parliament Square, Westminster, London, semaphore-arms with red and green gas lamps for night use.
1925	Piccadilly Circus, London, police-operated.
1926	Wolverhampton, Staffordshire, modern type electric.
1932	First vehicle actuation sets introduced.

131

Road speed limits
mph

2	1865 Act	Town limit for steam-driven vehicles preceded by man on foot with red flag.
4	1865 Act	Country limit for steam-driven vehicles as above.
14	1897 Act	Red flag abolished. General limit.
20	1903 Act	General limit under Motor Car Act. Licensing introduced on 1 Jan. 1904.
—	1930 Act	Unlimited. Motor cyclist age limit raised from 14 to 16.
30	1934 Act	Limit in built-up areas. Introduced in N Ireland on 1 Oct. 1956.
40	1957 Reg.	Experimentally introduced, confirmed 1958. N Ireland on 27 Mar. 1961.
50	1960 Reg.	Experimentally introduced on designated main roads, confirmed 1961.
70	1965 Reg.	Overall limit including motorways (experimental until September 1967).
70		Limit on motorways.
60	1974 Reg.	Limit on dual-carriageway roads.
50		Limit on hitherto decontrolled single carriageway roads.

MAJOR NATIONAL RAILWAY SYSTEMS

Country	Year of first railway	Length (miles)	Length (km)	Remarks
Great Britain	1825*	11 326	18 190	*Excluding early mineral lines
Ireland (total)	1834	1564	2285	
Czechoslovakia	1839	13 226	21 285	
France	1832	21 627	34 812	
Germany	1835			
Deutsche Bundesbahn		18 318	29 479	
Deutsche Reichsbahn		8938	14 384	
Hungary	1846	5047	8122	
Italy	1839	9950	16 014	
Poland	1842	14 553	23 421	
Spain	1828	10 191	16 401	All gauges
Sweden	1856	7059	11 361	
Canada	1836	44 794	72 089	CPR 16 588 miles, 23 518 km CNR 24 575 miles, 39 550 km
USA	1830	201 300	323 962	
Mexico	1850	15 204	24 468	
Argentina	1857	24 908	40 177	All gauges
Brazil	1854	19 893	32 015	
Chile	1851	6040	9721	
USSR	1837	84 691	136 294	
China	1883	23 900	38 500	
India Pakistan Bangladesh	1853	42 176	67 876	
Japan	1872	16 953	27 285	
Turkey	1856	5128	8253	
Australia	1854	24 900	40 073	Including Tasmania 530 miles, 853 km
South Africa	1860	12 496	22 199	

LOCOMOTIVES

Steam locomotive types are generally denoted by the system of wheel arrangements invented in 1900 by Frederic M Whyte (1865–1941), an official of the New York Central Railroad. It can easily be worked out from the examples below. All locomotives are imagined facing to the left.

2–2–2	4–6–2 (Pacific)
2–4–0	2–8–0 (Consolidation)
4–4–2 (Atlantic)	2–10–4
0–4–0	2–8–8–4
0–6–0	

The European continental countries use an axle system, thus a 4–6–2 is a 2C1. Germany and Switzerland denote the number of driving axles as a fraction of the total number of axles: for example a 4–6–2 is a 3/6, a 2–8–0 a 4/5. By this system, however, a 3/5 could be a 4–6–0, a 2–6–2 or a 0–6–4.

In the wheel arrangements of diesel, gas-turbine and electric locomotives the number of driving axles in one frame is denoted by a letter: A = 1, B = 2, C = 3, D = 4, E = 5. Idle axles are denoted by figures, 1 and 2. Axles individually driven are denoted by a small o after the letter, e.g.: Co–Co denotes a locomotive with two 3-axle bogies with all axles individually driven. A locomotive with two 3-axle bogies of which the middle axles are not driven is A1A–A1A. Axles coupled by rods or gears are denoted by a letter only, e.g. 2–D–2 denotes a locomotive with four coupled driving axles and a 4-wheeled bogie at each end. 1C–1C denotes a locomotive with two bogies each with three coupled axles and an idle axle, e.g. the Swiss 'Crocodiles'. Buffing or drag stresses taken through a form of articulation between the bogies are indicated by a + sign, e.g. Bo + Bo, such as the Furka-Oberalp and Brig-Visp-Zermatt locomotives in Switzerland.

WORLD'S MAJOR AIRPORTS (1974)

Name and Location	Terminal Passengers (000's)	Aircraft Movements (000's)	Date Opened to Scheduled Traffic
O'Hare, Chicago, USA	37 893	695	1 Oct. 1955
Atlanta, USA	25 606	439	3 May 1961
Los Angeles, USA	23 585	461	25 June 1961
Haneda, Tokyo, Japan	21 587	NA	July 1952
John F Kennedy, New York, USA	20 216	310	1 July 1948
Heathrow, London, UK	20 076	288	31 May 1946
San Francisco, USA	17 411	333	7 May 1927
La Guardia, New York, USA	13 703	287	2 Dec. 1939
Orly, Paris, France	12 688	188	1946
Miami, USA	12 444	300	1 Feb. 1959

Below: The heaviest aircraft in the world, a Swissair-owned Boeing 747 Jumbo Jet, with seating for 500 passengers.

Main commercial aircraft in airline service 1975

Aircraft*	Nationality	Number in Service (end 1975)	Wingspan	Length	Maximum cruising speed	Range	Maximum Take-off Weight	Maximum Seating Capacity
Boeing 727	USA	1131	108 ft 0 in (32,90 m)	152 ft 2 in (46,70 m)	523 knots (969 km/h)	3190 naut miles (5911 km)	209 000 lb (95 000 kg)	189
Antonov An-24–An-26	USSR	785+	95 ft 10 in (29,20 m)	77 ft 3 in (23,50 m)	270 knots (498 km/h)	1300 naut miles (2092 km)	46 300 lb (21 000 kg)	50
McDonnell Douglas DC-9	USA	741	93 ft 5 in (28,50 m)	125 ft 7 in (38,30 m)	488 knots (903 km/h)	1772 naut miles (3281 km)	114 000 lb (51 800 kg	125
Boeing 707	USA	626	145 ft 9 in (44,40 m)	152 ft 9 in (46,60 m)	516 knots (956 km/h)	6500 naut miles (12 000 km)	333 000 lb (161 454 kg)	219
Ilyushin 18	USSR	533+	NA	NA	NA	NA	NA	NA
Yakovlev YAK-40	USSR	523	82 ft 0 in (25,00 m)	66 ft 9 in (20,30 m)	301 knots (560 km/h)	1126 naut miles (2080 km)	35 280 lb (16 000 kg)	33
McDonnell Douglas DC-8	USA	481	148 ft 5 in (45,20 m)	157 ft 6 in (48,00 m)	518 knots (958 km/h)	6150 naut miles (11 400 km)	350 000 lb (159 000 kg)	189
Boeing 737	USA	398	93 ft 0 in (28,30 m)	100 ft 0 in (30,50 m)	494 knots (915 km/h)	2720 naut miles (5050 km)	117 000 lb (53 000 kg)	130
Ilyushin 14	USSR	299+	NA	NA	NA	NA	NA	NA
Fokker F-27	Netherlands	282	95 ft 2 in (29,00 m)	77 ft 4 in (23,50 m)	295 knots (480 km/h)	2230 naut miles (4130 km)	45 000 lb (20 410 kg)	48
Tupolev Tu-134	USSR	259+	95 ft 2 in (29,00 m)	114 ft 8 in (34,90 m)	486 knots (898 km/h)	2536 naut miles (4670 km)	99 200 lb (45 000 kg)	72
Boeing 747 (Jumbo)	USA	256	195 ft 8 in (59,60 m)	231 ft 4 in (70,50 m)	520 knots (965 km/h)	6960 naut miles (12 897 km)	710 000 lb (322 100 kg)	500

* Note: There are many variants of the basic models of these aircraft.

MAJOR WORLD AIRLINES
(1974 data)

Airline	Passenger km (000)	Aircraft km (000)	Passengers Carried (000)	Aircraft Departures	Scheduled Route Network (km)
Aeroflot, USSR	108 577 000	NA	87 500	NA	800 000
United, USA	47 145 930	578 856	30 588	521 060	30 319
Trans-World Airlines (TWA), USA	36 872 000	454 000	15 614	299 000	349 054
American, USA	34 578 410	440 818	20 645	349 824	92 375
Pan-American, USA	32 428 000	322 000	8627	147 000	651 771
Eastern, USA	28 918 530	403 780	27 614	488 762	56 610
Delta, USA	25 991 809	332 535	26 637	482 100	54 327
British Airways, UK*	24 171 272	289 433	13 349	225 856	749 869
Air Canada	17 476 844	188 853	10 516	202 855	238 209
Japan Air Lines (JAL)	17 325 594	137 185	9063	74 700	191 820
Air France	16 865 610	176 476	7545	150 585	508 742
Northwest, USA	16 031 089	177 833	NA	175 478	NA
Lufthansa, Germany	12 758 571	173 257	8887	181 019	425 013
Western, USA	10 854 523	139 779	NA	146 317	NA
KLM, Netherlands	10 848 520	103 487	3120	74 958	360 454
Alitalia, Italy	10 568 853	122 782	6135	113 733	307 211
Braniff, USA	10 402 731	162 368	8298	190 888	45 004
Iberia, Spain	9 916 069	121 848	9483	159 135	262 478
Qantas, Australia	9 880 685	68 393	1343	19 506	230 352
Continental, USA	9 124 564	122 441	6663	139 293	38 742†
SAS, Scandinavia	7 709 816	114 740	6287	151 830	257 655
Swissair, Switzerland	7 175 901	80 840	4573	88 174	230 769
Allegheny, USA	5 495 600	121 789	10 900	330 315	7527
South African Airways	5 460 970	53 663	2709	50 949	218 834
Varig, Brazil	5 166 275	87 792	2570	75 966	197 875

* 1974/75 data.
† 1973

Milestones in civil aviation

1785 (7 Jan.)	First crossing of English Channel by balloon Jean Pierre Blanchard (FRA) and Dr John J Jeffries (USA).
1852 (24 Sept.)	First flight by navigable airship, in France
1900 (2 July)	First flight by German Zeppelin airship
1903 (17 Dec.)	First sustained flight in an aeroplane, by Wright Brothers, in United States.
1906 (12 Nov.)	First public aeroplane flight in Europe. Alberto Santos-Dumont covers a distance of 38 m near Paris, France.
1909 (25 July)	Louis Blériot (FRA) completes first aeroplane crossing of the English Channel.
1910 (27–8 Aug.)	Louis Paulhan completes first flight from London to Manchester, in 4 hr 12 min with an overnight stop.
1919 (14–15 June)	Capt John William Alcock and Lieut Arthur Whitten Brown complete first non-stop crossing of the Atlantic.
1919 (12 Nov.–10 Dec.)	Capt Ross Smith and Lieut Keith Smith complete first flight from United Kingdom (Hounslow) to Australia (Darwin).
1924 (1 Apr.)	Imperial Airways formed in Great Britain.
1928 (31 May–9 June)	First trans-Pacific flight from San Francisco to Brisbane, by Capt Charles Kingsford Smith and C T P Ulm.
1949 (21 June)	First flight of commercial jet, the De Havilland Comet (Entered service 2 May 1952).
1968 (31 Dec.)	Flight of first supersonic airliner, the Russian Tupolev TU-144.
1969 (9 Feb.)	First flight of Boeing 747, the Jumbo. (Entered service 21 Jan. 1970).
1969 (2 Mar.)	First flight of BAC/Aerospatiale Concorde. (Entered service 21 Jan. 1976).

Engineering

Seven wonders of the world

The seven Wonders of the World were first designated by Antipater of Sidon in the second century AD. They are, or were:

	Name	Location	Built (circa)	Fate
1.	Three Pyramids of Gîza (El Gîzeh)*	near El Gîzeh, Egypt	from 2580 BC	still stand
2.	Hanging Gardens of Semiramis, Babylon	Babylon, Iraq.	600 BC	no trace
3.	Statue of Zeus (Jupiter) by Phidias	Olympia, Greece	post 432 BC	destroyed by fire
4.	Temple of Artemis (Diana) of the Ephesians	Ephesus, Turkey	ante 350 BC	destroyed by Goths AD 262
5.	Tomb of King Mausolus of Caria	Halicarnassus, (now Bodrum), Turkey	post 353 BC	fragments survive
6.	Statue of Helios (Apollo) by Chares of Lindus, called the Colossus of Rhodes (117 ft 36 m tall).	Rhodes, Aegean Sea	292–280 BC	destroyed by earthquakes 224 BC
7.	Lighthouse (400 ft 122 m) on island of Pharos	off Alexandria, Egypt	200 BC	destroyed by earthquakes AD 400 and 1375

* Built by the Fourth Dynasty Pharaohs, Hwfw (Khufu or Cheops), Kha-f-Ra (Khafrē or Khefren) and Menkaure (Mycerinus). The Great pyramid ('Horizon of Khufu') originally had a height of 480 ft 11 in *147 m* (now, since the loss of its topmost stone or pyramidion, reduced to 449 ft 6 in *137 m*), Khafrē's pyramid was 470 ft 9 in *143 m*, and Menkaure's was 218 ft *66 m* tall.

The world's tallest inhabited buildings

Height (ft)	Height (m)	No of stories	Building	Location
1454	443	110	Sears Tower (1974)	Wacker Drive, Chicago, Illinois
1350	381	110	World Trade Centre (1973)	Barclay and Liberty Sts, New York City
1250	412	102	Empire State Building (1930)*	5th Av and 34th St, New York City
1136	346	80	Standard Oil Building (1973)	Chicago, Ilinois
1127	343	100	John Hancock Center (1968)	Chicago, Ilinois
1046	319	77	Chrysler Building (1930)	Lexington Av and 42nd St, New York City
950	290	67	60 Wall Tower	70 Pine St, New York City
949	289	72	First Canadian Place, (1976†)	Toronto, Ontario
927	282	71	40 Wall Tower (1900)	New York City
900	274	71	Bank of Manhattan	40 Wall St, New York City
858	261	62	United California Bank (1974)	Los Angeles, California
853	259	48	Transamerica Pyramid	San Francisco, California
850	259	60	First National Bank of Chicago (1969)	Chicago, Illinois
850	259	74	Water Tower Plaza (1975)	Chicago, Illinois
850	259	70	RCA Building	Rockefeller Centre, 5th Av, New York City
813	248	60	Chase Manhattan Building	Liberty St and Nassau St, New York City
808	246	59	Pan American Building (1963)	Park Av, and 43rd St, New York City
841	256	64	US Steel Building (1971)	Pittsburg, Pennsylvania
792	241	60	Woolworth Building (1911–13)	233 Broadway, New York City
790	241	60	John Hancock Tower	Boston, Mass
787	240	28	Mikhail Lomonosov University	Moscow, USSR
784	238	57	Commerce Court	Toronto, Ontario
778	237	52	Bank of America	San Francisco, California
764	232	57	One Penn Plaza	New York City
756	230	33	Palace of Culture and Science	Warsaw, Poland
753†	229	64	MLC Office Tower	Sydney, Australia
750	228	52	Prudential Tower	Boston, Mass

* The Empire State Building was completed in 1930 to a height of 1250 ft. Between 27 July 1950 and 1 May 1951 a 222 ft TV tower was added.
† Under construction

World's tallest structures

Height (ft)	Height (m)	Structure	Location
2117	645	Warszawa Radio Mast (May 1974)	Konstantynow, nr Plock, Poland
2063	628	KTHI-TV (December 1963)	Fargo, North Dakota, USA
1898	578	KSLA-TV	Shreveport, Louisiana, USA
1815	553	CN Tower, Metro Centre (April 1975)	Toronto, Canada
1762	537	Ostankino TV Tower (1967) (4 m added in 1973)	near Moscow, USSR
1749	533	WRBL-TV & WTVM (May 1962)	Columbus, Georgia, USA
1749	533	WBIR-TV (September 1963)	Knoxville, Tennessee, USA
1676	510	KFVS-TV (June 1960)	Cape Girardeau, Missouri, USA
1638	499	WPSD-TV	Paducah, Kentucky, USA
1619	493	WGAN-TV (September 1959)	Portland, Maine, USA
1610*	490	KSWS-TV (December 1956)	Roswell, New Mexico, USA
1600	487	WKY-TV	Oklahoma City, Okla, USA
1572	479	KWTV (November 1954)	Oklahoma City, Okla, USA
1521	463	BREN Tower (unshielded atomic reactor) (April 1962)	Nevada, USA

Other tall structures

Height (ft)	Height (m)	Structure	Location
1345	410	Danish Govt Navigation Mast	Greenland
1312	399	Peking Radio Mast	Peking, China
1272†	387	Anglia TV Mast (1965–September 1967)	Belmont, Lincolnshire
1271	387	Tower Zero	North West Cape, W Australia
1253	382	Lopik Radio Mast	Netherlands
1251	381	International Nickel Co Chimney (1970)	Sudbery, Ontario, Canada
1206	368	Mitchell Power Station chimney (1969)	Cresap, West Virginia, USA
1212	369	Thule Radio Mast (1953)	Thule, Greenland
1200	366	Kennecott Copper Corp chimney (1975)	Magna, Utah, USA
1093	333	CHTV Channel II Mast	Hamilton, Ontario, Canada
1092	332	Tokyo Television Mast	Tokyo, Japan
1080	329	IBA Transmitter Tower (September 1971)	Emley Moor, West Yorkshire
1060	323	Leningrad TV Mast	Leningrad, USSR
1052	320	La Tour Eiffel (1887–9)	Paris, France

* Fell in a gale, 1960; re-erected.
† Highest structure in Great Britain.

Tallest Smokestacks and Towers in the United Kingdom

Height (ft)	Height (m)	Building	Location
800	243	Drax Power Station	Drax, Yorkshire
700	213	Pembroke Power Station	Pembroke, Pembrokeshire
650	198	Eggbrough Power Station (1 chimney)	Eggbrough, Yorkshire
650	198	Ferrybridge 'C' Power Station (2 chimneys) (1 completed, 1966)	Ferrybridge, Yorkshire
650	198	Ironbridge 'B' Power Station (1 chimney)	Ironbridge, Shropshire
650	198	Kingsnorth Power Station (1 chimney)	Kingsnorth, Kent
650	198	Fawley Power Station (1 chimney)	Fawley, Hampshire
c. 650	c. 198	West Fife Power Station (2 chimneys)	West Fife
619	188	GPO Tower (1963)	Cleveland Mews, London, W1
600	182	West Burton Power Station (2 chimneys)	West Burton, Nottinghamshire
550	167	Blyth 'B' Power Station (2 chimneys)	Blyth, Northumberland

The 77-storey Chrysler Building, New York City: currently the tallest inhabited building in the world.

Longest bridge spans in the world

Suspension Bridges

The suspension principle was introduced in 1741 with a 70 ft *21 m* span iron bridge over the Tees, England. Ever since 1816 the world's largest span bridges have been of this construction except for the reign of the Forth Bridge (1889–1917) and Quebec Bridge (1917–29).

Length (ft)	Length (m)	Name	Year of completion	Location
5840	1780	*Akashi-Kaikyo	1988	Honshu–Shikoku, Japan
4626	1410	*Humber Estuary Bridge	1978	Humber, England
4260	1298	Verrazano–Narrows (6 lanes)	1964	Brooklyn–Staten Is, USA
4200	1280	Golden Gate	1937	San Francisco Bay, USA
3800	1158	Mackinac Straits	1957	Straits of Mackinac, Mich, USA
3524	1074	Atatürk Bridge	1973	Bosphorus, Istanbul, Turkey
3500	1067	George Washington (2 decks, each 7 lanes since 1962)	1931	Hudson River, NY City, USA
3323	1013	Ponte do 25 Abril (Tagus) (2 lanes and rail)	1966	Lisbon, Portugal
3300	1006	Firth of Forth Road Bridge	1964	Firth of Forth, Scotland
3240	988	Severn–Wye River (4 lanes)	1966	Severn Estuary, England
2800	853	Tacoma Narrows II	1950	Washington, USA
2336	712	Angostura	1967	Ciudad Bolivar, Venezuela
2336	712	Kanmon Straits	1973	Shimonoseki, Japan
2310	704	Transbay (2 spans)	1936	San Francisco–Oakland, Calif, USA
2300	701	Bronx–Whitestone (Belt Parkway)	1939	East River, NY City, USA
2190	668	Pierre Laporte Bridge	1970	Quebec, City, Canada
2150	655	Delaware Memorial I	1951	Wilmington, Delaware, USA
2150	655	Delaware Memorial II	1968	Wilmington, Delaware, USA
2000	610	Melville Gaspipe	1951	Atchafalaya River, Louisiana, USA
2000	610	Walt Whiteman	1957	Philadelphia, Pennsylvania, USA
1995	608	Tancarville	1959	Seine, Le Havre, France
1968	600	Lillebaelt	1970	Lillebaelt, Denmark

* Under construction.

Cantilever Bridges

The term cantilever came in only in 1883 (from *cant* and *lever*, an inclined or projecting lever). The earlier bridges of this type were termed Gerber bridges from Heinrich Gerber, engineer, of the 425 ft *129,5 m* Hassfurt am Main, Germany, bridge completed in 1867.

Length (ft)	Length (m)	Name	Completion	Location
1800	548,6	*Quebec	1917	St Lawrence, Canada
1710	521,2	*Firth of Forth	1889	Firth of Forth, Scotland
1644	501,0	Delaware River	1971	Chester, Pennsylvania, USA
1575	480,0	Greater New Orleans	1958	Algiers, Mississippi River, Louisiana, USA
1500	457,2	Howrah	1943	Calcutta, India
1400	426,7	Transbay (Oakland)	1936	San Francisco, California, USA
1250	381,0	Yokohama	1954	Yokohama, Japan
1235	376,4	Baton Rouge	1968	Mississippi River, Louisiana, USA
1212	369,4	Nyack–Tarrytown (Tappen Zee)	1955	Hudson River, NY, USA
1200	365,7	Longview	1930	Columbia River, Washington, USA
1182	360,2	Queensboro	1909	East River, NY City, USA
1164	354,7	Muscaline	1892	Mississippi River, Louisiana, USA
1160	353,5	Savanna–Sabvia	1932	Mississippi River, Illinois, USA
1100	335,2	†Carquinez Strait	1927	nr San Francisco, California, USA
1100	335,2	New Narrows	1959	Burrard Inlet, Vancouver, BC, Canada

* Rail bridge.　† New parallel bridge completed 1958.

Steel Arch Bridges

Steel was first used in bridge construction in 1828 (Danube Canal bridge, Vienna) but the first all-steel bridge was not built until the Chicago and Alton Railway Bridge over the Missouri at Glasgow, South Dakota, USA, in 1878. The longest concrete arch bridge is the Gladesville Bridge, Sydney, Australia, with a span of 1000 ft *304 m*.

Length (ft)	Length (m)	Name	Year of completion	Location
1652	503,5	Bayonne (Kill Van Kull)	1931	Bayonne, NJ–Staten Is, NY, USA
1650	502,9	Sydney Harbour	1932	Sydney, Australia
1255	382,5	Fremont	1971	Portland, Oregon, USA
1200	365,7	Port Mann	1964	Vancouver, BC, Canada
1128	343,8	Thatcher Ferry	1962	Balbao, Panama
1100	335,2	Laviolette	1967	Trois-Rivières, Quebec, Canada
1090	332,2	Zdakov	1967	Vltava River, Czechoslovakia
1082	330,0	Runcorn–Widnes	1961	Runcorn, Cheshire–Widnes, Lancashire, England
1080	329,2	Birchenough	1935	Sabi River, Rhodesia

Longest Bridging

Length (miles)	Length (km)	Name	Date Built	Location
23·87	38,422	Lake Pontchartrain Causeway II	1969	Mandeville–Jefferson, Louisiana, USA
23·83	38,352	Lake Pontchartrain Causeway I	1956	Mandeville–Jefferson, Louisiana, USA
17·65	28,400	Chesapeake Bay Bridge-Tunnel	1964	Delmarva Peninsula–Norfolk, Virginia, USA
15·0	24,5	Sunshine Skyway	1954	Lower Tampa Bay, Florida, USA
11·85*	19,070	Great Salt Lake Viaduct (Lucin cut-off)	1904	Great Salt Lake, Utah, USA
8·7	13,9	Ponte Presidente Costa e Silva	1974	Niteroi, Brazil
8·0	12,9	Chesapeake Bay I	1952	Virginia, USA
8·0	12,9	Chesapeake Bay II	1972	Virginia, USA
7·0	11,27	San Mateo–Hayward	1967	San Francisco, California, USA

Canals

A canal, from the Latin *canalis*—a water channel—is an artificial channel used for purposes of drainage, irrigation, water supply, navigation or a combination of these purposes.

Navigation canals were originally only for specially designed barges, but were later constructed for sea-going vessels. This important latter category consists either of improved barge canals or, since the pioneering of the Suez in 1859–69, canals specially constructed for ocean-going vessels.

The world's major deep-draught ship canals (of at least 5 m or 16·4 ft depth) in order of length

Length of Waterway (miles)	Length of Waterway (km)	Name	Year Opened	Minimum Depth (ft)	Minimum Depth (m)	No of Locks	Achievement and Notes
141	227	White Sea (Beloye More)–Baltic (formerly Stalin) Canal	1933	16·5	5,0	19	Links the Barents Sea and White Sea to the Baltic with a chain of a lake, canalised river, and 32 miles 51,5 km of canal.
100·6	162	Suez Canal	1869	39·3	12,9	Nil	Eliminates the necessity for 'rounding the Cape'. Deepening in progress.
62·2	100	V I Lenin Volga–Don Canal	1952	—	—	13	Interconnects Black, Azov and Caspian Seas.
60·9	98	North Sea (or Kiel) Canal	1895	45	13,7	2	Shortens the North-Sea-Baltic passage; south German–Danish border. Major reconstruction 1914.
56·7	91	Houston (Texas) Canal	1940	34	10,4	Nil	Makes Houston, although 50 miles from the coast, the United States' eighth busiest port.
53	85	Alphonse XIII Canal	1926	25	7,6	13	Makes sea access to Seville safe. True canal only 4 miles 6,4 km in length.
50·71	82	Panama Canal	1914	41	12,5	6	Eliminates the necessity for 'rounding the Horn'. 49 miles 78,9 km of the length was excavated.
39·7	64	Manchester Ship Canal	1894	28	8,5	4	Makes Manchester, although 54 miles 86,9 km from the open sea, Britain's third busiest port.
28·0	45	Welland Canal	1931	29	8,8	7	Circumvents Niagara Falls and Niagara River rapids.
19·8	32	Brussels or Rupel Sea Canal	1922	21·0	6,4	4	Makes Brussels an inland port.

Notes: (1) The Volga–Baltic canal system runs 1850 miles *2300 km* from Leningrad *via* Lake Ladoga, Gor'kiy, Kuybysev and the Volga River to Astrakhan. The Grand Canal of China, completed in the 13th century over a length of 1107 miles *1780 km* from Peking to Hangchou had silted up to a maximum depth of 6 ft *1,8 m* by 1950 but is now being reconstructed.

(2) The world's longest inland navigation route is the St Lawrence Seaway of 2342 miles *3769 km* from the North Atlantic up the St Lawrence estuary and across the Great Lakes to Duluth, Minnesota, USA. It was opened on 26 Apr. 1959.

World's highest dams

Name	River	Country	Completion	Height (ft)	Height (m)
Nurek	Vakhsh	USSR	1975	1040	317
Grand Dixence	Dixence-Rhôde	Switzerland	1962	935	285
Ingurskayi	Inguri	USSR	Building	889	271
Vaiont	Piave	Italy	1961	858	262
Moa	Colombia	Canada	Building	794	242

Longest non-vehicular tunnels

Miles	km		
105	168,9	Delaware Aqueduct 1937–44	New York State, USA
51·2	82,42	Orange-Fish Irrigation 1974	South Africa
31	50	Central Outfall 1975	Mexico City, Mexico
29·8	48	Arpa-Sevan hydro-electric u.c.	Armenia, USSR
18·8	30,3	Thames-Lea Water Supply 1960	Hampton-Walthamstow, London

World's longest vehicular tunnels

Miles	km		
33·47	53,85	Seikan (rail) 1972–82	Tsugaru Channel, Japan
17·30	27,84	Northern Line (Tube) 1939	East Finchley-Morden, London
12·31	19,82	Simplon II (rail) 1918–22	Brigue, Switzerland-Iselle, Italy
12·30	19,80	Simplon I (rail) 1898–1906	Brigue, Switzerland-Iselle, Italy
11·6	18,7	New-Kanmon (rail) 1974	Kanmon Strait, Japan
11·49	18,49	Great Appennine (rail) 1923–34	Vernio, Italy
10·1	16,3	St Gotthard (road) 1971–78	Goschenen-Airolo, Switzerland
9·85	15,8	Henderson (rail) 1975	Röcky, Mts, Colorado, USA
9·26	14,9	St Gotthard (rail) 1872–82	Göschenen-Airolo-Switzerland

World's most massive earth and rock dams

Name	Volume (millions of cubic yards)	Volume (millions of cubic metres)
Tarbela, Indus, Pakistan (1975)	186·0	142,2
Mangla, Jhelum, Pakistan (1967)	139·4	106,6
Fort Peck, Missouri, Montana, USA (1940)	125·6	96
Oahe, Missouri, S Dakota, USA (1963)	92·0	70
Gardiner, South Saskatchewan, Canada (1968)	86	66
Oroville, Featherville, Calif, USA	78·0	60
San Luis, Calif, USA	77·0	59
Nurek, Vakhsh, Tadjikistan, USSR†	76	58
Garrison, Missouri, N Dakota, USA (1956)	67	51
Gorky, Volga, USSR (1955)	58·0	44
Kiev, Drieper, Ukraine, USSR (1964)	58·0	44
Aswan High Dam, Nile river, (Sadd-el-Aali), Egypt	57·0	44
W A C Bennett (formerly Portage Mt) Peace River, BC Canada (1968)	57	44

† Under construction.

Inventions

The invention and discovery of drugs, explosives and musical instruments are treated separately (see Index)

Object	Year	Inventor	Notes
Adding Machine	1623	Wilhelm Schickard (Ger)	Earliest commercial machine invented by William Burroughs (US) in St Louis, Missouri, in 1885
Aeroplane	1903	Orville (1871–1948) and Wilbur Wright (1867–1912) (US)	Kitty Hawk, North Carolina (17 Dec.)
Airship (non-rigid)	1852	Henri Giffard (Fr) (1825–82)	Steam-powered propeller, near Paris (24 Sept.)
(rigid)	1900	Graf Ferdinand von Zeppelin (Ger) (1838–1917)	Bodensee (2 July)
Bakelite	1907	Leo H Baekeland (Belg/US) (1863–1944)	First use, electrical insulation by Loando & Co, Boonton, New Jersey
Balloon	1783	Jacques (1745–99) and Joseph Montgolfier (1740–1810) (Fr)	Tethered flight, Paris (15 Oct.) manned free flight, Paris, (21 Nov.) by François de Rozierr and Marquis d'Arlandes. Father Bartolomeu de Gusmão (né Lourenço) (b. Brazil, 1685) demonstrated hot air balloon in Portugal on 8 Aug. 1709.
Ball-Point Pen	1888	John J Loud (US)	First practical models by Lazlo and Georg Biro (Hungary) in 1938
Barbed Wire	1867	Lucien B Smith (patentee) (25 June)	Introduced to Britain in 1880 by 5th Earl Spencer in Leicestershire
Barometer	1644	Evangelista Torricelli (It) (1608–47)	Referred to in a letter of 11 June
Bicycle	1839	Kirkpatrick Macmillan (Scot) (1810–78)	Pedal-driven cranks. First direct drive in March 1861 by Ernest Michaux (Fr)
Bicycle Tyres (pneumatic)	1888	John Boyd Dunlop (GB) (1840–1921)	Principle patented but undeveloped by Robert William Thomson (GB), 10 June 1845. First motor car pneumatic tyres adapted by André and Edouard Michelin (Fr) 1895 (see Rubber tyres)
Bifocal Lens	1780	Benjamin Franklin (1706–90) (US)	His earliest experiments began c. 1760
Bunsen Burner	1855	Robert Willhelm von Bunsen (1811–99) (Ger) at Heidelberg	Michael Faraday (1791–1867) (UK) had previously designed an adjustable burner
Burglar Alarm	1858	Edwin T Holmes (US)	Electric installed, Boston, Mass (21 Feb.)
Car (steam)	c. 1769	Nicolas Cugnot (Fr) (1725–1804)	Three-wheeled military tractor. Oldest surviving is Italian Bordino (1854) in Turin
Car (petrol)	1855	Karl Benz (Ger) (1844–1929)	First run Mannheim Nov. or Dec. Patented 29 Jan. 1886. First powered hand cart with internal combustion engine was by Siegfried Marcus (Austria), c. (1864)
Carburettor	1876	Gottlieb Daimler (Ger) (1834–1900)	Carburettor spray: Charles E Duryea (US) (1892)
Carpet Sweeper	1876	Melville R Bissell (US)	Grand Rapids, Mich (Patent, 19 Sept.)
Cash Register	1879	James Ritty (US) (Patent 4 Nov.)	Built in Dayton, Ohio. Taken over by National Cash Register Co 1884
Cellophane	1908	Dr Jacques Brandenberger (Switz), Zurich	Machine production not before 1911
Celluloid	1861	Alexander Parkes (GB) (1813–90)	Invented in Birmingham, Eng; developed and trade marked by J W Hyatt (US) in 1870
Cement	1824	Joseph Aspdin (GB)	Wakefield, Yorkshire (21 Oct.)
Chronometer	1735	John Harrison (GB) (1693–1776)	Received in 1772 Government's £20 000 prize on offer since 1714
Cinema	1895	Auguste Marie Louis Nicolas Lumière (1862–1954) and Louis Jean Lumière (1864–1948) (Fr)	Development pioneers were Etienne Jules Marey (Fr) (1830–1903) and Thomas A Edison (US) (1847–1931). First public showing, Blvd. des Capucines, Paris (28 Dec.)
Clock (mechanical)	725	I-Hsing and Liang Ling-Tsan (China)	Earliest escapement, 600 years before Europe
Clock (pendulum)	1656	Christaan Huygens (Neth) (1629–95)	
Dental Plate	1817	Anthony A Plantson (US) (1774–1837)	
Dental Plate (rubber)	1855	Charles Goodyear (US) (1854–1921)	
Diesel Engine	1895	Rudolf Diesel (Ger) (1858–1913)	Lower pressure oil engine patent by Stuart Akroyd, 1890. Diesel's first commercial success, Augsberg, 1897
Disc Brake	1902	Dr F Lanchester (GB)	First used on aircraft 1953 (Dunlop Rubber Co)
Dynamo	1832	Hypolite Pixii (Fr), demonstrated, Paris 3 Sept.	Rotative dynamo, demonstrated by Joseph Saxton, Cambridge, England June 1833
Electric Blanket	1883	Exhibited Vienna, Austria Exhibition	
Electric Flat Iron	1882	H W Seeley (US)	New York City, USA (Patent 6 June)
Electric Lamp	1879	Thomas Alva Edison (US) (1847–1931)	First practical demonstration at Menlo Park, New Jersey, USA, 20 Dec.
Electric motor (DC)	1873	Zénobe Gramme (Belg) (1826–1901)	Exhibited in Vienna. Patent by Thomas Davenport (US) of Vermont, 25 Feb. 1837
Electric motor (AC)	1888	Nikola Tesla (US) (1856–1943)	
Electromagnet	1824	William Sturgeon (GB) (b. 1783)	Improved by Joseph Henry (US), 1831
Electronic Computer	1942	J G Brainerd, J P Eckert, J W Mauchly (US)	ENIAC (Electronic numerical integrator and calculator), University of Pennsylvania, Philadelphia, USA. Point-contact transistor announced by John Bardeen and Walter Brattain, July 1948. Junction transistor announced by R. L. Wallace, Morgan Sparks and Dr. William Shockley in early 1951.
Film (musical sound)	1923	Dr Lee de Forest (US)	New York demonstration (13 Mar.)
(talking)	1926	Warner Bros. (US)	First release Don Juan, Warner Theatre, New York (5 Aug.)
Fountain Pen	1884	Lewis E Waterman (US) (1837–1901)	Patented by D Hyde (US), 1830, undeveloped
Gas Lighting	1792	William Murdock (GB) (1754–1839)	Private house in Cornwall, 1792; Factory Birmingham, 1798; London Streets, 1807

Object	Year	Inventor	Notes
Glass (stained)	c. 1080	Augsberg, Germany	Earliest English, c. 1170, York Minster
Glassware	c. 1500 BC	Egypt and Mesopotamia	Glass blowing Syria, c. 50 BC
Glider	1853	Sir George Cayley (GB) (1773–1857)	Near Brompton Hall, Yorkshire. Passenger possibly John Appleby. Emanuel Swedenborg (1688–1772) sketches dated c. 1714
Gramophone	1878	Thomas Alva Edison (US) (1847–1931)	Hand-cranked cylinder at Menlo Park, NJ. Patent, 19 Feb. First described on 30 Apr 1877 by Charles Cros (1842–88) (Fr)
Gyro-compass	1911	Elmer A Sperry (US) (1860–1930)	Tested on USS *Delaware*, (28 Aug.). Gyroscope devised 1852 by Foucault (Fr)
Helicopter	1924	Etienne Ochmichen (Fr)	First FAI world record set on 14 Apr. 1924. Earliest drawing of principal Le Mans Museum, France c. 1460. First serviceable machine by Igor Sikorsky (US), 1939.
Hovercraft	1955	C S Cockerell (GB)	Patented 12 Dec. Earliest air-cushion vehicle patent was in 1877 by J I Thornycroft (1843–1928) (GB). First 'flight' Saunders Roe SR-NI at Cowes, England, 30 May 1959
Iron Working	c. 100 BC	Hallstatt, Austria	Introduced into Britain, c. 550 BC
Jet Engine	1937	Sir Frank Whittle (GB) (b. 1907)	First test bed run (12 Apr.). Principles announced by Merconnet (Fr) 1909 and Maxime Guillaume (Fr) 1921. First flight 27 Aug. 1939 by Heinkel He-178
Laser	1960	Dr Charles H Townes (US). First demonstration by Theodore Maiman (US)	Demonstrated at Hughes Research, Malibu, California in July. Abbreviation for Light amplification by stimulated emission of radiation Fort Worth, Texas (18 Apr.)
Launderette	1934	J F Cantrell (US)	Fort Worth, Texas (18 Apr.)
Lift (Mechanical)	1852	Elisha G Otis (US) (1811–61)	Earliest elevator at Yonkers, NY
Lightning Conductor	1752	Benjamin Franklin (US) (1706–90)	Philadelphia, Pennsylvania, USA in Sept.
Linoleum	1860	Frederick Walton (GB)	
Locomotive	1804	Richard Trevithick (GB) (1771–1833)	Penydarren, Wales, 9 miles *14,4 km* (21 Feb.)
Loom, power	1785	Edmund Cartwright (GB) (1743–1823)	
Loudspeaker	1900	Horace Short (GB) Patentee in 1898	A compressed air Auxetophone. First used atop the Eiffel Tower, Summer 1900. Earliest open-air electric public address system used by Bell Telephone on Staten Island, NY on 30 June 1916.
Machine Gun	1718	James Puckle (GB) patentee, 15 May 1718. White Cron Alley factory in use 1721	Richard Gatling (US) (1818–1903) model dates from 1861.
Maps	c. 3500 BC	Sumerian (clay tablets of river Euphrates)	Earliest world map by Eratosthenes c. 220 BC. Earliest printed map printed in Bologna, Italy, 1477.
Margarine	1869	Hippolyte Mège-Mouries (Fr)	Patented 15 July
Match, safety	1826	John Walker, (GB) Stockton, Teeside	
Microphone	1876	Alexander Graham Bell (1847–1922) (US)	Name coined 1878 by Prof David Hughes, who gave demonstration in London in January 1878.
Microscope	1590	Zacharias Janssen (Neth)	Compound convex-concave lens.
Motor Cycle	1885	Gottlieb Daimler of Candstatt, Germany, patent 29 Aug.	First rider Paul Daimler (10 Nov. 1885); first woman rider Mrs Edward Butler near Erith, Kent, 1888
Neon Lamp	1910	Georges Claude (Fr) (1871–1960)	First installation at Paris Motor Show (3 Dec.)
Night Club	1843	Paris, France	First was Le Bal des Anglais, Paris 5me. (Closed c. 1960)
Nylon	1937	Dr Wallace H Carothers (US) (1896–1937) at Du Pont Labs, Seaford, Delaware, USA (Patent, 16 Feb.)	First stockings made about 1937. Bristle production 24 Feb. 1938. Yarn production December 1939
Paper	AD 105	Mulberry based fibre, China	Introduced to West *via* Samarkand, 14th century
Parachute	1797	André-Jacques Garnerin (Fr) (1769–1823)	First descent (from 2230 ft *620 m* over Paris, 22 Oct.) Earliest jump from aircraft 1 Mar. 1912 by Albert Berry (US) over St Louis, Missouri, USA
Parchment	c. 1300 BC	Egypt	Modern name from Pergamam, Asia Minor, c. 250 BC
Parking Meter	1935	Carlton C Magee (US)	Oklahoma City (16 July)
Photography (on metal)	1826	J Nicéphore Niépce (Fr) (1765–1833)	Sensitised pewter plate, 8 hr exposure at Chalon-sur-Saône, France
(on paper)	1835	W H Fox Talbot (GB) (1807–1877)	Lacock Abbey, Wiltshire (August)
(on film)	1888	John Carbutt (US)	Kodak by George Eastman (US) (1854–1932), August 1888
Porcelain	851	Earliest report from China	Reached Baghdad c. 800
Potter's Wheel	c. 6500 BC	Asia Minor	Used in Mesopotamia c. 3000 BC
Printing Press	c. 1455	Johann Gutenberg (Ger) (c. 1400–68)	Hand printing known in India in 868
Printing (rotary)	1846	Richard Hoe (US) (1812–86)	Philadelphia Public Ledger rotary printed, 1847
Propellor (ship)	1837	Francis Smith (GB) (1808–74)	
Pyramid	c. 2685 BC	Egypt	Earliest was Zoser step pyramid, Saqqara
Radar	1922	Dr Albert H Taylor and Leo C Young	Radio reflection effect first noted. First harnessed by Dr Rudolph Kühnold, Kiel, Germany 20 Mar. 1934. Word coined in 1940 by Cdr S M Tucker USN
Radio Telegraphy	1864	Dr Mahlon Loomis (US) demonstrated over 14 miles *22 km* Bear's Den, Loudoun County, Virginia (October)	First advertised radio broadcast by Prof R A Fessenden (b. Canada, 1868–1932) at Brant Rock, Massachusetts on 24 Dec. 1906
Radio Telegraphy (Transatlantic)	1901	Guglielmo Marconi (It) (1874–1937)	From Poldhu, Cornwall, to St John's, Newfoundland (12 Dec.)
Rayon	1883	Sir Joseph Swan (1828–1917) (GB)	Production at Courtauld's Ltd, Coventry, England November 1905. Name 'Rayon' adopted in 1924

Object	Year	Inventor	Notes
Razor (electric)	1931	Col Jacob Schick (US)	First manufactured Stamford, Conn (18 Mar.)
Razor (safety)	1895	King C Gillette (US) Patented 2 Dec. 1901	First throw-away blades. Earliest fixed safety razor by Kampfe
Record (long-playing)	1948	Dr Peter Goldmark (US)	Micro-groove developed in the CBS Research Labs and launched 21 June, so ending the 78 rpm market supremacy
Refrigerator	1850	James Harrison (GB) and Alexander Catlin Twining (US)	Simultaneous development at Rodey Point, Victoria Australia and in Cleveland, Ohio. Earliest domestic refrigerator 1913 in Chicago, Illinois
Rubber (latex foam)	1928	Dunlop Rubber Co (GB)	Team led by E A Murphy at Fort Dunlop, Birmingham
Rubber (tyres)	1846	Thomas Hancock (GB) (1786–1865)	Introduced solid rubber tyres for vehicles (1847) (see also bicycle)
Rubber (vulcanised)	1841	Charles Goodyear (US) (1800–60)	
Rubber (waterproof)	1823	Charles Macintosh (GB) (1766–1843) Patent	First experiments in Glasgow with James Syme. G. Fox in 1821 had marketed a Gambroon clock of which no detail has survived
Safety Pin	1849	William Hunt (US)	First manufactured New York City, NY (10 Apr.)
Self-Starter	1911	Charles F Kettering (US) (1876–1958)	Developed at Dayton, Ohio, sold to Cadillac
Sewing Machine	1829	Barthélemy Thimmonnier (Fr) (1793–1854)	A patent by Thomas Saint (GB) dated 17 July 1790 for an apparently undeveloped machine was found in 1874. Earliest practical domestic machine by Isaac M Singer (1811–75) of Pittstown, NY, USA, in 1851
Ship (sea-going)	c. 7250 BC	Grecian ships	Traversed from mainland to Melos.
Ship (steam)	1775	J C Périer (Fr) (1742–1818)	On the Seine, near Paris. Propulsion achieved on river Saône, France by Marquis d'Abbans, 1783.
Ship (turbine)	1894	Hon Sir Charles Parsons (GB) (1854–1931)	SS Turbinia attained 34·5 knots on first trial. Built at Heaton, County Durham.
Silk Manufacture	c. 50 BC	Reeling machines devised, China	Silk mills in Italy c. 1250, world's earliest factories
Skyscraper	1882	William Le Baron Jenny (US)	Home Insurance Co Building, Chicago, Ill, 10 storey (top 4 steel beams)
Slide Rule	1621	William Oughtred (1575–1660) (Eng)	Earliest slide between fixed stock by Robert Bissaker, 1654
Spectacles	1289	Venice, Italy (convex)	Concave lens for myopia not developed till c. 1450
Spinning Frame	1769	Sir Richard Arkwright (GB) (1732–92)	
Spinning Jenny	1764	James Hargreaves (GB) (d. 1778)	
Spinning Mule	1779	Samuel Crompton (GB) (1753–1827)	
Steam Engine	1698	Thomas Savery (GB) (c. 1650–1715)	
Steam Engine (piston)	1712	Thomas Newcomen (GB) (1663–1729)	Recorded on 25 July
Steam Engine (condenser)	1765	James Watt (Scot) (1736–1819)	
Steel Production	1855	Henry Bessemer (GB) (1813–1898)	At St Pancras, London. Cementation of wrought iron bars by charcoal contact known to Chalybes people of Asia minor c. 1400 BC
Steel (stainless)	1913	Harry Brearley (GB)	First cast at Sheffield (Eng) (20 Aug.). Krupp patent, Oct. 1912 for chromium carbon steel; failed to recognise corrosion resistance
Submarine	1776	David Bushnell (US), Saybrook, Conn	Hand propelled screw, one man crew, used off New York. A twelve man wooden and leather submersible devised by Cornelius Drebbel (Neth) demonstrated in Thames in 1624.
Tank	1914	Sir Ernest Swinton (GB) (1868–1951)	Built at Leicester, designed by William Trilton. Tested 8 Sept. 1915
Telegraph	1787	M. Lammond (Fr) demonstrated a working model, Paris	
Telegraph Code	1837	Samuel F B Morse (USA) (1791–1872)	The real credit belonged largely to his assistant Alfred Vail (US) who first transmitted at Morristown, NJ on 8 Jan. 1838
Telephone	1849	Antonio Meucci (It) in Havana, Cuba	Caveat not filed until 1871. Instrument worked imperfectly by electrical impulses
	1876	Alexander Graham Bell (US) (1847–1922) Patented 9 Mar. 1876	First exchange at Boston, Mass, 1878
Telescope	1608	Hans Lippershey (Neth)	(2 Oct.)
Television	1926	John Logie Baird (GB) (1888–1946)	First public demonstration 27 Jan., London, of moving image with gradations of light and shade at 22 Frith Street, London. First successful experiment 30 Oct. 1925. First transmission in colour on 3 July 1928 at 133 Long Acre, London
Terylene	1941	J R Whinfield (1901–1966), J T Dickson (GB) at Accrington, Lancashire	First available 1950, marketed in USA as 'Dacron'
Thermometer	1593	Galileo Galilei (It) (1564–1642)	
Transformer	1831	Michael Faraday (GB)	Built at Royal Institution, London (29 Aug.)
Transistor	1948	John Bardeen, William Shockley and Walter Brattain (US)	Researched at Bell Telephone Laboratories. First application for a patent was by Dr Julius E Lilienfeld in Canada on October 1925 (see Electronic Computer).
Typewriter	1808	Pellegrine Tarri (It)	First practical 27 character keyed machine with carbon paper built in Reggio Emilia, Italy
Washing Machine (electric)	1907	Hurley Machine Co (US)	Marketed under name of 'Thor' in Chicago, Illinois, USA
Watch	1462	Bartholomew Manfredi (It)	Earliest mention of a named watchmaker (November) but in reference to an earlier watchmaker
Water Closet	1589	Designed by Sir John Harington (GB)	Installed at Kelston, near Bath. Built by 'T C' (full name unknown)

Object	Year	Inventor	Notes
Welder (electric)	1877	Elisha Thomson (US) (1853–1937)	
Wheel	c. 330 BC	Sumerian civilisation	Spoked as opposed to solid wheels intro. c. 1900 BC
Windmill	c. 600	Persian corn grinding	Oldest known English port mill, 1191, Bury St Edmunds
Writing	c. 3400 BC	Sumerian civilisation	Earliest evidence found at Warka, Iraq, in 1952
X-Ray	1895	Wilhelm von Röntgen (Ger)	University of Wurzburg (8 Nov.)
Zip Fastener	1891	Whitcomb L Judson (US) Exhibited 1893 at Chicago Exposition	First practical fastener invented in USA by Gideon Sundback (Sweden) in 1913

Astronomy

A guide to the scale of the Solar System and the Universe

If the Sun were reduced to the size of a peach ball of twelve in. (30,4 cm) in diameter, following on the same scale relatively the nine planets would be represented relatively thus:

1) Mercury = a grain of mustard seed 50 ft 15,2 m away
2) Venus = a pea 78 ft 23,7 m away
3) Earth = a pea 106 ft 32,3 m away
   Moon = a grain of mustard seed 3½ in 8,5 cm out from the Earth
4) Mars = a currant 164 ft 49,9 m away
5) Jupiter = an orange 560 ft 170,6 m away
6) Saturn = a tangerine 1024 ft 312,1 m away
7) Uranus = a plum 2060 ft 627,8 m away
8) Neptune = a plum 3230 ft 984,5 m away
9) Pluto = a pinhead up to a mile 1,6 km away.

The utter remoteness of the solar system from all other heavenly bodies is stressed by the fact that, still using this same scale of a one-foot (30,48 cm) Sun, which for this purpose we shall place in the centre of London, the nearest stars, the triple Centauri system, would lie 5350 miles (8609,9 km) away, say near San Francisco with the largest member having a two-foot (60,96 cm) diameter. Only the next six nearest stars in our Milky Way galaxy could, even on this scale, be accommodated on the Earth's surface.

Human imagination must boggle at distances greater than these, so it is necessary to switch to a much vaster scale of measurement.

Light travels at 186,282·3970 miles/s or 299 792,458 km/s in vacuo. Thus, in the course of a tropical year (i.e. 365·242 198 78 mean solar days at January 0·12 hours Ephemeris time in AD 1900) light will travel 5 878 499 814 000 miles or 9 460 528 405 000 km. This distance is conveniently called a light year.

Light will thus travel to the Earth from the following heavenly bodies in the approximate times given:

From the Moon (reflected light)	1·25 s
From the Sun (at perihelion)	8 min 10·6 s
From Pluto (variable)	about 6 hrs
From nearest star (excepting the Sun)	4·28 yrs
From Rigel	900 yrs
From most distant star in Milky Way	75 000 yrs
From nearest major extra-galactic body (Larger Magellanic cloud)	160 000 yrs
From Andromeda (limit of naked eye vision)	2 200 000 yrs
By radio telescope, galaxies may be detectable up to about	12 000 000 000 yrs

Number of stars

There are 5776 stars visible to the naked eye. It is estimated that our own galaxy, the Milky Way galaxy, contains some 100 000 million (10^{11}) stars and that there are between 100 000 and 1 000 000 million (10^{11} to 10^{12}) galaxies in the detectable universe. This would indicate a total of 10^{22} to 10^{23} stars. The Milky Way galaxy is of a lens-shaped spiral form with a diameter of some 100 000 light years. The Sun is some 32 000 light years from the centre and hence the most distant star in our own galaxy is about 75 000 light years distant.

Age of stars

Being combustible, stars have a limited life. The Sun, which is classified as a Yellow Dwarf, functions like a controlled hydrogen bomb, losing four million tons in mass each second. It has been estimated that it has less than 10 000 million years to burn. It is difficult to give anything like a precise value for the age of the universe, as we are still very uncertain as to its early history. However, the Earth is over 4500 million years old, and the universe itself must be at least 12 000 million years old—very possibly much older still.

The brightest and nearest stars (excluding the Sun)

Magnitude—a measure of stellar brightness such that the light of a star of any magnitude bears a ratio of 2·511886 to that of the star of the next magnitude. Thus a fifth magnitude star is 2·511886 times as bright, whilst one of the first magnitude is exactly 100 (or $2·511886^5$) times as bright as a sixth magnitude star. In the case of such exceptionally bright bodies as Sirius, Venus, the Moon (magnitude −12·7) or the Sun (magnitude −26·8) the magnitude is expressed as a minus quantity. Such a value for the Sun is its 'apparent magnitude' (m_v) which is the brightness as seen from the Earth, but for comparison the intrinsic brightness needs to be known and which is defined as the 'absolute magnitude' (M_v), the magnitude that would be observed if the star was placed at a distance of ten parsecs. On this basis the magnitude of the Sun is reduced to +4·8 or a four billionfold reduction in brightness.

The absolute magnitude of a star is related to its apparent magnitude and its distance in parsecs (d) by means of the equation:

$$M_v = m_v + 5 - 5 \log_{10}(d)$$

Brightest Stars

Name	Magnitude		Distance	
	Apparent	Absolute	Light years	Parsecs
Sirius	−1·46	+1·4	8·7	2·7
Canopus★	−0·73	−4·6	200	60
Alpha Centauri★	−0·29	+4·1	4·4	1·3
Arcturus	−0·06	−0·3	36	11
Vega	+0·04	+0·5	26	8·1
Capella	+0·08	−0·5	42	13
Rigel	+0·10	−7·0	850	250
Procyon	+0·35	+2·6	11	3·5
Achernar★	+0·48	−2·5	127	39
Beta Centauri★	+0·60	−4·6	360	110
Altair	+0·77	+2·3	16	5·0
Betelgeuse	+0·85 v	−5·7 v	650	200
Aldebaran	+0·85	−0·7	65	21
Alpha Crucis	+0·90	−3·7	270	85
Spica	+0·96	−3·6	260	80
Antares	+1·08	−4·5	430	130
Pollux	+1·15	+1·0	35	11
Fomalhaut	+1·16	+1·9	23	7·0
Deneb	+1·25	−7·1	1500	500
Beta Crucis	+1·25	−5·1	530	160
Regulus	+1·35	−0·7	85	26
Adhara	+1·50	−4·4	490	150

★ Not visible from British Isles
v = very variable apparent magnitude, average figure.

The Sun

The Sun (for statistics see Solar System table) is a yellow dwarf star with a luminosity of 3×10^{27} candle power such that each square inch of the surface emits 1.5×10^6 candle power. Sun spots appear to be darker because they are 2700 °F (1500 °C) cooler than the surface temperature of 11 000 °F (6000 °C) These may measure up to 7×10^9 miles² and have to be 5×10^8 miles² to be visible to the (protected) naked eye. During 1957 a record 263 were noted. Solar prominences may flare out to some 300 000 miles from the Sun's surface.

EARTH-MOON SYSTEM
Creation of the Moon

It was once believed that the Moon used to be part of the Earth, and that the original combined body broke in two as a result of tidal forces. This is not now believed to be the case. It may be that the Moon was once an independent body which was captured by the Earth; however, most authorities believe that it has always been associated with the Earth. Certainly the rocks brought back by the Apollo astronauts confirm that the age of the Moon is approximately the same as that of the Earth (about 4 600 million years).

Creation of the Earth

The long-popular theory that the Earth and other planets were globules thrown out from a molten Sun has long been discarded. Spectroscopic analysis has shown that the Sun consists of 98 per cent hydrogen and helium whereas the planets are a composite of heavy non-gaseous elements.

It is now concluded that c. 10 000 million years ago the Sun, like so many stars, was a binary system with a companion star 500 million miles distant. It is from this star, Sun B, that our planets agglomerated.

Nearest Stars

Name	Distance		Magnitude			
	Light years	Parsecs	Apparent		Absolute	
Proxima Centauri	4·28	1·31	11·0		15·4	
Alpha Centauri	4·38	1·34	A 0·0 B 1·3		A 4·4 B 5·7	
Barnard's Star	5·91	1·81	9·5		13·2	
Wolf 359	7·60	2·33	13·5		16·7	
Lalande 21185	8·13	2·49	7·5		10·5	
Sirius	8·65	2·65	A −1·5 B 8·7		A 1·4 B 11·6	
Luyten 726-8**	8·89	2·72	A 12·5 B 13·0		A 15·3 B 15·8	
Ross 154	9·45	2·90	10·6		13·3	
Ross 248	10·3	3·15	12·3		14·8	
Epsilon Eridani	10·8	3·30	3·7		6·1	
Luyten 789-6	10·8	3·30	12·2		14·6	
Ross 128	10·8	3·32	11·1		13·5	
61 Cygni	11·1	3·40	A 5·2 B 6·0		A 7·6 B 8·4	
Epsilon Indi	11·2	3·44	4·7		7·0	
Procyon	11·4	3·50	A 0·4 B 10·7		A 2·6 B 13·0	
Sigma 2398	11·5	3·53	A 8·9 B 9·7		A 11·2 B 11·9	
Groombridge 34	11·6	3·55	A 8·1 B 11·0		A 10·3 B 13·3	
Lacaille 9352	11·7	3·58	7·4		9·6	
Tau Ceti	11·8	3·62	3·5		5·7	
Luyten's Star	12·2	3·73	9·8		12·0	
Luyten 725-32	12·5	3·83	11·5		13·6	
Lacaille 8760	12·5	3·85	6·7		8·8	
Kapteyn's Star	12·7	3·91	8·8		10·8	
Kruger 60	12·9	3·95	A 9·9 B 11·3		A 11·9 B 13·3	
Ross 614	13·0	4·00	A 11·2 B 14·8		A 13·2 B 16·8	

** The B star component is known as UV Ceti.

Constellations

There are 31 accepted constellations in the northern and 52 in the southern hemispheres and 5 which appear at times in both hemispheres, making 88 in all. The International Astronomical Union completed the now accepted arc codification by 1945. The rectangular constellation Orion includes 3 of the 24 brightest stars in its great quadrilateral—Rigel (bottom left, Mag. 0·1), Betelgeuse (top right, Mag. 0·85 variable) and Bellatrix (top left, Mag. 1·7).

Elements of the planetary orbits

Planet	Mean Distance From Sun miles km	Perihelion Distance miles km	Aphelion Distance miles km	Orbital Eccentricity	Orbital Inclination ° ' "	Sidereal Period days	Orbital Velocity Mean mph km/h	Maximum mph km/h	Minimum mph km/h
Mercury	35 983 100 / 57 909 100	28 584 000 / 46 001 000	43 382 000 / 69 817 000	0·205 630	7 00 15	87·9693	105 950 / 170 500	131 930 / 212 310	86 920 / 139 890
Venus	67 237 900 / 108 208 900	66 782 000 / 107 475 000	67 694 000 / 108 943 000	0·006 783	3 23 39	224·7008	78 340 / 126 070	78 870 / 126 930	77 810 / 125 220
Earth	92 955 800 / 149 597 900	91 402 000 / 117 097 000	94 510 000 / 152 099 000	0·016 718	———	365·2564	66 620 / 107 220	67 750 / 109 030	65 520 / 105 450
Mars	141 635 700 / 227 940 500	128 410 000 / 206 656 000	154 862 000 / 249 226 000	0·093 380	1 50 59	686·9797	53 860 / 86 680	59 270 / 95 390	49 150 / 79 100
Jupiter	483 634 000 / 778 333 000	460 280 000 / 740 750 000	506 990 000 / 815 920 000	0·048 286	1 18 16	4332·62	29 210 / 47 000	30 670 / 49 360	27 840 / 44 810
Saturn	886 683 000 / 1 426 978 000	837 000 000 / 1 347 020 000	936 370 000 / 1 506 940 000	0·056 037	2 29 21	10 759·06	21 560 / 34 700	22 820 / 36 730	20 400 / 32 830
Uranus	1 783 951 000 / 2 870 991 000	1 701 660 000 / 2 738 560 000	1 866 230 000 / 3 003 400 000	0·046 125	0 46 23	30 707·79	15 200 / 24 460	15 930 / 25 630	14 520 / 23 370
Neptune	2 794 350 000 / 4 497 070 000	2 766 270 000 / 4 451 880 000	2 822 430 000 / 4 542 270 000	0·010 050	1 46 20	60 199·63	12 150 / 19 560	12 270 / 19 750	12 030 / 19 360
Pluto	3 674 490 000 / 5 913 510 000	2 761 600 000 / 4 444 400 000	4 587 300 000 / 7 382 600 000	0·248 432	17 08 22	90 777·61	10 430 / 16 790	13 660 / 21 980	8220 / 13 230

NOTES ON THE PLANETS
Mercury

The closest of the planets to the Sun, Mercury, is never visible with the naked eye except when close to the horizon. Surface details are hard to see from Earth, even with powerful telescopes, but in 1974 the US probe Mariner 10 disclosed that the surface features are remarkably similar to those of the Moon, with mountains, valleys and craters. Mercury is virtually devoid of atmosphere, but it does have a weak but appreciable magnetic field.

Venus

Venus, almost identical in size with the Earth, is surrounded by a cloud-laden atmosphere, so that its actual surface is never visible telescopically. Research with unmanned probes has shown that the surface temperature exceeds 900 °F 480 °C, that the atmospheric ground pressure is about 100 times that on Earth, and that the main atmospheric constituent is carbon dioxide; the clouds contain corrosive sulphuric acid. The pictures sent back in 1975 by two Russian probes have shown rocks strewn on the surface. Venus rotates very slowly in a retrograde direction (i.e. in a sense opposite to that of the Earth).

Mars

Mars was long thought to be the one planet in the Solar System, apart from Earth, to be capable of supporting life, but results from space-probes are not encouraging. Mariner 9 (1971–2) sent back thousands of high-quality pictures, showing that Mars is a world of mountains, valleys, craters and giant volcanoes; one volcano, Olympus Mons, is some 15 miles high *over 24 000 m* and is crowned by a caldera 40 miles *64 km* in diameter. The Martian atmosphere is made up chiefly of carbon dioxide, and is very tenuous, with a ground pressure which is everywhere below ten millibars (cf. Earth's 1013 mb). The famous dark areas are certainly not due to vegetation tracts, and even the polar caps are composed principally of solid carbon dioxide. The two dwarf satellites, Phobos and Demos, were discovered by A Hall in 1877; Mariner 9 pictures show that each is an irregular, crater-pitted lump of rocky material.

Jupiter

Jupiter is the largest planet in the Solar System. The outer layers are gaseous, composed of hydrogen and hydrogen compounds; it is now thought that most of the planet is liquid, and that hydrogen predominates. The famous Great Red Spot has proved to be a kind of whirling storm, as was shown by the close-range photographs sent back by the US probes Pioneer 10 and 11. Jupiter has a strong magnetic field, and is surrounded by zones of lethal radiation.

Saturn

Saturn is basically similar to Jupiter, but is less dense and is, of course, colder. The rings which make Saturn unique are composed of pieces of material (probably ices, or at least ice-covered) moving round the planet in the manner of dwarf satellites; the ring-system is 169 000 miles *270 000 km* wide, but less than 10 miles *16 km* thick. There are four main rings, two bright, one dusky and the newly detected D Ring. The main bright rings are separated by a gap known as Cassini's Division. It has been suggested that the rings were formed by the break-up of a former satellite. Opinions differ, but at least Saturn has 10 satellites left, one of which (Titan) is 3440 miles *5530 km* in diameter, and has an appreciable atmosphere which may well contain clouds.

Uranus

Just visible to the naked eye, Uranus has the same low density as Jupiter and has a diameter nearly four times that of the Earth. Its axis is tilted at 98° compared with our 23° 45' which means that the night and day must at some points last up to 21 years each.

Neptune

Neptune is rather denser and 1400 miles *2250 km* less in equatorial diameter than Uranus. It requires nearly 165 years to make one revolution of the Sun against the 84 years of Uranus. Its axial tilt at 28° 48' conforms more closely to those of the Earth (23° 57'), Mars (25° 12'), and Saturn (26° 44').

Pluto

Discovered by systematic photography in 1930. The 248-year orbit of this faint planet with only 8 per cent of the volume of the Earth is so eccentric that at perihelion it will come inside Neptune on 21 Jan. 1979.

Eclipses

An eclipse (derived from the Greek *ekleipsis* 'failing to appear') occurs when the sight of a celestial body is either obliterated or reduced by the intervention of a second body.

There are two main varieties of eclipse.

(i) Those when the eclipsing body passes between the observer on Earth and the eclipsed body. Such eclipses are those of the Sun by the Moon; occultations of various stars by the moon; transits of Venus or Mercury across the face of the Sun; and the eclipses of binary stars.

(ii) Those when the eclipsing body passes between the Sun and the eclipsed body. These can only affect planets or satellites which are not self-luminous. Such are eclipses of the Moon (by the Earth's shadow); and the eclipses of the satellites of Jupiter.

There is nothing in all the variety of natural phenomena that is quite so impressive as a total eclipse of the Sun.

Eclipses of the Sun (by the Moon) and of the Moon (by the Earth) have caused both wonder and sometimes terror since recorded history.

The element of rarity enhances the wonder of this event, which should on average only be seen from a given city or town once in about four hundred years. More specifically, Londoners saw no such eclipse between 20 March 1140 and 3 May 1715—that is, about nineteen generations later. The next will be on 14 June 2051. The next total eclipse of the Sun visible from Great Britain will occur on 11 Aug. 1999 on the Cornish coast. Eclipses of the Sun are in fact commoner than those of the Moon but the area from which they can be seen is so much smaller that the number of possible spectators is infinitely smaller.

The places from which and the times at which solar eclipses have been seen have been worked out back as far as the year 4200 BC and can be worked out far into the future, with of course an increasing, but still slight, degree of inaccuracy, for centuries ahead. The precise date of actual historical events in the Assyrian, Chinese, Greek and Roman empires have been fixed or confirmed by eclipses. For example, the battle between the Lydians and the Medes, which is reported by Herodotus, can be fixed exactly as occurring on 28 May 585 BC, because a solar eclipse caused such awe that it stopped the fight. Modern astronomy has benefited from the study of ancient eclipses because they help to determine 'secular accelerations', that is, the progressive changes in celestial motions.

Solar Eclipses (i.e. of the Sun by the Moon)

Solar eclipses are of three sorts—Total, Partial and Annular. A *total* eclipse occurs when the Moon, which, of course, must be new, comes completely between the Sun's disc and the observer on Earth. The Moon's circular shadow—its umbra—with a maximum diameter of 170 miles, *273 km* sweeps across the face of the Earth. The maximum possible duration of totality is 7 min 58 sec.

The dramatic events at the moment of totality are: sunlight vanishes in a few seconds; sudden darkness (but *not* as intense as that during a night even under a full moon); the brightest stars become visible; the Sun's corona is seen; there is a hush from the animal and bird world; cocks have been noted to crow when the light floods back.

The moon's partial shadow—its penumbra—which forms a much larger circle of about 2000 miles *3200 km* in diameter, causes a *partial* eclipse. Partial eclipses, of course, vary in their degree of completeness. There must be a minimum of two Solar eclipses each year.

An *annular* eclipse occurs when—owing to variations in the Sun's distance—the Moon's disc comes inside the Sun. In other words, the Moon's umbra stops short of the Earth's surface and an outer rim of the Sun surrounds the Moon. The maximum possible duration of containment is 12 min 24 s.

Lunar Eclipses (i.e. of the Moon by the Earth's shadow)

Lunar eclipses are caused when the Moon—which, of course must be full—passes through the shadow of the Earth and so loses its bright direct illumination by the Sun. A

Physical Parameters of the sun and the planets

Sun or Planet		Diameters miles	km	Equatorial Sidereal Rotation Period d h m s	Equatorial Inclination	Mass tons	kg	Density g/cm³	Escape Velocity mps	km/s	Surface Temperature °C	On Scale Earth = 1 Equatorial Diameter	Volume	Mass	Surface Gravity	Mean Apparent Magnitude
Sun		864 940	1 391 980	25 09 07	7° 15'	$1{,}958 \times 10^{27}$	$1{,}989 \times 10^{30}$	1·409	383·73	617·55	5530	109·12	1 303 700	332 946	27·90	−26·8
Mercury	Equ.	3031	4878	58 15 30 32	0°	$3{,}250 \times 10^{20}$	$3{,}302 \times 10^{23}$	5·433	2·64	4·25	−180 to +420	0·3824	0·0561	0·055 27	0·3771	0·0
Venus	Equ.	7519	12 100	*243 00	178°	$4{,}792 \times 10^{21}$	$4{,}869 \times 10^{24}$	5·249	6·44	10·36	475	0·9486	0·8563	0·815 00	0·9038	−4·4
Earth	Equ.	7926	12 756	23 56 04·091	23° 27'	$5{,}884 \times 10^{21}$	$5{,}974 \times 10^{24}$	5·515	6·95	11·19	−88 to +58	1·0000	1·0000	1·000 00	1·0000	—
	Polar	7900	12 714													
Mars	Equ.	4221	6793	24 37 22·655	25° 12'	6318×10^{20}	$6{,}419 \times 10^{23}$	3·934	3·12	5·03	−125 to +30	0·5325	0·1507	0·107 45	0·3795	−2·0
	Polar	4196	6753													
Jupiter	Equ.	88 780	142 880	9 50 30·003	3° 04'	$1{,}869 \times 10^{24}$	$1{,}899 \times 10^{27}$	1·330	37·42	60·23	−25	11·201	1318	317·89	2·644	−2·6
	Polar	82 980	133 540													
Saturn	Equ.	74 600	120 000	10 14	26° 44'	$5{,}596 \times 10^{23}$	$5{,}686 \times 10^{26}$	0·705	22·52	36·25	−110	9·407	744	95·17	1·159	+0·7
	Polar	66 400	106 900													
Uranus	Equ.	31 600	50 800	10 49	97° 53'	$8{,}602 \times 10^{22}$	$8{,}740 \times 10^{25}$	1·31	13·38	21·53	−160	3·98	62	14·63	0·938	+5·5
	Polar	30 700	49 400	*												
Neptune	Equ.	30 200	48 600	15 48	28° 48'	$1{,}013 \times 10^{23}$	$1{,}029 \times 10^{26}$	1·75	14·82	23·84	−160	3·81	54	17·22	1·200	+7·8
	Polar	29 500	47 500													
Pluto		3400	5500	6 09 17	0°	$2{\cdot}6 \times 10^{20}$	$2{\cdot}6 \times 10^{23}$	3·0	2·21	3·56	−220	0·43	0·08	0·05	0·235	+15·0

* Retrograde

lunar eclipse is *partial* until the whole Moon passes into the Earth's umbra and so becomes *total*. After the Moon leaves the umbra it passes through the Earth's penumbra, which merely dims the moonlight so little that it is scarcely visible and is not even worth recording.

Comets

Comets are Solar System bodies moving in orbits about the Sun. Records go back to the 7th century BC. The speeds of the estimated 2 000 000 comets vary from only 700 mph in the outer reaches to 1 250 000 mph (*1100–2 million km/h*) when near the Sun. The periods of revolution vary, according to the ellipticity of orbit, from 3·3 years (Encke's comet) to millions of years as in the case of Comet 1910a (the letter 'a' indicating that it was the first classified during that year).

Comets are tenuous to the point that 10 000 cubic miles *41 000 km³* of tail might embrace only a cubic inch of solid matter. Comets are not self luminous, hence only visible only when in the inner part of the Solar System. They consist mainly of a head of dirty ice particles and a tail which may obey the laws of light pressure. In May 1910 the Earth probably passed through the tail of the famous Halley's Comet which is next due to return in 1986.

Telescopes

The prototype of modern refracting telescopes was that made in 1608 by the Dutchman Hans Lippershey (or Lippersheim) after an accidental discovery of the magnifying power of spectacle lens when held apart. The principle of the reflecting telescope was expounded by the Scot James Gregory in 1633 and the first reflector was built with a one-inch diameter mirror by Sir Isaac Newton in 1672.

The world's most powerful astronomical telescopes are now:

Diameter of Refractors (Lens) Inches	Completion Date
40·0 Yerkes, Williams Bay, Wisconsin, USA	1897
36·0 Lick, Mt Hamilton, Cal., USA	1888
32·7 Paris Observatory, Meudon, France	1893
32·0 Astrophysical Observatory, Potsdam, Germany	1899
30.0 Nice Observatory Nice, France	1880
30·0 Alleghany Observatory, Pittsburgh, Penn., USA	1914

Diameter of Reflectors (Mirror) Inches	
236·2 Mount Semirodriki, Caucasus, USSR	1976
200 Hale, Mt Palomar, nr Pasadena, Cal., USA	1948
158 Kitt Peak Nat. Observatory, Tucson, Arizona	1970
158 Cerro Tololo, Chile	1970
153 Siding Spring, Australia	1974
150 Mount Strumlo, Canberra, Australia	1972
120 Lick, Mt Hamilton, Cal., USA	1959
107 McDonald Observatory, Fort Davis, Texas	1968
104 Crimean Astrophysical Lab., Nauchny, USSR	1960
100 Hooker, Mt Wilson, Cal., USA	1917
98 Newton, Herstmonceux, Sussex, England	1967
88 Mauna Kea Observatory, Hawaii	1970

The Russian 6 m *236·2 in* reflector is now the largest in the world; it may well

The 20 Largest Asteroids

Asteroid		Diameter miles	km	Year of Discovery
(1)	Ceres	593	955	1801
(2)	Pallas	347	558	1802
(4)	Vesta	313	503	1807
(10)	Hygiea	237	382	1849
(15)	Eunomia	168	270	1851
(511)	Davida	165	265	1903
(16)	Psyche	158	254	1852
(324)	Bamberga	143	230	1892
(3)	Juno	140	226	1804
(19)	Fortuna	137	221	1852
(624)	Hektor	130	210	1907
(6)	Hebe	122	197	1847
(7)	Iris	120	193	1847
(29)	Amphitrite	116	187	1854
(747)	Winchester	116	187	1913
(9)	Metis	105	169	1848
(22)	Kalliope	104	168	1852
(68)	Leto	95	153	1861
(89)	Julia	95	153	1866
(8)	Flora	93	150	1847

Meteorite Craters

The most spectacular of all dry craters is the Coon Butte or Barringer crater near Canyon Diablo, Winslow, North Arizona, USA, discovered in 1891, which is now 575 ft *175 m* deep and 4150 ft *1265 m* in diameter. The next largest craters are Wolf's Creek, Western Australia (3000 ft *914 m* diameter, 170 ft *52 m* deep) and a crater discovered in N Chile in 1965 (1476 ft *450 m* diameter, 100 ft *30 m* deep). The New Quebec (formerly Chubb) 'crater' in North Ungava, Canada, discovered in June 1943, is 1325 ft *404 m* deep and 2·2 miles *3,5 km* in diameter, but is now regarded as a water-filled vulcanoid.

Ancient and oblique meteoric scars are much less spectacular though of far greater dimensions. These phenomena are known as astroblemes (Gk *astron*, a star; *blemma*, a glance).

Name	Diameter miles	km
Vredefort Ring, South Africa (meteoric origin disputed, 1963)	24·8	39,9
Nordlinger Ries, Germany	15·5	24,9
Deep Bay, Saskatchewan, Canada (discovered 1956)	8·5	13,6
Lake Bosumtibi, Ghana	6·2	9,9
Serpent Mound, Ohio, USA	3·98	6,4
Wells Creek, Tennessee, USA	2·97	4,7
Al Umchaimin, Iraq	1·98	3,1

Meteorites

The term meteorite must now be confined to a fallen meteor, a meteoric mass of stone (aerolite) or nickel-iron (siderite). It is loosely and incorrectly used of a meteor or shooting star which is usually only the size of a pinhead. The existence of meteorites, owing to a religious bias, was first admitted as late as 26 Apr. 1803, after a shower of some 2500 aerolites fell around L'Aigle, near Paris, France.

The majority of meteorites inevitably fall into the sea (70·8 per cent of the Earth's surface) and are not recovered. Only eight meteorites exceeding ten tons have been located. All these are of the iron-nickel type. The largest recorded stone meteorite is the one which fell in the Kivin Province, Manchuria on 8 Mar. 1976 weighing 3,894 lb *1766 kg*.

		Approximate tonnage
Hoba	nr Grootfontein, South West Africa	60
Tent (Abnighito)	Cape York, West Greenland	30·4
Bacuberito	Mexico	27
Mbosi	Tanganyika	26
Williamette (1902)	Oregon, USA	14
Chupaero	Chihuahua, Mexico	14
Campo de Cielo	Argentina	13
Morito	Chihuahua, Mexico	11
The largest recorded in other continents are:		
Australia	Cranbourne	3·5
Asia	Sikhote-Alin, USSR	1·7
Europe	Magura, Czechoslovakia	1·5

The total number of strikes recorded since the mid-17th century is nearly 1700, including 22 in the British Isles.

continued top of page 145

The largest British Isles meteorites of the 22 recorded have been:

Country	*Location*	*Date*	*Weight*	
Ireland	Adare, Limerick	10 Sept. 1813	65 lb (total 106 lb)	*29,5 kg* (*total 48 kg*)
England	World Cottage, nr Scarborough, Yorks	13 Dec. 1795	56 lb	*25,4 kg*
	Barwell, Leicestershire	24 Dec. 1965	17⅜ lb (total 102 lb)	*7,8 kg* (*total 46,25 kg*)
Scotland	Strathmore, Perthshire	3 Dec. 1917	22¼ lb	*10,1 kg*
Wales	Beddgelert, Caernarvonshire	21 Sept. 1949	25½ oz	*723 g*

remain so, as it is quite likely that future emphasis will be upon telescopes in space. The largest telescope in Great Britain in 1976 was the 98 in *248 mm* reflector at the Royal Greenwich Observatory, Herstmonceux, known as the Isaac Newton Telescope or INT. However, plans are now being made to move this telescope to the proposed Northern Hemisphere Observatory, expected to be set up on the island of La Palma in the Canaries.

Radio Telescope
The world's largest dish radio telescope is the non-steerable £3¾ million ionospheric apparatus at Arecibo, Puerto Rico, completed in November 1963. It utilises a natural crater which is spanned by a dish 1000 ft *305 m* in diameter. covering an area of 18½ acres *7,28 ha*. Improvements and re-plating cost a further £4½ million in 1974.

Radio Astronomy
Radio astronomy became possible with the discovery in 1887 of radio waves by Heinrich Hertz (Germany). The earliest suggestion that extra-terrestrial radio waves might exist and be detected came from Thomas Edison (USA), who corresponded with Prof A E Kennelly on the subject on 2 Nov. 1890.

It was not until 1932 that Karl Guthe Jansky (1905–49) a US scientist of Czech descent first detected radio signals from the Sagittarius constellation at Holmdel, New Jersey. This 'cosmic static' was recorded on a 15-m wave length. The pioneer radio astronomer was Grote Reber (USA) (b. 1911), who built the world's first radio telescope, a 31 ft 5-in parabolic dish, in his backyard at Wheaton, Illinois, in 1937. His first results were published in 1940.

Dr J S Hey (GB) discovered during war-time radar jamming research that sun spots emitted radio waves; that radio echoes come from meteor trails; and that the extra-galatic nebula Cygnus A was a discrete source of immense power.

In 1947 John G Bolton in Australia found that the Crab Nebula (M.1), a supernova remnant, is a strong radio source. Since then many more discrete sources have been found; some are supernova remnants in our Galaxy, while others are external galaxies and the mysterious, very remote quasars. Young science though it may be, radio astronomy is now of fundamental importance in our studies of the universe, and it has provided information which could never have been obtained in any other way.

Some milestones in astronomy
Aristotle (*c.* 385–325 BC) advanced the first argument against the flat Earth hypothesis.
Eratosthenes of Cyrene (*c.* 276–194 BC) made the earliest estimate of the Earth's circumference: very good at 24 662 miles *39 689 km.*
Ptolemy in *c.* AD 180 established the Ptolemic System i.e. Earth was the centre of the universe
Copernicus (1473–1543) established that both the Earth and Mars orbit the Sun.
Johannes Kepler published his first two laws of planetary motion in 1609: the third in 1619.
Galileo Galilei (1564–1642) discovered in 1609 the use of the telescope and made astronomical observations with it. He was summonsed by the Roman Church to abjure his heresy that the Earth went round the Sun.
Christiaan Huygens (1629–95) built a 210 ft *64 m* refractor. In 1665 he described Saturn's rings later observing the markings on Mars.
In 1663 James Gregory put forward the principle of the reflecting telescope and *c.* 1668 Sir Isaac Newton built the first one with a 1 in *2,5 cm* metal mirror.
In the 1670's Cassini recalculated the Sun's distance at 86 million miles *138 million km.*
In 1675 Romer measured the velocity of light. His inspired answer, ignored for more than 100 years and not believed by himself, was 186 000 miles per sec *300 000 km per sec.*
Sir Isaac Newton (1642–1727) published his *Principia* in 1687.
In 1705 Halley predicted the return of Halley's comet in 1758. This was confirmed in that year by Palitzsch.
Herschel discovered Uranus in 1781.
Giuseppe Piazzi observed the first asteroid in 1801, confirmed in 1802 and named *Ceres.*
Friedrich Bessel was one of the first to realise the vastness of our galaxy discovering the star *61 Cygni* 60 million miles distant.
The steady-state or continuous creation theory was postulated in 1948 by Professors H. Bondi and T. Gold. Other theories of the universe currently under discussion are the evolutionary or "big bang" theory due originally to the Abbè Lemaitre and the oscillating theory of 1965 supported by Professor A. Sandage of the USA.

Anthropology

The classification of the various races of mankind is intensely complex. There is much debate as to whether the best criterion for classification is the cranial form, skin colour, stature and nose form, or hair form.

The most modern research indicates that there are possibilities in another basis of classification—namely the blood group.

There are obvious objections to any method of classification. The main reason for difficulty is that, with the possible exception of the people inhabitating the Andaman Islands in the Indian Ocean, there is no such thing as a pure race. The inter-breeding between racial types blurs every boundary distinction so far devised. Probably the most convenient method of classification is still based on hair form.

There are three main types. The straight haired groups, the woolly haired groups and the curly haired groups.

The straight haired groups
The straight haired peoples correspond mainly to the Mongoloid or 'yellow-brown' races. In general these people possess prominent cheek bones, flat faces, and are brachycephalic. The main two divisions of straight haired people are: (1) The Asiatic groups and (2) The Amerinds (i.e. the American aborigines).

The Asiatic Groups
There are three main sub-divisions:

(1) The north or arctic group, who inhabit the circum-polar regions stretching from the Lapps in the west to the Koreans in the east.

(2) The central group known as the Pareoeans, who are distinguishable by their less prominent cheek bones and their broader noses. In the north of China they are often tall but lose stature the further south they live. The Japanese, who have mixed with the distinctive Ainu type, are a special variety of the Pareoean people.

(3) The third group is known as the southern Mongoloids, 'Oceanic Mongols' or Indonesians and are considerably mixed, but their broader heads sometimes distinguish them. An outcrop of the straight haired Asiatic group are the Polynesians who live in the Pacific islands, including New Zealand. Their origins are believed to be an ancient mixture of Proto-Malays with Nesiots (see below).

The Amerinds
This group consists of the Eskimos, stretching from the northern coasts of Asia across Canada to Greenland. They have exceptionally long skulls and surprisingly broad faces but with narrow noses. Coming further south there are the various Red Indian people with the Sioux being a well-known example. The Aztecs and the Mayas were from this group. The ethnology of the South American aborigines is still in dispute but there are similarities with the Maya people and a distinctive round headed type of tall stature is observed in Patagonia. The Fuegians are a branch of the latter division. The picture is confused by traces of curly haired types in this area.

The woolly haired groups
The woolly haired groups are divided into two, an eastern group that people parts of Asia and Oceania and a western group who populate the greater part of Africa. The common characteristic, besides woolly hair, is dark, often almost black, skin, broad noses, and a tendency to a small brain in relation to physical height. Both groups contain Pygmy divisions.

Eastern Group
The taller members are Papuans and Melanesians and the shorter the Negritos. This latter group is in four separate areas: the Andaman Is; central Malaya and eastern Sumatra, with the Semang; parts of the Philippine Islands (the people commonly known as the Aeta), the western

mountains of New Guinea and parts of Melanesia inhabited by the Tapiro people. The Papuans and Melanesians have narrower heads than the Negritos. The extinct Tasmanian aboriginals (but not Australian aboriginals) seem to have been connected with this Eastern group.

Western Group
This group is dominated by the negroes. True negroes come from the Guinea coast where they are tall with black or dark brown skin, long narrow heads, retreating foreheads and pronounced jaws. The lips are thickened and everted and the nose is strikingly broad. The negroes have mixed with other races, a notable example being the Nilotes, who inhabit the Upper Nile Valley. The African Pygmies or Negrillos, besides their smallness of stature, have lightly coloured skins and even broader noses than the negroes.

A striking division is the Bushmen and their close allies the Hottentots. Bushmen are now only found in the Kalahari Desert. They have yellowish skin and a massive development of the buttocks (staetopygia).

The curly haired groups
All the remaining races of the world come from this group, which has a world-wide distribution and includes both highly differentiated groups and undifferentiated groups. The hair colour varies strikingly from jet black to fair straw. This group is mainly large brained, with a prominent forehead, but the skin colour is fairly variable. The range of civilisation also differs widely, from the more primitive Australian aboriginals up to the most sophisticated white people in the world.

Other primitive peoples in this group are the Proto-Nordics, who include the inhabitants of the Turkoman steppes, and the Ainu, who survive in the most northern parts of Japan and are totally distinct from the Japanese, especially in that they lack their epicanthic fold.

The Proto-Indics are in four divisions, as follows: first, the jungle tribes of southern India; secondly, the most primitive inhabitants of Ceylon, known as the Vedda; thirdly, the primitive peoples of Malaya known as the Sakai, and fourthly, some scattered tribes in Sumatra and the Celebes. The Australian aboriginals are believed to stem from this Proto-Indic stock, but their long isolation has produced some special characteristics, such as their massive skulls, and the Cherisots (the mainlanders) are scattered throughout southern Asia, including India where they are rounder headed. The curly haired races populate the horn of Africa, the Nile and Red Sea areas and some have surprisingly pale skins. Three groups of these are the Eurafricans, the Bedouin Arabs and the Mediterranean races. The Nordic people predominate in Scandinavia but form a strong element of the British Isles, northern France, the Low Countries, and northern parts of Germany.

Finally, the round headed, wavy haired people conveniently called Eurasiatic, stretch across Europe and Asia from central France to the Himalayas in the east. An important branch of this group is the Alpine people, distinguishable by the extreme flatness and height of the head. A separate branch is the Pamiri, who inhabit the high areas of Asia and India. Locally, in western Europe, there are isolated groups of Beaker Folk.

The whole question of whether human cultures spread across oceans (diffusionism)

or developed independently in parallel (independent inventionism) has to be reconsidered in the light of recent demonstrations that highly intelligent elements existed among Neolithic Man (perhaps in the period vaguely remembered in historical times as the 'Golden Age'). Dr Thor Heyerdahl has shown that trans-Pacific and trans-Atlantic voyages are feasible in authentic replicas of ancient vessels. Dr Alexander Thom has interpreted many western European megalithic monuments as lunar observatories based on detailed mathematical and astronomical knowledge, some of which has only been re-discovered in the last 200 years. Archaeological finds near the Atlantic coasts of Canada, the USA and Brazil indicate that seafarers bearing Semitic cultures crossed the Atlantic at least as far back as 500 BC. Interpretations of cultural history based on the 'independent inventionist' theory, which has been predominant from about 1920, need to be received with caution in the light of Heyerdahl's and Thom's work.

Origin of the races
In his *Origin of the Races* (1964) Dr Carlton S Coon (USA) makes the hypothesis that man has devolved into five basic races thus:

Australoid	from	Java Man *c.* 400 000 BC
Capoid	from	Ternifine-Tangier Man *c.* 500 000 BC
Caucasoid	from	Heidelberg Man *c.* 450 000 BC
Congoid	from	Rhodesian Man *c.* 50 000 BC
Mongoloid	from	Peking Man *c.* 400 000 BC

The 25 civilisations of man

If the duration of man's evolution, now estimated at 1 750 000 years, is likened to a single year, then the earliest of all history's civilisations began after 5 p.m. on 30 Dec. Put another way, 289/290ths of man's existence has been uncivilised.

Few historians have attempted to classify the world's civilisations because of the natural tendency to specialise. An early attempt was that of the Frenchman, Count de Gobineau, in his four-volume *L'Inégalité des Races Humaines* (Paris, 1853–5). His total was ten. Since that time western archaeologists have rescued five more ancient civilisations from oblivion—the Babylonic, the Hittite, the Mayan, the Minoan, and the Sumeric. This would have brought his total to 15 compared with a more modern contention of 25.

The most authoritative classification now available is the revised twelve-volume life work of Professor Arnold Toynbee, *A Study of History*, published between 1921 and 1961. This concludes that there have been 21 civilisations of which seven still survive. Those surviving are the Arabic (Islamic), the Far Eastern (begun in AD 910 and now split into two), the Orthodox Christian (now also split into two), the Hindu (begun *c.* AD 775) and the Western civilisation.

Recent (1960) researches indicate that the Yucatec and Mayan civilisations had the same cradle. The compilation below gives details. The Eskimo, Spartan, Polynesian, and Ottoman civilisations have been listed though Toynbee excludes these from his total on the grounds that they were 'arrested civilisations'.

No.	Name	Dawn	Final Collapse	Duration in Centuries	Cradle	Universal States	Religion and Philosophy	Derivation
1.	Egyptiac	ante 4000 BC	*c.* AD 280	*c.* 43	Lower Nile	Middle Empire *c.* 2065–1660 BC	Osiris-worship Philosophy of Atonism	Spontaneous
2.	Sumeric or Sumerian	ante 3500 BC	*c.* 1700 BC	*c.* 18	Euphrates-Tigris Delta	Sumer and Akkad Empire *c.* 2298–1905 BC	Tammuz-worship	Spontaneous
3.	Indic	ante 3000 BC	*c.* AD 500	35	Mohenjo-Daro, Harappa Indus and Ganges valleys	Mauryan Empire 322–185 BC Gupta Empire AD 390–475	Hinduism Jainism Hinayāna Buddhism	Possibly of Sumeric origin
4.	Minoan	ante 2000 BC	*c.* 1400 BC	6	Cnossus, Crete and the Cyclades	Thalassocracy of Minos *c.* 1750–1400 BC	?Orphism	Spontaneous
5.	Hittite	2000 BC	*c.* 1200 BC	8	Boghazköi, Anatolia, Turkey	—	Pantheonism	Related to Minoan
6.	Mayan[1]	post 2000 BC	AD 1550	*c.* 35 ?	Guatemalan forests	First Empire AD *c.* 300–690	Human sacrifice and human penitential self-mortification	Spontaneous[2]
7.	Sinic	*c.* 1600 BC[3]	AD 220	18	Yellow River Basin	Ts'in and Han Empire 221 BC–AD	Mahāyāna Buddhism, Taoism, Confucianism	Believed unrelated
8.	Babylonic	*c.* 1500 BC	538 BC	10	Lower Mesopotamia	Babylonian Empire 610–539 BC	Judaism, Zoroastrianism Astrology	Related to Sumeric

9.	Hellenic	c. 1300 BC	AD 558	18½	Greek mainland and Aegean Is	Roman Empire 31 BC–AD 378	Mithraism, Platonism Stoicism, Epicureanism Christianity	Related to Minoan
10.	Syriac	c. 1200 BC	AD 970	22	Eastern Cilicia	Achaemenian Empire c. 525–332 BC	Islam and Philosophy of Zervanism	Related to Minoan
11.	Eskimo	c. 1100 BC	c. AD 1850	c. 30	Umnak Aleutian Islands	Thule AD c. 1150–1850	Includes Sila, sky god; Sedna, seal goddess	—
12.	Spartan	c. 900 BC	AD 396	13	Laconia	620–371 BC	—	Hellenic
13.	Polynesian	c. 500 BC	c. AD 1775	22½	Samoa and Tonga	—	Ancestor spirits Mana—supernatural power	—
14.	Andean	c. 100 BC	AD 1783	19	Chimu, N Peru and Nazca, S Peru	Inca Empire AD 1430–1533	Philosophy of Viracochaism	Spontaneous
15.	Khmer[4]	c. AD 100	AD 1432	13	Cambodian coast	Ankor Kingdom AD 802–1432	—	Possibly related to Indic and Sinic
16.	Far Eastern (main)	AD 589	Scarcely survives	14 to date	Si Ngan (Sian-fu) Wei Valley	Mongol Empire AD 1280–1351 Manchu Empire AD 1644–1853	Muhayaniah Buddhism	Related to Sinic
17.	Far Eastern (Japan and Korea)	AD 645	Survives	13 to date	Yamato, Japan via Korea	Tokugawa Shogunate AD 1600–1868	Mikado-worship; Shintoism; Buddhism and Zen Philosophy	Related to Sinic
18.	Western	c. AD 675	Survives	13 to date	Ireland	Habsburg Monarchy AD 1526–1918 and Napoleonic Empire AD 1797–1815	Philosophy of Christianity	Related to Hellenic
19.	Orthodox Christian (main)	c. AD 680	Survives	13 to date	Anatolia, Turkey	Ottoman Empire AD 1372–1768	Bedreddinism Orthodox Church, Imâmî	Related to Hellenic and Western
20.	Hindu	c. AD 810	Survives	11 to date	Kanauj, Jamna-Ganges Duab	Mughal Raj AD c. 1572–1707 British Raj 1818–1947	Hinduism, Sikhism	Related to Indic
21.	Orthodox Christian (Russia)	c. AD 950	Scarcely survives	10 to date	Upper Dnieper Basin	Muscovite Empire AD 1478–1881	Orthodox Church Sectarianism	Related to Hellenic
22.	Arabic	c. AD 975	AD 1525	5½	Arabia, Iraq, Syria	Abbasid Caliphate of Baghdad	Islâm (post AD 1516) 1516)	Related to Syriac
23.	Mexic	c. AD 1075	AD 1821	7½	Mexican Plateau	Aztec Empire AD 1375–1521	Quetzalcoatl	Related to Mayan
24.	Ottoman	c. AD 1310	AD 1919	6	—	—	Islâm	—
25.	Iranic (now Islamic)	c. AD 1320	Survives	6½ to date	Oxus-Jaxartes Basin	—	Islam (post AD 1516)	Related to Syriac

1. Toynbee regards a Yucatec civilisation (c. AD 1075–1680) as a separate entity. Archaeological discoveries in 1960 indicate that Dzibilchaltan, on the Yucatan Peninsula, was in fact the cradle of the whole Mayan civilisation.
2. There have been attempts to link aspects with Egyptiac. The early classic period at Tikal dates from c. AD 250–550.
3. The earliest archaeologically acceptable dynasty was that of Shang, variously dated 1766–1558 BC. The historicity of the First or Hsia dynasty, allegedly founded by Yü in 2205 BC, is in decided jeopardy.
4. Not regarded by Toynbee as a separate civilisation but as an offshoot of the Hindu civilisation. Modern evidence shows, however, that the Khmer origins antedate those of the Hindu civilisation by 7 centuries.

Major anthropological discoveries

Year	Scientific Name	Period and Estimated Date BC	Location	Description	Anthropologist
1856[1]	Homo neanderthalensis	Late middle Palaeolithic 120 000	Neander Valley, nr Düsseldorf, Germany	skull, bones	Fuhlrott
1868[2]	Homo sapiens (Cromagnon man)	Upper Palaeolithic 35 000	Cromagnon, Les Eyzies, France	4 skeletons, 1 foetus	Lartet
1890	Pithecanthropus erectus	Upper Pleistocene 400 000	Kedung Brebus, Java	mandible, tooth	Dubois
1907	Homo heidelbergensis	Lower Palaeolithic 450 000	Mauer, nr Heidelberg, Germany	lower jaw	Schoetensack
1912[3]	Eoanthropus dawsonii	Holocene (Recent) (fraud)	Piltdown, Sussex	composite skull	Dawson
1921	Homo rhodesiensis	Upper Pleistocene 50 000	Broken Hill, N Rhodesia	skull	Armstrong
1924	Australopithecus africanus	Early Pleistocene 1 000 000	Taung, Bechuanaland	skull	Dart (Izod)
1926[4]	Proconsul nyanzae	Miocene c. 25 000 000	Koru, Kenya	fragments (non-hominoid)	Hopwood
1927	Pithecanthropus pekinensis	Lower Palaeolithic 400 000	Choukoutien, nr Peking, China	tooth	Bohlin
1929–34	Neanderthaloid man	Middle Palaeolithic or Mousterian 120 000	Mt Carmel, Israel	part 16 skeletons	Garrod
1935[5]	Homo sapiens fossilis	Lower Palaeolithic 250 000	Boyn Hill, Swanscombe, Kent	parts skull	Marston
1935[6]	Gigantopithecus blacki	Middle Pleistocene 450 000	from Kwangsi, China (Hong Kong druggist)	teeth only	von Koenigswald
1936	Pleisianthropus transvaalensis	Early Pleistocene 1 000 000	Sterkfontein, Transvaal	skull, part femur	Broom (Barlow)
1938	Paranthropus robustus	Early Pleistocene 700 000	Kromdraai, Transvaal	skull part, bones	Broom (Terblanche)
1947	Homo sapiens fossilis	Middle Palaeolithic or Mousterian 125 000	Fontéchevade, France	2 callottes	Martin
1949	Australopithecus prometheus	Early Pleistocene 900 000	Makapansgat, Transvaal	fragments[7]	Dart
1953	Telanthropus capensis	Early Pleistocene 800 000	Swartkrans, Transvaal	jaw, skull parts	Broom
1954	Atlanthropus	Chelleo-Acheulian 500 000	Ternifine, Algeria	parietal, 3 mandibles	Arambourg
1957	Neanderthaloid man	Upper Palaeolithic 45 000	Shanidar, Iraq	skeletons	Solecki
1959	Zinjanthropus boisei	Late Pliocene c. 1 750 000	Olduvai, Tanganyika	skull	Leakey (Mrs Leakey)
1960	Homo habilis	Late Pliocene ante supra	Olduvai, Tanganyika	fragments	Leakey
1961	Kenyapithecus wickeri	Mid Miocene c. 14 000 000	Fort Ternan, Kenya	palate, teeth (non-hominoid)	Leakey (Mukiri)
1963	Australopithecus robustus	Middle Pleistocene 450 000	Chenchiawo, Lantien, NW China	jaw	
1964	Sinanthropus lantianensis	Middle Pleistocene c. 500 000	Kungwangling, Lantien, Shensi, China	skull cap and female jaw in 1963	Wu Ju Kang
1969	Homo erectus	Middle Pleistocene 500 000–1 000 000	Sangiran, Java	skull	Sartono
1972	Homo ?	Plio-Pleistocene 2 000 000	East Turkana, Kenya	skull	Leakey
1974/5	Australopithecus or Homo	Plio–Pleistocene 3 000 000	Hadar Afar region, Ethiopia	skull parts, jaws, teeth, skeleton	Johanson and Taieb

1 Female skull discovered in Gibraltar in 1848 but unrecognised till 1864.
2 Earliest specimen found at Engis, near Liége, Belgium, in 1832 by Schmerling.
3 Exposed by X-Ray and radio-activity tests in Nov 1953 as an elaborate fraud.
4 Non-hominoid. Complete skull discovered 1948 by Mrs Leakey.
5 Further part discovered 1955.
6 Since 1957 all the evidence is that these relate to a non-hominoid giant ape.
7 Complete skull in 1958 (Kitching).

Metrology

In essence, measurement involves *comparison*: the measurement of a physical quantity entails comparing it with an agreed and clearly defined *standard*. The result is expressed in terms of a *unit*, which is the name for the standard, preceded by a number which is the *ratio* of the measured quantity to the appropriate fixed unit.

A *system of units* is centred on a small number of *base units*. These relate to the fundamental standards of length, mass and time, together with a few others to extend the system to a wider range of physical measurements, e.g. to electrical and optical quantities.

These few base units can be combined to form a large number of *derived units*. For example, units of area, velocity and acceleration are formed from units of length and time. Thus, very many different kinds of measurement can be made and recorded employing only about half a dozen base units.

For convenience, *multiples* and *sub-multiples* of both base and derived units are frequently used: kilometres and millimetres; miles, feet and inches.

Historically, several systems of units have evolved: in Britain, the imperial system: in the United States, the US customary units; and forms of the metric system (CGS and MKS), employed universally in science and generally in very many countries of the world.

The International System of Units (Système International d'Unités or SI) is a modern form of the metric system. It was finally agreed at the Eleventh General Conference of Weights and Measures in October 1960 and is now being adopted throughout most of the world.

Base units

Quantity	Unit	Symbol	Definition	Other non-SI units
length	metre	m	the length equal to 1 650 763·73 wavelengths in vacuum of the radiation corresponding to the transition between the levels $2p_{10}$ and $5d_5$ of the krypton-86 atom.	1 mile $= 1·609\ 344$ km 1 UK nautical mile $= 1·853\ 184$ km 1 foot $= 0·3048$ m 1 in (inch) $= 25·4$ mm 1 Å (angstrom) $= 10^{-10}$ m 1 micron $= 10^{-6}$ m
mass	kilogram	kg	the mass of the international prototype of the kilogram, which is in the custody of the Bureau International des Poids et Mésures (BIPM) at Sèvres near Paris, France.	1 ton $= 1016·05$ kg 1 t (tonne) $= 1$ Mg 1 lb $= 0·453\ 592\ 37$ kg 1 oz $= 28·3495$ g 1 dr (dram) $= 1·771\ 85$ g 1 gr (grain) $= 64·7989$ g
time	second	s	the duration of 9 192 631 770 periods of the radiation corresponding to the transition between the two hyperfine levels of the ground state of the caesium-133 atom.	
electric current	ampere	A	that constant current which, if maintained in two straight parallel conductors of infinite length of negligible circular cross-section, and placed 1 metre apart in vacuum, would produce between these conductors a force equal to 2×10^{-7} newton per metre of length.	
thermodynamic temperature	kelvin	K	the fraction $1/273·16$ of the thermodynamic temperature of the triple point of water. The triple point of water is the point where water, ice and water vapour are in equilibrium.	
luminous intensity	candela	cd	the luminous intensity, in the perpendicular direction, of a surface of 1/600 000 square metre of a black body at the temperature of freezing platinum under a pressure of 101 325 newtons per square metre.	
amount of substance	mole	mol	the amount of substance of a system which contains as many elementary entities as there are atoms in 0·012 kilogram of carbon-12.	

Supplementary units

Quantity	Unit	Symbol	Definition	Other non-SI units
plane angle	radian	rad	the plane angle between two radii of a circle which cut off on the circumference an arc equal in length to the radius.	$1° = \pi/180$ rad 1^g(grade) $= \pi/200$ rad
solid angle	steradian	sr	the solid angle which having its vertex in the centre of a sphere, cuts off an area of the surface of the sphere equal to that of a square having sides of length equal to the radius of the sphere.	

Derived units

Quantity	Unit	Symbol	Expression in terms of other SI units	Other non-SI units
area	square metre	m²	—	1 mile² $= 2·589\ 99$ km² 1 acre $= 0·404\ 686$ ha 1 yd² $= 0·836\ 127$ m² 1 ft² $= 0·092\ 903$ m² 1 ha (hectare) $= 10^4$ m²
volume	cubic metre	m³	—	1 gal $= 4·546\ 091\ 879$ dm³ 1 US gal $= 3·785\ 41$ dm³ 1 pt (pint) $= 0·568\ 261$ dm³ 1 ft³ (cubic foot) $= 28·3168$ dm³ 1 litre $= 1$ dm³
velocity	metre per second	m·s⁻¹	—	1 mph $= 1·609\ 34$ km h⁻¹ $= 0·447\ 04$ m s⁻¹ 1 UK knot $= 1·852\ 00$ km h⁻¹ $= 0·514\ 444$ ms⁻¹ 1 kph $= 0·277\ 778$ m s⁻¹
angular velocity	radian per second	rad s⁻¹	—	
acceleration	metre per second squared	m·s⁻²	—	1 ft s⁻² $= 0·3048$ m s⁻²
angular acceleration	radian per second squared	rad s⁻²	—	
frequency	hertz	Hz	s⁻¹	
density	kilogram per cubic metre	kg·m⁻³	—	1 lb ft⁻³ (pound per cubic foot) $= 16·018\ 5$ kg·m⁻³ 1 g l⁻¹ (gram per litre) $= 1$ kg·m⁻³
momentum	kilogram metre per second	kg·m·s⁻¹	—	
angular momentum	kilogram metre squared per second	kg·m²·s⁻¹	—	
moment of inertia	kilogram metre squared	kg·m²	—	
force	newton	N	kg·m·s⁻²	1 lb f $= 4·448\ 22$ N 1 pdl (poundal) $= 0·138\ 255$ N 1 kgf or kp (kilopound) $= 9·806\ 65$ N 1 dyn (dyne) $= 10^{-5}$ N

Quantity	Unit	Symbol	Expression in terms of other SI units	Other non-SI units
pressure, stress	pascal	Pa	$N \cdot m^{-2} = kg \cdot m^{-1} \cdot s^{-2}$	1 lbf in^{-2} (psi) $= 6894 \cdot 76$ Pa 1 inHg $= 3386 \cdot 39$ Pa 1 atm (atmosphere) $= 101 \cdot 325$ kPa 1 mbar (millibar) $= 100$ Pa
work, energy, quantity of heat	joule	J	$N \cdot m = kg \cdot m^2 \cdot s^{-2}$	1 therm $= 105 \cdot 506$ MJ 1 kWh (kilowatt hour) $= 3 \cdot 6$ MJ 1 cal (international calorie) $= 4 \cdot 1868$ J 1 Btu (British thermal unit) $= 1 \cdot 055\ 66$ kJ 1 erg $= 10^{-7}$ J 1 eV (electron volt) $= 1 \cdot 602 \times 10^{19}$ J
power	watt	W	$J \cdot s^{-1} = kg \cdot m^2 \cdot s^{-3}$	1 hp $= 0 \cdot 745\ 700$ kW
surface tension	newton per metre	$N \cdot m^{-1}$	$kg \cdot s^{-2}$	1 dyn cm$^{-1} = 10^{-3}$ N m^{-1}
dynamic viscosity	newton second per metre squared	$N \cdot s \cdot m^{-2}$	$kg \cdot m^{-1} \cdot s^{-1}$	1 cP (centipoise) $= 0 \cdot 001$ N s m^{-2}
kinematic viscosity	metre squared per second	$m^2 \cdot s^{-1}$	—	1 cSt (centistokes) $= 10^{-6}$ m^2 s^{-1}
temperature	degree Celsius	°C	—	
thermal coefficient of linear expansion	per degree Celsius, per kelvin	°C^{-1}, K^{-1}	—	
thermal conductivity	watt per metre degree C	$W \cdot m^{-1} \cdot {}^{\circ}C^{-1}$	$kg \cdot m \cdot s^{-3} \cdot {}^{\circ}C^{-1}$	1 cal cm cm^{-2} s^{-1} °C$^{-1} = 418 \cdot 68$ Wm^{-1}°C^{-1}
heat capacity	joule per kelvin	$J \cdot K^{-1}$	$kg \cdot m^2 \cdot s^{-2} \cdot K^{-1}$	
specific heat capacity	joule per kilogram kelvin	$J \cdot kg^{-1} \cdot {}^{\circ}K^{-1}$	$m^2 \cdot s^{-2} \cdot K^{-1}$	1 kcal kg^{-1}°C$^{-1} = 4 \cdot 1868$ J·g^{-1}°C^{-1}
specific latent heat	joule per kilogram	$J \, kg^{-1}$	$m^2 \cdot s^{-2}$	1 Btu lb$^{-1} = 2326$ J kg^{-1}
electric charge	coulomb	C	$A \cdot s$	
potential difference, electromotive force	volt	V	$W \cdot A^{-1} = kg \cdot m^2 \cdot s^{-3} \cdot A^{-1}$	
electric resistance	ohm	Ω	$V \cdot A^{-1} = kg \cdot m^2 \cdot s^{-3} \cdot A^{-2}$	
electric conductance	siemens	S	$A \cdot V^{-1} = kg^{-1} \cdot m^{-2} \cdot s^3 \cdot A^2$	
electric capacitance	farad	F	$A \cdot s \cdot V^{-1} = kg^{-1} \cdot m^{-2} \cdot s^4 \cdot A^2$	
inductance	henry	H	$V \cdot s \cdot A^{-1} = kg \cdot m^2 \cdot s^{-2} \cdot A^{-2}$	
magnetic flux	weber	Wb	$V \cdot s = kg \cdot m^2 \cdot s^{-2} \cdot A^{-1}$	
magnetic flux density	tesla	T	$wb \cdot m^{-2} = kg \cdot s^{-2} \cdot A^{-1}$	
magnetomotive force	ampere	A	—	
luminous flux	lumen	lm	$cd \cdot sr$	
illumination	lux	lx	$lm \cdot m^{-2} = cd \cdot sr \cdot m^{-2}$	
radiation activity	becquerel	Bq	s^{-1}	
radiation absorbed dose	gray	Gy	$J \cdot kg^{-1} = m^2 \cdot s^{-2}$	

Units of length

	Inches	Feet	Yards	Rods, Poles or Perches*	Chains	Furlongs	Miles
1 inch	1	0·083 33	0·027 78	0·005	0·001 26	0·000 126	0·000 015 783
1 foot	12	1	0·33333	0·06	0·015	0·001 5	0·000 189 39
1 yard	36	3	1	0·18	0·045	0·004 5	0·000 568 18
1 rod, pole or perch	198	16·5	5·5	1	0·25	0·025	0·003 125
1 chain	792	66	22	4	1	0·10	0·0125
1 furlong	7920	660	220	40	10	1	0·125
1 mile	63 360	5280	1760	320	80	8	1

* Obsolescent 15th-century terms. Perch from French *perche*, a measuring rod or pole. Now mainly used to express fractions (1/160th part) of an acre (see below).

Units of area

	Sq. Inches	Sq. Feet	Sq. Yards	Sq. Rods, Perches or Poles	Roods	Acres	Sq. Miles
square inch	1	0·006 944	0·000 771 6	$2 \cdot 551 \times 10^{-5}$	$6 \cdot 377 \times 10^{-7}$	$1 \cdot 594 \times 10^{-7}$	$2 \cdot 491 \times 10^{-10}$
square foot	144	1	0·1111	$3 \cdot 673 \times 10^{-3}$	$9 \cdot 183 \times 10^{-5}$	$2 \cdot 296 \times 10^{-5}$	$3 \cdot 587 \times 10^{-8}$
square yard	1296	9	1	$33 \cdot 058 \times 10^{-2}$	$8 \cdot 264 \times 10^{-4}$	$2 \cdot 066 \times 10^{-4}$	$3 \cdot 228 \times 10^{-7}$
square rod	39 204	272·25	30·25	1	0·025	$6 \cdot 25 \times 10^{-3}$	$97 \cdot 656 \times 10^{-7}$
rood	1 568 160	10 890	1210	40	1	0·025	$3 \cdot 906 \times 10^{-4}$
acre	6 272 640	43 560	4840	160	4	1	$15 \cdot 625 \times 10^{-4}$
square mile	4 014 489 600	27 878 400	3 097 600	102 400	2560	640	1

The square link (62·7264 in²) and the square chain (0·10 of an acre) are still sometimes used.

Other units of length employed are:

animal stature	the hand $= 4$ in. *NB*—a horse of 14 hands 3 in to the withers is often written 14·3 hands.
surveying	the link $= 7 \cdot 92$ in or a hundredth part of a chain.
approximate	the span $= 9$ in from the span of the hand.
biblical	the cubit $= 18$ in.
approximate	the pace $= 30$ in (from the stride).
nautical	the cable $= 120$ fathoms or 240 yd.
navigation	the UK nautical mile $= 6080$ ft at the Equator.
navigation	the International nautical mile (adopted also by the USA on 1 July 1954) $= 6076 \cdot 1$ ft (0·99936 of a UK nautical mile).

Units of volume

		Cubic Inches	Cubic Feet	Cubic Yards
cubic inch		1	57.87×10^{-5}	21.43×10^{-6}
cubic foot		1728	1	0.037 037
cubic yard		46 656	27	1

Units of weight (Avoirdupois measure)

		Grains	Drams	Ounces	Pounds
1 grain	gr	1	0.036571	0.002 285 7	0.000 142 857
1 dram	dr	27.343 75	1	0.0625	0.003 906 25
1 ounce	oz	437.5	16	1	0.0625
1 pound	lb	7000	256	16	1

		Pounds	Stones	Quarters	Centals	Hundredweights	Short tons	Long tons
1 pound	lb	1	0.071 43	0.035 71	0.01	0.008 929	0.0005	0.000 446
1 stone	st	14	1	0.5	0.14	0.125	0.007	0.006 25
1 quarter	qtr	28	2	1	0.28	0.25	0.014	0.0125
1 cental	—	100	7.143	3.571 4	1	0.892 26	0.05	0.044 64
1 hundredweight	cwt	112	8	4	1.12	1	0.056	0.05
1 short ton	—	2000	142.857	71.428 6	20	17.857	1	0.89286
1 long ton	—	2240	160	80	22.4	20	1.12	1

Apothecaries' and Troy measures

		Grains	Scruples	Pennyweights	Drachms	Ounces	Pounds
1 grain	gr	1	0.05	0.041 667	0.166 67	0.002 083	0.000 173 611
1 scruple	scr	20	1	0.833	0.333	0.041 666	0.003 472
1 pennyweight	tr dwt	24	1.2	1	0.4	0.05	0.004 167
1 drachm	tr drm	60	3	2.5	1	0.125	0.010 417
1 ounce	tr oz	480	24	20	8	1	0.083 333
1 pound	tr lb	5760	288	240	96	12	1
(obsolete since 1878)							

The use of the metric system was legalised in the United Kingdom in 1897. The Halsbury Committee recommend the introduction of decimal currency in September 1963. The intention to switch to the metric system was declared on 24 May 1965 by the President of the Board of Trade 'within ten years'. The date for the official adoption of the metric system was announced on 1 Mar. 1966 to be 'February 1971.' On Tuesday, 23 Mar. 1976, the Government decided not to proceed with the second reading of the Weights and Measures (Metrication) Act.

Multiples and Sub-Multiples
In the metric system the following decimal multiples and sub-multiples are used:

Prefix	Symbol	British Equivalent	Factor
atto- (Danish *atten* = eighteen)	a	trillionth part	$\times 10^{-18}$
femto- (Danish *femten* = fifteen)	f	thousand billionth part	$\times 10^{-15}$
pico- (L. *pico* = miniscule)	p	billionth part	$\times 10^{-12}$
nano- (L. *nanus* = dwarf)	n	thousand millionth part	$\times 10^{-9}$
micro- (Gk. *mikros* = small)	μ	millionth part	$\times 10^{-6}$
milli- (L. *mille* = thousand)	m	thousandth part	$\times 10^{-3}$
centi- (L. *centum* = hundred)	c	hundredth part	$\times 10^{-2}$
deci- (L. *decimus* = tenth)	d	tenth part	$\times 10^{-1}$
deca- (Gk. *deka* = ten)	da	tenfold	$\times 10$
hecto- (Gk. *hekaton* = hundred)	h	hundredfold	$\times 10^{2}$
kilo- (Gk. *chilioi* = thousand)	k	thousandfold	$\times 10^{3}$
mega- (Gk. *megas* = large)	M	millionfold	$\times 10^{6}$
giga- (Gk. *gigas* = mighty)	G	thousand millionfold	$\times 10^{9}$
tera- (Gk. *teras* = monster)	T	billionfold	$\times 10^{12}$
peta- (Gk. *penta* = five)	P	thousand billionfold	$\times 10^{15}$
exa- (Gk. *hexa* = six)	E	million billionfold	$\times 10^{18}$

Physics

Newton's laws of motion
These three self-evident principles were discovered experimentally before Newton's time but were first formulated by him.

Law 1. The law of inertia
A particle will either remain at rest or continue to move with uniform velocity unless acted upon by a force.

Law 2
The acceleration of a particle is directly proportional to the force producing it and inversely proportional to the mass of the particle.

Law 3. The law of action and reaction
Forces, the results of interactions of two bodies, always appear in pairs. In each pair the forces are equal in magnitude and opposite in direction.

Equations of motion
Where
u is the initial velocity of a body;
v is its final velocity after time t;
s is the distance it travels in this time;
a is the uniform acceleration it undergoes.
then

$$v = u + at$$
$$s = ut + \tfrac{1}{2}at^2$$
$$v^2 = u^2 + 2as$$

Laws of Thermodynamics
Thermodynamics (Greek, *thermos*, hot; *dynamis*, power) is the quantitative treatment of the relation of heat to natural and mechanical forms of energy.

There are three Laws of Thermodynamics.

The **First Law**, derived from the principle of Conservation of Energy, may be stated 'Energy can neither be created nor destroyed, so that a given system can gain or lose energy only to the extent that it takes it from or passes it to its environment'. This is expressed as

$$E_f - E_i = \Delta$$

where E_i is the initial energy, E_f the final content of energy and Δ the change of energy. The impossibility of perpetual motion follows directly from this. The law applies only to systems of constant mass.

The **Second Law** concerns the concept of entropy (Gk. *en*, into; *tropos*, a changing) which is the relation between the temperature of and the heat content within any system. A large amount of lukewarm water may contain the same amount of heat as a little boiling water. The levelling out (equalising) of heat within a system (i.e. the pouring of a kettle of boiling water into a lukewarm bath) is said to increase the entropy of that system of two vessels. Any system, including the Universe, naturally tends to increase its entropy, i.e. to distribute its heat. If the Universe can be regarded as a closed system, it follows from the Law that it will have a finite end, i.e. when it has finally dissipated or unwound itself to the point that its entropy attains a maximal level —this is referred to as the 'Heat Death' of the Universe. From this it would also follow that the Universe must then have had a finite beginning for if it had had a creation an infinite time ago heat death would by now inevitably have set in. The second Law, published in Berlin in 1850 by Rudolf Clausius (1822–88), states 'Heat cannot of itself pass from a colder to a warmer body'. This is mathematically expressed by the inequality

$$\Delta > O$$

i.e. the change of entropy in any heat exchanging system and its surroundings taken together is always greater than zero.

The **Third Law** is not a general law but applies only to pure crystalline solids and states that at absolute zero the entropies of such substances are zero.

Celsius and Fahrenheit Compared
The two principal temperature scales are Celsius and Fahrenheit. The former was devised in 1743 by J P Christen (1683–1755) but is referred to by its present name because of the erroneous belief that it was invented by Anders Celsius (1701–44). The latter is named after Gabriel Daniel Fahrenheit (1686–1736), a German physicist. In a meteorological context the scale is still referred to in the United Kingdom as Centigrade though the name was otherwise abandoned in 1948.

To convert C to F, multiply the C reading by 9/5 and add 32.

To convert F to C, subtract 32 from the F reading and multiply by 5/9.

Useful comparisons are:

(1) Absolute Zero	=	$-273\cdot15\,°C$	$= -459\cdot67\,°F$
(2) Point of Equality	=	$-40\cdot0\,°C$	$= -40\cdot0\,°F$
(3) Zero Fahrenheit	=	$-17\cdot8\,°C$	$0\cdot0\,°F$
(4) Freezing Point of Water	=	$0\cdot0\,°C$	$32\,°F$
(5) Normal Human Blood Temperature	=	$36\cdot9\,°C$	$98\cdot4\,°F$
(6) 100 Degrees F	=	$37\cdot8\,°C$	$100\,°F$
(7) Boiling Point of Water (at standard pressure)	=	$100\,°C$	$= 212\,°F$

The Fundamental Particles
Particle types
Particles are classified into four basic classes: *gravitons* (the supposed theoretical massless exchange particles involved in gravitational forces); *photons* (the familiar massless exchange particles involved in electromagnetism); *leptons* (the electron and muon and their respective massless neutrinos); and *hadrons* (all other particles). Hadrons can be further subdivided into *mesons* and *baryons*, and baryons further subdivided into *nucleons* (the proton and the neutron) and *hyperons* (all other baryons).

All mesons are defined as having a baryon number $B = 0$ and baryons as $B = +1$ (or -1 for anti-baryons). Originally baryons were thought to be all hadrons with masses in excess of that of the K-mesons (kaons) but the recent discovery of very heavy mesons requires a revision of this definition and it is now possible to state that mesons are particles consisting of two quarks and baryons three quarks (see below).

Resonances
Nearly all of the multitude of new particles discovered since the early 60's are known as *resonances* and are so called because they have very short lifetimes of the order

The fundamental physical constants
The constants are called 'fundamental' since they are used universally throughout all branches of science. Because of the unprecedented amount of new experimental and theoretical work being carried out, thorough revisions are now being published about once every four years, the last being in 1973. Values are reported such that the figure in brackets following the last digit is the estimated uncertainty of that digit, i.e. the speed of light $c = 2\cdot997\,924\,58\,(1) \times 10^8$ m s^{-1} could be written $c = (2\cdot997\,924\,58 \pm 0\cdot000\,000\,01) \times 10^8$ m s^{-1}. The unit m s^{-1} represents m/s or metres per second.

	Quantity	Symbol	Value	Units
general constants	Speed of light in vacuo	c	$2\cdot99792458\,(1) \times 10^8$	m·s^{-1}
	elementary charge	e	$1\cdot6021892\,(46) \times 10^{-19}$	C
	Planck's constant	h	$6\cdot626176\,(36) \times 10^{-34}$	J·s
		$\hbar = h/2\pi$	$1\cdot0545887\,(57) \times 10^{-34}$	J·s
	gravitational constant	G	$6\cdot6720\,(41) \times 10^{-11}$	m^3·s^{-2}·kg^{-1}
matter in bulk	Avogadro constant	N_A	$6\cdot022045\,(31) \times 10^{23}$	mol^{-1}
	atomic mass unit	$u = 1/N_A$	$1\cdot6605655\,(86) \times 10^{-27}$	kg
			$9\cdot315016\,(26) \times 10^2$	Mev
	faraday	$F = N_A e$	$9\cdot648456\,(27) \times 10^4$	C·mol^{-1}
	normal volume of ideal gas	V_m	$2\cdot241383\,(70) \times 10^{-2}$	m^3·mol^{-1}
	gas constant	R	$8\cdot31441\,(26)$	J·mol^{-1}·K^{-1}
			$8\cdot20568\,(26) \times 10^{-5}$	m^3·atm·mol^{-1} K^{-1}
	Boltzmann constant	$k = R/N_A$	$1\cdot380662\,(44) \times 10^{-23}$	J·K^{-1}
electron	electron rest mass	m_e	$9\cdot109534\,(47) \times 10^{-31}$	kg
			$0\cdot5110034\,(14)$	Mev
	electron charge to mass ratio	e/m_e	$1\cdot7588047\,(49) \times 10^{11}$	C·kg^{-1}
proton	proton rest mass	m_p	$1\cdot6726485\,(86) \times 10^{-27}$	kg
			$9\cdot382796\,(27) \times 10^2$	Mev
neutron	neutron rest mass	m_n	$1\cdot6749543\,(86) \times 10^{-27}$	kg
			$9\cdot395731\,(27) \times 10^2$	Mev
energy conversion	million electron volt unit	Mev	$1\cdot7826758\,(51) \times 10^{-30}$	kg
			$1\cdot6021892\,(46) \times 10^{-13}$	J

Properties of the particles
These are reviewed annually by the 'Particle Data Group' which is an 'ad hoc' committee of nuclear physicists.

Notes to the tables
1. Since their principal quantum numbers are all zero, the graviton, the photon, the neutral pion, and the eta resonance are their own anti-particles.
2. Leptons conserve lepton number (1) which is $+1$ for leptons, -1 for anti-leptons, and zero for all other particles. Since only electron neutrinos (v_e) are associated with electrons then they are assigned the electron number (1_e) of ±1 (zero for all other particles) and the muon and muon neutrino (v_μ) are assigned the muon number (1_μ) of ±1 (zero for all other particles).
3. Both the neutral kaon and anti-neutral kaon can be considered to be a linear mixture of two states which have 'CP' (charge conjugation × space parity) values of $+1$ and -1 respectively. These states are named 'short' (K_s) and 'long' (K_L) based on their respective lifetimes.

Particle Name	Particle Symbol	Anti-particle Symbol	Isospin I	Spin Parity J^P	Baryon Number B	Strangeness S	Hypercharge Y	Mass (Mev)	Mean Life (seconds)	Year of Discovery
graviton	g	Note 1	—	2	0	0	0	0	Stable	—
photon	γ	Note 1	—	1	0	0	0	0	Stable	1902
LEPTONS										
electron neutrino	v_e	$\bar{v}_e$	—	$\frac{1}{2}$	Note 2		0		Stable	1956
muon neutrino	v_μ	$\bar{v}_\mu$	—	$\frac{1}{2}$	Note 2		0		Stable	1962
electron	e^-	e^+	—	$\frac{1}{2}$	Note 2		0·511003		Stable	1897
muon	μ^-	μ^+	—	$\frac{1}{2}$	Note 2		105·659		$2\cdot197 \times 10^{-6}$	1937
MESONS										
charged pion	π^+	π^-	1	0^-	0	0	0	139·569	$2\cdot603 \times 10^{-8}$	1947
neutral pion	$\pi^°$	Note 1	1	0^-	0	0	0	134·965	$8\cdot28 \times 10^{-17}$	1950
charged kaon	K^+	K^-	$\frac{1}{2}$	0^-	0	±1	±1	493·71	$1\cdot237 \times 10^{-8}$	1947
neutral kaon	$K^°$	$\bar{K}^°$	$\frac{1}{2}$	0^-	0	±1	±1	497·70	$50\% \; K_s + 50\% \; K_L$	(Note 3)
									$K_s \; 8\cdot93 \times 10^{-11}$	1947
									$K_L \; 5\cdot18 \times 10^{-8}$	1956
eta (Note 4)	$\eta^°$	Note 1	0	0^-	0	0	0	548·8	$7\cdot7 \times 10^{-19}$	1961
NUCLEONS										
proton	p^+	p^-	$\frac{1}{2}$	$\frac{1}{2}^+$	±1	0	±1	938·280	Stable	1911
neutron	$n^°$	$\bar{n}^°$	$\frac{1}{2}$	$\frac{1}{2}^+$	±1	0	±1	939·573	918	1932
HYPERONS										
lambda	$\Lambda^°$	$\bar{\Lambda}^°$	0	$\frac{1}{2}^+$	±1	∓1	0	1115·60	$2\cdot58 \times 10^{-10}$	1951
positive sigma	Σ^+	$\bar{\Sigma}^-$	1	$\frac{1}{2}^+$	±1	∓1	0	1189·37	$0\cdot80 \times 10^{-10}$	1953
neutral sigma	$\Sigma^°$	$\bar{\Sigma}^°$	1	$\frac{1}{2}^+$	±1	∓1	0	1192·48	$<1\cdot0 \times 10^{-14}$	1957
negative sigma	Σ^-	$\bar{\Sigma}^+$	1	$\frac{1}{2}^+$	±1	∓1	0	1197·35	$1\cdot48 \times 10^{-10}$	1954
neutral xi	$\Xi^°$	$\bar{\Xi}^°$	$\frac{1}{2}$	$\frac{1}{2}^+$	±1	∓2	∓1	1314·9	$2\cdot96 \times 10^{-10}$	1959
negative xi	Ξ^-	$\bar{\Xi}^+$	$\frac{1}{2}$	$\frac{1}{2}^+$	±1	∓2	∓1	1321·3	$1\cdot65 \times 10^{-10}$	1954
negative omega	Ω^-	$\bar{\Omega}^+$	0	$\frac{3}{2}^+$	±1	∓3	∓2	1672·2	$1\cdot30 \times 10^{-10}$	1964

(Hadrons comprise the Mesons, Nucleons (Baryons) and Hyperons sections above.)

of 10^{-22} s or less (this is because they decay via the strong interaction over nuclear distances of the order of 10^{-13} cm) and are therefore not able to be detected directly but only as an enhancement through a correlation between the behaviour of the initial reacting particles and the resonance's decay products. Unfortunately a large number of different resonances may be produced in a reaction and it is a deciphering of this data which is a major preoccupation of high energy physics.

Conservation Laws
All processes involving the production and decay of fundamental particles are subject to the usual conservation laws of charge, energy, and angular momentum, but in addition several other quantum parameters have to be conserved including the number of baryons, the number of leptons, and the vector sum of the spins of all of the particles involved in the reaction. Particles with half integral spin ($\mathcal{J} = 1/2$, $3/2$, $5/2$, etc.) (such as leptons and baryons) are called fermions, obey Fermi–Dirac statistics, and their numbers must be conserved, but particles with zero or integral spin ($\mathcal{J} = 0$, 1, 2, etc.) (such as pions, kaons, and photons) are called bosons, obey Bose–Einstein statistics, and their numbers need not be conserved.

Strangeness and hypercharge
However there exist conservation laws which need not necessarily be obeyed and in 1953 one of these was named *strangeness* (S) by M Gell-Mann and A Pais (both US) and K Nishijima (Japan) to explain the behaviour of charged kaons, i.e. if strangeness is conserved then the reaction can proceed quickly, but if it is not conserved (as in the decay of $S = 1$ kaons into $S = 0$ pions) then the decay can proceed only with difficulty and slowly (in about 10^{-8} instead of 10^{-23} s). However modern nomenclature relates not to strangeness but to its product with baryon number known as *hypercharge* (Y) such that $Y = S + B$, and conservation of strangeness is now known as conservation of hypercharge.

Multiplets and isospin
There is obviously a close relationship between particles which have similar quantum numbers and similar masses and appear to differ only in their electric charge. Thus such closely associated particles as the proton and neutron or the three sigma (Σ) baryons form groups known as *multiplets* and the number of particles in a multiplet can be calculated from a quantity known as *isospin* (I) such that $2I + 1$ particles of similar mass and quantum numbers (but differing in electric charge) comprise the multiplet. Thus the nucleons have $I = 1/2$ so that two particles can exist (the proton and the neutron but equally the anti-proton and the anti-neutron form the corresponding antimultiplet) whilst the delta (Δ) baryon resonances have $I = 3/2$ so that four particle states can exist (Δ^-, Δ°, Δ^+, and Δ^{++}).

Parity
Space parity (P) is the assumption that a physical system behaves in exactly the same way as its mirror image but in this context it is in fact an expression of the behaviour of the *wave function* of the particle when transformed from a right-handed to a left-handed system (or vice-versa) and if the wave function remains unchanged as a result of this reflection it is said to have *even* parity but if it changes sign the parity is said to be *odd*. In any system, parity is conserved in strong (rapid) reactions, but in 1956 T D Lee and C N Yang (both US) showed that it may not be conserved in weak (relatively slow) interactions.

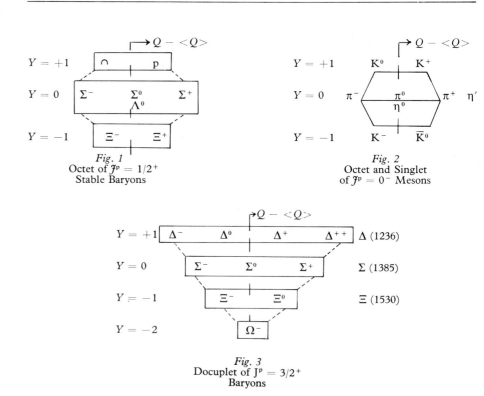

Fig. 1
Octet of $\mathcal{J}^p = 1/2^+$
Stable Baryons

Fig. 2
Octet and Singlet
of $\mathcal{J}^p = 0^-$ Mesons

Fig. 3
Docuplet of $J^p = 3/2^+$
Baryons

The quarks and charm
The regular patterns exhibited by the supermultiplets led to the conclusion that hadrons were composed of three primitive elements fitted together in an orderly manner, and which were named *quarks* (q) by M Gell-Mann (US). These, together with their equivalent anti-particles, have the general properties of hadrons except that they all have baryon number $B = 1/3$ and two quarks have electric charge $Q = -1/3$ and the other $Q = +2/3$ (N.B. the normal electric charge for particles is 0 or ± 1). Thus in order to preserve baryon number mesons must consist of a quark–anti-quark state and baryons must consist of three quarks. Quarks are considered as being point-like components which in a hadron are bound together by a strong interaction force envisaged as the exchange of particles for which the name *gluon* has been applied. The properties of the three quarks are tabulated below together with a fourth quark which was predicted in 1964 by B Bjorken and S Glashow to have the property known as *charm* (c). In spite of numerous discovery claims quarks have not been identified and their existence is still speculative but the use of quark theory to account for the fact that the SU3 meson octet shown in figure 2 is in fact an octet and a singlet (which was identified in 1964 to be the eta prime (η') resonance) and the apparent non-existence of baryons which cannot be manufactured from three quarks (i.e. the strangeness $S = +1:Z$ baryon resonances), is strong evidence in their favour.

Quark	Charge	Baryon Number	Strangeness	Hypercharge	Spin	Parity	Charm
q	Q	B	S	Y	$\mathcal{J}$	P	c
u	$+2/3$	$+1/3$	0	$+1/3$	$1/2$	$+$	0
d	$-1/3$	$+1/3$	0	$+1/3$	$1/2$	$+$	0
s	$-1/3$	$+1/3$	-1	$-2/3$	$1/2$	$+$	0
c	$+2/3$	$+1/3$	0	$+1/3$	$1/2$	$+$	$+1$
$\bar{u}$	$-2/3$	$-1/3$	0	$-1/3$	$1/2$	$-$	0
$\bar{d}$	$+1/3$	$-1/3$	0	$-1/3$	$1/2$	$-$	0
$\bar{s}$	$+1/3$	$-1/3$	$+1$	$+2/3$	$1/2$	$-$	0
$\bar{c}$	$-2/3$	$-1/3$	0	$-1/3$	$1/2$	$-$	-1

The discovery late in 1974 of two very heavy resonances, now known as the *psions* (symbol ψ), with lifetimes 10 000 times longer than other particles of similar mass, led to the speculation that these particles were mesons consisting of a mixture of a charmed quark and an anti-charmed quark in an 'atom' of 'charmonium' so that charm properties are neutralised, but the decay is delayed because of the need to conserve charm. This is only one theory for the existence of these neutral psion particles (although all of the theories require that the long lifetime be explained by the need to conserve a previously unobserved property) but it is predicted that the heavier psion, ψ (3684), is only the excited state of the lower mass ψ_0 (3094) 'charmonium' and that several other excited states should exist. The discovery of three such states in 1975 (represented by the symbol chi (χ)) indicates that the charm theory may be a correct assumption and the acceptance of the existence of at least four quarks and their anti-quarks may eventually solve the enigma of the proliferation of hadron resonances.

SU3 Theory

In order to explain the chaos of an ever increasing number of particles, the system of multiplets was resolved into a more coherent pattern in early 1961 by M Gell-Mann (US) Y Ne'eman (Israel), and Y Ohnuki (Japan) and this became known as the Symmetry Unitary SU3 or 'eightfold way' theory. Although based on a complex mathematical derivation, it was found that if the hypercharge (Y) of the stable baryon particles known in 1961 (which all had angular momentum parity values of $J^P = 1/2^+$) were plotted graphically against the charge of individual particles (Q) less the average charge of the multiplet ($\langle Q \rangle$) (i.e. for the nucleons $\langle Q \rangle$ is $\dfrac{1+0}{2}$ or $\frac{1}{2}$ so the net charge is $-1/2$ for the neutron and $+1/2$ for the proton), then the hexagon, or octet, shown in figure 1 results. Applying the same process to the seven mesons known at that time (all $J^P = 0^-$) (figure 2) then a second octet resulted with a missing neutral particle being predicted. This was discovered later in 1961 and named the eta (η) resonance.

However the major triumph of the SU3 theory was the prediction of the existence of a negatively-charged heavy baryon known as the omega minus (Ω^-). Since the delta (Δ) baryons of mass 1236 Mev (which were discovered in 1952) exist as a four-membered multiplet then they cannot be fitted into a hexagon but into the base of a triangle known as a docuplet of ten particles (figure 3). If, since both have $J^P = 3/2^+$, the delta multiplet is plotted together with the second baryon resonance Σ (1385) (discovered 1960) then this can be used to predict the existence first of an $I = 1/2$ two membered multiplet of mass 1530 Mev (from the fact that the difference in the masses of Δ(1236) and Σ(1385) is 149 Mev so the addition $1385 + 149$ is approximately 1530 Mev) which was identified in 1962 and is known as Ξ (1530), and secondly, of the omega minus baryon of mass approximately *1675* Mev (i.e. *1530* + 149 Mev) which has $I = 0$ so that corresponding neutral and positively charged omega particles cannot exist (although the anti-omega minus particle has the symbol Ω^+). The discovery of the omega minus in 1964 confirmed the principles of the SU3 theory, and many other meson and baryon multiplets have been fitted into octet and docuplet 'supermultiplets'.

Theory of Relativity

The velocity of sound was first measured by the Frenchman, Marin Mersenne (1588–1648) by means of cannon and a pendulum. His result was 700 mph compared with the now accepted value of 760·98 mph*.

Unable to believe that light waves could travel through the vacuum of interstellar space, scientists pre-supposed that light waves must be carried in luminiferous ether (from the Greek *aitho*, to glow). All attempts to detect this luminiferous agent failed. The Great Dilemma of Science up to 1905 was this:

'If ether existed, why could it not be detected? If ether did not exist, how could light waves travel *in vacuo*?'

The frustration of scientists was at last appeased by the genius of the Bavarian Jew, Albert Einstein (1879–1955). He published first in 1905 his Special (or Restricted) Theory of Relativity and on 20 Mar. 1916 his General Theory of Relativity (*Die Grundlage der allgemeinen Relativitätstheorie*). For the layman, however, frustration was in fact intensified because the new theory, hailed by scientists the world over, was to him not merely incomprehensible, but defied common sense. In fact its results were not so much difficult to understand as difficult to believe! Now, however, many of Einstein's equations have been experimentally proved.

The name 'Relativity' comes from the first of the two fundamental postulates of the Special Theory.
1. All motion is relative, i.e. we cannot speak of the Earth possessing an absolute velocity of 66 690 mph but only such a motion *relative* to some other object, e.g. the Sun.
2. The velocity of light is always constant relative to an observer, i.e. the light leaving a nebula will travel towards the observer at 186 282 miles per second regardless of the fact that the nebula may be receding, as some do, at over 100 000 miles per second.

Thus a stationary ether would defy the first postulate because it would possess *absolute* motion, since it would be the one motionless thing in the Universe. Thus at a stroke Einstein showed that science need no longer continue its useless search to detect ether. His Special Theory did not use or need to use the concept.

The basic concepts of relativity are:
1. A body contracts in length in the direction of its motion according to the equation (1)

$$L' = L\sqrt{1 - \frac{v^2}{c^2}}$$

Where L' is the length of the body, as seen by an observer, moving at a relative velocity of v, L is the body's original length at rest (when v equalled zero) and c is the velocity of light. Thus if a 20-ft-long rocket came past you in space at 93 141 miles per second (i.e. $0.5c$) it would (if you could measure it) be only about 17 ft long.
2. The mass of a body increases with its velocity according to the equation (2)

$$M' = \frac{M}{\sqrt{1 - \frac{v^2}{c^2}}}$$

where M' is the mass of the body, as detected by an observer, moving with a relative velocity v and M is the mass of the body at rest (when v equalled zero). In July 1952 the Californian Institute of Technology discovered that by accelerating electrons close to the speed of light ($0.999999c$) their mass in fact increased 300 fold, as predicted.

3. The closing speed of two high-speed objects A and B is not the sum of their velocities relative to a stationary observer, viz. the equation $V_{ab} = V_a + V_b$ is only an approximation. The true relative velocity is given by the equation:

$$V_{ab} = \frac{V_a + V_b}{1 + \dfrac{V_a V_b}{c^2}}$$

Thus if two 100 000 mps ion rockets crossed just above the earth from opposite directions their closing speed would appear to be not 200 000 mps (i.e. faster than the speed of light) but only 155 000 mps.

4. Since a heavier object possesses more innate energy than a lighter one and since the mass of an object increases with its relative velocity, it follows that there is an inter-relationship between energy, mass and velocity. This is expressed by the classic equation (4)
   $E = mc^2$ where E is equivalent energy, m is the mass of the object and c, again, the velocity of light.
   The most convincing proof of this verity was provided at Alamogordo, New Mexico, USA, on 16 July 1945, with the explosion of the prototype atomic bomb.

5. If two observers are moving at a constant velocity relative to each other, it appears to each that the other's time processes are slowed down as expressed by the equation (5):

$$T' = T\sqrt{1 - \frac{v^2}{c^2}}$$

where T' is one observer's time as read by the other, T is his own time as read by himself, v is the constant relative velocity of the two observers and c again equals the velocity of light. This gives rise to the famous Clock Paradox.

An ion space rocket sets out for the nearest star (*Proxima Centauri*) 4·28 light years distant at, say, one-fifth the speed of light, viz. $0.2c$ or 134 123 326 mph. The time spent in travelling there and back would be 43·00 Earth years but the spacemen would in fact age only 42·14 years.

If however the rocket is much faster and has a speed nine-tenths that of light ($0.9c$) and the distance of the star to be rounded is much farther, say *Arcturus* at 36 light years, the space travellers would apparently return to earth to find their wives or sweethearts probably dead of old age! The practical fallacy in this state of affairs is the word *constant* velocity. The phenomenon is diluted by the fact that to complete such a mission the rocket would have to accelerate at take-off and decelerate on landing and change direction in rounding *Arcturus*.

The equation is nonetheless valid though it was not verified until Ives's Experiment in 1938, or 33 years after it was propounded by Einstein. He showed that the frequency of the vibration of hydrogen atoms accelerated to a velocity of 1100 mps ($0.006c$) decreased by an amount exactly predicted.

Chemistry

TABLE OF THE CHEMICAL ELEMENTS

Atomic Number	Symbol	Name of Element	Derived From	Discoverers	Year	Atomic Weight (Note 3)	Density at 20°C (unless otherwise stated) (Note 4)	Melting Point °C (Note 5)	Boiling Point °C (Note 5)	Physical Description	Valency Number	Number of Nuclides
1	H	Hydrogen	Greek, 'hydor genes' = water producer	H Cavendish (UK)	1766	1·0079	0·0867 (solid at mp) 0·00008989 (gas at 0°C)	−259·194	−252·753	Colourless gas	1	3
2	He	Helium	Greek, 'helios' = sun	J N Lockyer (UK) and P- J- C Janssen (France)	1868	4·00260	0·1908 (solid at mp) 0·0001785 (gas at 0°C)	−272·375 at 24·985 atm (Note 6)	−268·926	Colourless gas	0	6
3	Li	Lithium	Greek, 'lithos' = stone	J A Arfwedson (Sweden)	1817	6·941	0·5334	180·57	1344	Silvery-white metal	1	5
4	Be	Beryllium	Greek, 'beryllion' = beryl	N- L Vauquelin (France)	1798	9·01218	1·846	1289	2476	Grey metal	2	7
5	B	Boron	Persian, 'burah' = borax	L- J Gay Lussac and L- J Thenard (France) and H Davy (UK)	1808	10·81	2·297 (β Rhombohedral) 2·465 (α Rhombohedral) 2·396 (β Tetragonal)	2130	3825	Dark brown powder	3	6
6	C	Carbon	Latin, carbo = charcoal	Prehistoric	—	12·011	2·266 (Graphite) 3·515 (Diamond)	4500 at 103 atm	3800 sublimes	Colourless solid (diamond) or black solid (graphite)	2 or 4	9
7	N	Nitrogen	Greek, 'nitron genes' = saltpetre producer	D Rutherford (UK)	1772	14·0067	0·9443 (solid at mp) 0·001250 (gas at 0°C)	−210·002	−195·806	Colourless gas	3 or 5	7
8	O	Oxygen	Greek, oxys genes' = acid producer	C W Scheele (Sweden) and J Priestley (UK)	1771-4	15·9994	1·350 (solid at mp) 0·001429 (gas at 0°C)	−218·789	−182·962	Colourless gas	2	8
9	F	Fluorine	Latin, fluo = flow	H Moissan (France)	1886	18·99840	1·780 (solid at mp) 0·001696 (gas at 0°C)	−219·669	−188·2C0	Pale greenish-yellow gas	1	6
10	Ne	Neon	Greek, 'neos' = new	W Ramsay and M W Travers (UK)	1898	20·179	1·433 (solid at mp) 0·0008999 (gas at 0°C)	−248·589	−246·047	Colourless gas	0	8
11	Na	Sodium (Natrium)	English, soda	H Davy (UK)	1807	22·98977	0·9688	97·86	884	Silvery-white metal	1	7
12	Mg	Magnesium	Magnesia, a district in Thessaly	H Davy (UK)	1808	24·305	1·737	649	1096	Silvery-white metal	2	9
13	Al	Aluminium	Latin, alumen = alum	H C Oersted; (Denmark) F Wöhler (Germany)	1825-7	26·98154	2·699	660·46	2525	Silvery-white metal	3	7
14	Si	Silicon	Latin, silex = flint	J J Berzelius (Sweden)	1824	28·086	2·329	1414	3225	Dark grey solid	4	8
15	P	Phosphorus	Greek, phosphoros' = light bringing	H Brand (Germany)	1669	30·97376	1·825 (white) 2·361 (violet) 2·708 (black)	44·14 597 at 45 atm 606 at 48 atm	277 431 sublimes 453 sublimes	White to yellow, violet to red, or black solid	3 or 5	7
16	S	Sulfur (Note 1)	Sanskrit, 'solvere'; Latin, sulfurum	Prehistoric	—	32·06	2·068 (rhombic) 2·038 (solid at mp)	115·21	444·674	Pale yellow solid	2,4, or 6	10
17	Cl	Chlorine	Greek, 'chloros' = green	C W Scheele (Sweden)	1774	35·453	0·003214 (gas at 0°C)	−100·97	−34·03	Yellow-green gas	1,3,5, or 7	9
18	Ar	Argon	Greek, 'argos' = inactive	W Ramsay and Lord Rayleigh (UK)	1894	39·948	0·001784 (gas at 0°C)	−189·352	−185·855	Colourless gas	0	12
19	K	Potassium (Kalium)	English, potash	H Davy (UK)	1807	39·098	0·8591	63·50	760	Silvery-white metal	1	12
20	Ca	Calcium	Latin, calx = lime	H Davy (UK)	1808	40·08	1·526	840	1491	Silvery-white metal	2	15
21	Sc	Scandium	Scandinavia	L F Nilson (Sweden)	1879	44·9559	2·989	1541	2835	Metallic	3	11
22	Ti	Titanium	Latin, Titanes = sons of the earth	M H Klaproth (Germany)	1795	47·90	4·506	1670	3295	Silvery metal	3 or 4	12
23	V	Vanadium	Vanadis, a name given to Freyja, the Norse goddess of beauty and youth	N G Sefström (Sweden)	1830	50·9414	6·119	1920	3425	Silvery-grey metal	2,3,4, or 5	9
24	Cr	Chromium	Greek, 'chromos' = colour	N- L Vauquelin (France)	1798	51·996	7·193	1860	2687	Silvery metal	2,3, or 6	10
25	Mn	Manganese	Latin, magnes = magnet	J G Gahn (Sweden)	1774	54·9380	7·472	1246	2065	Reddish-white metal	2,3,4,6, or 7	9
26	Fe	Iron (Ferrum)	Anglo-Saxon, iren	Prehistoric	—	55·847	7·874	1538	2865	Silvery-white metal	2 or 3	11
27	Co	Cobalt	German, kobold = goblin	G Brandt (Sweden)	1737	58·9332	8·834	1495	2900	Reddish-steel metal	2 or 3	11
28	Ni	Nickel	German, abbreviation of kupfernickel (devil's copper') or niccolite	A F Cronstedt (Sweden)	1751	58·70	8·907	1455	2920	Silvery-white metal	2 or 3	12
29	Cu	Copper (Cuprum)	Cyprus	Prehistoric (earliest known use)	c. 8000 BC	63·546	8·934	1084·88	2568	Reddish-bronze metal	1 or 2	12
30	Zn	Zinc	German, zink	A S Marggraf (Germany)	1746	65·38	7·140	419·58	908	Blue-white metal	2	17
31	Ga	Gallium	Latin, Gallia = France	L de Boisbaudran (France)	1875	69·72	5·912	29·74	2209	Grey metal	2 or 3	18
32	Ge	Germanium	Latin, Germania = Germany	C A Winkler (Germany)	1886	72·59	5·327	938·3	2835	Grey-white metal	4	20
33	As	Arsenic	Latin, arsenicum	Albertus Magnus (Germany)	c. 1220	74·9216	5·781	817 at 38 atm	603 sublimes	Steel-grey solid	3 or 5	19
34	Se	Selenium	Greek, 'selene' = moon	J J Berzelius (Sweden)	1818	78·96	4·810 (trigonal) 4·398 (α monoclinic) 4·352 (β monoclinic)	221·18	685	Greyish solid	2,4, or 6	21
35	Br	Bromine	Greek 'bromos' = stench	A- J Balard (France)	1826	79·904	3·119 (solid at mp) 3·937 (liquid at 20°C)	−7·25	59·09	Red-brown liquid	1,3,5, or 7	18
36	Kr	Krypton	Greek, 'kryptos' = hidden	W Ramsay and M W Travers (UK)	1898	83·80	2·801 (solid at mp) 0·003749 (gas at 0°C)	−157·38	−153·35	Colourless gas	0	23
37	Rb	Rubidium	Latin, rubidus = red	R W Bunsen and G R Kirchhoff (Germany)	1861	85·4678	1·529	39·30	688	Silvery-white metal	1	23
38	Sr	Strontium	Strontian, a village in Strathclyde, Scotland	H Davy (UK)	1808	87·62	2·582	768	1384	Silvery-white metal	2	20
39	Y	Yttrium	Ytterby, in Sweden	J Gadolin (Finland)	1794	88·9059	4·468	1522	3320	Steel-grey metal	3	17
40	Zr	Zirconium	Persian, 'zargun' = gold coloured	M F Klaproth (Germany)	1789	91·22	6·506	1855	4340	Steel-white metal	4	21
41	Nb	Niobium	Latin, Niobe, daughter of Tantalus	C Hatchett (UK)	1801	92·9064	8·595	2477	4860	Grey metal	3 or 5	14
42	Mo	Molybdenum	Greek, 'molybdos' = lead	P J Hjelm (Sweden)	1781	95·94	10·22	2623	4650	Silvery metal	2,3,4,5, or 6	19
43	Tc	Technetium	Greek, 'technetos' = artificial	C Perrier (France) and E Segré (Italy/USA)	1937	(96·9064)	11·28	2180	4270	Silvery-grey metal	2,3,4,6, or 7	16
44	Ru	Ruthenium	Ruthenia (The Ukraine, in USSR)	K K Klaus (Estonia/USSR)	1844	101·07	12·37	2300	4160	Bluish-white metal	3,4,6, or 8	18
45	Rh	Rhodium	Greek, 'rhodon' = rose	W H Wollaston (UK)	1804	102·9055	12·42	1963	3705	Steel-blue metal	3 or 4	16
46	Pd	Palladium	The asteroid Pallas (discovered 1802)	W H Wollaston (UK)	1803	106·4	12·01	1554	2970	Silvery-white metal	2 or 4	21
47	Ag	Silver (Argentum)	Anglo-Saxon, seolfor	Prehistoric (earliest silversmithery)	c. 4000 BC	107·868	10·50	961·93	2167	Lustrous white metal	1	24
48	Cd	Cadmium	Greek, 'kadmeia' = calamine	F Stromeyer (Germany)	1817	112·40	8·648	321·108	768	Blue-white metal	2	23
49	In	Indium	Its indigo spectrum	F Reich and H T Richter (Germany)	1863	114·82	7·289	156·634	2076	Bluish-silvery metal	1 or 3	28
50	Sn	Tin (Stannum)	Anglo-Saxon, tin	Prehistoric (intentionally alloyed with Cu to make Bronze	c. 3500 BC	118·69	7·288	231·968	2608	Silvery-white metal	2 or 4	26
51	Sb	Antimony (Stibium)	Lower Latin, antimonium	Near Historic	c. 1000 BC	121·75	6·693	630·76	1589	Silvery metal	3 or 5	26
52	Te	Tellurium	Latin, tellus = earth	F J Muller (Baron von Reichenstein) (Austria)	1783	127·60	6·237	449·87	989	Silvery-grey solid	2,4, or 6	30

Number	Symbol	Name of Element	Derived From	Discoverers	Year	(Note 3)	(g/cm³) (Note 4)	(Note 5)	(Note 5)	Physical Description	Number Nuclides
53	I	Iodine	Greek, 'iodes' = violet	B Courtois (France)	1811	126·9045	4·947	113·6	185·3	Grey-black solid	1,3,5, or 7
54	Xe	Xenon	Greek, 'xenos' = stranger	W Ramsay and M W Travers (UK)	1898	131·30	3·399 (solid at mp) 0·005897 (gas at 0°C)	-111·76	-108·09	Colourless gas	0
55	Cs	Caesium	Latin, caesius = bluish-grey	R W von Bunsen and G R Kirchhoff (Germany)	1860	132·9054	1·896	28·5	671	Silvery-white metal	1
56	Ba	Barium	Greek, 'barys' = heavy	H Davy (UK)	1808	137·34	3·595	729	1880	Silvery-white metal	2
57	La	Lanthanum	Greek, 'lanthano' = conceal	C G Mosander (Sweden)	1839	138·9055	6·145	921	3460	Metallic	3
58	Ce	Cerium	The asteroid Ceres (discovered 1801)	J J Berzelius and W Hisinger (Sweden); M H Klaproth (Germany)	1803	140·12	6·688 (beta) 6·770 (gamma)	799	3430	Steel-grey metal	3 or 4
59	Pr	Praseodymium	Greek, 'prasios didymos' = green twin	C Auer von Welsbach (Austria)	1885	140·9077	6·772	934	3520	Silvery-white metal	3
60	Nd	Neodymium	Greek, 'neos didymos' = new twin	C Auer von Welsbach (Austria)	1885	144·24	7·006	1021	3070	Yellowish-white metal	3
61	Pm	Promethium	Greek demi-god 'Prometheus'—the fire stealer	J Marinsky, L E Glendenin and C D Coryell (USA)	1945	(144·9128)	7·135	1042	2430	Metallic	3
62	Sm	Samarium	The mineral Samarskite, named after Col M Samarski, a Russian engineer	L de Boisbaudran (France)	1879	150·4	7·519	1077	1794	Light-grey metal	2 or 3
63	Eu	Europium	Europe	E A Demarçay (France)	1901	151·96	5·243	822	1599	Steel-grey metal	2 or 3
64	Gd	Gadolinium	Johan Gadolin (1760-1852)	J-C- G de Marignac (Switzerland)	1880	157·25	7·899	1313	3270	Silvery-white metal	3
65	Tb	Terbium	Ytterby, in Sweden	C G Mosander (Sweden)	1843	158·9254	8·228	1356	3230	Silvery metal	3
66	Dy	Dysprosium	Greek, 'dysprositos'—hard to get at	L de Boisbaudran (France)	1886	162·50	8·549	1412	2567	Metallic	3
67	Ho	Holmium	Holmia, a Latinised form of Stockholm	J-L Soret (France) and P T Cleve (Sweden)	1878-9	164·9304	8·794	1474	2700	Silvery metal	3
68	Er	Erbium	Ytterby, in Sweden	C G Mosander (Sweden)	1843	167·26	9·064	1529	2865	Greyish-silver metal	3
69	Tm	Thulium	Latin and Greek, 'Thule' = Northland	P T Cleve (Sweden)	1879	168·9342	9·319	1545	1950	Metallic	2 or 3
70	Yb	Ytterbium	Ytterby, in Sweden	J-C- G de Marignac (Switzerland)	1878	173·04	6·967	817	1228	Silvery metal	2 or 3
71	Lu	Lutetium	Lutetia, Roman name for the city of Paris	G Urbain (France)	1907	174·97	9·839	1665	3400	Metallic	3
72	Hf	Hafnium	Hafnia = Copenhagen	D Coster (Netherlands) and G C de Hevesy (Hungary/Sweden)	1923	178·49	13·28	2230	4630	Steel-grey metal	4
73	Ta	Tantalum	'Tantalus', a mythical Greek king	A G Ekeberg (Sweden)	1802	180·9479	16·67	3020	5520	Silvery metal	3 or 5
74	W	Tungsten (Wolfram)	Swedish, tung sten = heavy stone	J J de Elhuyar and F de Elhuyar (Spain)	1783	183·85	19·26	3422	5730	Grey metal	2,4,5, or 6
75	Re	Rhenium	Latin, Rhenus = the river Rhine	W Noddack, Fr I Tacke, and O. Berg, (Germany)	1925	186·207	21·01	3385	5610	Whitish-grey metal	1,4, or 7
76	Os	Osmium	Greek, 'osme' = odour	S Tennant (UK)	1804	190·2	22·59	3100	5020	Grey-blue metal	2,3,4,6, or 8
77	Ir	Iridium	Latin, iris = a rainbow	S Tennant (UK)	1804	192·22	22·56	2447	4730	Silvery-white metal	3 or 6
78	Pt	Platinum	Spanish, platina = small silver	A de Ulloa (Spain)	1748	195·09	21·45	1769	3835	Bluish-white metal	2 or 4
79	Au	Gold (Aurum)	Anglo-Saxon, gold	Prehistoric		196·9665	19·29	1064·43	2860	Lustrous yellow metal	1 or 2
80	Hg	Mercury (Hydrargyrum)	Assigned the alchemical sign of the Greek god 'Hermes' (Latin Mercurius), the divine patron of the occult sciences	Near Historic	c. 1600 BC	200·59	14·17 (solid at mp) 13·55 (liquid at 20°C)	-38·836	356·66	Silvery metallic liquid	1 or 2
81	Tl	Thallium	Greek, 'thallos' = a budding twig	W Crookes (UK)	1861	204·37	11·87	304	1475	Blue-grey metal	1 or 3
82	Pb	Lead (Plumbum)	Anglo-Saxon, lead	Prehistoric		207·2	11·35	327·502	1753	Steel-blue metal	2 or 4
83	Bi	Bismuth	German, weissmuth = white matter	C-F Geoffroy (France)	1753	208·9804	9·807	271·442	1566	Reddish-silvery metal	2 or 5
84	Po	Polonium	Poland	Mme M S Curie (Poland/France)	1898	(208·9824)	9·155	254	948	Metallic	2,3, or 4
85	At	Astatine	Greek, 'astatos' = unstable	D R Corson (USA), K R Mackenzie (USA), and E Segrè (Italy/USA)	1940	(209·9870)	~7·0	302	377	Metallic	1,3,5, or 7
86	Rn	Radon	Latin, radius = ray	F E Dorn (Germany)	1900	(222·0176)	~4·7 (solid at mp) 0·01005 (gas at 0°C)	-64·9	-61·2	Colourless gas	0
87	Fr	Francium	France	Mlle M Perey (France)	1939	(223·0197)	~2·8	23	657	Metallic	1
88	Ra	Radium	Latin, radius = ray	P Curie (France), Mme M S Curie (Poland/France), and M G Bemont (France)	1898	(226·0254)	5·503	707	1530	Silvery metal	2
89	Ac	Actinium	Greek, 'aktinos', genitive of 'aktis' = a ray	A Debierne (France)	1899	(227·0278)	10·06	1050	3450	Metallic	3
90	Th	Thorium	Thor, the Norse god of thunder	J J Berzelius (Sweden)	1829	232·0381	11·72	1760	4790	Grey metal	4
91	Pa	Protactinium	Greek, 'protos' = first, plus actinium	O Hahn (Germany) and Fr L Meitner (Austria); F Soddy and J A Cranston (UK)	1917	(231·0359)	15·37	1570	4530	Silvery metal	4 or 5
92	U	Uranium	The planet Uranus (discovered 1781)	M H Klaproth (Germany)	1789	238·029	19·05	1134	4250	Bluish-white metal	3,4,5, or 6
93	Np	Neptunium	The planet Neptune	E M McMillan and P H Abelson (USA)	1940	(237·0482)	20·47	637	4030	Silvery metal	3,4,5, or 6
94	Pu	Plutonium	The planet Pluto	G T Seaborg, E M McMillan, J W Kennedy, and A C Wahl (USA)	1940	(244·0642)	20·26	640	3360	Metallic	3,4,5, 6
95	Am	Americium	America	G T Seaborg, R A James, L O Morgan, and A Ghiorso (USA)	1944	(243·0614)	13·77	1176	1900	Metallic	3,5, or 6
96	Cm	Curium	The Curies—Pierre (1859-1906) and Marie (1867-1934)	G T Seaborg, R A James, and A Ghiorso (USA)	1944	(247·0703)	13·69	1340	3110	Metallic	3
97	Bk	Berkelium	Berkeley, a town in California, USA	S G Thompson, A Ghiorso, and G T Seaborg (USA)	1949	(247·0703)	14·67	986	—	Metallic	3 or 4
98	Cf	Californium	California, USA	S G Thompson, K Street Jr, A Ghiorso, and G T Seaborg (USA)	1950	(251·0796)	15·23	900	—	Metallic	2 or 3
99	Es	Einsteinium	Dr Albert Einstein (1879-1955)	A Ghiorso, S G Thompson, G H Higgins, G T Seaborg, M H Studier, P R Fields, S M Fried, H Diamond, J F Mech, G L Pyle, J R Huizenga, A Hirsch, W M Manning, C I Browne, H L Smith, and R W Spence (USA)	1953	(254·0880)	—	—	—	Metallic	2 or 3

Continued over page

Chemical Elements, continued

Atomic Number	Symbol	Name of Element	Derived From	Year	Discoverers	Atomic Weight (Note 3)	Density at 20°C (unless otherwise stated) (g/cm³) (Note 4)	Melting Point °C (Note 5)	Boiling Point °C (Note 5)	Physical Description	Valency Number	Number of Nuclides
100	Fm	Fermium	Dr Enrico Fermi (1901–54)	1953	A Ghiorso, S G Thompson, G H Higgins, G T Seaborg, M H Studier, P R Fields, S M Fred, H Diamond, J F Mech, G L Pyle, J R Huizenga, A Hirsch, W M Manning, C I Browne, H L Smith, and R W Spence (USA)	(257·0951)	—	—	—	Metallic	2 or 3	15
101	Md	Mendelevium	Dmitriy I Mendeleyev (1834–1907)	1955	A Ghiorso, B G Harvey, G R Choppin, S G Thompson, and G T Seaborg (USA)	(258·)	—	—	—	Metallic	2	10
102	No	Nobelium	Alfred B Nobel (1833–96)	1958	A Ghiorso, T Sikkeland, J R Walton, and G T Seaborg (USA)	(259·)	—	—	—	Metallic	2	9
103	Lr	Lawrencium	Dr Ernest O Lawrence (1901–58)	1961	A Ghiorso, T Sikkeland, A E Larsh, and R M Latimer (USA)	(260·)	—	—	—	Metallic	3	8
104	Ku	Kurchatovium (Note 2)	Dr Igor V Kurchatov (1903–60)	1964	G N Flerov, Yu Ts Oganesyan, Yu V Lobanov, V I Kuznetsov, V A Druin, V P Perelygin, K A Gavrilov, S P Tretyakova, and V M Plotko (USSR)	(261·)	—	—	—	Metallic	4	5
105	Rf Rutherfordium (Note 2) or Ns Nielsbohrium (Note 2)	Lord (Ernest) Rutherford (1871–1937) or Prof Niels Bohr (1885–1962)	1969, 1970	A Ghiorso, M Nurmia, J Harris, K Eskola, and P Eskola (USA), 1969; or G N Flerov, Yu Ts Oganesyan, Yu V Lobanov, Yu A Lasarev, S P Tretyakova, I V Kolesov, and V M Plotko (USSR), 1970	(262·)	—	—	—	Metallic	5	3
	Ha	Hahnium (Note 2)	Prof Otto Hahn (1879–1968)	1970								
106	—	(Note 2)	(Note 2)	1974	A Ghiorso, J M Nurmia, K Eskola, J Harris, and P Eskola (USA) or Yu Ts Oganesyan, Yu P Tretyakov, A S Iljinov, A G Demir, A A Pleve, S P Tretyakova, V M Plotko, M P Ivanov, N A Danilov, Yu S Korotkin, and G N Flerov (USSR)	(263·)	—	—	—	Metallic	6	2?

Note 1: The former spelling 'sulphur' is disallowed under International Union of Pure and Applied Chemistry rules on nomenclature.
Note 2: Because the discoveries of elements 104, 105, and 106 are disputed, under International Union of Pure and Applied Chemistry have not yet assigned official names to these elements.
Note 3: A value in brackets is the atomic mass of the isotope with the longest known half-life (i.e. the period taken for its radioactivity to fall to half of its original value).
Note 4: For the highly radioactive elements the density value has been calculated for the isotope with the longest known half-life.
Note 5: All temperature values have been corrected to the International Practical Temperature Scale of 1968.
Note 6: This value is the minimum pressure under which liquid helium can be solidified.

INORGANIC CHEMISTRY

The nomenclature of inorganic chemistry is governed by the International Union of Pure and Applied Chemistry whose latest detailed and authoritative guidance was published in 1970 and was followed by a definite interpretation by the Association of Science Education in 1972.

Because of the difficulties in trying to produce a systematic nomenclature which will adequately cover all aspects of inorganic chemistry, trivial names have not yet been completely discarded although, for example, the use of the familiar endings 'ous' and 'ic' to denote the lower and higher valency states of metal cations is to be discouraged in favour of the Stock System in which the oxidation number of the less electronegative constituent is indicated by Roman numerals in parentheses placed immediately after the name of the atom concerned, thus $FeCl_2$ is iron (II) chloride rather than ferrous chloride and $FeCl_3$ is iron (III) chloride rather than ferric chloride. For compounds consisting of simple molecules of known composition the stoichiometry determines the name using Greek or Roman multiplying affixes (see table below), thus P_4O_{10} is tetraphosphorus decaoxide. Trivial names for acids are still in use although such alchemical leftovers as 'Aquafortis' for nitric acid, 'Oil of Vitriol' for sulfuric acid, and 'Spirit of Salt' for hydrochloric acid have long (hopefully) been discarded.

Multiplying Affixes

½	hemi	8	octa	15 pentadeca
1	mono	9	nona (Latin)	16 hexadeca
1½	sesqui		ennea (Greek)	17 heptadeca
2	di	10	deca	18 octadeca
3	tri	11	undeca (Latin)	19 nonadeca
4	tetra		henadeca (Greek)	20 eicosa
5	penta	12	dodeca	24 tetracosa
6	hexa	13	trideca	30 triaconta
7	hepta	14	tetradeca	40 tetraconta

STABLE INORGANIC ACIDS OF THE NON-METALLIC ELEMENTS

Boron
boric acid (crystals) H_3BO_3

Arsenic
arsenious acid★ H_3AsO_3
arsenic acid★ H_3AsO_4

Bromine
hydrobromic acid (45%)   HBr
hypobromous acid★   HBrO
bromic acid★ $HBrO_3$

Carbon
carbonic acid★ H_2CO_3

Chlorine
hydrochloric acid (35%)   HCl
hypochlorous acid★   HClO
chlorous acid★ $HClO_2$
chloric acid★ $HClO_3$
perchloric acid (60%) $HClO_4$

Fluorine
hydrofluoric acid (40%)   HF
fluoroboric acid (40%) HBF_4
fluorosilicic acid (40%) H_2SiF_6
fluorosulfonic acid (liquid) HSO_3F

Iodine
hydriodic acid (55%)   HI
hypoiodic acid★   HIO
iodic acid (crystals) HIO_3
periodic acid (crystals) HIO_4

Nitrogen
hyponitrous acid★ $H_2N_2O_2$
nitrous acid★ HNO_2
nitric acid (70%) HNO_3

Phosphorus
phosphinic acid (50%) H_3PO_2
(hypophosphorous acid)
phosphonic acid (crystals) H_3PO_3
(orthophosphorous acid)
diphosphonic acid (crystals) $H_4P_2O_5$
(pyrophosphorous acid)
diphosphoric acid (crystals) $H_4P_2O_6$
(hypophosphoric acid)
metaphosphoric acid (solid) $(HPO_3)_n$
orthophosphoric acid (85%) H_3PO_4
diphosphoric acid (crystals) $H_4P_2O_7$
(pyrophosphoric acid)

Selenium
selenious acid (crystals) H_2SeO_3
selenic acid (crystals) H_2SeO_4

Silicon
metasilicic acid (solid) $(H_2SiO_3)_n$
orthosilicic acid★ H_4SiO_4

Sulfur
sulfurous acid★ H_2SO_3
sulfuric acid (liquid) H_2SO_4
peroxomonosulfuric acid (crystals) H_2SO_5
(Caro's Acid)
dithionic acid★ $H_2S_2O_6$
disulfuric acid (crystals) $H_2S_2O_7$
(pyrosulfuric acid)
peroxodisulfuric acid (crystals) $H_2S_2O_8$
(persulfuric acid)

Tellurium
tellurous acid (crystals) H_2TeO_3
orthotelluric acid (crystals) H_6TeO_6

★ Stable only in aqueous solution
Values in parentheses indicate the concentration in aqueous solution of the usual commercial grades of the acid.

ORGANIC CHEMISTRY

Organic chemistry is the chemistry of hydrocarbons and their derivatives. The original division between organic chemical compounds (meaning those occurring in the Animal and Plant Kingdoms) and inorganic chemical compounds (meaning those occurring in the mineral world) was made in 1675 by Lémery. This oversimplified division was upset when in 1828 Wöhler produced urea ($NH_2.CO.NH_2$) in an attempt to produce ammonium cyanate ($NH_4.CNO$) from inorganic sources and was ended with the synthesis of acetic acid (ethanoic acid) from its elements by Kolbe in 1845, and the synthesis of methane by Berthelot in 1856. Carbon has a valency number (from the Latin *valens* = worth) of 4, i.e. a combining power expressed in terms of the number of hydrogen atoms with which the atom of carbon can combine. In addition the carbon atom has the unique property of being able to join one to another to form chains, rings, double bonds and triple bonds.

Thus there are almost limitless numbers of organic compounds and since nearly four million are known then the transition to a strict system of nomenclature from the plethora of trivial names is an essential aim of the International Union of Pure and Applied Chemistry. When all the carbon valencies are utilised in bonding with other carbon or hydrogen atoms, with all the carbon linkages as single bonds, the hydrocarbons are said to be *saturated* and may be in the form of chains or rings. When the carbon atoms are joined together by double or triple bonds then these bonds are potentially available for completion of saturation and therefore such hydrocarbons are said to be *unsaturated*. Open chain compounds are called aliphatic from the Greek *aliphos*, fat, since the first compounds in this class to be studied were the so-called fatty acids.

Saturated hydrocarbons

Straight chain hydrocarbons necessarily conform to the formula C_nH_{2n+2} and are known collectively as **alkanes** or by their trivial name paraffins (from the Latin *parvum affinis*, small affinity, which refers to their low combining power with other substances). The first four alkanes retain their semi-trivial names:

methane (CH_4)   ethane (C_2H_6)

propane (C_3H_8)

butane (C_4H_{10})

The higher alkanes are named by utilising the recommended multiplying affixes listed in the Inorganic Section to indicate the number of carbon atoms in the chain, i.e. C_5H_{12} is pentane, C_7H_{16} is heptane, and C_9H_{20} is nonane.

Ring compounds, in which the carbon atoms form a closed ring, are known as the **napthene** family and of the formula C_nH_{2n}.

They take their names from the corresponding alkanes by adding the prefix *cyclo-*, e.g.

cyclopropane (C_3H_6)   cyclobutane (C_4H_8)

cyclopentane (C_5H_{10})   cyclohexane (C_6H_{12})

Unsaturated hydrocarbons

Compounds with one double bond are of the structure type $>C=C<$ and are of the formula C_nH_{2n}. They are known as **alkenes** or by the trivial name olefins (from the Latin *oleum*, oil, *faceo* = to make). They are named after their alkane equivalents by substituting the ending *-ene* to the root of the name, although the old system was to substitute the ending *-ylene*, e.g.

ethene (ethylene) (C_2H_4)   propene (propylene) (C_3H_6)

The higher alkenes are similarly named:
C_4H_8 butene (butylene)
C_5H_{10} pentene (pentylene)
C_6H_{12} hexene (hexylene) et seq.

where the letter ending 'a' in buta, penta, hexa, etc. is dropped for ease of pronunciation. When more than one double bond is present the endings *diene*, *triene* etc. are used with the positions of the double bonds being carefully noted, i.e. $CH_2=CH-CH=CH_2$ is buta-1,3-diene.

Compounds with one triple bond are called **alkynes** or by their trivial name acetylenes (from the Latin *acetum* = vinegar) and are of the general formula C_nH_{2n-2}. The same rules for nomenclature are used with the ending *-yne* being added to the root of the name of the equivalent alkane. The first member of the group is named ethyne although the more common name acetylene still has a semi-trivial standing. Typical group members include:

ethyne (C_2H_2)   propyne (C_3H_4)

butyne (C_4H_6)

Aromatic hydrocarbons

Substances based on the hydrocarbon benzene C_6H_6 have the family name **aromatic** (from the Greek *aroma*, fragrant smell). They are characterised by the six membered ring represented as having alternating or conjugate double bonds as shown on the left below, although because the double bonds have no fixed positions it is usual to symbolise the structure as shown on the right:

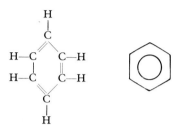

It is possible to produce multiple rings based on the benzene structure, e.g.

napthalene ($C_{10}H_8$)

anthracene ($C_{14}H_{10}$)

Organic radicals

Removal of a hydrogen atom from hydrocarbon molecules forms a radical which is named by replacing the suffix *-ane* by *-yl*, e.g.
$(CH_3)^-$ *methyl*; from Greek *methy*, wine, *hyle* = wood
$(C_2H_5)^-$ *ethyl*; from Greek *aither*, clean air (i.e. odourless)
$(C_3H_7)^-$ *propyl*; from Greek *pro*, before, and *peon*, fat, hence radical of fatty acid
$(C_4H_9)^-$ *butyl*; from Greek *butyrum* = butter (rancid smell)

Higher radicals are again based on the use of multiplying affixes, i.e. pentane becomes pentyl $(C_5H_{11})^-$ and hexane becomes hexyl $(C_6H_{13})^-$. These radicals are generically known as **alkyls** and being covalent they can be substituted for hydrogen in other molecules.

The general designation for radicals of aromatic hydrocarbons is **aryl** and the monovalent radical formed from benzene $(C_6H_5)^-$ is called *phenyl* and not *benzyl* which is reserved for the radical $(C_6H_5CH_2)^-$. The use of these radical names leads to a better description of a molecule's structure, i.e. the semi-trivial name toluene does not immediately convey an indication of molecular structure but its systematic equivalent methyl benzene indicates the replacement of one of the hydrogen atoms in the benzene ring by a methyl group.

Isomers and organic nomenclature

It is evident that except in the cases of the simplest organic molecules, it is possible to rearrange the positions of carbon atoms along the molecule skeleton (chain isomerism), or to a limited extent reposition double and triple bonds along the chain, or substitute radicals for hydrogen atoms at specific points along the chain (position isomerism).

In the case of the alkanes (paraffins) methane, ethane, and propane exist only as single molecular species, but butane exists in two—the normal straight chain (n) and a branched isomeric chain (iso), and pentane in three—normal, isomeric, and neopentane:

$$CH_3CH_2CH_2CH_3$$
n-butane

$$CH_3\overset{\overset{\displaystyle CH_3}{|}}{C}HCH_3$$
isobutane

$$CH_3CH_2CH_2CH_2CH_3$$
n-pentane

$$CH_3\overset{\overset{\displaystyle CH_3}{|}}{C}HCHCH_3$$
iospentane

$$CH_3\overset{\overset{\displaystyle CH_3}{|}}{\underset{\underset{\displaystyle CH_3}{|}}{C}}CH_3$$
neopentane

From then on there is a rapid increase with the alkane $C_{15}H_{32}$ exhibiting no less than 4347 possible isomeric states!

However in the IUPAC system of nomenclature the use of these prefixes becomes unnecessary since the longest possible chain is chosen as the *parent* chain and the positions of sites on the chain are indicated by numbers, the direction of numbering being so chosen as to give the lowest series of numbers for the *side* chains. Thus isobutane becomes 2-methyl propane (since the methyl radical is attached to the second carbon atom in the chain), isopentane becomes 2-methyl butane for the same reason, and neopentane becomes 2,2-dimethyl propane (since two of the methyl radicals are regarded as forming a 'chain' with the central carbon atom and the two other methyl radicals are both attached to the 'second' carbon atom). For single bonding the treatment of more complex molecules is a simple extension of this principle with apparent side chains being regarded as belonging to the parent chain where necessary, e.g. the structure below is 3-methyl hexane and *not* 2-propyl butane:

$$CH_3\overset{\overset{\displaystyle |}{\underset{\underset{\underset{\underset{\displaystyle CH_3}{|}}{CH_3}}{|}}{CH_2}}}{C}HCH_2CH_3$$

For alkenes (olefins) and alkynes (acetylenes) the chain is always numbered from the end closest to the double or triple bond and the positions of these bonds are also specified:

$$CH_3CH_2CH=CH_2$$
but-1-ene
(α butylene)

$$CH_3CH=CHCH_3$$
but-2-ene
(β butylene)

$$CH_3\diagdown_{CH_3}C=CH_2$$
2-methyl propene
(isobutylene)

$$CH_3CH_2C\equiv CH$$
but-1-yne

$$CH_3C\equiv CCH_3$$
but-2-yne

In compounds containing mixed bonds the double bond takes preference over triple bonds in numbering the chain and double and triple bonds take preference over single bonds in deciding the length of the parent chain.

When there is more than one type of radical attached to the parent chain then these are listed in strict alphabetical order without regard to the position on the chain, e.g. for the first five radicals the order will be: butyl, ethyl, methyl, pentyl, and propyl. The multiplying affixes used to indicate the total number of a particular type of radical are ignored in this sequence, e.g. ethyl still precedes dimethyl and triethyl before methyl.

For radicals the same rules apply and apart from the prefixes *normal*, *iso*, and *neo* discussed previously, the old system also includes *secondary* (*sec*) isomers (so called because two hydrogen atoms have been repositioned from the principal carbon atom and their bonds replaced by two of the carbon bonds) and *tertiary* (*tert*) isomers (so called because three hydrogen atoms have been repositioned). In the IUPAC system these prefixes are no longer required since the longest chain principal is applied and numbering specified from the carbon atom which has the free valency. In the examples of the propyl and butyl isomers listed below the names isopropyl and isobutyl are still retained on a semi-trivial basis:

Trivial Name	Structure	I.U.P.A.C. Name
n-propyl	$CH_3CH_2CH_2-$	propyl
iso-propyl	$CH_3\overset{\overset{\displaystyle |}{}}{C}HCH_3$	1-methylethyl
n-butyl	$CH_3CH_2CH_2CH_2-$	butyl
iso-butyl	$(CH_3)_2CHCH_2-$	2-methylpropyl
sec-butyl	$CH_3CH_2\overset{\overset{\displaystyle |}{}}{C}HCH_3$	1-methylpropyl
tert-butyl	$(CH_3)_3C-$	1,1-dimethylethyl

In the case of aromatic hydrocarbons, when two or more substituents are present in the benzene ring, the old nomenclature technique was to assign prefixes ortho, meta, and para to the name of the compound to indicate the differences in the positions of the radicals, i.e.

ortho (o)   *meta* (m)   *para* (p)

where ortho = neighbouring positions
meta = one position between the groups
para = opposite positions

In the IUPAC system these prefixes are again rendered unnecessary by simply numbering the benzene ring as shown below with the main functional group substituted usually assigned to position 1:

Thus a comparison of the different naming systems for the above examples clearly indicates the superiority of the IUPAC system:

Trivial Name	Semi-Trivial Name	I.U.P.A.C. Name
o-xylene	o-dimethylbenezene	1,2-dimethylbenzene
m-xylene	m-dimethylbenzene	1,3-dimethylbenzene
p-xylene	p-dimethylbenzene	1,4-dimethylbenzene

Substitution radicals

(a) *Alcohols.* Replacement of hydrogen atoms by hydroxyl groups (OH) leads to the **alcohols**. If the hydroxyl radical is the *principal* group (see end of this section) then the alcohol molecule is named after the hydrocarbon base with the ending *-ol* substituted for the ending *-e*, e.g. methanol (methyl alcohol) CH_3OH and ethanol (ethyl alcohol) C_2H_5OH. However, with longer chains the position of the attachment has to be specified and this is achieved by selecting the longest chain containing the hydroxy group and assigning the lowest possible number to this side chain hydroxyl radical using the suffix *-ol*, e.g.

$$CH_3CH_2CH_2OH$$ propan-1-ol (propyl alcohol)

$$CH_3\overset{\overset{\displaystyle |}{\underset{\underset{\displaystyle OH}{|}}{}}}{C}HCH_3$$ propan-2-ol (isopropyl alcohol)

This simplified procedure can be extended to much more complex alcohols provided that the hydroxyl radical is the principal group. To represent a number of alcohols present in a single molecule the multiplying affixes are used to obtain the endings *-diol*, *-triol*, etc.

In the case of aromatic hydrocarbons the single hydroxyl attachment is known as *phenol* whilst multi-hydroxyl groups are named on the *benzene . . . ol* system, even though the true aromatic alcohols are compounds containing the hydroxyl group in a side chain and may be regarded as aryl derivatives of the aliphatic alcohols, i.e. benzyl alcohol $C_6H_5CH_2OH$ is a true aromatic alcohol. Use of the new nomenclature gives a clearer understanding of molecular structure, e.g.

benzene-1,2-diol (catechol)   benzene-1,3-diol (resorcinol)   benzene-1,4-diol (quinol)

(b) *Ethers.* Derivatives of alcohols in which the hydrogen atoms in the hydroxyl groups are replaced by carbon are known as **ethers**. Thus $(C_6H_5)_2O$ is diphenyl ether and $CH_3.O.C_2H_5$ is ethylmethyl ether (using the rule that where there is no preference then the radicals are named alphabetically) but there is a tendency to treat the ether radical as a group (O.R) where 'R' is an alkyl radical part of the ether compound, so the above mixed radical compound would be methoxyethane since the group are known generically as **alkoxy** groups. Similarly $(C_2H_5)_2O$ becomes ethoxyethane rather than diethyl ether. When the two alkyl groups are the same the ether is said to be symmetrical or simple (i.e. ethoxyethane) but if the two alkyl groups are different the ether is said to be unsymmetrical or mixed (i.e. methoxyethane).

(c) *Aldehydes.* The substitution by the radical (CHO) leads to compounds known as the **aldehydes** although the suffix *carbaldehyde* is used if the carbon atom in the radical is not part of the base hydrocarbon, i.e. C_6H_5CHO is benzene carbaldehyde rather than its former name benzaldehyde. Where the carbon in the aldehyde is part of the original base hydrocarbon then the compound is named by substituting the ending -al for the hydrocarbon containing the same number of atoms in the parent group. Thus HCHO is methanal (formerly formaldehyde) and CH_3-CHO is ethanal (formerly acetaldehyde)

(d) *Ketones.* Ketones are based on the double bonded (>CO) radical. The trivial naming technique is to add the name ketone to the ends of the names of the radicals connected by the bond, i.e. $(CH_3)_2CO$ is dimethyl ketone and $CH_3.CO.C_2H_5$ is ethyl methyl ketone. However the new recommended technique is to name the molecule after the longest structural chain by adding the ending -one. Thus dimethyl ketone or acetone is in reality propanone. For similar reasons ethylmethyl ketone becomes butanone, etc.

(e) *Acids.* The functional group (COOH) is known as carboxylic acid and is used as such if the carbon atom is not part of the main base hydrocarbon, e.g.

benzene carboxylic acid (benzoic acid)

benzene-1,2-dicarboxylic acid (phthalic acid)

However if the carbon atom is part of the base chain then the acid molecule is named by substituting the ending -oic to the name of the hydrocarbon containing the same number of carbon atoms, i.e.

HCOOH — methanoic acid (formic acid)

CH_3COOH — ethanoic acid (acetic acid)

CH_3CH_2COOH — propanoic acid

$CH_3CH_2CH_2COOH$ — butanoic acid

(f) *Amines.* Amines are formed by substituting (NH_2) groups in place of hydrogen and the class name is added to the alkyl radical, i.e. CH_3NH_2 is methylamine. Further substitution can take place leading to dimethylamine $(CH_3)_2NH$ and even trimethylamine $(CH_3)_3N$. The aromatic amine $C_6H_5NH_2$ is phenylamine (aniline).

(g) *Principal Groups.* Since a large number of different radicals can attach to the base hydrocarbon it is important to produce an order of preference for listing these radicals. With a mixture of radicals the principal group is named as described above but the secondary groups are now named using prefixes to identify the type. Thus for hydroxy groups as secondary groups the ending -ol is dropped in favour of the prefix hydroxy. This occurs for many alcoholic compounds since this group is towards the bottom of the list. The carboxylic radical (COOH) heads the list and ethers, aldehydes, and ketones are intermediate.

Stereoisomerism

Where the carbon atoms are linked by double bonds, rotation of the kind exhibited by chain and position isomerism is not possible. In this case isomerism can occur geometrically. For example, dichloroethene which has a double bond may occur in a *cis* form (from the Latin *cis*, on the near side) which indicates that the chlorine atoms are on

the same side of the molecule, and a *trans* form (from the Latin *trans*, on the far side) which indicates that the atoms are diagonally opposed across the double bond, i.e.

cis-dichlorethene   *trans*-dichloroethene

The third class of isomerism is optical isomerism. In this the molecule of one is in one form but the molecule of the other is laterally inverted as in a mirror image. Using the instrument known as a *polarimeter* it can be shown that one isomer has the effect of twisting the plane of light shone through it to the right while its isomer twists to the left. These optically active forms are known as the *d*-form (*dextro* or right rotating) and the *l*-form (*laevo* or left rotating). When the isomers are mixed in equal proportions the rotating effect is cancelled out to give an optically inactive or *racemic* form (from the Latin *racemus* = a bunch of grapes, because the mother liquid of fermented grape juice exhibits this characteristic). The practical importance of this phenomenon can be illustrated by the ability of yeast to convert *d*-grape sugar to alcohol and its powerlessness to affect the *l*-compound.

Carbohydrates

These are an important source of energy for living organisms as well as a means by which chemical energy can be stored. The name originally indicated the belief that compounds of this group could be represented as hydrates of carbon of general formula $C_x(H_2O)_y$, but it is now realised that many important carbohydrates do not have the required 2 to 1 hydrogen to oxygen ratio whilst other compounds which conform to this structure, such as methanal (formaldehyde) (CH_2O) and ethanoic acid (acetic acid) $(C_2H_4O_2)$ are obviously not of this group. Further, other carbohydrates contain sulfur and nitrogen as important constituents. Carbohydrates can be defined as polyhydroxy aldehydes or ketones or as a substance which yield these compounds on hydrolysis. Glucose and fructose (both of general formula $C_6H_{12}O_6$) are typical examples, respectively of an 'aldose' and a 'ketose', e.g.

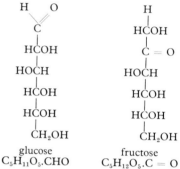

glucose $C_5H_{11}O_5.CHO$

fructose $C_5H_{12}O_5.C = O$

COMMON ORGANIC COMPOUNDS		
Common Name	*Recommended Name*	*Formula*
Acetaldehyde	Ethanal	$CH_3.CHO$
Acetic acid	Ethanoic acid	$CH_3.COOH$
Acetone	Propanone	$CH_3.CO.CH_3$
Acetylene	Ethyne	$CH\equiv CH$
Alcohol (ethyl)	Ethanol	$CH_3.CH_2.OH$
Alcohol (wood)	Methanol	$CH_3.OH$
Amyl acetate	Pentyl ethanoate	$CH_3.COO.C_5H_{11}$
Aniline	Phenylamine	$C_6H_5.NH_2$
Anthracene	no change	$C_{14}H_{10}$
Ascorbic acid (Vitamin C)	no change	$O.CO.C(OH)=C(OH).CH.CHOH.CH_2OH$
Aspirin	Acetyl o-salicylic acid	$CH_3.COO.C_6H_4.COOH$
Aspirin (soluble)	Calcium salt of acetyl o-salicylic acid	$(CH_3.COO.C_6H_4.COO)_2Ca.2H_2O$
Benzaldehyde	Benzenecarbaldehyde	$C_6H_5.CHO$
Benzene	no change	C_6H_6
Benzoic acid	Benzenecarboxylic acid	$C_6H_5.COOH$
Bromoform	Tribromomethane	$CHBr_3$
Butane	no change	C_4H_{10}
Butylene	Butene	C_4H_8
Camphor	no change	$CO.CH_2.CH[C(CH_3)_2].(CH_2)_2.C.CH_3$
Carbon tetrachloride	Tetrachloromethane	CCl_4
Celluloid	Poly (cellulose nitrate)	$[—C_7H_9O_2(OH)(ONO_2)_2—]_n$
Chloroform	Trichloromethane	$CHCl_3$
Citric acid	2-hydroxypropane-1,2,3-tricarboxylic acid	$C(OH)(COOH)(CH_2.COOH)_2.H_2O$
Cyanogen	no change	NC.CN
Cyclohexane	no change	$CH_2.(CH_2)_4.CH_2$
Decane	no change	$C_{10}H_{22}$
Dimethylglyoxime	Butanedione dioxime	$(CH_3.C=N.OH)_2$
Diphenylamine	no change	$(C_6H_5)_2.NH$
Ethane	no change	C_2H_6
Ether (diethyl)	Ethoxyethane	$(CH_3.CH_2)_2O$
Ether (dimethyl)	Methoxymethane	$(CH_3)_2O$
Ethylene	Ethene	$CH_2=CH_2$
Ethyl mercaptan	Ethanethiol	$CH_3.CH_2SH$
Formaldehyde (Formalin)	Methanal	H.CHO
Formic acid	Methanoic acid	H.COOH
Fructose (Fruit Sugar)	no change	$O.CH_2(CHOH)_3C(OH).CH_2OH$
Glucose (Dextrose or Grape Sugar)	no change	$O.(CHOH)_4.CH.CH_2OH$
Glycerine (Glycerol)	Propane-1,2,3-triol	$CH_2OH.CHOH.CH_2OH$
Glycol	Ethane-1,2-diol	$CH_2OH.CH_2OH$
Heptane	no change	C_7H_{16}
Hexane	no change	C_6H_{14}
Indigo	Indigotin	$NH.C_6H_4.CO.C=C.CO.C_6H_4.NH$
Ketone, diethyl	Pentan-3-one	$(CH_3.CH_2)_2CO$
Ketone, ethylmethyl	Butanone	$CH_3.CH_2.CO.CH_3$
Lactic acid	2-hydroxypropanoic acid	$CH_3.CHOH.COOH$
Lactose (Milk Sugar)	no change	$C_{12}H_{22}O_{11}.H_2O$
Lead, tetraethyl	Tetraethyl lead (IV)	$(CH_3.CH_2)_4Pb$
Maltose (Malt Sugar)	no change	$C_{12}H_{22}O_{11}.H_2O$
Melamine	Tricyanodiamide	$NH_2.C=N.C(NH_2)=N.C(NH_2)=N$
Methane (Marsh Gas)	no change	CH_4
Mustard Gas	Dichlorodiethyl sulfide	$(ClCH_2.CH_2)_2S$
Naphthalene	no change	$C_{10}H_8$
Naphthol	Naphthalenol	$C_{10}H_7.OH$
Neoprene	Poly (2-chlorobuta-1,3-diene)	$[—CH_2.C(Cl)=CH.CH_2—]_n$
Nitroglycerine	Propane-1,2,3-triyl trinitrate	$(O_2N.O)_3C_3H_5$
Nonane	no change	C_9H_{20}

Continued over page

Carbohydrates are defined by the number of carbon atoms in the molecule using the usual multiplying affixes, i.e. tetrose for 4 carbon atoms, pentose for 5, hexose for 6, etc. They are divided into two main groups known as sugars and polysaccharides, where the former is subdivided into monosaccharides of general formula $C_nH_{2n}O_n$ (where $n = 2$ to 10) which cannot be hydrolysed into smaller molecules, and oligosaccharides such as disaccharides ($C_{12}H_{22}O_{11}$), trisaccharides ($C_{18}H_{32}O_{16}$), and tetrasaccharides ($C_{24}H_{42}O_{21}$) which yield two, three, and four monosaccharide molecules respectively on hydrolysis.

The polysaccharides yield a large number of monosaccharides on hydrolysis and have molecular weights ranging from thousands to several million. The most widely spread polysaccharides are of the general formula $(C_6H_{10}O_5)_n$ and include *starch*, which occurs in all green plants and is obtained from maize, wheat, barley, rice and potatoes, and from which dextrins are produced by boiling with water under pressure; *glycogen*, which is the reserve carbohydrate of animals and is often known as 'animal starch'; and *cellulose*, the main constituent of the cell walls of plants.

Of the naturally-occurring sugars (which are all optically active), the most familiar monosaccharides are the dextrorotary (D+) aldohexose *glucose* (dextrose or grape sugar) and the laevorotary (D—) ketohexose *fructose* (laevulose or fruit sugar), both of formula $C_6H_{12}O_6$.

The most important disaccharides are those of the formula $C_{12}H_{22}O_{11}$ and include *sucrose* (cane sugar or beet sugar) obtained from sugar cane or sugar beet after chemical treatment; *maltose* (malt sugar) produced by the action of malt on starch; and *lactose* (milk sugar) which occurs naturally in the milk of all animals.

Common Organic Compounds, continued

Name		Formula
Nylon	no change	$[—CO.(CH_2)_4.CO.NH.(CH_2)_6.NH—]_n$
Octane	no change	C_8H_{18}
Oxalic acid	Ethanedioic acid	$(COOH)_2$
Pentane	no change	C_5H_{12}
Phenol (Carbolic Acid)	no change	$C_6H_5.OH$
Phenolphthalein	no change	$O.CO.C_6H_4.C(C_6H_4.OH)_2$
Phosgene	Carbonyl chloride	$COCl_2$
Phthalic acid	Benzene-1,2-dicarboxylic acid	$C_6H_4(COOH)_2$
Picric acid	2,4,6-trinitrophenol	$(NO_2)_3.C_6H_2.OH$
Polystyrene	Poly (phenylethene)	$[—CH(C_6H_5).CH_2—]_n$
PTFE (Polytetrafluoroethylene) (Teflon)	Poly (tetrafluoroethene)	$[—CF_2.CF_2—]_n$
Polythene	Poly (ethene)	$[—CH_2.CH_2—]_n$
PVC (Polyvinyl chloride)	Poly (chloroethene)	$[—CH_2.CHCl—]_n$
Propane	no change	C_3H_6
Propionic acid	Propanoic acid	$CH_3.CH_2.COOH$
Propylene	Propene	C_3H_6
Prussic acid	Hydrocyanic acid	$HN=CH.NC$
Pyridine	no change	C_6H_5N
Rayon (Viscose)	Sodium cellulose xanthates	$S=C(OR).SNa$ (R = cellulose)
Rochelle Salt	Potassium sodium 2,3-dihydroxy butanedioate	$COOK.(CHOH)_2COONa.4H_2O$
Saccharin (soluble)	Sodium salt of o-sulfobenzoicimide	$CO.C_6H_4.SO_2.NNa.2H_2O$
Salicylic acid	2-hydroxybenzenecarboxylic acid	$C_6H_4(OH).COOH$
Soap	Sodium or potassium salts of high molecular weight fatty acids such as palmitic acid (hexadecanoic acid) ($C_{15}H_{31}.COOH$) and stearic acid (octadecanoic acid) ($C_{17}H_{35}.COOH$)	$C_{15}H_{31}.COOR$ or $C_{17}H_{35}.COOR$ where R = Na or K
Succinic acid	Butanedioic acid	$(CH_2.COOH)_2$
Sucrose (Cane Sugar or Beet Sugar)	no change	$C_{12}H_{22}O_{11}$
Tartaric acid	2,3-dihydroxybutanedioic acid	$(CHOH.COOH)_2$
Toluene	Methylbenzene	$C_6H_5.CH_3$
Trichloroethylene	Trichloroethene	$ClHC=CCl_2$
TNT (Trinitrotoluene)	Methyl-2,4,6-nitrobenzene	$(NO_2)_3.C_6H_2.CH_3$
Urea	Carbamide	$NH_2.CO.NH_2$
Valeric acid	Pentanoic acid	$CH_3.CH_2.CH_2.CH_2.COOH$
Xylene	Dimethylbenzene	$C_6H_5(NH_3)_2$

Alloys Mixtures or compounds of a metal with one or more other metal or non-metal

Name	Composition expressed as percentages	Properties and uses
Alnico	Fe 60, Ni 20, Al 10, Co 10	Permanent magnet
Babbit Metal	Sn (predominates), Sb, Cu (+Pb)	Used for bearings, anti-friction metal
Brass	Cu with 20–35 Zn	Decorative, condenser tubes
Bronze	Cu with 5–8 Sn	Primitive tools, coinage
Carboloy	W_2C_3, with 10 Co	Very hard alloy, grinding tools
Cast Iron	Impure Fe, C up to $4\frac{1}{2}$ with Mn, P, Si and S traces	Decorative work, weights
Cupronickel	Cu 80, Ni 20 (coinage 75–25)	Marine condenser tubes, Imperial 'silver' coinage
Delta Metal	Cu 55–60, Zn c. 40, Fe 2–4	Bearings, marine propellers
Dow Metal	Al, Mg	Aircraft and car parts
Dental Alloy	Ag_3, Sn ground with Hg	Tooth fillings
Duralumin	Al 93–$95\frac{1}{2}$, Cu $3\frac{1}{2}$–$5\frac{1}{2}$, Mn $\frac{1}{4}$–$\frac{3}{4}$, Mg $\frac{1}{4}$–$\frac{3}{4}$	Aircraft frames
Dutch Metal	Cu with 30–35 Zn	Bronze in 'gold' leaf form
E-Alloy	Al 78, Zn 20, Cu 2; or Al 96, Zn 2, Cu 2	Castings
Electrum	Au with 15–45 Ag	Coinage (ancient times)
Frary Metal	Pb 97, Ba 2, Ca 1	Bearings
German Metal	Cu 56–65, Zn 24–28, Ni 7–20	Metal fittings, metal ware (often electroplated)
Gun Metal	Cu 88, Sn 8–10, Zn 2–4	Ordnance
Hiduminium	Al with small Cu, Ni, Mg, Si additions	Aircraft parts
Illium	Complex of Co, Cr, Fe, Mn, Mb, Ni and W	Acid resistant
Invar	Fe 64, Ni 35, some C and Mn	Very low expandibility, pendulum rods, steel tape measures
Jae Metal	Ni 70, Cu 30	Shunts on magnetic instruments
Lipowitz's Alloy	Bi 50, Pb 27, Sn 13, Cd 10	Very low melting point (60 °C)
Magnolia Metal	Pb 80, Sb 15, Sn 5	Medium duty bearings
Monel Metal	Ni 68, Cu $29\frac{1}{2}$, Fe $1\frac{1}{4}$, Mn $1\frac{1}{4}$	Resistant to steam corrosion
Muntz Metal	Cu 60, Zn 40	Resistant to sea-water corrosion
Nichrome	Ni 60, Fe 20, Cr 20	Filament wires
Nickel Silver	Cu 55–63, Ni 10–30, Zn 7–35	Electroplated articles, hence EPNS
Nimonic 80	Ni with Cr 19–22, Fe up to 5, Ti $1\frac{1}{2}$–3, Al $\frac{1}{2}$–$1\frac{1}{2}$, Mn < 1, C < 0.1	Non-creep at high temperatures gas turbine rotor blades
Pewter	Sn 80, Pb 20, trace of Sb. Tu and Bi (traces)	Modern pewter Pb replaced by Sb.
Permalloy	Ni 77.5, Fe 22.5 (sometimes with traces of Co, Cr, Cu and Mo)	Magnetic properties, transformers, submarine cable parts
Phosphorbronze	Cu 90, Sn $9\frac{1}{2}$, P $\frac{1}{2}$	Castings, bearings and resilient strip
Pinchbeck	Cu 89–93, Zn 7–11	Imitation gold, jewellery
'Silver' Alloy	Hg-Sn amalgam	'Silver' backing for mirrors. Powdered Al also now used

Continued

Solder	Sn 66⅔, Pb 33⅓	Plumbing
Speculum	Cu 60–70, Sn 30–40	High polish surfaces, plating
Stainless Steel	Fe 78–86, Cr 12–20, Ni 2	Corrosion resistant culinary, sterile vessels, decorative
Steel	Essentially Fe with C½–1½ with special purpose additives of Cr, Mn, Mb, Ni, Si, Al, Cu, Co, Ti, W, V	Multifarious
Stellite	Co 43, Cr 43, W 14 *et al.*	Surgical and other cutting tools
Tombac	Cu 71–90, Zn 10–29	Condenser tubes, cartridge cases
Type Metal	Pb 80–86, Sb 11–20, Sn 3–11	Lino-, mono- and stereotype fonts
White Gold	Au with Ni	Platinum substitute
Woods Metal	Bi 50, Pb 25, Sn 12½, Cd 12½	Low melting point, fire sprinklers
X-40	Co 55, Cr 25, Ni 9, W 7, C ½, Fe ½, traces of Mn, Si	Non-creep at high temperatures, gas turbine rotor blades
Y-Alloy	Al 93, Cu 4, Ni 2, Mn 1	
Yellow Metal	alternative name for Muntz metal, *q.v.*	

Explosives

Name	Introduced	Description	Inventor
Gun powder	c. 965	Charcoal 15%, sulphur 10%, potassium nitrate 75%	Sung dynasty of China (Europe c. 1280)
Mercuric fulminate	1799	Detonating agent $Hg(ONC)_2$	(Germany)
Gun cotton	1845	Nitro cellulose	Schonbein
Nitroglycerin	1846	Glyceryl trinitrate	A Sobrero (Italy)
TNT	1863	Trinitrotoluene $C_7H_5O_6N_3$	Wilbrand
Dynamite	1866	Nitroglycerin absorbed in kieselguhr or charcoal	A Nobel (Sweden)
Gelignite	1878	Trinitrocellulose plus nitroglycerin, wood pulp and potassium nitrate	—
Lyddite	1882	Picric acid, trinitrophenol	Woulfe (1771)
Cordite	1888	Gelignite plasticised with acetone solvent	—
Lox (Liquid oxygen)	1895	Porous combustible, e.g. charcoal soaked in liquid oxygen	Linde
RDX	1899	Cyclotrimethylenetrinitramine	Henning
PETN	1901	Pentaergthritol tetranitrate $C_5H_8N_9O_{12}$	Vignon and Gerin
Amatol	1916	Ammonium nitrate (4 pts) to 1 pt TNT	—
Torpex	1939	RDX plus TNT with aluminium powder	Admiralty research
Atomic fission	1945 (16 July)	Fission of uranium isotope 235	E Fermi (USA)
Atomic fusion	1952 (1 Nov.)	Hydrogen–helium fusion triggered by U_{235} or plutonium fission	K Fuchs and J von Neumann

An atom bomb of the "Littleboy" type, which was detonated over Hiroshima. (Copyright Camera Press)

Mathematics

Mensuration

Triangle
area $= \frac{1}{2}ah$

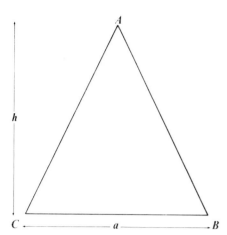

Ellipse
area $= \pi ab$

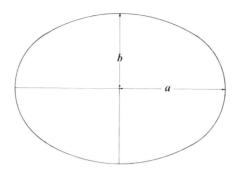

Cone
volume $= \frac{1}{3}\pi r^2 h$
surface area $= \pi rl$

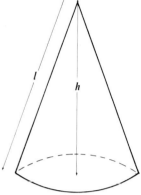

Trapezium
area $= \frac{1}{2}(m + n)h$

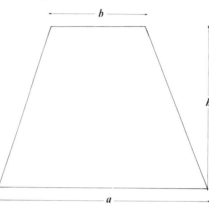

Cylinder
volume $= \pi r^2 h$
curved surface area $= 2\pi rh$
total surface area $= 2\pi rh + 2\pi r^2$
$\qquad\qquad\qquad = 2\pi r(h + r)$

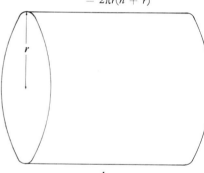

Square
area $= a^2$

Cube
volume $= a^3$
surface area $= 6a^2$

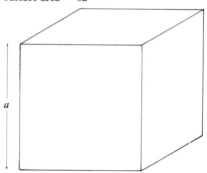

Pyramid
volume $= \frac{1}{3}a^2 h$
surface area $= a^2 + 2la$

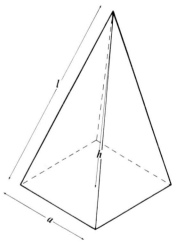

Circle
$d = 2r$
circumference $= 2\pi r$
area $= \pi r^2$

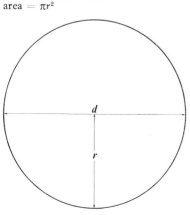

Sphere
volume $= \frac{4}{3}\pi r^3$
surface area $= 4\pi r^2$

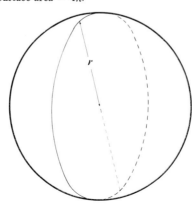

Regular polygons
area $= \frac{1}{4}na^2 \cot(180/n)$
where n is the number of sides and a the
length of one side

	number of sides	area
pentagon	5	$1{\cdot}721a^2$
hexagon	6	$2{\cdot}598a^2$
heptagon	7	$3{\cdot}634a^2$
octagon	8	$4{\cdot}829a^2$

Mathematical symbols

$=$	equal to
$\neq$	not equal to
$\equiv$	identically equal to
$>$	greater than (or remainder)
$<$	less than
$\not>$	not greater than
$\not<$	not less than
$\geqslant$	equal to or greater than
$\leqslant$	equal to or less than
$\simeq$	approximately equal to
$+$	plus
$-$	minus
$\pm$	plus or minus
$\times$	multiplication (times)
$\div$	divided by
( ) [ ] { }	brackets, square brackets, enveloping brackets
$\parallel$	parallel
$\nparallel$	not parallel
$\#$	numbers to follow (USA)
$\%$	per cent(um) (hundred)
$\%_0$	per mille (thousand)
$\propto$	varies with
∞	infinity
$r!$	factorial r
r or $\lfloor r$	
$\sqrt{}$	square root
$^n\sqrt{}$	nth root
r^n	r to the power n
$\triangle$	triangle or increment
or $\sim$	difference
Σ	summation
$\int$	integration sign
$^\circ$ $'$ $''$	degree, minute second ($1^\circ = 60'$, $1' = 60''$)
$\rightarrow$	appropriate limit of
$\therefore$	therefore
$\because$	because
$\varnothing$	diameter

Algebra

$x^m \times x^n = x^{m+n}$
$x^m \div x^n = x^{m-n}$
$(x^m)^n = x^{mn}$

$y = \log_n x$ means $x = n^y$
$\log(xy) = \log x + \log y$
$\log(x/y) = \log x - \log y$
$\log x^n = n \log x$
$\log(^n\sqrt{x}) = \dfrac{1}{n} \log x$

$\log_m x = \log_n x \times \log_m n$
so that
$\log_{10} x = \log_e x \times \log_{10} e$
$\qquad = 0.4343 \log_e x$

$x^2 - a^2 = (x + a)(x - a)$
$x^3 \pm a^3 = (x \pm a)(x^2 \mp ax + a^2)$
$(x \pm a)^2 = x^2 \pm 2ax + a^2$
$(x \pm a)^3 = x^3 \pm 3x^2a + 3xa^2 \pm a^3$
$(x + a)^n = {}_nC_0 x^n + {}_nC_1 x^{n-1}a$
$\qquad + {}_nC_2 x^{n-2}a^2 + \cdots$
$\qquad + {}_nC_r x^{n-r}a^r + \cdots + {}_nC_n a^n$
where ${}_nC_r = n!/(n - r)!r!$ and
$\qquad n! = n(n - 1)(n - 2)\ldots3.2.1$
Note that $0! = 1$.

The roots of the quadratic equation
$ax^2 + bx + c = 0$
are $x = \dfrac{-b \pm \sqrt{(b^2 - 4ac)}}{2a}$
If the roots are α and β then
$\alpha + \beta = -(b/a)$
and $\alpha\beta = c/a$

The sum to n terms of the arithmetic series
$a, a + d, a + 2d, \ldots$
is $S_n = \frac{1}{2}n[2a + (n - 1)d]$
The sum to n terms of the geometric series
$a, ar, ar^2, \ldots$
is $S_n = \dfrac{a(1 - r^n)}{1 - r}$, where $r \neq 1$
$\qquad = na$, where $r = 1$

Trigonometry

Trigonometry (from the Greek *trigonon*, triangle; *metria*, measurement) as a science may be traced back to work attributed to Hipparchus (*fl.* 150 BC), the Greek astronomer. Further contributions were made in India, Iraq, Italy and Persia between AD 800 and 1400. The six ratios received their standard names *c.* 1550. The earliest complete trigonometrical tables were published by Rhaeticus in 1596. The word trigonometry in English dates from 1614.

The division of the circle into 360 degrees dates from Ptolemy (AD 85–165) but at that time it was the circumference which was divided into 360 equal arcs. The sexagesimal sub-divisions of the degree are named after the latin *pars minuta prima* for the primary sub-division into 1/60th parts of a degree and *pars minuta secunda* for a second sub-division into 1/3600th parts of a degree, hence the modern terms minute $'$ and second $''$. The systematic use of decimals *c.* 1580 and of negative numbers *c.* 1610 greatly facilitated the science.

Trigonometry depends upon the fact that the corresponding sides of equiangular triangles are proportional. The three principal ratios are:
The sine (sin) of an angle
$$= \frac{\text{side opposite angle}}{\text{hypotenuse}}$$
The cosine (cos) of an angle
$$= \frac{\text{side adjacent to angle}}{\text{hypotenuse}}$$
The tangent (tan) of an angle
$$= \frac{\text{side opposite angle}}{\text{side adjacent to angle}}$$

Mnemonics
Opposite over Adjacent means Tangent (O/AMT)—Old and Ancient Motor Transport
Opposite over Hypotenuse means Sine (O/HMS)—On Her Majesty's Service
Adjacent over Hypotenuse means Cosine (A/HMC)—Algebra Helps Mental Clarity

Formulae
$\sin(A \pm B) = \sin A \cos B \pm \sin B \cos A$
$\cos(A \pm B) = \cos A \cos B \mp \sin A \sin B$
$\tan(A \pm B) = \dfrac{\tan A \pm \tan B}{1 \mp \tan A \tan B}$

$\sin A \pm \sin B$
$\qquad = 2 \sin\left(\dfrac{A \pm B}{2}\right) \cos\left(\dfrac{A \mp B}{2}\right)$
$\cos A + \cos B$
$\qquad = 2 \cos\left(\dfrac{B - A}{2}\right) \cos\left(\dfrac{B + A}{2}\right)$
$\cos A - \cos B$
$\qquad = 2 \sin\left(\dfrac{B - A}{2}\right) \sin\left(\dfrac{B + A}{2}\right)$

$\sin 2A = 2 \sin A \cos A$
$\cos 2A = \cos^2 A - \sin^2 A = 2\cos^2 A - 1$
$\qquad = 1 - 2\sin^2 A$

$\sin^2 A + \cos^2 A = 1$ (Pythagoras)
$\tan^2 A = \sec^2 A - 1$
$\cot^2 A = \mathrm{cosec}^2 A - 1$

Constants

$\pi = 3.14159\ldots \qquad e = 2.71828\ldots$
$\dfrac{1}{\pi} = 0.31831\ldots \qquad \log_{10} e = 0.43429\ldots$
$\log_{10} \pi = 0.49715\ldots$

In the triangle:

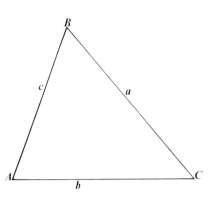

The sine rule:
$$\frac{a}{\sin A} = \frac{b}{\sin B} = \frac{c}{\sin C} = 2R$$
where R is the radius of the circumscribing circle.

$a^2 = b^2 + c^2 - 2bc \cos A$
$b^2 = c^2 + a^2 - 2ca \cos B$
$c^2 = a^2 + b^2 - 2ab \cos C$
and
$a = b \cos C + c \cos B$
$b = c \cos A + a \cos C$
$c = a \cos B + b \cos A$
If $s = \frac{1}{2}(a + b + c)$ then area of triangle
$\qquad = \sqrt{[s(s - a)(s - b)(s - c)]}$
$\qquad = \frac{1}{2}ab \sin C$

The Radian

The radian is the unit of angle being the angle subtended at the centre of a circle by an arc equal in length to the radius. Thus 2π radians correspond to 360° and so
$$1 \text{ radian} = \frac{360}{2\pi} \text{ degrees} = 57.3^\circ$$

Ratios greater than 90°

The sign of the three principal trigonometric ratios is shown in the accompanying diagram for the four quadrants. Those ratios which are *positive* are named in the given quadrant, the others being negative.

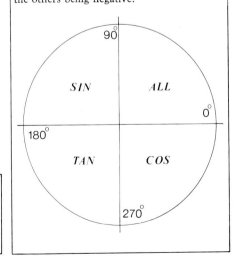

Calculus

y	$\dfrac{dy}{dx}$	$\displaystyle\int y\,dx$
x^n	nx^{n-1}	$\dfrac{x^{n+1}}{n+1} + C\ (n \neq -1)$
x^{-1}	$-x^{-2}$	$\log_e x + C$
e^{ax}	ae^{ax}	$\dfrac{1}{a}e^{ax} + C$
a^x	$a^x \log_e a$	$\dfrac{a^x}{\log_e a} + C$
$\log_e x$	$\dfrac{1}{x}$	$x(\log_e x - 1) + C$
$\sin ax$	$a \cos ax$	$-\dfrac{1}{a}\cos ax + C$
$\cos ax$	$-a \sin ax$	$\dfrac{1}{a}\sin ax + C$
$\tan ax$	$a \sec^2 ax$	$\dfrac{1}{a}\log_e \sec ax + C$
$\sinh ax$	$a \cosh ax$	$\dfrac{1}{a}\cosh ax + C$
$\cosh ax$	$a \sinh ax$	$\dfrac{1}{a}\sinh ax + C$
$\tanh ax$	$a \,\mathrm{sech}\, ax$	$\dfrac{1}{a}\log_e (\cosh x) + C$

Where u, v are functions of x:

if $y = uv$

then $\dfrac{dy}{dx} = u\dfrac{dv}{dx} + v\dfrac{du}{dx};$

if $y = \dfrac{u}{v}$

then $\dfrac{dy}{dx} = \dfrac{v\dfrac{du}{dx} - u\dfrac{dv}{dx}}{v^2}$

$\displaystyle\int u\dfrac{dv}{dx}\,dx = uv - \int v\dfrac{du}{dx}\,dx$

Series

Maclaurin's

$f(x) = f(0) + xf'(0) + \dfrac{x^2}{2!}f''(0)$
$+ \dfrac{x^3}{3!}f'''(0) + \cdots$

Taylor's

$f(x + h) = f(h) + xf'(h) + \dfrac{x^2}{2!}f''(h)$
$+ \dfrac{x^3}{3!}f'''(h) + \cdots$

$e^x = 1 + x + \dfrac{x^2}{2!} + \dfrac{x^3}{3!} + \cdots$

$\sin x = x - \dfrac{x^3}{3!} + \dfrac{x^5}{5!} - \dfrac{x^7}{7!} + \cdots$

$\cos x = 1 - \dfrac{x^2}{2!} + \dfrac{x^4}{4!} - \dfrac{x^6}{6!} + \cdots$

$\sinh x = x + \dfrac{x^3}{3!} + \dfrac{x^5}{5!} + \dfrac{x^7}{7!} + \cdots$

$\cosh x = 1 + \dfrac{x^2}{2!} + \dfrac{x^4}{4!} + \dfrac{x^6}{6!} + \cdots$

Odds on perfect deals

The number of possible hands with four players using a full pack of 52 cards is $\dfrac{52!}{(39!)(13!)}$ or 635 013 559 600. Thus the odds against picking up a specific complete suit are 635 013 559 599 to 1 or *any* complete suit 158 753 389 899 to 1.

The number of possible deals is $\dfrac{52!}{(13!)^4(4!)}$ or 2 235 197 406 895 366 368 301 560 000 or roughly $2 \cdot 23 \times 10^{27}$. A complete suit is thus to be expected once in every 39 688 347 497 deals.

Cases throughout the world of single complete suits are in practice reported about once per year. This being so, cases of two players receiving complete suits could be expected with the present volume of card playing once every 2000 million years and this has only once been recorded. Cases of all four players picking up complete suits might be expected once in 56 000 billion years. This latter occurrence was reported in New Zealand on 8 July 1958, in Illinois, USA, on 9 Feb. 1963, again in Illinois on 30 Mar. 1963 and again 3 days later in Greybull, Wyoming. This is so unlikely, not merely to strain credulity, but to be virtually certain evidence of rigged shuffling or hoaxing.

Sets

If A is a set and x is an element of (belongs to) A then this is written:

$x \in A$

The symbol $\in$ is used for 'is an element of'. The negation is:

$x \notin A$

x is not an element of A.

Subsets

Set B is a *subset* of set A if every element of B is an element of A. This is denoted

$B \subseteq A$

Sometimes the symbol $\subset$ is used instead of $\subseteq$

Note that a set A is always a subset of itself:

$A \subseteq A$

Intersection

The *intersection* of sets A and B is denoted:

$A \cap B$

and is the set of all elements which belong to both A and B.

If sets A, B have no element in common they are called *disjoint* sets, in which case:

$A \cap B = \varnothing$

Where $\varnothing$ is the *empty set* or *null set*, i.e. the set with no elements.

Union

The union of sets A, B is denoted

$A \cup B$

and is the set of *all* the elements of A together with *all* the elements of B.

For all sets A, B, C:

$A \cap B = B \cap A$

$A \cup B = B \cup A$

$A \cap (B \cup C) = (A \cup B) \cup (A \cap C)$

Properties of number systems

If n, a, b, c are any real or complex number then

$a + b = b + a$
Addition is *commutative*

$a + (b + c) = (a + b) + c$
and *associative*

$a \times b = b \times a$
Multiplication is *commutative*

$a \times (b \times c) = (a \times b) \times c$
and *associative*

$n \times (a + b) = (n \times a) + (n \times b)$
Multiplication is *distributive* over addition

Binary system

The numerical notation in ordinary use is the decimal or denary system with its ten symbols: 0, 1, 2, 3, 4, 5, 6, 7, 8 and 9.

The Imperial system of weights and measures utilises several other systems, viz. 3 ft to 1 yd (ternary), 12 in to 1 ft (duodenary), 20 fluid oz to 1 pint (vigesimal), etc. The most primitive notation is the unitary system of one symbol as used for instance by a cricket scorer.

Because electric switches have two essential positions, 'on' or 'off', the binary system is ideally suited to the programming of computers and is being used increasingly.

To convert the denary number, say 17, to its binary form it is necessary to divide successively through by two, recording the remainders which can only be 1 or 0 thus:
$2\,\overline{\smash{)}17} = 8 > 1$ which $\div 2 = 4 > 0$ which $\div 2 = 2 > 0$ which $\div 2 = 1 > 0$, thus 17 (decimal) is 10001 binary.

This represents 1×2^4 which is 16, 0×2^3, 0×2^2, 0×2^1 and 1×2^0 which is 1, giving a total of 17.

To convert a binary number to its decimal or denary form, it is simplest to regard the rightermost column as the 2^0 column, thence reading to the left 2^1, 2^2, 2^3, 2^4, etc. columns.

Thus 11101 reads $1 \times 2^4 = 16$, $+1 \times 2^3 = 8$, $+1 \times 2^2 = 4$, $+0 \times 2^1 = 0$, $+1 \times 2^0 = 1$, i.e. 29.

A binary conversion scale thus reads:

Denary	Binary	Denary	Binary
1	1	16	10000
2	10	17	10001
3	11	18	10010
4	100	19	10011
5	101	20	10100
6	110	32	100000
7	111	64	1000000
8	1000	100	1100100
9	1001	128	10000000
10	1010	144	10010000
11	1011	150	10010110
12	1100	200	11001000
13	1101	250	11111010
14	1110	500	111110100
15	1111	1000	1111101000

Fractions are also recorded in the binary notation, thus:

Denary	Binary
$\cdot 5$	$= \cdot 1$
$\cdot 25$	$= \cdot 01$
$\cdot 125$	$= \cdot 001$
$\cdot 0625$	$= \cdot 0001$
$\cdot 03125$	$= \cdot 00001$
$\cdot 015625$	$= \cdot 000001$

Thus the binary fraction $\cdot 10011$ is $\cdot 5 + 0 + 0 + \cdot 0625 + 0 \cdot 03125 = \cdot 59375$.

Media and Communications

The Cinema
The milestones of the cinema industry are the first public showing in the Hotel Scribe, Boulevard des Capucines, Paris, on 28 Dec. 1895; and the earliest sound film motion picture demonstrated in New York City on 13 Mar. 1923.

The leading countries in the production of full-length films (1972 figures unless otherwise indicated) are:

India	414
Japan	390
Italy	294
USA	280[1]
USSR	234
Philippines	208[2]
France	169
South Korea	143
Greece	142
Hong Kong	133[3]
Spain	103
Mexico	98

The United Kingdom produced 89 in the year ending 31 Mar. 1972.

[1] 1970 data.
[2] 1965 data.
[3] Year ending 31 Mar. 1972.

Number of cinemas
These figures for 1972 include, where known, mobile cinemas, drive-in cinemas and those only used in certain seasons.

USSR	156 300
USA	18 320[1]
China	12 000[2]
Italy	11 843
Rumania	6213
Spain	6064
India	4787
France	4218
Hungary	3697
Czechoslovakia	3469
East Germany	3206
Brazil	3196[3]

The United Kingdom had 1450, Canada—1734[1], Australia—1217, and New Zealand—244.

[1] 1970 data. [2] 1960 data. [3] 1967 data.

Cinema attendances
The highest attendances, by country, are (1972 data unless otherwise indicated):

USSR	4 569 000 000
China	4 000 000 000 (1960)
India	3 490 000 000
USA	920 600 000 (1970)
Italy	555 000 000
Spain	293 100 000

Comparative figures include the United Kingdom—156 600 000 (by 1974 it was 143 500 000); Canada—92 300 000 (1970); Australia—32 000 000; and New Zealand—14 300 000.

But the highest attendances per capita per annum are: Brunei 20·4; USSR 18·5; Lebanon (1970) 18·0 and Hong Kong 17·5. By comparison the United Kingdom was 2·8 and Canada 4·3.

Radio
The first advertised broadcast was on 24 Dec. 1906 from Brant Rock, Mass., USA. The first regular broadcast entertainment in the United Kingdom started on 14 Feb. 1922.

The estimated world total of radio sets in 1974 was 987 000 000. In the United States there were 383 000 000 sets, and in the USSR the number was 110 300 000. The next countries in order were: Japan, 87 000 000; China, 50 000 000; the United Kingdom, 39 100 000; and West Germany 20 767 000. Other figures include: Canada with 21 100 000; Australia, 12 300 000; and New Zealand, 2 700 000.

In 1974 the United States had an ownership ratio of 1·8 sets per inhabitant; the next highest was Canada with 0·9 sets per inhabitant.

Television
The estimated world total of television receivers in 1974 was 358 000 000. Transmissions were receivable in 127 countries in 1972.

Television receivers by country (1974 data):

USA	112 000 000
USSR	50 000 000
Japan	25 500 000
West Germany	18 730 000
United Kingdom	17 294 000[1]
France	12 335 000
Italy	11 380 000
Brazil	8 650 000
Canada	8 513 000
Spain	6 510 000
Poland	6 142 000

Other countries include: Australia, 3 600 000 and New Zealand, 760 847.

(Of large countries with television China has only 750 000 receivers and India, 60 000).

[1] By December 1975, 17 584 000.

In the United Kingdom colour receivers constituted only 7·8 per cent of the total in 1971, but by November 1975 the figure had risen to 46·1 per cent.

Telephones
In 1973 there were 336 297 000 telephones in use in the world.

USA	138 286 000
Japan	38 698 000
United Kingdom	19 095 000
West Germany	17 803 000
USSR	14 261 000[1]
Italy	12 612 000
Canada	11 665 000
France	11 337 000
Spain	5 713 000

Other comparative totals include: Australia—4 659 000 and New Zealand—1 444 000.

[1] Excludes military systems.

The principality of Monaco has the highest availability rate with 82·6 telephones per 100 inhabitants. Comparative figures include 65·7—USA, 52·8—Canada, 47·5—New Zealand, 35·5—Australia, and 34·0—United Kingdom.

United Kingdom National Press
The principal national newspapers in order of circulation are:

Name	Year Established	Circulation (Apr.–Sept. 1975)
Morning Newspapers		
Daily Mirror	1903	3 943 629
The Sun (prior to 1964 The Daily Herald)	1912	3 476 621
Daily Express	1900	2 798 629
Daily Mail (incorporating the News Chronicle)	1896	1 724 515
Daily Telegraph	1855	1 323 730
The Times	1785	315 094
The Guardian	1821	314 868
Financial Times	1888	180 201

Name	Year	Circulation
Sunday Newspapers		
News of the World	1843	5 467 089
Sunday Mirror	1915	4 267 025
The People	1881	4 184 848
Sunday Express	1918	3 726 389
Sunday Times	1822	1 347 691
Sunday Post (Glasgow)	1914	[1] [2]
Sunday Mail (Glasgow)	1919	752 337[1]
Sunday Telegraph	1961	751 858
The Observer	1791	730 832
Evening Newspapers		
Evening News and Star	1881	589 291[3]
Evening Standard	1827	442 535[3]
Media Journals		
Radio Times	1923	3 528 922[1] [4]
TV Times	1955	3 351 164[1] [4]

(*Source:* Audit Bureau of Circulations).
[1] January–June 1975.
[2] Estimated over 1 million.
[3] Monday–Friday issues.
[4] UK and Republic of Ireland only.

World Press
(Source: United Nations Statistical Yearbook 1974—data for 1972 unless otherwise stated).

The total of daily newspapers published in the world is 8375.

Greatest number of daily newspapers

USA	1761
West Germany	1223[1]
India	793
USSR	647[2]
Turkey	433
China	392
Brazil	261[2]
Mexico	216
Japan	172
Argentina	162
Chile	128
Canada	121

United Kingdom, 109; Australia, 62; New Zealand, 40.

[1] Includes 810 general editions.
[2] 1971 data.

Largest total circulation of daily newspapers[1]

USSR	84 953 000
USA	62 510 000
Japan	55 845 000
United Kingdom	29 557 000
West Germany	18 126 000
France	12 160 000[2]
India	8 873 000
Poland	7 553 000
Italy	7 267 000
East Germany	7 236 000
Australia	5 282 000
Canada	5 074 000

In 1970 Sweden had the highest sale rate of 534 per 1000 inhabitants. Other comparable figures (1972 data) include United Kingdom—528; Australia—408, New Zealand—376, and Canada—230.

[1] No data available for China
[2] 1971 data.

EUROPE

European Economic Community (EEC or Common Market) was established by the treaty signed in Rome (the Treaty of Rome) on 25 Mar. 1957 by Belgium, France, West Germany, Luxembourg, Italy and the Netherlands (known as The Six). Denmark, the Irish Republic and the United Kingdom became members on 1 Jan. 1973, having signed the Treaty of Accession to the Community on 22 Jan. 1972. On 25 Sept. 1972 a referendum in Norway rejected membership with a vote of 53·5% in a 77·7% poll.

The object is to weld a complete customs union between The Nine (as was forged by 1 July 1968 between The Six) by 1 July 1977. A common transport and external trade policy and co-ordination of financial, commercial, economic and social policy is a target. Economic and monetary union is scheduled for the end of 1980 and the extension of the Common Agricultural Policy to The Nine by 1 July 1977.

North Atlantic Treaty Organisation —NATO

NATO, an idea first broached by the Secretary of State for External Affairs for Canada on 28 Apr. 1948, came into existence on 4 Apr. 1949 and into force on 24 Aug. 1949 with Belgium, Canada, Denmark, France, Iceland, Italy, Luxembourg, the Netherlands, Norway, Portugal, the United Kingdom and the USA. In February 1952 Greece and Turkey were admitted and West Germany on 5 May 1955 bringing the total of countries to 15. In 1966 France withdrew from NATO's military affairs and the HQ was moved from Paris to Brussels. Greece withdrew her military forces in August 1974.

Organisation for Economic Co-operation and Development (OECD)

Founded as a European body of 30 Sept. 1961 (OEEC) the Organisation after 14 years was reconstituted to embrace other Western countries. It now comprises 24 countries: Australia, Austria, Belgium, Canada, Denmark, Finland, France, Greece, Iceland, Ireland, Italy, Japan, Luxembourg, the Netherlands, New Zealand, Norway, Portugal, Spain, Sweden, Switzerland, Turkey, United Kingdom, USA and West Germany, with Yugoslavia (special status).

Headquarters are in Paris. The aims are to achieve the highest sustainable economic growth and level of employment with a rising standard of living compatible with financial stability.

	West Germany	UK	Italy	France	Netherlands	Belgium	Denmark	Republic of Ireland	Luxembourg
Population	62 041 000	55 969 000	55 361 000	52 507 000	13 541 000	9 770 000	5 050 000	3 086 000	357 000
Area km²	248 577	244 034	301 225	551 000	41 160	30 513	43 069	70 283	2586
Capital	Bonn	London	Rome	Paris	Amsterdam	Brussels	Copenhagen	Dublin	Luxembou
Capital's Pop (million)	·282	7·168	2·800	8·182	1·002	1·069	1·357	·680	·078
Pop Density (per km²)	250	594	184	95	329	322	117	44	138
Av Income per Head (£)	2336	1303	937	1769	1673	1742	2041	819	1829
No of Vehicles	18 282 000	15 407 000	14 625 000	16 600 000	3 550 00	2 586 00	1 502 000	635 234	142 253
Telephone per 1000	287	341	227	217	320	257	278	125	377
TV and Radio per 1000	630	992	435	566	542	619	613	173 (TV only)	784
Currency	1 Deutsche mark = 100 Pfennig	£1 = 100 New Pence	1 Lire = 100 Centesimi	1 Franc = 100 Centimes	1 Guilder or florin = 100 Cents	1 Franc = 100 Centimes	1 Krone = 100 Øre	1 Pound = 100 New Pence	1 Franc = 100 Centim
Merchant Shipping Vessels Owned (grt)	7 980 000	31 566 000	9 322 000	8 835 000	5 501 000	1 215 000	4 250 176	210 000	—
Of Which—Oil Tankers	2 141 000	15 203 000	3 670 000	5 509 000	2 514 000	334 000	2 160 000	5688	—
Crude Steel (tonnes)	53 226 000	22 428 000	23 839 000	27 015 000	5 838 000	16 233 000	535 000	110 000	6 447 000
Housing (Dwellings Completed)	604 000	278 000	181 000	670 000	147 000	61 000	49 000	25 000	2000

European Free Trade Association (EFTA)

With the departure of the United Kingdom and Denmark EFTA comprised six countries viz. Austria, Iceland, Norway, Portugal, Sweden and Switzerland with Finland as an associate member. EFTA was established on 27 Mar. 1961.

The EFTA countries (except Norway) signed a free trade agreement with the EEC on 22 July 1972 and Norway did so on 14 May 1973.

South-East Asia Collective Defence Treaty (Seato)

On 8 Sept. 1954 eight countries (Australia, France, New Zealand, Pakistan, the Philippines, Thailand, United Kingdom and USA) signed a collective defence system on South-East Asia in Manila with the acronym SEATO.

Central Treaty Organisation (Cento)

The Baghdad mutual defence pact between Iraq and Turkey was signed on 24 Feb. 1955. This was joined by the United Kingdom, Pakistan and Iran within nine months and the USA joined the military committee in March 1957. In October 1958 the HQ was transferred to Ankara, Turkey with the post-revolution withdrawal of Iraq in July 1958.

Organisation of African Unity (OAU)

In Addis Ababa, Ethiopia on 25 May 1963, 30 African countries established the organisation for common defence of independence, the elimination of colonialism and the co-ordination of economic policies. English and French are recognised as official languages in addition to African languages.

THE UNITED NATIONS

'A general international organisation . . . for the maintenance of international peace and security' was recognised as desirable in Clause 4 of the proposals of the Four-Nation Conference of Foreign Ministers signed in Moscow on 30 Oct. 1943 by R Anthony Eden, now the Earl of Avon (UK), Cordell Hull (1871–1955) (USA), Vyacheslav M Skryabin, *alias* Molotov (USSR), and Ambassador Foo Ping-Sheung (China).

Ways and means were resolved at the mansion of Dumbarton Oaks, Washington, DC, USA, between 21 Aug. and 7 Oct. 1944. A final step was taken at San Francisco, California, USA between 25 Apr. and 26 June 1945 when delegates of 50 participating states signed the Charter (Poland signed on 15 Oct. 1945). This came into force on 24 Oct. 1945, when the four above-mentioned states, plus France and a majority of the other 46 states, had ratified the Charter. The first regular session was held in London on 10 Jan.–14 Feb. 1946.

Of the 159 *de facto* sovereign states of the world 139 are now in membership plus the two USSR republics of Byelorussia and the Ukraine which have separate membership. The non-members are:

Andoora
China (Taiwan)
Korea, Republic of
Korea, Democratic People's Republic of
Liechtenstein
Monaco
Nauru
San Marino
South Africa★
Switzerland
Tonga
Vatican City (Holy See)
Western Samoa

★ Credentials rejected on 30 Sept. 1974. Suspended from General Assembly 12 Nov. 1974.

The United Nations' principal organs are:

The General Assembly consisting of all member nations, each with up to five delegates but one vote, and meeting annually in regular sessions with provision for special sessions. The Assembly has seven main committees, on which there is the right of representation by all member nations. These are (1) Political Security, (2) Economic and Financial, (3) Social, Humanitarian and Cultural, (4) Trust and Non-Self-Governing Territories, (5) Administration and Budgetary, (6) Legal, and the Special Political.

The Security Council, consisting of 15 members, each with one representative, of whom there are five permanent members (China, France, UK, USA and USSR) and ten elected members serving a two-year term. Apart from procedural questions, an affirmative majority vote of at least nine must include that of all five permanent members. It is from this stipulation that the so-called veto arises.

The Economic and Social Council, consisting of 54 members elected for three-year terms, is responsible for carrying out the functions of the General Assembly's second and third Committees, viz. economic, social, educational, health and cultural matters. It had the following Functional Commissions in 1974: (1) Statistical (2) Population (3) Social Development (4)

Narcotic Drugs (5) Human Rights (and its sub-commission on the Prevention of Discrimination and the Protection of Minorities) (6) Status of Women. The Council has also established Economic Commissions, as follows: (1) for Europe (ECE), (2) for Asia and the Far East (ESCAP), (3) for Latin America (ECLA), (4) for Africa (ECA) and (5) for Western Asia (ECWA).

The International Court of Justice, comprising 15 Judges (quorum of nine) of different nations, each serving a nine-year term and meeting at 's Gravenhage (The Hague), Netherlands. Only states may be parties in contentious cases. In the event of a party's failing to adhere to a judgment, the other party may have recourse to the Security Council. Judgements are final and without appeal but can be reopened on grounds of a new decisive factor within ten years.

The Secretariat. The principal administrative officer is the Secretary General who is appointed by the General Assembly for a five-year term. This office has been held thus: Trygve Halvdan Lie (1896–1968) (Norway) 1 Feb. 1946–10 Nov. 1952.
Dag Hjalmar Agne Carl Hammarskjöld (1905–61) (Sweden) 10 Apr. 1953–18 Sept. 1961.
U Maung Thant 1909–1974 (Burma) (acting) 3 Nov. 1961–30 Nov. 1962, (permanent) 30 Nov. 1962–31 Dec. 1971.
Kurt Waldheim (b. 21 Dec. 1918) (Austria) 1 Jan. 1972 (in office).

Agencies in Relationship with the United Nations
There are 15 specialised agencies, which in order of absorption or creation are as follows:

ILO
International Labour Organisation (Headquarters—Geneva). Founded 11 Apr. 1919 in connection with The League of Nations. Re-established as the senior UN specialised agency, 14 Dec. 1946. Especially concerned with social justice, hours of work, unemployment, wages, industrial sickness, and protection of foreign workers.

FAO
Food and Agriculture Organisation of the United Nations (Headquarters—Rome). Established, 16 Oct. 1945. Became UN agency, 14 Dec. 1946. Objects: to raise levels of nutrition and standards of living; to improve the production and distribution of agricultural products. FAO provides an Intelligence Service on Agriculture, Forestry and Fisheries.

UNESCO
United Nations Educational, Scientific and Cultural Organisation (Headquarters—Paris). Established, 4 Nov. 1946. Objects: to stimulate popular education and the spread of culture, and to diffuse knowledge through all means of mass communication; to further universal respect for justice, the rule of law, human rights, and fundamental freedoms. Became a UN agency, 14 Dec. 1946.

ICAO
International Civil Aviation Organisation (Headquarters—Montreal). Established, 4 Apr. 1947. Objects: to study the problems of international civil aviation; to encourage safety measures and co-ordinate facilities required for safe international flight. A UN agency from 13 May 1947.

IBRD
International Bank For Reconstruction and Development (The World Bank) (Headquarters—Washington). Established, 27 Dec. 1945. Objects: to assist in the reconstruction and development of territories of members by aiding capital investment. Became a UN agency, 15 Nov. 1947. The *International Development Association* Headquarters—Washington) is affiliated to the IBRD. Established 24 Sept. 1960. Object: Making special term loans to less developed countries. Membership limited as in IFC.

IMF
International Monetary Fund (Headquarters—Washington). Established, 27 Dec. 1945. Objects: to promote international monetary co-operation, the expansion of international trade and stability of exchange rates. A UN agency from 15 Nov. 1947.

GATT
General Agreement on Tariffs and Trade (Headquarters—Geneva). Established, 1 Jan. 1948. Objects: to reduce or stabilise customs duties and assist the trade of developing countries. A major advancement of its aims was the establishment of the European Economic Community (EEC) or Common Market by The Treaty of Rome (signed, 21 Mar. 1957).

UPU
Universal Postal Union (Headquarters—Berne, Switzerland). Established, 1 July 1875, became UN specialised agency 1 July 1948. Objects: to unite members in a single postal territory.

IAEA
International Atomic Energy Agency (Headquarters—Vienna). Established 29 July 1957.

Objects: to accelerate and enlarge the contribution of non-military atomic energy to peace, health and prosperity. A UN agency from 14 Nov. 1957.

WHO
World Health Organisation (Headquarters—Geneva). Established, 7 Apr. 1948. Objects: to promote the attainment by all peoples of the highest possible standard of health. Its services are both advisory and technical. A UN agency from 10 July 1948.

ITU
International Telecommunication Union (Headquarters—Geneva). Founded 17 May 1865; incorporated in the United Nations, 10 Jan. 1949. Objects: to seek the standardisation of procedures concerning greater efficacy of telecommunications and to allocate frequencies.

WMO
World Meteorological Organisation (Headquarters—Geneva). Established 23 Mar. 1950. Objects: to standardise meteorological observations; to secure their publication, and apply the information for the greater safety of aviation and shipping and benefit of agriculture, etc. A UN agency from 20 Dec. 1951.

IFC
International Finance Corporation (Headquarters—Washington). Established 24 July 1956. Objects: to promote the flow of private capital internationally and to stimulate the capital markets. Membership is open only to those countries that are members of the World Bank. A UN agency from 20 Feb. 1957.

IMCO
Inter-Governmental Maritime Consultative Organisation (Headquarters—London). Established 17 Mar. 1958. Objects: to co-ordinate safety at sea and to secure the freedom of passage. A UN agency from 13 Jan. 1959.

The League of Nations
The League of Nations was established in Geneva, Switzerland among 42 nations on 10 Jan. 1920 and was disbanded on 10 Jan. 1946, the opening day of the First General Assembly of the United Nations in London.

Its creation has been regarded as an event of pioneering importance in the history of collective security and of international relations. Its efficacy was impaired by the withdrawal of crucial members. Japan withdrew in March 1933, Germany in October 1933, Italy in December 1937, Spain in May 1939, and the USSR, which joined in Sept. 1934, resigned on 14 Dec. 1939.

Albania was annexed by Italy in April 1939 and Austria by Germany in March 1938. Of the total of 63 nations who had been in membership 19 had withdrawn by 1940. Achievements of the League included the settlement of a crisis in Yugoslavia (October 1934), the ending of the Peru–Colombia war of 1934, and the international force which invigilated the Franco-German plebiscite in the Saar.

The Japanese aggression in Manchuria in Sept. 1931 in violation of the Covenant followed by Japan's circumvention of her obligations by the creation of the puppet state of Manchoukuo, was the first blow against the League's efficacy. The unilateral action of the French and British governments in lifting the oil sanctions against Italy two months after the invasion of Ethiopia in October 1935 proved a death blow.

The Trusteeship Council administers territories under UN trusteeship. Twelve territories have been under UN trusteeship:

Original Trust Territory	Subsequent Status
Tanganyika (UK)	Independent, 9 Dec. 1961; merged with Zanzibar, 26 Apr. 1964
Ruanda–Urundi (Belgium)	Two independent states, 1 July 1962
Somaliland (Italy)	Independent, 1 July 1960
Cameroons (UK)	Northern part joined Nigeria, 1 June 1961; southern part joined Cameroon, 1 Oct. 1961
Cameroons (France)	Independent republic of Cameroon, 1 Jan. 1960
Togoland (UK)	United with Gold Coast, to form Ghana, 6 Mar. 1957
Togoland (France)	Independent republic of Togo, 27 Apr. 1960
Western Samoa (NZ)	Independent, 1 Jan. 1962
Nauru (Australia, NZ and UK)	Independent 31 Jan. 1968
Papua New Guinea (Australia)	Self-Government, 1 Dec. 1973
Pacific Islands (USA) comprising the Carolines, Marshalls and Marianas (excepting Guam)	

167

COUNTRIES OF THE WORLD

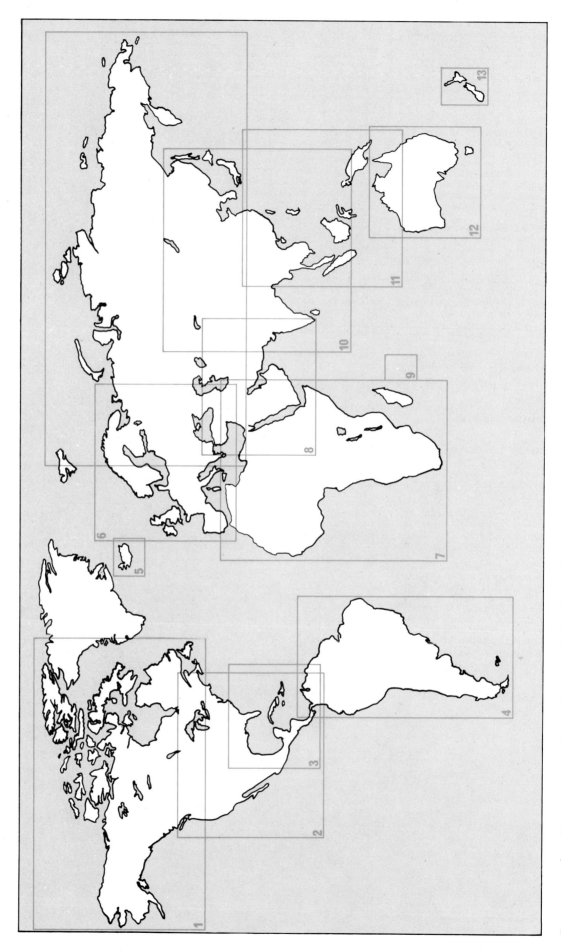

By autumn of 1976, there were 158 sovereign countries in the world. In this book the United Kingdom has been treated separately and in the pages which follow the salient details of both non-sovereign territories and the 157 other sovereign countries are given. Where a map appears for an individual country, it is based on one of the thirteen areas indicated on the above map of the world. The individual maps are intended as guides only to the position of the country concerned.

NON-SOVEREIGN COUNTRIES

The trend towards full national Sovereign status has substantially reduced the total number of non-sovereign territories. With few obvious exceptions these territories now tend to have too small a population and/or resources to sustain statehood.

The non-sovereign territories are divided below into four parts:

(a) Territories administered by the United Kingdom.
(b) Territories administered by Australia or New Zealand.
(c) Territories administered by the United States of America.
(d) Other non-sovereign territories.

TERRITORIES ADMINISTERED BY THE UNITED KINGDOM (excluding the Channel Islands and the Isle of Man)

Antigua
Location: An island about 20 miles *32 km* to the north-east of Montserrat, in the Leeward Islands, West Indies. The dependencies are Barbuda, 25 miles *40 km* north of Antigua, and Redonda, 25 miles *40 km* west-south-west of Antigua.
Area: 171 miles² *443 km²* (Antigua 108 miles² *279 km²*, Barbuda 62 miles² *160 km²*, Redonda 1 mile² *2½ km²*).
Population (Census 7 Apr. 1970): 65 525; (1974 estimate) 70 000.
Capital: St John's (St John City) (14 000), on north-west coast.

Belize (formerly British Honduras)
Location: On the east (Caribbean) coast of the Yucatán Peninsula, Central America. Bordered on the north by Mexico, on the west and south by Guatemala.
Area: 8867 miles² *22 965 km²*, including offshore islands (212 miles² *549 km²*).
Population (Census 7 Apr. 1970): 191 934. Latest estimate is 136 000 (1 July 1974).
Capital (population, 1973): Belmopan (3500)

Bermuda
Location: The Bermudas (or Somers Islands) are a group of islands in the western North Atlantic Ocean, about 570 miles *917 km* east of Cape Hatteras in North Carolina, USA.
Area: 20·59 miles² *53,3 km²*.
Population: Latest estimate is 55 000 (1 July 1974) excluding tourists. 20 islands are inhabited.
Capital (population 1970): Hamilton (3000), on Bermuda I.

British Antarctic Territory (Constituted 3 Mar. 1962)
Location: Comprises all the land south of latitude 60° south, situated between longitude 20° and 80° west. This includes the South Shetland Islands, the South Orkney Islands, Graham Land and a part of the mainland of Antarctica.
Area: The total area within the sector is about 2 200 000 miles² *5 698 000 km²* of which land (excluding ice-shelves) occupies about 150 000 miles² *388 498 km²*. The South Shetland Is. are about 130 miles² *336 km²* and the South Orkney Is 240 miles² *621 km²*.
Population: There are no permanent inhabitants. The only occupants are scientific workers, of whom UK personnel numbered 79 in the winter of 1972.
Capital: There being no settlements the Territory is administered from Stanley, Falkland Is (q.v.).

British Indian Ocean Territory (Constituted 8 Nov. 1965)
Location: The territory is now confined to the Chagos Archipelago (or Oil Islands) which is 1180 miles *1899 km* northeast of (and formerly administered by) Mauritius. The islands of Aldabra, Farquhar, and Desroches (originally parts of the territory) were restored to the Seychelles when the latter became independent on 29 June 1976.
Area: about 20 miles² *52 km²*
Population: n.a. (a floating population of contract labourers).

British Virgin Islands
Location and Composition: Comprises the eastern part of the Virgin Islands group (the western part is a US colony), and lies to the east of Puerto Rico, in the West Indies.
Area: About 59 miles² *153 km²* (Tortola 21 miles² *54 km²*, Virgin Gorda 8¼ miles² *21 km²*, Anegada 15 miles² *39 km²*, Jost van Dyke 3¼ miles² *8 km²*).
Population (Census 7 Apr. 1970): 10 484 (Tortola 8954, Virgin Gorda 1030, Anegada 270, Jost van Dyke 120, other islands (seven inhabited) 110). Latest estimate is 11 000 (1974).
Capital (Census 7 Apr. 1970): Road Town (2183), on Tortola.

The State of Brunei
Location: On the north-west of the East Indian island of Borneo, completely surrounded on the landward side by Sarawak, a state of Malaysia.
Area: 2226 miles² *5765 km²*.
Population (Census 10 Aug. 1971): 136 256. Latest estimate 150 000 (1 July 1974).
Capital: Bandar Seri Begawan (36 989 in 1971).

Canton and Enderbury Islands
Location: In the north of the Phoenix Islands, in the mid-Pacific Ocean.
Area: 27 miles² *70 km²*.
Population: uninhabited.
Status and Government: A condominium, administered jointly by the UK and the USA.

Cayman Islands
Location: A group of three islands, in the Caribbean Sea, south of Cuba. The principal island, Grand Cayman, is 178 miles *286 km* west of Jamaica.
Area: approximately 100 miles² *259 km²* (Grand Cayman 76 miles² *197 km²*, Cayman Brac 14 miles² *36 km²*, Little Cayman 10 miles² *26 km²*).
Population (Census 7 Apr. 1970): 10 249 (Grand Cayman 8932); Latest estimate 11 000 (1 July 1974).
Capital (Census 7 Apr. 1970): George Town (3975).

Dominica
Location: An island about 20 miles *32 km* north of Martinique, in the West Indies.
Area: 289·8 miles² *750 km²*.
Population (Census 7 Apr. 1970): 70 302. Latest estimate 74 000 (1 July 1974).
Capital (Census 7 Apr. 1970): Roseau (10 157).

Falkland Islands and Dependencies
Location: A group of islands in the south-western Atlantic Ocean, about 480 miles *772 km* north-east of Cape Horn, South America. The Dependencies are South Georgia, an island 800 miles *1287 km* to the east, and the South Sandwich Islands, 470 miles *756 km* south-east of South Georgia.
Area: approximately 6280 miles² *16 265 km²*, of which the Falklands are approximately 4700 miles² *12 173 km²* (East Falkland and adjacent islands 2610 miles² *6760 km²*, West Falkland, etc., 2090 miles² *5413 km²*). South Georgia is 1450 miles² *3755 km²* and the Sandwich Is 130 miles² *336 km²*.
Population: Falkland Islands (estimated 31 Dec. 1974): 1874. South Georgia has a small population which is highest during the summer whaling season.
Capital: Port Stanley (1083), on East Falkland.

City of Gibraltar
Location: A narrow peninsula on the south coast of Spain, commanding the north side of the Atlantic entrance to the Mediterranean Sea.
Area: 2¼ miles² *5,8 km²* (2¾ miles *4,4 km* long, greatest breadth nearly 1 mile *1,6 km*).
Population: 26 833 (Census 6 Oct. 1970 excluding armed forces). Latest estimate 29 000 (1 July 1974).
Chief (and only) Town: Gibraltar, at north-western corner of the Rock.

Gilbert Islands
Location: A group of 33 atolls within an area of more than 1 600 000 miles² *4 144 000 km²* in the mid-Pacific Ocean. Comprises the Gilbert Isands (16 atolls), Phoenix Islands (8), the Northern Line Islands (3: Washington Is, Fanning Is and Christmas Is), the Central and Southern Line Islands (5) and Ocean Island (Banaba), about 240 miles *386 km* south-west of Tarawa Atoll, Gilbert Islands.
Area: 253 miles² *655 km²* (Gilbert Is 114 miles² *295 km²*, Christmas Island 135 miles² *350 km²*)
Population (Census 8 Dec. 1973): 51 929 (Gilbert Is 47 714, Ocean Is 2314).
Headquarters: A residency on island of Bairiki, in the south of the Tarawa Atoll, Gilbert Islands.

Hong Kong
Location: A peninsula in the central south coast of the Kwangtung province of southern China, the island of Hong Kong and some 235 other islands, the largest of which is Lantao (58 miles² *150 km²*).
Area: 403.8 miles² *1046 km²* (Hong Kong Island 29.2 miles² *76 km²*, Kowloon peninsula 3.85 miles² *10 km²*, Stonecutters Island ¼ mile² *0,6 km²*, New Territories (leased) 370.5 miles² *960 km²*). It includes all islands within an approximately rectangular area of 738 miles² *1911 km²*.
Population: 4 249 000 (estimated, 1 July 1974). Over 98% are Chinese, many being British subjects by virtue of birth in the Colony.
Languages: mainly Chinese (Cantonese); English 8·5%.
Religion: Predominantly Buddhist.
Capital City and Other Principal Towns (population at Census, 1971): Victoria (520 932), on Hong Kong Island; Kowloon; New Kowloon; North Point; Tsuen Wan; Cheung Chau (an island).
Status and Government: A Crown Colony with the Governor assisted by an Executive Council (14 in 1974) and a Legislative Council (30 in 1974). There is also an urban council of 26 members (ten elected).
Recent History: British colony, 1841. New Territories leased in 1898 for 99 years. Attacked by Japan, 8 Dec. 1941. Surrendered, 25 Dec. 1941. Recaptured by UK forces, 30 Aug. 1945. UK military administration, 3 Sept. 1945 to May 1946. Formal Japanese surrender, 16 Sept. 1945. Many refugees during Chinese civil war 1948–50, and subsequently, notably on 1–25 May 1962.
Economic Situation: The principal occupations are manufacturing (notably cotton piece goods, shirts, electric products, cameras, toys and games, footwear), services

169

and commerce. Agriculture (poultry and pigs), fishing and mining (notably iron) are carried on.
Currency: 100 cents = 1 Hong Kong dollar (U.S. $1 = H.K. $4.99 in February 1976).
Climate: The sub-tropical summer (82° F July) is hot and humid with the winter cool and dry (59° F February). The average annual rainfall is 85 in, three-quarters of which falls from June to August in the south-west monsoon season.

Montserrat
Location: An island about 35 miles *56 km* north of Basse Terre, Guadeloupe, in the Leeward Islands, West Indies.
Area: 38 miles² *98 km²*.
Population (1 July 1974): 12 000.
Capital: Plymouth (3000), on south-west coast.

The Anglo-French Condominium of the New Hebrides (Nouvelles-Hebrides)
Location: In the south-western Pacific Ocean about 500 miles *804 km* west of Fiji. Includes the New Hebrides, Banks Islands and Torres Islands.
Area: Approximately 5700 miles² *14 763 km²*, of which Espiritu Santo Island (Ile Marina) is approximately 1500 miles² *3885 km²*.
Population (28 May 1967): 77 988. Latest estimate is 93 000 (1 July 1974).
Administrative Headquarters: Vila (Fila) (population approximately 3500), on south coast of Efate (Ile Vaté).

Pitcairn Islands Group
Location: Four islands in the south Pacific Ocean, about 3000 miles *4828 km* east of New Zealand and 3500 miles *5632 km* south-west of Panama: Pitcairn, Henderson, Dulcie, Oeno.
Area: 18.5 miles² *48 km²*, including Pitcairn 1.75 miles² *4,5 km²*.
Population: (31 Dec. 1973): all on 74, Pitcairn.
Principal settlement: Adamstown.
Status and Government: Administered by the British High Commissioner in New Zealand, assisted by an Island Council of 10 (including 3 elected).

St Christopher (St Kitts), Nevis and Anguilla
Location: In the northern part of the Leeward Islands, in the West Indies. The main island is St Christopher (or St Kitts), with Nevis 3 miles *5 km* to the south-east, Anguilla (with Scrub I and other offshore islands) some 60 miles *96 km* to the north-west and Sombrero 30 miles *48 km* north of Anguilla.
Area: 141 miles² *365 km²* (St Christopher 68 miles² *[176 km²]*, Nevis 36 miles² *[93 km²]*, Anguilla 35 miles² *[90 km²]*, Sombrero 2 miles² *[5 km²]*).
Population (Census 7 Apr. 1970): 64 000. Latest estimate is 65 000 (1 July 1974).
Capital: Basse-terre (population 15 897), on south coast of St Christopher.

St Helena and Dependencies
Location and Composition: An island in the South Atlantic Ocean, 1200 miles *1931 km* west of Africa. The dependencies are: (*a*) Ascension, an island 700 miles *1126 km* to the north-west; (*b*) the Tristan da Cunha group, comprising: Tristan da Cunha, 1320 miles *2124 km* south-west of St Helena; Inaccessible Islands, 20 miles *32 km* west of Tristan; Nightingale Islands, 20 miles *32 km* south of Tristan; Gough Island (Diego Alvarez), 220 miles *354 km* south of Tristan.
Area: 162 miles² *419 km²* (St Helena 47.3 miles² *122 km²*, Ascension 34 miles²

88 *km²*, Tristan da Cunha 38 miles² *98 km²*, Gough 35 miles² *90 km²*, Inaccessible 4 miles² *10 km²*, Nightingale ¾ mile² *2 km²*).
Population: (Census 24 July 1966): St Helena 4649, Ascension 476. Latest estimates (1973) St Helena 5159, Ascension 1206, Tristan da Cunha 292.
Capital: Jamestown (population 1475 in 1966).
Principal Settlements: Ascension—Georgetown (or Garrison); Tristan da Cunha—Edinburgh.

St Lucia
Location: An island about 20 miles *32 km* south of Martinique in the Windward Islands. West Indies.
Area: 238 miles² *616 km²*.
Population (Census 7 Apr. 1970): 99 806. Latest estimate 107 000 (mid 1974).
Capital: Castries (40 000).

St Vincent
Location: An island about 25 miles *40 km* south of St Lucia. The colony includes, as dependencies, the St Vincent Grenadines, the northerly part of a group between St Vincent and Grenada.
Area: 150·3 miles² *389 km²* (St Vincent 133 miles² *344 km²*, Grenadines 17 miles² *44 km²*).
Population (Census 7 April 1970): 89 129. Latest estimate is 100 000 (31 Dec. 1973).
Capital (Census 7 April 1970): Kingstown (population including suburbs 22 000).

Solomon Islands
Location: In the south-western Pacific Ocean. Comprises the Solomon Islands group to the south of Bougainville (the islands to the north being part of Papua New Guinea) plus the Ontong Java Islands (Lord Howe Atoll), Rennell Island and the Santa Cruz Islands, about 300 miles *483 km* to the east.
Area: 11 500 miles² *29 785 km²*, of which Guadalcanal is about 2 500 miles² *6 475 km²*.
Population: 160 998 (census of 7 Feb. 1970); 185 000 (estimate, 1 July 1974).
Capital: Honiara (population 11 191 in 1970), on north coast of Guadalcanal.

Turks and Caicos Islands
Location: Two groups of islands at the south-eastern end of the Bahamas, 120 miles *193 km* north of Hispaniola (Haiti and Dominican Republic), in the West Indies.
Area: 192 miles² *497 km²*.
Population (Census 29 Oct. 1970): 5558, comprising Turks Islands (Grand Turk, Salt Cay) and Caicos Islands (North Caicos, South Caicos, Middle Caicos, Providenciales). Latest estimate is 6000 (1 July 1974).
Capital (population 1970): Cockburn Town, on Grand Turk Island (2400).

Tuvalu
Location: A group of 9 atolls, formerly called the Ellice (Lagoon) Islands, in the western Pacific Ocean, south of the Gilbert Islands (from which Tuvalu was separated on 1 Oct. 1975).
Area: 9·5 miles² *24,6 km²*.
Population: 5 887 (census of 8 Dec. 1973).
Capital: Funafuti.

TERRITORIES ADMINISTERED BY AUSTRALIA OR NEW ZEALAND

The Australian Antarctic Territory

Australian Dependencies
Location: Comprises all land south of latitude 60° S, between 45° E and 160° E, except for French territory of Terre Adélie,

whose boundaries were fixed on 1 Apr. 193 as between 136° E and 142° E.
Area: 2 333 624 miles² *6 044 058 km²* o land and 29 251 miles² *75 759 km²* of ic shelf.

Christmas Island
Location: In the Indian Ocean, 223 mile *359 km* south of Java Head.
Area: Approximately 52 miles² *134 km²*.
Population (30 June 1973): 2884.
Chief Settlement: Flying Fish Cove.

Territory of Cocos (Keeling) Islands
Location: In the Indian Ocean, abou 1720 miles *2768 km* north-west of Perth North Keeling Is lies about 15 miles *24 kn* north of the main group.
Area: Approximately 5 miles² *13 km²*.
Population (Census 30 June 1971): 618 Latest estimate (30 June 1974) is 643. Th three inhabited islands are Home Island West Island and Direction Island.
Chief Settlement: Bantam Village or Home Is.

Coral Sea Islands Territory
Location: East of Queensland, between th Great Barrier Reef and 157° 10′E. longitude
Population: 3 meteorologists.

Territory of Heard and McDonald Islands
Location: In the southern Indian Ocean south-east of the Kerguélen Islands, an about 2500 miles *4023 km* south-west o Fremantle.
Area: 113 miles² *292 km²*. No permanen inhabitants.

Norfolk Island
Location: In south-west Pacific Ocean about 930 miles *1496 km* from Sydney and 400 miles *643 km* from New Zealand. Philip Island is about 4 miles *6 km* south of Norfoll Island.
Area: 8528 acres (13·3 miles² *34 km²*).
Population (Census 30 June 1971): 1683 Latest estimate 1894 (30 June 1974).
Seat of Government: Kingston.

New Zealand Dependencies Island Territories

Cook Islands
Location: In the southern Pacific Ocean between about 1750 miles *2816 km* and 2350 miles *3782 km* north-east of New Zealand between 8° S and 23° S, and 156° W and 167° W. Comprises 15 atolls or islands (Northern group 8, Lower group 7).
Area: 93 miles² *240 km²*. Main islands (with area in acres) are Rarotonga (16 602), Mangaia (12 800), Atiu (6654), Mitiaro (5500), Mauke (Parry Is) (4552), Aitutaki (4461) and Penrhyn (Tongareva) (2432).
Population (Census 1 Dec. 1971): 21 317 (Rarotonga 11 388). Latest estimate 19 000 (1 July 1974).

Niue
Location: Niue (or Savage) Island is in the southern Pacific Ocean, 1343 miles *2161 km* north of Auckland, New Zealand, between Tonga and the Cook Islands.
Area: 64 028 acres (100·04 miles² *[259 km²]*).
Population (Census 31 Dec. 1973): 4142. Latest estimate 4000 (1 July 1974).
Capital: Alofi.

Tokelau Islands
Location: The Tokelau (formerly Union) Islands consist of three atolls in the central Pacific Ocean, about 300 miles *483 km* north of Western Samoa.
Area: Approximately 2500 acres (Nukunonu 1350, Fakaofo 650, Atafu 500), or about 4

miles² *10 km².*
Population (Census 26 Sept. 1973): 1587.
Latest estimate: 2000 (1 July 1974).

The Ross Dependency
Location: All the land between 160° E and 150° W longitude (moving eastward) and south of 60° S latitude, comprising a sector of the mainland of Antarctica, including the Ross Ice Shelf, and some off-shore islands.
Area: The mainland area is estimated at 160 000 miles² *414 398 km²* and the permanent ice shelf at 130 000 miles² *336 698 km².*

Population: No permanent inhabitants, but some bases are permanently occupied by scientific personnel.

TERRITORIES ADMINISTERED BY THE UNITED STATES OF AMERICA

Territory	Area (miles²)	Area (km²)	Population	Capital
North America				
Canal Zone	553	*1432*	46 000 (est 1/7/73)	Balboa Heights
Commonwealth of Puerto Rico	3435	*8897*	3 031 000 (est 1/7/74)	San Juan
Virgin Islands of the United States	133	*344*	83 000 (est 1/7/73)	Charlotte Amalie
Oceania				
American Samoa	76	*197*	31 000 (1/7/74)	Pago Pago
Guam	212	*549*	97 000 (1/7/74)	Agaña
Johnston and Sand Islands	<½	*1*	1000	—
Midway Islands	2	*5*	2000	—
Wake Island	3	*8*	2000	—
Trust Territory of the Pacific Islands	687★	*1779★*	114 782 (18/9/73)	Saipan

★ Inhabited dry land only.

OTHER NON-SOVEREIGN TERRITORIES

Territory	Administering Country	Area (miles²)	Area (km²)	Population	Capital
Europe					
Faeroe Islands	Denmark	540	*1399*	40 000 (1/7/74)	Thorshavn
Svalbard and Jan Mayen Islands	Norway	24 101	*62 421*	3000 (31/12/65)★	Ny Alesund
Asia					
Macau (or Macao)	Portugal	6	*16*	266 000 (1/7/74)	Macau
Portuguese Timor	Portugal	5763	*14 925*	637 000 (1/7/72)	Dili
Africa					
French Southern and Antarctic Territories	France	2918	*7557*	190 (1/7/74)	—
French Territory of the Afars and the Issas	France	8500	*22 000*	104 000 (1/7/74)	Djibouti
Namibia†	UN Protectorate	317 836	*823 191*	862 000 (1/7/74)	Windhoek
La Réunion	France	969	*2510*	490 000 (1/7/74)	St Denis
North America					
Greenland	Denmark	840 000	*2 175 600*	49 000 (1/7/74)	Godthaab
St Pierre and Miquelon	France	93	*242*	5000 (1/7/74)	St Pierre
Central America					
Guadeloupe and dependencies	France	687	*1780*	349 000 (1/7/74)	Pointe-a-Pitre
Martinique	France	425	*1100*	358 000 (1/7/74)	Fort-de-France
Netherlands Antilles	Netherlands	371	*961*	238 000 (1/7/74)	Willemstad
South America					
French Guiana	France	35 000	*91 000*	58 000 (1/7/74)	Cayenne
Oceania					
French Polynesia	France	c. 1500	*4000*	124 000 (1/7/74)	Papeete
New Caledonia and Dependencies	France	7300	*19 000*	132 000 (1/7/74)	Nouméa
Wallis and Futuna Islands	France	77	*200*	9000 (1/7/73)	Mata-Uta

★ Inhabited only during winter season.
† Including data for Walvis Bay (area 434 miles² *1124 km²*, population 23 461), an integral part of South Africa.

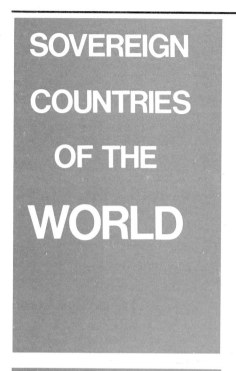

SOVEREIGN COUNTRIES OF THE WORLD

AFGHANISTAN

Official name: Doulat i Jumhouri ye Afghanistan *or* De Afghānistān Jamhouriat (the Republic of Afghanistan).
Population: 18 293 841 (1973 est)
Area: 250 000 miles² *647 494 km²*
Languages: Dari Persian, Pashtu (Pakhto).
Religion: Muslim.
Capital City: Kabul, population 318 094 (1971 est); Greater Kabul 534 350 (1973 est).
Other principal towns (1973): Kandahar (Quandahar) 140 024; Baghlan 110 874; Herat 108 750; Tagab 106 777; Charikar 100 443.

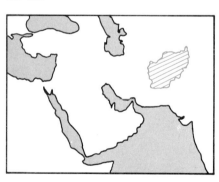

Highest point: Noshaq, 24 581 ft *7492 m* (first climbed 17 Aug. 1960).
Principal mountain ranges: Hindu Kush, Koh-i-Baba, Band-i-Baian, Band-i-Baba, Paropamisus, Paghman.
Principal rivers: Helmand, Bandihala-Khoulm, Kabul, Murghab, Kunduz, Hari Rud, Farah Rud, Ab-i-Panja.
Head of State: Lt-Gen Mohammad Da'ud (b. 18 July 1909), President and Prime Minister.
Climate: Wide variations between highlands and lowlands. Average annual rainfall 12 in. In Kabul July (61 °F to 92 °F) and August (59 °F to 91 °F) hottest; Jan. (18 °F to 36 °F) coldest; March rainiest (7 days). Maximum temperature up to 120 °F; minimum below −10 °F.
Crops: Wheat, maize, rice, barley, grapes, cotton.

Monetary unit: Afghani. 1 afghani = 100 puls.
Denominations:
Coins 1, 2, 5 afghani, 25, 50 puls.
Notes 10, 20, 50, 100, 500, 1000 afghani.
Exchange rate to US dollar: 45.00 (official rate, February 1976); free rate was 57·50 per US dollar in January 1976.
Political history and government: A republic, established by military *coup* on 17 July 1973. Government is by a 13-member Central Committee of the Republic, presided over by the Head of State, and a Cabinet. There are 28 provinces.
Telephones: 20 492 (1974).
Daily newspapers: 18
Total circulation: 101 000
Radio: 450 000 (1972).
Length of roadways: 4164 miles *6700 km.*
Universities: 2.
Adult illiteracy: Over 90% (1963).
Expectation of life: Males 37·4 years; females 38·1 years (1965–70).
Defence: Military service two years; Total armed forces 88 000; Defence expenditure 1973–4 $45 million.
Wildlife: Mountain sheep, goat, fox, wolves, bears, leopards, partridge and other game birds.
Cinemas: 24 (seating capacity 12 000) in 1970.

ALBANIA

Official name: Republika Popullóre e Shqipërisë (People's Republic of Albania), abbreviated to Shqipëri (Shqipni), 'the land of the eagles'. A new draft constitution, published on 21 Jan. 1976, proposes that the country be renamed the Socialist People's Republic of Albania.
Population: 1 626 315 (1960 census); 2 296 800 (1973 est).
Area: 11 101 miles² *28 748 km².*
Language: Albanian.
Religions: Muslim; Eastern Orthodox; Roman Catholic.
Capital city: Tiranë (Tirana), population 182 500 (1973 est).
Other principal towns: Shkodër (Scutari) 59 100; Durrës (Durezzo) 57 300; Vlorë (Valona) 53 200; Korçë (Koritsa) 49 200; Elbasan 45 500; Berat 28 400; Fier 25 800.
Highest point: Mount Korabi, 9028 ft *2751 m.*
Principal mountain ranges: Albanian Alps, section of the Dinaric Alps.
Principal rivers: Semani (157 miles *253 km*), Drini (174 miles *280 km*), Vjosa (147 miles *236 km*), Mati (65 miles *105 km*), Shkumbini (91 miles *146 km*).
Head of State: Haxhi Lleshi (b. 1913), President of the Presidium of the People's Assembly.
Political leader: Enver Hoxha (b. 16 Oct. 1908), First Secretary of the Central Com-

mittee of the Albanian Party of Labour.
Head of Government: Mehmet Shehu (b. 10 Jan. 1913), Chairman of the Council of Ministers.
Climate: Mild, wet winters and dry, hot summers along coast; rainier and colder inland. Maximum temperature 45,3 °C (113·5 °F) Lezhe 23 Aug. 1939; minimum −25,0 °C (−13·0 °F), Voskopje 29 Jan. 1942.
Crops: Maize, wheat, sugarbeet, potatoes, grapes, olives.
Monetary unit: Lek. 1 lek = 100 qintars.
Denominations:
Coins 5, 10, 20, 50 qintars, 1 lek.
Notes 1, 3, 5, 10, 25, 50 leks.
Exchange rate to US dollar: 4.145 (February 1976).
Political history and government: An independent republic with a single-chamber People's Assembly of 264 deputies. Ruled by the (Communist) Albanian Party of Labour. Comprises 26 districts.
Telephones: 10 150 (1963).
Daily Newspapers: 2
Total circulation: 136 000
Radio: 172 000 (1973).
TV: 4000 (1973).
Length of roadways: 1926 miles *3100 km.*
Length of railways: 125 miles *201 km.*
Universities: One.
Adult illiteracy: 28·5% (males 20·1%; females 36·9%) in 1955 (population aged 9 and over).
Expectation of life: Males 65·3 years; females 67·8 years (1965–70).
Defence: Military service: Army two years, Air Force, Navy and special units three years. Total armed forces 38 000 (21 000 conscripts) Defence expenditure 1975 $127 million.
Wildlife: Mountain goats and sheep, wild pigs.
Cinemas: 93 (seating capacity 23 700) in 1969.

ALGERIA

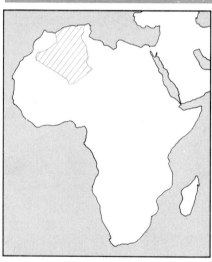

Official name: El Djemhouria El Djazaïria Demokratia Echaabia, or la République algérienne démocratique et populaire (the Democratic and Popular Republic of Algeria).
Population: 12 090 547 (1966 census); 16 275 000 (1974 est).
Area: 919 595 miles² *2 381 741 km².*
Languages: Arabic 80·4%; Berber 18·7%; French 0·6% (1966).
Religion: Muslim.
Capital city: El Djazair or Alger (Algiers), population 1 839 000 (1970 est).
Other principal towns (1966): Ouahran (Oran) 328 257; Constantine 253 649; Annaba (Bône) 168 790; Sidi-Bel-Abbès 101 000;

Sétif 98 000; Tlemcen 96 000; Blida 87 000.
Highest point: Mt Tahat, 9573 ft *2918 m.*
Principal mountain ranges: Atlas Saharien, Ahaggar (Hoggar), Hamada de Tinchert.
Principal river: Chéliff (430 miles *692 km*]).
Head of State: Col Houari Boumédienne (b. 23 Aug. 1927), President of the Revolutionary Council and President of the Council of Ministers.
Climate: Temperate (hot summers, fairly mild winters, adequate rainfall) along the coast, more extreme inland, hot and arid in the Sahara. In Algiers, August hottest (71 °F to 85 °F), January coldest (49 °F to 59 °F), December rainiest (12 days). Maximum temperature 53,0 °C (127·4 °F), Ouargla 27 Aug. 1884.
Crops: Wheat, barley, potatoes, grapes, oranges, dates, olives.
Monetary unit: Dinar. 1 dinar = 100 centimes.
Denominations:
  Coins 1, 2, 5, 20, 50 centimes, 1 dinar.
  Notes 5, 10, 50, 100, 500 dinars.
Exchange rate to US dollar: 4.13 (January 1976).
Political history and government: A former French possession, independent since 3 July 1962. Now ruled by a Revolutionary Council. A one-party state comprising 15 departments.
Telephones: 220 814 (1973).
Daily Newspapers: 4 (1972).
  Total circulation: 254 000.
Radio: 725 000 (1973).
TV: 260 000 (1973).
Length of roadways (1973): 48 720 miles *78 408 km.*
Length of railways: 2531 miles *4074 km.*
Universities: 4.
Adult illiteracy: 81·2% (males 70·1%; females 92·1%) in 1966.
Expectation of life: Males 49·3 years; females 52·2 years (1965–70).
Defence: Military service voluntary; Total armed forces 63 000; Defence expenditure 1975 $285 million.
Wildlife: Jackal, hyena, ape, antelope, red deer, wild goat; eagle, vulture, hawk, owl, snipe.
Cinemas: 440 (seating capacity 184 000) and 200 part-time (capacity 35 000) in 1970.

ANDORRA

Official name: Les Valls d'Andorra (Catalán); also Los Valles de Andorra (Spanish), or Les Vallées d'Andorre (French)
Population: 26 558 (1975 est).
Area: 175 miles² *453 km².*
Languages: Catalán (official), French, Spanish.
Religion: Roman Catholic.

Capital city: Andorra la Vella, population 9659.
Highest point: Pla del'Estany, 9678 ft *3011 m.*
Principal mountain ranges: Pyrenees.
Principal rivers: Valira.
Head of State: Co-Princes (the Bishop of Urgel and The President of France) each represented by a Permanent Delegate and by the Viguier Episcopal and the Viguier de France.
Head of government: Julià Reig Ribo, First Syndic.
Climate: Mild (cool summers, cold winters) and dry. May–October are rainiest months.
Crops: Potatoes, tobacco, barley.
Monetary unit: French and Spanish currencies (*q.v.*)
Political history and government: An autonomous principality divided into six parishes, each of which has four Councillors elected to sit in the 24-member General Council of the Valleys.
Daily Newspapers: 1.
  Total circulation: 4000.
Radio: 6000 (1972).
TV: 1700 (1969).
Wildlife: Hare, chamois, rabbit, quail, partridge.
Cinemas: 7 (seating capacity 2900) in 1969.

ANGOLA

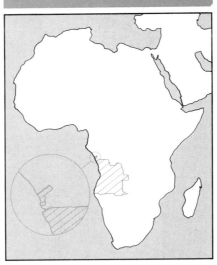

Official name: A República Popular de Angola (The People's Republic of Angola).
Population: 5 646 166 (1970 census); 6 000 000 (1975 est).
Area: 481 354 miles² *1 246 700 km².*
Languages: Portuguese (official), Bantu languages.
Religions: Catholic 38%; Protestant 12%; traditional beliefs 50%.
*Capital city: São Paulo de Luanda, population 480 613 (1970).
*Other principal towns (1970): Huambo (Nova Lisboa) 61 885; Lobito 59 258; Benguela 40 096; Lubango (Sá de Bandeira) 31 674; Malange 31 559.
Highest point: Serra Môco, 8563 ft *2610 m.*
Principal mountain ranges: Rand Plateau, Benguela Plateau, Bié Plateau, Humpata Highlands, Chela mountains.
Principal rivers: Cuanza, Cuando, Cubango, Zambezi, Cunene (587 miles *944 km*) Congo or Zaire.
Head of State: Dr Antônio Agostinho Neto (b. 17 Sept. 1922), President.
Prime Minister: Lopo do Nascimento.
Climate: A tropical climate with 2 distinct seasons. Average annual temperature decreases inland and towards the South. In Santo Antonio do Zaire average 79 °F

(26 °C); Huambo 67 °F (*19 °C*). There is but little seasonal fluctuation (2 °F to 5 °F). Rainy season October to mid-May, maximum Cabinda 70 in pa, minimum Lobito 11 in.
Crops: Cassava, sugar cane, maize, bananas, coffee, cotton, sisal.
Monetary unit: Angolan escudo. 1 escudo = 100 centavos.
Denominations:
  Coins 10, 20, 50 centavos, 1, 2½, 5, 10, 20 escudos.
  Notes 20, 50, 100, 500, 1000 escudos.
Exchange rate to US dollar: 27·75 (February 1976).
Political history and government: A former Portuguese territory, independent since 11 Nov. 1975. Before and after independence, rival nationalist groups fought for control of the country. By February 1976 the dominant group was the *Movimento Popular de Libertação de Angola* (MPLA), the Popular Movement for the Liberation of Angola, supported by troops from Cuba. Under the MPLA constitution for Angola, the supreme organ of state is the elected People's Assembly but, until Angola is completely under MPLA rule, power is held by a Revolutionary Council, led by the President. The Council comprises members of the MPLA's Political Bureau, the High Command of the armed forces and Provincial Commissars. Executive authority rests with the President, who appoints a Prime Minister and a Cabinet.
Telephones: 38 000 (1973).
Radio: 116 000 (1975).
Length of roadways: 43 500 miles *70 000 km.*
Length of railways: 2200 miles *3540 km.*
Universities: 1.
Adult illiteracy: 70% plus.
Expectation of life: Males 34·5 years; females 37·5 years (1965–70).
Defence: MPLA forces plus 10 000 Cuban 'advisers'.
Wildlife: Giant black antelope, elephant, hippopotamus, white and black rhinoceros, giraffe, zebra, gazelle, gorilla, lion, cheetah, crocodile and many bird species.
Cinemas: 47 (1972).

*As a result of the civil war there have been large-scale movements of population. Recent (March 1976) estimates suggest that Luanda has 800 000 inhabitants, Huambo over 100 000 and Lobito over 70 000.

ARGENTINA

Official name: La República Argentina (the Argentine Republic).
Population: 23 362 204 (1970 census); 25 050 000 (1974 est).
Area: 1 072 163 miles² *2 776 889 km².*
Language: Spanish.
Religion: Roman Catholic.
Capital city: Buenos Aires, population 2 972 453 (1970).
Other principal towns (1970): Rosario 810 840; Córdoba 798 663; La Plata 506 287; Mendoza 470 896; San Miguel de Tucumán 365 757; Mar del Plata 299 700; Santa Fé 244 579; San Juan 224 000.
Highest point: Cerro Aconcagua, 22 834 ft *6960 m* (first climbed 14 Jan. 1897).
Principal mountain range: Cordillera de los Andes.
Principal rivers: Paraná (2500 miles *4023 km*), Negro, Salado.
Head of State: Lt.-Gen. Jorge Rafael Videla (b. 1925), President.
Climate: Sub-tropical in Chaco region (north), sunny and mild in pampas, cold and windy in southern Patagonia. In Buenos Aires, January hottest (63 °F to 85 °F), June coldest (41 °F to 57 °F), August, October

173

and November rainiest (each 9 days). Absolute maximum temperature 48,8 °C (119·8 °F), Rivadavia, 27 Nov. 1916; absolute minimum −33,0 °C (−27·4 °F) Sarmiento.
Crops: Maize, wheat, sugar-cane.
Monetary unit: Peso. 1 peso = 100 centavos.
Denominations:
  Coins 1, 5, 10, 20, 50 centavos.
    1, 5, 10, 25 old pesos.
  Notes 50, 100, 500, 1000, 5000, 10 000 old pesos.
    1, 5, 10, 50, 100, 500, 1000 pesos.
Exchange rate to US dollar: 74.30 (February 1976).
Political history and government: A federal republic of 22 states and two centrally administered territories. Lt.-Gen. Juan Perón was elected President on 23 Sept. 1973 and took office on 12 Oct. 1973. Gen. Perón died on 1 July 1974 and was succeeded by his wife, the former Vice-President. She was deposed by an armed forces *coup* on 24 March 1976, when a three-man military junta took power. The bicameral Congress (a Senate and a Chamber of Deputies) and provincial legislatures were dissolved and political activities suspended. The junta's leader, Lt.-Gen. Jorge Videla, was inaugurated as President on 29 March 1976. Each province is administered by an appointed Governor.

Telephones: 2 065 273 (1973).
Daily newspapers: 162 (1972).
  Total circulation: 3 677 000 (148 dailies).
Radio: 6 100 000 (1974).
TV: 3 950 000 (1973).
Length of roadways (1972): 176 329 miles *283 775 km.*
Length of railways: 24 747 miles *39 827 km.*
Universities: 37 (12 national, 2 provincial, 23 private).
Adult illiteracy: 7·4% (males 6·5%; females 8·3%) in 1970.
Expectation of life: Males 64·06 years; females 70·22 years (1965–70).
Defence: Military service, army and air force one year, navy 14 months. Total armed forces 133 500; Defence budget 1975 $1031 million.
Wildlife: Anteater, jaguar, puma, woolly monkey, llama, fox, deer. Great variety of birds, including the condor in the Andes.
Cinemas: 2158, with seating capacity of 1 100 000.

AUSTRALIA

Official name: The Commonwealth of Australia.
Population: 12 755 638 (1971 census); 13 542 000 (1975 est).
Area: 2 966 150 miles² *7 682 300 km.*
Language: English.
Religions: Church of England; Roman Catholic; Methodist; Presbyterian.
Capital city: Canberra, population 190 000 (1975).
Other principal towns (metropolitan areas, 1974): Sydney 2 898 330; Melbourne 2 620 400; Brisbane 940 800; Adelaide 885 400; Perth 760 000; Newcastle 360 090; Wollongong 208 550; Hobart 161 320; Geelong 128 370.
Highest point: Mt Kosciusko, 7316 ft *2230 m.*
Principal mountain ranges: Great Dividing Range, Macdonnell Ranges, Flinders Ranges, Australian Alps.
Principal rivers: Murray (with Darling), Flinders, Ashburton, Fitzroy.
Head of State: HM Queen Elizabeth II, represented by the Rt Hon Sir John Robert Kerr, KCMG (b. 24 Sept. 1914), Governor-General.
Prime Minister: The Rt Hon John Malcolm Fraser (b. 21 May 1930).
Climate: Hot and dry, with average temperatures of about 80 °F. Very low rainfall in interior. In Sydney, January and February warmest (each average 65 °F to 78 °F). July coldest (46 °F to 60 °F), each month has an average of between 11 and 14 rainy days. In Perth, average daily maximum of 63 °F (July) to 85 °F (January, February), minimum 48 °F (July, August) to 63 °F (January, February), July and August rainiest (each 19 days), January and February driest (each 3 days). In Darwin, average maximum 87 °F (July) to 94 °F (November), minimum 67 °F (July) to 78 °F (November, December), January rainiest (20 days), no rainy days in July or August. Absolute maximum temperature 127·5 °F (53,1 °C), Cloncurry, 13 Jan. 1889; absolute minimum −8·0 °F (−22,2 °C) Charlotte Pass, 14 July 1945 and 22 Aug. 1947.
Crops: Wheat, barley, oats, sugar-cane, pineapples, bananas, citrus fruit, grapes.
Monetary unit: Australian dollar ($A). 1 dollar = 100 cents.
Denominations:
  Coins 1, 2, 5, 10, 20, 50 cents.
  Notes 1, 2, 5, 10, 20, 50 dollars.
Exchange rate to US dollar: 0.794 (February 1976).
Political history and government: Executive power is vested in the Queen and exercised by her representative, the Governor-General, advised by the Federal Executive Council led by the Prime Minister. Legisla-

tive power is vested in a Federal Parliament. This consists of the Queen, represented by the Governor-General, an elected Senate (64 members, 10 from each State and two from each of the federal territories) and a House of Representatives (127 members, chosen in proportion to population). Australia comprises six states (each with its own Government and judicial system) and two federally-administered territories.
Telephones: 4 999 982 (1974).
Daily newspapers: 62 (1972)
  Total circulation: 5 282 000
Radio: 2 851 230 (1974)
TV: 3 022 006 (1974).
Length of roadways: 549 501 miles *884 336 km.*
Length of railways: 25 027 miles *40 277 km.*
Universities: 18.
Expectation of life: Males 67·92 years; females 74·18 years (1960–62).
Defence: Military service voluntary; Total armed forces 69 100; Defence expenditure 1974–5 $2331 million.
Wildlife: Kangaroo, koala, wombat, Tasmanian wolfdevil, platypus, echidna (spiny anteater), lizards, snakes, salt-water crocodile, wild horses, wild pigs, camel, water buffalo; kookaburra, lyre bird, emu.
Cinemas: 735 (seating capacity 478 400) and 241 drive-in (1972).

NEW SOUTH WALES
Population: 4 601 180 (1971 census) 4 743 442 (1974 est).
Area: 309 500 miles² *801 600 km².*
Capital city: Sydney, population 2 898 330 (1974).
Other principal towns (1974): Newcastle 360 090; Wollongong 208 550; Albury 31 350; Wagga Wagga 31 160; Broken Hill 28 310.
Highest point: Mt Kosciusko, 7316 ft *2230 m.*
Principal mountain ranges: Great Dividing Range, Australian Alps, New England Range, Snowy Mountains, Blue Mountains, Liverpool Range.
Principal rivers: Darling, Murray.
Governor: Sir (Arthur) Roden Cutler, VC, KCMG, KCVO, CBE (b. 24 May 1916).
Premier: The Hon Neville Kenneth Wran, QC, LLB, MLA.
Climate: Most of the state has hot summers and mild winters, with rainfall well distributed, but in the east drought and storms sometimes occur.
Crops: Wheat, maize, oats, barley, tobacco, cotton, rice, sugar-cane, bananas.
Telephones: 1 299 620 (1974).
Radio: 996 248 (1974).
Length of roadways: 129 745 miles *208 804 km.*
Length of railways: 6061 miles *9754 km.*
Universities: 6.

VICTORIA
Population: 3 502 351 (1971 census); 3 631 877 (1974 est).
Area: 87 875 miles² *227 600 km².*
Capital city: Melbourne, population 2 620 400 (1974).
Other principal towns: Geelong 128 370 (1974); Ballarat 58 620 (1971); Bendigo 45 936 (1971).
Principal mountain ranges: Australian Alps, Great Dividing Range.
Principal rivers: Murray, Yarra-Yarra.
Governor: Sir Henry Arthur Winneke, KCMG, OBE (b. 29 Oct. 1908).
Premier: Rupert James Hamer, ED (b. 29 July 1916).
Crops: Wheat, oats, barley, potatoes, fruit.
Length of roadways: 101 598 miles *163 506 km.*
Length of railways: 4170 miles *6711 km.*
Universities: 3.

QUEENSLAND

Population: 1 827 065 (1971 census); 1 967 941 (1974 est).
Area: 666 875 miles² *1 727 200 km².*
Capital city: Brisbane, population 940 800 (1974).
Other principal towns (1974): Townsville 79 500; Gold Coast 78 600; Toowoomba 52 250; Rockhampton 51 100; Cairns 34 350.
Highest point: Mt Bartle Frere 5287 ft *1611 m.*
Principal mountain ranges: Great Dividing Range, Selwyn, Kirby.
Principal rivers: Brisbane, Mitchell, Fitzroy, Barcoo, Flinders.
Governor: Air Marshal Sir Colin Thomas Hannah, KCMG, KBE, CB (b. 22 Dec. 1914).
Premier: Johannes Bjelke-Petersen (b. 13 Jan. 1911).
Crops: Sugar-cane, wheat, maize, sorghum, peanuts, fodder crops, citrus fruit, apples, grapes, bananas.
Radio: 429 000 (1974).
TV: 424 090 (1974).
Length of roadways: 120 076 miles *193 243 km.*
Length of railways: 5797 miles *9329 km.*
Universities: 3.

SOUTH AUSTRALIA

Population: 1 173 707 (1971 census); 1 218 156 (1974 est).
Area: 379 925 miles² *984 000 km².*
Capital city: Adelaide, population 885 400 (1974).
Other principal towns (1971): Whyalla 32 109; Mount Gambier 17 934; Port Pirie 15 456.
Principal mountain ranges: Middleback, Mt Lofty Range.
Principal river: Murray.
Governor: Sir Douglas Ralph Nicholls, OBE (b. 9 Dec. 1906).
Premier: Donald Allan Dunstan (b. 21 Sept. 1926).
Climate: Mediterranean type.
Crops: Wheat, barley, oats, fruit, grapes.
Telephones: 298 300 (1974).
Radio: 339 516 (1974).
TV: 347 453 (1974).
Length of roadways: 75 517 miles *121 533 km.*
Length of railways: 3756 miles *6044 km.*
Universities: 2.

WESTERN AUSTRALIA

Population: 1 030 469 (1971 census) 1 094 721 (1974 est).
Area: 975 100 miles² *2 525 500 km².*
Capital city: Perth, population 760 000 (1974), incl Fremantle.
Other principal towns: Fremantle 32 100; Kalgoorlie-Boulder 20 600; Bunbury 18 550; Geraldton 15 800; Albany 12 300.
Highest point: Mt Meharry 4082 ft *1244 m.*
Principal mountain ranges: Darling, Hamersley.
Principal rivers: Fitzroy, Ashburton, Fortescue, Swan, Murchison.
Governor: Air Chief Marshal Sir Wallace Hart Kyle, GCB, CBE, DSO, DFC (b. 22 Jan. 1910).
Premier: Sir Charles Walter Michael Court, OBE (b. 29 Sept. 1911).
Crops: Wheat, barley, oats, hay, citrus fruit, grapes.
Telephones: 304 044 (1972).
Radio: 205 230 (1972).
TV: 218 782 (1972).
Length of roadways: 58 237 miles *93 723 km.*
Length of railways: 3837 miles *6175 km.*
Universities: 2.

TASMANIA

Population: 390 413 (1971 census); 400 431 (1974 est).
Area: 26 175 miles² *67 800 km².*
Capital city: Hobart, population 161 320 (1974).
Other principal towns (1974): Launceston 63 210; Burnie-Somerset 20 610; Devonport 19 730.
Highest point: Cradle Mountain, 5069 ft *1545 m.*
Principal mountain range: Highlands.
Principal rivers: Derwent, Gordon, Tamar
Governor: Sir Stanley Charles Burbury, KBE, (b. 2 Dec. 1909).
Premier: William Arthur Neilson (b. 27 Aug. 1925).
Crops: Hay, barley, oats, wheat, apples, pears, hops.
Length of roadways: c. 12 847 miles *20 675 km.*
Universities: 1

AUSTRIA

Official name: Republik Österreich (Republic of Austria).
Population: 7 456 403 (1971 census); 7 528 000 (1974 est).
Area: 32 375 miles² *83 850 km².*
Language: German
Religions: Roman Catholic, Protestant minority.
Capital city: Wien (Vienna), population 1 614 841 (1971).
Other principal towns (1971): Graz 248 500; Linz 202 874; Salzburg 128 845; Innsbruck 115 197; Klagenfurt 82 512.
Highest point: Grossglockner, 12 462 ft *3798 m* (first climbed in 1800).
Principal mountain range: Alps.
Principal rivers: Donau (Danube) (1770 miles *2848 km*), Inn, Mur.
Head of State: Dr Rudolf Kirchschläger (b. 20 Mar. 1915), Federal President.
Head of Government: Dr Bruno Kreisky (b. 22 Jan. 1911), Federal Chancellor.
Climate: Generally cold, dry winters and warm summers, with considerable variations due to altitude. Average annual temperature 45 °F to 48 °F. Most of rain in summer. In Vienna, July hottest (59 °F–75 °F), January coldest (26° F to 34 °F), August rainiest (10 days). Absolute maximum temperature 39,4 °C (102·9 °F), Horn, 5 July 1957; absolute minimum −36,6 °C (−33·9 °F), Zwettl, 11 Feb. 1929.
Crops: Barley, potatoes, wheat, rye, maize, oats, sugar-beet.
Monetary unit: Schilling. 1 Schilling = 100 Groschen.
Denominations:
Coins 1, 2, 5, 10, 50 Groschen, 1, 5, 10, 25, 50 and 100 Schilling.
Notes 20, 50, 100, 500, 1000 Schilling.

Exchange rate to US dollar: 18.31 (February 1976).
Political history and government: A federal republic, divided into nine provinces. The bicameral federal parliament comprises the *Nationalrat* (National Council) of 183 members, directly elected for four years, and the *Bundesrat* (Federal Council) of 58 members representing the provincial assemblies.
Telephones: 1 841 234 (1973).
Daily newspapers: 31 (1972).
   Total circulation: 2 460 000.
Radio: 2 169 939 (1974).
TV: 1 856 096 (1974).
Length of roadways: 59 962 miles *96 500 km.*
Length of railways: 3656 miles *5883 km* (state); 395 miles *636 km* (private).
Universities: 16.
Expectation of life: Males 64·9 years; females 67·0 years (1972).
Defence: Military service six months, followed by 60 days reservist training. Total armed forces 17 000 (regular); Defence expenditure 1975 $410 million.
Wildlife: Fox, marten, marmot, deer.
Cinemas: 679 (seating capacity 228 000) and 1 drive-in (1972).

BAHAMAS

Official name: The Commonwealth of the Bahamas.
Population: 175 192 (1970 census); 197 000 (1974 est).
Area: 5 382 miles² *13 939 km².*
Languages: English.
Religions: Anglican, Baptist, Roman Catholic, Methodist, Saints of God and Church of God.
Capital city: Nassau (on New Providence Island), population of island 101 503 (1970).
Other principal islands (1970): Grand Bahama 25 859; Andros 8845; Abaco 6501; Eleuthera 6247; Long Island 3861; Harbour Island and Spanish Wells 3221; Cat Island 2657; Inagua 1109.
Highest point: Mount Alvernia, Cat Island.
Head of State: HM Queen Elizabeth II, represented by Sir Milo Boughton Butler, GCMG (b. 11 Aug. 1906), Governor-General.
Prime Minister: The Rt Hon Lynden Oscar Pindling (b. 22 Mar. 1930).
Climate: Equable. Winter averages of 70 °F to 75 °F (21 °C to 24 °C). Summer averages of 80 °F to 90 °F (26 °C to 32 °C). Highest recorded temperature is 94 °F and lowest 51 °F. Rainfall mainly between May and September.
Crops: Citrus fruit, pineapples, tomatoes, okras, onions, bananas.
Monetary unit: Bahamian dollar (B$). 1 dollar = 100 cents.
Denominations:
Coins 1, 5, 10, 15, 25, 50 cents, B$ 1, 2, 5.
Notes 50 cents, B$ 1, 3, 5, 10, 20, 500, 1000.

Exchange rate to US dollar: 1.00 (February 1976).
Political history and government: A member of the Commonwealth, independent since 10 July 1973. Executive power is vested in the Queen, represented by a Governor-General who is advised by the Cabinet. Legislative power is vested in a Senate (16 members) and a House of Assembly (38 members).
Telephones: 54 097 (1973).
Daily newspapers: 3 (1972).
Total circulation: 30 000.
Radio: 85 000 (1974).
TV: 4500 (1964).
Length of roadways: 700 miles *1126 km.*
Adult illiteracy: 10·2% (males 9·8%; females 10·5%) in 1963.
Expectation of life: Males 64·0 years; females 67·3 years (1969–71).
Wildlife: Racoon, iguana, chameleon, turtle. Over 200 species of bird including parrots and flamingoes.
Cinemas: 19 and 3 drive-ins (1972).

BAHRAIN

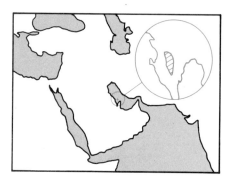

Official name: Daulat al Bahrain (State of Bahrain).
Population: 216 815 (1971 census); 266 078 (1975 est).
Area: 240 miles² *622 km².*
Language: Arabic.
Religions: Muslim, Christian minority.
Capital city: Manama, population 98 300 (1974).
Other principal towns: Muharraq 41 143 (1971); Rifa'a 9403 (1965); Hidd 5230 (1965).
Highest point: Jabal ad Dukhan, 440 ft *134 m.*
Head of State: H H Shaikh Isa ibn Sulman al-Khalifa, Hon KCMG (b. 3 July 1933), Amir.
Prime Minister: Shaikh Khalifa ibn Sulman al-Khalifa (b. 1935).
Climate: Very hot and humid. Average maximum 68 °F (January) to 100 °F (August), minimum 57 °F (January) to 85 °F (July, August), December and February rainiest (each two days).
Crops: Vegetables, dates.
Monetary unit: Bahrain dinar. One dinar = 1000 fils.
Denominations:
Coins 1, 5, 10, 25, 50, 100, 500 fils.
Notes 100 fils, ¼, ½ 1, 5, 10 dinars.
Exchange rate to US dollars: 0·396 (February 1976).
Political history and government: A shaikhdom under British protection from 1882 until full independence on 15 Aug. 1971. Now an amirate, with a Cabinet appointed by the Ruler. The National Assembly, containing Cabinet ministers and 30 elected members, was dissolved in August 1975.

Telephones: 17 657 (1973).
Daily newspapers: 1
Total circulation: 1000
Radio: 80 000 (1973).
TV: 18 000 (1973).
Adult illiteracy: 59·8% (males 50·7%; females 71·5%) in 1971.
Defence: Total armed forces 1100.
Wildlife: Wild ass, gazelle, jerboa, hare, lizard, mongoose, raven, bulbul, pigeon, flamingo, sparrow.
Cinemas: 9 (seating capacity 9800) in 1970.

BANGLADESH

Official name: Gana Praja Tantri Bangla Desh (People's Republic of Bangladesh).
Population: 71 316 517 (census of 1 Mar. 1974, excluding underenumeration); 74 991 000 (estimate for 1 July 1974).
Area: 55 598 miles² *143 998 km².*
Language: Bengali.
Religions: Muslim with Hindu, Christian and Buddhist minorities.
Capital city: Dhaka (Dacca), population 1 310 976 (1974).
Other principal towns: (1973): Chittagong 492 153; Khulna 467 881; Narayanganj 442 673.
Principal rivers: Ganges, Jumna, Meghna.
Head of State: Abusadat Mohammed Sayem (b. 1 Mar. 1916), President and Chief Martial Law Administrator.
Climate: Tropical and monsoon. Summer temperature about 86 °F (30 °C); winter 68 °F (20 °C). Rainfall is heavy, varying from 50 in to 135 in in different areas, and most falling from June to September (the monsoon season).
Crops: Rice, sugar cane, jute, potatoes, sweet potatoes, tea.
Monetary unit: Taka. 1 taka = 100 paisa.
Denominations:
Coins 1, 2, 5, 10, 25, 50 paisa.
Notes 1, 5, 10, 100 taka.
Exchange rate to US dollar: 14.82 (February 1976).
Political history and government: Formerly East Pakistan, declared independence 26 Mar. 1971. Secession became effective on 16 Dec. 1971. Joined the Commonwealth on 18 Apr. 1972. Under martial law, with political parties banned, since 15 Aug. 1975. Parliament was dissolved on 6 Nov. 1975.
Telephones: 48 000 (1972).
Daily newspapers: 5 (1975).
Radio: 531 000 (1969).
Length of roadways: 14 913 miles *c. 24 00 km.*
Length of railways: 1776 miles *2858 km.*
Universities: 6.
Adult illiteracy: approx. 85%.

Expectation of life: Males 43·5 years; females 43·0 years (1965–70).
Defence: Military service voluntary. Total armed forces 36 000; Defence expenditure 1973–4 $65 million.
Wildlife: Tiger, elephant, buffalo, samba deer, clouded leopard, jackal, bear; wide variety of birds.

BARBADOS

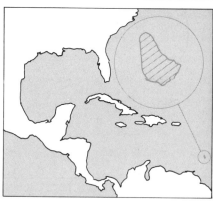

Population: 238 141 (1970 census); 251 237 (1974 est).
Area: 166 miles² *430 km².*
Languages: English.
Religions: Anglican with Methodist, Roman Catholic and Moravian minorities.
Capital city: Bridgetown, population 8789 (1970); parish of Bridgetown and St Michael 96 886.
Other principal town: Speightstown.
Highest point: Mount Hillaby, 1115 ft *340 m.*
Head of State: HM Queen Elizabeth II, represented by Sir (Arleigh) Winston Scott, GCMG, GCVO (b. 27 Mar. 1900), Governor-General.
Prime Minister: The Rt Hon Errol Walton Barrow (b 21 Jan 1920)
Climate: Pleasant, with temperatures rarely rising above 86 °F (30 °C) or falling below 67 °F (18 °C). Average rainfall, which varies from district to district, 50 in to 75 in (1270 mm to 1778 mm). Subject to earthquakes and hurricanes.
Crops: Sugar, cotton, tobacco, coffee.
Monetary unit: Barbados dollar (B$). 1 dollar = 100 cents.
Denominations:
Coins 1, 5, 10, 25 cents, B$1
Notes B$ 1, 5, 10, 20, 100.
Exchange rate to US dollar: 2.00 (February 1976).
Political history and government: A member of the Commonwealth, independent since 30 Nov. 1966. The legislature comprises a Senate (21 appointed members) and a House of Assembly (24 elected members). Executive power is effectively held by the Prime Minister and the Cabinet.
Telephones: 39 445 (1973).
Daily newspapers: One.
Total circulation: 25 642 weekdays; 35 746 Sundays.
Radio: 110 000 (1972).
TV: 42 000 (1974).
Length of roadways: 840 miles *1352 km.*
Universities: 1
Expectation of life: Males 62·74 years; Females 67·43 years (1959–61).
Defence: A small volunteer force but no standing armed forces.
Wildlife: Monkeys, mongoose, hare, racoon, tree frog; humming bird, 'Barbados' sparrow, dove.
Cinemas: 6 (seating capacity 4700) in 1972; also two drive-ins for 568 cars.

BELGIUM

Official name: Royaume de Belgique (in French) or Koninkrijk België (in Dutch) (Kingdom of Belgium).
Population: 9 650 944 (census of 31 Dec. 1970); 9 788 248 (estimate, 31 Dec. 1974).
Area: 11 781 miles² *30 513 km²*.
Languages: Dutch (Flemish), French, German.
Religion: Roman Catholic.
Capital city: Brussels, population 1 054 970 (1974), incl. suburbs.
Other principal towns: Antwerp 672 703; Liège 440 447; Ghent 224 728; Charleroi 218 089; Bruges 118 023.
Highest point: Baraque Michel, 2303 ft *702 m*.
Principal mountain ranges: Ardennes.
Principal rivers: Schelde, Meuse (575 miles *925 km*).
Head of State: HM Baudouin Albert Charles Léopold Axel Marie Gustave, KG (b. 7 Sept. 1930), King of the Belgians.
Prime Minister: Léo Tindemans (b. 16 Apr. 1922).
Climate: Mild and humid on coast. Hotter summers, colder winters inland. In Brussels, January coldest (31 °F to 42 °F), July hottest 54 °F to 73 °F) December rainiest (13 days). Absolute maximum temperature 40,0 °C (*104 °F*) on the coast, 27 June 1947; absolute minimum −29,8 °C (−21·6 °F) Vielsalm, 10 Dec. 1879.
Crops: Potatoes, wheat, barley, maize, flax, sugar-beet, hops.
Monetary unit: Belgian franc (frank). 1 franc = 100 centimes (centiemen).
Denominations:
Coins 25, 50 centimes, 1, 5, 10, 50, 100 francs.
Notes 20, 50, 100, 500, 1000, 5000 francs.
Exchange rate to US dollar: 39.14 (February 1976).
Political history and government: A constitutional monarchy. Legislative power is vested in the King, the Senate (181 members, including 106 directly elected) and the Chamber of Representatives (212 members chosen by proportional representation). Members of both Houses are elected for up to four years. There are nine provinces.
Telephones: 2 503 036 (1973).
Daily newspapers: 47 (1971).
Radio: 3 768 491 (1974).
TV: 2 464 201 (1974).
Length of roadways: 57 576 miles *92 660 km*.
Length of railways: 2536 miles *4081 km*.
Universities: 6.
Expectation of Life: Males 67·73 years; females 73·51 years (1959–63).
Defence: Military service 10–12 months; Total armed forces 87 000; Defence expenditure 1975 $1821 million.
Wildlife: Boar, badger, fox.

Cinemas: 678 with seating capacity of 366 856 (1971).

BENIN

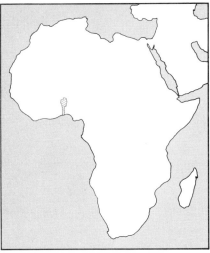

Official name: La République populaire du Bénin (the People's Republic of Benin).
Population: 3 029 000 (1974 est).
Area: 43 484 miles² *112 622 km²*.
Languages: French (official), Fon, Adja, Bariba, Yoruba.
Religions: Animist, with Christian and Muslim minorities.
Capital city: Porto-Novo, population 100 000 (1972).
Other principal towns: Cotonou 175 000 (1972); Abomey 42 100; Ouidah 19 600; Parakou 16 300.
Highest point: 2083 ft *635 m*.
Principal mountain ranges: Châine de l'Atakora.
Principal rivers: Ouémé, Niger (2600 miles [*4184 km*]) on frontier.
Head of State: Lt-Col Mathieu Kerekou (b. 2 Sept. 1933), President and Head of the Government.
Climate: Tropical (hot and humid). Average temperatures 68 °F to 93 °F. Heavy rainfall near the coast, hotter and drier inland. In Cotonou the warmest month is April (daily average high 83 °F), coldest is August (73 °F).
Crops: Yams, cassava, maize, palm kernels and palm oil, cotton, groundnuts.
Monetary unit: Franc de la Communauté financière africaine.
Denominations:
Coins 1, 2, 5, 10, 25, 50, 100 CFA francs.
Notes 50, 100, 500, 1000, 5000 CFA francs.
Exchange rate to US dollar: 224.24 (February 1976).
Political history and government: Formerly part of French West Africa, became independent as the Republic of Dahomey on 1 Aug. 1960. Under military rule since 26 Oct. 1972. Government is controlled by a cabinet of army officers. On 1 Sept. 1973 the President announced the creation of a National Council of the Revolution (69 members, including 30 civilians), under his leadership, to develop state policy. Since 28 Nov. 1974 the Council has been directed by a 14-member National Political Bureau, also chaired by the President. The military government advocates Marxist-Lenninist principles and introduced the country's present name on 1 Dec. 1975.
Telephones: 8326 (1974).
Daily newspapers: 2 (1972).
Total circulation: 2000.
Radio: 150 000 (1972).
TV: 100 (1972).

Length of roadways: 4310 miles *6937 km* (1973).
Length of railways: 360 miles *579 km*.
Universities: 1.
Adult illiteracy: 95·4% (males 92·3%; females 98·2%) in 1961.
Expectation of life: Males 36·9 years; females 40·1 years (1965–70).
Defence: Total armed forces 1650.
Wildlife: Elephant, buffalo, warthog, antelope, leopard, lion.
Cinemas: 6 (seating capacity 9000) in 1972.

BHUTAN

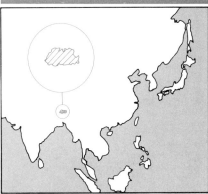

Official name: Druk-yul or, in Tibetan, Druk Gyalkhap (Realm of the Dragon). The name Bhutan is Tibetan for 'the End of the Land'.
Population: 1 034 774 (1969 census); 1 173 000 (UN estimate, mid-1975).
Area: 18 000 miles² *47 000 km²*.
Languages: Dzongkha, Bumthangka, Sarchapkkha.
Religions: Buddhist with Hindu minority.
Capital city: Thimbu (Thimphu).
Other principal towns: Paro Dzong; Punakha; Tongsa Dzong.
Highest point: Khula Kangri 1, 24 784 ft *7554 m*.
Principal mountain range: Himalaya.
Principal rivers: Amo-Chu, Wang-chu, Ma-chu, Manas.
Head of State: Jigme Singhye Wangchuk (b. 11 Nov. 1955), Druk Gyalpo ('Dragon King').
Climate: Steamy hot in lowland. foothills Cold most of the year in higher areas.
Crops: Rice, wheat, maize, potatoes, oranges, apples.
Monetary unit: Ngultrum. 1 ngultrum = 100 chetrums (Indian currency is also legal tender).
Denominations:
Coins 5, 10, 20, 25 chetrums, 1 ngultrum.
Notes 1, 5, 10 ngultrums.
Exchange rate to US dollar: 8.9284 (February 1976).
Political history and government: A monarchy under Indian protection. The National Assembly members can remove the King by a two-thirds vote, and can outvote any government bills or proposals of the King. There are nine provinces.
Telephones: 570 (1974).
Length of roadways: 621 miles *1000 km*.
Expectation of life: Males 39·2 years, females 42·0 years (1965–70).
Defence: Army: 5000 men, Indian trained.
Wildlife: Deer, wild hog, bear, elephant, tiger, leopard.
Cinemas: 3 (seating capacity 1500) in 1971.

BOLIVIA

Official name: La República de Bolivia.
Population: 5 470 000 (1974 est).

177

Area: 424 164 miles² *1 098 581 km.²*
Languages: Spanish Amyará, Quéchua.
Religion: Roman Catholic.
Capital City: La Paz de Ayacucho, population 697 480 (1974).
Other principal towns (1974): Santa Cruz de la Sierra 263 260; Cochabamba 245 230; Potosí 209 850; Oruro 145 410; Sucre 88 040.
Highest point: Nevado Sajama, 21 391 ft *6520 m* (first climbed in 1937).
Principal mountain ranges: Cordillera de los Andes, Cordillera Real, Cordillera Oriental, Cordillera Central.
Principal rivers: Beni, Mamoré, Pilcomayo, Paraguai (Paraguay) (1500 miles *2414 km*) on frontier.
Head of State: Gen Hugo Banzer Suárez (b. 10 May 1926), President.
Climate: Dry, with cold winds on Antiplano, hot and humid in eastern lowlands. In La Paz, average maximum 62 °F (June, July) to 67 °F (November), minimum 33 °F (July) to 43 °F (January, February), January, rainiest (21 days).
Crops: Sugar-cane, rice, maize, cotton, potatoes, coffee.
Monetary unit: Bolivian peso. 1 peso = 100 centavos.
Denominations:
  Coins 5, 10, 20, 25, 50 centavos, 1 peso.
  Notes 1, 5, 10, 20, 50, 100 pesos.
Exchange rate to US dollar: 20.00 (February 1976).
Political history and government: A republic, divided into nine departments. Under military rule since September 1969, sometimes with the participation of political parties. An all-military Cabinet has held office since June 1974. The government announced a state of siege in November 1974 and banned political activity until 1980.

Telephones: 48 950 (1974).
Daily newspapers: 17 (1972).
  Total circulation: 194 000.
Radio: 1 350 000 (1968).
TV: 11 000 (1972).
Length of roadways: 15 930 miles *25 637 km.*
Length of railways: 2190 miles *3524 km.*
Universities: 9.
Adult illiteracy: 60% (1960 estimate).
Expectation of life: Males 44·3 years, females 46·3 years (1965–70).

Defence: Military service 12 months selective. Total armed forces 27 000; Defence expenditure 1974 $35 million.
Wildlife: Llama, alpaca, vicuna, monkeys, jaguar, puma, anteater, deer; many kinds of snake. Parrots, ducks, geese, rhca.
Cinemas: 90 with seating capacity of *c.* 42 500 (1970).

BOTSWANA

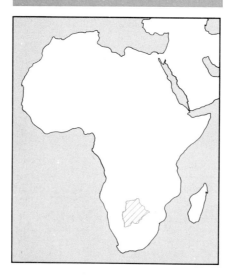

Official name: The Republic of Botswana.
Population: 608 656 (1971 census); 661 000 (1974 est).
Area: 231 805 miles² *600 372 km².*
Languages: Se-Tswana, English.
Religions: Christian, ancestral beliefs.
Capital city: Gaborone, population 18 436 (1971).
Other principal towns (1971): Serowe 43 186; Kanye 39 200; Molepolole 31 986; Mochudi 21 382; Francistown 19 903.
Principal rivers: Chobe, Shashi.
Head of State: Sir Seretse Khama, KBE (b. 1 July 1921), President.
Climate: Sub-tropical but variable. Hot summers. In winter, warm days and cold nights in higher parts. Average annual rainfall 18 in, varying from 25 in in north, to 9 in or less in western Kalahari. Sand and dust blown by westerly wind in August.
Crops: Sorghum, maize, millet, groundnuts, tobacco, cotton.
Monetary unit: South African currency (*q.v.*).
Political history and government: Formerly the Bechuanaland Protectorate, an independent republic within the Commonwealth since 30 Sept. 1966. Executive power is vested in the President, who leads the Cabinet. They are responsible to the National Assembly, which has 38 members (32 chosen by general election).
Telephones: 6699 (1974).
Daily newspapers: 2 (1971).
  Total circulation: 14 000.
Radio: 11 602 (1972).
Length of roadways (1972): 12 923 miles *20 798 km.*
Length of railways: 392 miles *630 km.*
Universities: 1.
Adult illiteracy: 67·1% (males 69·7%; females 65·0%) unable to read in 1964.
Expectation of life: Males 39·4 years, females 42·6 years (1965–70).
Defence: A paramilitary police force of about 1500.
Wildlife: Hartebeest, springbok, eland, zebra, gemsbok, hippopotamus, giraffe, buffalo, crocodile; numerous snakes including cobras and puff adders. Vulture, ostrich, bustard, pelican.
Cinemas: 11 (est seating capacity 3000) in 1971.

BRAZIL

Official name: República Federativa do Brasil (the Federative Republic of Brazil).
Population: 92 341 556 (1970 census); 104 243 000 (1974 est).
Area: 3 286 488 miles² *8 511 965 km².*
Language: Portuguese.
Religion: Roman Catholic.
Capital city: Brasília, population 271 570 (1970).
Other principal towns (1975): São Paulo 7 198 608; Rio de Janeiro 4 857 716; Belo Horizonte 1 557 446; Recife (Pernambuco) 1 249 821; Salvador (Bahia) 1 237 373; Fortaleza 1 109 837; Pôrto Alegre 1 043 964.
Highest point: Pico da Bandeira, 9482 ft *2890 m.*
Principal mountain ranges: Serra do Mar, Serra Geral, Serra de Mantiqueira.
Principal rivers: Amazonas (Amazon) (3910 miles *6292 km*) and tributaries, Paraná, São Francisco.
Head of State: Gen Ernesto Geisel (b. 3 Aug. 1907), President.
Climate: Hot and wet in tropical Amazon basin; sub-tropical in highlands; temperate (warm summers and mild winters) in southern uplands. In Rio de Janeiro, average maximum 75 °F (July, September) to 85 °F (February), minimum 63 °F (July) to 73 °F (January, February), December rainiest (14 days). In São Paulo maximum 71 °F (June, July) to 82 °F (February), minimum 49 °F (July) to 64 °F (February), January rainiest (19 days). Absolute maximum temperature 43·9 °C (*111·0 °F*), Ibipetuba, 16 Sept. 1927: absolute minimum −11° C (+12·2 °F), Xanxerê, 14 July 1933.
Crops: Beans, cassava, coffee, cotton, maize, sugar-cane, rice, sweet potatoes, citrus fruit, bananas, tobacco, cocoa.
Monetary unit: Cruzeiro. 1 cruzeiro = 100 centavos.
Denominations:
  Coins 1, 2, 5, 10, 20, 50 centavos, 1 cruzeiro.
  Notes 1, 5, 10, 50, 100, 500 cruzeiros.
Exchange rate to US dollar: 9.395 (February 1976).

Political history and government: Military rule since April 1964. Under the 1969 constitution, Brazil is a federal republic comprising 21 States, four Territories and a Federal District (Brasília). Executive power is exercised by the President, chosen by an electoral college. Legislative power is exercised by the National Congress, comprising the Chamber of Deputies (364 members, elected for four years) and the Federal Senate (66 members, elected for eight years). Only two political parties have been legalised.
Telephones: 2 415 000 (1973).
Daily newspapers: 261 (1971).
Total circulation: 3 498 000.
Radio: 6 250 000 (1974).
TV: 6 600 000 (1972).
Length of roadways (1972): 783 133 miles *1 260 331 km.*
Length of railways: 19 381 miles *31 191 km*
Universities: 64.
Adult illiteracy: 33·8% (males 30·6%; females 36·8%) in 1970.
Expectation of life: Males 57·1 years; females 62·4 years (1965–70).
Defence: Military service one year; Total armed forces 254 000; Defence expenditure 1975 $1283 million.
Wildlife: Cayman, ocelot, tapir, armadillo, many reptiles including boa constrictor, anaconda (world's largest snake), insects and birds including about 200 kinds of humming bird. Turtles and, among the fish, the piranha.
Cinemas: 3194 (seating capacity 1 911 200) and one drive-in (1967).

BULGARIA

Official name: Narodna Republika Bulgaria (People's Republic of Bulgaria).
Population: 8 227 866 (1965 census); 8 678 699 (1974 est).
Area: 42 823 miles² *110 912 km².*
Languages: Bulgarian with Turkish and Macedonian minorities.
Religions: Eastern Orthodox with Muslim, Roman Catholic and Protestant minorities.
Capital city: Sofiya (Sofia), population 946 305 (1973).
Other principal towns: Plovdiv 287 744; Varna 260 129; Russe 166 971; Burgas 143 977; Stara Zagora 119 246.
Highest point: Musala, 9596 ft *2925 m.*
Principal mountain ranges: Balkan Mountains.
Principal rivers: Dunav (Danube) (1770 miles *2848 km*), Iskŭr (Iskar) (229 miles *368 km*), Maritsa (326 miles *524 km*), Tundzha.
Head of State: Todor Zhivkov (b. 7 Sept. 1911), President of the State Council and First Secretary of the Central Committee of the Bulgarian Communist Party.

Head of Government: Stanko Todorov (b. 10 Dec. 1920), Chairman of the Council of Ministers.
Climate: Mild in the south, more extreme in the north. In Sofia, July (57 °F to 82 °F), August (56 °F to 82 °F), hottest, January (22 °F to 34 °F), coldest, May rainiest (11 days).
Crops: Wheat, maize, barley, grapes, tomatoes, sunflower seed, sugar-beet (also world's principal supplier of attar of roses).
Monetary unit: Lev. 1 lev = 100 stotinki.
Denominations:
Coins 1, 2, 5, 10, 20, 50 stotinki, 1, 2 leva
Notes 1, 2, 5, 10, 20 leva.
Exchange rate to US dollar: 0.96 (February 1976).
Political history and government: A people's republic. Supreme power is vested in the single-chamber National Assembly consisting of 400 deputies elected for five years from areas of equal population. The Assembly elects the State Council to be the leading organ of state power, performing both executive and legislative functions. Administrative responsibility is held by the Council of Ministers.
Telephones: 640 842 (1973).
Daily newspapers: 13.
Total circulation: 2 434 000.
Radio: 2 265 821 (1973).
TV: 1 489 640 (1975).
Length of roadways (1972): 22 186 miles *35 706 km.*
Length of railways: 3830 miles *6164 km.*
Universities: 3.
Adult illiteracy: 9·8% (males 4·8%; females 14·7%) in 1965.
Expectation of life: Males 68·81 years; females 72·67 years (1965–7).
Defence: Military service, army and air force two years, navy three years. Total armed forces 152 000; Defence expenditure 1975 $392 million.
Wildlife: Wolf, fox, wildcat, elk, bear, squirrel and other rodents.
Cinemas: 3106 (seating capacity 707 100) in 1972.

BURMA

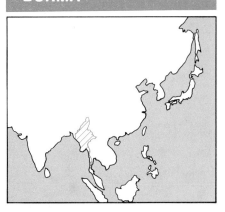

Official name: Pyidaungsu Socialist Thammada Myanma Nainggnan (The Socialist Republic of the Union of Burma).
Population: 28 885 867 (1973 census); 30 170 000 (1974 est).
Area: 261 790 miles²; *678 033 km².*
Languages: Burmese, English.
Religions: Buddhist with Muslim, Hindu and Animist minorities.
Capital city: Rangoon, population 3 186 886 (1973).
Other principal towns: Mandalay 417 266; Bassein 335 588; Henzada 283 658; Pegu 254 761; Myingyan 220 129; Moulmein 202 967 (1973).
Highest point: Hkakado Razi, 19 296 ft *5881 m.*

Principal mountain ranges: Arakan Yoma, Pegu Yoma.
Principal rivers: Irrawaddy (including Chindwin), Salween, Sittang, Mekong (2600 miles [*4184 km*]) on frontier.
Head of State: U Ne Win (b. 24 May 1911), President.
Prime Minister: U Sein Win.
Climate: Hot March–April, monsoon May–October, cool November–February. In Rangoon, average maximum 85 °F (July, August) to 97 °F (April), minimum 65 °F (January) to 77 °F (May). July (26 days) and August (25 days) rainiest. Absolute maximum temperature 114 °F (*45 °C* to *56 °C*), Mandalay, 29 April 1906, Monywa 15 May 1934; absolute minimum 31 °F (*−0,56 °C*), Maymyo, 29 Dec. 1913.
Crops: Rice, sugar-cane, pulses, groundnuts, sesame seed, jute.
Monetary unit: Kyat. 1 kyat = 100 pyas.
Denominations:
Coins 1, 5, 10, 25, 50 pyas, 1 kyat.
Notes 1, 5, 10, 20, 25 kyats.
Exchange rate to US dollar: 6.567 (February 1976).
Political history and government: A former British dependency, independent since 4 Jan. 1948. Under military rule since 2 Mar. 1962. Under the 1974 constitution, the People's Assembly (450 representatives) is the highest authority, while the 29-member Council of State, of which the President is Chairman, has executive powers. The senior administrative body is the Council of Ministers. A one-party state since 28 Mar. 1964.
Telephones: 29 411 (1974).
Daily newspapers: 7 (1972).
Total circulation: 264 000.
Radio: 627 000 (1973).
Length of roadways: *c.* 15 534 miles *c. 25 000 km.*
Length of railways: 1925 miles *3098 km.*
Universities: 2.
Expectation of life: Males 46·1 years; females 49·0 years (1965–70).
Defence: Military service voluntary; Total armed forces 167 000; Defence expenditure 1972–3 $101 million.
Wildlife: Tiger, elephant, leopard, many types of monkey, jackal, great variety of birds, bats, insects, moths and butterflies.
Cinemas: 418 (seating capacity 302 600) in 1972.

BURUNDI

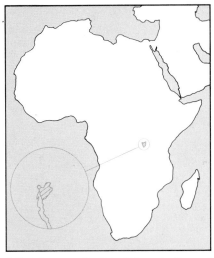

Official name: La République du Burundi or Republika y'Uburundi (the Republic of Burundi).
Population: 3 600 000 (1973 est).

179

Area: 10 747 miles² *27 834 km²*.
Languages: French, Kirundi, Kiswahili.
Religions: Roman Catholic with Animist and Protestant minorities.
Capital city: Bujumbura (formerly Usumbura), population 78 810 (1970).
Other principal towns: Kitega population 5000 (1970).
Highest point: 8809 ft *2685 m*.
Principal rivers: Kagera, Ruzizi.
Head of State: Lt-Gen Michel Micombero (b. 1940), President and Prime Minister.
Climate: Hot and humid in lowlands, cool in highlands.
Crops: Coffee, cassava (manioc), bananas, maize, sweet potatoes.
Monetary unit: Burundi franc. One franc = 100 centimes.
Denominations:
  Coins 1, 5, 10 francs.
  Notes 10, 20, 50, 100, 500, 1000, 5000 francs.
Exchange rate to US dollar: 78.75 (February 1976).
Political history and government: Formerly part of the Belgian-administered Trust Territory of Ruanda-Urundi. Burundi became independent, with the Mwami (King) as Head of State, on 1 July 1962. A one-party state since 24 Nov. 1966. The monarchy was overthrown, and a republic established, by a military *coup* on 28 Nov. 1966. A constitution was adopted in July 1974. The Council of Ministers is directly responsible to the Party.
Telephones: 4797 (1974).
Daily newspapers: 1.
  Total circulation: 300.
Radio: 100 000 (1972).
Length of roadways: 1856 miles *2987 km*.
Universities: 1.
Expectation of life: Males 36·9 years, females 40·1 years (1965–70).
Defence: Total forces (army and police) about 3000.
Wildlife: Hippopotamus, crocodile, okapi, gorilla. Fish eagle.
Cinemas: 4 (seating capacity 1000) in 1970.

CAMBODIA

Official name: Democratic Kampuchea.
Population 5 728 771 (1962 census); 8 110 000 (UN estimate for mid-1975).
Area: 69 898 miles², *181 035 km²*.
Languages: Khmer (official), French.
Religions: Buddhist.
Capital city: Phnom-Penh, population 393 995 (1962).
Other principal towns: Battambang, Kompong Chhnang, Kompong Cham, Kompong Som (Sihanoukville).
Highest point: Mt Ka-Kup 5722 ft *1744 m*.
Principal mountain ranges: Chaîne des Cardamomes.
Principal rivers: Mekong 2600 miles *4184 km*.
Head of State: Khieu Samphan (b. 1932), President of the State Presidium.
Prime Minister: Pol Pot.
Climate: Tropical and humid. Rainy season June–November. In Phnom-Penh, average maximum 86 °F (November, December) to 94 °F (April), minimum 70 °F (January) to 76 °F (April–October), September rainiest (19 days).
Crops: Rice, maize, sugar-cane, rubber.
Monetary unit: Riel. One riel = 100 sen.
Denominations:
  Coins 10, 20, 50 sen.
  Notes 1, 5, 10, 20, 50, 100, 500 riels.
Exchange rate to US dollar: 1675 (April 1975).
Political history and government: On 18 Mar. 1970 Prince Sihanouk was deposed

as Head of State by his Prime Minister, Lt-Gen (later Marshal) Lon Nol, who proclaimed the Khmer Republic on 8 Oct. 1970. Sihanouk went into exile and formed a Royal Government of National Union, supported by the pro-Communist *Khmers Rouges*. Sihanoukists and the *Khmers Rouges* formed the National United Front of Cambodia (NUFC). Their combined forces defeated the republicans and Phnom-Penh surrendered on 17 April 1975, when the Royal Government took power. On 14 Dec. 1975 a congress of the NUFC approved a new republican constitution, promulgated on 5 Jan. 1976. Elections for a new Assembly were held on 20 Mar. 1976 and Prince Sihanouk resigned as Head of State on 4 Apr. 1976.

Legislative power is vested in the People's Representative Assembly, with 250 members elected for 5 years by universal adult suffrage. The Assembly elects a three-man State Presidium and appoints the Council of Ministers.

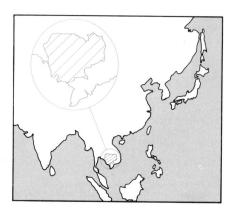

Telephones: 9000 (1972).
Radio: 111 000 (1974).
TV: 25 500 (1974).
Length of roadways: *c.* 6836 miles, *c. 11 000 km*.
Length of railways: 851 miles *1370 km*.
Adult illiteracy: 59·0% (males 30·1%; females 87·3%) in 1962.
Expectation of life: Males 44·0 years; females 46·9 years (1965–70).
Defence: Position of 'Liberation Army' (about 80 000 men) unclear.
Wildlife: Elephant, panther, tiger, leopard, honey bear, buffalo, sumatran rhinoceros, crocodile, several varieties of snakes.
Cinemas: 52 (seating capacity 28 800) in 1967.

CAMEROON

Official name: La République unie du Cameroun (the United Republic of Cameroon).
Population: 6 539 000 (1975 est).
Area: 183 569 miles² *475 442 km²*.
Languages: French, English (both official).
Religions: Animist with Christian and Muslim minorities.
Capital city: Yaoundé, population 274 399 (1975).
Other principal towns (1975): Douala 485 797; Foumban 59 701; Maroua 46 077; Bafoussam 45 998; Garoua 36 661; Victoria 31 222.
Highest point: Cameroon Mt 13 350 ft *4069 m*.
Principal mountain ranges: Massif de Ladamaoua.
Principal rivers: Sanaga, Nyong.
Head of State: Ahmadou Ahidjo (b. 24 Aug. 1924), President.

Prime Minister: Paul Biya (b. 13 Feb. 1933).

Climate: Hot and rainy on the coast; cooler and drier inland. Average temperature 80 °F. In Yaoundé average maximum 80 °F to 85 °F, minimum around 66 °F.
Crops: Cassava, sweet potatoes, maize, millet, sorghum, groundnuts, cocoa beans, coffee.
Monetary unit: Franc de la Communauté financière africaine (CFA).
Denominations:
  Coins 1, 2, 5, 10, 25, 50, 100 CFA francs
  Notes 100, 500, 1000, 5000, 10 000 CFA francs.
Exchange rate to US dollar: 224.24 (February 1976).
Political history and government: The former German colony of Cameroon was divided into British and French zones, both parts becoming UN Trust Territories. The French zone became independent as the Republic of Cameroon on 1 Jan. 1960. The northern part of the British zone joined Nigeria on 1 June 1961 and the southern part became West Cameroon when it joined the former French zone (renamed East Cameroon) to form a federal republic on 1 Oct. 1961. A one-party state since 8 Sept. 1966. After approval by a referendum on 21 May 1972, the federal arrangement ended and Cameroon became a unitary state on 2 June 1972. The legislature is a unicameral National Assembly of 120 members elected for five years by universal suffrage. The President, elected by the people every five years, appoints the Prime Minister, other Ministers and a governor for each of the seven provinces.
Telephones: 21 811 (1973).
Daily newspapers: 1 (1975).
  Total circulation: 20 000.
Radio: 225 000 (1973).
Length of roadways (1972): 14 136 miles *22 750 km*.
Length of railways: 723 miles *1164 km*.
Universities: 1.
Expectation of life: Males 39·4 years; females 42·6 years (1965–70).
Defence: Total armed forces 5600; paramilitary forces 10 000.
Wildlife: Antelope, elephant, monkeys, gorilla; many insects and birds.
Cinemas: 41 (seating capacity 15 600) in 1972.

CANADA

Official name: The Dominion of Canada.
Population: 21 568 310 (1971 census); 22 800 000 (1975 est).
Area: 3 851 809 miles² *9 976 139 km²*.

Languages: English 60·1%; French 26·9%; German 2·6%; Italian 2·5%; Ukrainian 1·4% (1971).
Religions: Roman Catholic, United Church of Canada, Anglican.
Capital city: Ottawa, population 626 000 (metropolitan area) in 1974.
Other principal towns: Montreal 2 798 000; Toronto 2 741 000; Vancouver 1 137 000; Winnipeg 570 000; Edmonton 529 000; Hamilton 520 000; Quebec 499 000; Calgary 444 000 (metropolitan areas, 1974).
Highest point: Mt Logan 19 850 ft 6050 m (first climbed 23 June 1925).
Principal mountain ranges: Rocky Mts. Coast Mts, Mackenzie Mts.
Principal rivers: Mackenzie (2635 miles 4240 km including Peace 1195 miles 1923 km), Yukon, (1979 miles 3185 km) St. Lawrence (1900 miles 3058 km), Nelson (1600 miles 2575 km, including Saskatchewan 1205 miles 1939 km), Columbia (1150 miles 1850 km), Churchill (1000 miles 1609 km).
Head of State: HM Queen Elizabeth II, represented by Jules Léger (b. 4 Apr. 1913), Governor-General.
Prime Minister: The Rt Hon Pierre Elliott Trudeau (b. 18 Oct. 1919).

Climate: Great extremes, especially inland. Average summer temperature 65 °F, very cold winters. Light to moderate rainfall, heavy snowfalls. Below are listed a selection of towns showing the extreme monthly variations in average maximum and minimum daily temperatures and the month with the maximum number of rainy days.
Calgary: Average maximum 24 °F (January) to 76 °F (July), Average minimum 2 °F (January) to 47 °F (July). Rainiest month (rainy days) June (12).
Halifax: Average maximum 31 °F (February) to 74 °F (July, August). Average minimum 15 °F (January, February) to 56 °F (August). Rainiest month (rainy days) January (17).
Ottawa: Average maximum 21 °F (January) to 81 °F (July). Average minimum 3 °F (January, February) to 58 °F (July). Rainiest month (rainy days) December (14).
St John's: Average maximum 28 °F (February) to 69 °F (August). Average minimum 16 °F (February) to 53 °F (August). Rainiest month (rainy days) November, December (17).
Vancouver: Average maximum 41 °F (January) to 74 °F (July). Average minimum 32 °F (January) to 54 °F (July, August). Rainiest month (rainy days) December (22).
Winnipeg: Average maximum 7 °F (January) to 79 °F (July). Average minimum −13 °F (January) to 55 °F (July). Rainiest month (rainy days) January, June (12).

Yellowknife: Average maximum −10 °F (January) to 69 °F (July). Average minimum −26 °F (January) to 52 °F (July). Rainiest month (rainy days) December (13).
Absolute maximum temperature 115 °F (46,1 °C), Gleichen, Alberta, 28 July 1903; absolute minimum −81 °F (−62,8 °C), Snag, Yukon, 3 Feb. 1947.
Crops: Wheat, barley, oats, maize, potatoes.
Monetary unit: Canadian dollar. One dollar = 100 cents.
Denominations:
  Coins 1, 5, 10, 25, 50 cents, $1.
  Notes $ 1, 2, 5, 10, 20, 50, 100, 1000.
Exchange rate to US dollar: 1.0318 (July 1975).
Political history and government: A federal parliamentary state and member of the Commonwealth. Executive power is vested in the Queen and exercisable by her representative, the Governor-General, whom she appoints on the advice of the Canadian Prime Minister. The Federal Parliament comprises the Queen, a nominated Senate (104 members, appointed on a regional basis) and a House of Commons (264 members elected by universal adult suffrage). A Parliament may last no longer than 5 years. Canada contains 10 provinces (each with a Lieutenant-Governor and a legislature from which a Premier is chosen) and two centrally-administered territories.
Telephones: 11 668 292 (1974).
Daily newspapers: 121 (1972).
  Total circulation: 5 074 000 (116 dailies)
Radio: 19 133 000 (1973).
TV: 7 705 000 (1973).
Length of roadways: 516 893 miles 831 858 km.
Length of railways: 44 162 miles 71 071 km.
Universities: 45 (also 22 other degree-awarding institutions).
Expectation of life: Males 68·75 years; females 75·18 years (1965–7).
Defence: Military service voluntary; Total armed forces 77 000; Defence expenditure 1975–6 $2665 million.
Wildlife: Wolf, coyote, beaver, mink, moose, caribou, black bear, otter, red fox, mountain sheep, mountain goat, grizzly bear, elk, white-tailed and mule deer, pronghorn antelope, gopher, polar bear, puma. Garter snake.
Jay, oriole, American robin, junco, horned lark, blue-backed Heron, humming bird, snowy owl.
Cinemas: 1128 with seating capacity of 651 899; 284 drive-ins for 117 858 cars.

ALBERTA
Population: 1 627 875 (1971 census); 1 768 000 (1975 est).
Area: 255 285 miles² 661 188 km².
Languages: English, German, Ukrainian, French.
Religions: United Church of Canada, Roman Catholic, Anglican, Lutheran.
Capital city: Edmonton, population 529 000 (metropolitan area) in 1974.
Other principal towns (1974): Calgary 433 389; Lethbridge 43 612; Red Deer 28 079; Medicine Hat 27 430; Grande Prairie 15 359.
Principal mountain range: Rocky Mountains.
Principal rivers: Peace, Athabasca.
Lieutenant-Governor: Ralph Garvin.
Premier: (Edgar) Peter Lougheed (b. 26 July 1928).
Crops: Wheat, barley, oats.
Telephones: 969 280 (1973).
Length of roadways: 86 347 miles 138 962 km.
Length of railways: 6244 miles 10 048 km.
Universities: 3.

BRITISH COLUMBIA
Population: 2 184 625 (1971 census); 2 457 000 (1975 est).
Area: 366 255 miles² 948 600 km².
Languages: English, German.
Religion: United Church of Canada, Anglican, Roman Catholic, Lutheran.
Capital city: Victoria, population 199 000 (1972).
Other principal towns (1971): Vancouver 1 071 081; New Westminster 42 835; Prince George 33 101; North Vancouver 31 847; Kamloops 26 168.
Principal mountain range: Rocky Mountains.
Principal rivers: Fraser, Thompson, Kootenay, Colombia.
Lieutenant-Governor: Col Walter Stewart Owen.
Premier: William R. Bennett.
Crops: Apples.
Telephones: 1 160 333 (1972).
Length of roadways: 28 120 miles 45 254 km.
Length of railways: 4826 miles 7766 km.
Universities: 4.

MANITOBA
Population: 988 250 (1971 census); 1 019 000 (1975 est).
Area: 251 000 miles² 652 218 km².
Languages: English, Ukrainian, German, French.
Religions: United Church of Canada, Roman Catholic, Anglican, Lutheran.
Capital city: Winnipeg, population 570 000 (metropolitan area) in 1974.
Other principal towns: (1971) St James–Assinabora 71 800; St Boniface 46 661; St Vital 32 613; Brandon 31 150; East Kildonian 29 722.
Highest point: Duck Mountain 2727 ft 831 m.
Lieutenant-Governor: William John McKeag (b. 17 Mar. 1928).
Premier: Edward Richard Schreyer (b. 21 Dec. 1935).
Crops: Wheat, oats, barley.
Telephones: 433 598 (1970).
Length of roadways: 11 300 miles 18 185 km.
Length of railways: 4900 miles 7886 km.
Universities: 3.

NEW BRUNSWICK
Population: 634 555 (1971 census); 657 000 (1975 est).
Area: 28 354 miles² 72 000 km².
Languages: English, French.
Religions: Roman Catholic, Baptist, United Church of Canada, Anglican.
Capital city: Fredericton, population 42 000 (1973).
Other principal towns (1971): Saint John 106 744; Moncton 71 416; Bathurst 19 784; Edmundston 17 331; Campbellton 12 443.
Highest point: Mt Carleton, 2690 ft 820 m.
Principal rivers: St John.
Lieutenant-Governor: Hédard J Robichaud (b. 2 Nov. 1911).
Premier: Richard Bennett Hatfield (b. 9 Apr. 1931).
Crops: Potatoes, oats, hay, fruit.
Telephones: 260 050 (1972).
Length of roadways: 12 854 miles 20 686 km.

NEWFOUNDLAND (Terre-Neuve)
Population: 522 105 (1971 census); 549 000 (1975 est).
Area: 156 185 miles² 383 300 km².
Language: English.
Religions: Roman Catholic, Anglican, United Church of Canada, Salvation Army.
Capital city: St John's, population 101 161 (1971).

Other principal towns (1971): Corner Brook 26 309; Stephenville 7770; Gander 7748; Grand Falls 7677; Windsor 6644.
Highest point: Mt Gras Morne 2666 ft *812 m.*
Principal mountain ranges: Long range mountains.
Principal rivers: Humber, Exploits, Gander.
Lieutenant-Governor: Gordon Arnaud Winter (b. 6 Oct. 1912).
Premier: Frank Duff Moores (b. 18 Feb. 1933).
Telephones: 100 655 (1972).
Length of railways: 1085 miles *1746 km.*
Universities: 1.

NOVA SCOTIA

Population: 788 960 (1971 census); 822 000 (1975 est).
Area: 21 425 miles² *55 000 km².*
Language: English.
Religions: Roman Catholic, United Church of Canada, Anglican, Baptist.
Capital city: Halifax, population 122 035 (1971).
Other principal towns (1971): Dartmouth 64 770; Sydney 33 230; Glace Bay 22 440; Truro 12 047; New Glasgow 10 849.
Lieutenant-Governor: Dr Clarence L Gosse.
Premier: Gerald Augustine Regan (b. 13 Feb. 1928).
Crops: Apples, tobacco, blueberries, strawberries.
Length of roadways 15 443 miles *24 853 km* (excluding cities and towns).
Length of railways: 1750 miles *2816 km.*
Universities: 6.

ONTARIO

Population: 7 703 105 (1971 census); 8 226 000 (1975 est).
Area: 412 582 miles² *1 068 587 km².*
Languages: English, French, Italian, German.
Religions: Roman Catholic, United Church of Canada, Anglican, Presbyterian.
Capital city: Toronto, population 712 786 (city) in 1971; 2 741 000 (metropolitan area) in 1974.
Other principal towns (1971): Hamilton 309 173; Ottawa 302 341; London 223 222; Windsor 203 300.
Principal rivers: St Lawrence, Ottawa.
Lieutenant-Governor: Mrs Pauline M McGibbon (b. 20 Oct. 1910).
Premier: William Grenville Davis (b. 30 July 1929).
Crops: Fruit, soybeans, maize, oats, tobacco, sugar-beet.
Telephones: 4 561 693 (1973).
Length of roadways: 12 990 miles *20 900 km.*
Length of railways: 10 045 miles *16 166 km*
Universities: 15.

PRINCE EDWARD ISLAND

Population: 111 640 (1971 census); 119 000 (1975 est).
Area: 2184 miles² *5656 km².*
Languages: English, French.
Religions: Roman Catholic, United Church of Canada, Presbyterian.
Capital city: Charlottetown, population 19 133 (1971).
Other principal town: Summerside, 9439 (1971).
Lieutenant-Governor: Gordon Lockhart Bennett.
Premier: Alexander Bradshaw Campbell (b. 1 Dec. 1933).
Crops: Potatoes.
Telephones: 42 314 (1973).
Length of roadways: 3360 miles *5406 km.*
Length of railways: 283 miles *455 km.*
Universities: 1.

QUEBEC

Population: 6 027 765 (1971 census); 6 188 000 (1975 est).
Area: 594 860 miles² *1 540 668 km².*
Languages: French, English.
Religion: Roman Catholic.
Capital city: Quebec, population 187 400 (city); 499 000 (metropolitan area) in 1974.
Other principal towns (1971): Montreal 1 466 500; Laval 237 918; Sherbrooke 81 881; Verdun 76 832; Trois-Rivières 64 000; Hull 63 720.
Highest point: 4160 ft *1268 m* Mt Jacques Cartier.
Principal mountain ranges: Notre Dame, Appalachian.
Principal rivers: St Lawrence.
Lieutenant-Governor: Lt-Col Hugues Lapointe (b. 3 Mar. 1911).
Premier: Jean Robert Bourassa (b. 14 July 1933).
Crops: Oats, maize, potatoes, barley, hay.
Telephones: 1 500 000 (1970).
Length of roadways: 45 994 miles *74 020 km.*
Length of railways: 5360 miles *8626 km.*
Universities: 7.

SASKATCHEWAN

Population: 926 240 (1971 census); 918 000 (1975 est).
Area: 251 700 miles² *651 903 km².*
Languages: English, German, Ukrainian.
Religions: United Church of Canada, Roman Catholic, Lutheran, Anglican.
Capital city: Regina, population 146 950 (1973).
Other principal towns (1973): Saskatoon 132 200; Moose Jaw 31 854; Prince Albert 29 150; Swift Current 15 950; Yorkton 14 500.
Highest point: 4546 ft *1385 m.*
Principal rivers: N Saskatchewan, Cree, Geokie.
Lieutenant-Governor: Dr Stephen Worobetz, MC (b. 26 Dec. 1914).
Premier: Allan Emrys Blakeney (b. 7 Sept. 1925).
Crops: Wheat, oats, barley, rye, rape seed, flax.
Telephones: 416 163 (1973).
Length of roadways: 128 125 miles *206 197 km.*
Length of railways: 8690 miles *13 985 km*
Universities: 2.

NORTHWEST TERRITORIES

Population: 34 805 (1971 census); 38 000 (1975 est).
Area: 1 304 903 miles² *3 379 700 km².*
Languages: Eskimo and Indian languages, English, French.
Religions: Roman Catholic, Anglican, United Church of Canada.
Capital city: Yellowknife, population 8000 (1975).
Other principal towns (1971): Inuvik 2672; Hay River 2420; Fort Smith 2372; Frobisher Bay 2014.
Principal mountain ranges: Mackenzie.
Principal rivers: Mackenzie.
Commissioner: Stuart Milton Hodgson (b. 1 Apr. 1924).

YUKON TERRITORY

Population: 18 390 (1971 census); 21 000 (1975 est).
Area: 207 076 miles² *536 000 km².*
Languages: English, Indian languages.
Religions: Anglican, Roman Catholic, United Church of Canada.
Capital city: Whitehorse, population 12 000 (1971).
Other principal towns: Watson Lake 1115; Dawson City 500; Mayo 500;

Highest point: Mt Logan, 19 850 ft *6050 m.*
Principal mountain ranges: St Elias.
Principal rivers: Yukon.
Commissioner: James Smith.
Length of roadways: 2332 miles *3752 km.*

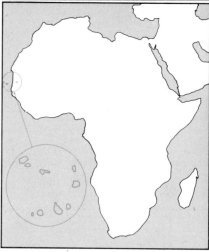

CAPE VERDE

Official name: A República de Cabo Verde.
Population: 272 071 (1970 census); 294 425 (1974 est). There has been wide-scale migration from Angola (autumn 1975–spring 1976). Recent estimates suggest a population of 360 000, largely as a result of this.
Area: 1557 miles² *4033 km².*
Languages: Portuguese, Crioulo (a patois).
Religions: Roman Catholic 98·7% (1965).
Capital city: Praia, population 21 000 (1970).
Other principal towns: Mindelo 29 000; São Filipe 29 500.
Highest point: Pico ? (Fogo Island), 9285 ft *2829 m.*
Head of State: Aristides Maria Pereira (b. 17 Nov. 1924), President.
Prime Minister: Major Pedro Pires.
Climate: Oceanic and temperate; subject to NE Trades; little temperature difference—hottest month September 79·8 °F; coolest February 70·8 °F. Dense sand mist (from Sahara) is a hazard. Rain is scarce (falling almost entirely between August and October) and drought sometimes chronic.
Crops: Maize, purgueira (physic nut), sugar-cane, beans.
Monetary unit: Cape Verde escudo. 1 escudo = 100 centavos.
Denominations:
Coins 5, 10, 20, 50 centavos, 1, 2½, 5, 10 escudos.
Notes 20, 50, 100, 500 escudos.
Exchange rate to US dollar: 27.75 (February 1976).
Political history and government: Until 1879 the islands were part of Portuguese Guinea, and formed a separate colony from then until independence on 5 July 1975. One-party government (Partido Africano da Independência da Guiné e Cabo Verde). A People's Assembly is elected by universal suffrage (all those over 17 years of age). The Constitution pledges the nation to full political union with Guinea-Bissau, but sets neither method nor timetable to do this.
Telephones: 1482 (1971).
Radio: 31 000 (1975).
Length of roadways: 611 miles *984 km.*
Adult illiteracy: 73·2% (males 61·4%; females 82·8%) in 1960 (population aged 10 and over).
Expectation of life: Males 44·4 years;

females 47·6 years (1965–70).
Defence: Popular Revolutionary Armed Forces.
Wildlife: Limited owing to aridity but includes lizards, skinks, butterfly, rose flamingo, cape verde kite, wild goats, Senegal green monkey.
Cinemas: 6 (seating capacity 2800) in 1971.

CENTRAL AFRICAN REPUBLIC

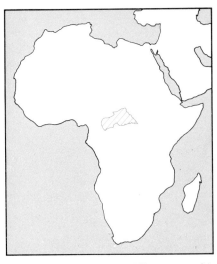

Official name: La République centrafricaine.
Population: 2 255 536 (1968 census); 2 370 000 (1970 est).
Area: 240 535 miles² *622 984 km².*
Languages: Sangho, French (official).
Religions: Protestant, Roman Catholic, Animist.
Capital city: Bangui, population 301 793 (1968).
Other principal towns (1964): Bouar 20 700; Bambari 19 700.
Highest point: Mt Gaou, 4659 ft *1420 m.*
Principal mountain ranges: Chaîne des Mongos.
Principal rivers: Oubangui.
Head of State: Marshal Jean-Bédel Bokassa (b. 22 Feb. 1921), President and Prime Minister.
Climate: Tropical (hot and humid). Heavy rains June to October, especially in southwestern forest areas. Average temperature 79 °F. Daily average high temperature 85 °F to 93 °F, low 66 °F to 71 °F.
Crops: Cassava, bananas, groundnuts, cotton, coffee.
Monetary unit: Franc de la Communauté financière africaine.
Denominations:
Coins 1, 2, 5, 10, 25, 50, 100 CFA francs.
Notes 100, 500, 1000, 5000, 10 000 CFA francs.
Exchange rate to US dollar: 224.24 (February 1976).
Political history and government: Formerly Oubangui-Chari, part of French Equatorial Africa. Took present name on achieving self-government, 1 Dec. 1958. Independent since 13 Aug. 1960. A one-party state since November 1962. Under military rule since 31 Dec. 1965. National Assembly dissolved on 1 Jan. 1966. Constitution revoked, 4 Jan. 1966. The president has assumed full powers and rules with a Council of Ministers.
Telephones: 5000 (1972).
Daily newspapers: 1 (1972).
Total circulation: 500.

Radio: 65 000 (1973).
Length of roadways (1973): 13 639 miles *21 950 km.*
Universities: 1.
Adult illiteracy: 97·9% (males 95·6%; females 99·8%) in 1959–60 (aged 14 and over).
Expectation of life: Males 37·5 years; females 40·6 years (1965–70).
Defence: Armed forces about 3000.
Wildlife: Monkeys, giant squirrel, gorilla, chimpanzee, hippopotamus, crocodile, hyena, lion, white rhinoceros; various types of snake; many types of bird.
Cinemas: 8 (1971).

CHAD

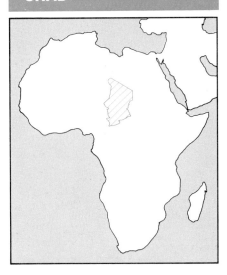

Official name: La République du Tchad.
Population: 3 949 000 (1974 est).
Area: 495 750 miles² *1 284 000 km²*
Languages: French (official), Arabic, some African languages.
Religions: Muslim, Animist, Christian.
Capital city: N'Djamena (formerly Fort-Lamy), population 193 000.
Other principal towns (1972): Sarh (Fort-Archambault) 43 700; Moundou 39 600; Abéché 28 100.
Highest point: Emi Koussi, 11 204 ft *3415 m.*
Principal mountain ranges: Tibesti, Ennedi.
Principal rivers: Chari, Bahr Kéita.
Head of State: Gen Félix Malloum (b. 1932), President of the Supreme Military Council and President of the Council of Ministers.
Climate: Hot and dry in the Sahara desert (in the north) but milder and very wet (annual rainfall 196 in) in the south. In N'Djamena, average maximum 87 °F (August) to 107 °F (April), minimum 57 °F (December, January) to 77 °F (May), August rainiest (22 days).
Crops: Millet, sorghum, cotton.
Monetary unit: Franc de la Communauté financière africaine.
Denominations:
Coins 1, 2, 5, 10, 25, 50, 100 CFA francs.
Notes 100, 500, 1000, 5000, 10 000 CFA francs.
Exchange rate to US dollar: 224.24 (February 1976).
Political history and government: Former province of French Equatorial Africa, independent since 11 Aug. 1960. Under military rule since 13 Apr. 1975. Provisional constitution announced, 16 Aug. 1975. The Supreme Military Council chooses a President who has executive and legislative powers.
Telephones: 5096 (1974).

Daily newspapers: 1.
Total circulation: 1500.
Radio: 70 000 (1972).
Length of roadways (1973): 19 091 miles *30 725 km.*
Universities: 1.
Adult illiteracy: 94·4% (males 87·9%; females 99·4%) in 1963–4.
Expectation of life: Males 36·5 years; females 39·6 years (1965–70).
Defence: Total armed forces 4200; paramilitary forces 6000.
Wildlife: Elephant, warthog, crocodile, hippopotamus, black rhinoceros; buzzards, guinea-fowl.
Cinemas: 9 (seating capacity 5900) in 1968.

CHILE

Official name: La República de Chile.
Population: 8 834 820 (1970 census, excl 8·5% underenumeration); 10 405 103 (1974 est).
Area: 292 258 miles² *756 945 km².*
Language: Spanish.
Religions: Roman Catholic, Protestant minority.
Capital city: Santiago, population 3 435 900
Other principal towns (1970): Valparaíso 292 847; Concepción 196 317; Viña del Mar 153 085; Antofagasta 137 968; Talcahuano 115 568; Temuco 104 372.
Highest point: Ojos del Salado, 22 539 ft *6870 m* (first climbed 1937).
Principal mountain ranges: Cordillera de los Andes.
Principal rivers: Loa (273 miles *439 km*), Maule, Bio-Bio, Valdiva.
Head of State: Gen Augusto Pinochet Ugarte (b. 25 Nov. 1915), President.
Climate: Considerable variation north (annual rainfall 0·04 in) to south (105 in). Average temperatures 53°F winter, 63 °F summer. In Santiago, December (51 °F to 83 °F), January (53 °F to 85 °F), and February (52 °F to 84 °F) hottest, June (37 °F to 58 °F) and July (37 °F to 59 °F) coldest and rainiest (6 days each). Absolute maximum temperatures 41,6 °C (*106·9 °F*), Los Angeles, February 1944; absolute minimum −21,2 °C (*−6·16 °F*) Longuimay, July 1933.
Crops: Wheat, maize, potatoes, sugar beet.
Monetary unit: Chilean peso. 1 peso = 100 centavos.

183

Denominations:
Coins 1, 5, 10, 50 centavos, 1 peso.
Notes 1, 5, 10, 50 pesos.
Exchange rate to US dollar: 10.30 (February 1976).
Political history and government: A republic, divided into 25 provinces. Under military control, with constitutional rule suspended, since 11 Sept. 1973. A 'state of siege' was proclaimed; the bicameral National Congress (a Senate and a Chamber of Deputies) was dissolved on 13 Sept. 1973; and the activities of political parties were suspended on 27 Sept. 1973. Power is held by the *Junta Militar de Gobierno*, whose leader is Head of State. The junta rules through a cabinet of ministers.
Telephones: 433 682 (1974).
Daily newspapers: 128 (1972).
Total circulation: 803 000.
Radio: 1 500 000 (1972).
TV: 525 000 (1974).
Length of roadways (1972): 39 553 miles *63 656 km.*
Length of railways: 6723 miles *10 820 km.*
Universities: 8.
Adult illiteracy: 11·9% (males 11·0%; females 12·7%) in 1970.
Expectation of life: Males 60·48 years; females 66·01 years (1969–70).
Defence: Military service one year; Total armed forces 73 800; Defence expenditure $213 million.
Wildlife: Puma, vicuna, quanaco, wolf, deer; condor.
Cinemas: 360 (seating capacity 245 700) in 1971.

CHINA (mainland)

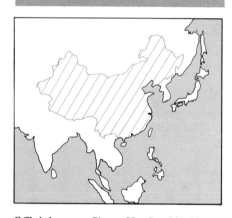

Official name: Chung-Hua Jen-Min Kung-Ho Kuo (the People's Republic of China).
Population: 582 603 417 (1953 census), excluding Taiwan; 838 803 000 (UN estimate for mid-1975), including Taiwan (approx 16 million).
Area: 3 691 500 miles² *9 561 000 km².*
Language: Chinese (predominantly Mandarin dialect).
Religions: Confucianism, Buddhism, Taoism, Roman Catholic and Muslim minorities.
Capital city: Peking, population 7 570 000 (1970 est.)
Other principal towns (1970): Shanghai 10 820 000; Tientsin 4 280 000; Shenyang 2 800 000; Wuhan 2 560 000; Kwangchow (Canton) 2 500 000; Chungking 2 400 000; Nanking 1 750 000; Harbin 1 670 000; Luta 1 650 000; Sian 1 600 000; Lanchow 1 450 000.
Highest point: Mt Everest (on Tibet-Nepal border), 29 028 ft *8848 m* (first climbed 29 May 1953).
Principal mountain ranges: Himalayas, Kunlun Shan, Tien Shan, Nan Shan, Astin Tagh.
Principal rivers: Yangtze (Ch'ang Kiang)

(3436 miles *5530 km*), Huang (Yellow), Mekong.
Political Leader: Mao Tse-tung (b. 26 Dec. 1893), Chairman of the Central Committee of the Communist Party of China.

Head of Government: Hua Kuo-feng, Premier of the State Council.
Climate: Extreme variations. Warm, humid summers and long cold winters in north (annual average below 50 °F); sub-tropical in extreme south; monsoons in the east; arid in the north-west. In Peking July hottest (71 °F to 89 °F) and rainiest (13 days), January coldest (15 °F to 35 °F).
Crops: Rice, wheat, maize, millet, barley, sweet potatoes, potatoes, sugar-cane, soybeans, cotton, tobacco, tea, jute, kenaf, groundnuts, sesame seed.
Monetary unit: Yüan. 1 yüan = 10 chiao = 100 fen.
Denominations:
Coins 1, 2, 5 fen.
Notes 1, 2, 5 chiao, 1, 2, 5, 10 yüan.
Exchange rate to US dollar: 1.95 (February 1976).
Political history and government: Under Communist rule since September 1949. The People's Republic was inaugurated on 1 Oct. 1949. The present constitution was adopted on 17 Jan. 1975. China is a unitary state comprising 21 provinces, 5 'autonomous' regions (including Tibet) and 3 municipalities. The Communist Party is 'the core of leadership' and the Chairman of the Party's Central Committee commands the People's Liberation Army (PLA), which includes naval and air forces. The highest organ of state power is the National People's Congress, with (in 1975) 2885 deputies indirectly elected for 5 years by provinces, regions, municipalities and the PLA. The Congress, under the leadership of the Party, elects a Standing Committee to be its permanent organ. There is no Head of State but the equivalent functions are exercised by this Committee. The executive and administrative arm of government is the State Council (a Premier, Vice-Premiers and other ministers), appointed by and accountable to the Congress.
Telephones: 255 000 (1951).
Daily newspapers: n/a.
Total circulation: 12 million (est.)
Radio: c. 12 000 000 (1970).
TV: c. 300 000 (1969).
Length of roadways: c. 497 097 miles *c. 800 000 km.*
Length of railways: (1965) c. 22 369 miles *c. 36 000 km.*
Universities: 24.
Adult illiteracy: 33% (1960 claim).
Expectation of life: Males 57·3 years; females 60·8 years (1965–70, incl Taiwan).
Defence: Military service: army two–four

years, air force three–five years, navy four–six years. Total regular forces 3 250 000. Defence expenditure—not made public.
Wildlife: Arctic fox, snow rabbit, reindeer, bear, mink, marten, ermine, sable, otter, fox, moose, giant panda, Chinese alligator, large Indian civet, monkey, elephant, tiger, leopard, wild horse, camel; several tropical birds including the wild peacock.
Cinemas: 1386 (1958).

CHINA (Taiwan)

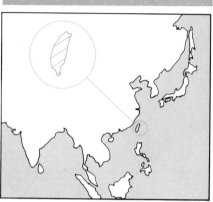

Official name: Chung-Hua Min-Kuo (the Republic of China).
Population: 14 990 000 (1971 census); 16 092 160 (1975 est.)
Area: 13 893 miles² *35 981 km².*
Language: Northern Chinese (Amoy dialect).
Religions: Buddhist with Muslim and Christian minorities.
Capital city: Taipei, population 2 038 199 (1975).
Other principal towns (1975): Kaohsiung 993 010; Taichung 543 152; Tainan 522 575; Keelung 341 917.
Highest point: Yü Shan (Mt Morrison) 13 113 ft *3997 m.*
Principal mountain range: Chunyang Shanmo.
Principal rivers: Hsia-tan-shui Chi, Cho-shui Chi, Tan-shui Ho, Wu Chi.
Head of State: Dr Yen Chia-kan (b. 23 Oct. 1905), President.
Prime Minister: Gen Chiang Ching-kuo (b. 18 Mar. 1910).
Climate: Rainy summers and mild winters, average temperature 73 °F, average annual rainfall 101 in. In Taipei, July (76 °F to 93 °F) and August (75 °F to 91 °F) warmest, January (54 °F to 66 °F) and February (53 °F to 65 °F) coolest, April rainiest (14 days).
Crops: Rice, sweet potatoes, sugar-cane.
Monetary unit: New Taiwan dollar (NT $). 1 dollar = 100 cents.
Denominations:
Coins 10, 20, 50 cents, 1, 5 dollars.
Notes 1, 5, 10, 50, 100 dollars.
Exchange rate to US dollar: 38.00 (February 1976).
Political history and government: After the Republic of China was overthrown by Communist forces on the mainland, the government withdrew to Taiwan on 8 Dec. 1949. As it claims to be the legitimate administration for all China, the regime continues to be dominated by mainlanders who came to the island in 1947–9. The first elections since the Communist victory were held in Taiwan on 23 Dec. 1972. There are five governing bodies (*yuans*). The highest legislative organ is the Legislative Yuan, comprising (in 1975) 396 life members and 36 elected for 3 years. This body submits proposals to the National Assembly (1299 life members and 53 elected for 6 years),

which elects the President and Vice-President for 6 years. The Executive Yuan (Council of Ministers) is the highest administrative organ and is responsible to the Legislative Yuan.
Telephones: 742 304 (1974).
Daily newspapers: 32 (1963).
 Total circulation: 750 000.
Radio: 1 484 095 (1975).
TV: 911 849 (1975).
Length of roadways: 10 193 miles *16 404 km.*
Length of railways: 3116 miles *5014·6 km.*
Universities: 11.
Adult illiteracy: 27·6% (males 15·2%; females 42·0%) in 1966.
Expectation of life: 68·2 years (1965–70).
Defence: Military service two years. Total armed forces 494 000 (1975). Defence expenditure 1975–6 US $1000 million.
Wildlife: Deer, black bear; yellow-throated marten, pheasants.
Cinemas: 734 (capacity 734 000) in 1967.

COLOMBIA

Official name: La República de Colombia.
Population 21 070 115 (1973 census).
Area: 439 737 miles² *1 138 914 km².*
Language: Spanish.
Religion: Roman Catholic.
Capital city: Santa Fe de Bogotá, population 2 855 065 (1973).
Other principal towns (1973): Medellín 1 100 082; Cali 923 446; Barranquilla 661 920; Cartagena de Indias 313 305; Bucaramanga 298 051; San José de Cúcuta 269 565.
Highest point: Pico Cristobal Colón, 18 947 ft *5775 m* (first climbed 1939).
Principal mountain range: Cordillera de los Andes.
Principal rivers: Magdalena, Cauca, Amazonas (Amazon 4007 miles *6448 km*) on frontier.
Head of State: Dr Alfonso López Michelsen (b. 30 June 1913), President.
Climate: Hot and humid on the coasts and in the jungle lowlands, temperate in the Andean highlands, with rainy seasons March–May and September–November. In Bogotá, daily average low temperature 48 °F to 51 °F, high 64 °F to 68 °F, April and October rainiest (20 days).
Crops: Rice, yucca, potatoes, sugar-cane, maize, coffee, cotton.
Monetary unit: Colombian peso. 1 peso = 100 centavos.
Denominations:
 Coins 1, 5, 10, 20, 50 centavos.
 Notes 1, 2, 5, 10, 20, 50, 100, 500 pesos.
Exchange rate to US dollar: 33.51 (February 1976).

Political history and government: A republic. Legislative power is vested in Congress which is composed of the Senate (112 members) and the House of Representatives (199 members). Members of both Houses are elected for 4 years. Executive power is exercised by the President (elected for 4 years by universal adult suffrage), assisted by a Cabinet. The country is divided into 22 departments, 5 intendencies and 4 commissaries.
Telephones: 1 079 645 (1973).
Daily newspapers: 36 (1971).
 Total circulation: 2 369 000.
Radio: 2 792 700 (1973).
TV: 809 632 (1974).
Length of roadways (1971): 28 504 miles *45 873 km.*
Length of railways: 2128 miles *3424 km*
Universities: 38 (21 state, 17 private).
Adult illiteracy: 27·1% (males 25·2%; females 28·9%) in 1964.
Expectation of life: Males 56·9 years; females 60·2 years (1965–70).
Defence: Military service two years; Total armed forces 64 300; Defence expenditure $102 million.
Wildlife: Jaguar, ocelot, puma (all in decreasing numbers), guinea-pig; great variety of birds (more species than in any other country).
Cinemas: 726 (seating capacity 431 400) in 1968.

THE COMOROS

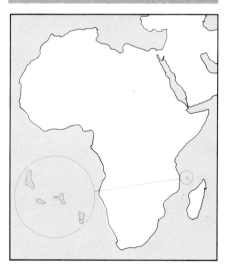

Official name: Etat Comorien (Comoran State).
Population: 243 948 (1966 census), including 32 494 in Mayotte prefecture; 284 000 (1973 est).
Area: 838 miles² *2 171 km²* (including Mayotte, 144 miles² *374 km²*).
Languages: French (official), Comoran (a blend of Swahili and Arabic).
Religions: Muslim, with a Christian minority (a majority on Mayotte).
Capital city: Moroni, population 15 900 (1973).
Other principal towns: Dzaoudzi (on Mayotte), Mutsamudu.
Highest point: Mt Kartala, 7746 ft *2361 m.*
Head of State: Ali Soilih, President.
Prime Minister: Abdallah Mohamed.
Climate: Tropical climate with two distinct seasons. Dry between May and October, hot and humid from November to April. Most rain in January (up to 15 in). Cyclones, waterspouts and tidal waves occur in the summer. The November monsoon brings the maximum temperature of 82 °F (28 °C),

while the minimum temperature (July) falls to 68 °F (*20 °C*).
Crops: Cassava, coconuts, rice, sweet potatoes, yams, maize, vanilla, cloves.
Monetary unit: Franc de la Communauté financière africaine (French currency is used on Mayotte).
Denominations:
 Coins 1, 2, 5, 10, 20 CFA francs.
 Notes 50, 100, 500, 1000, 5000 CFA francs.
Exchange rate to US dollar: 224.24 (February 1976).
Political history and government: Formerly attached to Madagascar, the Comoro Islands became a separate French Overseas Territory in 1947. The Territory achieved internal self-government by a law of 29 Dec. 1961, with a Chamber of Deputies (in place of the territorial Assembly) and a Government Council to control local administration. Ahmed Abdallah, President of the Council from 26 Dec. 1972, was restyled President of the Government on 15 June 1973. In a referendum on 22 Dec. 1974 the Comorans voted 95·6% in favour of independence, though on the island of Mayotte the vote was 65% against. The French Government wanted each island to ratify a new constitution separately by referendum. To avoid the expected separation of Mayotte, the Chamber of Deputies voted for immediate independence on 6 July 1975. A unilateral declaration of independence was made on the same day. On 7 July the Chamber elected Abdallah as President of the Comoros and constituted itself as the National Assembly. France kept its hold on Mayotte but the three other main islands achieved *de facto* independence. On 3 Aug. 1975 Abdallah was deposed in a *coup* by a group, led by Ali Soilih, who wished to maintain the unity of the islands. The next day a National Revolutionary Council, led by Prince Said Mohamed Jaffer, took office and abolished the National Assembly. Prince Said became President of the National Executive Council on 10 Aug. 1975. Government came under the control of a coalition of four parties, previously in opposition, but they proved equally unsuccessful at achieving a reconciliation with Mayotte. France recognized the independence of the three islands on 31 Dec. 1975. On 2 Jan. 1976 the Executive and Revolutionary Councils elected Soilih to be President, with full executive authority, and he took office the next day. He appointed a new Council of Ministers, headed by a Prime Minister. The Revolutionary Council was replaced by a National Institutional Council to oversee the actions of the government. A referendum on Mayotte on 8 Feb. 1976 resulted in a 99·4% vote for retaining links with France. In a second referendum, on 11 Apr. 1976, Mayotte voted against remaining a French Overseas Territory. The majority there want Mayotte to be a French Overseas Department and France has agreed to implement their wishes.
Telephones: 1378 (1975).
Radio: 36 000 (1975).
Length of roadways: 466 miles *750 km.*
Expectation of life: Males 38·5 years; females 41·6 years (1965–70).
Cinemas: 4 (seating capacity 1300) in 1969.

THE CONGO

Official name: La République populaire du Congo (The People's Republic of the Congo).
Population: 1 300 106 (1974 census).
Area: 132 047 miles² *342 000 km².*
Languages: French (official), Bantu languages.

Religions: Animist, Christian minority.
Capital city: Brazzaville, population 289 700 (1974).
Other principal towns (1974): Pointe-Noire 141 700; Jacob 30 600; Loubomo (Dolisie) 29 600.
Highest point: 3412 ft *1040 m.*
Principal mountain range: Serro do Crystal.
Principal rivers: Congo (2718 miles *4374 km*), Oubangui.
Head of State: Major Marien Ngouabi (b. 1938), President.
Prime Minister: Major Louis Sylvain Goma.
Climate: Tropical (hot and humid). Equatorial rains for seven to eight months per year. In Brazzaville, daily average low temperature 63 °F to 70 °F, high 82 °F to 91 °F.
Crops: Cassava, sugar-cane, sweet potatoes.
Monetary unit: Franc de la Communauté financière africaine.

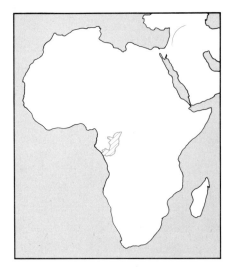

Denominations:
Coins 1, 2, 5, 10, 25, 50, 100 CFA francs.
Notes 100, 500, 1000, 5000 10 000 CFA francs.
Exchange rate to US dollar: 224.24 (February 1976).
Political history and government: Formerly, as Middle Congo, a part of French Equatorial Africa. Became independent as the Republic of the Congo on 15 Aug. 1960. A one-party state on 2 July 1964. Present name adopted on 3 Jan. 1970. A new constitution was approved by referendum on 24 June 1973, when a People's National Assembly of 115 members was elected (from a single list of candidates) to be the main legislative body. Executive power rests with the Council of State (led by the President), which is responsible to the Party. The President is elected for 5 years by the National Congress of the Party and is Chairman of its Central Committee. He appoints the Prime Minister and the Council of Ministers. The National Assembly is responsible to the Prime Minister.
Telephones: 10 181 (1974).
Daily newspapers: 3 (1971).
Radio: 75 000 (1973).
TV: 3800 (1973).
Length of roadways: 6836 miles *11 000 km.*
Length of railways: 494 miles *795 km.*
Universities: 1.
Adult illiteracy: 83·5% (males 76·2%; females 92·7%) in 1960–1.
Expectation of life: Males 39·4 years; females 42·6 years (1965–70).
Defence: Military service voluntary; Total armed forces 5500; Defence expenditure $19 million.
Wildlife: Buffalo, mountain gorilla, elephant, giraffe, lion, hippopotamus, zebra, rhinoceros, chimpanzee; many species of antelope and monkey; large variety of birds, reptiles and insects.
Cinemas: 10 (seating capacity 6500) in 1970.

COSTA RICA

Official name: República de Costa Rica (the 'rich coast').
Population: 1 871 780 (1973 census); 1 921 000 (1974 est).
Area: 19 600 miles² *50 700 km².*
Language: Spanish.
Religion: Roman Catholic.
Capital city: San José, population 218 717 (1974).
Other principal towns (1974): Alajuela 33 645; Limón 30 208; Puntarenas 26 864; Cartago 26 073; Heredia 23 133.
Highest point: Chirripó, 12 533 ft *3820 m.*
Principal mountain ranges: Cordillera del Guanacaste, Cordillera de Talamanca.
Principal river: Río Grande.
Head of State: Lic. Daniel Oduber Quirós (b. 25 Aug. 1921), President.
Climate: Hot and wet on Caribbean coast, hot but drier on Pacific coast, cooler on central plateau. In San José, May hottest (62 °F to 80 °F), December and January coolest (58 °F to 75 °F), rainy season May–November, October rainiest (25 days). Absolute maximum temperature 42 °C (*107·6 °F*), Las Cañas de Guanacaste, 26 Apr. 1952; absolute minimum −1.1 °C (*30 °F*) Cerro Buena Vista, 11 Jan. 1949.
Crops: Coffee, bananas, sugar-cane, cocoa.

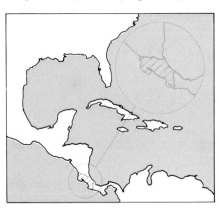

Monetary unit: Costa Rican colón. 1 colón = 100 céntimos.
Denominations:
Coins 5, 10, 25, 50 céntimos, 1, 2, colones
Notes 5, 10, 20, 50, 100, 500, 1000 colones
Exchange rate to US dollar: 8.57 (February 1976).
Political history and government: A republic. Legislative power is vested in the unicameral Legislative Assembly (57 deputies elected for four years by compulsory adult suffrage). Executive power is vested in the President, similarly elected for four years. He is assisted by two Vice-Presidents and a Cabinet. There are 7 provinces, each administered by an appointed governor.
Telephones: 88 563 (1974).
Daily newspapers: 8 (1972).
Total circulation: 174 000.
Radio: 140 000 (1973).
TV: 122 000 (1973).
Length of roadways: 10 936 miles *17 600 km.*
Length of railways: 496 miles *799 km.*
Universities: 1.
Adult illiteracy: 15·6% (males 15·2%; females 16·0%) in 1963. Highest rate of literacy in Central America.
Expectation of life: Males 61·87 years, females 64·83 years (1962–4).
Defence: There have been no armed forces since 1948. Paramilitary forces number about 5000.
Wildlife: Deer, monkey, puma; numerous snakes; numerous of species of bird.
Cinemas: 132 with seating capacity of 90 000 (1969).

CUBA

Official name: La República de Cuba.
Population: 8 569 121 (1970 census); 9 090 000 (1974 est).
Area: 42 827 miles² *110 922 km².*
Languages: Spanish, English.
Religions: Roman Catholic, Protestant minority.
Capital city: San Cristóbal de la Habana (Havana), population 1 755 360 (incl suburbs) in 1970.
Other principal towns (1970): Santiago de Cuba 292 251; Santa Clara 213 296; Camagüey 196 854; Holguín 183 115; Cienfuegos 164 061.
Highest point: Pico Turquino, 6467 ft *1971 m.*
Principal mountain range: Sierra Maestra.
Principal river: Cáuto (155 miles [*249 km*])
Head of State: Dr Osvaldo Dorticós Torrado (b. 17 Apr. 1919), President.
Prime Minister: Dr Fidel Castro Ruz (b. 13 Aug. 1927).
Climate: Semi-tropical. Rainy season May–October. High winds, hurricanes frequent. In Havana July and August warmest (75 °F to 89 °F), January and February coolest (65 °F to 79 °F), September and October rainiest (11 days each).
Crops: Sugar-cane, rice, sweet potatoes, cassava, maize, tobacco, citrus fruits.
Monetary unit: Cuban peso. 1 peso = 100 centavos.
Denominations:
Coins 1, 2, 5, 20, 40 centavos.
Notes 1, 5, 10, 20, 50, 100 pesos.
Exchange rate to US dollar: 0.829 (February 1976).
Political history and government: On 1 Jan. 1959 the dictatorship of Gen Fulgencio Batista was overthrown by revolutionary forces, led by Dr Fidel Castro. The constitution was suspended and a Fundamental Law of the Republic was instituted from 7 Feb. 1959. Executive and legislative authority was vested in the Council of Ministers, led by a Prime Minister, which appoints the Head of State. A 'Marxist-Leninist programme' was proclaimed on 2 Dec. 1961 and revolutionary groups merged into a single political movement, called the Communist Party since 2 Oct. 1965. It is the only permitted party. On 24 Nov. 1972 the government established an Executive

Committee (including the President and Prime Minister) to supervise State administration. The first elections since the revolution were held for municipal offices in one province on 30 June 1974. A new constitution, approved by referendum on 15 Feb. 1976 and in force from 24 Feb. 1976, lays down that Cuba is a socialist state in which the Communist Party is the leading force. The supreme organ of state is to be the National Assembly of People's Power, composed of deputies elected for 5 years by universal suffrage. The Assembly is to elect from its members a Council of State to be its permanent organ. The Council's President is to be Head of State and Head of Government and will also lead the Council of Ministers, the executive and administrative arm of government, appointed by the Assembly on the President's proposal. Existing bodies will continue to function until December 1976, when the new organs become operative. The country comprises 6 provinces.

Telephones: 281 000 (1973).
Daily newspapers: 10 (1972).
 Total circulation: 834 000.
Radio: 1 800 000 (1974).
TV: 370 000 (1974).
Length of roadways: 8291 miles *13 343 km.*
Length of railways: 9006 miles *14 494 km.*
Universities: 4.
Adult illiteracy: 22·1% (males 24·2%; females 20·0%) in 1953.
Expectation of life: Males 67·5 years; females 70·9 years (1965–70).
Defence: Military service three years; Total armed forces 117 000 (1975); Defence expenditure (1971 est) $290 million.
Wildlife: Snakes (two species, both harmless), cayman, iguana, chameleon; many species of birds (incl world's smallest—Helena's humming bird) and frogs (also incl world's smallest, the Arrow-poison frog).
Cinemas: 439 (seating capacity 294 300) and one drive-in (1972).

CYPRUS

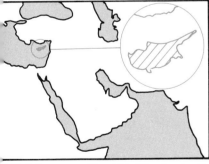

Official name: Kypriaki Dimokratia (in Greek), or Kibris Cumhuriyeti (in Turkish), meaning Republic of Cyprus.
Population: 631 778 (1973 census); 639 000 (1974 est).
Area: 3572 miles² *9251 km².*
Languages: Greek 77%; Turkish 18%; English 3% (1960).
Religions: Greek Orthodox 77%; Muslim 18% (1960).
Capital city: Levkosia (Nicosia), population 116 100 (1973).
Other principal towns (1973): Lemesos (Limassol) 79 000; Famagusta 39 100; Larnaca 19 700; Paphos 9000; Kyrenia (Girne) 3900.
Highest point: Mt Olympus (Troödos), 6403 ft *1951 m.*
Principal mountain ranges: Troödos Kyrenian Mts.

Principal rivers: Seranhis, Pedieas.
Head of State: Archbishop Makarios III (b. 13 Aug. 1913), President.
Climate: Generally equable. Average rainfall is about 15 in but the summers are often rainless. The average high temperature in Nicosia is 97 °F (July) and the average daily low 42 °F (January).
Crops: Citrus fruit, potatoes, grapes, barley, wheat.
Monetary unit: Cyprus pound. C£1 = 1000 mils.
Denominations:
 Coins 1, 3, 5, 25, 50, 100 mils.
 Notes 250, 500 mils, £1, £5.
Exchange rate to US dollar: 0.3965 (February 1976).
Political history and government: A former British dependency, independent since 16 Aug. 1960 and a member of the Commonwealth since 13 Mar. 1961. Under the 1960 constitution, Cyprus is a unitary republic with executive authority vested in the President (who must be a Greek Cypriot) and the Vice-President (who must be a Turkish Cypriot). They are elected for 5 years by universal suffrage (among the Greek and Turkish communities respectively) and jointly appoint a Council of Ministers (seven Greeks, three Turks). The National legislature is the unicameral House of Representatives, comprising 50 members (35 Greek and 15 Turkish, separately elected for 5 years). Each community was also to have a communal chamber. The President proposed amendments to the constitution on 30 Nov. 1963. These were unacceptable to the Turks, who have ceased to participate in the central government since December 1963. After the Turkish withdrawal, the all-Greek House of Representatives abolished the Greek communal chamber and the separate electoral rolls. The Turkish community continued to elect a Vice-President for Cyprus (not recognised by the Greeks) and established separate administrative, legal and judicial organs. After the temporary overthrow of President Makarios in July 1974, the armed forces of Turkey intervened and occupied northern Cyprus. On 17 Feb. 1975 the Turkish Cypriots unilaterally proclaimed this area the Turkish Federated State of Cyprus, for which a constitution was approved by referendum on 8 June 1975.
Telephones: 62 492 (1973).
Daily newspapers: 12 (1972).
 Total circulation: 80 000.
Radio: 205 000 (1973).
TV: 80 000 (1973).
Length of Roadways (1971): 5170 miles *8319 km*
Adult illiteracy: 24·1% (males 11·8%; females 35·6%) in 1960.
Expectation of life: Males 63.6 years; females 68.8 years.
Defence: Greek community has a National Guard; Turkish community has a Fighters' Army.
Wildlife: Hare, moufflon.
Cinemas: 150 (seating capacity 88 000) and 180 part-time (capacity 97 000) in 1972.

CZECHOSLOVAKIA

Official name: Československá Socialistická Republika (Czechoslovak Socialist Republic).
Population: 14 344 986 (1970 census); 14 738 311 (1974 est).
Area: 49 373 miles² *127 876 km².*
Languages: Czech 64%; Slovak 30%; Hungarian 4%.
Religions: Roman Catholic 70%; Protestant 15%.

Capital city: Praha (Prague), population 1 161 226 (1974).
Other principal towns (1974): Brno (Brünn) 355 661; Bratislava (Pressburg) 333 131; Ostrava 293 454; Košice 168 000; Plzeň (Pilsen) 155 006; Hradec Kralové 85 585; Havířov 84 975.
Highest point: Gerlachovský Štit 8711 ft *2655 m.*
Principal mountain ranges: Bohemian massif, Low Tatras, High Tatras.
Principal rivers: Labe (Elbe, 525 miles *845 km*), Vltava (Moldau), Dunaj (Danube, 1770 miles *2850 km*), Morava, Váh, Nitra, Hron.
Head of State: Dr Gustáv Husák (b. 10 Jan. 1913), President; also General Secretary of the Communist Party of Czechoslovakia.
Prime Minister: Dr Lubomír Štrougal (b. 19 Oct. 1924).

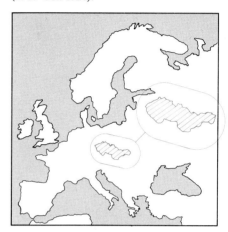

Climate: A mixed climate with continental influences often masked by relief. Mean annual temperatures reach 25·4 °F in the High Tatras and 50·9 °F in the Danube Lowlands. Maximum over 68 °F in the lowlands; minimum (January) −40 °F in mountain basins. Rainfall: considerable range from 18 in in central Bohemia to 59 in in the Giant Mountains.
Crops: Flax, hops, potatoes, wheat, rye, barley.
Monetary unit: Koruna (Kčs) or Czechoslovak Crown. 1 koruna = 100 haléřů (singular haléř).
Denominations:
 Coins 1, 3, 5, 10, 20, 50 haléřů; 1, 2, 5 korunas.
 Notes 10, 20, 50, 100, 500 korunas.
Exchange rate to US dollar: 5.876 (February 1976).
Political history and government: Formerly part of Austria-Hungary, independent since 28 Oct. 1918. Under Communist rule since 25 Feb. 1948. A People's Republic was established on 9 June 1948. A new constitution, introducing the country's present name, was proclaimed on 11 July 1960. Czechoslovakia has been a federal republic since 1 Jan. 1969.

The country comprises two nations, the Czechs and the Slovaks, each forming a republic with its own elected National Council and government. Czechoslovakia comprises 10 administrative regions and two cities.

The supreme organ of state power is the bicameral Federal Assembly, elected for 5 years by universal adult suffrage. Its permanent organ is the elected Presidium. The Assembly comprises the Chamber of the People, with 200 members (138 Czechs and 62 Slovaks), and the Chamber of Nations, with 150 members (75 from each republic). The Assembly elects the President of the Republic for a 5-year term and he appoints

187

the Federal Government, led by the Prime Minister, to hold executive authority. Ministers are responsible to the Assembly.

Political power is held by the Communist Party of Czechoslovakia, which dominates the National Front (including four other minor parties). All candidates for representative bodies are sponsored by the Front. The Communist Party's highest authority is the Party Congress, which elects the Central Committee (121 members were elected on 16 April 1976) to supervise Party work. The Committee elects a Presidium (11 full members and two alternate members) to direct policy.

Telephones: 2 480 801 (1975).
Daily newspapers: 29.
  Total circulation: 3 987 000.
Radio: 3 916 375 (1975).
TV: 3 404 000 (1975).
Length of roadways: 90 670 miles *145 919 km.*
Length of railways: 15 032 miles *24 192 km*
Universities: 5 (plus 4 technical universities).
Adult illiteracy: under 1%.
Expectation of life: Males 67·4 years; females 73·7 years.
*Defence: Military service 2 years; Army c. 150 000, Air Force 40 000, Paramilitary 40 000, Soviet forces present c. 80 000. Czechoslovakia is a member of the Warsaw Pact.
Wildlife: Deer, roebuck, hare, pheasant.
Cinemas: 3469 (1972).

*Defence Budget 1971 estimated at c. $2 810 million

DENMARK

Official name: Kongeriget Danmark (Kingdom of Denmark).
Population: 4 937 579 (1970 census); 5 054 510 (estimate for 1 Jan. 1975).
Area: 16 629 miles² *43 069 km².*
Language: Danish.
Religions: Evangelical Lutheran 94%, other Christian minorities.
Capital city: København (Copenhagen), population 603 368 (1972); Greater Copenhagen 1 287 498 (1 Jan. 1975).
Other principal towns (1975): Århus (Aarhus) 246 298; Odense 168 542; Ålborg (Aalborg) 154 702; Frederiksberg 95 318; Esbjerg 78 751; Randers 64 529.
Highest point: Yding Skovhøj, 568 ft *173 m.*
Principal river: Gudenå.
Head of State: HM Queen Margrethe II (b. 16 Apr. 1940).
Prime Minister: Anker Jørgensen (b. 13 July 1922).

Climate: Changeable—west Oceanic, east more continental. Coldest month February, mean temperature 32 °F. Warmest month July, mean temperature 61 °F. Moist ranging from 32 in rain (SW Jutland) to 16 in (Sprøgo).
Crops: Potatoes, barley.
Monetary unit: Danish krone. 1 krone = 100 øre.
Denominations:
  Coins 5, 10, 25 øre, 1, 5 kroner.
  Notes 10, 50, 100, 500, 1000 kroner.
Exchange rate to US dollar: 6.156 (February 1976).
Political history and government: A constitutional monarchy since 1849. Under the constitutional charter (*Grundlov*) of 5 June 1953, legislative power is held jointly by the hereditary monarch (who has no personal political power) and the unicameral Parliament (*Folketing*), with 179 members (175 from metropolitan Denmark and two each from the Faeroe Islands and Greenland). Members are elected by universal adult suffrage for 4 years (subject to dissolution), using proportional representation. Executive power is exercised by the monarch through a Cabinet, led by the Prime Minister, which is responsible to Parliament. Denmark comprises 14 counties, one city and one borough.
Telephones: 2 183 847 (1975), including the Faeroes and Greenland.
Daily newspapers: 52.
  Total circulation: 1 792 000 (1974).
Radio: 1 672 000 (1975).
TV: 1 557 000 (1975).
Length of roadways: 38 295 miles *61 630 km.*
Length of railways: 3387 miles *5451 km.*
Universities: 5 (plus 3 technical universities).
Adult illiteracy: under 1%.
Expectation of life: Males 70·6 years; females 75·4 years.
Defence: NATO member. Military service 9 months; Army (standing force) 8500, Navy (standing force) 7500, Air Force (standing force) 9700.
Wildlife: Red deer; most British bird and animal species.
Cinemas: 356 (seating capacity 128 622) in 1973.

THE DOMINICAN REPUBLIC

Official name: La República Dominicana.
Population: 4 006 405 (1970 census); 4 696 793 (1975 est.).
Area: 18 816 miles² *48 734 km².*
Language: Spanish.
Religion: Roman Catholic.
Capital city: Santo Domingo de Guzmán, population 922 528 (1975).

Other principal towns (1975): Santiago de los Caballeros 209 179; San Pedro de Macorís 61 994; San Francisco de Macor: 58 174; Barahona 51 109; La Roman: 47 382.
Highest point: Pico Duarte (formerly Pic Trujillo), 10 417 ft *3175 m.*
Principal mountain ranges: Cordiller Central.
Principal river: Yacque del Norte.
Head of State: Dr Joaquín Balaguer (t 1 Sept. 1907), President.
Climate: Sub-tropical. Average tempera ture 80 °F. The west and south-west ar arid. In the path of tropical cyclones. F Santo Domingo August is hottest (73 ° to 88 °F), January coolest (66 °F to 84 °F June rainiest (12 days). Absolute maximum temperature 43 °C (109·4 °F), Valverde 31 Aug. 1954; absolute minimum −3,5 ° (+25·7 °F) Valle Nuevo, 2 Mar. 1959.
Crops: Sugar-cane, coffee, rice, coco: tobacco, bananas.
Monetary unit: Dominican Republic pesc 1 peso = 100 centavos.
Denominations:
  Coins 1, 5, 10, 25, 50 centavos, 1 peso.
  Notes 1, 5, 10, 20, 50, 100, 500, 1000 pesos
Exchange rate to US dollar: 1.0 (February 1976).
Political history and government: / republic comprising 26 provinces (eac administered by an appointed governor) an a *Distrito Nacional* (DN) containing th capital. Legislative power is exercised by th bicameral National Congress, with a Senat of 27 members (one for each province an one for the DN) and a Chamber of Deputie (91 members). Members of both houses ar elected for four years. Executive power lie with the President, elected by direct popula vote for four years. He is assisted by a Vice President and a Cabinet containing Secre taries of State.
Telephones: 83 066 (1974).
Daily newspapers: 7 (1972).
  Total circulation: 162 000.
Radio: 180 000 (1974).
TV: 155 000 (1973).
Length of roadways (1971): 6504 mile *10 467 km.*
Length of Railways: 1056 miles *1700 km*
Universities: 4.
Adult illiteracy: 32·8% (males 31·2% females 34·3%) in 1970.
Expectation of life: Males 57·15 years females 58·59 years (1959–61).
Defence: Military service one year, selective Total armed forces 15 800 (1974); Defenc expenditure $36 million (1974).
Wildlife: Ground sloth, bat, spiny ra shrew; dove, pigeon, duck, coot, flamingo spoonbill, parrot; many reptiles.
Cinemas: 80 (seating capacity 40 600), part-time (capacity 1345) and 2 drive-i (1971).

ECUADOR

Official name: La República del Ecuadc ('the equator').
Population: 6 500 845 (1974 census), ex cluding nomadic Indian tribes.
Area: 109 484 miles² *283 561 km².*
Language: Spanish.
Religion: Roman Catholic.
Capital city: Quito, population 557 11 (1974).
Other principal towns (1974): Guayaqu 814 064; Cuenca 104 667; Ambato 77 06: Machala 68 379; Esmeraldas 60 132; Porto viejo 59 404; Ríobamba 58 029.
Highest point: Chimborazo, 20 561 *6267 m* (first climbed 1879).
Principal mountain ranges: Cordiller de los Andes.

Principal rivers: Napo, Pastaza, Curaray, Daule.
Head of State: Vice-Admiral Alfredo Poveda Burbano, President.
Climate: Tropical (hot and humid) in coastal lowlands. Temperate (mild days, cool nights) in highlands, average temperature 55 °F, rainy season November–May. In Quito, average maximum 70 °F (April, May) to 73 °F (August, September), minimum 44 °F (July) to 47 °F (February–May), April rainiest (22 days). Absolute maximum temperature 38 °C (100·4 °F) Babahoyo, 4 Jan. 1954; absolute minimum −3,6 °C (25·5 °F) Cotopaxi, 9 Sept. 1962.
Crops: Bananas (World's leading exporter), potatoes, maize, rice, coffee, cocoa.
Monetary unit: Sucre. 1 sucre = 100 centavos.
Denominations:
  Coins 5, 10, 20, 50 centavos, 1 sucre.
  Notes 5, 10, 20, 50, 500, 1000 sucres.
Exchange rate to US dollar: 25.00 (February 1976).

Political history and government: A republic comprising 19 provinces (each administered by an appointed governor) and a National Territory, the Archipiélago de Colón (the Galapagos Islands). On 22 June 1970 the President dismissed the National Congress (a Senate of 54 members and a 72-member Chamber of Deputies) and assumed dictatorial powers. He was deposed by the armed forces on 15 Feb. 1972 and a National Military Government was formed. All political activity was suspended on 11 July 1974. A three-man military junta took power on 11 Jan. 1976 and appointed a new Cabinet.
Telephones: 131 000 (1973).
Daily newspapers: 22 (1972).
  Total circulation: 307 000.
Radio: 1 700 000 (1971).
TV: 300 000 (1971).
Length of roadways: 11 400 miles *18 345 km.*
Length of railways: 665 miles *107 km.*
Universities: 16.
Adult illiteracy: 32·7% (males 27·9%; females 36·9%) in 1962.
Expectation of life: Males 51·04 years; females 53·67 years (1961–3).
Defence: Military service two years, selective; Total armed forces 22 300 (1975); Defence expenditure $71 million (1974).

Wildlife: Elephant tortoise (Galapagos Islands), jaguar, ocelot, weasel, fox, puma, otter, skunk, racoon, kinkajou, deer, peccary, tapir, bat, various types of rodent, iguana, monkey; many species of snake; about 1500 species of bird including blue-winged teal, jackass penguin kingbird, scarlet tanager, barn swallow.
Cinemas: 113 (seating capacity 114 600) in 1972.

EGYPT

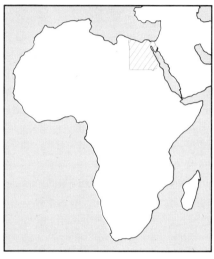

Official name: Jumhuriyat Misr al-Arabiya (Arab Republic of Egypt).
Population: 30 075 858 (1966 census); 36 417 000 (1974 est.).
Area: 386 662 miles² *1 001 449 km².*
Language: Arabic.
Religions: Muslim 92·6% Christian 7·3% (1960).
Capital city: El Qahira (Cairo), population 5 517 000 (1973 est.).
Other principal towns (1970): El Iskandariyah (Alexandria) 2 032 000; El Giza 711 900; El Suwais (Suez) 315 000; Bur Sa'id (Port Said) 313 000; El Mahalla el Kubra 255 800; Tanta 253 600; Subra-El Khema 252 500; El Mansura 212 300; Aswan 201 500.
Highest point: Jebel Katherina, 8651 ft *2609 m.*
Principal mountain ranges: Sinai, Eastern Coastal Range.
Principal river: Nile 4145 miles *6671 km.*
Head of State: Col Muhammad Anwar as-Sadat (b. 25 Dec. 1918), President.
Prime Minister: Gen Mamduh Muhammad Salem (b. 1918).
Climate: Hot and dry. Over 90% is arid desert. Annual rainfall generally less than 2 in, except on Mediterranean coast (maximum of 8 in around Alexandria). Mild winters. In Cairo average maximum 65 °F (January) to 96 °F (July), minimum 47 °F (January) to 71 °F (August). In Luxor average maximum 74 °F (January) to 107 °F (July), minimum 42 °F (January) to 73 °F (July, August), rain negligible.
Crops: Cotton, maize, rice, wheat, millet, sugar-cane, onions.
Monetary unit: Egyptian pound (£E). £E1 = 100 piastres = 1000 millièmes.
Denominations:
  Coins 1, 2, 5 millièmes, 1, 2, 5, 10 piastres.
  Notes 5, 10 piastres, ¼, ½, 1, 5, 10 pounds.
Exchange rate to US dollar: 0.391 (February 1976).

Political history and government: A former British protectorate, Egypt became independent, with the Sultan as King, on

28 Feb. 1922. Army officers staged a *coup* on 23 July 1952 and the King abdicated, in favour of his son, on 26 July 1952. Political parties were dissolved on 16 Jan. 1953. The young King was deposed, and a republic proclaimed, on 18 June 1953. Egypt merged with Syria to form the United Arab Republic on 1 Feb. 1958. Syria broke away and resumed independence on 29 Sept. 1961 but Egypt retained the union's title until the present name was adopted on 2 Sept. 1971. A new constitution, proclaiming socialist principles, was approved by referendum on 11 Sept. 1971. Legislative authority rests with the unicameral People's Assembly of 360 members (10 appointed, 12 representing occupied territories and 338 elected by universal adult suffrage for 5 years). Half the elected members must be workers or peasants. The Assembly nominates the President, who is elected by popular referendum for six years. He has executive authority and appoints one or more Vice-Presidents, a Prime Minister and a Council of Ministers to perform administrative functions. The Arab Socialist Union (ASU), created on 7 Dec. 1962, is the only recognised political organisation of the state. The President is Chairman of the ASU. The country is composed of 25 governorates (5 cities, 16 provinces, 4 frontier districts).
Telephones: 471 791 (1973).
Daily newspapers: 14 (1971).
  Total circulation: 745 000.
Radio: 5 100 000 (1973).
TV: 584 000 (1971).
Length of Roadways: 31 068 miles *50 000 km.*
Length of railways: 3111 miles *5006 km.*
Universities: 8.
Adult illiteracy: 73·7% (males 59·5%; females 87·6%) in 1960.
Expectation of life: Males 51·6 years; females 53·8 years (1960).
Defence: Military service three years; Total armed forces 322 500 (1975); Defence expenditure 1975-6 $ 6103 million.
Wildlife: Hyena, gazelle, hare, fennu fox, jackal, lynx, ibis, bat, horned viper, echis, hooded snake, lizard, mouse, rat, jerboa, ichneumon; over 300 species of bird including vultures, kites, eagles, barn owl, partridge, quail, pigeon, hoopoe, crane, heron, spoonbill, kingfisher.
Cinemas: 150 (seating capacity 137 900) and 89 part-time (capacity 77 086) in 1970.

EL SALVADOR

Official name: La República de El Salvador ('The Saviour').
Population: 3 549 260 (1971 census); 3 980 000 (1974 est.).
Area: 8124 miles² *21 040 km².*
Language: Spanish.
Religion: Roman Catholic.
Capital city: San Salvador, population 416 900 (1974 est.).
Other principal towns (1971): Santa Ana 172 300; San Miguel 110 966; Zacatecoluca 57 001; Santa Tecla 55 718; Ahuachapán 53 386; Sonsonate 48 821.
Highest point: 9200 ft *2804 m.*
Principal rivers: Lempa (250 miles [*402 km*]), San Miguel.
Head of State: Col Arturo Armando Molina Barraza (b. 6 Aug. 1927), President.
Climate: Tropical (hot and humid) is coastal lowlands, temperate in uplands. In San Salvador maximum temperature is 90 °F (April and May), minimum around 60 °F (December, January, February).
Crops: Maize, cotton, coffee, sugar cane.
Monetary unit: Salvadorian colón. 1 colón = 100 centavos.

189

Denominations:
Coins 1, 2, 3, 5, 10, 25, 50 centavos.
Notes 1, 2, 5, 10, 25, 100 colones.
Exchange rate to US dollar: 2.50 (February 1976).

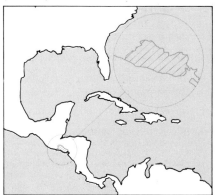

Political history and government: A republic composed of 14 departments. Legislative power is held by a single Legislative Assembly containing 52 members elected for two years by universal suffrage, using a system of proportional representation. Executive power is vested in the President, who is elected by popular vote for 5 years and may not be re-elected. The President is assisted by a Vice-President and a Council of Ministers.
Telephones: 45 684 (1974).
Daily newspapers: 12 (1971).
 Total circulation: 272 000.
Radio: 350 000 (1971).
TV: 125 000 (1971).
Length of roadways: 5216 miles *8394 km.*
Length of railways: 447 miles *720 km.*
Universities: 2.
Adult illiteracy: 43·1% (1971).
Expectation of life: Males 56·56 years; females 60·42 years (1960–1).
Defence: Total armed forces 5130 (1974).
Wildlife: Ocelot, coyote, jaguar, tapir, deer, iguana, cayman, crocodile; many species of waterfowl and land birds.
Cinemas: 57 (est seating capacity 57 000) in 1971.

EQUATORIAL GUINEA

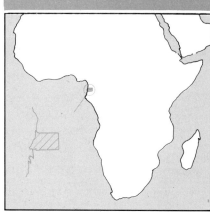

Official name: La República de Guinea Ecuatorial.
Population: 245 989 (1960 census); 286 000 (1969 est); 310 000 (UN est for mid-1975).
Area: 10 831 miles² *28 051 km².*
Languages: Spanish (official), Fang, Bubi.
Religions: Roman Catholic, Protestant minority.
Capital city: Malabo (formerly Santa Isabel), population 19 341 (1970 est).
Other principal town: Bata 3548.
Highest point: Pico de Moca (Moka),

9350 ft *2850 m.*
Principal rivers: Campo
 Benito ⎱ in Mbini
 Muni ⎰
Head of State: Francisco Macías Nguema (b. 1 Jan. 1924), President.
Climate: Tropical (hot and humid), with average temperatures of over 26 °C (*80 °F*) and heavy rainfall (about 80 in per year).
Crops: Cassava, sweet potatoes, bananas, cocoa, coffee, palm oil and palm kernels.
Monetary unit: Ekuele. 1 ekuele = 100 céntimos.
Denominations:
 Coins 5, 10, 50 céntimos, 1, 2½, 5, 25, 50, 100 ekuele.
 Notes 1, 5, 25, 50, 100, 500, 1000 ekuele.
Exchange rate to US dollar: 66.65 (February 1976).
Political history and government: Formed on 20 Dec. 1963 by a merger of two Spanish territories, Río Muni (now Mbini) on the African mainland and the islands of Fernando Póo (now Macías Nguema Biyogo). Became an independent republic, as a federation of two provinces, on 12 Oct. 1968. All political parties were merged into one on 2 Feb. 1970. The legislature, a unicameral National Assembly of 35 members, was dissolved in 1971. Executive power lies with the President (proclaimed President for Life on 14 July 1972), assisted by a Cabinet. A revised constitution, approved by referendum on 29 July 1973 and effective from 4 Aug. 1973, gave absolute power to the President and established a unitary state, abolishing the provincial autonomy of the islands.
Telephones: 1451 (1969).
Daily newspapers: 1 (1967).
 Total circulation: 1000
Radio: 76 000.
Length of roadways: 730 miles *1175 km.*
Expectation of life: Males 39·4 years; females 42·6 years (1965–70).
Wildlife: Baboon, monkey, hyena, antelope, mamba, cobra, crocodile, Goliath frog (world's largest).
Cinemas: 11 (seating capacity 6300) in 1967.

ETHIOPIA

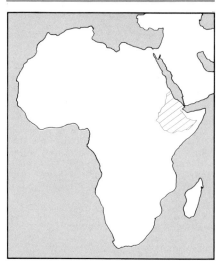

Official name: Republic of Ethiopia.
Population: 27 239 000 (1974 est).
Area: 471 800 miles² *1 221 900 km².*
Languages: Amharic, Galla, Somali.
Religions: Muslim 50%, Christian (mainly Coptic).
Capital city: Addis Ababa ('New Flower'), population 1 011 565 (1973).
Other principal towns (1972): Asmara

249 110; Dire Dawa 66 570, Dessie 49 750 Harar 48 440; Jimma 47 360; Nazret 45 280 Gondar 38 600.
Highest point: Ras Dashen, 15 158 *4620 m.*
Principal mountain ranges: Eritrea highlands, Tigre Plateau, Eastern Highlands, Semien mountains.
Principal rivers: Abbay, Tekeze, Awash Omo, Sagan, Webi, Shelebe.
Head of State: Brig-Gen. Teferi Bante (b 1921), Chairman of the Provisional Military Council.
Climate: Although tropical, the Ethiopian Plateau is temperate owing to altitude Temperatures in highland and lowland areas differ markedly, e.g. Addis Ababa (at 8000 ft) annual mean temperature 60 °F. Massawa (sea level) 87 °F. Coldest month usually January, hottest May. Rainy season —peak, June and July. Rainfall varie from 100 in in SW to 2 in in NE.
Crops: Barley, teff, sorghum, maize, wheat ensete, neug, coffee, sugar cane, sesame seed.
Monetary unit: Ethiopian dollar (E$). dollar = 100 cents.
Denominations:
 Coins 1, 5, 10, 25, 50 cents.
 Notes 1, 5, 10, 20, 50, 100, 500 dollars.
Exchange rate to US dollar: 2.072 (February 1976).
Political history and government: Formerly a monarchy, ruled by an Emperor with near-autocratic powers. Political parties were not permitted. The former Italian colony of Eritrea was merged with Ethiopia under a federal arrangement, on 15 Sept 1952. Its federal status was ended on 14 Nov. 1962.
 The last Emperor was deposed by the armed forces on 12 Sept. 1974. The constitution and the bicameral Parliament (a Senate and a Chamber of Deputies) were suspended. The *coup* was engineered by the Armed Forces Co-ordinating Committee (the Derg), which controls ultimate power. The Derg's original 120 members have been reduced to about 60. Since 28 Nov. 1974 executive authority has been held by the Provisional Military Council (PMC), whose Chairman is Head of State. Ethiopia was declared a socialist state on 20 Dec. 1974 and the monarchy was abolished on 21 Mar. 1975. On 21 Apr. 1976 the PMC announced plans for the eventual creation of a People's Democratic Republic. Ethiopia has 14 provinces.
Telephones: 65 987 (1975).
Daily newspapers: 8.
 Total circulation: 28 000.
Radio: 200 000 (1975).
TV: 20 000 (1975).
Length of roadways: 14 292 miles *23 000 km.*
Length of railways: 744 miles *1197 km.*
Universities: 2.
Adult illiteracy: 90% (esimate).
Expectation of life: Males 36·5 years; females 39·6 years (1965–70).
Defence: Total armed forces (including paramilitary) *c.* 64 000. Defence expenditure 1972–3 $46 million.
Wildlife: Walia ibex, hyena, jackal, wild dog, kudu, oryx, bushbuck, wild pig, vervet, baboon, lion, elephant, buffalo, zebra.
Cinemas: 28.

FIJI

Population: 476 727 (1966 census); 564 000 (1974 est).
Area: 7055 miles² *18 272 km².*
Languages: English, Fijian, Hindi.
Religions: Christian 50·8% (mainly Metho-

dist), Hindu 40·3%, Muslim 7·8% (1966).
Capital city: Suva, population 65 530 (1973 est).
Other principal towns: Lautoka, Vatukoula, Ba, Labasa, Levuka.
Highest point: Mt Victoria (Tomaniivi) on Viti Levu, 4341 ft *1323 m*.
Principal rivers: Rewa, Sigatoka, Navua, Nadi, Ba.
Head of State: HM Queen Elizabeth II, represented by Ratu Sir George Kandavulevu Cakobau, GCMG, OBE (b. 6 Nov. 1912), Governor-General.
Prime Minister: Ratu the Rt Hon Sir Kamisese Kapaiwai Tuimacilau Mara, KBE (b. 13 May 1920).
Climate: Temperate, with temperatures rarely falling below 60 °F (*15·5 °C*) or rising above 90 °F (*32,2 °C*). Copious rainfall on windward side; dry on leeward side.
Crops: Bananas, coconut, sugar-cane, rice, yams, pineapple.
Monetary unit: Fiji dollar ($F). 1 dollar = 100 cents.
Denominations:
Coins 1, 2, 5, 10, 20, 50 cents.
Notes 50 cents, 1, 2, 5, 10, 20 dollars.
Exchange rate to US dollar: 0.861 (February 1976).
Political history and government: A former British colony, an independent member of the Commonwealth since 10 Oct. 1970. Executive power is vested in the Queen and exercisable by her personal representative, the Governor-General, advised by the Prime Minister, who heads the Cabinet. The bicameral legislature comprises a Senate (22 members nominated for 6 years) and a House of Representatives (52 members elected for 5 years). Elections to the House are on three rolls: Fijian (22), Indian (22) and general (8). There are 14 provinces, each headed by a chairman.
Telephones: 22 523 (1973).
Daily newspapers: 1 (1972).
Total circulation: 19 000.
Radio: 53 000 (1972).
Length of roadways: 1568 miles *2523 km*.
Length of railways: 400 miles *644 km*.
Universities: 1.
Expectation of life: Males 66·4 years; females 69·9 years (1965–70).
Wildlife: Bat, rat, wild pig; parrot, pigeon.
Cinemas: 24 with seating capacity of 10 000 (1970).

FINLAND

Official name: Suomen Tasavalta (Republic of Finland).
Population: 4 698 000 (1974 est).
Area: 130 129 miles² *337 032 km²*.
Languages: Finnish 92·4%; Swedish 7·4%.
Religions: Lutheran 92·5%; Orthodox 1·3%.

Capital city: Helsinki (Helsingfors), population 502 383 (1974).
Other principal towns (1974): Tampere (Tammerfors) 165 293; Turku (Åbo) 163 162; Espoo (Esbo) 116 541; Vantaa (Vandu) 111 420; Lahti 94 617; Oulu (Uleåborg) 90 714; Pori (Björneborg) 80 198.
Highest point: Haltiatunturi, 4344 ft *1324 m*
Principal mountain ranges: Sualaselkä, Maanselkä.
Principal rivers: Paatsjoki, Torniojoki, Kemijoki, Kokemäenjoki.
Head of State: Dr Urho Kaleva Kekkonen, GCB (b. 3 Sept. 1900), President.
Prime Minister: Martti Juhani Miettunen (b. 17 Apr. 1907).
Climate: N Finland is in the Arctic Circle and therefore has a long, extreme winter, temperatures falling to −22 °F (−*30 °C*). In summer temperature can reach 80 °F (*27 °C*). Further S temperatures are less extreme. Rainfall about 24 in in S, less in N—⅓ falls as snow.
Crops: Oats, barley, potatoes, wheat.
Monetary unit: Markka (Finnmark). 1 markka = 100 penniä.
Denominations:
Coins 1, 5, 10, 20, 50 penniä, 1, 5 markkaa.
Notes 5, 10, 50, 100, 500 markkaa.
Exchange rate to US dollar: 3.825 (February 1976).
Political history and government: Formerly a Grand Duchy within the Russian Empire. After the Bolshevik revolution in Russia, Finland's independence was declared on 6 Dec. 1917. A republic was established by the constitution of 17 July 1919, This combines a parliamentary system with a strong presidency. The unicameral Parliament has 200 members elected by universal adult suffrage for 4 years (subject to dissolution by the President), using proportional representation. The President, entrusted with supreme executive power, is elected for 6 years by a college of 300 electors, chosen by popular vote in the same manner as members of Parliament. Legislative power is exercised by Parliament in conjunction with the President. For general administration the President appoints a Council of State (Cabinet), headed by a Prime Minister, which is responsible to Parliament. Finland has 12 provinces, each administered by an appointed Governor.
Telephones: 1 678 873 (1975).
Daily newspapers: 89.
Total circulation: 2 188 000.
Radio: 2 036 187 (1975).
TV: 1 440 337 (1975).
Length of roadways: 45 712 miles *73 567 km*.
Length of railways: 5487 miles *8831 km*.
Universities: 8 (plus 3 technical universities).
Adult illiteracy: Under 1%.
Expectation of life: Males 65·88 years; females 73·57 years (1966–70).
Defence: Neutral. Military service 240 to 330 days; Army 34 000, Navy 2500, Air Force 3000, size limited by the terms of the Peace Treaty (1947) concluded with UK and USSR.
Wildlife: Bear, wolf, wolverine, lynx, elk; wide variety of waterfowl.
Cinemas: 318 (1972).

FRANCE

Official name: La République française (the French Republic).
Population: 52 544 400 (1975 census).
Area: 211 208 miles² *547 026 km²*.
Language: French.

Religions: Roman Catholic, Protestant, Jewish.
Capital city: Paris, population 2 290 900 (1975).
Other principal towns (1975): Marseille 907 900; Lyon 457 000; Toulouse 383 200; Nice 344 500; Strasbourg 257 300; Nantes 257 300; Bordeaux 221 100; Saint-Etienne 220 000; Le Havre 219 100; Rennes 195 000; Montpellier 191 100; Toulon 181 800; Reims 177 600; Lille 169 500; Brest 167 200; Grenoble 167 000; Clermont-Ferrand 157 500; Le Mans 152 200; Dijon 151 600; Limoges 147 300; Tours 140 600; Angers 137 300; Amiens 131 000; Nîmes 127 700; Caen 122 500; Besançon 120 400.
Highest point: Mont Blanc, 15 771 ft *4807 m* (first climbed on 8 Aug. 1786).
Principal mountain ranges: Alps, Massif Central, Pyrenees, Jura Mts, Vosges, Cévennes.
Principal rivers: Rhône, Seine, Loire (625 miles [*1006 km*]), Garonne, Rhin (Rhine).
Head of State: Valéry Giscard d'Estaing (b. 2 Feb. 1926), President.
Prime Minister: Jacques René Chirac (b. 29 Nov. 1932).

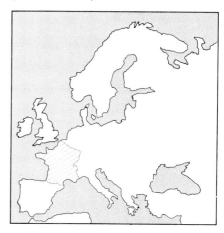

Climate: Generally temperate, with cool summers in the west and warm summers elsewhere. Mediterranean climate (warm summers, mild winters) in the south. In Paris, average maximum 42 °F (January) to 76 °F (July), minimum 32 °F (January) to 55 °F (July, August), December rainiest (17 days). Absolute maximum temperature 44,0 °C (111.2 °F), Toulouse, 8 Aug. 1923; absolute minimum −33 °C (−*27·4 °F*), Langres, 9 Dec. 1879.
Crops: Wheat, barley, maize, oats, potatoes, sugar-beet, grapes, apples.
Monetary unit: French franc. 1 franc = 100 centimes.
Denominations:
Coins 1, 5, 10, 20, centimes, 1, 2 old francs, ½, 1, 5, 10 francs.
Notes 10, 50, 100, 500 francs.
Exchange rate to US dollar: 4.485 (February 1976).
Political history and government: A republic whose present constitution (establishing the Fifth Republic and the French Community) was approved by referendum on 28 Sept. 1958 and promulgated on 6 Oct. 1958. Legislative power is held by a bicameral parliament. The Senate has 283 members (264 for metropolitan France, 13 for the overseas departments and territories and 6 for French nationals abroad) indirectly elected for 9 years (one third renewable every three years). The National Assembly has 490 members (473 for metropolitan France and 17 for overseas departments) directly elected by universal adult suffrage (using two ballots if necessary) for 5 years, subject

191

to dissolution. Executive power is held by the President. Since 1962 the President has been directly elected by universal adult suffrage (using two ballots if necessary) for 7 years. The President appoints a Council of Ministers, headed by the Prime Minister, which administers the country and is responsible to Parliament. Metropolitan France comprises 21 administrative regions containing 95 departments. There are also four overseas departments (French Guiana, Guadeloupe, Martinique and Réunion) which are integral parts of the French Republic. Each department is administered by an appointed Prefect.

Telephones: 12 405 054 (1973).
Daily newspapers: 105 (1971).
  Total circulation: 12 160 000.
Radio: 17 034 000 (1972).
TV: 12 955 000 (1973).
Length of roadways (1973): 493 260 miles *793 826 km.*
Length of railways (1973): 21 693 miles *34 912 km* (SNCF only).
Universities: 37.
Expectation of life: Males 68·5 years; females 76·1 years (1971).
Defence: Military service 12 months; Total armed forces 502 500 (1974); Defence expenditure, 1975: $10 838 million.
Wildlife: Pire vole, frog, hare, chamois, ibex, marmot, beaver; about 90 species of reptile including swamp snake, lizard; about 400 species of bird including flamingo, stilt, egret, heron, ducks, geese, warblers, bee eater, Corsican nuthatch, roller.
Cinemas: 4206 (seating capacity 1 936 900) and 6 drive-in (1972).

Climate: Tropical (hot and humid). Average temperature 79 °F. Heavy rainfall (annual average 98 in). In Libreville, average maximum 86 °F to 94 °F, minimum 65 °F to 71 °F.
Crops: Cassava, bananas, cocoa, palm oil.
Monetary unit: Franc de la Communauté financière africaine.
Denominations:
  Coins 1, 2, 5, 10, 25, 50, 100 CFA francs.
  Notes 100, 500, 1000, 5000, 10 000 CFA francs.
Exchange rate to US dollar: 224.24 (February 1976).
Political history and government: Formerly part of French Equatorial Africa, independent since 17 Aug. 1960. A one-party state since March 1968. The legislature is a unicameral National Assembly of 70 members, directly elected by universal adult suffrage for 7 years. Executive power is held by the President, also directly elected for 7 years. He appoints, and presides over, a Council of Ministers, including a Prime Minister. Gabon comprises 9 regions, each administered by an appointed Prefect.
Telephones: 11 000 (1973).
Radio: 65 000 (1972).
TV: 1300 (1972).
Length of roadways: 4256 miles *6848 km.*
Length of railways: 231 miles *372 km.*
Universities: 1.
Expectation of life: Males 36·9 years; females 40·1 years (1965–70).
Wildlife: Elephant, monkey, gorilla, antelope, forest buffalo, hippopotamus, Gaboon viper.
Cinemas: 2 (seating capacity 1700) in 1971.

40 in. on coast, less inland. Rainy season June to October. Average annual temperature Banjue 80 °F.
Crops: Groundnuts, rice, millet, sorghum
Monetary unit: Dalasi. 1 dalasi = 10 butut.
Denominations:
  Coins 1, 5, 10, 25, 50 butut, 1 dalasi.
  Notes 1, 5, 10, 25 dalasi.
Exchange rate to US dollar: 1.97 (February 1976).
Political history and government: former British dependency, an independen member of the Commonwealth since 1 Feb. 1965. A republic since 24 April 1970 Legislative power is held by a unicameral House of Representatives containing 4 members (32 directly elected for 5 years b universal adult suffrage, 4 Chiefs' Representative Members elected by the Chief in Assembly, 3 non-voting nominate members and the Attorney-General. Executive power is held by the President, the leade of the majority party in the House. H appoints a Vice-President (who is leader o government business in the House) and Cabinet from elected members of the House The country has four political parties.
Telephones: 1942 (1973).
Radio: 60 000 (1972).
Length of roadways (1974): 1858 miles *2990 km.*
Expectation of life: Males 37·0 years females 40·1 years (1965–70).
Defence: No armed forces.
Wildlife: Antelope, gazelle, monkey, crocodile, hippopotamus, numerous types of bird
Cinemas: 8 (1971).

GABON

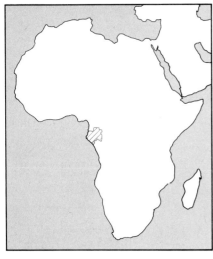

Official name: La République gabonaise (The Gabonese Republic).
Population: 448 564 (1961 census); 500 000 (1970 est).
Area: 103 347 miles² *267 667 km².*
Languages: French (official), Fang, Eshira, Mbété.
Religions: Christian 60%, Animist minority
Capital city: Libreville, population 105 080 (1970).
Other principal towns: Port-Gentil, Lambaréné.
Highest point: Mont Iboundji, 5185 ft *1580 m.*
Principal river: Ogooué (Ogowe).
Head of State: Albert-Bernard Bongo (b. 30 Dec. 1935), President and Head of Government.
Prime Minister: Léon Mebiame (b. 1 Sept. 1934).

THE GAMBIA

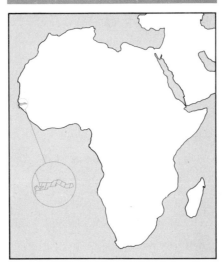

Official name: The Republic of the Gambia.
Population: 493 197 (1973 census); 510 000 (1974 est).
Area: 4361 miles² *11 295 km²*
Languages: English (official), Mandinka, Fula, Wollof.
Religions: Muslim, Christian minority
Capital city: Banjul (formerly Bathurst), population 39 476 (1973).
Other principal towns: Brikama; Salikeni; Bakau; Gunjur.
Principal river: Gambia.
Head of State: Sir Dawda Kairaba Jawara (b. 11 May 1924), President.
Climate: Long dry season, normally November to May, with pleasant weather on coast (best in West Africa) due to effect of harmattan. Hotter up-river, especially February to May. Average annual rainfall

GERMANY (East)

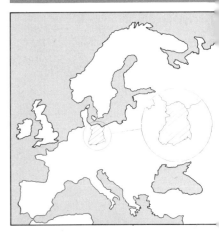

Official name: Deutsche Demokratisch Republik (German Democratic Republic
Population: 17 068 318 (1971 census 16 924 700 (1974 est).
Area: 41 768 miles² *108 178 km².*
Language: German.
Religions: Protestant, Roman Catholi minority.
Capital city: East Berlin, population 1 089 962 (1974).
Other principal towns (1974): Leipzig 572 976; Dresden 506 752; Karl-Marx Stadt (Chemnitz) 302 952; Magdeburg 274 146; Halle an der Saale 243 961 Rostock 208 640; Erfurt 202 477.
Highest point: Fichtelberg (3983 ft *[1214m]*
Principal mountain ranges: Thüringe Wald, Erz Gebirge.
Principal rivers: Elbe (525 miles *[845 km]* (with Havel and Saale), Oder (with Neisse)
Head of State: Willi Stoph (b. 9 Jul 1914), Chairman of the Council of State.
Political Leader: Erich Honecker (b. 2

Aug. 1912), First Secretary of the Central Committee of the Socialist Unity Party.
Head of Government: Horst Sindermann b. 5 Sept. 1915), Chairman of the Council f Ministers.
Climate: Temperate (warm summers, cool vinters), greater range inland. In Berlin, July warmest (55 °F to 74 °F), January oldest (26 °F to 35 °F), December rainiest 11 days). Absolute maximum temperature 39,3 °C (*102·7 °F*), Blankenberg, 7 July 957; absolute minimum −33,8 °C (−*28·8 F*), Zittau-Hirschfelde, 11 Feb. 1939.
Crops: Wheat, barley, rye, potatoes, sugar-beet.
Monetary unit: Mark der Deutschen Demokratischen Republik (DDR-Mark). Mark = 100 Pfennige.
Denominations:
  Coins 1, 5, 10, 20, 50 Pfennige, 1, 2, 5, 10, 20 M.
  Notes 5, 10, 20, 50, 100 M.
Exchange rate to US dollar: 2.40 (July 1975).
Political history and government: The territory was the USSR's Zone of Occupation in Germany from May 1945. The republic, a 'people's democracy' on the Soviet pattern, was proclaimed on 7 Oct. 1949. The present constitution was promulgated on 9 Apr. 1968. The supreme organ of state power is the *Volkskammer* (People's Chamber), containing 500 members, including 434 elected for 4 years by universal adult suffrage (from a single list of candidates) and 66 representatives from East Berlin, elected by the City Assembly. The Chamber elects a 24-member *Staatsrat* (Council of State) to be its permanent organ. The executive branch of government is the *Ministerrat* (Council of Ministers), under a Chairman (Minister-President) appointed by the Chamber, which also approves his appointed Ministers. The Council's work is directed by a Presidium of 15 members. Political power is held by the (Communist) Socialist Unity Party of Germany (SED), formed in 1946 by a merger of the Communist Party and the Social Democratic Party in the Soviet Zone. The SED dominates the National Front of Democratic Germany, which also includes four minor parties and four mass organisations. The country is divided into 14 districts (*Bezirke*) and the city of East Berlin.
Telephones: 2 326 027 (1973).
Daily newspapers: 40 (1972).
  Total circulation: 7 236 000.
Radio: 6 082 400 (1973).
TV: 4 966 500 (1973).
Length of roadways (1974): 78 859 miles *126 911 km.*
Length of railways (1974): 8856 miles *14 252 km.*
Universities: 7.
Expectation of life: Males 68·85 years; females 74·19 years (1969–70).
Defence: Military service 18 months; Total regular forces 143 000; Defence expenditure 1975 $2333 million.
Wildlife: Numerous mammals including deer, wolf, pine-marten, wildcat, wild boar, beaver, bat, hamster. Owls, woodpecker, warblers, great bustard, capercaillie.
Cinemas: 1197 (seating capacity 355 000) and 226 part-time (1972).

GERMANY (West)

Official name: Bundesrepublik Deutschland (Federal Republic of Germany).
Population: 60 650 599 (1970 census); 61 916 000 (1975 est).
Area: 95 989 miles² *248 611 km²*.
Language: German.

Religions: Protestant, Roman Catholic.
Capital city: Bonn, population 283 900 (1974 est).
Other principal towns (1974): Berlin (West) 2 002 615; Hamburg 1 751 620; München (Munich) 1 311 978; Köln (Cologne) 849 451; Essen 696 419; Frankfurt am Main 666 179; Düsseldorf 660 963; Dortmund 640 642; Stuttgart 634 202; Bremen 592 533; Hannover (Hanover) 521 003; Nürnberg (Nuremberg) 478 181; Duisberg 452 721; Wuppertal 417 694; Gelsenkirchen 347 074; Bochum 343 809; Mannheim 332 378; Kiel 271 042; Karlsruhe 259 091; Wiesbaden 250 715.

Highest point: Zugspitze, 9721 ft *2963 m* (first climbed 1820).
Principal mountain ranges: Alps, Schwarzwald (Black Forest).
Principal rivers: Rhein (Rhine) (820 miles [*1320 km*]), Ems, Weser, Elbe, Donau (Danube) (1770 miles [*2848 km*]).
Head of State: Walter Scheel (b. 8 July 1919), Federal President.
Head of Government: Helmut Heinrich Waldemar Schmidt (b. 23 Dec. 1918), Federal Chancellor.
Climate: Generally temperate (average annual temperature 48 °F) with considerable variations from northern coastal plain (mild) to Bavarian Alps (cool summers, cold winters). In Hamburg, July warmest (56 °F to 69 °F) January coolest (28 °F to 35 °F). January, July and December rainiest (each 12 days). Absolute maximum temperature 39,8 °C (*103·6 °F*), Amberg, 18 Aug. 1892; absolute minimum −35,4 °C (−*31·7 °F*), 12 Feb. 1929.
Crops: Potatoes, wheat, barley, oats, rye, sugar beet, grapes, hops.
Monetary unit: Deutsche Mark (DM). 1 Deutsche Mark = 100 Pfennige.
Denominations:
  Coins 1, 2, 5, 10, 50 Pfennige, 1, 2, 5, 10 DM.
  Notes 5, 10, 20, 50, 100, 500, 1000 DM.
Exchange rate to US dollar: 2.56 (February 1976).
Political history and government: The territory was the British, French and US Zones of Occupation in Germany from May 1945. A provisional constitution, the *Grundgesetz* (Basic Law), came into force in the three Zones (excluding Saarland) on 23 May 1949 and the Federal Republic of Germany (FRG) was established on 21 Sept. 1949. Sovereignty was limited by the continuing military occupation, and subsequent defence agreements, until 5 May 1955, when the FRG became fully independent. Saarland (under French occupation) was rejoined with the FRG administratively on 1 Jan. 1957 and economically incorporated on 6 July 1959. The FRG is composed of 10 states (*Länder*)—each *Land* having its

own constitution, parliament and government—plus the city of West Berlin which retains a separate status. The country has a parliamentary regime, with a bicameral legislature. The Upper House is the *Bundesrat* (Federal Council) with 45 seats, including 41 members of *Land* governments (which appoint and recall them) and 4 non-voting representatives appointed by the West Berlin Senate. The term of office varies with *Land* election dates. The Lower House, and the FRG's main legislative organ, is the *Bundestag*, with 518 deputies, including 496 elected for four years by universal adult suffrage (using a mixed system of proportional representation and direct voting) and 22 members (with limited voting rights) elected by the West Berlin House of Representatives. Executive authority rests with the *Bundesregierung* (Federal Government), led by the *Bundeskanzler* (Federal Chancellor) who is elected by an absolute majority of the *Bundestag* and appoints the other Ministers. The Head of State, who normally acts on the Chancellor's advice, is elected by a Federal Convention, consisting of the *Bundestag* and an equal number of members elected by the *Land* parliaments.
Telephones: 18 707 000 (1974).
Daily newspapers: 1223 (1972), incl 810 regional editions.
  Total circulation: 18 126 000.
Radio: 20 586 000 (1973).
TV: 18 486 000 (1973).
Length of roadways: 285 490 miles *459 452 km.*
Length of railways: 18 138 miles| *29 191 km* | federal

  2164 miles| other
  3482 km |
Universities: 54 (incl 9 technical universities).
Expectation of life: Males 67·24 years; females 73·44 years (1968–70).
Defence: Military service 15 months; Total armed forces 495 000 (1975); Defence expenditure 1975 $12 669 million.
Wildlife: Numerous mammals including deer, wolf, pine-marten, wild cat, wild boar, beaver, bat, hamster. Owls, woodpecker, warblers, great bustard, capercaillie.
Cinemas: 3171 (seating capacity 1 279 800) in 1972; also 19 drive-ins for 18 331 cars (1971).

GHANA

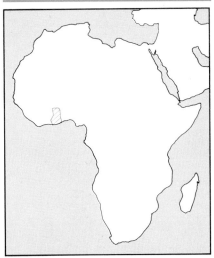

Official name: The Republic of Ghana ('land of gold').
Population: 8 559 313 (1970 census); 9 607 000 (1974 est).

Area: 92 100 miles² *238 537 km²*.
Languages: English (official), Asante, Ewe, Fante.
Religions: Christian, Muslim, Animist.
Capital city: Accra, population 636 067 (1970).
Other principal towns (1970): Kumasi 260 286; Tamale 83 653; Tema 60 767; Takoradi 58 161; Cape Coast 51 653; Sekondi 33 713.
Highest point: Vogag (2989 ft [*911 m*]).
Principal rivers: Volta (formed by the confluence of the Black Volta and the White Volta) and its tributaries (principally the Oti), Tano, Ofin.
Head of State: Gen Ignatius Kutu Acheampong (b. 23 Sept. 1931), Chairman of the Supreme Military Council.
Climate: Tropical. In north hot and dry. Forest areas hot and humid. Eastern coastal belt warm and fairly dry. In Accra average maximum 80 °F (August) to 88 °F (February to April and December), average minimum 71 °F (August) to 76 °F (March, April), June rainiest (10 days).
Crops: Cassava, taro, yams, maize, cocoa (world's leading producer), sugar cane, coconuts, groundnuts.
Monetary unit: New cedi. 1 cedi = 100 pesewas.
Denominations:
Coins ½, 1, 2½, 5, 10, 20 pesewas.
Notes 1, 2, 5, 10 cedis.
Exchange rate to US dollar: 1.1538 (February 1976).
Political history and government: On 6 Mar. 1957 the British dependency of the Gold Coast merged with British Togoland to become independent, and a member of the Commonwealth, as Ghana. Became a republic on 1 July 1960. The President, Dr Kwame Nkrumah, was deposed by a military *coup* on 24 Feb. 1966. Civilian rule was restored on 30 Sept. 1969 but again overthrown by the armed forces on 13 Jan. 1972. The 1969 constitution was abolished, the National Assembly dissolved and political parties banned. Power was assumed by the National Redemption Council (NRC), comprising military commanders and Commissioners of State with ministerial responsibilities. On 14 Oct. 1975 a 7-man Supreme Military Council was established, with full legislative and administrative authority, to direct the NRC.
Telephones: 51 938 (1973).
Daily newspapers: 7 (1970).
Total circulation: 415 000 (6 dailies).
Radio: 775 000 (1972).
TV: 25 000 (1973).
Length of roadways: 19 236 miles *30 957 km*.
Length of railways: 593 miles *954 km*.
Universities: 3.
Expectation of life: Males 39·9 years; females 43·1 years (1965–70).
Defence: Military service voluntary; Total armed forces 15 450; Defence expenditure 1974–5 $83 million.
Wildlife: Giant toad, tree frog, chimpanzee, antelope, forest elephant, leopard, bush pig, forest crocodile, hartebeest, hippopotamus (diminishing numbers), green mambas, vipers. Rock-fowl, hornbill, sunbird, weaver-bird, waxbill, parrot, pigeon, egret, kingfisher, flycatcher, shrike.
Cinemas: 57 (seating capacity 50 400) in 1969.

GREECE

Official name: The Hellenic Republic.
Population: 8 768 641 (1971 census); 8 962 023 (1974 est).
Area: 50 944 miles² *131 944 km²*.

Languages: Greek.
Religions: Eastern Orthodox Church, with Roman Catholic and other minorities.
Capital city: Athínai (Athens), population 867 023 (1971).
Other principal towns (1971): Thessaloniki (Salonika) 345 799; Piraeus 187 458; Pátrai (Patras) 112 228; Iráklion (Heraklion) 78 209; Lárisa 72 760; Vólos 51 290; Kaválla 46 887.
Highest point: Óros Ólimbos (Olympus) 9550 ft *2911 m*.
Principal mountain ranges: Pindus Mountains.
Principal rivers: Aliákmon (195 miles *314 km*), Piniós, Akhelóös.
Head of State: Konstantinos Tsatsos (b. 1 July 1899), President.
Prime Minister: Konstantinos G Karamanlis (b. 23 Feb. 1907).
Climate: Mediterranean (hot, dry summers and mild, wet winters). Colder in the north and on higher ground. In Athens, July and August hottest (72 °F to 90 °F), January coolest (42 °F to 54 °F), December and January rainiest (seven days each). Absolute maximum temperature (45,7 °C *114·3 °F*), Heraklion, Crete, 16 June 1914; absolute minimum −25 °C (−*13 °F*), Kaválla, 27 Jan. 1954.
Crops: Wheat, barley, maize, tomatoes, potatoes, citrus fruits, watermelons, cotton, olives, grapes, sugar beet, tobacco.
Monetary unit: Drachma. 1 drachma = 100 leptae.
Denominations:
Coins 5, 10, 20, 50 leptae, 1, 2, 5, 10, 20 drachmae.
Notes 50, 100, 500, 1000 drachmae.
Exchange rate to US dollar: 35.23 (February 1976).

Political history and government: While Greece was a monarchy a *coup* by army officers, led by Col Georgios Papadopoulos, deposed the constitutional government on 21 Apr. 1967. Parliament was suspended and political parties banned. Papadopoulos became Prime Minister on 13 Dec. 1967, a Regent was appointed and the King left the country the next day. A republic was proclaimed on 1 June 1973 and Papadopoulos became President. He was deposed by another military *coup* on 25 Nov. 1973. Civilian rule was re-established on 24 July 1974, when a Government of National Salvation took office. The ban on political parties was lifted and free elections for a Parliament were held on 17 Nov. 1974. A referendum on 8 Dec. 1974 rejected the return of the monarchy. A new republican constitution, providing for a parliamentary democracy, came into force on 11 June 1975. Executive power rests with the President, elected for 5 years by the legislature, a unicameral Parliament of 300 members directly elected by

universal adult suffrage for 4 years. The President appoints a Prime Minister and on his recommendation, the other Ministers to form a Cabinet to govern the country. The Cabinet is accountable to Parliament. The country is divided into 51 prefectures (*Nomoi*). The district of Mount Athos, with its autonomous monastic community, has a privileged status as a self-governing part of the Greek state.
Telephones: 1 670 132 (1973).
Daily newspapers: 104 (1972).
Radio: 1 000 000 (1972).
TV: 520 000 (1972).
Length of roadways: 24 233 miles *39 000 km*.
Length of railways: 1598 miles *2572 km*.
Universities: 6.
Adult illiteracy: 15·6% (males 6·9% females 23·7%) in 1971.
Expectation of life: Males 67·46 years; females 70·70 years (1960–2).
Defence: Military service 24 months; Total armed forces 161 200; Defence expenditure 1975 $1035 million.
Wildlife: Wolf, brown bear, roe deer, marten, jackal, porcupine, wild goat, turtle, lizard; several types of snake; pelican, stork, great spotted cuckoo, heron.
Cinemas: 691 (seating capacity 354 600) and 932 part-time (capacity 890 584) in 1961.

GRENADA

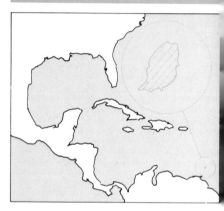

Official name: Grenada.
Population: 96 000 (1974 est).
Area: 133 miles² *344 km²*.
Language: English.
Religions: Christian.
Capital city: Saint George's, population 8644 (1971 est).
Highest point: Mount St Catherine's, 2756 ft *840 m*.
Head of State: H.M. Queen Elizabeth II, represented by Sir Leo Victor de Gale, GCMG, CBE (b. 28 Dec. 1921), Governor-General.
Prime Minister: Eric Matthew Gairy (b. 18 Feb. 1922).
Climate: Tropical maritime, with equable temperature averaging 82 °F (*28 °C*) in the lowlands. Rainfall averages 60 in (*1524 mm*) in coastal area and 150–200 in (*3810–5080 mm*) in mountain areas.
Crops: Cocoa, nutmeg, bananas, coconuts, citrus fruit, sugar-cane, mace.
Monetary unit: East Caribbean dollar (EC$). 1 dollar = 100 cents.
Denominations:
Coins 1, 2, 5, 10, 25, 50 cents.
Notes 1, 5, 20, 100 dollars.
Exchange rate to US dollar: 2.37 (February 1976).
Political history and government: A former British dependency. An Associated State, with internal self-government, from 3 Mar. 1967 until becoming fully independent,

within the Commonwealth, on 7 Feb. 1974. Executive power is vested in the Queen and exercised by the Governor-General, who acts on the advice of the Cabinet, led by the Prime Minister. Legislative power is vested in the bicameral Parliament, comprising a Senate (13 members appointed by the Governor-General) and a House of Assembly 15 members elected by universal adult suffrage). The Cabinet is responsible to Parliament.
Telephones: 4700 (1975).
Daily newspapers: 2 (1971).
　Total circulation: 3000 (1 daily).
Radio: 22 000 (1975).
Length of roadways: 577 miles *928 km.*
Expectation of life: Males 60·14 years; females 65·60 years (1959–61).
Wildlife: Turtle, iguana, mona monkey, manicou.
Cinemas: 3 (seating capacity 2000) in 1965.

GUATEMALA

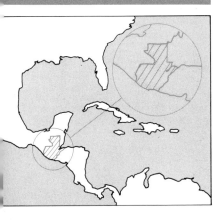

Official name: República de Guatemala.
Population: 5 175 400 (1973 census).
Area: 42 042 miles² *108 889 km².*
Languages: Spanish, with some twenty Indian dialects (most important is Quiché).
Religion: Mainly Roman Catholic.
Capital city: Ciudad de Guatemala (Guatemala City), population 700 504 (1973).
Other principal towns (1973): Quezaltenango 53 021; Escuintla 33 205; Mazatenango 23 285; Puerto Barrios 22 598; Retalhuleu 19 060; Chiquimula 16 126.
Highest point: Volcán Tajumulco, 13 845 ft *4220 m.*
Principal mountain ranges: Sierra Madre, Sierra de las Minas, Sierra de Los Cuchumatanes, Sierra de Chuacús.
Principal rivers: Motagua (249 miles *400 km*), Usumacinta (688 miles *1107 km.*)
Head of State: Gen Kjell Eugenio Laugerud García (b. 24 Jan. 1940), President.
Climate: Tropical (hot and humid) on coastal lowlands, with average temperature of 83 °F. More temperate in central highlands, with average of 68 °F. Mountains cool. In Guatemala City, average maximum 72 °F (December) to 84 °F (May), minimum 53 °F (January) to 61 °F (June), June rainiest (23 days). Absolute maximum temperature 45 °C (*113 °F*), Guatemala City, 17 Dec. 1957; absolute minimum −7,1 °C (*19·2 °F*), Quezaltenango, 15 Jan. 1956.
Crops: Maize, sugar cane, bananas, coffee, cotton.
Monetary unit: Quetzal. 1 quetzal = 100 centavos.
Denominations:
　Coins 1, 5, 10, 25 centavos.
　Notes 50 centavos, 1, 5, 10, 20, 50, 100 quetzales.
Exchange rate to US dollar: 1.00 (February 1976).

Political history and government: A republic comprising 22 departments. Under the constitution, promulgated on 15 Sept. 1965 and effective from 1 July 1966, legislative power is vested in the unicameral National Congress, with 61 members elected for 4 years by universal adult suffrage. Executive power is held by the President, also directly elected for 4 years. He is assisted by a Vice-President and an appointed Cabinet.
Telephones: 52 905 (1974).
Daily newspapers: 8 (1972).
　Total circulation: 212 000.
Radio: 262 000 (1975).
TV: 110 000 (1975).
Length of roadways: 8358 miles *13 449 km.*
Length of railways: 595 miles *957 km.*
Universities: 4.
Adult illiteracy: 62·0% (males 55·7%; females 68·4%) in 1964.
Expectation of life: Males 48·29 years; females 49·74 years (1963–65).
Defence: Total armed forces 11 400.
Wildlife: Coyote, armadillo, tapir, monkey, jaguar, manatee, crocodile, deer; wide variety of birds including quetzal, ducks, dove, pheasant, wild turkey.
Cinemas: 106 (seating capacity 75 200) and one drive-in (1972).

GUINEA

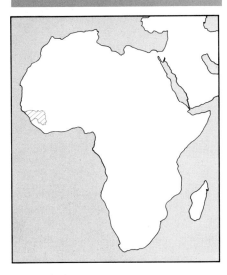

Official name: République de Guinée.
Population: 4 416 000 (UN estimate for mid-1975).
Area: 94 926 miles² *245 857 km².*
Languages: French (official), Fulani (Poular), Susu, Malinké.
Religions: Muslim, Animist minority.
Capital city: Conakry, population 525 671 (1972).
Other principal towns (1960): Kankan 29 100; Kindia 25 000; Siguiri 12 700; Labé 12 500; N'Zérékoré 8600.
Highest point: Mt Nimba, 5748 ft *1752 m.*
Principal mountain ranges: Fouta Djallon.
Principal rivers: Niger (2600 miles *4184 km*), Bafing, Konkouré, Kogon.
Head of State: Ahmed Sekou Touré (b. 9 Jan. 1922), President.
Prime Minister: Dr. Louis Lansana Beavogui (b. 1923).
Climate: Hot and moist, with heavy rainfall in coastal areas. Cooler in higher interior. In Conakry, average maximum 82 °F to 90 °F, minimum around 74 °F, annual rainfall 169 in.
Crops: Cassava, rice, maize, bananas, sweet potatoes, palm kernels and palm oil, ground-nuts, pineapples, coffee.
Monetary unit: Syli. 1 syli = 100 cauris (corilles).
Denominations:
　Coins 50 cauris, 1, 2, 5 sylis.
　Notes 10, 25, 50, 100 sylis.
Exchange rate to US dollar: 20.65 (December 1975).
Political history and government: Formerly French Guinea, part of French West Africa. Became independent, outside the French Community, on 2 Oct. 1958. A provisional constitution was adopted on 12 Nov. 1958. Legislative power is vested in the unicameral National Assembly, with 150 members elected by universal adult suffrage for 7 years. The Assembly elects a Commission to be its permanent organ. Full executive authority is vested in the President, also directly elected for 7 years. He appoints and leads a Cabinet, including a Prime Minister. Guinea has a single political party which exercises 'sovereign and exclusive control of all sections of national life'. The party's directing organ is the Central Committee, 25 members elected for 5 years at Congress.
Telephones: 9000 (1973).
Daily newspapers: 1 (1972).
　Total circulation: 46 000.
Radio: 110 000 (1975).
Length of roadways: All-weather roads 2175 miles *3500 km*, dry season 4350 miles *7000 km.*
Length of railways: 510 miles *820 km.*
Adult illiteracy: 90 to 95% (estimate).
Expectation of Life: Males 36·9 years; females 40·1 years (1965–70).
Defence: Total armed forces 5650.
Wildlife: Antelope, panther, buffalo, hartebeest, lion, crocodile.
Cinemas: 16 (1959).

GUINEA-BISSAU

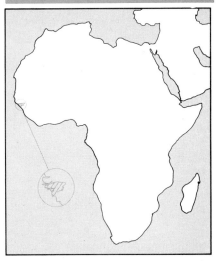

Official name: A República de Guiné-Bissau.
Population: 487 448 (1970 census); 482 000 (1972 est).
Area: 13 948 miles² *36 125 km².*
Languages: Portuguese (official), Creole, Balante, Fulani, Malinké.
Religions: Aminist, Muslim minority.
Capital city: Madina do Boé (population a few hundred).
Other principal towns: Bissau, 71 169, Bolama.
Principal rivers: Cacheu, Mansôa, Gêba, Corubel.
Head of State: Luiz de Almeida Cabral (b. 1929), President of the State Council.
Head of Government: Commdt Francisco

Mendes, Chief State Commissioner.
Climate: Tropical, with an average annual temperature of 77 °F. Rainy season June to November. In dry season (December to May) the northerly *harmattan*, a dust-laden wind, blows from the Sahara.
Crops: Cassava, rice, groundnuts, palm kernels and palm oil.
Monetary unit: Guinea peso. 1 peso = 100 centavos.
Denominations:
Coins 10, 20, 50 centavos, 1 2½, 5, 10, 20 pesos.
Notes 50, 100, 500 pesos.
Exchange rate to US dollar: 27.75 (February 1976).
Telephones: 2764 (1972).
Daily newspapers: 1 (1972).
Total circulation: 500.
Political history and government: Formerly Portuguese Guinea. Independence declared on 24 Sept. 1973, recognized by Portugal on 10 Sept. 1974. The independence movement was dominated by the *Partido Africano da Independencia da Guiné e Cabo Verde* (PAIGC), the African Party for the Independence of Guinea and Cape Verde. In 1973 the PAIGC established a National People's Assembly as the supreme organ of the state and formulated the independence constitution, which provides for the eventual union of Guinea-Bissau with Cape Verde (*qv*). The constitution proclaims the PAIGC, the only permitted party, to be 'the supreme expression of the sovereign will of the people'. Executive power is held by the State Council, with 15 members elected for 3 years from deputies to the Assembly. Administrative authority is exercised by the Council of State Commissioners, appointed by the Head of State.
Radio: 10 000 (1975).
Length of roadways: 2168 miles *3489 km.*
Expectation of life: Males 35·0 years; females 38·1 years (1965–70).
Cinemas: 8 (seating capacity 2900) in 1971.

GUYANA

Official name: The Co-operative Republic of Guyana.
Population: 774 000 (1974 est).
Area: 83 000 miles² *215 000 km².*
Languages: English (official), Hindi, Urdu.
Religions: Christian 56·7%; Hindu 33·4%;

Muslim 8·8% (1960).
Capital city: Georgetown, population 167 000.
Other principal cities: Linden 29 000; New Amsterdam 23 000; Mackenzie 20 000; Corriverton 17 000.
Highest point: Mt Roraima (9094 ft *2772 m*), on the Brazil-Venezuela frontier.
Principal mountain ranges: Pakaraima, Serra Acarai, Kanuku, Kamoa.
Principal rivers: Essequibo, Courantyne (on the frontier with Surinam). Mazaruni, Berbice, Demerara.
Head of State: Raymond Arthur Chung (b. 10 Jan. 1918), President.
Prime Minister: Linden Forbes Sampson Burnham (born 20 Feb. 1923).
Climate: Generally warm and pleasant. Average temperature 80 °F, with daily range of about 18 °F on coast, increasing inland. Average annual rainfall 93 in, 80 to 100 in on coast (mainly April to August and November to January), 60 in inland (May to August).
Crops: Rice, sugar cane, coconuts.
Monetary unit: Guyana dollar ($G). 1 dollar = 100 cents.
Denominations:
Coins 1, 5, 10, 25, 50 cents.
Notes 1, 5, 10, 20 dollars.
Exchange rate to US dollar: 2.55 (February 1976).
Political history and government: Formerly the colony of British Guiana. Became independent, within the Commonwealth, on 26 May 1966, taking the name Guyana. A republic since 23 Feb. 1970. Legislative power is held by the unicameral National Assembly, with 53 members elected for 5 years by universal adult suffrage, using proportional representation. The President, a constitutional Head of State, is elected by the Assembly for 6 years. Executive power is held by the Cabinet, led by the Prime Minister, which is responsible to the Assembly. Guyana comprises 6 administrative districts, each the responsibility of a Minister of State.
Telephones: 19 115 (1975).
Daily newspapers: 4 (1972).
Total circulation: 41 000.
Radio: 280 000 (1975).
Length of roadways: 1832 miles *2948 km.*
Length of railways: 55 miles *89 km* (government owned), 50 miles *80 km* (privately owned).
Universities: 1.
Expectation of life: Males 59·03 years; females 63·01 years (1959–61), excluding Amerindians.
Defence: Total armed forces 2500, including an Air Wing with 4 aircraft and 2 helicopters.
Wildlife: Tapir, monkeys, deer, ocelot, sloth, bush pig, great anteater, armadillo, giant anaconda, bushmaster, lizards, kingfisher, scarlet ibis, cock-of-the-rock, vulture, hummingbird, kiskadee, macaw, tinamou.
Cinemas: 50 with seating capacity of 37 500.

HAITI

Official name: République d'Haïti.
Population: 4 513 600 (1974 est).
Area: 10 714 miles² *27 750 km².*
Languages: French (official), Créole 90%.
Religions: Roman Catholic, Vodum (Voodoo).
Capital city: Port-au-Prince, population 458 680 (1971).
Other principal towns: Cap Haïtien 44 000; Gonaïves 29 000; Les Cayes 23 000; Jérémie 17 000.
Highest point: Pic La Selle, 8793 ft *2680 m.*

Principal mountain ranges: Massif de la Hotte.
Principal rivers: Artibonite.
Head of State: Jean-Claude Duvalier (b 3 July 1951), President.
Climate: Tropical, but cooled by sea winds. Rainy season May to September. North warmer than south. In Port-au-Prince average maximum 87 °F (December, January) to 94 °F (July), minimum 68 °F (January, February) to 74 °F.
Crops: Sugar cane, maize, sorghum, bananas, cassava, rice, coffee.
Monetary unit: Gourde. 1 gourde = 100 centimes.
Denominations:
Coins 5, 10, 20, 50 centimes.
Notes 1, 2, 5, 10, 50, 100, 250, 500 gourdes.
Exchange rate to US dollar: 5.00 (February 1976).
Political history and government: A republic comprising 9 departments. Dr François Duvalier was elected President in September 1957 and took office in October. Under the constitution of June 1964, the unicameral Legislative Chamber has 58 members elected for 6 years by universal adult suffrage. The constitution granted absolute power to the President, who took office for life on 22 June 1964. On 14 Jan. 1971 the constitution was amended to allow the President to nominate his own successor. The President named his son, Jean-Claude, to succeed him as President for life. Dr Duvalier died on 21 Apr. 1971 and his son was sworn in on the following day. Only one political party is officially recognised.

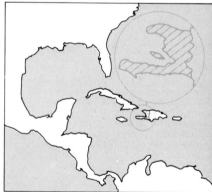

Telephones: 8852 (1974).
Daily newspapers: 7 (1972).
Total circulation: 82 000.
Radio: 93 000 (1975).
TV: 13 200 (1975).
Length of roadways: 1962 miles *3157 km.*
Universities: 1.
Adult illiteracy: 89·5% (males 87·2%; females 91·5%) in 1950.
Expectation of life: Males 47·0 years; females 48·5 years (1965–70).
Defence: Total armed forces 6550.
Wildlife: Lizards, crocodiles, turtle, oriole, dove, duck, flamingo, pigeons, roseate spoonbill.
Cinemas: 19 and 4 drive-ins in Port-au-Prince (1974).

HONDURAS

Official name: República de Honduras ('depths').
Population: 2 933 000 (1974 est).
Area: 43 277 miles² *112 088 km².*
Languages: Spanish, some Indian dialects.
Religion: Roman Catholic.
Capital city: Tegucigalpa, population 303 879 (1974).
Other principal towns: San Pedro Sula 102 129; La Ceiba 37 947; Puerto Cortés 27 757; Tela 12 395.

Highest point: Cerro Las Minas, 9400 ft *865 m*.
Principal rivers: Patuca, Ulúa.
Head of State: Colonel Juan Alberto Melgar Castro (b. 1929), President.
Climate: Tropical (hot and humid) and wet on coastal plains. Rainy season, May to November. More moderate in central highlands. In Tegucigalpa, average maximum 77 °F (December, January) to 86 °F June), September and October rainiest (each 14 days). Absolute maximum temperature 43,3 °C (*110 °F*), Nueva Octepeque, 3 March 1958; absolute minimum −0,6 °C *31 °F*), La Esperanza, 17 Feb. 1956.

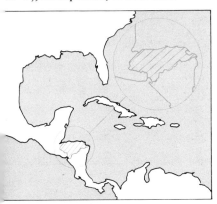

Crops: Bananas, citrus fruit, sugar cane.
Monetary unit: Lempira. 1 lempira = 100 centavos.
Denominations:
  Coins 1, 2, 5, 10, 20, 50 centavos, 1 lempira.
  Notes 1, 5, 10, 20, 50, 100 lempiras.
Exchange rate to US dollar: 2.00 (February 1976).
Political history and government: A republic comprising 18 departments. The last elected President was deposed on 4 Dec. 1972 by a military *coup*, led by a former President, Brig.-Gen. Oswaldo López Arellano. The military regime suspended the legislature, a unicameral Congress of Dputies, and introduced government by decree. On 22 Apr. 1975 Gen. López was overthrown by army officers and replaced by Col. Juan Melgar Castro. The President rules with the assistance of an appointed Cabinet.
Telephones: 14 984 (1975).
Daily newspapers: 12 (1971).
  Total circulation: 113 000 (6 dailies).
Radio: 160 000 (1975).
TV: 47 000 (1975).
Length of roadways: c. 3542 miles, c. *5700 km*.
Length of railways: 658 miles *1059 km*.
Universities: 1.
Adult illiteracy: 55·0% (males 51·3%; females 58·5%) in 1961.
Expectation of life: Males 48·0 years; females 50·9 years (1965–70).
Defence: Total armed forces 11 200.
Wildlife: Anteater, monkeys (many types), peccary, tapir, deer, jaguar, coyote, turtle, cayman, iguana, fer-de-lance, bushmaster. Hummingbird, Quetzal thrush, macaw, partridge.
Cinemas: About 46 with seating capacity of about 40 000 (1972).

HUNGARY

Official name: Magyar Népköztársaság (Hungarian People's Republic).
Population: 10 322 099 (census of 1 Jan. 1970); 10 546 000 (estimate for 1 July 1975).
Area: 35 920 miles², *93 032 km²*.
Language: Magyar.

Religions: Roman Catholic, Protestant, Orthodox and Jewish minorities.
Capital city: Budapest, population 2 055 646 (1975 est).
Other principal towns (1975): Miscolc 196 049; Debrecen 182 326; Szeged 167 220; Pécs 161 612; Győr 116 110; Székesfehérvár 91 737; Kecskemét 88 535; Nyírgyháza 88 222.
Highest point: Kékes 3330 ft *1015 m*.
Principal mountain ranges: Cserhát, Mátra, Bukk, Bakony.
Principal rivers: Duna (Danube) (1770 miles *2848 km*, 273 miles *439 km* in Hungary), with its tributaries (Drava, Tisza, Rába).
Head of State: Pál Losonczi (b. 18 Sept. 1919), President of the Presidential Council.
Political Leader: János Kádár (b. 22 May 1912), First Secretary of the Central Committee of the Hungarian Socialist Worker's Party.
Head of Government: György Lázár (b. 15 Sept. 1924), Chairman of the Council of Ministers.
Climate: Continental (long, dry, hot summers, cold winters). In Budapest, July warmest (61 °F to 82 °F), January coldest (26 °F to 35 °F), May and December rainiest (each nine days). Absolute maximum temperature 41,3 °C (*106·3 °F*), Pécs, 5 July 1950; absolute minimum −34,9 °C (*30·8 °F*), Alsófügöd, 16 Feb. 1940.
Crops: Maize, wheat, potatoes, sugar-beet, barley, grapes.
Monetary unit: Forint. 1 forint = 100 fillér.
Denominations:
  Coins 2, 5, 10, 20, 50 fillér, 1, 2, 5, 10 forints.
  Notes 10, 20, 50, 100 forints.
Exchange rate to US dollar: 8.513 (October 1975).

Political history and government: After occupation by Nazi Germany, a Hungarian provisional government signed an armistice on 20 Jan. 1945. Following elections in October 1945, a republic was proclaimed on 1 Feb. 1946. The Communist Party took power in May–June 1947. A new constitution was introduced on 18 Aug. 1949 and a People's Republic established two days later.
  The highest organ of state power is the unicameral National Assembly, with 352 members elected for 5 years by universal adult suffrage (at the last election, on 15 June 1975, 318 members were elected unopposed while 34 seats were each contested by two candidates). The Assembly elects from its members a Presidential Council (21 members) to be its permanent organ and the state's executive authority, responsible to the Assembly. The Council of Ministers, the

highest organ of state administration, is elected by the Assembly on the recommendation of the Presidential Council.
  Political power is held by the (Communist) Hungarian Socialist Workers' Party (HSWP), the only legal party, which dominates the Patriotic People's Front. The Front presents an approved list of candidates for elections to representative bodies. The HSWP's highest authority is the Party Congress, which elects a Central Committee to supervise Party work. The Central Committee elects a Political Committee (Politburo) of 15 members to direct policy.
  Hungary comprises 19 counties and 6 cities.
Telephones: 1 013 731 (1975).
Daily newspapers: 29 (1974).
  Total circulation: 2 640 000.
Radio: 2 538 000 (1975).
TV: 2 351 913 (1975).
Length of roadways: 68 133 miles *109 649 km*.
Length of railways: 5227 miles *8413 km*.
Universities: 4 (also 14 specialised).
Adult illiteracy: 2·0% (males 1·6%; females 2·4%) in 1970.
Expectation of life: Males 66·87 years; females 72·59 years.
Defence: Military service: 2 years. Total regular forces 103 000. Defence expenditure 1975: $485 million.
Wildlife: Deer, hare, roebuck, boar, heron, flamingo, partridge, pheasant, wild geese and ducks.
Cinemas: 3697 (seating capacity 580 900) in 1972.

ICELAND

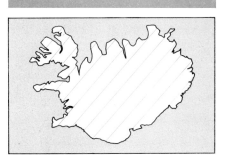

Official name: Lýðveldið Island (Republic of Iceland).
Population: 204 930 (1970) census); 216 628 (1974 est).
Area: 39 769 miles² *103 000 km²*.
Languages: Icelandic.
Religion: Lutheran.
Capital city Reykjavík ('Bay of Smokes'), population 84 772 (1974).
Other principal towns (1974): Kópavogur 12 090; Akureyri 11 698; Hafnarfjördur 11 372; Keflavík 6113; Akranes 4514; Vestmannaeyjar 4396
Highest point: Hvannadalshnúkur, 6952 ft *2119 m*.
Principal rivers: Thjórsá (120 miles *193 km*), Skjálfandafljót, Jökulsa á Fjöllum.
Head of State: Dr Kristján Eldjárn (b. 6 Dec. 1916), President.
Prime Minister: Geir Hallgrímsson (b. 16 Dec. 1925).
Climate: Cold. Long winters with average temperature of 34 °F. Short, cool summers with average of 50 °F. Storms are frequent. In Reykjavík, average maximum 36 °F (January) to 58 °F (July), minimum 28 °F (January, February) to 48 °F (July), December rainiest (21 days). Absolute maximum temperature 32,8 °C (*91·0 °F*), Módrudalur, 26 July 1901; absolute minimum −44,6 °C (−*48·2 °F*), Grímsstaoir, 22 Mar. 1918.
Crops: Hay, potatoes, turnips.

197

Monetary unit: Icelandic króna. 1 króna = 100 aurar.

Denominations:
  Coins 10, 50 aurar, 1, 5, 10, 50 krónur.
  Notes 100, 500, 1000, 5000 krónur.

Exchange rate to US dollar: 171.10 (February 1976).

Political history and government: Formerly ruled by Denmark. Iceland became a sovereign state, under the Danish Crown, on 1 Dec. 1918. An independent republic was declared on 17 June 1944. Legislative power is held jointly by the President (elected for 4 years by universal adult suffrage) and the Althing (Parliament), with 60 members elected by universal suffrage for 4 years (subject to dissolution by the President), using a mixed system of proportional representation. The Althing chooses 20 of its members to form the Upper House, the other 40 forming the Lower House. For some purposes the two Houses sit jointly as the United Althing. Executive power is held jointly by the President and the Cabinet he appoints. The Cabinet, led by the Prime Minister, is responsible to the Althing. Iceland has seven administrative districts.

Telephones: 81 288 (1975).

Daily newspapers: 5 (1971).
  Total circulation: 96 000.

Radio: 63 543 (1975).

TV: 50 854 (1975).

Length of roadways: 6920 miles *11 137 km*

Universities: 1.

Expectation of life: Males 70·7 years; females 76·3 years (1966–70).

Wildlife: Reindeer, mink, fox, seal, eagle, water-fowl, eider duck, falcon, ptarmigan.

Cinemas: 25 (seating capacity 9500) in 1970.

INDIA

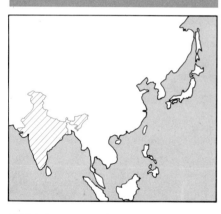

Official name: Bhartiya Ganrajya or Bharat ka Ganatantra (the Republic of India). India is called Bharat in the Hindi language.

Population: 548 154 569 (1971 census); 586 266 000 (1974 est).

Area: 1 269 346 miles² *3 287 590 km²*.

Languages: Hindi (official) 30·4%; Telugu 8·6%; Bengali 7·7%; Marathi 7·6%; Tamil 7·0%; Urdu 5·3%; Gujarati 4·6%; Kannada 4·0%; Malayalam 3·9%; Orija 3·1%; Punjabi 2·5%; Assamese 1·6% (1961).

Religions: Hindu 82·7%; Muslim 11·2%; Christian 2·6%; Sikh 1·9%; Buddhist 0·7%; Jain 0·5%; others 0·4% (1971).

Capital city: New Delhi, population 301 801 (1971).

Other principal towns (1971): Bombay 5 970 575; Dehli 3 287 883; Calcutta 3 148 746; Madras 2 469 449; Hyderabad 1 607 396; Ahmedabad 1 585 544; Bangalore 1 540 741; Kanpur (Cawnpore) 1 154 388; Nagpur 866 076; Pune (Poona) 856 105; Lucknow 749 239; Howrah

737 877; Jaipur 615 258; Agra 591 917; Varanasi (Banaras) 583 856; Madurai 549 114; Indore 543 381; Allahabad 490 622; Patna 473 001; Surat 471 656; Vadodara (Baroda) 466 696; Cochin 439 066; Jabalpur 426 224.

Highest point: Nanda Devi, 25 645 ft *7817 m* (first climbed 29 Aug. 1936), excluding Kashmir.

Principal mountain ranges: Himalayas, Gravalti, Sappura, Vindhya, Western Ghats, Chota Nagpur.

Principal rivers: The great rivers of India are the Ganges (1560 miles *2510 km*) and the Brahmaputra (1800 miles *2897 km,*) which drain the southern and northern slopes of the massive Himalayas respectively. The Narmeda and the Tapti drain the Vindhyas and the Satpura hills of mid-India into the Gulf of Cambay; the 3 principal southern rivers are the Godavari, the Kistna and the Cauvery, which all rise in the Western Ghats and flow eastwards across the peninsula to empty into the Bay of Bengal.

Head of State: Fakhruddin Ali Ahmed (b. 13 May 1905), President.

Prime Minister: Mrs Indira Priyadarshini Gandhi (b. 19 Nov. 1917).

Climate: Ranges from temperate in the north (very cold in the Himalayas) to tropical in the south. The average summer temperature in the plains is about 85 °F. The full weight of the monsoon season is felt in June and July but the rainfall figures vary widely according to locality. Average daily high temperature in Bombay 83 °F (January, February) to 91 °F (May); average daily low temperature 67 °F (January, February) 80 °F (May); rainiest month July (21 days). Average daily high temperature in Calcutta 79 °F (December) to 97 °F (April); average daily low 55 °F (December, January) to 79 °F (June, July); rainiest months July, August (each 18 days).

Crops: Rice, wheat, sorghum (jowar), cat-tail millet (bajra), maize, jute, cotton, groundnuts, chick-peas (gram), potatoes, sugar cane, tea.

Monetary unit: Indian rupee. 1 rupee = 100 paisa (singular: paise).

Denominations:
  Coins 1, 2, 3, 5, 10, 20, 25, 50 paisa, 1, 10 rupees.
  Notes 1, 2, 5, 10, 20, 100, 1000, 5000, 10 000 rupees.

Exchange rate to US dollar: 8.9284 (February 1976).

Political history and government: On 15 Aug. 1947 former British India was divided on broadly religious lines into two independent countries, India and Pakistan, within the Commonwealth.

India was formed as a Union of States, with a federal structure. A republican constitution was passed by the Constituent Assembly on 26 Nov. 1949 and India became a republic, under its present name, on 26 Jan. 1950. Sikkim, formerly an Associated State, became a State of India on 26 Apr. 1975.

Legislative power is vested in a Parliament, consisting of the President and two Houses. The Council of States (*Rajya Sabha*) has 243 members, including 231 indirectly elected by the State Assemblies for 6 years (one-third retiring every two years) and 12 nominated by the President for 6 years. The House of the People (*Lok Sabha*) has 524 members elected by universal adult suffrage for 5 years (subject to dissolution). The President is a constitutional Head of State elected for 5 years by an electoral college comprising elected members of both Houses of Parliament and the State legislatures. He exercises executive power on the advice of the Council of Ministers, which is

responsible to Parliament. The President appoints the Prime Minister and, on the latter's recommendation, other Ministers.

India comprises 22 self-governing States (including the disputed territory of Jammu-Kashmir) and 9 Union Territories. Each State has a Governor (appointed by the President for 5 years), a legislature elected for 5 years and a Council of Ministers. The Union Territories are administered by officials appointed by the President.

A state of emergency was declared on 26 June 1975 and certain constitutional rights have since been held in abeyance.

Telephones: 1 689 528 (1975).

Daily newspapers: 793 (1972).
  Total circulation: 8 873 000

Radio: 14 075 000 (1975).

TV: 162 724 (1975).

Length of roadways: 634 928 miles *1 021 819 km.*

Length of railways: 37 411 miles *60 208 km.*

Universities: 88.

Adult illiteracy: 72·2% (males 58·6%; females 86·8%) in 1961.

Expectation of Life: Males 47·8 years; females 46·5 years (1965–70).

Defence (1974): Authorised strength of Army 826 000 plus Territorial Army 50 000. Naval strength totalled 30 000 men and some 70 ships of various types, including one aircraft carrier, two cruisers, four submarines and three destroyers. The Indian Air Force comprise 80 000 personnel and over 2000 aircraft.

Wildlife: Elephant, jackal, hyena, tiger, wild boar, crocodile, gazelle, mongoose, monkey, porcupine, sloth, bear, black buck, giant squirrel, fox, hare, buffalo, swamp deer, civet, cobra, boiga, crane, jacana.

Cinemas: 4787 (seating capacity 3 430 000), excluding touring cinemas (about 2500), in 1972.

INDONESIA

Official name: Republik Indonesia.

Population: 119 383 285 (1971 census); 127 586 000 (1974 est), excluding West Irian (923 440 in 1971).

Area: 782 663 miles² *2 027 087 km².*

Languages: Bahasa Indonesia (official), Javanese, Madurese, Sundanese.

Religions: Muslim 85%; Christian, Buddhist and Hindu minorities.

Capital city: Jakarta, population 4 915 300 (1973 est).

Other principal towns: Surabaja 1 556 255; Bandung 1 201 730; Semarang 646 590; Medan 635 562; Palembang 582 961 (1971).

Highest point: Ngga Pulu (formerly Mt Sukarno, formerly Carstensz Pyramide), 16 500 ft *5030 m* (first climbed on 13 Feb. 1962).

Principal mountain ranges: Bukit, Barisan, Pegunungan Djajawidjaja.

Principal rivers: Kapuas (715 miles

50 km), Digul (557 miles *896 km*), Barito 60 miles *900 km*), Mahakam, Kajan, Hari.
Head of State: Gen. Suharto (b. 8 June 921), President and Prime Minister.
Climate: Tropical (hot and rainy). Average temperature 80 °F. Mountain areas cooler. Jakarta, average maximum 84 °F (January, February) to 88 °F (September), minimum 73 °F (July, August) to 75 °F (April, May), January rainiest (18 days).
Crops: Rice, cassava, maize, sweet potatoes, sugar cane, rubber, coconuts, soybeans, groundnuts, palm kernels and palm oil, coffee, tobacco.
Monetary unit: Rupiah. 1 rupiah = 100 sen.
Denominations:
  Coins 1, 2, 5, 10, 25, 50, 100 rupiahs.
  Notes 2½, 5, 10, 25, 50, 100, 500, 1000, 5000, 10 000 rupiahs.
Exchange rate to US dollar: 415.0 (February 1976).
Political history and government: Formerly the Netherlands East Indies. Occupied by Japanese forces in March 1942. On 17 Aug. 1945, three days after the Japanese surrender, a group of nationalists proclaimed the independence of the Republic of Indonesia. The Netherlands transferred sovereignty (except for West New Guinea) on 27 Dec. 1949. West New Guinea remained under Dutch control until 1962 and, following a brief period of UN administration, was transferred to Indonesia on 1 May 1963.

Military commanders, led by Gen. Suharto, assumed emergency executive powers on 11–12 Mar. 1966. The President handed all power to Suharto on 22 Feb. 1967. On 12 Mar. 1967 the People's Consultative Assembly removed the President from office and named Gen. Suharto as acting President. He became Prime Minister on 11 Oct. 1967 and, after being elected by the Assembly, was inaugurated as President on 27 Mar. 1968.

The highest authority of the state is the People's Consultative Assembly, with 920 members who serve for 5 years. The Assembly, which elects the President and Vice-President for 5 years, includes 460 members of the People's Representation Council (House of Representatives), which is the legislative organ. The Council has 100 appointed members, 351 directly elected and representatives from West Irian (West New Guinea) chosen in indirect elections. The remaining 460 members of the Assembly include 207 appointed by the government, 130 elected by regional assemblies, 121 allocated to parties and groups in proportion to their elected seats in the Council and 2 allocated to minor parties. The President is assisted by an appointed Cabinet.

Indonesia comprises 19 provinces.
Telephones: 284 831 (1975).
Daily newspapers: 11 (1970).
  Total circulation: 329 000 (est).
Radio: 5 010 000 (1975).
TV: 300 000 (1975).
Length of roadways: 52 748 miles *84 891 km*.
Length of railways: 4847 miles *7801 km*.
Universities: 51 (28 state, 23 private).
Adult illiteracy: 40·4% (males 29·2%; females 51·0%) in 1971 (population aged 10 and over).
Expectation of Life: Males 44·1 years; females 45·1 years (1965–70).
Defence: Military service: selective. Total armed forces 266 000. Defence expenditure 1975–6: $1108 million.
Wildlife: Elephant, tiger, rhinoceros, wild cattle, panther, orang utan, Malayan bear, tapir, crocodile, 400 varieties of snakes, many varieties of lizard, including the Komodo dragon. Parrot, cockatoo, bird of paradise, rhinoceros hornbill, bantam chicken.

Cinemas: 1011 with seating capacity of 470 000 (1962).

IRAN

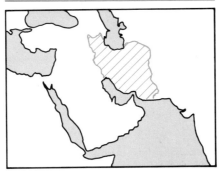

Official name: Keshvarē Shahanshahiyē Īrān (Empire of Iran).
Population: 32 139 000 (1974 est).
Area: 636 296 miles² *1 648 000 km²*.
Languages: Farsi (Persian), Kurdish.
Religions: Muslim 98%, Christian, Jewish, Zoroastrian minorities.
Capital city: Tehrān (Teheran), population 3 931 000 (1974).
Other principal towns (1974): Eşfahān (Isfahan) 601 000; Mashhad (Meshed) 586 000; Tabriz 559 000
Highest point: Qolleh-ye Damāvand (Mt Demavend), 18 386 ft *5604 m*.
Principal mountain ranges: Reshteh-ye Alborz (Elburz Mts), Kūhhā-ye Zāgros (Zagros Mts).
Principal rivers: Kārūn, Safid (Sefid Rud), Atrak, Karkheh, Zāyandeh.
Head of State: HIM Mohammad Rezā Pahlavi Aryamehr (b. 26 Oct. 1919), Shah (Emperor).
Prime Minister: Amir Abbās Huvaida (b. 18 Feb. 1919).
Climate: Extremely hot on Persian Gulf, cooler and dry on central plateau, subtropical on shore of Caspian Sea. In Teheran, July hottest (77 °F to 99 °F), January coldest (27 °F to 45 °F), March rainiest (5 days). Absolute maximum temperature 52 °C (*126 °F*), Abādān, 6 July 1951.
Crops: Wheat, sugar-beet, rice, dates, cotton, barley.
Monetary unit: Iranian rial. 1 rial = 100 dinars.
Denominations:
  Coins 1, 2, 5, 10, 20 rials.
  Notes 10, 20, 50, 100, 200, 500, 1000, 5000, 10 000 rials.
Exchange rate to US dollar: 69.275 (February 1976).
Political history and government: Formerly the Empire of Persia, renamed Iran on 21 Mar. 1935. The country was an absolute monarchy until the adoption of the first constitution, approved by the Shah on 30 Dec. 1906. On 31 Oct. 1925 the National Assembly deposed the Shah and handed power to the Prime Minister, Reza Khan. He was elected Shah on 13 Dec. 1925 and took the title Reza Shah Pahlavi. During the Second World War Reza Shah favoured Nazi Germany. British and Soviet forces entered Iran on 25 Aug. 1941, forcing the Shah to abdicate in favour of his son, Mohammed Reza Pahlavi, on 16 Oct. 1941.

Iran is a limited constitutional monarchy. Executive power rests with the Shah, who appoints the Prime Minister and other Ministers. Legislative power rests with the bicameral Parliament (*Majles*), comprising a Senate of 60 members (30 appointed by the Shah and 30 elected for 4 years) and a National Consultative Assembly of 269 members elected for 4 years. Parliament

must approve the Shah's nominee for Prime Minister. On 2 Mar. 1975 the Shah dissolved existing political parties and announced the formation of a single party.

Iran comprises 21 provinces, each administered by an appointed Governor-General.
Telephones: 805 560 (1975).
Daily newspapers: 39 (1972).
  Total circulation: 750 000.
Radio: 2 050 000 (1975).
TV: 1 700 000 (1975).
Length of roadways: 26 994 miles *43 442 km*.
Length of railways: 2859 miles *4601 km*.
Universities: 8.
Adult illiteracy: 77·3% (males 67·2%; females 87·8%) in 1966.
Expectation of life: Males 48·4 years; females 49·2 years (1965–70).
Defence: Military service 2 years. Total armed forces 250 000. Defence expenditure 1975–6: $10 405 million.
Wildlife: Over 100 species of mammals including: fox, wolf, hyena, brown bear, wild boar, cheetah, jackal, jerboa, mongoose, mouflon, ibex, gazelle, panther, wild cat, tortoise, lizards, snakes. Many hundreds of species of bird including: snipe, partridge, pelican, flamingo, owl, falcon, eagle, buzzard, kestrel.
Cinemas: 437 (seating capacity 282 000), 45 part-time (capacity 25 000) and one drive-in (1972).

IRAQ

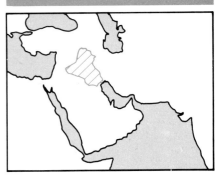

Official name: Al Jumhuriya al 'Iraqiya (Republic of Iraq).
Population: 8 047 415 (1965 census); 10 765 000 (1974 est.).
Area: 167 925 miles² *434 924 km²*.
Languages (1965): Arabic 81·1%; Kurdish 15·5%; Turkoman 1·7%.
Religions: Muslim, Christian minority.
Capital city: Baghdād, population 2 183 760 (1970 est).
Other principal towns (1965): Basra 310 950; Mosul 264 146; Kirkūk 175 303; Najaf 134 027.
Highest point: 12 000 ft *3658 m*.
Principal mountain ranges: Kurdistan Mts.
Principal rivers: Tigris, Euphrates (1700 miles [*2735 km*]).
Head of State: Field Marshal Ahmad Hassan al-Bakr (b. 1914), President and Prime Minister.
Climate: Extremely hot, dry summers; humid near coast. Cold damp winters with severe frosts in highlands. In Baghdad, average maximum 60 °F (January) to 110 °F (July, August), minimum 39 °F (January) to 76 °F (July, August), December rainiest (5 days). Absolute maximum temperature 52 °C (*125 °F*), Shaiba, 8 Aug. 1937; minimum −14 °C (6 °F), Ar Rutbah, 6 Jan. 1942.
Crops: Wheat, barley, dates.
Monetary unit: Iraqi dinar. 1 dinar = 5

199

riyals = 20 dirhams = 1000 fils.

Denominations:
 Coins 1, 5, 10, 25, 50, 100, 250, 500 fils,
 1, 5 dinars.
 Notes ¼, ½, 1, 5, 10 dinars.

Exchange rate to US dollar: 0.296 (February 1976).

Political history and government: Formerly part of Turkey's Ottoman Empire, captured by British forces during the 1914–18 war. After the war Iraq became a Kingdom under a League of Nations mandate, administered by Britain. The mandate was ended on 3 Oct. 1932, when Iraq became independent. In an army-led revolution on 14 July 1958 the King was murdered, the bicameral parliament dissolved and a republic established. Since then Iraq has been ruled by a succession of military regimes. The present regime was established on 17 July 1968. A new constitution, proclaiming socialist principles, was introduced on 16 July 1970.

 The constitution provides for the establishment of an elected National Assembly. Until the Assembly is formed the highest authority in the state is the Revolutionary Command Council (RCC), whose President is Head of State and Supreme Commander of the Armed Forces. The RCC, with up to 12 members, elects the President and the Vice-President. The President appoints and leads a Council of Ministers to control administration. The only authorized political organization is the National Progressive Front, a partnership between the Arab Socialist Renaissance (Ba'ath) Party and the Iraq Communist Party.

 Iraq comprises 16 provinces, each administered by an appointed Governor.

Telephones: 152 932 (1975).
Daily newspapers: 5 (1972).
Radio: 1 252 000 (1975).
TV: 352 000 (1975).
Length of roadways: 6726 miles *10 824 km.*
Length of railways: 1571 miles *2529 km.*
Universities: 5.
Adult illiteracy: 75·7% (males 64·4%; females 87·1%) in 1965.
Expectation of Life: Males 48·8 years; females 51·6 years (1965–70).
Defence: Military service: 2 years. Total armed forces 135 000. Defence expenditure 1974–5: $803 million.
Wildlife: Numerous reptiles, tortoise, bats, rats, jackal, wild cat, gazelle, eagle, hawk, bustard, partridge, grouse, raven, owl, kingfisher.
Cinemas: 84 (seating capacity 62 600) in 1965.

IRELAND

Official name: Poblacht na h'Eireann (Republic of Ireland), abbreviated to Eire (Ireland).
Population: 3 086 000 (1974 est).
Area: 26 600 miles² *68 893 km².*
Languages: English, Irish Gaelic.
Religions: Roman Catholic. Church of Ireland, Presbyterian, Methodist minorities.
Capital city: Dublin, population 567 866 (1971 census).
Other principal towns: Cork 128 235; Limerick 57 137; Dún Laoghaire 52 996; Waterford 31 695; Galway 26 896; Dundalk 21 718; Drogheda 19 744; Sligo 14 071; Bray 14 058; Tralee 12 227; Wexford 11 744; Clonmel 11 630; Kilkenny 10 292.
Highest point: Carrantuohill, 3414 ft *1041 m,* in Co Kerry.
Principal mountain ranges: Macgillycuddy's Reeks, Wicklow Mts.
Principal rivers: Shannon (224 miles *360 km*), Suir (85 miles *136 km*), Boyne

(70 miles *112 km*), Barrow (119 miles *191 km*), Erne (72 miles *115 km*).
Head of State: Carroll O'Daly (Cearbhall O Dálaigh) (born 12 Feb. 1911), *An Uachtaran* (President).
Head of Government: Liam Cosgrave (Liam Mac Cosgair) (b. 30 Apr. 1920), *Taoiseach* (Prime Minister).
Climate: Mild (generally between 32 °F and 70 °F). In Dublin, average maximum 47 °F (December, January, February) to 67 °F (July, August) minimum 35 °F (January, February) to 51 °F (July, August); July, August, December, January rainiest (each 13 days). Absolute maximum temperature 92 °F (*33 °C*), Dublin (Phoenix Park), 16 July 1876; absolute minimum −2 °F (*−19 °C*), Markee Castle, Co. Sligo, 16 Jan. 1881.
Crops: Turnips, potatoes, barley, wheat.
Monetary unit: Irish pound (I£). 1 pound = 100 pence.
Denominations:
 Coins ½, 1, 2, 5, 10, 50 pence.
 Notes 10s, 1, 5, 10, 20, 50, 100 pounds.
Exchange rate to US dollar: 0.494 (February 1976).
Political history and government: The whole of Ireland was formerly part of the United Kingdom. During an insurrection against British rule in April 1916 a republic was proclaimed but the movement was suppressed. After an armed struggle, beginning in 1919, a peace agreement was signed on 6 Dec. 1921 and became operative on 15 Jan. 1922. It provided that the six Ulster counties of Northern Ireland should remain part of the UK while the remaining 26 counties should become a dominion under

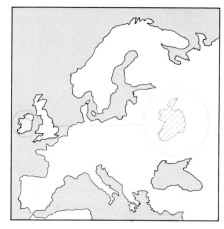

the British Crown. Southern Ireland duly achieved this status as the Irish Free State on 6 Dec. 1922. A new constitution, giving full sovereignty within the Commonwealth, became effective on 29 Dec. 1937. Formal ties with the Commonwealth were ended on 18 Apr. 1949, when the 26 counties became a republic.

 Legislative power is vested in the bicameral National Parliament: a Senate of 60 members (11 nominated by the Prime Minister, 49 indirectly elected for 5 years) with restricted powers; and a House of Representatives (*Dáil Éireann*) with 144 members elected by universal adult suffrage for 5 years (subject to dissolution), using proportional representation. The President is a constitutional Head of State elected by universal adult suffrage for 7 years. Executive power is held by the Cabinet, led by a Prime Minister appointed by the President on the nomination of the *Dáil*. The President appoints other Ministers on the nomination of the Prime Minister with the previous approval of the *Dáil*. The Cabinet is responsible to the *Dáil*.

Telephones: 393 879 (1975).
Daily newspapers: 7 (1972).
 Total circulation: 702 000.
Radio: 865 000 (1975).
TV: 600 000 (1975).
Length of roadways: 54 792 mil *88 180 km.*
Length of railways: 1361 miles *2190 km.*
Universities: 2.
Expectation of life: Males 68·58 year females 72·85 years (1965–67).
Wildlife: Red deer (diminishing numbers badger, stoat, hedgehog.
Cinemas: 183 with seating capacity 152 000 (1961).

ISRAEL

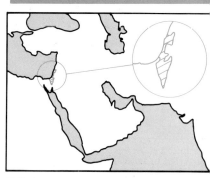

Official name: Medinat Israel (State o Israel).
Population: 3 371 000 (1975 est).
Area: 7992 miles² *20 700 km².*
Languages (1961): Hebrew (official) 65·9% Arabic 15·9%; Yiddish 4·8%.
Religions (1961): Jewish 88·7%; Muslim 7·8%.
Capital city: Yerushalayim (Jerusalem) population 344 200 (1974) including Eas Jerusalem (Jordanian territory under Israel occupation since 1967).
Other principal towns (1974): Tel Aviv Yafo (Jaffa) 357 600; Haifa 225 000; Rama Gan 120 000; Holon 110 300; Petah Tiqv (Petach Tikva) 103 000; Be'er Sheva (Beer sheba) 93 400; Benei Beraq (Bnei Brak 81 000.
Highest point: Mt Atzmon (Har Meron) 3963 ft *1208 m.*
Lowest point: The Dead Sea, 1302 f *397 m* below sea level.
Principal mountain ranges: Mts o Judea.
Principal rivers: Jordan (200 mile *321 km*), Qishon.
Head of State: Ephraim Katzir (b. 16 May 1916), President.
Prime Minister: Maj-Gen Yitzhak Rabir (b. 1 Mar. 1922).
Climate: Mediterranean (hot, dry, summer and mild rainy winters). More extreme ir the south. Subtropical on coast. In Jerusalem average maximum 55 °F (January) to 87 °F (July, August), minimum 41 °F (January) to 64 °F (August), February rainiest (1 days). Absolute maximum temperature 54 °C (*129 °F*), Tirat Tseri, 22 June 1942 absolute minimum −16 °C (*2 °F*), Tel ha Tanim, 8 Nov. 1950.
Crops: Oranges, grapefruit, wheat, potatoes
Monetary unit: Israeli pound (I£). 1 pound = 100 agorot (singular: agora).
Denominations:
 Coins 1, 5, 10, 25, 50, 100, 250 prutot, 1, 5, 10, 25 agorot.
 Notes 50, 100, 250, 500 prutot, ½ 1, 5, 10 50, 100 pounds.
Exchange rate to US dollar: 7.38 (February 1976).
Political history and government: Palestine (of which Israel forms part) was formerly

rt of Turkey's Ottoman Empire. During
e First World War (1914–18) Palestine
as occupied by British forces. After the war
was administered by Britain as part of a
eague of Nations mandate, established in
»22. The British Government terminated
; Palestine mandate on 14 May 1948, when
wish leaders proclaimed the State of
rael. After armed conflict with neigh-
»uring Arab states, Israel's borders were
ked by armistice agreements in 1949.
uring the war of 5–10 June 1967 Israeli
rces occupied parts of Egypt, Syria and
»rdan, including East Jerusalem (which
rael has unilaterally incorporated into its
rritory).

Israel is a republic. Supreme authority
sts with the unicameral Parliament
(nesset), with 120 members elected by
iiversal suffrage for 4 years, using propor-
»nal representation. Parliament elects the
esident, a constitutional Head of State,
r 5 years. Executive power rests with the
abinet, led by the Prime Minister. The
abinet takes office after receiving a vote of
»nfidence in Parliament, to which it is
sponsible. Israel comprises 6 administra-
ve districts.

elephones: 735 156 (1975).
aily newspapers: 27 (1974).
adio: 450 000 (1975).
V: 579 000 (1975).
ength of roadways: 5779 miles *9300 km.*
ength of railways: 503 miles *809 km.*
niversities: 5 (plus 2 specialized).
dult illiteracy: 15·8% (males 9·5%;
males 22·3%) in 1961 (population aged 14
d over).
xpectation of life: Males 70·14 years;
males 72·83 years (1972).
efence: Military service: men 36 months,
»men 24 months (Jews and Druses only):
uslims and Christians may volunteer.
nnual training for reservists thereafter up
age 40/41 for men, up to age 30 for women.
»tal armed forces 34 000 (regular). Defence
penditure 1975–6: $3503 million.
ildlife: Gazelle, wolf, wild boar, ibex.
»me 400 species of birds.
inemas: 260 with seating capacity of
5 000.

ITALY

fficial name: Repubblica Italiana (Italian
epublic), abbreviated to Italia.
opulation: 54 136 547 (1971 census);
5 731 000 (1975 est).
rea: 116 318 miles² *301 262 km².*
anguage: Italian.
eligion: Roman Catholic.
apital city: Roma (Rome), population
856 309 (1974).
ther principal towns (1974): Milano
Milan) 1 732 451; Napoli (Naples)
224 274; Torino (Turin) 1 202 846; Genova

(Genoa) 807 138; Palermo 661 233; Bologna
492 700; Firenze (Florence) 464 897; Catania
399 635; Bari 374 521; Venezia (Venice)
365 431; Trieste 271 536; Verona 270 815;
Messina 259 858.
Highest point: On Monte Bianco (Mont
Blanc), 15 616 ft *4759 m.*
Principal mountain range: Appennini
(Appennines), Alps.
Principal rivers: Po (418 miles *672 km*),
Tevere (Tiber), Arno, Volturno, Garigliano.
Head of State: Giovanni Leone (b. 3 Nov.
1908), President.
Head of Government: Giulio Andreotti
(b. 14 Jan. 1919), President of the Council of
Ministers (Prime Minister).
Climate: Generally Mediterranean, with
warm, dry summers (average maximum
80 °F) and mild winters. Cooler and rainier
in the Po Valley and the Alps. In Rome,
average maximum 54 °F (January) to 88 °F
(July, August), minimum 39 °F (January,
February) to 64 °F (July, August), February
rainiest (11 days). Absolute maximum
temperature, 46 °C (*114 °F*), Foggia, 6 Sept.
1946; absolute minimum −34 °C (−*29 °F*),
Pian Rosa, 14 Feb. 1956.
Crops: Grapes, wheat, sugar-beet, maize,
olives, citrus fruit.
Monetary unit: Italian lira. 1 lira = 100
centesimi.
Denominations:
  Coins 1, 2, 5, 10, 20, 50, 100, 500, 1000
    lire.
  Notes 500, 1000, 5000, 10 000, 50 000,
    100 000 lire.
Exchange rate to US dollar: 783.0
(February 1976).
Political history and government: For-
merly several independent states. The
Kingdom of Italy, under the House of
Savoy, was proclaimed in 1861 and the
country unified in 1870. Italy was under
Fascist rule from 28 Oct. 1922 to 25 July
1943. A referendum on 2 June 1946 voted
to abolish the monarchy and Italy became
a republic on 10 June 1946. A new constitu-
tion took effect on 1 Jan. 1948.

Legislative power is held by the bicameral
Parliament, elected by universal adult
suffrage for 5 years (subject to dissolution),
using proportional representation. The
Senate has 315 elected members (seats allo-
cated on a regional basis) and 7 life Senators.
The Chamber of Deputies has 630 members.
The President of the Republic is a constitu-
tional Head of State elected for 7 years by an
electoral college comprising both Houses of
Parliament and 58 regional representatives.
Executive power is exercised by the Council
of Ministers. The Head of State appoints the
President of the Council (Prime Minister)
and, on the latter's recommendation, other
Ministers. The Council is responsible to
Parliament.

Italy has 20 administrative regions, each
with an elected legislature and a regional
executive.
Telephones: 13 695 006 (1975).
Daily newspapers: 78 (1972).
  Total circulation: 7 267 000.
Radio: 12 400 000 (1975).
TV: 11 500 000 (1975).
Length of roadways: 179 236 miles
288 453 km.
Length of railways: 12 458 miles *20 050
km.*
Universities: 35 (28 state, 7 private).
Adult illiteracy: 9·3% (males 7·3%;
females 11·2%) in 1961 (aged 14 and over).
Expectation of life: Males 67·87 years;
females 73·36 years (1964–67).
Defence: Military service: Army and Air
Force 12 months; Navy 18 months. Total
armed forces 421 000 (regulars). Defence
expenditure 1975: $3891 million.
Wildlife: Deer, wolf, chamois, ibex, wild

boar, fox, badger, polecat, otter, weasel,
hedgehog, dormouse, hare, rabbit, porcupine,
moles, lizards, capercaillie, partridge, grouse,
ptarmigan, golden eagle, vultures.
Cinemas: 9324 with seating capacity of
about 5 000 000 (1971).

IVORY COAST

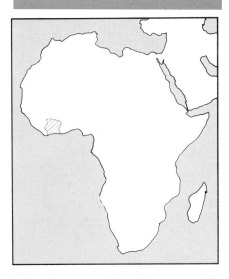

Official name: La République de la Côte
d'Ivoire.
Population: 6 673 013 (1975 census).
Area: 124 504 miles² *322 463 km².*
Languages: French (official), many African
languages.
Religions: Animist, Muslim, Christian.
Capital city: Abidjan, population 650 000
(1970 est).
Other principal towns (1969): Bouaké
100 000; Gagnoa 45 000.
Highest point: Monts de Droupole, *c.*
6900 ft *2103 m.*
Principal rivers: Bandama, Sassandra,
Komoé.
Head of State: Félix Houphouët-Boigny
(b. 18 Oct. 1905), President.
Climate: Generally hot, wet and humid.
Temperatures from 57 °F to 103 °F. Rainy
seasons May to July, October to November.
In Abidjan, average maximum 82 °F to
90 °F, minimum around 74 °F.
Crops: Yams, plantains, cassava, rice,
coffee, pineapples, bananas, cocoa, taro, palm
oil, cotton.
Monetary unit: Franc de la Communauté
financière africaine.
Denominations:
  Coins 1, 2, 5, 10, 25, 50, 100 CFA francs.
  Notes 100, 500, 1000, 5000 CFA francs.
Exchange rate to US dollar 224·24
(February 1976).
Political history and government: Formerly part of French West Africa, independent since 7 Aug. 1960. The ruling *Parti
démocratique de la Côte d'Ivoire* has been the
only organised political party since its
establishment in 1946.

Legislative power is vested in the unicameral National Assembly, with 120
members elected for 5 years by universal
adult suffrage. Executive power is held by
the President, also directly elected for 5
years. He rules with the assistance of an
appointed Council of Ministers, responsible
to him. The country comprises 24 departments.
Telephones: 25 185 (1974).
Daily newspapers: 3 (1972).
  Total circulation: 44 000.
Radio: 206 000 (1975).
TV: 100 500 (1975).

Length of roadways: 20 269 miles *32 620 km.*
Length of railways: 405 miles *c. 652 km.*
Universities: 1.
Adult illiteracy: 80% (est.)
Expectation of life: Males 39·4 years; females 42·6 years (1965–70).
Wildlife: Antelope, forest hog, lion, elephant, pygmy hippopotamus.
Cinemas: 80 (seating capacity 80 000) in 1972.

JAMAICA

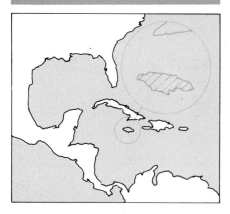

Population: 1 865 400 (1970 census); 2 025 000 (1974 est).
Area: 4244 miles² *10 991 km².*
Language: English.
Religions: Christian (Anglican and Baptist in majority).
Capital city: Kingston, population 169 800 (1974 est).
Other principal towns: Montego Bay 42 800; Spanish Town 41 600.
Highest point: Blue Mountain Peak (7402 ft *2256 m*).
Principal mountain range: Blue Mountains.
Head of State: H.M. Queen Elizabeth II, represented by Florizel Augustus Glasspole (b. 25 Sept. 1909), Governor-General.
Prime Minister Michael Norman Manley (b. 10 Dec. 1923).
Climate: The average rainfall is 77 in, and the rainfall is far greater in the mountains than on the coast. In Kingston, average maximum 86 °F (January to March) to 90 °F (July, August), minimum 67 °F (January, February) to 74 °F (June), wettest month is October (nine days). In the uplands the climate is pleasantly equable. Hurricanes tend to miss the island, but there were severe storms on 20 Aug. 1944 and 17–18 Aug. 1951 (over 150 killed).
Crops: Sugar cane, coconuts, bananas, citrus fruits, coffee, cocoa, tobacco.
Monetary unit: Jamaican dollar. 1 dollar = 100 cents.
Denominations:
Coins 1, 5, 10, 20, 25, 50 cents, 1 $.
Notes 50 cents, 1, 2, 5, 10 $.
Exchange rate to US dollar: 0.9091 (February 1976).
Political history and government: A former British colony. Became independent, within the Commonwealth, on 6 Aug. 1962. Executive power is vested in the Queen and exercised by the Governor-General, who is guided by the advice of the Cabinet. Legislative power is held by the bicameral Parliament: the Senate has 21 members, appointed by the Governor-General (13 on the advice of the Prime Minister and 8 on that of the Leader of the Opposition), and the House of Representatives has 53 members elected by universal adult suffrage for 5 years (sub-

ject to dissolution). The Governor-General appoints the Prime Minister and, on the latter's recommendation, other Ministers. The Cabinet is responsible to Parliament. Jamaica has three counties.
Telephones: 92 548 (1975).
Daily newspapers: 3 (1972).
Total circulation: 192 000.
Radio: 550 000 (1975).
TV: 110 000 (1975).
Length of roadways: 2682 miles *4315 km.*
Length of railways: 205 miles *330 km.*
Universities: 1.
Adult illiteracy: 18·1% (males 21·4%; females 15·2%) in 1970.
Expectation of life: Males 62·65 years; females 66·63 years (1959–61).
Defence: Total forces about 1400.
Wildlife: Crocodile, numerous lizards including iguana, bats, turtle, toad, frogs. (There are 55 species of amphibians and reptiles). Long-tailed humming bird, parrots, tanager, pigeon.
Cinemas: 42 (seating capacity 39 400) and one part-time (1972).

JAPAN

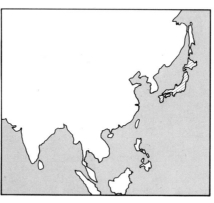

Official name: Nippon or Nihon (Land of the Rising Sun).
Population: 104 665 171 (1970 census); 110 049 000 (1974 est).
Area: 143 751 miles² *372 313 km².*
Language: Japanese.
Religions: Shintō, Buddhist.
Capital city: Tōkyō, population 8 678 642 (1974).
Other principal towns (1974): Osaka 2 802 065; Yokohama 2 562 291; Nagoya 2 082 235; Kyōto 1 438 714 Kōbe 1 351 651; Sapporo 1 178 224; Kitakyushu 1 052 133; Kawasaki 1 004 455.
Highest point: Fuji 12 388 ft *3776 m.* First climbed before AD 806.
Principal mountain range: Hida.
Principal rivers: Tone (200 miles *321 km*), Ishikari (227 miles *365 km*), Shinano (229 miles *368 km*), Kitakami.
Head of State: H.I.M. Hirohito (b. 29 Apr. 1901) *Nihon-koku Tennō* (Emperor of Japan).
Prime Minister: Takeo Miki (b. 17 Mar. 1907).
Climate: Great variation, from north (warm summers with long, cold winters) to south (hot, rainy summers with mild winters). In Tokyo, August warmest (72 °F to 86 °F), January coldest (20 °F to 47 °F), June and September rainiest (each 12 days). Absolute maximum temperature 41 °C (*105 °F*), Yamagata, 25 July 1933; absolute minimum −41,0 °C (*−42 °F*), Asahikawa, 25 Jan. 1902.
Crops: Rice, barley, wheat, soybeans, peaches, pears, apples, grapes, persimmons, mandarins, soya beans.

Monetary unit: Yen. 1 yen = 100 sen.
Denominations:
Coins 1, 5, 10, 50, 100 yen.
Notes 100, 500, 1000, 5000, 10 000 ye
Exchange rate to US dollar: 302.▪ (February 1976).
Political history and government: A hereditary monarchy, with an Emperor Head of State. After being defeated in t Second World War, Japanese forces s rendered on 14 Aug. 1945 and the count was placed under US military occupation. new constitution took effect from 3 M 1947 and, following the peace treaty of Sept. 1951, Japan regained its sovereignty 28 Apr. 1952. The Bonin Islands we restored on 26 June 1968 and the Ryuk Islands (including Okinawa) on 15 M 1972.
Japan is a constitutional monarchy, wi the Emperor as a symbol of the state. He h formal prerogatives but no power relating government. Legislative power is vested the bicameral Diet, elected by univers adult suffrage. The House of Councillors h 252 members elected for 6 years (half retirir every three years) and the House of Repr sentatives has 491 members elected for years (subject to dissolution). Executi power is vested in the Cabinet. The Prin Minister is appointed by the Emperor (c designation by the Diet) and himself appoin the other Ministers. The Cabinet is respo sible to the Diet.
Japan has 47 prefectures, each admini tered by an elected Governor.
Telephones: 41 904 960 (1975).
Daily newspapers: 172 (1972).
Total circulation: 55 845 000.
Radio: 25 600 000 (1975).
TV: 26 030 000 (1975).
Length of roadways: 652 259 mil *1 049 710 km.*
Length of railways: 17 348 miles *27 919 k*
Universities: 121 (41 national, 13 oth public, 67 private) plus 21 technologic universities.
Expectation of life: Males 70·49 year females 75·92 years (1972).
Defence: Military service: voluntary. Tot armed forces 236 000. Defence expenditu 1975–6: $4484 million.
Wildlife: Monkey, bear, fox, deer, badge marten, weasel. Sparrow, robin, wagta jay, wren, swallow, swift, woodpecke kingfisher, magpie, crow, rook, lark, thrus bull-finch, nightingale, pheasant, wood-coc snipe, plover, grouse, quail, duck, te falcon, eagle, kestrel, owl.
Cinemas: 2673 (seating capacity 1 249 00 and one drive-in (1972).

JORDAN

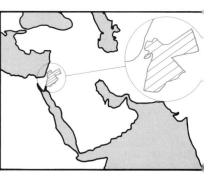

Official name: Al Mamlaka al Urduniya Hashimiyah (The Hashemite Kingdom Jordan).
Population: 2 620 000 (1974 est).

Area: 36 909 miles² *95 594 km².*
Language: Arabic.
Religions: Muslim, Christian minority.
Capital city: Ammān, population 615 000 (1974 est).
Other principal towns: Az Zarqa (Zraka) 220 000 (1972); Irbid 116 000 (1973); Bait Lahm (Bethlehem) 68 009 (1961); Ariha (Jericho) 66 839 (1961); Al Quds ash Sharif (Jerusalem) 60 337 (Jordanian sector, 1961).
Highest point: Jabal Ramm 5755 ft *1754 m.*
Principal rivers: Jordan (200 miles *321 km).*
Head of State: H.M. King Husain ibn Talal, GCVO (b. 14 Nov. 1935).
Prime Minister: Mudar Badran (b. 1934).
Climate: Hot and dry, average temperature 60 °F with wide diurnal variations. Cool winters, rainy season December to March. In Ammān, August hottest (average maximum 90 °F), January coolest (average minimum 39 °F). Absolute maximum temperature 51 °C (*124 °F*), Dead Sea North, 22 June 1942; absolute minimum −7 °C (*18 °F*), Ammān, 28 Feb. 1959.
Crops: Wheat, barley, tomatoes, citrus fruits.
Monetary unit: Jordanian dinar. 1 dinar = 1000 fils.
Denominations:
 Coins 1, 5, 10, 20, 25, 50, 100, 250 fils.
 Notes ½, 1, 5, 10 dinars.
Exchange rate to US dollar: 0.332 February 1976).
Political history and government: Formerly part of Turkey's Ottoman Empire. Turkish forces were expelled in 1918. Palestine and Transjordan were administered by Britain under League of Nations mandate, established in 1922. Transjordan became an independent monarchy, under an Amir, on 22 Mar. 1946. The Amir became King, and the country's present name was adopted, on 25 May 1946. In the Arab-Israeli war of 1948 Jordanian forces occupied part of Palestine, annexed in December 1949 and fully incorporated on 24 Apr. 1950. This tory was captured by Israel in the war of 5–10 June 1967.

Under the constitution, adopted on 7 Nov. 1951, legislative power is held by a bicameral National Assembly, comprising a Chamber of Notables (30 members appointed by the King for 8 years, half retiring ever 4 years) and a Chamber of Deputies with 60 members (50 Muslims and 10 Christians) elected by universal adult suffrage for 4 years (subject to dissolution). Executive power is vested in the King, who rules with the assistance of an appointed Council of Ministers, responsible to the Assembly. The only authorized political organization is the Arab National Union, established on 7 Sept. 1971.

Jordan comprises 8 administrative districts, including 3 on the West Bank (under Israeli occupation since June 1967).
Telephones: 40 511 (1974).
Daily newspapers: 4 (1972).
 Total circulation: 58 000.
Radio: 529 000 (1975).
TV: 205 000 (1975).
Length of roadways: 3672 miles *5909 km.*
Length of railways: 310 miles *500 km.*
Universities: 1.
Adult illiteracy: 67·6% (males 49·9%; females 84·8%) in 1961.
Expectation of life: Males 52·6 years; females 52.0 years (1959–63).
Defence: Military service: voluntary. Total armed forces: 80 250. Defence expenditure 1975–6: $155 million.
Wildlife: Over 600 varieties of vertebrate species include: hyena, ibex, mole rat, desert fox, mongoose. Golden eagle, bulbul, vulture.
Cinemas: 39 (seating capacity 22 000) in 1972 (excluding Israeli-occupied territory).

KENYA

Official name: Djumhuri ya Kenya (Republic of Kenya).
Population: 12 912 000 (1974 est).
Area: 224 961 miles² *582 646 km².*
Languages: Swahili (official), English, Kikuyu, Luo.
Religions: Christian 58% (1962).
Capital city: Nairobi, population 663 000 (1974 est).
Other principal towns: Mombasa 246 000; Nakuru 47 800; Kisumu 30 700; Thika 18 100; Eldoret 16 900.
Highest point: Mount Kenya (17 058 ft *5199 m).*
Principal mountain range: Aberdare Mountains.
Principal rivers: Tana, Umba, Athi, Mathioya.
Head of State: Johnstone Kamau (*né* Kamau wa Ngengi), *alias* Jomo Kenyatta (b. 20 Oct. 1891), President.
Climate: Varies with altitude. Hot and humid on coast, with average temperatures of 69 °F to 90 °F, falling to 45 °F to 80 °F on land over 5000 ft. Ample rainfall in the west and on highlands, but very dry in the north. In Nairobi, average maximum 69 °F (July) to 79 °F (February), minimum 51 °F (July) to 58 °F (April), May rainiest (17 days).
Crops: Maize, cassava, sweet potatoes, millet, pulses, potatoes, sugar cane, sisal, coffee, tea.
Monetary unit: Kenya shilling. 1 shilling = 100 cents.
Denominations:
 Coins 5, 10, 25, 50 cents, 1, 2 shillings.
 Notes 5, 10, 20, 50, 100 shillings.

Exchange rate to US dollar: 8.2865 (February 1976).
Political history and government: Formerly a British colony and protectorate. Became independent, within the Commonwealth, on 12 Dec. 1963 and a republic on 12 Dec. 1964. A one-party state since 30 Oct. 1969. Legislative power is held by the unicameral National Assembly, with 171 members (158 elected by universal adult suffrage, the Minister of Justice and 12 members nominated by the President) serving a term of 4 years (subject to dissolution). Executive power is held by the President, also directly elected for 4 years. He is assisted by an appointed Vice-President and Cabinet. Kenya has 7 provinces, each with an advisory Provincial Council.
Telephones: 113 688 (1975).
Daily newspapers: 4 (1970).
 Total circulation: 155 000.
Radio: 511 000 (1975).

TV: 37 500 (1975).
Length of roadways: 29 954 miles *48 206 km.*
Length of railways: 1286 miles *2070 km.*
Universities: 1.
Expectation of life: Males 46·9 years; females 51·2 years (1969).
Defence: Military service: voluntary. Total armed forces 7550. Defence expenditure 1974: $2·5 million.
Wildlife: Zebra, gazelle, antelope, hippopotamus, leopard, lion, elephant, rhinoceros, hyena, jackal, baboon, monkeys, over 100 species of snakes. Stork, pelican, flamingo, ostrich.
Cinemas: 32 (seating capacity 20 600) and 3 drive-in (1971).

KOREA (North)

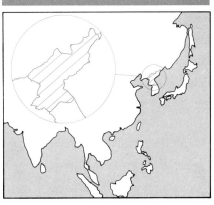

Official name: Chosun Minchu-chui Inmin Konghwa-guk (Democratic People's Republic of Korea).
Population: 15 852 000 (UN estimate for mid-1975).
Area: 46 540 miles², *120 538 km²* (excluding demilitarized zone).
Languages: Korean.
Religions: Buddhist, Confucian, Taoist.
Capital city: Pyongyang, population 1 500 000 (1974 est).
Other principal towns (1974): Ch'ŏngjin 300 000; Kaesong 240 000; Hungnam 200 000.
Highest point: Paektu San (Pait'ou Shan), 9003 ft *2744 m* (first climbed 1886).
Principal mountain range: Nangnim Sanmaek.
Principal rivers: Imjin, Ch'ongch'ŏn, Yalu (300 miles *482 km*) on frontier.
Head of State: Marshal Kim Il Sung (*ne* Kim Sung Chu, 15 Apr. 1912), President, also General Secretary of the Central Committee of the Korean Workers' Party.
Head of Government: Pak Sung Chul, Premier of the Administration Council.
Climate: Continental; hot, humid, rainy summers (average temperature 77 °F) and cold dry winters (average 21 °F).
Crops: Rice, maize, potatoes, millet, barley, sweet potatoes, soybeans, pulses.
Monetary unit: Won. 1 won = 100 jeon.
Denominations:
 Coins 1, 5, 10 jeon.
 Notes 50 jeon, 1, 5, 10, 50, 100 won.
Exchange rate to US dollar: 0.94 (February 1976).
Political history and government: Korea was formerly a kingdom, for long under Chinese suzerainty. Independence was established on 17 Apr. 1895. Korea was occupied by Japanese forces in November 1905 and formally annexed by Japan on 22 Aug. 1910, when the King was deposed. After Japan's defeat in the Second World War, Korea was divided at the 38th parallel into military occupation zones, with Soviet forces in the North and US forces in the

South. After the failure of negotiations in 1946 and 1947, the country remained divided. With Soviet backing, a Communist-dominated administration was established in the North. Elections were held on 25 Aug. 1948 and the Democratic People's Republic of Korea was proclaimed on 9 Sept. 1948. After the Korean War of 1950–53 a cease-fire line replaced the 38th parallel as the border between North and South.

In North Korea a new constitution was adopted on 27 Dec. 1972. The highest organ of state power is the unicameral Supreme People's Assembly, with 541 members elected (unopposed) for 4 years by universal adult suffrage. The Assembly elects for its duration the President of the Republic and, on the latter's recommendation, other members of the Central People's Committee to direct the government. The Assembly appoints the Premier and the Committee appoints other Ministers to form the Administration Council, led by the President.

Political power is held by the (Communist) Korean Workers' Party (KWP), which dominates the Democratic Front for the Reunification of the Fatherland (including two other minor parties). The Front presents an approved list of candidates for elections to répresentative bodies. The KWP's highest authority is the Party Congress, which elects a Central Committee to supervise Party work. The Committee elects the Politburo to direct policy.

North Korea comprises nine provinces and two cities, each with an elected People's Assembly.

Radio: 600 000 (1961).
Length of railways: 9320 miles *15 000 km.*
Universities: 1.
Adult illiteracy: 10% (est).
Expectation of life: Males 56·0 years; females 59·4 years (1965–70).
Defence: Military service: Army 5 years; Navy and Air Force 3 to 4 years. Total armed forces 467 000. Defence expenditure 1974: $770 million.
Wildlife: See Korea, South.

KOREA (South)

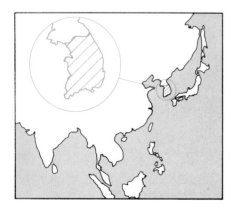

Official name: Daehen-Minkuk (Republic of Korea).
Population: 33 459 000 (1974 est).
Area: 38 131 miles² *98 758 km².*
Languages: Korean.
Religions: Buddhist, Christian, Confucian, Chundo Kyo.
Capital city: Sŏul (Seoul), population 5 536 377 (1970).
Other principal towns (1970): Pusan (Busan) 1 880 710; Taegu (Daegu) 1 082 750; Inchŏn (Incheon) 646 013; Kwangchu (Gwangju) 502 753; Taejŏn (Daejeon)

414 598; Chonchu (Jeonju) 262 816; Masan 190 992; Mokp'o 177 801; Suweon (Puwan) 170 518; Ulsan 159 340.
Highest point: Halla-san 6398 ft *1950 m.*
Principal rivers: Han, Naktong (with Nam), Kum, Somjin, Yongsan.
Head of State: Gen Pak Chung Hi, *also written* Park Chung Hee (b. 30 Sept. 1917), President.
Prime Minister: Ch'oi Kyu Ha (b. 16 July 1919).
Climate: Hot, humid summers (average temperature 77 °F) and cold, dry winters (average 21 °F). In Seoul, August hottest (71 °F to 87 °F), January coldest (15 °F to 32 °F), July rainiest (16 days). Absolute maximum temperature 40 °C (*104 °F*), Taegu, 1 Aug. 1942; absolute minimum −43,6 °C (*−46·5 °F*), Chungkangjin, 12 Jan. 1933.
Crops: Rice, barley, sweet potatoes, cabbages, potatoes, soybeans, apples, water melons, tobacco.
Monetary unit: Won. 1 won = 100 jeon.
Denominations:
   Coins 1, 5, 10, 100 won.
   Notes 10, 50 jeon, 1, 5, 10, 50, 100, 500, 5000 won.
Exchange rate to US dollar: 484 (February 1976).
Political history and government: (For events before partition, *see* North Korea, above). After UN-supervised elections for a National Assembly on 10 May 1948, South Korea adopted a constitution and became the independent Republic of Korea on 15 Aug. 1948. North Korean forces invaded the South on 25 June 1950 and war ensued until 27 July 1953, when an armistice established a cease-fire line (roughly along the 38th parallel) between North and South. This line has become effectively an international frontier.

On 16 May 1961 South Korea's government was overthrown by a military *coup*, led by Maj-Gen Pak Chung Hi, who assumed power and dissolved the National Assembly. A new constitution was approved by referendum on 17 Dec. 1962. Gen. Pak was elected President on 15 Oct. 1963 and inaugurated on 17 Dec. 1963, when a newly-elected National Assembly was convened. Martial law was imposed in October 1972 and another constitution approved by referendum in November 1972.

Executive power is held by the President, indirectly elected for 6 years by the National Conference for Unification (NCU), which comprises 2359 delegates elected for 6 years by direct popular vote on 22 Dec. 1972. The President rules with the assistance of an appointed State Council (Cabinet), led by a Prime Minister. Legislative power is vested in the unicameral National Assembly, with 219 members (146 elected for 6 years by universal adult suffrage and 73 elected for 3 years by the NCU). An emergency decree of 13 May 1975 banned virtually all opposition activities.

South Korea comprises nine provinces and two cities.
Telephones: 1 014 016 (1974).
Daily newspapers: 33 (1972).
   Total circulation: 4 400 000.
Radio: 3 105 000 (1975).
TV: 1 184 000 (1975).
Length of roadways: 27 079 miles *43 580 km.*
Length of railways: 3511 miles *5650 km.*
Universities: 26.
Adult illiteracy: 12·4% (males 5·6%; females 19·0%) in 1970.
Expectation of life: Males 59·74 years; females 64·07 years (1966).
Defence: Military service: Army and Marines 2½ years; Navy and Air Force 3 years. Total armed forces 625 000. Defence expenditure 1975: $719 million.

Wildlife: Tiger, snow leopard, musk deer bear, wolf, red deer, roe deer, frogs, lizards snakes. Red-necked pheasant.
Cinemas: 786 (seating capacity 446 400) in 1972.

KUWAIT

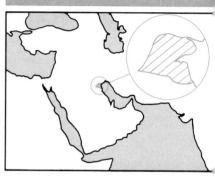

Official name: Daulat al Kuwait (State of Kuwait). Kuwait means 'little fort'.
Population: 990 389 (1975 census).
Area: 6880 miles² *17 818 km².*
Language: Arabic.
Religions: Muslim, Christian minority.
Capital city: Kuwait City, population 93 050 (1973 est).
Other principal towns (1970): Hawalli 106 542; Salmiya 67 346.
Highest point: 951 ft *289 m.*
Head of State: H.H. Shaikh Sabah as-Salim as-Sabah (b. 1913), Amir.
Prime Minister: H.H. Shaikh Jabir al-Ahmad al-Jabir as-Sabah (b. 1928).
Climate: Humid, average temperature 75 °F. In Kuwait City, maximum recorded temperature 51 °C (*123·8 °F*), July 1954; minimum −2,6 °C (*+27·3 °F*), January 1964.
Crop: Dates.
Monetary unit: Kuwaiti dinar. 1 dinar = 1000 fils.
Denominations:
   Coins 1, 5, 10, 20, 50, 100 fils.
   Notes ¼, ½, 1, 5, 10 dinars.
Exchange rate to US dollar: 0.2935 (February 1976).
Political history and government: A monarchy formerly ruled by a Shaikh. Under British protection from 23 Jan. 1899 until achieving full independence, with the ruling Shaikh as Amir, on 19 June 1961. Present constitution adopted on 16 Dec. 1962. Executive power is vested in the Amir (chosen by and from members of the ruling family) and is exercised through a Council of Ministers. The Amir appoints the Prime Minister and, on the latter's recommendation, other Ministers. Legislative power is held by the unicameral National Assembly, with 50 members elected for 4 years (subject to dissolution) by literate civilian adult male Kuwaiti citizens. Political parties are not legally permitted. Kuwait comprises three governorates.
Telephones: 108 587 (1975).
Daily newspapers: 6 (1971).
   Total circulation: 55 000.
Radio: 500 000 (1975).
TV: 135 000 (1975).
Length of roadways: 1193 miles *1920 km.*
Universities: 1.
Adult illiteracy: 45·0% (males 36·6%; females 58·1%) in 1970.
Expectation of life: Males 66·14 years; females 71·82 years (1970).
Defence: Military service: conscription. Total armed forces 10 200. Defence expenditure 1974: $162 million.
Cinemas: 7 (seating capacity 11 300), one part-time (capacity 780) and one drive-in (1972).

LAOS

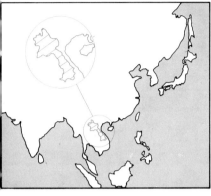

Official name: The Lao People's Democratic Republic.
Population: 3 257 000 (1974 est).
Area: 91 400 miles² *236 800 km²*.
Languages: Lao (official), French, English.
Religions: Buddhist, tribal.
Capital city: Vientiane, population 176 637 (1973).
Other principal towns (1973): Savannakhet 50 690; Pakse 44 860; Luang Prabang 44 244.
Highest point: Phou Bia, 9252 ft *2820 m.*
Principal mountain range: Annamitic Range.
Principal river: Mekong (2600 miles [*4184 km*]).
Head of State: Prince Souphanouvong (b. 1902), President.
Prime Minister: Kaysone Phomvihan (b. 1920), also General Secretary of the Lao People's Revolutionary Party.
Climate: Tropical (warm and humid). Rainy monsoon season May–October. In Vientiane average maximum 83 °F (December to January) to 93 °F (April), minimum 57 °F (January) to 75 °F (June to September), July and August rainiest (each 18 days). Maximum recorded temperature 44,8 °C (*112·6 °F*), Luang Prabang, January 1924.
Crops: Rice, maize, tobacco, cotton, coffee.
Monetary unit: Liberation kip. 1 kip = 100 at.
Denominations:
Notes 10, 20, 50, 100, 200, 500 kips.
Exchange rate to US dollar: 750.00 (October 1975).
Political history and government: Formerly the three principalities of Luang Prabang, Vientiane and Champassac. Became a French protectorate in 1893. The three principalities were merged in 1946 and an hereditary constitutional monarchy, under the Luang Prabang dynasty, was established on 11 May 1947. The Kingdom of Laos became independent, within the French Union, on 19 July 1949. Full sovereignty was recognized by France on 23 Oct. 1953. After nearly 20 years of almost continuous civil war between the Royal Government and the *Neo Lao Hak Sat* (Lao Patriotic Front or LPF), a Communist-led insurgent movement whose armed forces were known as the *Pathet Lao*, a peace agreement was signed on 21 Feb. 1973. A joint administration was established on 5 Apr. 1974 but the LPF became increasingly dominant. The National Assembly was dissolved on 13 Apr. 1975. The King abdicated on 29 Nov. 1975 and on 1 Dec. 1975 a National Congress of People's Representatives (264 delegates elected by local authorities) proclaimed the Lao People's Democratic Republic, with Prince Souphanouvong, Chairman of the LPF, as President. The Congress installed a Council of Ministers, led by a Prime Minister, and appointed a People's Supreme Council of 45 members, chaired by the President, to draft a new constitution.
Telephones: 5506 (1974).
Daily newspapers: 2 (1975).
Radio: 51 000 (1971).
Length of roadways: 4536 miles *7 300km.*
Universities: 1.
Adult illiteracy: 75% (estimate).
Expectation of life: Males 39·1 years; females 41·8 years (1965–70).
Defence: Military service: 18 months. Total armed forces: 52 500. Defence expenditure, 1974–5: $27 million.
Wildlife: Elephant, gaur, leopard, tiger, numerous types of reptile, panther. Many varieties of birds.
Cinemas: 16 (seating capacity 8200) in 1969.

LEBANON

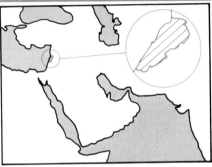

Official name Al-Jumhuriya al-Lubnaniya (the Lebanese Republic), abbreviated to al-Lubnan.
Population: 2 854 325 (1970 survey), excluding Palestinian refugees (187 529 in 1973).
Area: 3950 miles² *10 400 km².*
Languages: Arabic (official), French, Armenian, English.
Religions: Christian, Muslim 34%.
Capital city: Beirut, population 800 000 (1972).
Other principal towns: Tripoli 175 000; Zahlé 46 800; Saida (Sidon) 24 740; Tyre 14 000; Aley 13 800.
Highest point: Qurnat as-Sadwā, 10 131 ft *3088 m.*
Principal mountain ranges: Lebanon, Jabal ash Sharqi (Anti-Lebanon).
Principal rivers: Nahr al Litāni (Leontes).
Head of State: Sulaiman Franjieh (b. 14 June 1910), President.
Prime Minister: Rashid Abdul Hamid Karami (b. 1921).
Climate: Coastal lowlands are hot and humid in summer, mild (cool and damp) in winter. Mountains cool in summer, heavy snowfall in winter. In Beirut, average maximum 62 °F (January) to 89 °F (August), minimum 51 °F (January, February) to 74 °F (August), January rainiest (15 days).
Crops: Citrus fruit, apples, grapes, potatoes, sugar-beet, olives, bananas, wheat.
Monetary unit: Lebanese pound (£L). 1 pound = 100 piastres.
Denominations:
Coins 1, 2, 5, 10, 25, 50 piastres.
Notes 1, 5, 10, 25, 50, 100 pounds.
Exchange rate to US dollar: 2.425 (February 1976).
Political history and government: Formerly part of Turkey's Ottoman Empire. Turkish forces were expelled in 1918 by British and French troops, with Arab help. Administered by France under League of Nations mandate from 1 Sept. 1920. Independence declared on 26 Nov. 1941. A republic was established in 1943 and French powers transferred on 1 Jan. 1944. All foreign troops left by December 1946.

Legislative power is held by the unicameral Chamber of Deputies, with 99 members elected by universal adult suffrage for 4 years (subject to dissolution), using proportional representation. Seats are allocated on a religious basis (53 Christian, 45 Muslim). Executive power is vested in the President, elected for 6 years by the Chamber. He appoints a Prime Minister and other Ministers to form a Cabinet, responsible to the Chamber. By convention, the President is a Maronite Christian and the Prime Minister a Sunni Muslim.
Telephones: 227 000 (1970).
Daily newspapers: 52 (1972).
Radio: 1 321 000 (1975).
TV: 410 000 (1975).
Length of roadways: 4598 miles *7400 km.*
Length of railways: 259 miles *417 km.*
Universities: 5.
Adult illiteracy: 20% (estimate).
Expectation of life: Males 59·0 years; females 62·9 years (1965–70).
Defence: Military service: 12 months selective. Total armed forces 15 300. Defence expenditure 1975: $144 million.
Wildlife: Deer, hedgehog, squirrel, dormouse, hare, wild cat, lizards, chameleon. Flamingo, pelican, duck, cormorant, heron, snipe, eagle, buzzard, falcon, hawk, kite, owl, cuckoo, kingfisher, woodpecker.
Cinemas: 170 (seating capacity 86 600) and 2 drive-in (1970).

LESOTHO

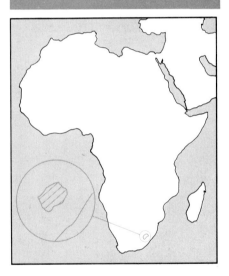

Official name: Kingdom of Lesotho (formerly Basutoland).
Population: 1 155 700 (1974 est).
Area: 11 720 miles² *30 355 km².*
Languages: Sesotho, English.
Religions: Christian 73·4% (1966).
Capital city: Maseru, population 18 800 (1972 est).
Highest point: Thabana Ntlenyana (Thadentsonyane), 11 425 ft *3482 m.*
Principal mountain range: Drakensberg.
Principal rivers: Orange, Caledon (on northern frontier).
Head of State: King Motlotlehi Moshoeshoe II (b. 2 May 1938).
Prime Minister: Chief Joseph Leabua Jonathan (b. 30 Oct. 1914).
Climate: In lowlands, maximum temperature in summer 90 °F, winter minimum 20 °F. Range wider in highlands. Average annual rainfall 29 in. Rainy season October–April.
Crops: Wheat, maize, sorghum.
Monetary unit: South African currency (*qv*).

Political history and government: An hereditary monarchy, formerly the British colony of Basutoland. Granted internal self-government, with the Paramount Chief as King, on 30 April 1965. Became independent (under present name), within the Commonwealth, on 4 Oct. 1966. Under the constitution, legislative power was vested in a bicameral Parliament, comprising a Senate of 33 members (22 Chiefs and 11 Senators nominated by the King for 5-year terms) and a National Assembly of 60 members elected by universal adult suffrage for 5 years (subject to dissolution). Executive power is exercised by the Cabinet, led by the Prime Minister, which is responsible to Parliament. The Assembly elections of 27 Jan. 1970 were annulled three days later by the Prime Minister, who declared a state of emergency and suspended the constitution. The Cabinet assumed full power. No more elections have been held but an interim National Assembly of 93 members (the former Senate and 60 nominated members) was inaugurated on 27 Apr. 1973. Lesotho comprises 9 administrative districts, each under an appointed District Administrator.
Telephones: 3726 (1975).
Radio: 22 000 (1975).
Length of roadways: *c.* 960 miles *c. 1545 km.*
Length of railways: 1 mile *2 km.*
Universities: 1.
Adult illiteracy: 41·2% (males 55·9%; females 32·2%) in 1966 (excl. absentee workers).
Expectation of life: Males 41·9 years; females 45·1 years (1965–70).
Wildlife: Antelope, hare.
Cinemas: 2 (seating capacity 800) in 1971.

LIBERIA

Official name: The Republic of Liberia.
Population: 1 016 443 (1962 census); 1 496 000 (1974).
Area: 43 000 miles² *111 369 km².*
Languages: English (official), tribal languages.
Religion: Mainly Animist.
Capital city: Monrovia, population 180 000 (1974).
Other principal towns: Harbel, Buchanan, Greenville (Sinoe), Harper (Cape Palmas).
Highest point: On Mt Nimba, 4500 ft *1372 m.*
Principal mountain range: Guinea Highlands.
Principal rivers: St Paul, St John, Cess.
Head of State: William Richard Tolbert, Jr. (b. 13 May 1913), President.

Climate: Tropical (hot and humid) with temperatures from 55 °F to 120 °F. Rainy season April to October. In Monrovia, average maximum 80 °F (July, August) to 87 °F (March, April), minimum 72 °F to 74 °F all year round, June and September rainiest (each 26 days).
Crops: Cassava, rice, rubber, bananas.
Monetary unit: Liberian dollar. 1 dollar = 100 cents.
Denominations:
  Coins 1, 2, 5, 10, 25, 50 cents, 1 Liberian dollar.
  Notes 1, 5, 10, 20 US dollars (There are no Liberian banknotes).
Exchange rate to US dollar: 1.00 (February 1976).
Political history and government: Settled in 1822 by freed slaves from the USA. Became independent on 26 July 1847. The constitution was modelled on that of the USA. The bicameral legislature, elected by universal adult suffrage, comprises a Senate, with 18 members (two from each of the 9 counties) serving overlapping 6-year terms, and a House of Representatives (65 members serving 4 years). Executive power is held by the President, directly elected (with a Vice-President) for 8 years. The President rules with the assistance of an appointed Cabinet.
Telephones: 3400 (1974).
Daily newspapers: 1 (1971).
  Total circulation: 7000.
Radio: 264 000 (1975).
TV: 8800 (1975).
Length of roadways: 62 298 miles *100 260 km.*
Length of railways: 291 miles *468 km.*
University: 1.
Adult illiteracy: 91·1% (males 86·1%; females 95·8%) illiterate in English in 1962.
Expectation of life: Males 45.8 years; females 44·0 years (1971).
Defence: Total armed forces 5220.
Wildlife: Monkeys, lizard, snakes, squirrel, pygmy hippopotamus, anteater, crocodile, leopard, bat. Many hundreds of species of birds.
Cinemas: 26 (seating capacity 15 000) in 1971.

LIBYA

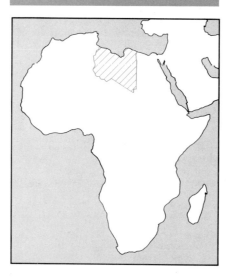

Official name: Al Jumhuriya al-Arabiya al-Libiya (The Libyan Arab Republic).
Population: 2 346 000 (1974 est).
Area: 679 363 miles² *1 759 540 km².*
Language: Arabic.
Religion: Muslim.
Capital city: Tripoli, population 551 477

(1973 census).
Other principal towns: Benghazi 140 000; Misurata 103 302; Homs-Cussabat 88 695; Zawia 72 207; Gharlan 65 439; Tobruk 58 869.
Highest point: Pico Bette 7500 ft *2286 m.*
Principal mountain ranges: Jabal a Sawdā, Al Kufrah, Al Harūj al Aswad, Jaba Nafūsah, Hamada de Tinrhert.
Principal river: Wādī al Fārigh.
Head of State: Col Muammar Muhamma al-Qaddafi (b. 1938), Chairman of th Revolutionary Command Council.
Prime Minister: Maj Abdul Salam Ahma Jalloud (b. 1942).
Climate: Very hot and dry, with averag temperatures between 55 °F and 100 °F Coast cooler than inland. In Tripoli, Augus hottest (72 °F to 86 °F), January cooles (47 °F to 61 °F). Absolute maximum temperature 57,3 °C *(135·1 °F)* Al 'Aziziyah (el Azizia), 24 Aug. 1923. Absolute minimun −9 °C *(−15·8 °F)* Hon, 10 Jan. 1938.
Crops: Barley, tomatoes, olives, potatoes wheat, dates.
Monetary unit: Libyan dinars. 1 dinar = 1000 dirhams.
Denominations:
  Coins 1, 5, 10, 20, 50, 100 dirhams.
  Notes ¼, ½, 1, 5, 10 dinars.
Exchange rate to US dollar: 0.296 (February 1976).
Political history and government: Formerly part of Turkey's Ottoman Empire Became an Italian colony in September 1911 Italian forces were expelled in 1942–43 and the country was under British and French administration from 1943 until becoming an independent kingdom, under the Amir of Cyrenaica, on 24 Dec. 1951. The monarchy was overthrown by an army *coup* on 1 Sept. 1969, when a Revolutionary Command Council (RCC) took power and proclaimed the Libyan Arab Republic. The bicameral Parliament was abolished and political activity suspended. A provisional constitution, proclaimed in December 1969, vests supreme authority in the RCC, which appoints a Council of Ministers. The only legal political party is the Arab Socialist Union, established on 11 June 1971. Libya is divided into 10 governorates.
Telephones: 42 000 (1971).
Daily newspapers: 6 (1972).
Radio: 106 000 (1975).
TV: 10 000 (1975).
Length of roadways: *c.* 3232 miles *c. 5200 km.*
Length of railways: 108 miles *174 km.*
Universities: 2.
Adult illiteracy: 78·3% (males 62·5%; females 95·8%) in 1964.
Expectation of life: Males 49·0 years; females 51·8 years (1965–70).
Defence: Military service: voluntary. Total armed forces 32 000. Defence expenditure 1975: $203 million.
Wildlife: Jerboa, hyena, fox, wild cat, lizards, snakes. Numerous migrating birds in spring and autumn.

LIECHTENSTEIN

Official name: Fürstentum Liechtenstein (Principality of Liechtenstein).
Population: 22 000 (1974 est).
Area: 62 miles², *160 km².*
Language: German.
Religions: Roman Catholic, Protestant minority.
Capital city: Vaduz, population 4326 (1973 est).
Other principal towns (1973): Schaan 4302; Balzers 2903; Triesen 2898; Mauren

2279; Eschen 2194.
Highest point: Grauspitze 8526 ft *2599 m*.
Principal mountain ranges: Alps.
Principal rivers: Rhein (Rhine) (820 miles *1319 km*, 17 miles *27 km* in Liechtenstein), Samina.
Head of State: Prince Franz Josef II (b. 16 Aug. 1906)
Head of Government: Dr Walter Kieber (b. 20 Feb. 1931).
Climate: Alpine, with mild winters. Temperature extremes for Sargans, in Switzerland, a few miles from the Liechtenstein border: Absolute maximum 38,0 °C (*100·4 °F*), 29 July 1947; absolute minimum −25,6 °C (*−14·1 °F*), 12 Feb. 1929.
Crops: Maize, potatoes, grapes.
Monetary unit: Swiss currency (*qv*).
Political history and government: An hereditary principality, independent since 1866. Present constitution adopted on 5 Oct. 1921. Legislative power is exercised jointly by the Sovereign and the unicameral Diet (*Landtag*), with 15 members elected (by men only) for 4 years, using proportional representation. A 5-man Government (*Regierung*) is elected by the Diet for its duration and confirmed by the Sovereign.

Telephones: 14 745 (1975).
Daily newspapers: 1 (1972).
  Total circulation: 6000.
Radio: 5398 (1973).
TV: 4467 (1973).
Length of railways: 11 miles *18 km*.
Cinemas: 3 (seating capacity 900) in 1971.

LUXEMBOURG

Official name: Le Grand-Duché de Luxembourg, Grousherzogdem Lezebuurg or Grossherzogtum Luxemburg (Grand Duchy of Luxembourg).
Population: 332 434 (1970 census); 357 400 (1975 est).
Area: 999 miles² *2586 km²*.
Languages: Letzeburgesch (Luxembourgois), French, German.
Religion: Roman Catholic.
Capital city: Luxembourg-Ville, population 78 400 (1975).
Other principal towns (1973): Esch-sur-Alzette 27 539; Differdange 17 976; Dudelange 14 625; Petange 11 903.
Highest point: Bourgplatz 1833 ft *559 m*.
Principal mountain range: Ardennes.
Principal rivers: Mosel (Moselle), Sûre (107 miles [*172 km*], 99 miles [*159 km*] in Luxembourg), Our, Alzette.
Head of State: H.R.H. Prince Jean Benoît Guillaume Marie Robert Louis Antoine Adolphe Marc d'Aviano (b. 5 Jan. 1921), Grand Duke.
Head of Government: Gaston Thorn (b. 3

Sept. 1928), President of the Government (Prime Minister).
Climate: Temperate (cool summers and mild winters). Absolute maximum temperature, 37,0 °C (*98·6 °F*), Luxembourg-Ville, 28 July 1895, and Grevenmacher, 6 July 1957; absolute minimum −24,3 °C (*−11·7 °F*), Wiltz, 5 Feb. 1917.
Crops: Potatoes, barley, beet, oats, wheat, grapes.
Monetary unit: Luxembourg franc. 1 franc = 100 centimes.
Denominations:
  Coins 25, 50 centimes, 1, 5, 10, 100, 250 Luxembourg francs.
  Notes 10, 20, 50, 100 Luxembourg francs; 20, 50, 100, 500, 1000, 5000 Belgian francs.
Exchange rate to US dollar: 39·14 (February 1976).

Political history and government: An hereditary grand duchy, independent since 1867. Luxembourg is a constitutional monarchy. Legislative power is exercised by the unicameral Chamber of Deputies, with 59 members elected by universal adult suffrage for 5 years (subject to dissolution). Some legislative functions are also entrusted to the advisory Council of State, with 21 members appointed by the Grand Duke, but the Council can be overridden by the Chamber. Executive power is vested in the Grand Duke but is normally exercised by the Council of Ministers, led by the President of the Government. The Grand Duke appoints Ministers but they are responsible to the Chamber. Luxembourg is divided into 12 cantons.
Telephones: 141 686 (1975).
Daily newspapers: 7 (1972).
  Total circulation: 161 000 (6 dailies).
Radio: 175 500 (1975).
TV: 82 000 (1975).
Length of roadways: 3083 miles *4962 km*.
Length of railways: 168 miles *271 km*.
Expectation of life: Males 66·8 years; females 73·2 years (1965–70).
Defence: Military service: voluntary. Total armed forces 550. Defence expenditure 1975 $19 million.
Cinemas: 27 (seating capacity 13 700) in 1972.

MADAGASCAR

Official name: La République démocratique de Madagascar (The Democratic Republic of Madagascar).
Population: 8 080 900 (1974 est).
Area: 226 658 miles², *587 041 km²*.
Languages: Malagasy, French (both official).
Religions: Animist, Christian, Muslim.
Capital city: Tananarive (Antananarivo), population 366 530 (1972).

Other principal towns (1972): Majunga 67 458; Tamatave 59 503; Fianarantsoa 58 818; Diégo-Suarez 45 487; Tuléar 38 978; Antsirabé 33 287.
Highest point: Maromokotro 9436 ft *2876 m*.
Principal mountain ranges: Massif du Tsaratanana, Ankaratra.
Principal rivers: Ikopa, Mania, Mangoky.
Head of State: Lt-Cdr Didier Ratsiraka (b. 4 Nov. 1936), President.
Prime Minister: Justin Rakotoniaina (b. 1933).
Climate: Hot on coast (average daily maximum 90 °F), but cooler inland. Fairly dry in south, but monsoon rains (December to April) in north. In Tananarive average maximum 68 °F (July) to 81 °F (November), minimum 48 °F (July, August) to 61 °F (January, February), January rainiest (21 days). Absolute maximum temperature 44,4 °C (*111·9 °F*), Behara, 20 Nov. 1940; absolute minimum −6,3 °C (*−20·7 °F*), Antsirabé, 18 June 1945.
Crops: Rice, cassava, sweet potatoes, bananas, potatoes, maize, sugar cane, coffee, cloves, vanilla.

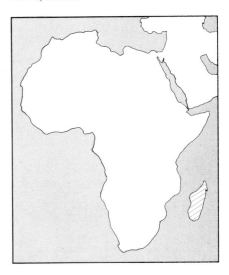

Monetary unit: Franc malgache (Malagasy franc). 1 franc = 100 centimes.
Denominations:
  Coins 1, 2, 5, 10, 20 francs
  Notes 50, 100, 500, 1000, 5000 francs.
Exchange rate to US dollar: 224.24 (February 1976).
Political history and government: Formerly a French colony. Became independent, as the Malagasy Republic, on 26 June 1960. Following disturbances, the President handed over full powers to the army commander on 18 May 1972, when Parliament was dissolved. A National Military Directorate was formed on 12 Feb. 1975 and suspended all political parties. On 15 June 1975 the Directorate elected Lt-Cdr Didier Ratsiraka to be Head of State, as President of the Supreme Revolutionary Council (SRC). A referendum on 21 Dec. 1975 approved a draft constitution and the appointment of Ratsiraka as Head of State for 7 years. The Democratic Republic of Madagascar was proclaimed on 30 Dec. 1975 and Ratsiraka took office as President of the Republic on 4 Jan. 1976.

Executive power is vested in the President, who rules with the assistance of the SRC and an appointed Council of Ministers. The constitution provides for a legislative National People's Assembly to be elected (within 18 months) by universal adult suffrage for 5 years. It also envisages the creation of a single political party. The country is divided into 6 provinces.

Telephones: 29 324 (1974).
Daily newspapers: 13 (1972).
 Total circulation: 103 000.
Radio: 608 000 (1975).
TV: 7500 (1975).
Length of roadways: 16 789 miles *27 019 km.*
Length of railways: 549 miles *884 km.*
University: 1.
Adult illiteracy: 66·5% (males 59·2%; females 73·0%) illiterate in Malagasy in 1953 (indigenous population aged 14 and over).
Expectation of life: Males 39·4 years; females 42·6 years (1965–70).
Defence: Total armed forces 4760.
Wildlife: Tenrec, chameleons, tortoise, lizard, lemurs (over 40 species), aye-aye, hedgehog, bat, crocodile. Egret, owl, guinea fowl, heron, partridge, pigeon, ibis, flamingo.
Cinemas: 46 with seating capacity of 21 000.

MALAWI

Official name: The Republic of Malawi.
Population: 4 916 000 (1974 est).
Area: 45 747 miles² *118 484 km².*
Languages: English (official), Nyanja.
Religions: Mainly traditional beliefs. Christian minority.
Capital city: Lilongwe, population 19 178 (1966).
Other principal towns (1966): Blantyre 109 795; Zomba 19 616; Mzuzu 8490; Salima 2307.
Highest point: Mount Sapitwa 9843 ft *3000 m.*
Principal river: Shire.
Head of State: Dr. Hastings Kamuzu Banda (b. 14 May 1906), President.
Climate: In the low-lying Shire valley temperatures can rise to 115 °F in October and November, but above 3000 ft the climate is much more temperate and at the greatest heights the nights can be frosty. The dry season is May to September with the very wet season from late December to March. Rainfall in the highlands is about 50 in, and in the lowlands 35 in.
Crops: Maize, groundnuts, cotton, tobacco, tea, beans, millet, rice.
Monetary unit: Malawi kwacha. 1 kwacha = 100 tambala.
Denominations:
 Coins 1, 2, 5, 10, 20 tambala.
 Notes 50 tambala, 1, 2, 5, 10 kwacha.
Exchange rate to US dollar: 0.8994 (February 1976).
Political history and government: Formerly the British protectorate of Nyasaland.

Became independent, within the Commonwealth, on 6 July 1964, taking the name Malawi. Became a republic, and a one-party state, on 6 July 1966, when Dr. Hastings Banda (Prime Minister since independence) became President. On 6 July 1971 he became President for life. Legislative power is held by the unicameral National Assembly, with 75 members (60 elected by universal adult suffrage for 5 years, subject to dissolution, and 15 nominated by the President). All members must belong to the ruling Malawi Congress Party (at the 1971 election, no voting took place as there were no opposition candidates). Executive power is vested in the President, who rules with the assistance of an appointed Cabinet. Malawi has three administrative regions, each the responsibility of a Cabinet Minister.
Telephones: 19 353 (1975).
Radio: 127 000 (1975).
Length of roadways: 7342 miles *11 814 km.*
Length of railways: 352 miles *566 km.*
University: 1.
Adult illiteracy: 77·9% (males 66·2%; females 87·7%) in 1966.
Expectation of life: Males 37·0 years; females 40·1 years (1965–70).
Defence: Total armed forces 1600.
Wildlife: Elephant, bush baby, monkeys, lion, cheetah, leopard, civet, genet, jackal, mongoose, badger, zoril, anteater, pangolin, hippopotamus, eland, waterbuck, hartebeest, zebra, otter, numerous reptiles. Over 600 species of birds.
Cinemas: 13 (seating capacity 5000) and one drive-in (1971).

MALAYSIA

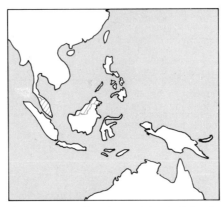

Official name: Persekutuan Tanah Melaysiu (Federation of Malaysia).
Population: 10 319 324 (1970 census); 11 700 000 (1974 est).
Area: 127 316 miles² *329 747 km².*
Languages: Malay (official), Chinese, Tamil, Iban, English.
Religions (1970): Muslim 50·0%; Buddhist 25·7%; Hindu; Christian.
Capital city: Kuala Lumpur, population 451 977 (1970).
Other principal towns (1970): George Town (Penang) 269 603; Ipoh 247 953; Johore Bahru 136 234; Klang 113 611.
Highest point: Mount Kinabalu, 13 455 ft *4101 m*, in Sabah.
Principal mountain range: Trengganu Highlands.
Principal rivers: Pahang, Kelantan.
Head of State: Tuanku Yahya Petra ibni al-Marhum Sultan Ibrahim (b. 10 Dec. 1917), Sultan of Kelantan, *Yang di-Pertuan Agong* (Supreme Head of State).
Prime Minister: Datuk Hussein bin Dato Onn (b. 12 Feb. 1922).

Climate: Average daily temperatures range between 70 °F to 90 °F, while rainfall averages about 100 in throughout the year, varying from area to area.
Crops: Rice, copra, rubber.
Monetary unit: Ringgit (Malaysian dollar). 1 ringgit = 100 cents (sen).
Denominations:
 Coins 1, 5, 10, 20, 50 cents, 1 ringgit.
 Notes 1, 5, 10, 50, 100, 1000 ringgit.
Exchange rate to US dollar: 2.56 (February 1976).
Political history and government: Peninsular (West) Malaysia comprises 11 states (nine with hereditary rulers, two with Governors) formerly under British protection. They were united as the Malayan Union on 1 Apr. 1946 and became the Federation of Malaya on 1 Feb. 1948. The Federation became independent, within the Commonwealth, on 31 Aug. 1957. On 16 Sept. 1963 the Federation (renamed the States of Malaya) was merged with Singapore (*qv*), Sarawak (a British colony) and Sabah (formerly the colony of British North Borneo) to form the independent Federation of Malaysia, still in the Commonwealth. On 9 Aug. 1965 Singapore seceded from the Federation. On 5 Aug. 1966 the States of Malaya were renamed West Malaysia, now known as Peninsular Malaysia.
 Malaysia is an elective monarchy. The nine state rulers of Peninsular Malaysia choose from their number a Supreme Head of State and a Deputy, to hold office for 5 years. Executive power is vested in the Head of State but is normally exercised on the advice of the Cabinet. Legislative power is held by the bicameral Parliament. The Senate has 58 members, including 32 appointed by the Head of State and 26 (two from each state) elected by State Legislative Assemblies. The House of Representatives has 154 members elected by universal adult suffrage for 5 years. The Head of State appoints the Prime Minister and, on the latter's recommendation, other Ministers. The Cabinet is responsible to Parliament.
 Malaysia comprises 13 states and, since 1 Feb. 1974, the Federal Territory of Kuala Lumpur. Each state has a unicameral Legislative Assembly, elected by universal adult suffrage.
Telephones: 259 405 (1975).
Daily newspapers: 39 (1972).
 Total circulation: 927 000.
Radio: 450 000 (1975).
TV: 2 612 400 (1975).
Length of roadways: 15 155 miles *24 389 km.*
Length of railways: 1127 miles *1814 km.*
Universities: 5.
Adult illiteracy: 42·0% (males 30·9%; females 53·2%) in 1970 (population aged 10 and over): Peninsular Malaysia 39·2%; Sabah 55·7%; Sarawak 61·7%.
Expectation of life: Males 55·0 years; females 58·5 years (1965–70).
Defence: Military service: voluntary. Total armed forces 61 100. Defence expenditure 1975: $445 million.
Wildlife: Elephant, rhinoceros, monkeys, tiger, leopard, snakes, lizards. Many varieties of birds.
Cinemas: 550 (seating capacity 385 000) in 1972.

MALDIVES

Official name: Divehi Jumhuriya (Republic of Maldives).
Population: 122 673 (1972 census); 128 697 (1974 est).
Area: 115 miles² *298 km².*
Languages: Divehi (Maldivian).

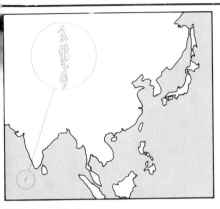

Religion: Muslim.
Capital city: Malé, population 15 740 (1974).
Head of State: Amir Ibrahim Nasir (b. 2 Sept. 1926), President and Prime Minister.
Climate: Very warm and humid. Average temperature 27 °C (80 °F), with little daily variation. Annual rainfall from 100 inches to 150 inches.
Crops: Coconuts, fruit, maize, millet.
Monetary unit: Maldivian rupee. 1 rupee = 100 larees (cents).
Exchange rate to US dollar: 7.707 (February 1976).
Political history and government: Formerly an elective sultanate, called the Maldive Islands. Under British protection, with internal self-government, from December 1887 until achieving full independence, outside the Commonwealth, on 26 July 1965. Following a referendum in March 1968, the islands became a republic on 11 Nov. 1968, with Ibrahim Nasir (Prime Minister since 1954) as President. Name changed to Maldives in April 1969. Legislative power is held by the unicameral People's Council (*Majlis*), with 48 members (40 elected for 5 years by universal adult suffrage and 8 appointed by the President). Executive power is vested in the President, elected by universal adult suffrage for 5 years. He rules with the assistance of an appointed Cabinet, responsible to the *Majlis*. The country has 19 administrative districts.
Telephones: 343 (1975).
Radio: 2457 (1975).
Wildlife: Rat, turtle, flying fox, snakes. Various types of birds.
Cinemas: 2 (seating capacity 800) in 1969.

MALI

Official name: République du Mali (Republic of Mali).
Population: 5 376 000 (1973 est).
Area: 478 822 miles² *1 240 142 km²*.
Languages: French (official language); Bambara 60%; Fulah.
Religions: Sunni Muslim 65%; traditional beliefs 30%.
Capital city: Bamako, population 310 000 (1975 est).
Other principal towns: Mopti 35 000 (1975 est); Ségou 30 000 (1975 est).
Highest point: Hombori Tondo, 3789 ft *1155 m*.
Principal mountain ranges: Mandingue Plataeu, Adrar des Iforas.
Principal rivers: Sénégal, Niger, Falémé.
Head of State: Col Moussa Traoré (b. 25 Sept. 1936), President of the Military Committee for National Liberation; also President of the Government (Prime Minister).
Climate: Hot dry climate with 2 seasons—the dry (November–June): high temperature, harmattan winds and a cool spell (77 °F *25 °C*) in December and February; wet (June to October): 'monsoon' wind from SW, main rainfall August. Sahara (N) average mean temperature 117 °F to 140 °F; rain under 2 in. Sudan (S) average mean temperature 75 °F to 86 °F; rain 20 in to 5 in. Sahel (centre) average mean temperature 73 °F to 97 °F; rain 8 in to 20 in.
Crops: Millet, rice, maize, yams, cassava, cotton, groundnuts.
Monetary unit: Franc malien.
Denominations:
  Coins 5, 10, 25 francs.
  Notes 50, 100, 500, 1000, 5000, 10 000 francs.
Exchange rate to US dollar: 448.47 (February 1976).

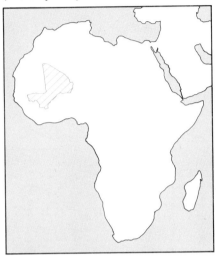

Political history and government: Formerly French Sudan, part of French West Africa. Joined Senegal to form the Federation of Mali on 4 Apr. 1959. By agreement with France, signed on 4 Apr. 1960, the Federation became independent on 20 June 1960. Senegal seceded on 20 Aug. 1960 and the remnant of the Federation was proclaimed the Republic of Mali on 22 Sept. 1960. The elected National Assembly was dissolved on 17 Jan. 1968. The government was overthrown by an army *coup* on 19 Nov. 1968, when a Military Committee for National Liberation (CMLN) was established. The constitution was abrogated and political parties banned. The CMLN rules by decree with the assistance of an appointed Council of Ministers. The President of the CMLN became also Prime Minister on 19 Sept. 1969. A new constitution, approved by referendum in June 1974, provides for a one-party state with an elected President and National Assembly, but the CMLN will remain in power for a transitional period until 1979. Mali has 19 administrative districts.
Telephones: 5062 (1969).
Daily newspapers: 3.
  Total circulation: 3000.
Radio: 81 000 (1975).
Length of roadways: 7507 miles *12 081 km*.
Length of railways: 400 miles *645 km*.
Universities: None. There is a polytechnic.
Adult illiteracy: 97·8%.
Expectation of life: Males 36·5 years; females 38·0 years (1965–70).
Defence: Total armed forces 4200.
Wildlife: Gazelle, giraffe, elephant, lion, wide variety of reptiles and birds.

MALTA

Official name: Repubblika ta Malta (Republic of Malta).

Population: 315 765 (1967 census); 325 000 (1975 est).
Area: 122 miles² *316 km²*, including Gozo (25·9 miles² *67 km²*) and Comino (1·07 miles² *2,77 km*).
Languages: Maltese, English, Italian.
Religion: Mainly Roman Catholic.
Capital city: Valletta, population 14 150 (1973 est).
Other principal town: Sliema 20 120.
Highest point: 816 ft *249 m*.
Head of State: Sir Anthony Joseph Mamo, OBE (b. 9 Jan. 1909), President.
Prime Minister: Dominic Mintoff (b. 6 Aug. 1916).
Climate: Basically healthy without extremes. The temperature rarely drops below 40 °F, and in most years does not rise above 100 °F. The average annual rainfall in Valletta is 22·7 in. In the summer the nights are cool except when the *Sirocco* desert wind blows from the south-east.
Crops: Potatoes, tomatoes, other vegetables, fruit.
Monetary unit: Maltese pound (£M). 1 pound = 100 cents = 1000 mils.
Denominations:
  Coins 2, 3, 5 mils, 1, 2, 5, 10, 50 cents
  Notes 1, 5, 10 pounds.
Exchange rate to US dollar 0.4075 (February 1976)

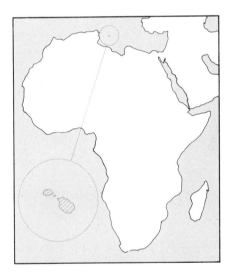

Political history and government: A former British colony. Became independent, within the Commonwealth, on 21 Sept. 1964. A republic since 13 Dec. 1974, when the Governor-General became President. Legislative power is held by the unicameral House of Representatives, with 55 members elected for 5 years (subject to dissolution) by universal adult suffrage, using proportional representation. The President is a constitutional Head of State, elected by the House, and executive power is exercised by the Cabinet. The President appoints the Prime Minister and, on the latter's recommendation, other Ministers. The Cabinet is responsible to the House.
Telephones: 48 984 (1975).
Daily newspapers: 6 (1972).
Radio: 80 000 (1975).
TV: 62 000 (1975).
Length of roadways: 774 miles *1245 km*.
Universities: 1.
Expectation of life: Males 68·64 years; females 73·06 years (1970–72).
Wildlife: Shrews, bats, weasel, rabbit, rat, mouse. Blue rock thrush, Manx shearwater, jackdaw, spectacled warbler, owls, linnet,

bunting, rock dove and many passage migrants.
Cinemas: 37 seating 30 317 (1973).

MAURITANIA

Official name: République Islamique de Mauritanie (Islamic Republic of Mauritania).
***Population:** 1 290 000 (1974 est.).
***Area:** 398 000 miles², *1 030 700 km².*
Languages: French, Arabic.
Religion: Muslim.
Capital city: Nouakchott, population 55 000 (1972 est.).
Other principal towns (1972): Nouadhibou (Port-Etienne) 20 000; F'Derik (Fort-Gouraud) 18 000; Kaédi 13 000; Rosso 13 000; Atar 10 000.
Highest point: Kediet Ijill 3002 ft *915 m.*
Principal river: Sénégal.
Head of State: Moktar Ould Daddah (b. 20 Dec. 1924), President.
Climate: Hot and dry with breezes on coast. In Nouakchott, average maximum 83 °F to 93 °F. In interior, F'Derik has average July maximum of 109 °F.
Crops: Millet, sorghum, dates, cow peas.
Monetary unit: Ouguiya. 1 ouguiya = 5 khoums.
Denominations:
Coins 1 khoum, 1, 5, 10, 20 ouguiya.
Notes 100, 200, 1000 ouguiya.
Exchange rate to US dollar: 44.20 (October 1975).
Political history and government: Excluding its share of the former Spanish Sahara, Mauritania was formerly part of French West Africa and became independent on 28 Nov. 1960. The constitution was promulgated on 20 May 1961. Since 1964 the *Parti du peuple mauritanien* (PPM) has been the only legal political party. Executive power is held by the President, elected for 5 years by universal adult suffrage (the sole candidate is appointed by the PPM). The President decides and conducts the policy of the government, assisted by an appointed Council of Ministers. Legislative power is held by the unicameral National Assembly, with 50 members elected by universal adult suffrage for 5 years from a single list of PPM candidates. On 28 Feb. 1976 Spain ceded Spanish Sahara to Mauritania and Morocco, to be apportioned between them.
Telephones: 1318 (1968).
Daily newspapers: 1.
Radio: 82 000 (1975).
Length of roadways: 4290 miles *6904 km.*
Length of railways: 404 miles *650 km.*
Adult illiteracy: 88·9%.
Expectation of life: Males 39·4 years; females 42·6 years (1965–70).

Defence: Total armed forces 1250.
Cinemas: 10 (seating capacity 1000) in 1971.
*Figures exclude Mauritania's section of the former Spanish Sahara, partitioned between Mauritania and Morocco in April 1976.

MAURITIUS

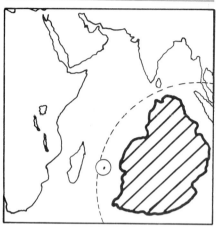

Population: 850 968 (1972 census); 872 000 (1974 est.). Figures exclude Agalega Islands and St Brandon Islands (315 in 1962).
Area: 787·5 miles² *2040 km².*
Languages (1962): Hindi 35·5%; Creole 31·0%; Urdu 13·2%; French 6·8%; Tamil 6·3%; Chinese 2·8%; Telegu 2·3%; Marathi 1·6%. The official language is English.
Religions (1962): Hindu 47·6%; Christian 35·4%; Muslim 15·8%.
Capital city: Port Louis, population 136 802 (1974 est.).
Other principal cities (1974): Beau Bassin-Rose Hill 80 829; Curepipe 52 709; Quatre Bornes 51 638; Vacoas-Phoenix 48 809.
Highest point: Piton de la Rivière Noire (Black River Mountain), 2711 ft.
Head of State: H.M. Queen Elizabeth II, represented by Sir Abdul Rahman Muhammad Osman, GCMG, CBE. (b. 29 Aug. 1902), Governor-General.
Prime Minister: The Rt. Hon Sir Seewoosagur Ramgoolam (b. 18 Sept. 1900).
Climate: Generally humid, with south-east trade winds. Average temperatures between 19 °C (66 °F) at 2,000 ft and 23 °C (75 °F) at sea-level. At Vacoas (1394 ft) maximum 37 °C (98·6 °F), minimum 8 °C (46·4 °F). Average annual rainfall between 35 in and 200 in on highest parts. Wettest months are Jan. to Mar. Tropical cyclones between Sept. and May.
Crops: Sugar cane, tea.
Monetary unit: Mauritian rupee. 1 rupee = 100 cents.
Denominations:
Coins 1, 2, 5, 10, 25, 50 cents, 1 rupee.
Notes 5, 10, 25, 50 rupees.
Exchange rate to US dollar: 6.602 (February 1976).
Political history and government: A former British colony. Became independent, within the Commonwealth, on 12 Mar. 1968. Executive power is held by the Queen and exercisable by the Governor-General, who is guided by the advice of the Cabinet. Legislative power is held by the unicameral Legislative Assembly, with 71 members: the Speaker, 62 members elected by universal adult suffrage for 5 years and 8 'additional' members (the most successful losing candidates of each community). The Governor-General appoints the Prime Minister and, on the latter's recommendation, other Ministers. The Cabinet is responsible to the Assembly.

Telephones: 22 593 (1974).
Daily newspapers: 8 French, 3 Chinese.
Total circulation: 82 000; 8250.
Radio: 84 000 (1975).
TV: 40 236 (1975).
Length of roadways: 1232 miles *1984 km.*
Universities: 1.
Adult illiteracy: 39·2% (males 28·5%; females 49·9%) in 1962 (population aged 13 and over).
Expectation of life: Males 58·66 years; females 61·86 years (island of Mauritius only) in 1961–63.
Wildlife: Monkeys, deer, wild dog, Wide variety of birds.
Cinemas: 53 (seating 52 000) in 1972.

MEXICO

Official Name: Estados Unidos Mexicanos (United Mexican States).
Population: 48 225 238 (1970 census); 60 145 258 (1975 est.).
Area: 761 605 miles² *1 972 547 km².*
Language: Spanish.
Religion: mainly Roman Catholic.
Capital city: Ciudad de México (Mexico City), population 8 591 750 (Federal District) in 1975.
Other principal towns (1975): Guadalajara 1 560 805; Monterrey 1 049 959; Ciudad Juárez 520 539; León 496 598; Puebla de Zaragoza 482 155; Tijuana 386 852; Acapulco de Juárez 352 673, Chihuahua 346 003; Mexicali 331 059; San Luis Potosí 281 534; Cuernavaca 273 986; Veracruz Llave 266 255; Torreón 251 294; Hermosillo 247 887; Culiacán Rosales 244 645; Mérida 239 222.
Highest point: Pico de Orizaba (Volcán Citlaltépetl), 18 865 ft *5750 m* (first climbed in 1848).
Principal mountain ranges: Sierra Madre Occidental, Sierra Madre Oriental, Sierra Madre del Sur.
Principal rivers: Rio Bravo del Norte (Rio Grande) (1885 miles *[3033 km]*), Balsas (Mexcala), Grijalva, Pánuco.
Head of State: Luis Echeverría Alvarez (b. 17 Jan. 1922), President.
Climate: Tropical (hot and wet) on coastal lowlands and in south, with average temperature of 64 °F. Temperate on highlands of central plateau. Arid in north and west. In Mexico City, average maximum 66 °F (December, January) to 78 °F (May), minimum 42 °F (January) to 55 °F (June), July and August rainiest (27 days each). Absolute maximum temperature 58,0 °C (*136·4 °F*), San Luis Potosí, 11 Aug. 1933; absolute minimum −28 °C (−19·3 °F), Balerio, 30 Jan. 1949.

Crops: Maize, wheat, beans, coffee, sorghum, sugar-cane, rice, cotton.
Monetary unit: Peso. 1 peso = 100 centavos.
Denominations:
Coins 1, 5, 10, 20, 50 centavos, 1, 5, 10, 25 pesos.
Notes 1, 5, 10, 20, 50, 100, 500, 1000, 10 000 pesos.
Exchange unit to US dollar: 12.50 (February 1976).
Political history and government: A federal republic of 31 states and a Federal District (around the capital). Present constitution was proclaimed on 5 Feb. 1917. Legislative power is vested in the bicameral National Congress. The Senate has 60 members (to be 64 at the next election)—two from each state and the Federal District—elected by universal adult suffrage for 6 years. The Chamber of Deputies has 222 members elected by universal adult suffrage for 3 years. Executive power is held by the President, elected for 6 years by universal adult suffrage at the same time as the Senate. He appoints and leads a cabinet to assist him. Each state is administered by a Governor (elected for 6 years) and an elected Chamber of Deputies.
Telephones: 2 546 186 (1975).
Daily newspapers: 208 (1971).
Total circulation: Nearly 5 000 000.
Radio: 16 870 000 (1973).
TV: 4 050 000 (1975).
Length of roadways: 96 126 miles *154 700 km.*
Length of railways: 12 113 miles *19 494 km.*
Universities: 42.
Adult illiteracy: 25·8% (males 21·8%; females 29·6%) in 1970.
Expectation of life: Males 61·03 years; females 63·73 years.
Defence: Military service: voluntary, with part-time conscript militia. Total armed forces 82 500 (regular). Defence expenditure 1974: $423 million.
Wildlife: Tapir, monkeys, deer, coyote, opossum, lynx, badger, sloth, armadillo, deer, bats, buffalo, jaguar, puma. Many species of birds including: Parrots, macaw, parakeets, toucan, cormorant, curlew, woodpecker, cuckoo, quail, buzzard.
Cinemas: 1726 (seating capacity 1 481 800) and 3 drive-in (1972).

MONACO

Official name: Principauté de Monaco (Principality of Monaco).
Population: 24 000 (1974 est).
Area: 0·73 miles² *1,89 km².*
Language: French.
Religion: Mainly Roman Catholic.
Capital city: Monaco-Ville, population 2422.

Other principal town: Monte Carlo 9948 (1968).
Highest point: On Chemin de Révoirés, 533 ft *162 m.*
Principal river: Vésubie.
Head of State: H.S.H. Prince Rainier III (b. 31 May 1923).
Minister of State: André Saint-Mleux.
Climate: Mediterranean, with warm summers (average July maximum 83 °F) and very mild winters (average January minimum 37 °F), 62 rainy days a year (monthly average maximum seven days in winter). Absolute maximum temperature 34 °C (*93·2 °F*) 29 June 1945 and 3 Aug. 1949; absolute minimum −2,3 °C (*27·8 °F*).
Crops: Fruit.
Monetary unit: French franc.
Political history and government: An hereditary principality, in close association with France since 2 Feb. 1861. Monaco became a constitutional monarchy on 5 Jan. 1911. The present constitution was promulgated on 17 Dec. 1962. Legislative power is held by the unicameral National Council, with 18 members elected by universal adult suffrage for 5 years. Executive power is vested in the Sovereign and exercised by a 4-man Council of Government, headed by a Minister of State. Monaco comprises 3 *quartiers.*
Telephones: 20 612 (1975).
Radio: 7500 (1975).
TV: 16 200 (1975).
Length of railways: 1 mile *1,6 km.*
Cinemas 2 (seating capacity 1100) in 1970.

MONGOLIA

Official name: Bügd Nairamdakh Mongol Ard Uls (Mongolian People's Republic).
Population: 1 403 000 (1974 est).
Area: 604 000 miles² *1 565 000 km².*
Languages: Khalkha Mongolian.
Religion: Buddhist Lamaism.
Capital city: Ulan Bator (Ulaan Baatar), population 310 000 (1974).
Other principal town: Darkhan 30 000.
Highest point: Mönh Hayrhan Uul 14 311 ft *4362 m.*
Principal mountain ranges: Altai Mts, Hangayn Nuruu.
Principal rivers: Selenge (Selenga) with Orhon, Hereleng (Kerulen).
Head of State: Marshal Yumzhagiyin Tsedenbal (b. 17 Sept. 1916), Chairman of the Presidium of the People's Great Hural and First Secretary of the Central Committee of the Mongolian People's Revolutionary Party.
Head of Government: Zhambyn Batmunkh, Chairman of the Council of Ministers.
Climate: Dry. Summers generally mild,

winters very cold. In Ulan Bator, July warmest (51 °F to 71 °F) and rainiest (10 days), January coldest (−26 °F to −2 °F).
Crops: Wheat, oats.
Monetary unit: Tugrik. 1 tugrik = 100 möngö.
Denominations:
Coins 1, 2, 10, 15, 20, 50 möngö, 1 tugrik.
Notes 1, 3, 10, 25, 50, 100 tugrik.
Exchange rate to US dollar: 3.36 (February 1976).
Political history and government: Formerly a province of China. With backing from the USSR, the Mongolian People's (Communist) Party—called the Mongolian People's Revolutionary Party (MPRP) since 1924—established a Provisional People's Government on 31 Mar. 1921. After nationalist forces, with Soviet help overthrew Chinese rule in the capital, independence was proclaimed on 11 July 1921. The USSR recognized the People's Government on 5 Nov. 1921. The Mongolian People's Republic was proclaimed on 26 Nov. 1924 but was not recognized by China. A plebiscite on 20 Oct. 1945 voted 100% for independence, recognized by China on 5 Jan. 1946. A new constitution was adopted on 6 July 1960.
The supreme organ of state power is the People's Great Hural (Assembly), with 287 members elected (unopposed) by universal adult suffrage for 4 years. The Assembly elects a Presidium (11 members) to be its permanent organ. The highest executive body is the Council of Ministers, appointed by (and responsible to) the Assembly.
Political power is held by the MPRP, the only legal party. The MPRP's highest authority is the Party Congress, which elects the Central Committee (91 full members and 61 candidate members were elected in 1976) to supervise Party work. The Committee elects a Political Bureau (8 full members and 2 candidate members) to direct its policy.
Mongolia is divided into 18 provinces and 3 municipalities.
Telephones: 27 410 (1974).
Daily newspapers: 2 (1970).
Total circulation: 133 000.
Radio: 114 000 (1975).
TV: 3500 (1975).
Length of roadways: *c.* 46 602 miles *c. 75 000 km.*
Length of railways: 885 miles *1425 km.*
Universities: 1.
Adult illiteracy: 4·6% (population aged 9 to 50) in 1956.
Expectation of life: Males 56·3 years; females 59·8 years (1965–70).
Defence: Military service: 2 years. Total armed forces 30 000. Defence expenditure 1975: $112 million.
Wildlife: Przewalski's horse (diminishing species of wild horse), elk, lynx, hare, antelope, wild ass, gazelle. Snowy owl, golden eagle, grouse, quail, sparrow hawk, finch, waxwing.
Cinemas: 17 fixed, 446 mobile (1970).

MOROCCO

Official name: al-Mamlaka al-Maghrebia (Kingdom of Morocco).
*Population: 16 880 000 (1974 est).
*Area: 177 116 miles² *458 730 km².*
Languages: Arabic, Berber.
Religions: Muslim, Christian minority.
Capital city: Rabat, population 435 510 (1971), including Salé.
Other principal cities (1971): Casablanca (Ad Dar al Baida) 1 371 330; Merrakech (Marrakesh) 330 400; Fès (Fez) 321 460; Meknès 244 520; Tanger (Tangier) 185 850; Oujda 155 800; Tétouan 137 080; Kénitra 135 960; Safi 129 100.

Highest point: Jebel Toubkal, 13 665 ft *4165 m* (first climbed in 1923).
Principal mountain ranges: Haut (Grand) Atlas, Moyen (Middle) Atlas, Anti Atlas.
Principal rivers: Oued Dra (335 miles *539 km*), Oued Oum-er-Rbia, Oued Moulouya (320 miles *515 km*), Sebou (280 miles *450 km*).
Head of State: H.M. King Hassan II (b. 9 July 1929).
Prime Minister: Dr. Ahmed Osman (b. 3 Jan. 1930).
Climate: Semi-tropical. Warm and sunny on coast, very hot inland. Rainy season November to March. Absolute maximum temperature 51,7 °C (*125·0 °F*), Agadir, 17 Aug. 1940; absolute minimum −24 °C (*−11·2 °F*), Ifrane, 11 Feb. 1935.
Crops: Barley, wheat, citrus fruit, tomatoes pulses, maize, grapes, olives, potatoes, sugar beet.
Monetary unit: Dirham. 1 dirham = 100 centimes.
Denominations:
Coins 1, 2, 5, 10, 20, 50 centimes, 1 dirham.
Notes 5, 10, 50, 100 dirhams.
Exchange rate to US dollar: 4.253 (February 1976).
Political history and government: An hereditary monarchy, formerly ruled by a Sultan. Most of Morocco (excluding the former Spanish Sahara) became a French protectorate on 30 Mar. 1912. A smaller part in the north became a Spanish protectorate on 27 Nov. 1912. Tangier became an international zone on 18 Dec. 1923. The French protectorate became independent on 2 Mar. 1956 and was joined by the Spanish protectorate on 7 Apr. 1956. The Tangier zone was abolished on 29 Oct. 1956. The Sultan became King on 18 Aug. 1957. The northern strip of Spanish Sahara was ceded to Morocco on 10 Apr. 1958 and the Spanish enclave of Ifni was ceded on 30 June 1969. On 28 Feb. 1976 the rest of Spanish Sahara was ceded to Morocco and Mauritania, to be apportioned between them.

A new constitution, approved by referendum on 1 Mar. 1972 and promulgated on 10 Mar. 1972, provides for a modified constitutional monarchy. Legislative power is vested in a unicameral Chamber of Representatives, with 240 members elected for 4 years (160 by direct universal adult suffrage and 80 by an electoral college). The former Chamber was dissolved in 1972 but no date has been set for elections to the new Chamber. Executive power is vested in the King, who appoints (and may dismiss) the Prime Minister and other members of the Cabinet. The King can also dissolve the Chamber.

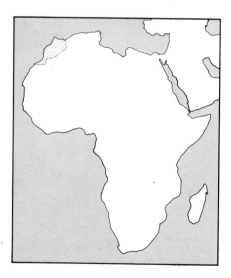

Telephones: 189 000 (1975).
Daily newspapers: 11 (1972).
Total circulation: 234 000 (8 dailies)
Radio: 1 600 000 (1975).
TV: 459 700 (1975).
Length of roadways: 15 792 miles *25 414 km.*
Length of railways: 1091 miles *1756 km.*
Universities: 2.
Adult illiteracy: 78·6% (males 66·4%; females 90·2%) in 1971.
Expectation of life: Males 49.0 years; females 51·8 years (1965–70).
Defence: Military service: 18 months. Total armed forces 61 000. Defence expenditure 1974: $190 million.
Wildlife: Gazelle, jackal, reptiles and rodents.
Cinemas: 196 (seating 107 700) in 1967.

*Figures exclude Morocco's section of the former Spanish Sahara, partitioned between Mauritania and Morocco in April 1976.

MOZAMBIQUE

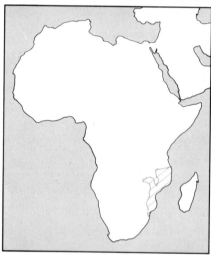

Official name: A República Popular de Moçambique (The People's Republic of Mozambique).
Population: 8 233 978 (1970 census); 8 519 000 (1972 est.).
Area: 302 329 miles²; *783 030 km²*
Languages: Portuguese (official), many African languages.
Religions: Animist, Christian and Muslim minorities.
Capital city: Maputo (formerly Lourenço Marques), population 500 000 (1974 est.).
Other principal towns: Sofala (formerly Beira) 150 000 plus; Nacala, Moçambique.
Highest point: Monte Binga, 7992 ft *2436 m.*
Principal mountain range: Lebombo Range.
Principal rivers: Limpopo, Zambezi, Rovuma, Shire.
Head of State: Samora Moïsés Machel (b. Oct. 1933), President.
Climate: Varies from tropical to sub-tropical except in a few upland areas. Rainfall is irregular but the rainy season is usually from November to March, with an average temperature of 83 °F in Maputo. In the dry season, average temperatures are from 65 °F to 68 °F.
Crops: Maize, sugar cane, cashew nuts (world's leading producer), rice, cotton.
Monetary unit: Mozambique escudo, 1 escudo = 100 centavos.
Denominations:
Coins 10, 20, 50 centavos, 1, 2½, 5, 10, 20 escudos.
Notes 50, 100, 500, 1000 escudos.

Exchange rate to US dollar: 27.75 (February 1976).
Political history and government: Formerly a Portuguese colony, independent since 25 June 1975. The independence movement was dominated by the *Frente de Libertação de Moçambique* (FRELIMO), the Mozambique Liberation Front. Before independence FRELIMO was recognized by Portugal and its leader became the first President. The independence constitution proclaims that FRELIMO is the directing power of the state and of society. Legislative power is vested in the People's Assembly, with 210 members, mainly FRELIMO officials, to be indirectly elected during the year after the third FRELIMO Congress. The President appoints and leads a Council of Ministers. Mozambique has 11 provinces.
Telephones: 55 708 (1975).
Daily newspapers: 4.
Total circulation: 45 000.
Radio: 200 000 (1975).
TV: 1000 (1974).
Length of roadways: 23 043 miles *37 085 km.*
Length of railways: 2301 miles *3703 km.*
Universities: 1
Adult illiteracy: 85–95% (est.).
Expectation of life: Males 39·4 years; females 42·6 years (1965–70).
Defence: National Defence Force.
Wildlife: Lion, other large cats, elephant, hippopotamus, rhinoceros, buffalo, zebra, wide variety of antelope, snakes and birds.
Cinemas: 31 (seating capacity 20 195) in 1971.

NAURU

Official name: The Republic of Nauru.
Population: 6057 (1966 census); 6768 (1972 est.).
Area: 8·2 miles² *21 km².*
Languages: English, Nauruan.
Religions: Protestant, Roman Catholic.
Highest point: 225 ft *68 m.*
Head of State: Hammer de Roburt, OBE (b. 25 Sept. 1922), President.
Monetary unit: Australian currency (*qv*).
Political history and government: Annexed by Germany in October 1888. Captured by Australian forces in November 1914. Administered by Australia under League of Nations mandate (17 Dec. 1920) and later as a UN Trust Territory. Independent since 31 Jan. 1968. The Head Chief was elected President on 19 May 1968. Legislative power is held by a unicameral Parliament, with 18 members elected by universal adult suffrage for up to 3 years. Executive power is held by the President, who is elected by Parliament for its duration and rules with the assistance of an appointed Cabinet, responsible to Parliament. Nauru is a 'special member' of the Commonwealth.
Length of roadways: 12 miles *19 km.*
Length of railways: 3¼ miles *5 km.*
Cinemas: 3 (seating capacity 1000) in 1970.
Radio: 3600 (1975)

NEPAL

Official name: Sri Nepāla Sarkār (Kingdom of Nepal).
Population: 11 555 983 (1971 census); 12 321 000 (1974 est.).
Area: 54 362 miles² *140 798 km².*
Languages (1971): Nepali (official) 52·4%; Maithir 11·5%; Bhojpuri 7·0%; Tamang 4·8%; Tharu 4·3%; Newari 3·9%; Abadhi 2·7%; Magar 2·5%; Raikirati 2·0%.
Religions (1971): Hindu 89·4%; Buddhist 7·5%; Muslim 3·0%.

Capital city: Katmandu, population 150 402 (1971); 353 756 (incl. suburbs).
Other principal towns (1971, including suburbs): Morang 301 557; Lalitpur 154 998; Patan 135 230; Bhaktapur 110 157.
Highest point: Mount Everest, 29 028 ft *8848 m* (on Chinese border). First climbed 29 May 1953.
Principal mountain range: Nepal Himalaya (Mahabharat Range).
Principal rivers: Karnali, Naryani, Kosi.
Head of State: H.M. King Birenda Bir Bikram Shah Dev (b. 28 Dec. 1945).
Prime Minister: Dr. Tulsi Giri (b. Sept. 1926).
Climate: Varies sharply with altitude, from Arctic in Himalaya to humid subtropical in the central Vale of Katmandu (annual average 52 °F), which is warm and sunny in summer. Rainy season June to October. In Katmandu, average maximum 65 °F (January) to 86 °F (May), minimum 35 °F (January) to 68 °F (July, August), July (21 days) and August (20 days) rainiest. Maximum temperature recorded in Katmandu is 99 °F (2 May 1960) and minimum is 26 °F (20 Jan. 1964).
Crops: Rice, maize, millet, wheat, herbs.

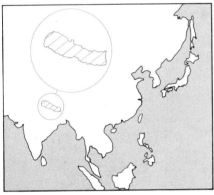

Monetary unit: Nepalese rupee. 1 rupee = 100 paisa.
Denominations:
   Coins 1, 2, 5, 10, 25, 50 paisa, 1 rupee.
   Notes 1, 5, 10, 100, 500, 1000 rupees.
Exchange rate to US dollar: 12.525 (February 1976).
Political history and government: A hereditary kingdom. A limited constitutional monarchy was proclaimed on 18 Feb. 1951. Political parties were banned in December 1960. Present constitution adopted on 16 Dec. 1962. Executive power is vested in the King but is normally exercised on the advice of an appointed Council of Ministers. Legislative power is held by the unicameral National Panchayat, with 135 members (112 indirectly elected by zonal assemblies for staggered 4-year terms and 23 nominated by the King). All Ministers must be members of the National Panchayat. Nepal comprises 14 zones, each administered by an appointed Commissioner.
Telephones: 9162 (1974).
Daily newspapers: 26 (1972).
   Total circulation: c. 39 000.
Radio: 80 000 (1975).
Length of roadways: *c.* 500 miles *c. 804 km.*
Length of railways: 63 miles *101 km.*
Universities: 1.
Adult illiteracy: 87·5% (males 77·6%; females 97·4%) in 1971.
Expectation of life: Males 39·2 years; females 42·0 years (1965–70).
Defence: Military service; voluntary. Total armed forces 20 000. Defence expenditure, 1973–74: $8 million.
Wildlife: Antelope, wild boar, panther, elephant, crocodile, rhinoceros, bear, mountain sheep.

THE NETHERLANDS (Holland)

Official name: Koninkrijk der Nederlanden (Kingdom of the Netherlands).
Population: 13 045 785 (1971 census); 13 654 000 (1975 est).
Area: 15 892 miles² *41 160 km².*
Language: Dutch.
Religions: Roman Catholic, Dutch Reformed Church.
Capital city: Amsterdam, population 757 958 (1975). The seat of government is 's Gravenhage (Den Haag or The Hague), population 482 879 (1975).
Other principal towns (1975): Rotterdam 620 867; Utrecht 256 016; Eindhoven 192 042; Haarlem 165 861; Groningen 164 726; Tilburg 152 112; Nijmegen 147 810; Enschede 141 061; Apeldoorn 132 028; Arnhem 126 235; Zaanstad 124 549; Maastricht 111 588; Breda 110 001; Dordrecht 101 117.
Highest point: Vaalserberg, 1053 ft *321 m.*
Principal rivers: Maas (Meuse), Waal (Rhine) (820 miles *1319 km*), IJssel.
Head of State: H.M. Queen Juliana Louise Emma Marie Wilhelmina, KG (b. 30 Apr. 1909).
Prime Minister: Dr Johannes ('Joop') Marten den Uyl (b. 9 Aug. 1919).
Climate: Temperate, generally between 0 °F and 70 °F. Often foggy and windy. In Amsterdam, average maximum 40 °F (January) to 69 °F (July), minimum 34 °F (January, February) to 59 °F (July, August). November, December, January rainiest (each 19 days). Absolute maximum temperature 38,6 °C (*101·5 °F*), Warnsveld, 23 Aug. 1944; absolute minimum −27,4 °C (−17·3 °F), Winterswijk, 27 Jan. 1942.
Crops: Sugar-beet, potatoes, wheat, rye, oats, barley.
Monetary unit: Netherlands gulden (guilder) or florin. 1 guilder = 100 cents.
Denominations:
   Coins 1, 5, 10, 25 cents, 1, 2½, 10 guilders.
   Notes 1, 2½, 5, 10, 25, 100, 1000 guilders.
Exchange rate to US dollar: 2.67 (February 1976).
Political history and government: A constitutional and hereditary monarchy. Legislative power is held by the bicameral States-General. The First Chamber has 75 members indirectly elected for 6 years (half retiring every 3 years) by members of the 11 Provincial Councils. The Second Chamber has 150 members directly elected by universal suffrage for 4 years (subject to dissolution), using proportional representation. The Head of State has mainly formal prerogatives and executive power is exercised by the Council of Ministers, led by the Prime Minister, which is responsible to the States-General. Each of the 11 provinces is administered by an appointed Governor and an elected Council.
Telephones: 4 678 945 (1975).
Daily newspapers: 93 (1971).
   Total circulation: 4 100 000.
Radio: 3 845 000 (1974).
TV: 3 601 020 (1975).
Length of roadways: 51 497 miles *82 877 km.*
Length of railways: 1760 miles *2834 km.*
Universities: 7 (plus 3 technical universities and 4 colleges of university standing).
Expectation of life: Males 70·8 years; females 76·8 years (1972).
Defence: Military service: Army 16–18 months, Navy and Air Force 18–21 months. Total armed forces 112 500 (regular). Defence expenditure 1975: $2936 million.
Wildlife: Deer, fox, pine marten, tree frog, dormouse, lizard, red deer. Marsh and water birds, including purple heron, bearded tit.
Cinemas: 381 with seating capacity of 176 500 (1973).

NEW ZEALAND

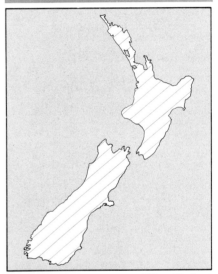

Official name: Dominion of New Zealand.
Population: 2 862 631 (1971 census); 3 076 000 (1975 est).
Area: 103 736 miles² *268 675 km².*
Languages: English, Maori.
Religions: Church of England, Presbyterian, Roman Catholic.
Capital city: Wellington, population 141 800 (1974 est); 354 660, including suburbs, in 1975.
Other principal towns (including suburbs, 1974): Auckland 775 460; Christchurch 320 530; Hamilton 147 450; Dunedin 119 870; Napier-Hastings 105 460; Palmerston North 85 270.
Highest point: Mt Cook, 12 349 ft *3764 m.*
Principal mountain range: Southern Alps.
Principal rivers: Waikato, Clutha (210 miles [*338 km*]), Waihou, Rangitaiki, Mokau, Wanganui, Rangitikei, Manawatu.
Head of State: H.M. Queen Elizabeth II, represented by Sir (Edward) Denis Blundell, GCMG, GCVO, KBE (b. 29 May 1907), Governor-General.
Prime Minister: The Rt Hon Robert David Muldoon (b. 21 Sept. 1921).
Climate: Temperate and moist. Moderate temperatures (annual average 52 °F) except in the hotter far north. Small seasonal variations. In Wellington, January and February warmest (56 °F to 69 °F), July coolest (42 °F to 53 °F) and rainiest (18 days), February driest (nine days). In Auckland,

213

average maximum 56 °F (July) to 73 °F (January, February), minimum 46 °F (July, August) to 60 °F (January, February), July rainiest (21 days).

Crops: Wheat, barley, potatoes, maize.

Monetary unit: New Zealand dollar ($NZ). 1 dollar = 100 cents.

Denominations:
Coins 1, 2, 5, 10, 20, 25, 50 cents.
Notes 1, 2, 5, 10, 20, 100 dollars.

Exchange rate to US dollar: 0.955 (February 1976).

Political history and government: A former British colony. Became a dominion under the British crown, on 26 Sept. 1907. Fully independent, within the Commonwealth, under the Statute of Westminster, passed by the British Parliament in December 1931 and accepted by New Zealand on 25 Nov. 1947. Executive power is vested in the Queen and exercisable by the Governor-General, who must be guided by the advice of the Executive Council (Cabinet), led by the Prime Minister. Legislative power is held by the unicameral House of Representatives, with 87 members (including 4 Maoris) elected for 3 years by universal adult suffrage. The Governor-General appoints the Prime Minister and, on the latter's recommendation, other Ministers. The Cabinet is responsible to the House.

Telephones: 1 494 587 (1975).

Daily newspapers: 40 (1972).

Radio: 2 704 000 (1975).

TV: 798 778 (1975).

Length of roadways: 57 169 miles 92 005 km.

Length of railways: 2982 miles 4799 km.

Universities: 6.

Expectation of life: Males 68·19 years; females 74·30 years.

Defence: Military service: voluntary, supplemented by Territorial service of 12 weeks for the Army. Total armed forces 12 685. Defence expenditure 1975–6 $233 million.

Wildlife: Lizards, opossom, bats, turtles. Birds decreasing in number; the kiwi now very rare.

Cinemas: 239 (seating capacity 144 000) and 5 part-time (capacity 500) in 1972.

Principal mountain ranges: Cordillera Isabelia, Cordillera de Darién.

Principal rivers: Coco (Segovia) (300 miles [482 km]), Rio Grande, Escondido, San Juan.

Head of State: Gen. Anastásio Somoza Debayle (b. 5 Dec. 1925), President.

Climate: Tropical (hot and humid) with average annual temperature of 78 °F. Rainy season May–December. Annual rainfall 100 in on east coast. In Managua, annual average over 80 °F all year round.

Crops: Maize, cotton, sugar cane, beans, rice, coffee.

Monetary unit: Córdoba. 1 córdoba = 100 centavos.

Denominations:
Coins 5, 10, 25, 50 centavos, 1 córdoba.
Notes 1, 5, 10, 20, 50, 100, 500, 1000 córdobas.

Exchange rate to US dollar: 7.026 (February 1976).

Political history and government: A republic comprising 16 departments and one territory. A new constitution was promulgated in April 1974 but constitutional guarantees were suspended in 1975. Legislative power is vested in the bicameral Congress, comprising a Senate of 30 members and a Chamber of Deputies (70 members). Executive power is held by the President, elected by universal adult suffrage for 6 years. He appoints and leads a Council of Ministers.

Telephones: 20 447 (1975).

Daily newspapers: 7.
Total circulation: 75 000.

Radio: 700 000 (1975).

TV: 70 000 (1975).

Length of roadways: 8169 miles 13 147 km.

Length of railways: 198 miles 318 km.

Universities: 2.

Adult illiteracy: 50·2% (males 49·9%; females 50·4%) in 1963.

Expectation of life: Males 48·9 years; females 52·1 years (1965–70).

Defence: Total armed forces 7100.

Wildlife: Jaguar, peccary, armadillo, deer, alligator; many species of snakes and monkeys. Macaw.

Cinemas: Over 100 with seating capacity of over 60 000 (1965).

Religions: Muslim 85%; Animist, Christian.

Capital city: Niamey, population 121 900 (1973 est).

Other principal towns (1972: Zinder 39 000; Maradi 37 000; Tahoua 31 000.

Highest point: Mont Gréboun 6562 ft 2000 m.

Principal mountain ranges: Aïr ou Azbine, Plateau du Djado.

Principal rivers: Niger (370 miles 595 km in Niger) Dillia.

Head of State: Lt-Col Seyni Kountché (b. 1930), President of the Supreme Military Council.

Climate: Hot and dry. Average temperature 84 °F. In Niamey, average maximum 93 °F (January) to 108 °F (April).

Crops: Millet, sorghum, cassava, groundnuts, beans.

Monetary unit: Franc de la Communauté financière africaine.

Denominations:
Coins 1, 2, 5, 10, 25, 50, 100 CFA francs.
Notes 100, 500, 1000, 5000 CFA frans.

Exchange rate to US dollar: 224.24 (February 1976).

Political history and government: Formerly part of French West Africa, independent since 3 Aug. 1960. Under military rule since 15 Apr. 1974, when the constitution was suspended and the National Assembly dissolved. Niger is ruled by a Supreme Military Council, composed of army officers, which has appointed a provisional government. The country has 16 administrative districts.

Telephones: 4000 (1971).

Daily newspapers: 1 (1971).
Total circulation: 2000.

Radio: 100 000 (1975).

Length of roadways: 4349 miles 6998 km.

Universities: 1.

Adult illiteracy: 96% (est).

Expectation of life: Males 37·0 years; females 40·2 years (1965–70).

Defence: Total armed forces 2100.

Cinemas: 4 (seating capacity 3800) in 1970.

NICARAGUA

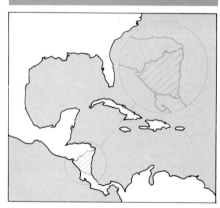

Official name: República de Nicaragua.

Population: 1 877 952 (1971 census); 2 084 000 (1974 est).

Area: 49 759 miles² 128 875 km².

Language: Spanish.

Religion: Roman Catholic.

Capital city: Managua, population 398 514 (1971).

Other principal towns: León 119 347; Granada 100 334; Masaya 96 830; Chinandega 95 437; Matagalpa 65 928.

Highest point: Pico Mogotón (6913 ft 2107 m).

NIGER

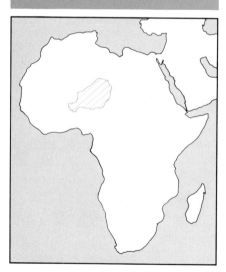

Official name: République du Niger.

Population: 4 476 000 (1974 est).

Area: 458 075 miles² 1 186 408 km².

Languages: French (official), Hausa, Tuareg, Djerma, Fulani.

NIGERIA

Official name: The Federal Republic of Nigeria.

Population: 62 925 000 (UN estimate for mid-1975).

Area: 356 669 miles² 923 768 km².

Languages: English (official), Hausa, Ibo, Yoruba and other linguistic groups.

Religions: Muslim, Christian.

Capital city: Lagos, population 900 969 (with suburbs 1 476 837) in 1971.

Other principal towns (1971): Ibadan 758 332; Ogbomosho 386 650; Kano 357 098; Oshogbo 252 583; Ilorin 252 076; Abeokuta 226 361; Port Harcourt 217 043; Zaria 200 850; Ilesha 200 434; Onitsha 197 062; Iwo 191 684; Ado-Ekiti 190 398; Kaduna 181 201; Mushin 176 446.

Highest point: Dimlang, 6700 ft 2042 m.

Principal rivers: Niger (2600 miles [4184 km] in total length), Benue, Cross.

Head of State: Lt-Gen Olusegun Obasanjo (b. 1937), Head of the Federal Military Government and Commander-in-Chief of the Armed Forces.

Climate: On the coast it is hot (average daily maximum temperature at Lagos 89 °F) and unpleasantly humid. In the north it is drier and semi-tropical. Annual rainfall ranges from 25 to 150 inches.

Crops: Yams, cassava, sorghum, millet, taro, maize, cow peas, palm kernels and oil, groundnuts, cocoa.

Monetary unit: Naira. 1 naira = 100 kobo.
Denominations:
  Coins ½, 1, 5, 10, 25 kobo.
  Notes 50 kobo, 1, 5, 10 naira.
Exchange rate to US dollar: 0.619 (February 1976). ·
Political history and government: Formerly a British dependency. Independent, within the Commonwealth, since 1 Oct. 1960. Became a republic on 1 Oct. 1963. Under military rule since 15 Jan. 1966, when the bicameral Federal Parliament was abolished. Political parties were banned on 24 May 1966. Legislative and executive functions are vested in the Supreme Military Council (SMC), which rules by decree. The SMC's Chairman is Head of State and Government. The SMC delegates powers to the Federal Executive Council, with Commissioners in charge of government Ministries. Nigeria comprises 12 States, each administered by a Military Governor.
Telephones: 111 478 (1975).
Daily newspapers: 17 (1972).
  Total circulation: 238 000 (8 dailies).
Radio: 5 000 000 (1975).
TV: 100 000 (1975).

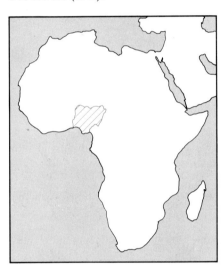

Length of roadways: 55 240 miles *88 900 km.*
Length of railways: 2178 miles *3505 km.*
Universities: 6.
Adult illiteracy: 88·5% in 1952–53 (population aged 7 and over).
Expectation of life: Males 36·9 years; females 40·1 years (1965–70).
Defence: Military service: voluntary. Total armed forces 208 000. Defence expenditure 1975–6: $1786 million.
Wildlife: Lion, leopard, lizard, crocodile, black cobra, green mamba, gorilla, chimpanzee, monkeys, hippopotamus, manatee, elephant, giraffe, gazelle, hartebeest. Many hundreds of species of birds including: parrots, weaver bird, snowbird, hornbill, ostrich, storks, bustards, guinea fowl, ducks, geese.
Cinemas: 105 with seating capacity of 106 000 (1967).

NORWAY

Official name: Kongeriket Norge (Kingdom of Norway).
Population: 3 874 133 (1970 census); 4 003 000 (1975 est).
Area: 125 053 miles² *323 886 km².*
Languages: Norwegian; small Lappish minority.

Religion: Lutheran.
Capital city: Oslo, population 464 900 (1975).
Other principal towns (1975): Bergen 213 992; Trondheim 134 037; Stavanger 85 613; Kristiansand 59 258; Drammen 50 776.
Highest point: Glittertinden (8110 ft *2472 m*).
Principal mountain range: Langfjellene.
Principal rivers: Glomma (Glama) (380 miles *611 km*), Lågen (224 miles *360 km*), Tanaelv (213 miles *342 km*).
Head of State: HM King Olav V, KG, KT, GCB, GCVO (b. 2 July 1903).
Prime Minister: Odvar Nordli (b. 3 Nov. 1927).

Climate: Temperate on coast, but cooler inland. In Oslo, average maximum 30 °F (January) to 73 °F (July), minimum 20 °F (January, February) to 56 °F (July), August rainiest (11 days). Absolute maximum temperature 35,0 °C (*95·0 °F*), Oslo, 21 July 1901, and Trondheim, 22 July 1901; absolute minimum −51,4 °C (*−60·5 °F*), Karasjok, 1 Jan. 1886.
Crops: Potatoes, barley, oats.
Monetary unit: Norwegian krone. One krone = 100 øre.
Denominations:
  Coins 1, 2, 5, 10, 25, 50 øre. 1, 5 kroner.
  Notes 5, 10, 50, 100, 500, 1000 kroner.
Exchange rate to US dollar: 5.532 (Feb. 1976).
Political history and government: Formerly linked with Sweden. Independence declared on 7 June 1905; union with Sweden ended on 26 Oct. 1905. Norway is a constitutional monarchy, headed by an hereditary King. Legislative power is held by the unicameral Parliament (*Storting*), with 155 members elected for 4 years by universal adult suffrage, using proportional representation. The members choose one quarter of their number to form the *Lagting* (upper house), the remainder forming the *Odelsting* (lower house). Executive power is nominally held by the King but is exercised by the Council of Ministers, appointed by the King in accordance with the will of the *Storting*, to which the Council is responsible. Norway comprises 19 counties.
Telephones: 1 355 142 (1975).
Daily newspapers: 75 (1974).
  Total circulation: 1 566 000.
Radio: 1 276 784 (1974).
TV: 1 021 004 (1974).
Length of roadways: 46 476 miles *74 796 km.*
Length of railways: 2635 miles *4240 km.*
Universities: 4, and 6 institutions equivalent to universities.
Expectation of life: Males 71·24 years; females 77·43 years.

Defence: Military service: Army 12 months, Navy and Air Force 15 months. Total armed forces 35 000 (regular); Defence expenditure 1975: $871 million.
Wildlife: Hare, fox, deer, bear, lynx, wolf and elk, all rapidly diminishing. Lemming, seal. Wood fowl, black grouse, woodcock, snipe, partridge, snowy owl, puffin, kittiwake.
Cinemas: 450 (seating capacity 145 100) in 1971.

OMAN

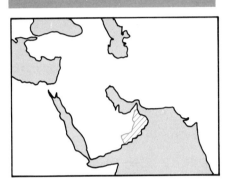

Official name: Sultanat 'Uman.
Population: 600 000 (1972 est).
Area: 82 000 miles² *212 457 km²* (est).
Language: Arabic.
Religion: Muslim.
Capital city: Masqat (Muscat), population 25 000 (with port of Matrah).
Other principal towns: Matrah (14 000 in 1960); Salalah.
Highest point: Jabal ash Sham 10 400 ft *3170 m.*
Principal mountain range: Jabal Akhdas ('Green Mountains').
Head of State: Sultan Qaboos bin Said (b. 18 Nov. 1940).
Climate: Extremely hot summers (temperatures rising to 130 °F) and mild winters. Cooler in the mountains. Average annual rainfall 3 to 6 in.
Crops: Dates, limes.
Monetary unit: Rial Omani. 1 rial = 1000 baiza.
Denominations:
  Coins 2, 5, 10, 25, 50, 100 baiza.
  Notes 100, 250, 500 biaza, 1, 5, 10 rials.
Exchange rate to US dollar: 0.3454 (February 1976).
Political history and government: A sultanate, formerly called Muscat and Oman, under British influence since the 19th century. Full independence was recognised by the treaty of friendship with the UK on 20 Dec. 1951. The present Sultan deposed his father on 23 July 1970 and the country adopted its present name on 9 Aug. 1970. The Sultan is an absolute ruler and legislates by decree. He is advised by an appointed Cabinet. The country has no parliament and no political parties. Oman is divided into 37 *wilayet* (governorates).
Telephones: 4 300 (1975).
Length of roadways: 600 miles *965 km* (mainly minor roads).
Defence: Military service: voluntary. Total armed forces 14 100. Defence expenditure, 1975: $359 million.

PAKISTAN

Official name: The Islamic Republic of Pakistan ('Pakistan' means 'land of the pure' in the Urdu language).

215

*Population: 64 892 000 (1972 census); 68 214 000 (1974 est).
*Area: 310 403 miles² *803 943 km²*.
Languages: Punjabi, Urdu, Sindhi, Pushtu.
Religions: Muslim 97·1%; Hindu 1·6%; Christian 1·3% (1961).
Capital city: Islamabad, population 77 000 (1972).
Other principal towns (1972): Karachi 3 469 000; Lahore 2 148 000; Lyallpur 820 000; Hyderabad 624 000; Rawalpindi 615 000; Multan 544 000; Gujranwala 366 000; Peshawar 273 000.
Highest point: K2 (Mt Godwin Austen), 28 250 ft *8611 m* (first climbed 31 July 1954).
Principal mountain ranges: Hindu Kush, Pamirs, Karakoram.
Principal rivers: Indus and tributaries (Sutlej, Chenab, Ravi, Jhelum).

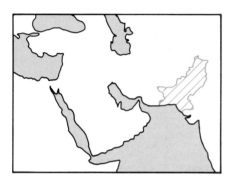

Head of State: Fazal Elahi Chaudhry (b. 1904), President.
Prime Minister: Zulfiqar Ali Bhutto (b. 5 Jan. 1928).
Climate: Dry, and generally hot, with average temperature of 80 °F except in the mountains, which have very cold winters. Temperatures range from 30 °F in winter to 120 °F in summer. In Karachi, June warmest (average 82 °F to 93 °F), January coolest (55 °F to 77 °F), rainfall negligible throughout the year. In Lahore, average maximum 69 °F (January) to 106 °F (June), minimum 40 °F (December, January) to 80 °F (July), July and August rainiest (each six days). Absolute maximum temperature 127·0 °F (*52,8 °C*), Jacobabad, 12 June 1919.
Crops: Wheat, rice, sugar cane, cotton.
Monetary unit: Pakistani rupee. 1 rupee = 100 paisa.
Denominations:
Coins 1, 2, 5, 10, 25, 50 paisa, 1 rupee.
Notes 1, 5, 10, 50, 100 rupees.
Exchange rate to US dollar: 9.894 (February 1976).
Political history and government: Pakistan was created as an independent dominion within the Commonwealth on 15 Aug. 1947, when former British India was partitioned. Originally in two parts, East and West Pakistan, the country became a republic on 23 Mar. 1956. Military rule was imposed on 27 Oct. 1958. Elections for a Constituent Assembly were held on 7 Dec. 1970, giving a majority to the Awami League, which sought autonomy for East Pakistan. After negotiations on a coalition government failed, East Pakistan declared independence as Bangladesh on 26 Mar. 1971. Following Indian intervention on behalf of the Bengalis, Pakistan's forces surrendered on 16 Dec. 1971, when Bangladesh's independence became a reality. Pakistan was confined to the former western wing. Military rule ended on 20 Dec. 1971. Pakistan left the Commonwealth on 30 Jan. 1972. A new constitution came into force on 14 Aug. 1973. Pakistan is a federal republic comprising four provinces (each under a Governor) plus the Federal Capital Territory and 'tribal areas' under federal administration. The bicameral Federal Legislature comprises a mainly advisory Senate (45 members, mostly elected by provincial assemblies) and a National Assembly of 210 members (200 directly elected by universal adult suffrage for 5 years and 10 women elected by the Assembly). The constitution provides for an increase in Senate membership to 63. The chief executive is the Prime Minister, elected by the Assembly. His advice is binding on the President, a constitutional Head of State elected at a joint sitting of the Legislature. The Prime Minister and his appointed Cabinet are answerable to the Legislature. Each province has its own elected Assembly, a Chief Minister and a Cabinet.
Telephones: 195 325 (1973).
Daily newspapers: 71 (1972).
Radio: 1 100 000 (1975).
TV: 250 000 (1975).
Length of roadways: 39 022 miles *62 800 km*.
Length of railways: 5475 miles *8811 km*.
Universities: 8.
Adult illiteracy: 81·2% (males 71·1%; females 92·6%) in 1961 (including Bangladesh).
Expectation of life: Males 47·4 years; females 47·3 years (1965–70).
Defence: Military Service: two years, selective. Total armed forces 392 000. Defence expenditure, 1975–6: $722 million.
Wildlife: Himalayan bear, snow leopard, buffalo.
Cinemas: 578 (seating capacity 300 000) and one drive-in (1972).
* Excluding the disputed territory of Jammu and Kashmir. The Pakistan-held part has an area of 32 358 sq miles (*83 807 sq km*).

PANAMA

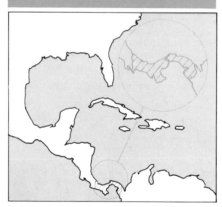

Official name: La República de Panamá.
*Population: 1 428 082 (1970 census); 1 667 700 (1975 est).
*Area: 29 209 miles² *75 650 km²*.
Language: Spanish.
Religions: Roman Catholic, Protestant minority.
Capital city: Panamá (City), population 392 000 (1974 est).
Other principal town: Colón 63 500 (1966).
Highest point: Volcán de Chiriquí, 11 410 ft *3477 m*.
Principal mountain ranges: Serrania de Tabasará, Cordillera de San Blas.
Principal rivers: Tuira (with Chucunaque), Bayano, Santa Maria.
Head of State: Demetrio Basilio Lakas Bahas (b. 29 Aug. 1925), President.
Chief of Government: Brig-Gen Omar Torrijos Herrera (b. 13 Feb. 1929).
Climate: Warm, humid days with cool nights. Little seasonal temperature change. Absolute maximum temperature 98·0 °F (*36,7 °C*) at Madden Dam, Canal Zone, 13 Apr. 1920, and Panamá (City), 16 Apr. 1958; absolute minimum 59·0 °F (*15,0 °C*) at Madden Dam, Canal Zone, 4 Feb. 1924.
Crops: Rice, maize, bananas, sugar, coffee.
Monetary unit: Balboa. 1 balboa = 100 centésimos.
Denominations:
Coins 1, 5, 10, 25, 50 centésimos, 1 and 100 balboas.
Notes US $1 2, 5, 10, 20, 50, 100 (there are no Panamanian bank notes).
Exchange rate to US dollar: 1.00 (February 1976).
Political history and government: Formerly part of Colombia, independence declared on 3 Nov. 1903. The elected President was deposed by a *coup* on 11–12 Oct. 1968, when power was seized by the National Guard, led by Col (later Brig-Gen) Omar Torrijos Herrera. A Provisional Junta was established, the National Assembly dissolved and political activity suspended. Political parties were abolished in February 1969. In August 1972 elections were held for a National Assembly of Community Representatives (505 members to hold office for six years) to approve a new constitution. The Assembly elects a President and Vice-President. For a transitional period of six years from 11 Oct. 1972, full executive authority is held by Gen Torrijos as Chief of Government and Supreme Leader of the Panamanian Revolution. He rules with an appointed Cabinet Council. Panama comprises nine provinces.
Telephones: 139 241 (1975).
Daily newspapers: 7 (1971).
Total circulation: 116 000.
Radio: 265 000 (1975).
TV: 185 000 (1975).
Length of roadways: 4413 miles *7102 km* (1973).
Length of railways: 447 miles *720 km*.
Universities: 2.
Adult illiteracy: 21·7% (males 21·1%; females 22·3%) in 1970.
Expectation of life: Males 57·62 years; females 60·88 years (1960–1).
Defence: National Guard of 11 000 men.
Wildlife: Armadillo, alligator, anteater, peccary, tapir, jaguar, monkeys.
Cinemas: 45 (seating capacity 39 800) and one drive-in (1971).
* Excluding the Canal Zone, area 553 sq miles (*1432 sq km*), population 44 198 (1970).

PAPUA NEW GUINEA

Official name: The Independent State of Papua New Guinea.
Population: 2 489 935 (1971 census); 2 693 000 (1974 est).
Area: 178 260 miles² *461 691 km²*.
Languages: English (official), Pidgin, Moru.
Religion: Christian 92·8% (1966).
Capital city: Port Moresby, population 76 507 (1971).
Other principal cities (1971): Lae 34 699; Rabaul 24 778; Madang; Wewak; Goroka.
Highest point: Mt Wilhelm, 15 400 ft *4694 m*.
Principal mountain range: Bismarck Range.
Principal rivers: Fly (with Strickland), Sepik (690 miles [*1110 km*]).
Head of State: HM Queen Elizabeth II, represented by Sir John Guise, GCMG, KBE (b. 29 Aug. 1914). Governor-General.
Prime Minister: Michael Thomas Somare (b. 9 Apr. 1936).
Climate: Generally hot and humid, cooler in highlands. Average annual rainfall between 40 and 250 in. In Port Moresby, average maximum temperature 82 °F (August) to 90 °F (December), minimum

73 °F (July, August) to 76 °F (November to March), rainiest month is March (9 days).
Crops: Bananas, coconuts, sweet potatoes, taro, yams, sugar cane, coffee, cocoa.
Monetary unit: Kina. 1 kina = 100 toea.
Denominations:
Coins 1, 2, 5, 10, 20 toea, 1 kina.
Notes 2, 5, 10 kina.
Exchange rate to US dollar: 0.794 (February 1976).
Political history and government: Formed by a merger of the Territory of Papua (under Australian rule from 1906) and the Trust Territory of New Guinea, administered by Australia from 1914, later under a trusteeship agreement with the United Nations. A joint administration for the two territories was established by Australia on 1 July 1949. The combined territory became independent, within the Commonwealth, on 16 Sept. 1975. Executive authority is vested in the Queen and exercisable by the Governor-General, whom she appoints on the advice of the Prime Minister, leader of the National Executive Council (the Cabinet). Legislative power is vested in the unicameral House of Assembly (100 members directly elected for four years by universal adult suffrage). The Council is responsible to the Assembly, where the Prime Minister, appointed by the Governor-General, must command majority support. The country comprises 19 districts.
Telephones: 16 949 (1975).
Daily newspapers: 1.
Radio: 110 000 (1975).
Length of roadways (1974): 7456 miles *12 000 km*.
Universities: 2.
Adult illiteracy: 67·9% (males 60·7%; females 75·6%) in 1971.
Expectation of life: Males 45·4 years; females 44·9 years (1965–70).
Defence: Total armed forces about 3500.
Wildlife: Over 100 species of mammal, all marsupial except for echidna, rodents and bats; snakes, lizards, crocodile, tortoise. Many bird species, including Bird of Paradise.
Cinemas: 28 (seating capacity 18 800) and one drive-in (1972).

PARAGUAY

Official name: La República del Paraguay.
Population: 2 354 071 (1972 census); 2 572 000 (1974 est).
Area: 157 048 miles² *406 752 km²*.
Languages: Spanish (official), Guaraní.
Religion: Roman Catholic.
Capital city: Asunción, population 417 152 (1973 est).

Other principal towns (1962): Coronel Oviedo 44 254; Encarnación 35 186; Concepción 33 886; Mariscal Estigarribia 33 478; Luque 30 780; Villarrica 30 761.
Highest point: Cerro Tatug, 2297 ft *700 m*.
Principal mountain ranges: Cordillera Amambay, Sierra de Maracaju.
Principal rivers: Paraguay (1500 miles [*2414 km*]), Paraná (2500 miles [*4023 km*]). Pilcomayo (1000 miles [*1609 km*]).
Head of State: Gen Alfredo Stroessner (b. 3 Nov. 1912), President.
Climate: Sub-tropical and humid, average temperatures 65 °F to 85 °F. Hot December–March. Cool season May–September. Wet season March–May. In Asunción, average maximum 72 °F (June) to 95 °F (January), minimum 53 °F (June, July) to 71 °F (January, February), October, November and January rainiest (each 8 days).
Crops: Cassava, maize, sweet potatoes, cotton, sugar cane, tobacco.
Monetary unit: Guaraní. 1 guaraní = 100 céntimos.
Denominations:
Coins (issued only for commemorative purposes).
Notes 1, 5, 10, 50, 100, 500, 1000, 5000, 10 000 guaraníes.
Exchange rate to US dollar: 126.00 (February 1976).

Political history and government: A republic comprising 16 departments. Gen. Alfredo Stroessner assumed power by a military *coup* on 5 May 1954. He was elected President on 11 July 1954 and re-elected in 1958, 1963, 1968 and 1973. A new constitution was promulgated on 25 Aug. 1967 and took effect in 1968. Legislative power is held by a bicameral National Congress, whose members serve for 5 years. The Senate has 30 members and the Chamber of Deputies 60 members. The party receiving the largest number of votes (since 1947 the National Republican Association, known as the Colorado Party) is allotted two-thirds of the seats in each chamber, the remaining seats being divided proportionately among the other contending parties. Executive power is held by the President, directly elected for 5 years at the same time as the Congress. He rules with the assistance of an appointed Council of Ministers.
Telephones: 34 531 (1975).

Daily newspapers: 11 (1972).
Total circulation: 99 000 (5 dailies).
Radio: 180 000 (1975).
TV: 54 000 (1975).
Length of roadways: 4347 miles *6996 km* (1973).
Length of railways: 309 miles *498 km*.
Universities: 2.
Adult illiteracy: 25·5% (males 19·0%; females 31·3%) in 1962.
Expectation of life: Males 58·6 years; females 61·7 years (1965–70).
Defence: Military Service: two years. Total armed forces 14 500. Defence expenditure, 1973: $19 million.
Wildlife: Jaguar, deer, water hog, opossum. partridge, duck, parrot, parakeet.
Cinemas: 65 in Asunción (1974).

PERU

Official name: La República del Perú.
Population: 13 572 052 (1972 census); 14 370 000 (1974 est).
Area: 496 224 miles² *1 285 216 km²*.
Languages: Spanish, Quechua, Aymará.
Religion: Roman Catholic.
Capital city: Lima, population 2 862 197 (1972).
Other principal towns (1972): Arequipa 304 653; Callao 296 220; Trujillo 241 882; Chiclayo 189 685; Chimbote 159 045; Piura 126 702; Cuzco 120 881.
Highest point: Huascarán 22 205 ft *6768 m*.
Principal mountain ranges: Cordillera de los Andes (C. Oriental, C. Occidental, C. Blanca).
Principal rivers: Amazonas (Amazon), with Ucayali.
Head of State: Gen Francisco Morales Bermúdez (b. 4 Oct. 1921), President.
Prime Minister: Gen Guillermo Arbulu Galliani.
Climate: Varies with altitude. Daily fluctuations greater than seasonal. Rainy season October–April. Heavy rains in tropical forests. In Lima, average maximum 66 °F (August) to 83 °F (February, March), minimum 56 °F (August) to 67 °F (February), August rainiest (two days). Absolute maximum temperature 38·5 °C (*101·3 °F*), Iquitos, 19 June 1948; absolute minimum −20,2 °C (−*4·4 °F*), Imata, 1 Aug. 1947.
Crops: Potatoes, sugar cane, maize, rice, cotton, coffee.

Monetary unit: Sol. 1 sol = 100 centavos.
Denominations:
Coins 5, 10, 25, 50 centavos, 1, 5, 10 soles.
Notes 5, 10, 50, 100, 200, 500, 1000 soles.
Exchange rate to US dollar: 45.00 (February 1976).
Political history and government: A republic comprising 23 departments and one province. A new constitution was promulgated on 9 April 1933. The last elected President was deposed by a military *coup* on 3 Oct. 1968. The bicameral National Congress was abolished, political activity suspended and a 'revolutionary government' of military officers took power. The constitution remains only partially in force. Executive and legislative powers are exercised by the armed forces through the President, who rules by decree with the assistance of an appointed Council of Ministers. Each department is administered by an appointed prefect.
Telephones: 333 346 (1975).
Daily newspapers: 56 (1971).
Radio: 2 050 000 (1975).
TV: 500 000 (1975).
Length of roadways (1973): 32 374 miles *52 102 km.*
Length of railways: 1305 miles *2100 km.*
Universities: 33.
Adult illiteracy: 38·9% (males 25·6%; females 51·6%) in 1961.
Expectation of life: Males 52·59 years; females 55·48 years (1960–5).
Defence: Military service: two years, selective. Total armed forces; 56 000. Defence expenditure 1974: $226 million.
Wildlife: Llama, jaguar, sloth, alligator, monkeys, snakes, puma, alpaca, chinchilla, vicuna, guanaco. Parrot. Piranha.
Cinemas: 276 and one drive-in (1972); seating capacity about 243 000 (1966).

PHILIPPINES

Official name: República de Filipinas (in Spanish) or Repúblika ñg Pilipinas (in Tagalog).
Population: 41 831 045 (1975 census).
Area: 115 800 miles² *300 000 km².*
Languages (1960): Cebuano 24·1% Tagalog 21·0%; Iloco 11·7%; Panay-Hiligaynon 10·4%; Bikol 7·8%; many others.
Religions (1960): Roman Catholic 84%; Aglipayan 5%, Muslim 5%, Protestant 3%.
Capital city: Quezon City, population 960 341 (1975).
Other principal towns (1975): Manila 1 454 352; Davao 482 233; Cebu 408 173; Caloocan 393 251; Zamboanga 261 978; Iloilo 227 374; Bacolod 222 735; Pasay 186 920.
Highest point: Mt Apo (on Mindanao), 9690 ft *2953 m.*
Principal mountain ranges: Cordillera Central (on Luzon), Diuata Range (on Mindanao).
Principal rivers: Cagayan (180 miles [*290 km*]), Pampanga, Abra, Agusan, Magat, Laoang, Agno.
Head of State: Ferdinand Edralin Marcos (b. 11 Sept. 1917), President and Prime Minister.
Climate: Tropical. Hot and humid, except in mountains. Heavy rainfall, frequent typhoons. In Manila, average maximum 86 °F (December, January) to 93 °F (April, May), minimum 69 °F (January, February) to 75 °F (May–August), July rainiest (24 days). Absolute maximum temperature 42,2 °C (*108·0 °F*), Tuguegarao, 29 Apr. 1912; absolute minimum 7,3 °C (*45·1 °F*), Baguio City, 1 Feb. 1930 and 11 Jan. 1932.
Crops: Rice, sugar cane, maize, copra.

Monetary unit: Philippine peso. 1 peso = 100 centavos.
Denominations:
Coins 1, 5, 10, 25, 50 centavos, 1 peso.
Notes 5, 10, 20, 50, 100 pesos.
Exchange rate to US dollar: 7.48 (February 1976).
Political history and government: Formerly a Spanish colony. After the Spanish-American War, Spain ceded the Philippines to the USA (10 Dec. 1898). A constitution, ratified by plebiscite on 14 May 1935, gave the Philippines self-government and provided for independence after 10 years. The islands were occupied by Japanese forces in 1942–45. After the restoration of US rule, the Philippines became an independent republic on 4 July 1946.
Ferdinand Marcos was elected President on 9 Nov. 1965 and inaugurated on 30 Dec. 1965. He was re-elected in 1969. Before completing his (then) maximum of two four-year terms, President Marcos proclaimed martial law, and suspended the bicameral Congress, on 23 Sept. 1972. Following a plebiscite, a new constitution was proclaimed on 17 Jan. 1973. This provides for a unicameral National Assembly and a constitutional President (both elected for 6 years), with executive power held by a Prime Minister, to be elected by the Assembly. Pending its full implementation, transitional provisions give the incumbent President the combined authority of the Presidency (under the 1935 constitution) and the Premiership under the new constitution, without any fixed term of office. The President should convene an interim National Assembly but this provision has been postponed indefinitely. Under martial law the definitive provisions of the constitution remain in abeyance. A referendum on 27–28 July 1973 approved the President's continuation in office beyond his elected term. Another referendum, in February 1975, approved the continuation of martial law, enabling the President to rule by decree. He appoints and leads a Cabinet and is Commander-in-Chief of the armed forces. The country is divided into 68 provinces.

Telephones: 446 262 (1975).
Daily newspapers: 24 (1974).
Total circulation: 1 196 239.
Radio: 1 850 000 (1975).
TV: 421 000 (1971).
Length of roadways: 57 647 miles *92 775 km* (1974).
Length of railways: 735 miles *1183 km.*
Universities: 42.
Adult illiteracy: 16·6% (males 15·4%; females 17·8%) in 1970 (population aged 10 and over).
Expectation of life: Males 54·0 years; females 57·3 years (1965–70).
Defence: Military Service: selective. Total armed forces 67 000. Defence expenditure, 1975–6: $407 million.
Wildlife: Dwarf deer, monkeys, rodents, water buffalo, porcupine, lizards, snakes. Almost 1000 species of birds.
Cinemas: 951 (1965).

POLAND

Official name: Polska Rzeczpospolita Ludowa (Polish People's Republic).
Population: 32 642 270 (1970 census); 33 992 000 (1975 est).
Area: 120 725 miles² *312 677 km².*
Language: Polish.
Religion: Roman Catholic.
Capital city: Warszawa (Warsaw), population 1 410 837 (1974 est).
Other principal towns (1974): Łódź 787 035; Kraków (Cracow) 668 275; Wrocław (Breslau) 568 928; Poznań (Posen) 506 191; Gdańsk (Danzig) 406 900; Szczecin (Stettin) 363 744; Katowice 321 900; Bydgoszcz (Bromberg) 313 500; Lublin 263 973.
Highest point: Rysy, 8199 ft *2499 m.*
Principal mountain ranges: Carpathian Mountains (Tatry range), Beskids.
Principal rivers: Wisła (Vistula) with Bug, Odra (Oder).
Head of State: Dr Henryk Jabłoński (b. 27 Dec. 1909), Chairman of the Council of State.
Political Leader: Edward Gierek (b. 6 Jan. 1913), First Secretary of the Central Committee of the Polish United Workers' Party.
Head of Government: Piotr Jaroszewicz (b. 8 Oct. 1909), Chairman of the Council of Ministers.
Climate: Temperate in west, continental in east. Short, rainy summers, but occasional dry spells; cold snowy winters. In Warsaw, average maximum 30 °F (January) to 75 °F (July), minimum 21 °F (January) to 56 °F (July), June, July and August rainiest (each 11 days). Absolute maximum temperature 40,2 °C (*104·4 °F*), Prószkow, 29 July 1921; absolute minimum −40,6 °C (*−41·1 °F*), Zgwiec, 10 Feb. 1929.
Crops: Potatoes, rye, wheat, barley, oats, sugar beet.
Monetary unit: Złoty. 1 złoty = 100 groszy.
Denominations:
Coins 1, 2, 5, 10, 20, 50 groszy, 1, 2, 5, 10, 50, 100 złotys.
Notes 20, 50, 100, 500, 1000 złotys.
Exchange rate to US dollar: 3.32 (October 1975).
Political history and government: Formerly partitioned between Austria, Prussia and Russia. After the First World War an independent republic was declared on 11 Nov. 1918. Parliamentary government was overthrown in May 1926 by military leaders who ruled until 1939, when invasions by Nazi Germany (1 Sept.) and the USSR (17 Sept.) led to another partition (29 Sept.).

After Germany declared war on the USSR (June 1941) its forces occupied the whole of Poland but they were driven out by Soviet forces in March 1945. With the end of the Second World War (May 1945) Poland's frontiers were redrawn. A provisional government was formed on 28 June 1945. A Communist regime took power after the elections of 19 Jan. 1947 and a People's Republic was established on 19 Feb. 1947. A new constitution was adopted on 22 July 1952.

The supreme organ of state power is the unicameral parliament (*Sejm*), with 460 members elected by universal adult suffrage for 4 years (in the elections of 21 March 1976 there were 631 candidates). The *Sejm* elects a Council of State (17 members) to be its permanent organ. The highest executive and administrative body is the Council of Ministers, appointed by (and responsible to) the *Sejm*.

Political power is held by the (Communist) Polish United Workers' Party (PUWP), which dominates the Front of National Unity (including two other smaller parties). The Front presents an approved list of candidates for elections to representative bodies. The PUWP's highest authority is the Party Congress, convened every 5 years. The Congress elects a Central Committee (140 full members and 111 candidate members were elected in December 1975) to supervise Party work. To direct its policy the Committee elects a Political Bureau (Politburo), with 14 full members (including the Committee's First Secretary) and 3 alternate members.

Poland is divided into 49 provinces (voivodships), each with a People's Council elected for 4 years.
Telephones: 2 399 249 (1975).
Daily newspapers: 44 (1974).
  Total circulation: 7 991 000.
Radio: 5 920 502 (1975).
TV: 6 100 412 (1975).
Length of roadways: 186 334 miles *299 876 km* (1973).
Length of railways: 16 596 miles *26 709 km* (1974).
Universities: 10.
Adult illiteracy: 2·3% (males 1·3%; females 3·1%) in 1970.
Expectation of life: Males 66·83 years; females 73·76 years (1970–2).
Defence: Military Service: Army, internal security forces and Air Force, two years; Navy and special services, three years. Total regular forces: 293 000; Defence expenditure 1975 $2170 million.
Wildlife: Lynx, elk, wild cats, bison, wild pony, bear. Eagle.
Cinemas: 2465 (seating capacity 575 500) and 32 part-time (capacity 16 396) in 1972.

PORTUGAL

Official name: República Portuguesa.
*Population: 8 447 790 (1970 census); 8 564 200 (1973 est).
*Area: 35 553 miles² *92 082 km²*.
Language: Portuguese.
Religion: Roman Catholic.
Capital city: Lisboa (Lisbon), population 757 700 (1973 est).
Other principal towns (1970): Pôrto (Oporto) 300 925; Amadora 65 870; Coímbra 55 985; Barreiro 53 690; Vila Nova de Gaia 50 805; Setúbal 49 670; Braga 48 735.
Highest point: Serra da Estréla, 6532 ft *1991 m*.
Principal mountain range: The Serra da Estréla.

Principal rivers: Rio Tejo (Tagus), Douro.
Head of State: Gen António des Santos Ramalho Eanes (b. 25 Jan. 1935), President.
Prime Minister: Dr. Mario Alberto Nobre Lopes Soares (b. 7 Dec. 1924).

Climate: Mild and temperate. Average annual temperature 61 °F, drier and hotter inland. Hot summers, rainy winters in central areas, warm and very dry in south. In Lisbon, average maximum 56 °F (January) to 80 °F (August), minimum 46 °F (January) to 64 °F (August); March, November and December rainiest (each 10 days). Absolute maximum temperature 45,8 °C (*114·4 °F*), Coímbra, 31 July 1944; absolute minimum −11,0 °C (*12·2 °F*), Penhas Douradas, 25 Jan. 1947.
Crops: Potatoes, wheat, maize, rice, rye, grapes.
Monetary unit: Portuguese escudo. 1 escudo = 100 centavos.
Denominations:
  Coins 10, 20, 50 centavos, 1, 2½, 5, 10, 20, 50 escudos.
  Notes 20, 50, 100, 500, 1000 escudos.
Exchange rate to US dollar: 27.75 (February 1976).
Political history and government: Formerly a kingdom. An anti-monarchist uprising deposed the King on 5 Oct. 1910, when a republic was proclaimed. The parliamentary regime was overthrown by a military *coup* on 28 May 1926. Dr. António Salazar became Prime Minister, with dictatorial powers, on 5 July 1932. A new constitution, establishing a corporate state, was adopted on 19 March 1933. Dr. Salazar retained power until illness forced his retirement on 26 Sept. 1968. His successor, Dr. Marcello Caetano, was deposed on 25 Apr. 1974 by a military *coup*, initiated by the Armed Forces Movement. Military leaders formed a Junta of National Salvation and appointed one of its members as President. He appointed a Prime Minister and, on the latter's recommendation, other Ministers to form a provisional government. The 1933 constitution was suspended and the bicameral Parliament dissolved.

On 14 Mar. 1975 the Junta was dissolved and three days later a Supreme Revolutionary Council (SRC) was established to exercise authority until a new constitution took effect. A Constitutional Assembly was elected on 25 Apr. 1975 to formulate a new constitution. After approval by the SRC, the constitution was promulgated on 2 Apr. 1976. It provides for a unicameral Legislative Assembly (elected by universal adult suffrage on 25 Apr. 1976) and an executive President (elected on 27 June 1976). The President appoints a Prime Minister to lead a Council of Ministers, responsible to the Assembly. Portugal has 22 administrative districts.

Telephones: 1 011 177 (1975).
Daily newspapers: 29 (1972).
  Total circulation: 745 000 (est).
Radio: 1 518 724 (1975).
TV: 674 686 (1974).
Length of roadways: 26 984 miles *43 426 km* (1972).
Length of railways: 2214 miles *3563 km.*
Universities: 8.
Adult illiteracy: 37·2% (males 30·0%; females 43·4%) in 1960.
Expectation of life: Males 65·30 years; females 71·02 years (1970).
Defence: Military Service: Army 24 months, Air Force 36 months, Navy 48 months. Total armed forces 217 000 (regular). Defence expenditure 1975: $701 million.
Wildlife: Boar, wolf.
Cinemas: 461 (seating capacity 261 329) in 1972.
  *Metropolitan Portugal, including the Azores and Madeira Islands.

QATAR

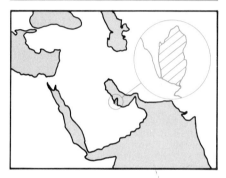

Official name: Daulat al-Qatar (State of Qatar).
Population: 180 000 (1975 est).
Area: 4250 miles² *11 000 km²*.
Language: Arabic.
Religion: Muslim.
Capital city: Ad Dauhah (Doha), population 130 000 (1975 est).
Other principal towns: Dukhan, Umm Said.
Highest point: 240 ft *73 m*.
Head of State: Shaikh Khalifa ibn Hamad al-Thani (b. 1934), Amir and Prime Minister.
Climate: Very hot, with high humidity on the coast. Temperatures reach 120 °F in summer.
Crop: Tomatoes.
Monetary unit: Qatar riyal. 1 riyal = 100 dirhams.
Denominations:
  Coins 1, 5, 10, 25, 50 dirhams.
  Notes 1, 5, 10, 100, 500 riyals.
Exchange rate to US dollar: 3.97 (February 1976).
Political history and government: Became part of Turkey's Ottoman Empire in 1872. Turkish forces evacuated Qatar at the beginning of the First World War. The UK entered into treaty relations with the ruling Shaikh on 3 Nov. 1916. A provisional constitution was adopted on 2 Apr. 1970. Qatar remained under British protection until achieving full independence on 1 Sept. 1971. On 22 Feb. 1972 the ruler was deposed by his deputy, the Prime Minister.

Qatar is an absolute monarchy, with full powers vested in the ruler (called Amir since independence). It has no parliament or political parties. The ruler appoints and leads a Council of Ministers to exercise executive power. The Ministers are assisted by a Consultative Council with 20 nominated members.

Telephones: 18 289 (1975).
Daily newspapers: 1.
 Total circulation: 7000.
TV: 29 000 (1975).
Defence: Total armed forces 2200.
Cinemas: 8 (seating capacity 7000) in 1973.

RHODESIA

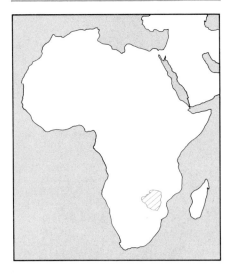

Official Name: The Republic of Rhodesia.
Population: 5 099 344 (1969 census);
6 200 000 (1974 est.).
Area: 150 804 miles². *390 580 km².*
Languages: English (official), Sindebele,
Chishona.
Religions: Tribal beliefs, Christian minority.
Capital city: Salisbury, population 555 000
(1974 est).
Other principal towns (1974): Bulawayo
339 000; Gwelo 62 000; Umtali 59 000; Que
Que 45 000; Gatooma 33 000; Wankie
27 000.
Highest point: Mount Inyangani, 8503 ft
2592 m.
Principal mountain ranges: Enyanga,
Melsetter.
Principal rivers: Zambezi and tributaries
(Shangani, Umniati), Limpopo and tribu-
taries (Umzingwani, Nuanetsi), Sabi and
tributaries (Lundi, Odzi).
Head of State: John James Wrathall (b. 28
Aug. 1913), President.
Prime Minister: Ian Douglas Smith (b. 8
Apr. 1919).
Climate: Tropical, modified by altitude.
Average temperature 65 °F to 75 °F. In
Salisbury, average daily maximum 70 °F
(June, July) to 83 °F (October), minimum
44 °F (June, July) to 60 °F (November–
February), January rainiest (18 days).
Crops: Maize, sugar-cane, millet, ground-
nuts, cotton, tobacco.
Monetary unit: Rhodesian dollar (R$).
1 dollar = 100 cents.
Denominations:
 Coins ½ 1, 2½, 5, 10, 20, 25 cents.
 Notes 1, 2, 5, 10 dollars.
Exchange rate to US dollar: 0.617
(February 1976).
Political history and government: The
British South Africa Company was granted a
Royal Charter over the territory on 29 Oct.
1889. On 12 Sept. 1923 Southern Rhodesia
(as it was known) was transferred from the
Company to the British Empire and became
a colony. It was granted full self-government
(except for African interests and some other
matters) on 1 Oct. 1923. The colony became

part of the Federation of Rhodesia and
Nyasaland (the Central African Federation),
proclaimed on 1 Aug. 1953. A new constitution, which removed most of the UK's legal
controls (except for foreign affairs), was
promulgated on 6 Dec. 1961 and made fully
operative on 1 Nov. 1962. This constitution
provided for a limited African franchise and
could have led to ultimate majority rule. The
Federation was dissolved on 31 Dec. 1963.
Ian Smith became Prime Minister on 13
Apr. 1964. Following unsuccessful negotiations with the British Government, Ian
Smith made a unilateral declaration of
independence (UDI) on 11 Nov. 1965. The
British Government regards Rhodesia's independence as unconstitutional and having no
legal validity, and no other country has
formally recognized it. A new constitution
was approved by referendum on 20 June
1969, adopted on 29 Nov. 1969 and took
effect on 2 Mar. 1970, when a republic was
proclaimed.
 Legislative power is held by the bicameral
Legislative Assembly. The House of Assembly has 66 members, including 50 Europeans
(whites) elected by non-African voters, 8
Africans directly elected by African voters
and 8 Africans elected by tribal electoral
colleges. The Senate (with delaying powers
only) has 23 members, including 10 Europeans elected by white members of the House,
10 Africans elected by an advisory Council of
Chiefs, and 3 members (of any race) appoint-
ed by the President. He is a constitutional
Head of State appointed on the nomination
of the Executive Council (Cabinet). The
Council, which directs the government, is
led by a Prime Minister, appointed by the
President. Other Ministers are appointed on
the Prime Minister's recommendation.
Telephones: 171 881 (1975).
Daily newspapers: 4 (1971).
 Total circulation: 85 000.
Radio: 250 000 (1975).
TV: 68 700 (1975).
Length of roadways: 49 045 miles
78 930 km.
Length of railways: 2109 miles *3394 km.*
Universities: 1.
Adult illiteracy: 95·3% (males 94·4%;
females 96·3%) in 1962 (Africans only).
Expectation of life: Males 47·3 years;
females 50·4 years (1965–70). Europeans:
Males 66·9 years; females 74·0 years.
Defence: Military service: 12 months
(White, Asian and Coloured population).
Total armed forces 5700. Defence expendi-
ture 1975–6 $102 million.
Wildlife: Elephant, leopard, etc. (all
decreasing in number).
Cinemas: 72 (seating capacity 53 900) and
5 drive-in (1971).

ROMANIA

Official name: Republica Socialistă Ro-
mânia (Socialist Republic of Romania).
Population: 19 103 163 (1966 census);
21 028 841 (1974 est).
Area: 91 699 miles² *237 500 km².*
Languages (1966): Romanian 87·8%;
Hungarian 8·6%; German 2·0%.
Religions: Romanian Orthodox (85% of
believers), Roman Catholic, Reformed
(Calvinist).
Capital city: Bucureşti (Bucharest), popu-
lation 1 507 295 (1972).
Other principal towns (1972): Cluj
208 125; Timişoara 199 987; Iaşi 193 998;
Braşov 188 828; Galaţi 187 101; Craiova
183 035; Constanţa 180 464; Ploieşti 168 642
Brăila 157 840.
Highest point: Moldoveanul, 8343 ft *2543
m.*

Principal mountain ranges: Carpathian
Mountains, Transylvanian Alps.
Principal rivers: Dunărea (Danube) (1777
miles [*2860 km*], 668 miles [*1075 km*] in
Romania), Mureş (446 miles [*718 km*]),
Prut (437 miles [*703 km*]).
Head of State: Nicolae Ceauşescu (b. 26
Jan. 1918), President.
Head of Government: Manea Mănescu
(b. 9 Aug. 1916), Chairman of the Council of
Ministers.

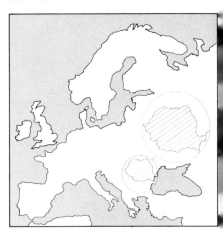

Climate: Hot and humid summers (average
temperatures 70 °F); cold, windy, snowy
winters (average 28 °F). Moderate rainfall.
Absolute maximum temperature 44,5 °C
(*112·1 °F*), Ion Sion, 10 Aug. 1951; minimum
−38,5 °C (−*37·3 °F*), Bod, near Braşov,
25 Jan. 1942.
Crops: Maize, wheat, potatoes, grapes,
barley.
Monetary unit: Leu (plural lei). 1 leu =
100 bani.
Denominations:
 Coins 5, 10, 15, 25 bani, 1, 3 lei.
 Notes 1, 3, 5, 10, 25, 50, 100 lei.
Exchange rate to US dollar: 5.01
(February 1976).
Political history and government: For-
merly a monarchy. Under the Fascist 'Iron
Guard' movement, Romania entered the
Second World War as an ally of Nazi
Germany. Soviet forces entered Romania in
1944. The Iron Guard regime was over-
thrown on 23 Aug. 1944 and a predominantly
Communist government took power on 6
March 1945. The King was forced to abdi-
cate on 30 Dec. 1947, when a People's
Republic was proclaimed. A new constitution
introducing the country's present name, was
adopted on 21 Aug. 1965.
 The supreme organ of state power is the
unicameral Grand National Assembly, with
349 members elected by universal adult
suffrage for 5 years (210 members were
elected unopposed in 1975). The assembly
elects from its members the State Council
(18 members) to be its permanent organ.
The President of the Republic, elected by the
Assembly for its duration, is also President
of the State Council. The Council of
Ministers, the highest organ of state administration, is elected by (and responsible
to) the Assembly.
 Political power is held by the Romanian
Communist Party (RCP), the only legal
party, which dominates the Front of Socialist
Unity. The Front presents an approved list
of candidates for elections to representative
bodies. The Head of State is General Secretary of the RCP and Chairman of the Front.
The RCP's highest authority is the Party
Congress, convened ever 5 years. The Congress elects a Central Committee (205 full
members and 156 alternate members were

elected in November 1974) to supervise party work. The Central Committee elects from its members an Executive Political Committee (23 full members and 13 alternate members) to direct policy. The Executive Committee has a five-man Permanant Bureau (including the President), which is the Party's most powerful policy-making body.

Romania comprises 40 administrative districts, each with a People's Council elected for 5 years.

Telephones: 1 076 566 (1975).
Daily newspapers: 58 (1972).
Total circulation: 3 634 000.
Radio: 3 111 000 (1975).
TV: 2 553 419 (1975).
Length of roadways: 48 317 miles *77 759 km* (1974).
Length of railways (1973): 6441 miles *10 366 km* plus 406 miles *653 km* (narrow-gauge).
Universities: 7.
Adult illiteracy: 11·4% (males 6·1%; females 16·3%) in 1956.
Expectation of life: Males 66·27 years; females 70·85 years (1970–72).
Defence: Military service: Army and Air Force 16 months, Navy 2 years. Total regular forces 171 000 (1975). Defence expenditure 1975 $647 million.
Wildlife: Chamois, brown bear, wolf, fox, wild boar, lynx, marten.
Cinemas: 6191 (1973).

RWANDA

Official name: La République Rwandaise (in French) *or* Republica y'u Rwanda (in Kinyarwanda).
Population: 4 123 000 (1974 est).
Area: 10 169 miles² *26 338 km²*.
Languages: French, Kinyarwanda (both official), Kiswahili.
Religions: Roman Catholic, Animist, Protestant and Muslim minorities.
Capital city: Kigali, population 54 403 (1970).
Other principal towns: Nyanzi, Gisenyi, Cyangugu, Sitarama.
Highest point: Mt Karisimbi, 14 787 ft *4507 m*.
Principal mountain ranges: Chaîne des Mitumba.
Principal rivers: Luvironza (headwaters of the Nile).
Head of State: Maj-Gen Juvénal Habyalimana (b. 3 Aug. 1937), President.
Climate: Tropical, tempered by altitude. Average temperature at 4800 ft *1463 m* is

73 °F. Hot and humid in lowlands, cool in highlands. Average annual rainfall 31 in. Main rainy season from February to May, dry season May to September.
Crops: Plantains, sweet potatoes, cassava, sorghum, potatoes, coffee.
Monetary unit: Rwanda franc. 1 franc = 100 centimes.
Denominations:
Coins 50 centimes, 1, 2, 5, 10 francs.
Notes 20, 50, 100, 500, 1000 francs.
Exchange rate to US dollar: 92.84 (February 1976).
Political history and government: Formerly a monarchy, ruled by a *Mwami* (King). Part of German East Africa from 1899. Occupied in 1916 by Belgian forces from the Congo (now Zaire). From 1920 Rwanda was part of Ruanda-Urundi, administered by Belgium under League of Nations mandate and later as a UN Trust Territory. Following a referendum in September 1961, the monarchy was abolished and the republic proclaimed on 28 Jan. 1961 was recognised by Belgium on 2 Oct. 1961. Rwanda became independent on 1 July 1962. On 5 July 1973 the government was overthrown by a military *coup*, led by Maj.-Gen. Juvénal Habyalimana, who became President in August 1973. The National Assembly was dissolved and political activity suspended. The President appoints and leads a Council of Ministers. In July 1975 a new ruling party was established.
Telephones: 2452 (1975).
Radio: 65 000 (1975).
Length of roadways: 3700 miles *5953 km*.
Universities: 1.
Adult illiteracy: 90% (estimate).
Expectation of life: Males 39·4 years; females 42·6 years (1965–70).
Defence: Total armed forces 3750.
Wildlife: Antelopes, leopard, zebra.
Cinemas: 4 (seating capacity 800) and 15 part-time (1968).

SAN MARINO

Official name: Serenissima Repubblica di San Marino (Most Serene Republic of San Marino).
Population: 19 621 (1975 est).
Area: 23·4 miles² *60,5 km²*.
Language: Italian.
Religion: Roman Catholic.
Capital city: San Marino, population 4512 (1975 est).
Highest point: Mt Titano, 2424 ft *739 m*.
Head of State: There are two co-regents (Capitani reggenti) appointed every six months.
Climate: Warm summers, average maximum 85 °F; dry, cold winters.
Crops: Wheat, grapes, maize, barley.

Monetary unit: Italian currency (*qv*).
Political history and government: Founded as a city-state in AD 301. In customs union with Italy since 1862. Legislative power is vested in the unicameral Great and General Council, with 60 members elected by universal adult suffrage for 5 years. The Council elects two of its members to act jointly as Captains-Regent, with the functions of Head of State and Government, for 6 months at a time. Executive power is held by the Congress of State, with 10 members elected by the Council for the duration of its term. San Marino has a multi-party political system.
Telephones: 4 736 (1975).
Radio: 4400 (1971).
TV: 3100 (1971).
Length of roadways: 137 miles *220 km*.
Cinemas: 9 (1971).

SÃO TOMÉ and PRÍNCIPE

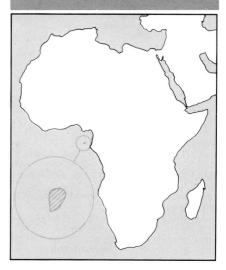

Official name: A República Democrática de São Tomé e Príncipe.
Population: 79 000 (1974 est).
Area: 372 miles² *964 km²*.
Languages: Portuguese.
Religion: Roman Catholic.
Capital city: São Tomé, population 5714 (1960).
Other principal towns: Santo António.
Highest point: Pico de Tomé 6640 ft *2024 m*.
Head of State: Dr. Manuel Pinto da Costa (b. 1910), President.
Prime Minister: Miguel Anjos da Cunha Lisboa Trovoada.
Climate: Warm and humid, with an average temperature of 80 °F.
Crops: Cocoa, copra, palm kernels.
Monetary unit: Guinea escudo. One escudo = 100 centavos.
Denominations:
Coins: 10, 20, 50 centavos, 1, 2½, 5, 10, 20 escudos.
Notes: 20, 50, 100, 500, 1000 escudos.
Exchange rate to US dollar: 27.75 (February 1976).
Political history and government: A former Portuguese territory, independent since 12 July 1975. Before independence, Portugal recognized the islands' Liberation Movement, whose leader became first President. A Constitutional Assembly, elected on 6 July 1975, is to approve a new constitution. Executive power is held by the President, who appoints and leads the Cabinet, including a Prime Minister.

221

Telephones: 677 (1975).
Radio: 10 000 (1975).
Length of roadways: 179 miles *288 km* (1972).

SAUDI ARABIA

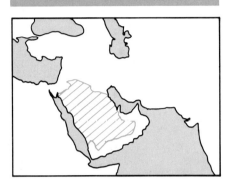

Official name: Al-Mamlaka al-'Arabiya as-Sa'udiya (Kingdom of Saudi Arabia).
Population: 8 966 000 (UN estimate for mid-1975).
Area: 830 000 miles² *2 149 690 km².*
Languages: Arabic.
Religion: Muslim.
Capital city: Riyadh, population 500 000 (1975 est).
Other principal towns (1975): Jidda (Jeddah) 400 000; Mecca 250 000; Medina 100 000; Dammam 60 000; Al-Khobar 60 000.
Highest point: Jebel Razikh, 12 002 ft *3658 m.*
Principal mountain range: Tihāmatash Shām.
Principal rivers: The flows are seasonal only.
Head of State and Prime Minister: HM King Khalid ibn Abdul-Aziz (b. 1912).
Climate: Very hot and dry. Mostly desert; frequent sandstorms. Average summer temperature 100 °F to 120 °F on coast, up to 130 °F inland. High humidity. Some places have droughts for years. In Riyadh, average maximum is 107 °F June–August; January coldest (40°F to 70 °F). In Jeddah, average maximum 84 °F (January, February) to 99 °F (July, August), minimum 65 °F (February) to 80 °F (August), rainiest month is November (two days).
Crops: Dates, sorghum, wheat, millet, tomatoes.
Monetary unit: Saudi riyal. 1 riyal = 20 qursh = 100 halalah.
Denominations:
  Coins 1, 5, 10, 25, 50 halalah, 1, 2, 4 qursh.
  Notes 1, 5, 10, 50, 100 riyals.
Exchange rate to US dollar: 3.5355 (February 1976).
Political history and government: Formerly part of Turkey's Ottoman Empire. In 1913 the Sultan of Nejd overthrew Turkish rule in central Arabia. Between 1919 and 1925 he gained control of the Hijaz and was proclaimed King there on 8 Jan. 1926. In September 1932 the Hijaz and Nejd were combined and named Saudi Arabia. The country is an absolute monarchy, with no parliament or political parties. The King rules in accordance with the *Sharia*, the sacred law of Islam. He appoints and leads a Council of Ministers, which serves as the instrument of royal authority in both legislative and executive matters. The King is also assisted by advisory councils, nominated or approved by him.
Telephones: 84 650 (1974).
Daily newspapers: 7 (1972).
  Total circulation: 61 000.

Radio: 255 000 (1975).
TV: 124 000 (1975).
Length of roadways: 9745 miles *15 680 km.*
Length of railways: 379 miles *610 km.*
Universities: 6.
Adult illiteracy: 85% (estimate).
Expectation of life: Males 41·4 years; females 43·3 years (1965–70).
Defence: Military service: voluntary. Total armed forces 47 000. Defence expenditure 1975–6 $6343 million.
Wildlife: Gazelle, oryx—diminishing in number.

SENEGAL

Official name: La République du Sénégal.
Population: 4 418 000 (UN estimate for mid-1975).
Area: 75 750 miles² *196 192 km².*
Languages: French (official), Wolof, several other local dialects.
Religions: Muslim, Christian minority.
Capital city: Dakar, population 667 400 (1973 est).
Other principal towns (1970): Kaolack 96 238; Thiès 90 456; Saint-Louis 81 204; Rufisque 48 101; Ziguinchor 45 772; Djourbel 40 230.
Highest point: Gounou Mt, 4970 ft *1515 m.*
Principal mountain ranges: Fouta Djallon.
Principal rivers: Gambia (Gambie), Casamance, Senegal.
Head of State: Léopold-Sédar Senghor (b. 9 Oct. 1906), President.
Prime Minister: Abdou Diouf (b. 7 Sept. 1935).
Climate: Tropical. Hot, with long dry season and short, wet season. Average annual temperature about 84 °F. Heavy rainfall on coast. Average maximum 90 °F to 108 °F in interior; average minimum about 60 °F. In Dakar, on coast, average maximum 79 °F (January) to 89 °F (September, October); minimum 63 °F (February) to 76 °F (July to October); rainiest month is August (13 days).
Crops: Groundnuts, millet, sorghum, cassava.
Monetary unit: Franc de la Communauté financière africaine.
Denominations:
  Coins 1, 2, 5, 10, 25, 50 and 100 CFA francs.
  Notes 50, 100, 500, 1000 and 5000 CFA francs.
Exchange rate to US dollar: 224.24 (February 1976).
Political history and government: Formerly part of French West Africa, Senegal

joined French Sudan (now the Republic of Mali) to form the Federation of Mali on April 1959. By agreement with France signed on 4 Apr. 1960, the Federation became independent on 20 June 1960. Senegal seceded, and became a separate independent republic, on 20 Aug. 1960. A new constitution was promulgated on 7 Mar. 1963. Senegal became a one-party state in 1966 but two legal opposition parties have since been formed (in July 1974 and February 1976). A constitutional amendment, approved by the government on 10 Mar. 1976, fixed the maximum number of permitted parties at three. Legislative power rests with the unicameral National Assembly, with 100 members elected for 5 years by universal adult suffrage (at the last election, in January 1973, all candidates were elected unopposed). Executive power is held by the President also elected for 5 years at the same time as the Assembly. He appoints and leads a Cabinet, including a Prime Minister. Senegal comprises 7 regions, each with an appointed Governor and an elected local assembly.
Telephones: 36 385 (1975).
Daily newspapers: 1 (1972).
  Total circulation: 25 000.
Radio: 287 000 (1975).
TV: 1800 (1975).
Length of roadways: 9582 miles *15 422 km* (1971).
Length of railways: 642 miles *1034 km.*
Universities: 1.
Adult illiteracy: 95% (estimate).
Expectation of life: Males 39·2 years; females 40·7 years (1965–70).
Defence: Total armed forces 5900.
Wildlife: Leopard, lion, wild cat, civet, cheetah, hyena, wild boar, gazelle, crocodile, Bustard, marabou, ostrich.
Cinemas: 77 (seating capacity 33 500) in 1965.

SEYCHELLES

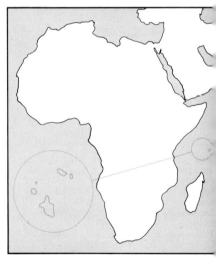

Official name: Republic of Seychelles.
Population: 52 650 (1971 census); 58 000 (1975 est).
Area: 156 miles² *404 km².*
Languages: Creole 94·4%; English 3·0%; French 1·9% (1971).
Religions: Christian (mainly Roman Catholic) 98·2% (1971).
Capital city: Victoria, population 13 736 (1971).
Other principal town: Takamaka.
Highest point: Morne Seychellois 2992 ft *912m.*

Head of State: James Richard Marie
Mancham (b. 11 Aug. 1939), President.
Prime Minister: France Albert René
b. 16 Nov. 1935).
Climate: Warm and pleasant, with tem-
peratures generally between 75 °F and
5 °F, cooler on high ground. Hottest during
north-west monsoon, December to May.
South-east monsoon is from June to Novem-
ber. Average annual rainfall on Mahé between 70 in and 135 in. In Port Victoria,
average annual temperature 84·5 °F, rainfall
4 in.
Crops: Copra, cinnamon.
Monetary unit: Seychelles rupee. 1 rupee
= 100 cents.
Denominations:
  Coins 1, 5, 25, 50 cents, 1, 5, 10 rupees.
  Notes 5, 10, 20, 50, 100 rupees.
Exchange rate to US dollar: 6.58
(February 1976).
Political history and government: Formerly a British colony, with internal self-
government from 1 Oct. 1975. At a constitutional conference on 19–22 Jan. 1976 it was
agreed that Seychelles would become an
independent republic, within the Commonwealth, on 29 June 1976. At the same time
three islands which formed part of the
British Indian Ocean Territory (established
in 8 Nov. 1965) would be returned to Seychelles. Legislative power lies with the
House of Assembly (25 elected members and
two official members), which will become the
National Assembly. The present Assembly
will continue its 5-year term, due to end in
June 1979. Executive authority rests with the
President, the post to be taken initially by
the pre-independence Prime Minister. Future
Presidents will be elected by universal adult
suffrage at the same time as the Assembly.
The President appoints, and presides over, a
Cabinet (including a Prime Minister).
Telephones: 2857 (1975).
Daily newspapers: 2 (1972).
  Total circulation: 3000.
Radio: 16 000 (1975).
Length of roadways: 127 miles *204 km.*
Adult illiteracy: 42·2% (males 44·3%;
females 40·2%) in 1971.
Expectation of life: Males 61·9 years;
females 68·0 years (1970–72).
Wildlife: Giant tortoise (on Aldabra);
many species of birds.
Cinemas: 2 (seating capacity 2400) in 1972.

SIERRA LEONE

Official name: The Republic of Sierra
Leone.
Population: 3 002 426 (1974 census).
Area: 27 699 miles² *71 740 km².*
Languages: English (official), Krio, Mende,
Temne.
Religions: Animist, Muslim, Christian
minorities.
Capital city: Freetown, population 274 000
(1974).
Other principal towns: Bo 26 000;
Kenema 13 000; Makeni 12 000.
Highest point: Bintimani and Kundukonko
peaks, 6390 ft *1948 m.*
Principal mountain range: Loma.
Principal rivers: Siwa, Jong, Rokel.
Head of State: Dr Siaka Probyn Stevens
b. 24 Aug. 1905), President.
Prime Minister: Christian Alusine
Kamara-Taylor (b. 3 June 1917).
Climate: Generally hot with two main
seasons: wet (May–October) when humidity
is tryingly high, and dry (November–April).
The average annual rainfall at Freetown is
138 in and the average daily high tempera-
ture nearly 85 °F.

Crops: Rice, citrus fruit, cassava, palm
kernels and palm oil, coffee, cocoa.
Monetary unit: Leone. 1 leone = 100
cents.
Denominations:
  Coins ½, 1, 5, 10, 20, 50 cents.
  Notes 50 cents, 1, 2, 5 leones.
Exchange rate to US dollar: 0.9875
(February 1976).
Political history of government: A
former British dependency which became
independent, within the Commonwealth, on
27 Apr. 1961. Following disputed elections,
the army assumed power on 21 Mar. 1967.
Two days later, in a counter-*coup*, another
group of officers established a National
Reformation Council (NRC), which suspended the constitution. The NRC was
overthrown on 17–18 Apr. 1968 by junior
officers who restored constitutional government and civilian rule on 26 Apr. 1968, when
Dr. Siaka Stevens, appointed Prime Minister
in 1967, was sworn in. A republic was established on 19 April 1971 and two days later
Dr Stevens was elected President and took
office. Legislative power is held by the
unicameral House of Representatives, with
100 members: 85 elected by universal adult
suffrage for 5 years, 12 Paramount Chiefs
(one from each District) and 3 members
appointed by the President. Executive power
is held by the President, elected by the
House for 5 years. He appoints and leads the
Cabinet, including a Vice President and a
Prime Minister. The country has 4 regions,
administered through the Ministry of the
Interior.

Telephones: 10 331 (1975).
Daily newspapers: 5 (1970).
  Total circulation: 45 000.
Radio: 62 000 (1975).
TV: 6100 (1975).
Length of roadways: 5135 miles *8262 km.*
Universities: 1.
Adult illiteracy: 93·3%.
Expectation of life: Males 39·4 years;
females 42·6 years (1965–70).
Defence: Total armed forces 2125.
Wildlife: Elephant, leopard, dwarf buffalo,
antelope, chimpanzee, civet, tiger cat,
monkeys, cave rats, hippopotamus, crocodile,
manatee. Numerous species of birds.
Cinemas: 10 (seating capacity 5500) in
1969.

SINGAPORE

Official name: The Republic of Singapore.
Population: 2 074 507 (1970 census);
2 249 900 (1975 est).

Area: 226·9 miles² *587,6 km².*
Languages: Malay, Mandarin Chinese,
Tamil, English.
Religion: Muslim, Buddhist, Hindu.
Capital city: Singapore City, population
1 327 500 (1974).
Highest point: Bukit Timah (Hill of Tin),
581 ft *177 m.*
Principal rivers: Sungei Seletar (9 miles
[*14 km*]).

Head of State: Sir Benjamin Henry
Sheares, GCB (b. 12 Aug. 1907), President.
Prime Minister: Lee Kuan Yew (b. 16
Sept. 1923).
Climate: Hot and humid throughout the
year, with average maximum of 86 °F to
89 °F, minimum 73 °F to 75 °F. Frequent
rainfall (between 11 and 19 days each
month).
Crops: Vegetables, coconuts.
Monetary unit: Singapore dollar (S$).
1 dollar = 100 cents.
Denominations:
  Coins 1, 5, 10, 20, 50 cents, 1 dollar.
  Notes 1, 5, 10, 25, 50, 100, 500, 1000,
  10 000 dollars.
Exchange rate to US dollar: 2.48
(February 1976).
Political history and government: A
former British colony, with internal self-
government from 3 June 1959. Singapore
became a constituent state of the independent
Federation of Malaysia, within the Commonwealth, on 16 Sept. 1963 but seceded and
became a separate independent country on
9 Aug. 1965. The new stated joined the
Commonwealth on 16 Oct. 1965 and became
a republic on 22 Dec. 1965. Legislative
power rests with the unicameral Parliament,
with 65 members elected by universal adult
suffrage from single-member constituencies
for 5 years (subject to dissolution). The
President is elected by Parliament for a 4-
year term as constitutional Head of State.
Effective executive authority rests with the
Cabinet, led by the Prime Minister, which is
appointed by the President and responsible
to Parliament.
Telephones: 280 280 (1975).
Daily newspapers: 10 (1973).
  Total circulation: 454 533.
Radio: 355 814 (1975).
TV: 268 671 (1975).
Length of roadways: 1339 miles *2155 km*
(1974).
Length of railways: 30 miles *48 km.*
Universities: 2.
Adult illiteracy: 31·1% (males 17·0%;
females 45·7%) in 1970.
Expectation of life: Males 65·1 years;
females 70·0 years (1970).
Defence: Military service: 24–36 months.
Total armed forces 30 000. Defence expen-
diture, 1975–6 $269 million.
Cinemas: 75 (seating capacity 62 900) and
one drive-in (1972).

223

SOMALIA

Official name: Jamhuriyadda Dimuqradiga Somaliya (Somali Democratic Republic).
Population: 2 941 000 (1972 est).
Area: 246 201 miles² *637 657 km²*.
Languages: Somali, Arabic, English, Italian
Religions: Sunni Muslim, Christian minority.
Capital city: Muqdisho (Mogadishu or Mogadiscio), population 230 000 (1972 est).
Other principal towns (1966): Hargeisa 60 000; Kisimayu 60 000; Merca 56 000; Berbera 50 000.
Highest point: Surud Ad, 7 894 ft *2406 m*.
Principal mountain range: Guban.
Principal rivers: Juba (Giuba) and Scebeli.
Head of State: Maj-Gen Muhammad Siyad Barrah (b. 1919), President of the Supreme Revolutionary Council.
Climate: Hot and dry. Average temperature of 80 °F. Average maximum over 90 °F in interior and on Gulf of Aden. Cooler on Indian Ocean coast. Average rainfall less than 17 inches. In Mogadiscio, average maximum 83 °F (July, August), to 90 °F (April), minimum 73 °F (January, July, August), to 78 °F (April), rainiest month is July (20 days).
Crops: Maize, sorghum, bananas, sugar-cane.
Monetary unit: Somali shilling. 1 shilling = 100 centesimi.
Denominations:
Coins 1, 5, 10, 50 centesimi, 1 shilling.
Notes 5, 10, 20, 100 shillings.
Exchange rate to US dollar: 6.295 (February 1976).
Political history and government: Formed on 1 July 1960 as an independent country, called the Somali Republic, by a merger of the Trust Territory of Somaliland, under Italian protection, with British Somaliland (a protectorate until 26 June 1960). Following the assassination of the President on 15 Oct. 1969, the government was overthrown by a military *coup* on 21 Oct. 1969, when the constitution and political parties were abolished and the National Assembly dissolved. A Supreme Revolutionary Council (SRC) was established and the country's present name adopted on 22 Oct. 1969. The SRC directs the government with the assistance of a Council of Secretaries of States, responsible for government ministries. Somalia comprises 15 regions.
Telephones: 5000 (1970).
Daily newspapers: 2 (1972).
Total circulation: 4000.
Radio: 68 000 (1975).
TV: (to be introduced in 1976).
Length of roadways: 10 702 miles

17 223 km (1971).
Universities: 1.
Adult illiteracy: 40% (claimed after the 1974–5 literacy campaign).
Expectation of life: Males 36·9 years; females 40·1 years (1965–70).
Defence: Military service: voluntary. Total armed forces 23 000. Defence expenditure, 1974 $15 million.
Wildlife: Lion, leopard, elephant, cheetah, wild cat, lizard, water buck, crocodile, turtle, dik-dik, zebra, hippopotamus, baboon, gazelle. Partridge, bustard, ostrich, duck, guinea fowl, heron.
Cinemas: 26 (seating capacity 23 000) in 1970.

SOUTH AFRICA

Official name: Republic of South Africa, or Republiek van Suid-Afrika.
Population: 21 448 172 (1970 census); 24 920 000 (1974 est).
Area: 471 445 miles² *1 221 037 km²* (exclusive of Walvis Bay 434 miles² *1124 km²*).
Languages: Afrikaans, English, Xhosa, Zulu, Sesuto, Tswana, Sepedi.
Religions: Christian, Muslim and Hindu minorities.
Capital city: Administrative: Pretoria, population 543 950 (1970).
Legislative: Cape Town (Kaapstad), 691 296 (1970).
Other principal towns (1970): Durban 729 857; Johannesburg 654 682; Port Elizabeth 386 577; Germiston 210 298; Vereeniging 169 553; Benoni 149 166; Bloemfontein 148 282; Springs 141 820.
Highest point: Injasuti, 11 182 ft *3408 m*.
Principal mountain range: Drakensberg.
Principal rivers: Orange (Oranje), 1300 miles *2092 km*; Limpopo; Vaal.
Head of State: Dr Nicolaas D Diederichs (b. 17 Nov. 1903), State President.
Prime Minister: Balthazar Johannes Vorster (b. 13 Dec. 1915).
Climate: Generally temperate (cool summers, mild winters). Average temperatures about 63 °F. In Cape Town, average maximum 63 °F (July) to 79 °F (February), minimum 45 °F (July) to 60 °F (January, February), rainiest month is July (10 days). In Johannesburg, average maximum 62 °F (June) to 78 °F (December, January), minimum 39 °F (June, July) to 58 °F (January, February), rainiest month is January (12 days). Absolute maximum temperature 124·8 °F (*51,56 °C*), Main, 28 Jan. 1903; absolute minimum 5·5 °F (*−14,7 °C*), Carolina, 23 July 1926.

Crops: Maize, wheat, sugar-cane, sorghum, potatoes, oranges, groundnuts.
Monetary unit: Rand. 1 rand = 100 cents
Denominations:
Coins ½, 1, 2, 5, 10, 20, 50 cents, 1 rand
Notes 10s, 1, 5, 10, 20, 100 South Africa pounds; 1, 2, 5, 10, 20 rand.

Exchange rate to US dollar: 0·8 (February 1976).
Political history and government: After the Boer War of 1899–1902 two former Boer republics, the Transvaal and the Orange Free State, became part of the British Empire. On 31 May 1910 they were merged with the British territories of Natal and Cape Colony (now Cape Province) to form the Union of South Africa, a dominion under the British crown. Under the Statute of Westminster, passed by the British Parliament in December 1931 and accepted by South Africa in June 1934, the Union was recognized as an independent country within the Commonwealth. Following a referendum among white voters on 5 Oct. 1960, South Africa became a republic, outside the Commonwealth, on 31 May 1961. Legislative power rests with the bicameral Parliament made up exclusively of European (white) members who hold office for 5 years (subject to dissolution). The Senate has 55 members: 42 elected by electoral colleges of the four provinces, two similarly elected for South West Africa (Namibia) and 11 nominated by the State President (two for each province and South West Africa and one representative of the Cape Coloured people). The House of Assembly has 171 members directly elected by Europeans: 165 for South Africa and 6 for South West Africa. Only Europeans may vote. Executive power rests with the State President, elected by a joint session of Parliament for a 7-year term as constitutional Head of State. He acts on the advice of the Executive Council (Cabinet), led by a Prime Minister, which is appointed by the President and responsible to Parliament. Each province has an Administrator appointed by the President for 5 years and a provincial council elected (by whites only) for 5 years.
Telephones: 1 935 831 (1975).
Daily newspapers: 22 (1970).
Radio: 2 336 750 (1975).
TV: 250 000 (1976 est).
Length of roadways: 198 838 miles *320 000 km*.
Length of railways: 12 373 miles *19 909 km*.
Universities: 16.
Adult illiteracy: 59·7% (males 59·3%, females 60·2%) in 1960 (Africans only).
Expectation of life:
All races: Males 47·8 years; females 50 years (1965–70). For non-Africans (1959–61):

224

siatic: Males 57·70 years; females 59·57 years.
oloured: Males 49·62 years; females 54·28 years.
'hite: Males 64·73 years; females 71·67 years.
efence: Military service: 12 months. Total ·gular forces 50 000. Defence expenditure 975–6 $1332 million.
Vildlife: Lion, elephant, leopard, water uffalo, giraffe, many kinds of antelope. ireat variety of birds.
Cinemas: 686 (seating capacity 498 000) nd 120 drive-in (1971).

SPAIN

Official name: El Estado Español (The Spanish State).
Population: 33 956 376 (1970 census); 35 472 000 (1975 est).
Area: 194 897 miles² *504 782 km².*
Languages: Spanish (Castilian), Catalán, Basque.
Religions: Roman Catholic.
Capital city: Madrid, population 3 146 071 (1970).
Other principal towns (1970): Barcelona 1 745 142; Valencia 653 690; Sevilla (Seville) 548 072; Zaragoza (Saragossa) 479 843; Bilbao 410 490; Málaga 374 452; Las Palmas 287 038; Murcia 243 759; Hospitalet 241 978; Valladolid 236 341; Córdoba 235 632; Palma de Mallorca 234 098.
Highest point: Mt Teide (Canary Is), 12 190 ft *3716 m.*
Principal mountain ranges: Pyrenees, Cordillera Cantábrica, Sierra Morena.
Principal rivers: Ebro (556 miles [895 *km*]) Duero (Douro), Tajo (Tagus), Guadiana, Guadalquivir.
Head of State: HM King Juan Carlos (b. 5 Jan. 1938).
Head of Government: Adolfo Suárez González (b. 25 Sept. 1932). President of the Government (Prime Minister).
Climate: Cool summers and rainy winters on north coast; hot summers and cold winters in interior; hot summers and mild winters on south coast. In Madrid, average maximum 47 °F (January) to 87 °F (July), minimum 33 °F (January) to 62 °F (July, August), rainiest month is March (11 days). In Barcelona, average maximum 56 °F (January) to 82 °F (August), minimum 42 °F (January) to 69 °F (July, August), rainiest months are April, May, October (each 8 days). Absolute maximum temperature 46,2 °C (*115·2 °F*), Gualulcacin, 17 July 1943; absolute minimum −32,0 °C (−*25. 6°F*), Estangento, 2 Feb. 1956.
Crops: Potatoes, grapes, wheat, barley, maize, oranges, tomatoes, onions, sugar-beet.

Monetary unit: Spanish peseta. 1 peseta = 100 céntimos.
Denominations:
 Coins 10, 50 céntimos, 1, 2½, 5, 25, 50, 100 pesetas.
 Notes 100, 500, 1000 pesetas.
Exchange rate to US dollar: 66.65 (February 1976).
Political history and government: In the civil war of 1936–39 the forces of the republic (established on 14 Apr. 1931) were defeated. Gen Francisco Franco, leader of the successful insurgent forces, acted as Head of State until his death on 20 Nov. 1975. In accordance with the 1947 Law of Succession, Prince Juan Carlos de Borbón, grandson of the last reigning monarch, became King on 22 Nov. 1975. Spain is now an hereditary monarchy, with the King as Head of State. He appoints the President of the Government (Prime Minister) and, on the latter's recommendation, other members of the Council of Ministers. The Council initiates legislation for discussion by the unicameral Legislative Assembly (*Cortes*) of 570 members (400 elected for 4 years, most of them indirectly, and others nominated). The King is advised by the Council of State (also partly elected and partly nominated) and by the Council of the Realm (16 members, including 10 elected by the *Cortes*). Spain comprises 50 provinces, each with its own Assembly (*Diputación Provincial*) and an appointed Civil Governor.
Telephones: 7 042 968 (1975).
Daily newspapers: 115 (1972).
 Total circulation: 3 396 000.
Radio: 8 075 000   **TV:** 6 525 000 (1975).
Length of roadways: 88 319 miles *142 136 km* (1974).
Length of railways: 12 016 miles *19 338 km* (1973).
Universities: 23 (plus 8 technical universities).
Adult illiteracy: 9·9% (males 5·7%; females 13·7%) in 1970.
Expectation of life: Males 67·32 years; females 71·90 years (1960).
Defence: Military service: 18 months. Total armed forces 302 300 (1975). Defence expenditure, 1974 $1372 million.
Wildlife: Pardel lynx, mongoose, genet, wild boar, beach marten, chamois.
Cinemas: 8486 (seating capacity about 5 million) in 1972.
* Figures refer to Metropolitan Spain, including the Canary Islands and Spanish North Africa (Ceuta and Melilla).

SRI LANKA

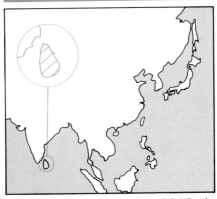

Official name: The Republic of Sri Lanka ('Exalted Ceylon').
Population: 12 711 143 (1971 census); 13 249 000 (1973 est).
Area: 25 332 miles² *65 610 km².*
Languages: Sinhala (official) 69%; Tamil 23%; English.
Religions: Buddhist 66·2%; Hindu 18·5%;

Christian 8·4%; Muslim 6·8% (1963).
Capital city: Colombo, population 618 000 (1973 est).
Other principal towns (1973): Dehiwala-Mt Lavinia 136 000; Jaffna 112 000; Kandy (1971) 93 602; Galle (1971) 72 720.
Highest point: Pidurutalagala, 8292 ft *2527 m.*
Principal rivers: Mahaweli Ganga (203 miles [*327 km*]), Kelani Ganga.
Head of State: William Gopallawa, MBE (b. 16 Sept. 1897), President.
Prime Minister: Mrs Sirimavo Ratwatte Dias Bandaranaike (b. 17 Apr. 1916).
Climate: Tropical, with average temperature of about 80 °F (*27 °C*). Monsoon strikes the south-west of the island. In Colombo average maximum 85 °F (June to December) to 88 °F (March, April); minimum 72 °F (December, January, February) to 78 °F (May), May and October rainiest (each 19 days).
Crops: Rice, coconuts, cassava, tea, rubber.
Monetary unit: Sri Lanka rupee. 1 rupee = 100 cents.
Denominations:
 Coins 1, 2, 5, 10, 25, 50 cents, 1 rupee.
 Notes 2, 5, 10, 50, 100 rupees.
Exchange rate to US dollar: 7.707 (February 1976).
Political history and government: Ceylon (now Sri Lanka) was a British dependency until achieving independence, within the Commonwealth, on 4 Feb. 1948. The country became a republic, under the present name, on 22 May 1972, when the Governor-General became President. Legislative and executive power is vested in the unicameral National State Assembly, with 157 members (151 elected for 6 years by universal adult suffrage and 6 appointed by the government). Direction of the government is vested in the Cabinet, headed by the Prime Minister, which is responsible to the Assembly. Ministers are appointed by the President, a constitutional Head of State appointed for 4 years on the nomination of the Prime Minister. The country is divided into 21 districts, each administered by an appointed government agent.
Telephones: 67 753 (1973).
Daily newspapers: 25 (1971).
 Total circulation: 536 000.
Radio: 530 000 (1975).
Length of roadways (1973): 13 883 miles *22 339 km.*
Length of railways: 954 miles *1535 km.*
Universities: 1 (with five campuses).
Adult illiteracy: 24·5% (males 14·4%; females 35·9%) in 1963.
Expectation of life: Males 64·8 years; females 66·9 years (1967).
Defence: Military service: voluntary. Total armed forces 13 600. Defence expenditure, 1975 $24 million.
Wildlife: Elephant, leopard, deer, buffalo, bear, wild boar, monkeys, Kabaragoya lizard, python, tic polonga, cobra. Over 400 species of birds.
Cinemas: 303 (seating capacity 128 500) in 1971.

SUDAN

Official name: Al Jumhuriyat as-Sudan al-Dimuqratiya (The Democratic Republic of Sudan).
Population: 14 171 732 (1973 census).
Area: 967 500 miles² *2 505 813 km².*
Languages: Arabic, Nilotic, others.
Religions: Muslim (in North), Animist (in South).
Capital city: Al Khurtum (Khartoum), population 321 666 (1973 est).
Other principal towns (1973): Omdurman

305 308; Khartoum North 161 278; Port Sudan 123 000; Wadi Medani 81 904; El Obeid 74 109.

Highest point: Mt Kinyeti, 10 456 ft *3187 m*.

Principal mountain ranges: Darfur Highlands, Nubian Mts.

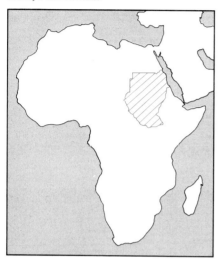

Principal rivers: Nile (the Blue Nile and White Nile join at Khartoum), 4145 miles *6670 km*.

Head of State: Maj-Gen Ga'afar Muhammad an-Numairi (b. 1 Jan. 1930), President and Prime Minister.

Climate: Hot and dry in desert areas of north (average maximum up to 111 °F); rainy and humid in tropical south. Average temperature about 70 °F. In Khartoum, average maximum 90 °F (January) to 1'07 °F (May), minimum 59 °F (January) to 79 °F (June); rainiest month is August (6 days). Absolute maximum 49,0 °C (*120·2 °F*), Wadi Halfa, 7 and 8 June 1932, 9 and 13 June 1933, 19 June 1941; absolute minimum —0,8 °C (*30·6 °F*), Zalingei, 6 Feb. 1957.

Crops: Sorghum, cassava, groundnuts, cotton, sweet potatoes, millet, water melons, sesame seed.

Monetary unit: Sudanese pound. 1 pound = 100 piastres = 1000 millièmes.

Denominations:
Coins 1, 2, 5, 10 millièmes, 2, 5, 10 piastres.
Notes 25, 50 piastres, 1, 5, 10 pounds.

Exchange rate to US dollar: 0.3482 (February 1976).

Political history and government: An Anglo-Egyptian condominium from 19 Jan. 1899 until becoming an independent parliamentary republic on 1 Jan. 1956. On 25 May 1969 the civilian government was overthrown by army officers, under Col. (promoted Maj-Gen) Ga'afar an-Numairi, who established a Revolutionary Command Council (RCC) and introduced the country's present name. Gen Numairi became Prime Minister on 28 Oct. 1969. On 13 Aug. 1971 the RCC promulgated a provisional constitution, proclaiming socialist principles. Gen Numairi was elected President (unopposed) in September 1971 and inaugurated for a 6-year term on 12 Oct. 1971. The RCC was dissolved and the Sudanese Socialist Union (SSU) established as the country's sole political party. A new definitive constitution was introduced on 8 May 1973. Executive power is vested in the President, nominated by the SSU, and he appoints a Council of Ministers. Legislative power is vested in the People's Assembly of 250 members (225 elected for 4 years by universal adult suffrage and 25 appointed by the President). The Southern Region also has an elected regional assembly. Sudan comprises 15 provinces.

Telephones: 56 146 (1975).

Daily newspapers: 22 (1970).
Total circulation: 127 000 (18 dailies).

Radio: 115 000 (1975).

TV: 100 000 (1975).

Length of roadways: *c.* 31 070 miles *c. 50 000 km*.

Length of railways: 2971 miles *4781 km*.

Universities: 2 (plus the Khartoum branch of Cairo University).

Adult illiteracy: 95·6% (males 92·6%; females 98·4%) in 1956.

Expectation of life: Males 44·9 years; females 47·3 years (1965–70).

Defence: Military service: voluntary. Total armed forces 48 600 (1975). Defence expenditure, 1975–6 $97 million.

Wildlife: Lion, cheetah, leopard, giraffe, zebra, antelope, buffalo, chimpanzee, baboon, hippopotamus, crocodile, lizard, snakes. Shoebill, guinea fowl, geese, crane, stork, bustard, pelican, weaver bird, starling, shrike.

Cinemas: 52 (seating capacity 84 000) in 1972.

SURINAM

Official name: Republic of Surinam.

Population: 384 903 (census of 31 Dec. 1971); 405 000 (estimate for 31 Dec. 1974).

Area: 63 037 miles² *163 265 km²*.

Languages: Dutch 37·1%; Hindustani 31·7%; Javanese 15·4%; Creole 13·8% (1964).

Religions: Christian 45·1%; Hindu 27·8%; Muslim 20·2% (1964).

Capital city: Paramaribo, population 151 500 (1971).

Other principal towns: Nieuw Nickerie, Nieuw Amsterdam.

Highest point: Julianatop 4218 ft *1286 m*.

Principal mountain ranges: Wilhelmina Gebergte, Kayser Gebergte.

Principal rivers: Corantijn, Nickerie, Coppename, Saramacca, Suriname, Commewijne, Maroni (Marowijne).

Head of State: Dr Johann Henri Eliza Ferrier (b. 12 May 1910), President.

Prime Minister: Henck A E Arron.

Climate: Sub-tropical, with fairly heavy rainfall and average temperatures of 21 °C 30 °C (*73 °F* to *88 °F*).

Crops: Rice, bananas, sugar-cane.

Monetary unit: Surinam gulden (guilder or florin. 1 guilder = 100 cents.

Denominations:
Coins 1, 5, 10, 25 cents, 1 guilder.
Notes 1, 2½, 5, 10, 25, 100, 1000 guilder

Exchange rate to US dollar: 1.7: (February 1976).

Political history and government: Formerly a Dutch possession, with full intern autonomy from 29 Dec. 1954. Surina became an independent republic on 25 No 1975. Legislative power is held by the Stat. (Legislative Assembly) of 39 member elected by universal adult suffrage for years. The Assembly elects the President an Vice-President. Executive power is vested the appointed Council of Ministers led b the Prime Minister, which is responsible the Assembly. Surinam comprises 9 district

Telephones: 13 000 (1973).

Daily newspapers: 6 (1972).
Total circulation: 24 000 (five dailies).

Radio: 110 000 (1975).

TV: 33 500 (1975).

Length of roadways: 2310 miles *3717 k*

Length of railways: 54 miles *86 km*.

Universities: 1.

Adult illiteracy: 20% (estimate).

Expectation of life: Males 62·5 years females 66·7 years (1963).

Cinemas: 31 (seating capacity 19 000) an one drive-in (1973).

SWAZILAND

Official name: The Kingdom of Swaziland

Population: 374 697 (1966 census) 494 000 (1975 est.).

Area: 6704 miles² *17 363 km²*.

Languages: English, Siswati.

Religions: Christian, Animist.

Capital city: Mbabane, population 20 755 (1973 est.).

Other principal towns Manzini 16 000; Havelock 5000; Big Bend 3500; Mhlame 2600; Pigg's Peak 2100.

Highest point: Emlembe, 6113 ft *1863 m*.

Principal mountain range: Lubombo.

Principal rivers: Usutu, Komati, Umbuluzi, Ingwavuma.

Head of State: HM King Sobhuza II, KBE (b. 22 July 1899).

Prime Minister: Col Maphevu Dlamini.

Climate: Rainy season October to March. Annual average at Mbabane, in high veld

in, in low veld 25 in. Average temperatures 52 °F to 72 °F at Mbabane, 56 °F to) °F at Manzini, warmer on low veld.
rops: Sugar-cane, maize, citrus fruits.
Monetary unit: Lilangeni (plural: emalangeni). 1 lilangeni = 100 cents.
enominations:
Coins 1, 2, 5, 10, 20, 50 cents, 1 lilangeni.
Notes 1, 2, 5, 10 emalangeni.
xchange rate to US dollar: 0·87 February 1976).
olitical history and government: A rmer British protectorate, with internal elf-government from 25 Apr. 1967 and full dependence, within the Commonwealth, om 6 Sept. 1968. Swaziland is a monarchy, ith executive authority vested in the King. e appoints a Cabinet, led by a Prime Minister. Under the constitution, legislative ower is vested in the bicameral Parliament: House of Assembly, with 30 voting members (24 elected and 6 nominated by the King) and the Attorney-General; and a enate of 12 members (6 appointed by the King and 6 nominated by the House). On 12 pr. 1973, in response to a motion passed by oth Houses, the King repealed the constitu-ion, suspended political activity and as-umed all legislative, executive and judicial owers. Swaziland has 4 districts, each dministered by an appointed District Commissioner.
Telephones: 6969 (1975).
Radio: 55 000 (1975).
ength of roadways: 1501 miles *2415 km.*
ength of railways: 139 miles *224 km.*
Universities: 1.
dult illiteracy: Males 68·7%; females '2·5% (1966).
xpectation of life: Males 39·4 years; emales 42·6 years (1965–70).
Defence: An army of 300 men (1974).
Cinemas: 4 (seating capacity 2400) and one rive-in (1971).
* South African currency is also legal tender.

SWEDEN

Official name: Konungariket Sverige (Kingdom of Sweden).
Population: 8 076 903 (1970 census); 8 195 000 (1975 est.)
Area: 173 732 miles² *449 964 km².*
Languages: Swedish; Finnish and Lapp in north.
Religion: Lutheran.
Capital city: Stockholm, population 671 226 (1974 est.)
Other principal towns (1974): Göteborg (Gothenburg) 445 704; Malmö 246 647; Uppsala 137 543; Norrköping 119 470; Västerås 118 044; Örebro 117 560.
Highest point: Kebnekaise, 6965 ft *2123 m.*
Principal mountain ranges: Norrland Mountains, Smaland Highlands.

Principal rivers: Ume (310 miles [*499 km*]), Torne (354 miles [*569 km*]), Angerman (279 miles [*449 km*]), Klar (304 miles [*489 km*]), Dal (323 miles [*520 km*]).
Head of State: King Carl XVI Gustaf (b. 30 Apr. 1946).
Prime Minister: Sven Olof Joachim Palme (b. 30 Jan. 1927).
Climate: Summers mild and warm; winters long and cold in north, more moderate in south. In Stockholm, average maximum 31 °F (January, February) to 70 °F (July), minimum 22 °F (February) to 55 °F (July), rainiest month is August (ten days). Absolute maximum temperature 38,0 °C (*100·4 °F*), Ultana, 9 July 1933; absolute minimum, −53,3 °C (*−63·9 °F*), Laxbacken, 13 Dec. 1941.
Crops: Barley, wheat, oats, potatoes, rye, sugar-beet.
Monetary unit: Swedish krona. 1 krona = 100 öre.
Denominations:
Coins 5, 10, 25, 50 öre, 1, 2, 5, 10 kronor.
Notes 5, 10, 50, 100, 1000, 10 000 kronor.
Exchange rate to US dollar: 4.379 (February 1976).
Political history and government: Sweden has been a constitutional monarchy, traditionally neutral, since the constitution of 6 June 1809. Parliamentary government was adopted in 1917 and universal adult suffrage introduced in 1921. A revised constitution was introduced in January 1975. The King is Head of State but has very limited formal prerogatives. Legislative power is held by the Parliament (*Riksdag*), which has been uni-cameral since 1 Jan. 1971. It has 350 members (to be reduced to 349 at the next elec-tion) elected by universal adult suffrage for 3 years, using proportional representation. Executive power is held by the Cabinet, led by the Prime Minister, which is responsible to the *Riksdag*. Under the 1975 constitution, the Prime Minister is nominated by the Speaker of the *Riksdag* and later confirmed in office by the whole House. After approval, the Prime Minister appoints other members of the Cabinet, Sweden is divided into 24 counties, each administered by a governor.
Telephones: 5 178 082 (1975).
Daily newspapers: 114 (1970).
Total circulation: 4 324 000.
Radio: Combined radio and TV licences:
TV: 2 881 694; radio only: 231 938 (1975).
Length of roadways: 60 577 miles *97 490 km* (1 Jan. 1974).
Length of railways: 7520 miles *12 102 km.*
Universities: 6 (plus 3 technical).
Expectation of life: Males 71·97 years; females 77·41 years (1972).
Defence: Military service: Army and Navy 7½ to 15 months; Air Force 9 to 14 months. Total regular armed forces 18 100. Defence expenditure, 1975–6 $2475 million.
Wildlife: Elk, deer, hare, mink, weasel, fox; bear, lynx, wolf (numbers diminishing) Lemming. Grouse, pheasant, woodcock, capercaillie, crane, ptarmigan, white owl, golden eagle.
Cinemas: 1329 (1974).

SWITZERLAND

Official name: Schweizerische Eidgenossenschaft (German), Confédération suisse (French), Confederazione Svizzera (Italian): The Swiss Confederation.
Population: 6 269 783 (1970 census); 6 431 000 (1973 est.)
Area: 15 943 miles² *41 293 km².*
Languages: German 64·9%; French 18·1%; Italian 11·9%; Spanish 2·0%; Romanche 0·8% (1970).

Religions: Roman Catholic 49·4%; Protestant 47·8% (1970).
Capital city: Bern (Berne), population 156 100 (1974 est.)
Other principal towns (1974): Zürich 404 300; Basel (Bâle or Basle) 201 000; Genève (Genf or Geneva) 164 300; Lausanne 137 400; Winterthur 92 000; St Gallen (Saint-Gall) 80 900; Luzern (Lucerne) 68 500.
Highest point: Dufourspitze (Monte Rosa), 15 203 ft *4634 m* (first climbed 1855).
Principal mountain ranges: Alps.
Principal rivers: Rhein (Rhine) and Aare, Rhône, Inn, Ticino.
Head of State: Rudolf Gnägi (b. 3 Aug. 1917), President for 1976.

Climate: Generally temperate, with wide variations due to altitude. Cooler in north, warm on southern slopes. In Zürich, average maximum 48 °F (January) to 86 °F (July), minimum 14 °F (January) to 51 °F (July), rainiest months are June and July (each 15 days). In Geneva, January coldest (29 °F to 39 °F), July warmest (58 °F to 77 °F). Absolute maximum temperature 38,7 °C (*101·7 °F*), Basel, 29 July 1947; absolute minimum −35,8 °C (*−34·4 °F*), Jungfraujoch, 14 Feb. 1940.
Crops: Wheat, rye, barley, potatoes, sugar-beet, vegetables.
Monetary unit: Schweizer Franken (Swiss franc). 1 franc = 100 Rappen (centimes).
Denominations:
Coins 1, 2, 5, 10, 20, 50 centimes, 1, 2, 5 francs.
Notes 5, 10, 20, 50, 100, 500, 1000 francs.
Exchange rate to US dollar: 2.559 (February 1976).
Political History and government: Since 1815 Switzerland has been a neutral con-federation of 19 cantons and 6 half-cantons. The present constitution, establishing a republican form of government, was adopted on 29 May 1874. The cantons hold all powers not specifically delegated to the federal authorities. Legislative power is held by the bicameral Federal Assembly: a Council of States with 44 members representing the cantons (two for each canton and one for each half-canton), elected for 3 to 4 years; and the National Council with 200 members directly elected by universal adult suffrage for 4 years, using proportional representa-tion. The two Houses have equal rights. A referendum on 7 Feb. 1971 approved women's suffrage in federal elections. Executive power is held by the Federal Council, which has 7 members (not more than one from any canton) elected for 4 years by a joint session of the Federal Assembly. Each member of the Council has ministerial responsibility as head of a Federal Depart-ment. The Council elects one of its members to be President of the Confederation (also

presiding over the Council) for one calendar year at a time. Each canton has a constitution, an elected unicameral legislature and an executive.

Telephones: 3 790 351 (1975).
Daily newspapers: 98 (1972).
Total circulation: 2 466 000.
Radio: 2 060 927 (1975).
TV: 1 746 357 (1975).
Length of roadways: 37 720 miles *60 705 km.*
Length of railways: 3084 miles *4963 km.*
Universities: 8 (plus 2 technical universities).
Expectation of life: Males 69·21 years; females 75·03 years (1960–70).
Defence: Military service: four months initial training; refresher training of three weeks a year for eight years, two weeks for three years, and one week for two years. Total regular armed forces 6500. Dcfcncc expenditure 1975 $1041 million.
Wildlife: Ibex, chamois, deer, boar, fox. Eagle, white grouse.
Cinemas: 554 (seating capacity 204 000) in 1972.

SYRIA

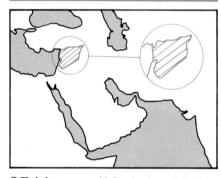

Official name: Al-Jumhuriya al-Arabiya as-Suriya (The Syrian Arab Republic).
Population: 6 304 685 (1970 census); 7 355 000 (1975 est).
Area: 71 498 miles² *185 180 km².*
Languages: Arabic (official); Kurdish; Armenian; Turkish; Circassian.
Religion: Muslim.
Capital city: Dimash'q (Damascus), population 836 668 (1970).
Other principal towns (1970): Halab (Aleppo) 639 428; Homs 215 423; Hama 137 421; Latakia 125 716; Deir-ez-Zor 66 000.
Highest point: Jabal ash-Shaikh (Mt Hermon), 9232 ft *2814 m.*
Principal mountain ranges: Ansariyah range, Jabal ar Ruwā.
Principal rivers: Al Furat (Euphrates headwaters) (420 miles *676 km* out of 1400 miles *2253 km*), Asi (Orontes).
Head of State: Lt-Gen Hafiz al-Assad (b. 1928), President.
Prime Minister: Maj-Gen Abdul-Rahman Khlai fawi (b. 1927).
Climate: Variable. Hot summers, mild winters and ample rainfall on coast. Inland it is arid with hot, dry summers and cold winters. In Damascus, average maximum 53 °F (January) to 99 °F (August), minimum 36 °F (January) to 64 °F (July, August), rainiest month is January (seven days).
Crops: Wheat, barley, cotton, tomatoes, grapes, olives.
Monetary unit: Syrian pound. 1 pound = 100 piastres.
Denominations:
Coins 2½, 5, 10, 25, 50 piastres, 1 pound.
Notes 1, 5, 10, 25, 50, 100, 500 pounds.

Exchange rate to US dollar: 3.675 (February 1976).
Political History and government: Formerly part of Turkey's Ottoman Empire. Turkish forces were defeated in the First World War (1914–18). In 1920 Syria was occupied by French forces, in accordance with a League of Nations mandate. Nationalists proclaimed an independent republic on 16 Sept. 1941. The first elected parliament met on 17 Aug. 1943, French powers were transferred on 1 Jan. 1944 and full independence achieved on 12 Apr. 1946. Syria merged with Egypt to form the United Arab Republic, proclaimed on 1 Feb. 1958 and established on 21 Feb. 1958. Following a military *coup* in Syria on 28 Sept. 1961, the country resumed separate independence, under its present name, on 29 Sept. 1961. Left-wing army officers overthrew the government on 8 Mar. 1963 and formed the National Council of the Revolutionary Command (NCRC), which took over all executive and legislative authority. The NCRC installed a cabinet dominated by the Arab Socialist Renaissance (Ba'ath) Party. This party has held power ever since. Lt-Gen Hafiz al-Assad became Prime Minister on 18 Nov. 1970 and assumed Presidential powers on 22 Feb. 1971. His position was approved by popular referendum on 12 Mar. 1971 and he was sworn in for a 7-year term as President on 14 Mar. 1971. Legislative power is held by the People's Council, originally comprising 173 members appointed for two years on 16 Feb. 1971 to draft a permanent constitution. The constitution, proclaiming socialist principles, was approved by referendum on 12 Mar. 1973 and adopted two days later. It declares that the Ba'ath Party is 'the leading party in the State and society'. A new People's Council, with 186 members, was elected by universal adult suffrage in May 1973. A majority of seats are held by the National Progressive Front, formed in March 1972 by a grouping of five parties. The Head of State is leader of the Ba'ath Party and President of the Front. Syria has 13 administrative districts.
Telephones: 143 320 (1973).
Daily newspapers: 5 (1972).
Radio: 878 200 (1975).
TV: 224 000 (1975).
Length of roadways: 10 383 miles *16 710 km.*
Length of railways: 713 miles *1148 km.*
Universities: 3.
Adult illiteracy: 60·0% (males 40·4%; females 80·0%) in 1970.
Expectation of life: Males 49·9 years; females 52·8 years (1965–70).
Defence: Military service: 30 months. Total armed forces 177 500. Defence expenditure 1975 $668 million.
Wildlife: Wolf, hyena, antelope, gazelle, porcupine, squirrel, hedgehog, otter, dormouse, rat, hare, lizard, chameleon, viper. Flamingo, pelican, eagle, kite, buzzard, falcon.
Cinemas: 112 (seating capacity 55 000) in 1967.

TANZANIA

Official name: The United Republic of Tanzania (Jamhuri ya Muungano wa Tanzania).
Population: 12 313 469 (1967 census); 14 763 000 (1974 est).
Area: 364 900 miles² *945 087 km².*
Languages: English, Swahili.
Religions: Traditional beliefs. Christian, Muslim.

Capital city: Dar es Salaam, population 517 000 (1975 est).
Other principal towns (1967): Tan 61 058; Mwanza 34 861; Grusha 32 45 Moshi 26 853; Dodoma 23 559; Irin 21 746.
Highest point: Mount Kilimanjar 19 340 ft *5894 m.*
Principal mountain range: Southe Highlands.
Principal rivers: Pangani (Ruvu), Ruf Rovuma.
Head of State: Dr Julius Kambara Nyerere (b. March 1922), President.
Prime Minister: Rashidi Mfaume Kawav (b. 1929).

Climate: Varies with altitude. Tropica (hot and humid) on Zanzibar, and on th coast and plains. Cool and semi-temperat in the highlands. In Dar es Salaam, averag maximum 83 °F to 88 °F, minimum 66 ° to 77 °F. In Zanzibar Town, averag maximum 82 °F (July) to 91 °F (February March), minimum 72 °F (July–September to 77 °F (March–April), average annua rainfall 62 in, April rainiest (16 days), Jul driest (four days).
Crops: Cassava, maize, bananas, coconuts cotton, sisal, cashew nuts, mangoes, coffee cloves.
Monetary unit: Tanzanian shilling. shilling = 100 cents.
Denominations:
Coins 5, 20, 50 cents, 1, 5 shillings.
Notes 5, 10, 20, 100 shillings.
Exchange rate to US dollar: 8.2865 (February 1976).
Political history and government: Tanganyika, a former United Nations Trus Territory under British administration, became an independent member of the Commonwealth on 9 Dec. 1961 and a republic on 9 Dec. 1962. Zanzibar, a sultanate under British protection, became an independent constitutional monarchy within the Commonwealth on 10 Dec. 1963. The Sultan was overthrown by revolution on 12 Jan. 1964 and the People's Republic of Zanzibar proclaimed. The two republics merged on 26 Apr. 1964 to form the United Republic of Tanganyika and Zanzibar (renamed Tanzania on 29 Oct. 1964) and remained in the Commonwealth. An interim constitution, declaring Tanzania a one-party state, was approved by the legislature on 5 July 1965 and received the President's assent three days later. Tanganyika and Zanzibar have separate ruling parties. Legislative power is held by the unicameral National Assembly, with 214 members: 96 (including four unopposed in 1975) elected

rom Tanganyika by universal adult suffrage or five years; 46 appointed from Zanzibar; 0 regional party secretaries; 8 nominated y the President; 9 appointed to the East African Legislative Assembly (an organ of he East African Community comprising Kenya, Tanzania and Uganda); and 35 elected by the National Assembly from other institutions. Executive power lies with he President, elected by popular vote for ive years. He appoints a First Vice-President who is Chairman of the Zanzibar Revolutionary Council), a Second Vice-President who is also Prime Minister) and a Cabinet. Zanzibar continues to have a separate administration, under the Afro-Shirazi Party, for internal affairs. On the mainland, government policy is directed by the Tanganyika African National Union (TANU), whose leading decision-making organ is the National Executive, elected by party members.

Telephones: 58 000 (1975).
Daily newspapers: 4 (1969).
 Total circulation: 61 000.
Radio: 230 000 (1973).
TV: 4000 (1969).
Length of roadways: 10 403 miles *16 742 km* (1969).
Length of railways: 1591 miles *2560 km.*
Adult illiteracy: 71·9% (males 57·3%; females 85·1%) in 1967.
Universities: 1.
Expectation of life: Males 40·2 years; females 43·4 years (1965–70).
Defence: Military service: voluntary. Total armed forces 14 600. Defence expenditure 1974–5 $42 million.
Wildlife: Elephant, hippopotamus, giraffe, monkeys, lemurs, bush pigs. Great variety of birds.
Cinemas: 29 (seating capacity 13 500) in 1971.

THAILAND

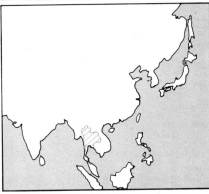

Official name: Prathet Thai (Kingdom of Thailand), also called Prades Thai or Muang-Thai (Thai means free).
Population: 35 103 000 (1970 census); 42 277 000 (1975 est.).
Area: 198 500 miles² *514 000 km².*
Language: Thai.
Religions: Buddhist, Muslim minority.
Capital city: Krungt'ep (Bangkok), population 1 867 297 (1970).
Other principal town (1970): Thonburi 627 989.
Highest point: Doi Inthanon, 8452 ft *2576 m.*
Principal rivers: Mekong (2600 miles *[4184 km]*) Chao Pyha (154 miles *[247 km]*).
Head of State: HM King Bhumibol Adulyadej (b. 5 Dec. 1927).
Prime Minister: Mom Rachawongse Seni Pramoj (b. 26 May 1905).
Climate: Tropical monsoon climate (humid). Three seasons–hot, rainy, and cool. Average temperature 85 °F. In Bangkok, average

maximum 87 °F (November, December) to 95 °F (April), minimum 68 °F (December, January) to 77 °F (April, May), rainiest month is September (15 days). Absolute maximum 44,1 °C *(111·4 °F)* Mae Sariang, 25 Apr. 1958; absolute minimum 0,1 °C *(32·2 °F).* Loey, 13 Jan. 1955.
Crops: Rice, cassava, maize, bananas, sugar-cane, coconuts, water melons, kenaf, rubber, groundnuts.
Monetary unit: Baht. 1 baht = 100 satangs.
Denominations:
 Coins ½, 1, 5, 10, 20, 25, 50 satangs, 1 baht.
 Notes 50 satangs, 1, 5, 10, 20, 100, 500 baht.
Exchange rate to US dollar: 20.40 (February 1976).
Political history and government: Thailand, called Siam before 1939, is a kingdom with an hereditary monarch as Head of State. The military regime established on 17 Nov. 1971 was forced to resign, following popular demonstrations, on 14 Oct. 1973. An interim government was formed and a new constitution, legalising political parties, was promulgated on 7 Oct. 1974. The country is a constitutional monarchy, with legislative power vested in the bicameral National Assembly, comprising a Senate (100 members appointed by the King for six years) and a House of Representatives (between 240 and 300 members, directly elected for four years by universal adult suffrage). Executive power is held by the Council of Ministers, led by the Prime Minister, which is appointed by the King but may be removed by the Assembly. Elections to the House of Representatives (271 members) were held on 26 Jan. 1975, when 42 political parties offered candidates, but the House was dissolved on 12 Jan. 1976. New elections, with 39 parties contesting 279 seats, were held on 4 April 1976. Thailand comprises 71 provinces.
Telephones: 270 840 (1975).
Daily newspapers: 28 in Bangkok (1974).
 Total circulation: over 800 000.
Radio: 3 009 000 (1973).
TV: 241 000 (1971).
Length of roadways: 10 989 miles *17 686 km* (1972).
Length of railways: 5115 miles *8233 km.*
Universities: 12.
Adult illiteracy: 21·3% (males 12·7%; females 29·5%) in 1970.
Expectation of life: Males 53·6 years; females 58·7 years (1960).
Defence: Military service: two years. Total armed forces 204 000. Defence expenditure 1975–6 $371 million.
Wildlife: Elephant, leopard, tiger, panther, deer, crocodile, sea turtle, snakes, lizards. Many varieties of birds including drongo, martin, babbler.
Cinemas: 565 (seating capacity 422 200) in 1970.

TOGO

Official name: La République togolaise (The Togolese Republic).
Population: 1 950 646 (1970 census); 2 171 000 (1974 est.).
Area: 21 600 miles² *56 000 km².*
Languages: French (official), Ewe.
Religions: Animist, Christian and Muslim minorities.
Capital city: Lomé, population 214 200 (1974 est.).
Other principal towns (1971): Sokodé 30 100; Palimé 20 900; Atakpamé 17 800; Bassari 16 000.
Highest point: 3018 ft *919 m.*
Principal rivers: Mono, Oti (Volta tributary).

Head of State: Major-Gen Etienne Gnassingbe Eyadéma (b. 1935), President.
Climate: Equatorial (hot and humid). On coast average temperatures 76 °F to 82 °F, higher inland (average 97 °F in drier north).
Crops: Cassava, yams, millet, sorghum, maize, taro, cocoa, coffee.

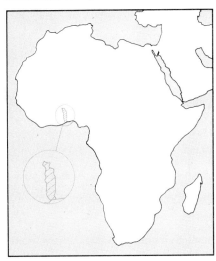

Monetary unit: Franc de la Communauté financière africaine.
Denominations:
 Coins 1, 2, 5, 10, 25, 50, 100, 500 CFA francs.
 Notes 100, 500, 1000, 5000 CFA francs.
Exchange rate to US dollar: 224.24 (February 1976).
Political history and government: Formerly a United Nations Trust Territory under French administration, an independent republic since 27 Apr. 1960. An army *coup* on 13 Jan. 1967 deposed the President and established military rule under Lieut-Col (later Major-Gen) Etienne Gnassingbe Eyadéma, who suspended the constitution and dissolved the National Assembly. Eyadéma proclaimed himself President on 14 Apr. 1967. Political parties were banned and the President rules by decree through an appointed Council of Ministers. On 29 Nov. 1969 the President established a single ruling party which mobilizes support for the government. Togo is divided into four regions, each administered by an appointed Inspector.
Telephones: 7000 (1973).
Daily newspapers: 3 (1972).
 Total circulation: 13 000.
Radio: 50 000 (1973).
TV: n/a.
Length of roadways: 4361 miles *7019 km.*
Length of railways: 309 miles *498 km.*
Universities: 1.
Adult illiteracy: 90–95% (estimate).
Expectation of life: Males 36·9 years; females 40·1 years (1965–70).
Defence: Total armed forces 1750.
Wildlife: Lion, leopard, elephant (in small numbers), crocodile, monkeys, hippopotamus, snakes, lizards. Rock-fowl.
Cinemas: 2 (seating capacity 2300) in 1964.

TONGA

Official name: The Kingdom of Tonga.
Population: 77 429 (1966 census); 94 000 (1973 est.).
Area: 270 miles² *699 km².*
Languages: Tongan, English.
Religions: Christian, mainly Wesleyan.
Capital city: Nuku'alofa, population 25 000 (1973 est.).

Highest point: Kao, 3380 ft *1030 m.*
Head of State: HM King Taufa'ahau Tupou IV, GCVO, KCMG, KBE (b. 4 July 1918).
Prime Minister: HRH Prince Fatafehi Tu'ipelehake, CBE (b. 7 Jan. 1922).
Climate: Mild. Temperature from May to November rarely exceeds 84 °F in the shade, with minimum temperature of 52 °F.
Crops: Coconuts, bananas.
Monetary unit: Pa'anga. 1 pa'anga = 100 seniti.
Denominations:
  Coins 1, 2, 5, 10, 20, 50 seniti; 1, 2 pa'anga.
  Notes ½, 1, 2, 5, 10 pa'anga.
Exchange rate to US dollar: 0.684 (February 1976).
Political history and government: Tonga is a kingdom ruled by an hereditary monarchy. It was under British protection from 18 May 1900 until becoming independent, within the Commonwealth, on 4 June 1970. The King is Head of State and Head of Government. He appoints, and presides over, a Privy Council which acts as the national Cabinet. Apart from the King, the Council includes six Ministers, led by the Prime Minister (currently the King's brother), and the Governors of two island groups. The uni-cameral Legislative Assembly comprises 23 members: the King, the Privy Council, seven hereditary nobles elected by their peers and seven representatives elected by the people. Elected members hold office for three years. There are no political parties.
Telephones: 1125 (1975).
Radio: 9100 (1973).
Length of roadways: 271 miles *436 km.*
Expectation of life: 55·2 years (both sexes) in 1965.
Defence: Defence budget, 1972–3; 74 100 pa'anga.
Cinemas: 5 (seating capacity 3600) in 1969.

TRINIDAD & TOBAGO

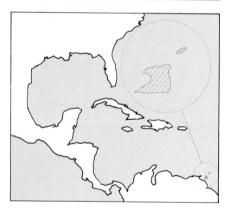

Official name: Trinidad and Tobago.
Population: 945 210 (1970 census); 1 062 000 (1973 est).
Area: 1980 miles² *5128 km².*
Languages: English (official), Hindi, French, Spanish.
Religions: Christian, Hindu, Muslim minorities.
Capital city: Port-of-Spain, population 65 400 (1972 est).
Other principal towns (1972): San Fernando 33 800; Arima 11 636.
Highest point: Mount Aripo, 3085 ft *940 m.*
Principal mountain ranges: Northern and Southern, Central.
Principal rivers: Caroni, Ortoire, Oro-puche.
Head of State: Sir Ellis Emmanuel Innocent Clarke, GCMG (b. 28 Dec. 1917), President.

Prime Minister: The Rt Hon Dr Eric Eustace Williams, CH (b. 25 Sept. 1911).
Climate: Tropical, with an annual average temperature of 84 °F. The dry season is January to May.
Crops: Sugar cane, cocoa, coconuts, citrus fruit, ronca beans.
Monetary unit: Trinidad and Tobago dollar. 1 dollar = 100 cents.
Denominations:
  Coins 1, 5, 10, 25, 50 cents, 1 dollar.
  Notes 1, 5, 10, 20 dollars.
Exchange rate to US dollar: 2.37 (February 1976).
Political history and government: Formerly a British dependency, an independent member of the Commonwealth since 31 Aug. 1962. Became a republic on 1 Aug. 1976. Legislative power is vested in a bicameral parliament, comprising a Senate (24 members appointed for up to five years) and a House of Representatives (36 members elected by universal adult suffrage for five years). The President is a constitutional Head of State elected by both Houses of Parliament. He appoints the Prime Minister to form a Cabinet from members of Parliament. The Cabinet has effective control of the government and is responsible to Parliament.
Telephones: 66 385 (1975).
Daily newspapers: 3.
  Total circulation: 135 000.
Radio: 256 000 (1971).
TV: 82 000 (1972).
Length of roadways: 2629 miles *4230 km.*
Universities: 1.
Expectation of life: Males 62·15 years; females 66·33 years (1959–61).
Defence: Army of about 1000.
Wildlife: Lizards, alligator, snakes. Bird of Paradise, scarlet Ibis.
Cinemas: 66 (seating capacity 42 700) and 5 drive-in (1972).

TUNISIA

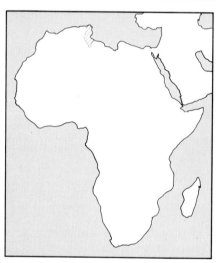

Official name: Al-Jumhuriya at-Tunisiya (The Republic of Tunisia).
Population: 4 533 351 (1966 census); 5 641 000 (1974 est).
Area: 63 170 miles² *163 610 km².*
Languages: Arabic, French.
Religions: Muslim, Jewish and Christian minorities.
Capital city: Tunis, population 468 997 (1966).
Other principal towns (1966): Sfax 100 000; Bizerta 95 023; Sousse 82 666; Kairouan 82 299; Gabés 76 356; Béja 72 034; Djerba 65 533.

Highest point: Djebel Chambi, 5066 *1544 m.*
Principal rivers: Medjerda (300 mil [*482 km*]).
Head of State: Habib Ben Ali Bourguib (b. 3 Aug. 1903), President.
Prime Minister: Hedi Nouira (b. 6 Ap 1911).
Climate: Temperate, with winter rain, o coast; hot and dry inland. In Tunis, Augu warmest (69 °F to 91 °F), January coole (43 °F to 58 °F) December rainiest (14 days Absolute maximum temperature 55,0 ° (*131·0 °F*), Kébili, 7 Dec. 1931; absolut minimum −9,0 °C (*15·8 °F*), Fort-Sain 22 Dec. 1940.
Crops: Wheat, olives, barley, tomatoe melons, grapes.
Monetary unit: Tunisian dinar. 1 dinar 1000 millimes.
Denominations:
  Coins 1, 2, 5, 10, 20, 50, 100, 500 millime
  Notes ½, 1, 5, 10 dinars.
Exchange rate to US dollar: 0.421 (February 1976).
Political history and government: For merly a monarchy, ruled by the Bey o Tunis. A French protectorate from 188 until independence on 20 Mar. 1956. Th campaign for independence was led by th Neo-Destour Party (founded by Habib Bourguiba), since October 1964 called th *Parti Socialiste Destourien* (PSD), th Destourian (Constitutional) Socialist Party Elections were held on 25 Mar. 1956 for Constitutional Assembly, which met on Apr. 1956 and appointed Bourguiba a Prime Minister two days later. On 25 Jul 1957 the Assembly deposed the Bey abolished the monarchy and established republic, with Bourguiba as President. new constitution was promulgated on 1 June 1959. Legislative power is vested in th unicameral National Assembly, first elected on 8 Nov. 1959. It has 112 members elected (unopposed in 1974) by universal adul suffrage for five years. Executive power i held by the President, elected for five years by popular vote at the same time as th Assembly (in March 1975 the Assembly proclaimed Bourguiba as President for life) The President, who is Head of State and Head of Government, appoints a Council o Ministers, headed by a Prime Minister which is responsible to him. Tunisia ha been a one-party state since 1963. The country is divided into 18 governorates.
Telephones: 114 250 (1975).
Daily newspapers: 4 (1972).
  Total circulation: 156 000.
Radio: 400 000 (1972).
TV: 80 000 (1972).
Length of roadways: 11 665 miles *18 774 km* (1973).
Length of railways: 1298 miles *2089 km* (1972).
Universities: 1.
Adult illiteracy: 76·0% (males 62·9%; females 89·4%) in 1966.
Expectation of life: Males 50·2 years; females 53·1 years (1965–70).
Defence: Military service: 12 months selective. Total regular armed forces 24 000. Defence expenditure 1975–6 $56 million.
Wildlife: Gazelle, fennec, antelope, gundi, jerboa, lizards.
Cinemas: 103 (seating capacity 44 800) in 1968.

TURKEY

Official name: Türkiye Cumhuriyeti (Republic of Turkey).
Population: 35 666 549 (1970 census); 39 180 000 (1975 est).

Area: 301 382 miles² *780 576 km²*.
Languages: Turkish 90·2%; Kurdish 6·9%; Arabic 1·2%; Zaza 0·5% (1965).
Religion: Muslim.
Capital city: Ankara (Angora), population 522 350 (1974 est.).
Other principal towns (1974): İstanbul 2 487 100; İzmir (Smyrna) 619 150; Adana 397 003; Bursa 335 498; Gaziantep 294 950; Eskişehir 254 169; Konya 238 946.
Highest point: Büyük Ağridaği (Mt Ararat), 17 011 ft *5185 m*.

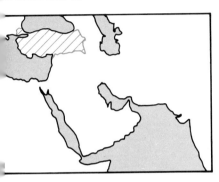

Principal mountain ranges: Armenian Plateau, Toros Dağlari (Taurus Mts), Kuzey Anadolu Dağlari.
Principal rivers: Firat (Euphrates), Dicle (Tigris), Kizilirmak (Halys), Sakarya.
Head of State: Admiral Fahri S Korutürk (b. 1903), President.
Prime Minister: Süleyman Demirel (b. 1924).
Climate: Hot, dry summers and cold, snowy winters in interior plateau; mild winters and warm summers on Mediterranean coast. In Ankara, average maximum 39 °F (January) to 87 °F (August), minimum 24 °F (January) to 59 °F (July, August), rainiest month is December (9 days). In Istanbul, average maximum 45 °F (January) to 81 °F (July, August), minimum 36 °F (January) to 66 °F (August), rainiest month is December (15 days). Absolute maximum temperature 46,2 °C (*115·2 °F*), Diyarbakir, 21 July 1937; absolute minimum −43,2 °C (−45·8 °F), Karaköse, 13 Jan. 1940.
Crops: Wheat, barley, maize, melons, grapes, potatoes, tomatoes, cotton, apples, citrus fruit, olives, sugar-beet, onions, hazelnuts, tobacco, figs.
Monetary unit: Turkish lira. 1 lira = 100 kuruş.
Denominations:
    Coins 1, 5, 10, 25, 50 kuruş, 1, 2, 5, 10 liras.
Notes 5, 10, 20, 50, 100, 500, 1000 liras.
Exchange rate to US dollar: 15.15 (February 1976).
Political history and government: Formerly a monarchy, ruled by a Sultan. Following the disintegration of the Ottoman Empire after the First World War, power passed to the Grand National Assembly, which first met on 23 Apr. 1920. The Assembly approved a new constitution on 20 Jan. 1921, vesting executive and legislative authority in itself. It abolished the sultanate on 1 Nov. 1922 and declared Turkey a republic on 29 Oct. 1923. The armed forces overthrew the government on 27 May 1960, the Assembly was dissolved and political activities suspended until 12 Jan. 1961. A new constitution was approved by referendum on 9 June 1961 and took effect on 25 Oct. 1961. Legislative power is vested in the bicameral Grand National Assembly, comprising the Senate of the Republic, with 183 members (150 elected by universal suffrage for staggered six-year terms, 15 appointed by the President and 18 holding life member-

ship in 1975), and the National Assembly (450 members elected by universal adult suffrage for four years). The Grand National Assembly elects one of its members to be President of the Republic for a seven-year term. The President appoints the Prime Minister from among members of the legislature. The Prime Minister, who should have the support of a majority in both houses, appoints a Council of Ministers to assist him in administering the government. Turkey is composed of 67 provinces.
Telephones: 899 923 (1975).
Daily newspapers: 433 (1972).
    Total circulation. n/a.
Radio: 4 091 142 (1974).
TV: 455 752 (1974).
Length of roadways: 82 130 miles *132 176 km* (1975).
Length of railways: 6108 miles *9831 km*.
Universities: 11.
Adult illiteracy: 48·6% (males 30·9%; females 66·4%) in 1970.
Expectation of life: Males 52·8 years; females 56·1 years (1965–70).
Defence: Military service: 20 months. Total regular armed forces 453 000. Defence expenditure, 1975–6 $2174 million.
Wildlife: Wolf, bear, jackal, deer, angora goat, mole.
Cinemas: 2424 (seating capacity 1 164 800) in 1970.

UGANDA

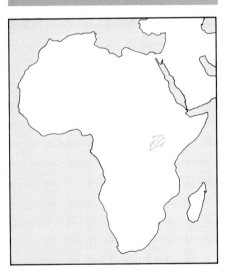

Official name: The Republic of Uganda.
Population: 9 548 847 (1969 census); 11 171 900 (1974 est.).
Area: 91 452 miles² *236 860 km²*.
Languages: English (official), Luganda, Ateso, Runyankore.
Religions: Christian, Muslim, traditional beliefs.
Capital city: Kampala, population 330 700 (1969).
Other principal towns (1969): Jinja-Njeru 52 509; Bugembe 46 884; Mbale 23 544; Entebbe 21 096.
Highest point: Mount Stanley, 16 763 ft *5109 m*.
Principal mountain ranges: Ruwenzori.
Principal rivers: Nile, Semliki.
Head of State: Field Marshal Idi Amin Dada (b. 1 Jan. 1928), President.
Climate: Tropical, with an average temperature of 71 °F. There is a seasonal variation of only 20 °F.
Crops: Cassava, sweet potatoes, yams,

millet, maize, sorghum, cotton, coffee, groundnuts, sugar-cane, tea.
Monetary unit: Uganda shilling. 1 shilling = 100 cents.
Denominations:
    Coins 5, 10, 20, 50 cents, 1, 2, 5 shillings.
    Notes 10, 20, 50, 100 shillings.
Exchange rate to US dollar: 8.2865 (February 1976).
Political history and government: Formerly a British dependency, an independent member of the Commonwealth since 9 Oct. 1962. Uganda became a republic, with a nominal President and an executive Prime Minister, on 9 Oct. 1963. A provisional constitution, effective from 15 Apr. 1966, ended the former federal system and introduced an executive President. A unitary republic was established on 8 Sept. 1967. The president was deposed on 25 Jan. 1971 by an army *coup*, led by Major-Gen (later Field Marshal) Idi Amin Dada, who assumed full executive powers as Head of the Military Government and suspended political activity. The National Assembly was dissolved on 2 Feb. 1971, when Amin declared himself Head of State, took over legislative powers and suspended parts of the 1967 constitution. He was proclaimed President on 21 Feb. 1971 and rules with the assistance of an appointed Council of Ministers. Uganda is divided into 10 provinces, each administered by a Governor.
Telephones: 42 903 (1975).
Daily newspapers: 7 (1972).
    Total circulation: 78 000 (6 dailies).
Radio: 275 000 (1972).
TV: 15 000 (1972).
Length of roadways: 14 927 miles *24 024 km*. (1974).
Length of railways: 808 miles *1301 km* (1974).
Universities: 1.
Adult illiteracy: 74·9% (males 63·2%; females 86·1%) in 1959 (African population aged 16 and over).
Expectation of life: Males 45·9 years; females 49·2 years (1965–70).
Defence: Military service: voluntary. Total armed forces 21 000. Defence expenditure 1974–5 $49 million.
Wildlife: Gorilla, chimpanzee, buffalo, elephant, rhinoceros, giraffe, eland, zebra, oryx, lion, leopard.
Cinemas: 16 (seating capacity 8700) and 1 drive-in (1971).

UNION OF SOVIET SOCIALIST REPUBLICS

map over page

Official name: Soyuz Sovyetskikh Sotsialisticheskikh Respublik. (Abbreviation in Cyrillic scriptis CCCP).
Population: 241 720 134 (census of 15 Jan. 1970); 253 259 000 (estimate, 1 Jan. 1975).
Area: 8 649 550 miles² *22 402 200 km²*.
Languages (1970): Russian (official) 58·7%; Ukrainian 14·6%; Uzbek 3·8%; Byelorussian 3·2%; Tatar 2·4%; Kazakh 2·2%; over 50 others.
Religions: No state religion. Christian with Jewish and Muslim minorities.
Capital city: Moskva (Moscow), population 7 635 000 (1975 est.).
Other principal towns (1974): Leningrad (St Petersburg) 4 243 000; Kiyev (Kiev) 1 887 000; Tashkent 1 552 000; Baku 1 359 000; Khar'kov 1 330 000; Gor'kiy (Nizhniy-Novgorod) 1 260 000; Novosibirsk (Novonikolayevsk) 1 243 000; Kuibyshev (Samara) 1 140 000; Sverdlovsk (Yekaterinburg) 1 122 000; Minsk 1 095 000.

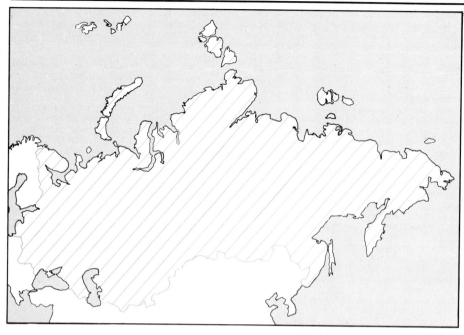

Highest point: Pik Kommunizma, 24 589 ft *7494 m* (first climbed 3 Sept. 1933).
Principal mountain ranges: Caucasus, Urals, Pamirs, Tien Shan.
Principal rivers: 14 rivers over 1000 miles *1609 km* in length.
Head of State: Nikolay Viktorovich Podgorny (b. 18 Feb. 1903), Chairman of the Presidium of the Supreme Soviet.
Political Leader: Leonid Ilyich Brezhnev (b. 19 Dec. 1906), General Secretary of the Communist Party of the Soviet Union.
Head of Government: Aleksey Nikolayevich Kosygin (b. 21 Feb. 1904), Chairman of the Council of Ministers.
Climate: Great variations. Summers generally short and hot, winters long and cold. Very hot in central Asia, extremely cold in north-east Siberia. Average maximum and minimum temperatures for selected places:
Moscow: Average maximum 21 °F (January) to 76 °F (July). Average minimum 9 °F (January) to 55 °F (July). Rainiest months July, August (each 12 days).
Archangel: Average maximum 9 °F (January) to 64 °F (July). Average minimum 0 °F (February) to 51 °F (July). Rainiest month October (12 days).
Odessa: Average maximum 28 °F (January) to 79 °F (July). Average minimum 22 °F (January) to 65 °F (July, August). Rainiest months January and June (each 7 days).
Yakutsk: Average maximum −45 °F (January) to 73 °F (July). Average minimum −53 °F (January) to 54 °F (July). Rainiest months September, October, November (each 10 days).
Absolute maximum temperature 50,0 °C (*122·0 °F*), Termez (Uzbekistan), July 1912; absolute minimum −71,1 °C (*−96·0 °F*). Oymyakon, 1964.
Crops: Wheat, barley, oats, rye, maize, potatoes, sugar beet, cotton, sunflower seed, grapes.
Monetary unit: Rubl' (ruble or rouble). 1 rouble = 100 kopeks.
Denominations:
Coins 1, 2, 3, 5, 10, 15, 20, 50 kopeks, 1 rouble.
Notes 1, 3, 5, 10, 25, 50, 100 roubles.
Exchange rate to US dollar: 0.758 (February 1976).
Political history and government: Formerly the Russian Empire, ruled by an hereditary Tsar (of the Romanov dynasty from 1613). Prompted by discontent with

autocratic rule and the privations caused by the First World War, a revolution broke out on 27 Feb. (12 March New Style) 1917, causing the abdication of the last Tsar three days later and the establishment of a provisional government. During the following months Soviets (councils) were elected by some groups of industrial workers and peasants. A republic was proclaimed on 1 Sept. (14 Sept. NS) 1917. A political struggle developed between government supporters and the Bolshevik Party (called the Communist Party from 1919), which advocated the assumption of power by the Soviets. On 25 Oct. (7 Nov. NS) 1917 the Bolsheviks led an insurrection, arrested the provisional government and transferred power to the All-Russian Congress of Soviets. The Bolsheviks won only 175 out of 707 seats in the elections of 25–27 Nov. 1917 for the Constituent Assembly. The Assembly met on 18 Jan. 1918 but was forcibly dissolved by the Bolsheviks, who proclaimed a 'dictatorship of the proletariat'. On 31 Jan. 1918 Russia was proclaimed a Republic of Soviets. A constitution for the Russian Soviet Federative Socialist Republic (RSFSR) was adopted on 10 July 1918. Armed resistance to Communist rule developed into civil war (1917–22) but was eventually crushed. During the war other Soviet Republics were set up in the Ukraine, Byelorussia and Transcaucasia. These were merged with the RSFSR by a Treaty of Union, establishing the USSR, on 30 Dec. 1922. By splitting the territory of the original four, two more Republics were added in 1925 and another in 1929. A new constitution was adopted on 5 Dec. 1936, when the number of Republics was raised from seven to eleven. On 31 Mar. 1940 territory ceded by Finland became part of the newly-formed Karelo-Finnish SSR. Territory ceded by Romania on 28 June 1940 became part of the new Moldavian SSR on 2 Aug. 1940. Lithuania, Latvia and Estonia were annexed on 3–6 Aug. 1940, raising the number of Union Republics to 16. This was reduced to the present 15 on 16 July 1956, when the Karelo-Finnish SSR was merged with the RSFSR.
The Soviet Union is formally a federal state comprising 15 Union (constituent) Republics of equal status, voluntarily linked and having the right to secede. Some of the 15 Union Republics contain Autonomous Republics and Autonomous

Regions. The RSFSR also includes National Areas. The highest organ of state power is the bicameral legislature, the Supreme Soviet of the USSR, comprising the Soviet (Council) of the Union, with 7[.] members elected from constituencies, and the Soviet (Council) of Nationalities, with 750 members (32 from each of the 15 Union Republics; 11 from each of the 20 Autonomous Republics; five from each of the eight Autonomous Regions; one from each of the 10 National Areas). Both houses have equal rights and powers and their terms run concurrently. Members are directly elected (from a single list of candidates) for four year terms by universal adult suffrage. At a joint session the members elect the Presidium of the Supreme Soviet (37 members) to be the legislature's permanent organ. The Supreme Soviet also appoints the Council of Ministers (called People's Commissars until 16 Mar. 1946), headed by a Chairman to form the executive and administrative branch of government, responsible to the Supreme Soviet. Each of the 15 Union Republics has a constitution and state structure on the same pattern as the central government, with a unicameral Supreme Soviet and a Council of Ministers to deal with internal affairs.
Throughout the whole country, real power is held by the highly centralised Communist Party of the Soviet Union (CPSU), the only legal party, which has an absolute monopoly of power in all political affairs and controls government at all levels. The Party had over 15 million members in 1976. Its highest authority is, in theory, the Party Congress, which should be convened at least every five years. The Congress elects the Central Committee (287 members and 139 alternate members were chosen in 1976) which supervises Party work and directs state policy. The Committee, which meets twice a year, elects a Political Bureau (Politburo), which is the Party's most powerful policy-making body. In 1976 the Politburo had 15 members (including the General Secretary) and six candidate members. Apart from the RSFSR, each Union Republic has its own Communist Party with a Central Committee led by a First Secretary, but they are subsidiary to, and subject to direction from, the CPSU.
Telephones: 15 782 000 (1975).
Daily newspapers: 647 (1971).
Total circulation: 84 953 000.
Radio: 110 300 000 (1973).
TV: 49 200 000 (1973).
Length of roadways: 868 676 miles *1 398 000 km.*
Length of railways: 159 754 miles *257 100 km.*
Universities: 63 (plus 58 technical universities).
Adult illiteracy: 0·3% (males 0·2%; females 0·3%) in 1970.
Expectation of life: Males 65 years; females 74 years (1968–9).
Defence: Military service: Army and Air Force 2 years; Navy and Border Guards 2–3 years. Total armed forces: 3 575 000 (1975). Defence expenditure (1975) $36 400 million.
Wildlife: Reindeer, Arctic fox, ermine, polar bear, brown bear, wolf, elk, fox, rodents, lemming, vole, vipers, dormouse, tree frog, toad, leopard, viper, turtle, suslik, jerboa, wild cat, wild ass.
Hawk, grey partridge, heron, snipe, goose, gull, grebe, capercailzie, owls, woodpecker, crossbill, bullfinch, jay, pigeon, golden oriole, nightingale, blackbird, chaffinch, greenfinch, bustards, eagles, lark, sandgrouse, house sparrow.
Cinemas: 146 300 permanent; 8800 mobile (1974).

UNITED ARAB EMIRATES

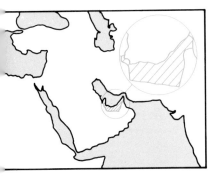

Official name: Ittihād al-Imārāt al-Arabiyah.
Population: 179 126 (1968 census); 342 000 (1975 est).

Area: 32 300 miles² *83 650 km².*
Languages: Arabic.
Religions: Muslim.
Capital city: Abu Dhabi, population 80 000 (1975 est).
Other principal town (1975): Dubai 100 000.
Highest point: Western Al-Hajar, 3900 ft *1189 m.*
Principal mountain ranges: Al-Hajar.
Head of State: Shaikh Zaid ibn Sultan an-Nahayan (b. 1918), President.
Prime Minister: Shaikh Makhtum ibn Rashid al-Makhtum.
Climate: Very hot and dry, with summer temperatures of over 100 °F; cooler in the eastern mountains.
Monetary unit: UAE dirham. 1 dirham = 10 dinars = 100 fils.
Denominations:
 Coins 1, 5, 10, 25, 50 fils, 1 dinar.
 Notes 1, 5, 10, 50, 100, 1000 dirhams.
Exchange rate to US dollar: 3.947 (February 1976).
Political history and government: Formerly the seven shaikhdoms of Trucial Oman (the Trucial States), under British protection. An independent federation (ori-

ginally of six states), under a provisional constitution, since 2 Dec. 1971. The seventh, Ras al Khaimah, joined the UAE on 11 Feb. 1972. The highest federal authority is the Supreme Council of the Union, comprising the hereditary rulers of the seven emirates (the rulers of Abu Dhabi and Dubai have the power of veto). From its seven members the Council elects a President and a Vice-President. The President appoints a Prime Minister and a Union (Federal) Council of Ministers, responsible to the Supreme Council, to hold executive authority. The legislature is the Union National Council, a consultative assembly (comprising 40 members appointed for two years by the emirates) which considers laws proposed by the Council of Ministers. There are no political parties. In local affairs each ruler has absolute power over his subjects.
Telephones: 34 282 (1975).
Daily newspapers: 3.
Radio: 50 000.
TV: 16 000.
Adult illiteracy: 79·1% (males 73·0%; females 91·1%) in 1968.
Defence: Total armed forces 15 000.
Cinemas: 2 (seating capacity 1500) in 1960.

UNITED STATES OF AMERICA

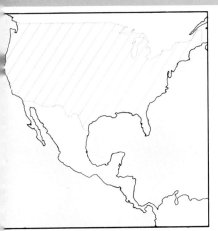

Official name: United States of America.
Population: 203 235 298 (1970 census); 212 300 000 (1975 est).
Area: 3 615 122 miles² *9 363 123 km².*
Language: English.
Religions: Protestant, Roman Catholic, Jewish, Orthodox.
Capital city: Washington DC. Population 723 000 (1974 est).
Head of State: Gerald Rudolph Ford (born 14 July 1913), President.
Monetary unit: US dollar ($). 1 dollar = 100 cents.

Denominations:
 Coins 1, 5, 10, 25, 50 cents, 1 dollar.
 Notes 1, 2, 5, 10, 20, 50, 100 dollars.
GNP: $ 1 498 800 million (1975).
Telephones: 143 972 000 (1975).
Daily newspapers: 1768 (1974)
 Total circulation: 61 877 000.
Radio: 368 600 000 (1973).
TV: 110 million (1973).
Length of roadways: 3 786 713 miles *6 094 108 km.*
Length of railways: 218 024 miles *350 875 km.*
Universities: 2606.
School leaving age: 16.
Adult illiteracy: 1·0%.
Expectation of life: Males 67·4 years; females 75·1 years (1972).
Defence: Military service voluntary. Total forces 2 130 000. Defence expenditure 1975 $92 800 million.
Wildlife: Mississippi Alligator, Californian Sea-lion, Rattlesnake, Ground Puma, Bear, Blue Jay, American Robin, Heron, Woodpecker.
Cinemas: 12 187 (1967).

The United States of America ranks fourth in size (3 615 122 miles² *9 363 123 km²*), fourth in population (212 300 000 estimated at 1975), and first in production of all the countries in the world (40%).
The area of the 48 conterminous states comprises 3 022 260 miles² *7 827 617 km².*

The principal mountain ranges are listed on pp. 80. The highest point is Mount McKinley (20 320 ft [*6193 m*]) in Alaska.
There are eight US river systems involving rivers in excess of 1000 miles *1609 km* in length of which by far the vastest is the Mississippi–Missouri.
The population is divided 88·3% white and 11·7% non-white. The population of foreign origin included at March 1972:

Jewish	6 460 000
Italian	8 764 000
German	25 543 000
British (UK)	29 548 000
Polish	5 105 000
Russian	2 188 000
Irish (Republic)	16 408 000
Spanish and Spanish origin	9 178 000
French	5 420 000

The principal religious denominations in 1972 were (in millions):

Roman Catholic	48·2
Baptist	27·3
Methodist	13·0
Lutheran	8·8
Jewish	5·6
Presbyterian	4·1
Protestant Episcopal Church	3·2
Eastern Orthodox	3·9
Mormon	2·0
United Church of Christ	1·9

THE 50 STATES OF THE UNITED STATES OF AMERICA

Name, with date and order of (original) admission into the Union. Nicknames	Area (inc inland water). Pop. at 1970 Census (with rankings). Population density per mile² per km². State Capital. Admin. divisions	Major Cities (with population, at 1970, unless later date given)
ALABAMA (Ala.) 14 Dec. 1819 (22nd) 'Heart of Dixie' 'Cotton State' 'Yellowhammer State'	51 609 miles² *133 667 km²* (29th) 3 444 165 (21st) 66·7 *25,8* Montgomery 67 counties	Birmingham (300 910) Mobile (190 026) Huntsville (139 282) Montgomery (133 386) Tuscaloosa (65 773) Gadsden (53 928) Prichard (41 578)
ALASKA (Aleut, 'Great Land') 3 Jan. 1959 (49th) 'The Last Frontier' 'Land of the Midnight Sun'	586 412 miles² *1 518 800 km²* (1st) 302 173 (50th) 0·5 *0,2* Juneau 19 election districts	Anchorage (48 081) Spenard (18 089) Fairbanks (14 771) Ketchikan (6994) Juneau (6050)

Name, with date and order of (original) admission into the Union. Nicknames	Area (inc inland water). Pop. at 1970 Census (with rankings). Population density per mile² per km². State Capital. Admin. divisions	Major Cities (with population, at 1970, unless later date given)
ARIZONA (Ariz) 14 Feb. 1912 (48th) 'Grand Canyon State' 'Apache State'	113 909 miles² 295 023 km² (6th) 1 772 482 (33rd) 15·6 6,0 Phoenix 14 counties	Phoenix (582 500) Tucson (262 933) Tempe (63 550) Mesa (62 853) Yuma (29 007)
ARKANSAS (Ark) 15 June 1836 (25th) 'Land of Opportunity' 'Wonder State' 'Bear State'	53 104 miles² 137 539 km² (27th) 1 923 295 (32nd) 36·2 14,0 Little Rock 75 counties	Little Rock (132 483) Fort Smith (65 393) North Little Rock (60 040) Pine Bluff (57 389) Hot Springs (35 631) El Dorado City (25 283)
CALIFORNIA (Cal) 9 Sept. 1850 (31st) 'Golden State' Nine other towns in California have a population of over 100,000: Riverside (140,089); Torrance (134,968); Glendale (132,664); Berkeley (116,716); Huntington Beach (115,960); Pasadena (112,951); Stockton (109,963); San Bernardino (106,869); E. Los Angeles (106,033).	158 693 miles² 411 013 km² (3rd) 19 953 134 (1st) 125·7 48,5 Sacramento 58 counties	Los Angeles City (2 809 813) San Francisco (715 674) San Diego (697 027) San Jose (445 779) Oakland (361 561) Long Beach (358 879) Sacramento (257 105) Anaheim (166 408) Fresno (165 972) Santa Ana (155 762)
COLORADO (Colo) 1 Aug. 1876 (38th) 'Centennial State'	104 247 miles² 269 998 km² (8th) 2 207 259 (30th) 21·2 8,2 Denver 63 counties	Denver (514 678) Colorado Springs (135 060) Pueblo (97 453) Aurora (75 974) Boulder (66 870) Fort Collins (43 337) Greeley (38 902) Englewood (33 695)
CONNECTICUT (Conn) 9 Jan. 1788 (5th) 'Constitution State' 'Nutmeg State'	5009 miles² 12 973 km² (48th) 3 032 217 (24th) 605·4 233,7 Hartford 8 counties	Hartford (158 017) Bridgeport (156 542) New Haven (137 707) Stamford (108 798) Waterbury (108 033) New Britain (83 441) Norwalk (79 113)
DELAWARE (Del) 7 Dec. 1787 (1st) 'First State' 'Diamond State'	2057 miles² 5327 km² (49th) 548 104 (46th) 266·5 102,9 Dover 3 counties	Wilmington (80 386) Newark (21 298) Dover (17 488) Elsmere (8415) Seaford (5537) Milford (5314)
FLORIDA (Fla) 3 Mar. 1845 (27th) 'Sunshine State' 'Peninsula State'	58 560 miles² 151 670 km² (22nd) 6 789 443 (9th) 115·9 44,8 Tallahassee 67 counties	Jacksonville (528 865) Miami (334 859) Tampa (277 753) St Petersburg (216 159) Fort Lauderdale (139 590) Hialeah (102 452) Orlando (99 006) Miami Beach (87 072)
GEORGIA (Ga) 2 Jan. 1788 (4th) 'Empire State of the South' 'Peach State'	58 876 miles² 152 488 km² (21st) 4 589 575 (15th) 77·9 30,1 Atlanta 159 counties	Atlanta (497 421) Columbus (155 028) Macon (122 423) Savannah (118 349) Albany (72 623) Augusta (59 864)
HAWAII 21 Aug. 1959 (50th) 'Aloha State'	6450 miles² 16 705 km² (47th) 769 913 (40th) 119·4 46,1 Honolulu (on Oahu) 5 counties	Honolulu (324 871) Kailua-Lanikai (33 783) Hilo (26 353) Wahiawa (17 598)
IDAHO 3 July 1890 (43rd) 'Gem State' 'Gem of the Mountains'	83 557 miles² 216 412 km² (13th) 713 008 (42nd) 8·5 3,3 Boise City 44 counties, plus small part of Yellowstone Park	Boise City (74 990) Pocatello (40 036) Idaho Falls (35 776) Twin Falls (21 914) Nampa (20 768) Coeur d'Alene (16 228)

Name, with date and order of (original) admission into the Union. Nicknames	Area (inc inland water). Pop. at 1970 Census (with rankings). Population density per mile² per km². State Capital. Admin. divisions	Major Cities (with population, at 1970, unless later date given)
ILLINOIS (Ill) 3 Dec. 1818 (21st) 'Prairie State'	56 400 miles² 146 075 km² (24th) 11 113 976 (5th) 197·1 76,1 Springfield 102 counties	Chicago (3 369 357) Rockford (147 370) Peoria (126 963) Springfield (91 753) Decatur (90 397) Evanston (80 113) East St Louis (69 996)
INDIANA (Ind) 11 Dec. 1816 (19th) Moosier State'	36 291 miles² 93 993 km² (38th) 5 193 669 (11th) 143·1 55,3 Indianapolis 92 counties	Indianapolis (746 302) Fort Wayne (178 021) Gary (175 415) Evansville (138 764) South Bend (125 580) Hammond (107 885) Terre Haute (70 335)
IOWA (Ia) 28 Dec. 1846 (29th) 'Hawkeye State'	56 290 miles² 145 790 km² (25th) 2 825 041 (25th) 50·2 19,4 Des Moines 99 counties	Des Moines (201 404) Cedar Rapids (110 642) Davenport (98 469) Sioux City (85 925) Waterloo (75 533) Dubuque (62 300) Council Bluffs (60 348)
KANSAS (Kan) 29 Jan. 1861 (34th) 'Sunflower State' 'Jayhawk State'	82 264 miles² 213 063 km² (14th) 2 249 071 (28th) 27·3 10,6 Topeka 105 counties	Wichita (276 554) Kansas City (168 213) Topeka (125 011) Lawrence (45 698) Salina (37 714) Hutchinson (36 885)
KENTUCKY (Ky) (officially the Commonwealth of Kentucky) 1 June 1792 (15th) 'Bluegrass State'	40 395 miles² 104 623 km² (37th) 3 219 311 (23rd) 79·7 30,8 Frankfort 120 counties	Louisville (361 706) Lexington (108 137) Covington (52 535) Owensboro (50 329) Paducah (31 627) Ashland (29 245)
LOUISIANA (La) 30 Apr. 1812 (18th) 'Pelican State' 'Creole State' 'Sugar State' 'Bayou State'	48 523 miles² 125 674 km² (31st) 3 643 180 (20th) 75·1 29,0 Baton Rouge 64 parishes (counties)	New Orleans (593 471) Shreveport (182 064) Baton Rouge (165 963) Lake Charles (77 998) Monroe (56 374)
MAINE (Me) 15 Mar. 1820 (23rd) 'Pine Tree State'	33 215 miles² 86 026 km² (39th) 993 663 (38th) 30·0 11,6 Augusta 16 counties	Portland (65 116) Lewiston (41 779) Bangor (33 168) Auburn (24 151)
MARYLAND (Md) 28 Apr. 1788 (7th) 'Old Line State' 'Free State'	10 577 miles² 27 394 km² (42nd) 3 922 399 (18th) 370·8 143,2 Annapolis 23 counties, plus the independent city of Baltimore	Baltimore (905 759) Dundalk (85 377) Silver Spring (77 411) Bethesda (71 621) Wheaton (66 280) Catonsville (54 812)
MASSACHUSETTS (Mass) 6 Feb. 1788 (6th) 'Bay State' 'Old Colony State'	8257 miles² 21 385 km² (45th) 5 689 170 (10th) 689·0 266,0 Boston 14 counties	Boston (641 071) Worcester (176 572) Springfield (163 905) New Bedford (101 777) Cambridge (100 361)
MICHIGAN (Mich) 26 Jan. 1837 (26th) 'Wolverine State'	58 216 miles² 150 779 km² (23rd) 8 875 083 (7th) 152·5 58,9 Lansing 83 counties	Detroit (1 513 601) Grand Rapids (197 649) Flint (193 317) Lansing (131 403) Dearborn (104 199)
MINNESOTA (Minn) 11 May 1858 (32nd) 'North Star State' 'Gopher State'	84 068 miles² 217 735 km² (12th) 3 805 069 (19th) 45·3 17,5 St Paul 87 counties	Minneapolis (434 400) St Paul (309 714) Duluth (100 578) Bloomington (81 970) St Louis Park (48 922)
MISSISSIPPI (Miss) 10 Dec. 1817 (20th) 'Magnolia State'	47 716 miles² 123 584 km² (32nd) 2 216 912 (29th) 46·5 17,9 Jackson 82 counties	Jackson (153 968) Biloxi (48 486) Meridian (45 083) Greenville (39 648) Hattiesburg (38 277)

Name, with date and order of (original) admission into the Union. Nicknames	Area (inc inland water). Pop. at 1970 Census (with rankings). Population density per mile² per km². State Capital. Admin. divisions	Major Cities (with population, at 1970, unless later date given)
MISSOURI (Mo) 10 Aug. 1821 (24th) 'Show Me State'	69 686 miles² 180 486 km² (19th) 4 677 399 (13th) 67·1 25,9 Jefferson City 114 counties, plus the independent city of St Louis	St Louis (622 236) Kansas City (507 330) Springfield (120 096) Independence (111 630) St Joseph (72 691) University City (47 527)
MONTANA (Mont) 8 Nov. 1889 (41st) 'Treasure State'	147 138 miles² 381 086 km² (4th) 694 409 (43rd) 4·7 1,8 Helena 56 counties, plus small part of Yellowstone National Park	Billings (61 581) Great Falls (60 091) Missoula (29 497) Butte (23 368) Helena (22 730)
NEBRASKA (Nebr) 1 Mar. 1867 (37th) 'Cornhusker State' 'Beef State' 'Tree Planter's State'	77 227 miles² 200 017 km² (15th) 1 483 791 (35th) 19·2 7,4 Lincoln 93 counties	Omaha (346 929) Lincoln (149 518) Grand Island (31 269) Hastings (23 580) Fremont (22 962)
NEVADA (Nev) 31 Oct. 1864 (36th) 'Sagebrush State' 'Silver State' 'Battle Born State'	110 540 miles² 286 297 km² (7th) 488 738 (47th) 4·1 1,7 Carson City 17 counties	Las Vegas (125 787) Reno (72 863) North Las Vegas (36 216) Sparks (24 187) Henderson (16 395)
NEW HAMPSHIRE (NH) 21 June 1788 (9th) 'Granite State'	9304 miles² 24 097 km² (44th) 737 681 (41st) 79·0 30,6 Concord 10 counties	Manchester (87 754) Nashua (55 820) Concord (30 022) Portsmouth (25 717)
NEW JERSEY (NJ) 18 Dec. 1787 (3rd) 'Garden State'	7836 miles² 20 295 km² (46th) 7 168 164 (8th) 914·7 353,2 Trenton 21 counties	Newark (381 930) Jersey City (260 350) Paterson (144 824) Trenton (104 786) Camden (102 551) Elizabeth (112 654)
NEW MEXICO (NM) 6 Jan. 1912 (47th) 'Land of Enchantment' 'Sunshine State'	121 666 miles² 315 113 km² (5th) 1 016 000 (37th) 8·4 3,2 Santa Fe 32 counties	Albuquerque (243 751) Sante Fe (41 167) Las Cruces (37 857) Roswell (33 908) Hobbs (26 025)
NEW YORK (NY) 26 July 1788 (11th) 'Empire State'	49 576 miles² 128 401 km² (30th) 18 190 740 (2nd) 366·9 141,7 Albany 62 counties	New York City (7 895 563) Buffalo (462 768) Rochester (296 233) Yonkers (204 297) Syracuse (197 297) Albany (115 781) Utica (91 340) Niagara Falls (85 615)
NORTH CAROLINA (NC) 21 Nov. 1789 (12th) 'Tar Heel State' 'Old North State'	52 586 miles² 136 197 km² (28th) 5 082 059 (12th) 96·6 37,3 Raleigh 100 counties	Charlotte (241 178) Greensboro (144 076) Winston-Salem (133 683) Raleigh (123 793) Durham (95 438) High Point (63 259) Asheville (57 681)
NORTH DAKOTA (ND) 2 Nov. 1889 (39th) 'Sioux State' 'Flickertail State'	70 665 miles² 183 022 km² (17th) 617 761 (45th) 8·7 3,4 Bismarck 53 counties	Fargo (53 365) Grand Forks (40 060) Bismarck (34 703) Minot (32 290) Jamestown (15 078)
OHIO 1 Mar. 1803 (17th) 'Buckeye State'	41 222 miles² 106 764 km² (35th) 10 652 017 (6th) 258·4 99,8 Columbus 88 counties	Cleveland (750 879) Columbus (540 025) Cincinnati (451 455) Toledo (383 105) Akron (275 425) Dayton (242 917) Youngstown (140 909) Canton (110 053)

Name, with date and order of (original) admission into the Union. Nicknames	Area (inc inland water). Pop. at 1970 Census (with rankings). Population density per mile² per km². State Capital. Admin. divisions	Major Cities (with population, at 1970, unless later date given)
OKLAHOMA (Okla) 16 Nov. 1907 (46th) 'Sooner State'	69 919 miles² *181 089 km²* (18th) 2 559 253 (27th) 36·6 *14,1* Oklahoma City 77 counties	Oklahoma City (368 377) Tulsa (330 350) Lawton (74 470) Midwest City (48 212) Enid (44 986) Muskogee (37 331)
OREGON (Ore) 14 Feb. 1859 (33rd) 'Beaver State'	96 981 miles² *251 180 km²* (10th) 2 091 385 (31st) 21·6 *8,3* Salem 36 counties	Portland (379 967) Eugene (79 028) Salem (68 480) Medford (28 454)
PENNSYLVANIA (Pa) 12 Dec. 1787 (2nd) 'Keystone State'	45 333 miles² *117 412 km²* (33rd) 11 793 909 (3rd) 260·2 *100,4* Harrisburg 67 counties	Philadelphia (1 949 996) Pittsburgh (520 117) Erie (129 231) Allentown (109 527) Scranton (103 564) Reading (87 643) Harrisburg (68 061)
RHODE ISLAND (RI) 29 May 1790 (13th) 'Little Rhody'	1214 miles² *3144 km²* (50th) 949 723 (39th) 782·3 *302,1* Providence 5 counties	Providence (179 116) Warwick (83 694) Pawtucket (76 984) Cranston (74 287) East Providence (48 207) Woonsocket (46 820) Newport (34 562)
SOUTH CAROLINA (SC) 23 May 1788 (8th) 'Palmetto State'	31 055 miles² *80 432 km²* (40th) 2 590 516 (26th) 83·4 *32,2* Columbia 46 counties	Columbia (113 542) Charleston (66 945) Greenville (61 436) Spartanburg (44 546) Anderson (27 556)
SOUTH DAKOTA (SD) 2 Nov. 1889 (40th) 'Coyote State' 'Sunshine State'	77 047 miles² *199 551 km²* (16th) 666 257 (44th) 8·6 *3,3* Pierre 67 counties (64 county governments)	Sioux Falls (72 488) Rapid City (43 836) Aberdeen (26 476) Huron (14 299) Mitchell (13 425) Watertown (13 388)
TENNESSEE (Tenn) 1 June 1796 (16th) 'Volunteer State'	42 244 miles² *109 411 km²* (34th) 3 924 164 (17th) 92·9 *35,9* Nashville 95 counties	Memphis (623 530) Nashville-Davidson (447 877) Knoxville (174 587) Chattanooga (119 923) Jackson (39 996) Johnson City (33 770)
TEXAS 29 Dec. 1845 (28th) 'Lone Star State'	267 338 miles² *692 402 km²* (2nd) 11 196 730 (4th) 41·9 *16,2* Austin 254 counties	Houston (1 232 802) Dallas (844 401) San Antonio (654 153) Fort Worth (393 476) El Paso (322 261) Austin (251 808) Corpus Christi (204 525) Lubbock (149 101) Amarillo (127 010) Beaumont (117 548) Wichita Falls (96 265) Waco (95 326) Abilene (89 653)
UTAH 4 Jan. 1896 (45th) 'Beehive State'	84 916 miles² *219 931 km²* (11th) 1 059 273 (36th) 12·5 *4,8* Salt Lake City 29 counties	Salt Lake City (75 885) Ogden (69 478) Provo (53 131) Bountiful (27 751) Orem (25 729) Logan (22 333) Kearns (17 247)
VERMONT (Vt) 4 Mar. 1791 (14th) 'Green Mountain State'	9609 miles² *24 887 km²* (43rd) 444 932 (48th) 46·3 *17,9* Montpelier 14 counties	Burlington (38 633) Rutland (19 293) Barre (10 209) Brattleboro (9055; township 12 239)

Name, with date and order of (original) admission into the Union. Nicknames	Area (inc inland water). Pop. at 1970 Census (with rankings). Population density per mile² per km². State Capital. Admin. divisions	Major Cities (with population, at 1970, unless later date given)
VIRGINIA (Va) (officially called the Commonwealth of Virginia) 26 June 1788 (10th) 'The Old Dominion' 'Cavalier State'	40 817 miles² 105 716 km² (36th) 4 648 494 (14th) 113·9 44,0 Richmond 98 counties, plus 32 independent cities	Norfolk (307 951) Richmond (249 431) Arlington County (174 284) (unincorporated) Newport News (138 177) Hampton (120 779) Portsmouth (110 963) Alexandria (110 927) Roanoke (92 115)
WASHINGTON (Wash) 11 Nov. 1889 (42nd) 'Evergreen State' 'Chinook State'	68 192 miles² 176 616 km² (20th) 3 409 169 (22nd) 49·9 19,3 Olympia 39 counties	Seattle (530 831) Spokane (170 516) Tacoma (154 407) Everett (53 622) Yakima (45 588) Vancouver (41 859) Bellingham (39 375) Bremerton (35 307) Walla Walla (23 619)
WEST VIRGINIA (W Va) 20 June 1863 (35th) 'Mountain State' 'Panhandle State'	24 181 miles² 62 629 km² (41st) 1 744 237 (34th) 72·1 27,8 Charleston 55 counties	Huntingdon (74 315) Charleston (71 505) Wheeling (48 188) Parkersburg (44 208) Weirton (27 131) Fairmont (26 093) Clarksburg (24 864)
WISCONSIN (Wisc) 29 May 1848 (30th) 'Badger State'	56 154 miles² 145 438 km² (26th) 4 417 933 (16th) 78·7 30,4 Madison 72 counties	Milwaukee (717 372) Madison (171 769) Racine (95 162) Green Bay (87 809) Kenosha (78 805) West Allis (71 649) Wauwatosa (58 676)
WYOMING (Wyo) 10 July 1890 (44th) 'Equality State'	97 914 miles² 253 596 km² (9th) 332 416 (49th) 3·4 1,3 Cheyenne 23 counties, plus most of Yellowstone National Park	Cheyenne (40 914) Casper (39 361) Laramie (23 143) Rock Springs (11 657) Sheridan (10 856) Rawlins (7855)

20th Century Presidents

Name	Dates of Birth and Death	Party	Dates in Office
Theodore Roosevelt	27 Oct. 1858 to 6 Jan. 1919	Republican	1901–09
William Howard Taft	15 Sept. 1857 to 8 Mar. 1930	Republican	1909–13
Thomas Woodrow Wilson	28 Dec. 1856 to 3 Feb. 1924	Democratic	1913–21
Warren Gamaliel Harding	2 Nov. 1865 to 2 Aug. 1923	Republican	1921–23
John Calvin Coolidge	4 July 1872 to 5 Jan. 1933	Republican	1923–29
Herbert Clark Hoover	10 Aug. 1874 to 20 Oct. 1964	Republican	1929–33
Franklin Delano Roosevelt	30 Jan. 1882 to 12 Apr. 1945	Democratic	1933–45
Harry S Truman	8 May 1884 to 26 Dec. 1972	Democratic	1945–53
Dwight David Eisenhower	14 Oct. 1890 to 28 Mar. 1969	Republican	1953–61
John Fitzgerald Kennedy	29 May 1917 to 22 Nov. 1963	Democratic	1961–63
Lyndon Baines Johnson	27 Aug. 1908 to 22 Jan. 1973	Democratic	1963–69
Richard Milhous Nixon	b. 9 Jan. 1913	Republican	1969–74
Gerald Rudolph Ford	b. 14 July 1913	Republican	1974–

Presidential Elections

US Presidential elections occur on the first Tuesday after the first Monday of November in every fourth year—these coincide with leap years. Election is not by popular majority but by majority of votes in the Electoral College which comprises 538 Electors divided between the States on the basis of one Elector for each of the 100 Senators (upper house) and the 435 Representatives (lower house) plus, since 1964, three Electors for the District of Columbia. Thus a Presidential election victory is achieved by securing at least 270 votes. Recent results have been:

Year	Republican	Democrat	Plurality
1944	99	432	Roosevelt (D) over Dewey (R) by 333
1948	189	303	Truman (D) over Dewey (R) by 114
1952	442	89	Eisenhower (R) over Stevenson (D) by 353
1956	457	73	Eisenhower (R) over Stevenson (D) by 384
1960	219	303	Kennedy (D) over Nixon (R) by 84
1964	52	486	Johnson (D) over Goldwater (R) by 434.
1968	301	191	Nixon (R) over Humphrey (D) by 110
1972	521	17	Nixon (R) over McGovern (D) by 504

The capital city is Washington, District Columbia, with a population (estimate 197 of 723 000. Greater Washington had population of 1 808 423 (Census of 1960) an the metropolitan area had 3 020 000 (197 estimate). The District of Columbia is th seat of the US Federal Government con prising 69 miles² from west central Marylar on the Potomac River opposite Virgini The site was chosen in October 1790 b President Washington and the Capit corner stone laid by him on 18 Sept. 179 Washington became the capital (Philadelph 1790–1800) on 10 June 1800. The othe principal cities (with populations at 1 Ap 1970) are listed in the separate entries fe each of the 50 States.

Historical Note: Evidence from the mos recent radiometric dating has backdate human habitation of North America to 35 000 BC. This occupation was probabl achieved via the Bering Bridge (now the 55 mile-wide Bering Strait) from NE Asia.

The continent derived its name from th Italian explorer Amerigo Vespucci (1454 1512), discoverer of the NE South America coastal regions in 1498. The German carto grapher Martin Waldseemüller named th New World 'Terra America' in his atla published in St Dié, France, in April 1507

The earliest European landing on presen US territory was on 27 Mar. 1513 by th Spaniard Juan Ponce de León in Florida The discovery of the US Pacific coast wa by Juan R Cabrillo who landed from Mexic on 28 Sept. 1542, near San Diego, California The oldest town of European origin is S Augustine, Florida, founded on 8 Sept. 156 on the site of Seloy by Pedro Menéndez d Avilés with 1500 Spanish colonists. The British exploration of what is now US terri tory began with Philip Amadas and Arthu Barlowe in Virginia in 1584. Henry Hudso sailed into New York harbour in Septembe 1609. The Plymouth Pilgrims reached Cap Cod 54 days out from Plymouth, England in the *Mayflower* (101 passengers and 48 crew) on 9 Nov. 1620. On 6 May 1626 Pete Minuit bought Manhattan island for som trinkets valued at $39. In 1664 the area wa seized by the British and granted to Charle II's brother, the Duke of York, and the city of New Amsterdam was renamed New York

The American revolution and the War o Independence (total battle deaths 4435 occupied the years 1763–83. The inciden of the Boston Tea Party occurred on 16 Dec. 1773 and the Battle of Bunker Hil on 17 June 1775. The Declaration of Inde pendence was made on 4 July 1776. This was recognised by Britain in March 1782. General George Washington was chosen President in February 1789 and the first US Congress was called on 4 Mar. 1789.

The War of 1812 between the US and Great Britain was declared by Congress on 18 June 1812, because Britain seized US ships running her blockade of France, im pressed 2800 seamen and armed Indians who raided US territory. In 1814 Maj-Gen Robert Ross burnt the Capitol and the White House in Washington. The war which inspired national unity cost only 2260 battle deaths. The Monroe Doctrine (the isola tionism of the Americas from Europe) was declared on 2 Dec. 1823.

On 1 Nov. 1835 Texas proclaimed inde pendence from Mexico. In the Alamo in San Antonio a US garrison was massacred (including Sen David Crockett) on 6 Mar. 1836.

The secession of States over the question of slave labour on cotton plantations began with South Carolina on 20 Dec. 1860. The Southern States of South Carolina, Georgia, Alabama, Mississippi, Louisiana and Florida formed the Confederate States of America

The Pentagon, Headquarters of the U.S. Department of Defense situated in Arlington County, Virginia. (U.S. Embassy)

on 8 Feb. 1861. War broke out on 12 Apr. 1861 with the bombardment of Fort Sumter in Charleston Harbor, South Carolina. The war culminated in the Battle of Gettysburg in July 1863 during which there was a total of 43 000 casualties. President A Lincoln was assassinated on 14 Apr. 1865. Slavery was abolished by the adoption of the 13th Amendment (to the Constitution) on 18 Dec. 1865.

The total fatal casualties in the Civil War were c. 547 000 of which the Union forces (North) lost 140 400 in the field and the Confederates (South) 74 500 in battle and c. 28 500 in Union prisons. The dates of the United States' entry into the World Wars of 1914–18 and 1939–45 respectively were 6 Apr. 1917 and 8 Dec. 1941.

Climate: Its continental dimensions ensure extreme variety, ranging in temperature between the 134 °F (56,7 °C) recorded in Death Valley, California, on 10 July 1913, and the −76 °F (−60,0 °C) at Tanana, Alaska, in January 1886. Mean annual averages range between 76·6 °F at Key West, Florida, and 10·1 °F at Barrow, Alaska. Excluding Alaska and Hawaii, rainfall averages 29 in per year and ranges between 55·6 in in Louisiana and 8·6 in in Nevada.

Climate in representative population centres are:

Anchorage, Alaska: Average daily high 65 °F July; 19 °F January. Average daily low 5 °F January; 49 °F July. Days with rain 15 in August; 4 in April.

San Francisco, Cal: Average daily high 69 °F September; 55 °F January. Average daily low 45 °F January; 55 °F September. Days with rain 11 in January–February; 0 in July–August.

Washington, DC: Average daily high 87 °F July; 42 °F January. Average daily low 27 °F January; 68 °F July. Days with rain 12 in March, May; 8 in September–October.

Chicago, Illinois: Average daily high 81 °F July; 32 °F January. Average daily low 18 °F January; 66 °F July. Days with rain 12 in March, May; 9 in July–October.

Honolulu, Hawaii: Average daily high 83 °F August–September; 76 °F January–February. Average daily low 67 °F February–March; 74 °F September–October. Days with rain 15 in December; 11 in February, May.

New York, NY: Average daily high 82 °F July; 37 °F January. Average daily low 24 °F January–February; 66 °F July–August. Days with rain 12 in January, March, July; 9 in September–November.

Miami, Florida: Average daily high 88 °F July–August; 74 °F January. Average daily low 61 °F January–February; 76 °F July–August. Days with rain 18 in September; 6 in February.

Exports and Imports of leading commodities (value in millions of dollars)

Exports: Total 1973 $70 223.
Some of the major commodities were:

Grains and preparations	8495
Maize (corn)	2837
Fruit and nuts	662
Tobacco, unmanufactured	681
Crude materials, inedible, other than fuels	8384
Animal and vegetable oils and fats	684
Chemicals	5748
Machinery and transport equipment	27 842
New motor vehicles	2666
Aircraft and parts	4124
Paper and manufactures	919
Metals and manufactures	1111
Iron and steel-mill products	1258
Textiles other than clothing	1225

Imports: Total 1973 $69 121.
Some of the major commodities were:

Meat	1668
Fish	1387
Coffee, green	1566
Alcoholic beverages	996
Ores and metal scrap	1291
Petroleum and products	7548
Textile and leather machinery	625
New motor vehicles	6479
Paper and manufactures	1457
Diamonds excluding industrial	827
Metals and manufactures	6885
Iron and steel-mill products	2769
Non-ferrous base metals	1994
Textiles other than clothing	1568
Clothing	2154

Exports by principal countries of consumption:

	Value $ million
Canada	15 073
Japan	8312
Latin America Free Trade Association	7708
Germany, Federal Republic of	3756
United Kingdom	3563
Netherlands	2860
France	2263
Italy	2119
Belgium and Luxembourg	1622
Australia	1439
Spain	1319
Korea, Republic of	1242
China, Republic of (Taiwan)	1168

Imports by principal countries of production:

	Value $ million
Canada	17 670
Japan	9645
Latin America Free Trade Association	6668
Germany, Federal Republic of	5318
United Kingdom	3642
Italy	1989
China, Republic of (Taiwan)	1772
France	1717
Hong Kong	1444
Belgium and Luxembourg	1261
Australia	1062

Flag: Seven red and six white alternating stripes with a dark blue canton in the upper hoist bears 50 white stars (in nine rows of 6 and 5 alternately).

UPPER VOLTA

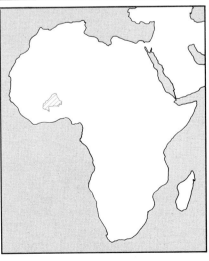

Upper Volta continued over page.

Official name: République de Haute-Volta.
Population: 6 144 013 (1975 census).
Area: 105 870 miles² *274 200 km²*.
Languages: French (official), Mossi, other African languages.
Religions: Animist, Muslim and Christian minorities.
Capital city: Ouagadougou, population 110 000 (1970 est).
Other principal towns (1970): Bobo-Dioulasso 78 478; Koudougou 41 200.
Highest point: Mt Tema, 2457 ft *749 m*.
Principal rivers: Volta Noire (Black Volta), Volta Rouge (Red Volta), Volta Blanche (White Volta).
Head of State: Gen Aboubakar Sangoulé Lamizana (b. 1916), President.
Climate: Hot (average temperature 83 °F). Dry from November to March. Very dry in north and north-east. Rainy season June to October in south. In Ouagadougou average maximum temperature 87 °F (August) to 104 °F (March), minimum 60 °F to 79 °F.
Crops: Sorghum, millet, groundnuts, cotton, karité nuts.
Monetary unit: Franc de la Communauté financière africaine.
Denominations:
  Coins 1, 2, 5, 10, 25, 50, 100 CFA francs.
  Notes 50, 100, 500, 1000, 5000 CFA francs.
Exchange rate to US dollar: 224.24 (February 1976).
Political history and government: Formerly a part of French West Africa, independent since 5 Aug. 1960. Army officers, led by Lt-Col (later Gen) Sangoulé Lamizana, took power in a *coup* on 3 Jan. 1966. Col Lamizana took office as President and Prime Minister, the constitution was suspended, the National Assembly dissolved and a Supreme Council of the Armed Forces established. Political activities were suspended on 21 Sept. 1966 but the restriction was lifted in November 1969. A new constitution was approved by popular referendum on 14 June 1970 and introduced on 21 June 1970. This provided for a four-year transitional regime, under joint military and civilian control, leading to the return of civilian rule. Elections for a unicameral National Assembly of 57 members were held on 20 Dec. 1970. The leader of the majority party was appointed Prime Minister by the President, took office on 13 Feb. 1971 and formed a mixed civilian and military Council of Ministers. On 8 Feb. 1974, after a dispute between the Premier and the Assembly, the President dismissed the former and dissolved the latter. The army again assumed power, with the constitution and political activity suspended. The Head of State also became President of the Council of Ministers on 11 Feb. 1974. Political parties were banned on 30 May 1974. The Assembly was replaced by a National Consultative Council for Renewal, formed on 2 July 1974, with 65 members nominated by the President. The country is divided into 10 departments, each under a military prefect.
Telephones: 4000 (1971).
Daily newspapers: 1 (1971).
  Total circulation: 2000.
Radio: 90 000 (1972).
TV: 6000 (1971).
Length of roadways: 10 353 miles *16 662 km*.
Length of railways: 321 miles *517 km*.
Universities: 1.
Adult illiteracy: 90 to 95% (estimate).
Expectation of life: Males 34·9 years; females 36·1 years (1965–70).
Defence: Total armed forces 2050.
Wildlife: Elephant, crocodile, monkeys, hippopotamus, gazelle, hartebeest. Wide variety of birds.

Cinemas: 6 (seating capacity 2000) and 3 part-time (capacity 700) in 1969.

URUGUAY

Official name: La República Oriental del Uruguay (The Eastern Republic of Uruguay)
Population: 2 763 964 (1975 census).
Area: 68 536 miles² *177 508 km²*.
Language: Spanish.
Religion: Roman Catholic.
Capital city: Montevideo, population 1 229 748 (1975).
Other principal towns (1975): Salto 80 000; Paysandú 80 000; Mercedes 53 000; Las Piedras 42 000; Rivera 42 000; Minas 40 000; Melo 38 000.
Highest point: Cerro de las Animas, 1643 ft *500 m*.
Principal mountain ranges: Sierra de las Animas.
Principal rivers: Uruguay (1000 miles [*1609 km*]).
Head of State: Dr Pedro Alberto Demichela Lizaso (b. 7 Aug. 1896), President.★
Climate: Temperate (average 61 °F). Warm summers and mild winters. Moderate rain. In Montevideo, average maximum 58 °F (July) to 83 °F (January), minimum 43 °F (June, July, August) to 62 °F. (January), rainiest months are August and December (each 7 days). Maximum recorded temperature 44 °C (*111·2 °F*), Rivera, February 1953; minimum −7 °C (*19·4 °F*), Paysandú, June 1945.
Crops: Wheat, maize, sorghum, rice, potatoes, grapes, sugar beet, sugar cane.
Monetary unit: New Uruguayan peso. 1 new peso = 100 centésimos.
Denominations:
  Coins 1, 2, 5, 10 centésimos.
  Notes 5, 10, 50 centésimos, 1, 5, 10 new pesos.
Exchange rate to US dollar: 2.955 (February 1976).
Political history and government: A republic comprising 19 departments. A new constitution, approved by plebiscite on 27 Nov. 1966 and taking effect on 1 Mar. 1967, provided that elections by universal adult suffrage be held every five years for a President, a Vice-President and a bicameral legislature, the General Assembly (Congress), comprising a Senate (30 elected members plus the Vice-President) and a 99-member

Chamber of Representatives. Elections to both Houses were by proportional representation. Executive power is held by the President, who appoints and leads an 11 member Council of Ministers. On 27 June 1973, after agreeing to political demands by the armed forces, the President dissolved both Houses of Congress. On 19 Dec. 1973 he appointed a new legislature, a 25-member Council of State, headed by a President, to control the executive and draft plans for constitutional reform. On 12 June 1976 the President was deposed by the armed forces and replaced by the Vice-President.
Telephones: 247 923 (1975)
Daily newspapers: 54 (1972).
  Total circulation: 790 000 (25 dailies).
Radio: 1 500 000 (1972).
TV: 305 000 (1973).
Length of roadways: 30 841 miles *49 634 km* (1973).
Length of railways: 1849 miles *2976 km*.
Universities: 2.
Adult illiteracy: 9·5% (males 9·8% females 9·3%) in 1963.
Expectation of life: Males 65·51 years; females 71·56 years (1963–4).
Defence: Military service: voluntary. Total armed forces 27 000 (1975). Defence expenditure 1973 $68 million.
Wildlife: Water hog, fox, armadillo, deer, alligator, puma, jaguar, cayman, lizard, viper, rattlesnake, tortoise, seal. Rhea, vulture, crow, quail, partridge, duck, owl, lapwing, hummingbird, cardinal.
Cinemas: 180 (seating capacity 124 700) in 1967 (35 mm cinemas only).
★On 14 July 1976 the Council of State elected Dr. Aparicio Méndez to be President from 1 Sept. 1976.

VATICAN CITY

Official name: Stato della Città del Vaticano (State of the Vatican City).
Population: 722 (1973 est).
Area: 108·7 acres *44 hectares*.
Languages: Italian, Latin.
Religions: Roman Catholic.
Head of State: Pope Paul VI (b. Giovanni Battista Montini, 26 Sept. 1897).
Head of Government: Cardinal Jean Villot (b. 11 Oct. 1905), Secretary of State.
Climate: See Italy for climate of Rome.
Monetary unit: Italian currency (*q.v.*).
Political history and government: An enclave in the city of Rome, established on 11 Feb. 1929 by the Lateran Treaty with Italy. The Vatican City is under the temporal jurisdiction of the Pope, the Supreme Pontiff elected for life by the College of Cardinals (137 in 1976). He appoints a Pontifical Commission, headed by the Secretary of State, to conduct the administrative affairs of the Vatican, which serves

as the international headquarters, and administrative centre, of the worldwide Roman Catholic Church.
Daily newspapers: 1.
Universities: There are 7 pontifical universities in Rome.

VENEZUELA

Official name: La República de Venezuela ('Little Venice').
Population: 10 721 522 (1971 census); 11 993 062 (1975 est).
Area: 352 144 miles² *912 050 km²*.
Languages: Spanish.
Religion: Roman Catholic.
Capital city: Santiago de León de los Caracas, population 2 105 578 (Federal District) in 1975.
Other principal towns (1970): Marracaibo 690 400; Barquisimeto 281 600; Valencia 224 800; Maracay 192 900; San Cristóbal 156 600; Cabimas 154 700.
Highest point: La Pico Columna (Pico Bolívar) 16 427 ft *5007 m*.
Principal mountain ranges: Cordillera de Mérida, Sierra de Perijá, La Gran Sabana.
Principal rivers: Orinoco (1700 miles [*2736 km*]).
Head of State: Carlos Andrés Pérez Rodríguez (b. 27 Oct. 1922), President.
Climate: Varies with altitude from tropical in steamy lowlands to cool in highlands. Maximum recorded temperature 38 °C (*100·4°F*), minimum −6 °C (*21·2 °F*). In Caracas, average temperature 69 °F, average maximum 75 °F (January) to 81 °F (April), minimum 56 °F (January, February) to 62 °F (May, June), rainiest months are July and August (each 15 days).
Crops: Sugar cane, bananas, maize, yucca, oranges, rice, potatoes, coffee, cotton.
Monetary unit: Bolívar. 1 bolívar = 100 céntimos.
Denominations:
  Coins 5, 12½, 25 and 50 céntimos, 1, 2, 5, 10, 20, 100 bolívares.
  Notes 5, 10, 20, 50, 100, 500 bolívares.
Exchange rate to US dollar: 4.285 (February 1976).
Political history and government: A federal republic of 20 states, two Federal Territories and a Federal District (containing the capital), each under a Governor. The

last military dictatorship was overthrown by popular revolt on 21–22 Jan. 1958, after which Venezuela returned to democratic rule. A new constitution was promulgated on 23 Jan. 1961. Legislative power is held by the bicameral National Congress, comprising a Senate (49 elected members plus ex-Presidents of the Republic) and a Chamber of Deputies (203 members). Executive authority rests with the President. Senators. Deputies and the President are all elected for 5 years by universal adult suffrage. The President has wide powers and appoints a Council of Ministers to conduct the government. He may not have two consecutive terms of office.
Telephones: 554 197 (1975).
Daily newspapers: 42 (1971).
  Total circulation: 998 000.
Radio: 2 000 000 (1972).
TV: 995 000 (1973).
Length of roadways: 27 514 miles *44 279 km*.
Length of railways: 107 miles *173 km* (1975).
Universities: 14.
Adult illiteracy: 36·7% (males 32·0%; females 41·6%) in 1961.
Expectation of life: Both sexes 66·41 years (1961).
Defence: Military service: two years selective. Total armed forces 44 000. Defence expenditure 1975 $494 million.
Wildlife: Anteater, sloth, tapir, bear, jaguar, margay, puma, ocelot, monkeys, bats (including Vampire), crocodile, boa constrictor, bushmaster, coral snake, tree frog, toad, salamander. Parrot, umbrella birds, macaw, crested coquette, water fowl, heron, guacharo, bellbird.
Cinemas: 436 and 20 drive-in (1971).

VIET-NAM (North)

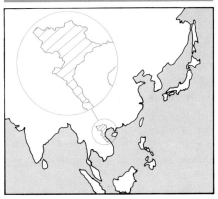

See note following South Viet-Nam.

Official name: Viêt-Nam Dan-Chu Công-Hoa (Democratic Republic of Viet-Nam).
Population: 23 787 375 (1974 census).
Area: 61 294 miles². *158 750 km²*.
Languages: Vietnamese.
Religions: Buddhist, Taoist, Confucian, Christian.
Capital city: Hà-nôi (Hanoi), population 1 378 335 (1974), incl suburbs.
Other principal towns (1960): Haiphong 182 490 (369 248, incl suburbs); Nam Dinh 86 132; Vinh 43 954.
Highest point: Fan si Pan 10 308 ft *3142 m*.
Principal rivers: Hong Ha (Red River) Nhi Ha, Lo, Gam, Da (Black River), Ma, Ca.
Head of State: Ton Duc Thang (b. 20 Aug. 1888), President.
Political Leader: Le Duan (b. 1908), First Secretary of the Central Committee of the Viet-Nam Workers' Party.
Prime Minister: Pham Van Dong (b. 1 Mar. 1906).

Climate: Hot and wet. Rainy monsoon season April to October. In Hanoi average maximum temperature 68 °F (January) to 92 °F (June), minimum 56 °F to 78 °F (June, July August); rainiest month August (16 days).
Crops: Rice, sweet potatoes, cassava, maize, sugar cane.
Monetary unit: Dông. 1 dông = 10 hào = 100 xu.
Denominations:
  Coins 1, 2, 5 xu.
  Notes 2 xu, 1, 2, 5, hào, 1, 2, 5, 10 dông.
Exchange rate to US dollar: 2.52 (December 1975).
Political history and government: Formerly part of French Indo-China, Viet-Nam was occupied by Japanese forces, with French co-operation, in September 1940. On 6 June 1941 nationalist and revolutionary groups, including the Communist Party of Indo-China, formed the *Viet-Nam Doc-Lap Dong Minh Hoi* (Revolutionary League for the Independence of Viet-Nam), known as the *Viet-Minh*, to overthrow French rule. On 9 Mar. 1945 French administrative control was ended by a Japanese *coup* against their nominal allies. After Japan's surrender in August 1945, *Viet-Minh* forces entered Hanoi and formed a provisional government under Ho Chi Minh, leader of the Communist Party. On 2 Sept. 1945 the new regime proclaimed independence as the Democratic Republic of Viet-Nam (DRV), with Ho as President. On 6 Mar. 1946, after French forces re-entered Viet-Nam, an agreement between France and the DRV recognised Viet-Nam as a 'free' state within the French Union. The DRV government continued to press for complete independence but negotiations broke down and full-scale hostilities began on 19 Dec. 1946. The war continued until cease-fire agreements were made on 20–21 July 1954. These provided that DRV forces should regroup north of latitude 17° N. Thus the DRV was confined to North Viet-Nam. The present constitution was adopted on 1 Jan. 1960. Legislative authority is vested in the unicameral National Assembly, with 420 members elected by universal adult suffrage for 4 years. The Assembly elects a Standing Committee to be its permanent organ and to supervise local government. The DRV's President and Vice-President are elected by the Assembly for 4 years. Executive authority lies with the Council of Ministers, headed by a Prime Minister, which is elected by, and responsible to, the Assembly. Political power is held by the (Communist) *Dang Lao Dong Viet-Nam* or Viet-Nam Workers' Party, formed in 1951. The party's highest policy-making body is the Central Committee's politburo, with 10 full and 2 alternate (candidate) members in 1975. The *Lao Dong* Party dominates the National Fatherland Front, which also includes two minor parties and other state organisations. The DRV is divided into 17 provinces. On 25 April 1976 elections were held in North and South Viet-Nam for a National Assembly of 492 members to draw up a new constitution for a reunified Viet-Nam.
Radio: 1 400 000 (1966).
Length of roadways: 8390 miles *c. 13 500 km*.
Length of railways: 485 miles *c. 780 km*.
Universities: 1.
Adult illiteracy: 35·5% (population aged 12 and over) in 1960.
Expectation of life: Males 44·0 years; females 46·9 years (1965–70).
Defence: Military service: two years minimum. Total armed forces 700 000. Defence expenditure 1970 (est) $584 million.
Wildlife: See Viet-Nam (South).
Cinemas: 41 (1961).

VIET-NAM (South)

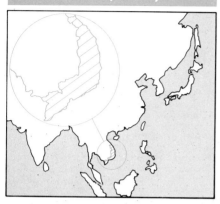

Official name: The Republic of South Viet-Nam.*
Population: 19 954 000 (1973 est).
Area: 67 108 miles² *173 809 km².*
Language: Vietnamese.
Religions: Buddhist, Taoist, Confucian, Christian.
Capital city: Saigon, population (1973 est) 1 825 297 (incl Cholon).
Other principal towns (1973): Da-Nhang (Tourane) 492 194; Nha-trang 216 227; Qui-Nhon 213 757; Hué 209 043; Can-Tho 182 424; Mytho 119 892; Cam-Ranh 118 111; Vungtau 108 436; Dalat 105 072.
Highest point: (Spot height) 8 524 ft *2598 m.*
Principal rivers: Mekong (2600 miles *4184 km*), Dong Nai.
Head of State: Huynh Tan Phat (b. 1913), President of the Provisional Revolutionary Government.
Climate: Tropical monsoon climate (warm and humid). Monsoon season May to October. In Saigon, average maximum 87 °F (November, December) to 95 °F (April), minimum 70 °F (January) to 76 °F (April, May), rainiest month is July (23 days). Absolute maximum temperature 42,1 °C (*107·8 °F*), Qui-Nhon, July 1908; absolute minimum −0,6 °C (*30·9 °F*), Dalat, February 1918.
Crops: Rice, cassava, sweet potatoes, sugar cane, bananas, rubber.
Monetary unit: New Viet-Nam piastre. 1 piastre = 100 centimes.
Exchange rate to US dollar: 1.51 (September 1975).
Political history and government: On 8 Mar. 1949, during the first Indo-China war, the French government made an agreement with anti-Communist elements for the establishment of the State of Viet-Nam, under Bao Dai, Emperor of Annam. Originally within the French Union, the State made an independence agreement with France on 4 June 1954. After the cease-fire agreements of 20–21 July 1954 French forces withdrew, leaving the State's jurisdiction confined to the zone south of latitude 17° N. Complete sovereignty was transferred by France on 29 Dec. 1954. Following a referendum, Bao Dai was deposed and the Republic of Viet-Nam proclaimed on 26 Oct. 1955. In 1959 an insurgent movement, supported by North Viet-Nam, launched guerrilla warfare to overthrow the Republic. The insurgents formed the National Liberation Front (NLF) on 20 Dec. 1960. From 1961 the USA supported the Republic with troops, numbering over 500 000 by 1969. From 1964 regular forces from North Viet-Nam, numbering about 250 000 by 1975, moved south to support the NLF. On 10 June 1969 the NLF announced the forma-tion of a Provisional Revolutionary Government (PRG) to administer 'liberated' areas. A 'peace' agreement on 27 Jan. 1973 led to the withdrawal of US forces but fighting continued until the Republic surrendered to the PRG on 30 Apr. 1975. The PRG is to administer South Viet-Nam until reunification with the North, under a constitution to be drafted by a single National Assembly (for both North and South) of 492 members elected on 25 April 1976. South Viet-Nam has 44 provinces.
Telephones: 46 509 (1973).
Radio: 2 200 000 (1970).
TV: 500 000 (1973).
Length of roadways: 13 000 miles *20 917 km.*
Length of railways: c. 423 miles *c. 680 km.* (1973).
Universities: 7.
Expectation of life: Males 39 1 years; females 41·8 years (1965–70).
Wildlife: Elephant, tiger, leopard, wild oxen, wild pig, deer, monkeys, tapirs, bears. Wide variety of birds.
Cinemas: 252 (seating capacity 134 800) in 1971.
*The National Assembly for North and South Viet-Nam met on 24th June 1976 and the country was reunified as the Socialist Republic of Viet-Nam, proclaimed on 2 July 1976. The capital is Hanoi and the North's political leaders continue in office in the new state.

WESTERN SAMOA

Official name: The Independent State of Western Samoa (Samoa i Sisifo)
Population: 146 627 (1971 census); 159 000 (1975 est).
Area: 1097 miles² *2842 km².*
Languages: Samoan, English.
Religions: Congregational, Roman Catholic, Methodist.
Capital city: Apia, population 30 266 (1971).
Highest point: Mauga Silisli, 6094 ft *1857 m.*
Head of State: H H,Malietoa Tanumafili II, CBE (b. 4 Jan. 1913).
Prime Minister: Tupuola Taisi Efi.
Climate: Warm all the year round. Rainy season November to April. In Apia, average maximum 84 °F to 86 °F, minimum 74 °F to 76 °F; rainiest month is January (22 days).
Crops: Coconuts, taro, bananas, cocoa.
Monetary unit: Tala. 1 tala = 100 sene.
Denominations:
Coins 1, 2, 5, 10, 20, 50 sene.
Notes 1, 2, 10 tala.
Exchange rate to US dollar: 0.6066 (September 1975).
Political history and government: Formerly a United Nations Trust Territory, administered by New Zealand. Independent since 1 Jan. 1962. The position of Head of State (*O le Ao o le Malo*) was held jointly by two tribal leaders, one of whom died on 5 Apr. 1963. The other remains Head of State for life. Future Heads of State will be elected for 5 years by the Legislative Assembly. The Assembly is a unicameral body of 47 members, including 45 Samoans elected by about 11 000 *matai* (elected clan chiefs) and two members popularly elected by voters (mainly Europeans) outside the *matai* system. Members hold office for 3 years. There are no political parties. Executive power is held by the Cabinet, comprising a Prime Minister and 8 other members of the Assembly. The Prime Minister, appointed by the Head of State, must have the support of a majority in the Assembly. Western Samoa joined the Commonwealth on 28 Aug. 1970.

Telephones: 2610 (1975).
Radio: 50 000 (1972).
TV: 80 (1972).
Length of roadways: 582 miles *936 km.*
Adult illiteracy: 2·6% (males 2·6%, females 2·5%) in 1966 (native language only).
Expectation of life: Males 60·8 years; females 65·2 years (1961–66).
Cinemas: 14 (1972).

THE YEMEN ARAB REPUBLIC

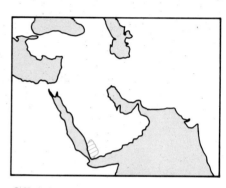

Official name: Al Jamhuriya al Arabiya al Yamaniya.
Population: 5 237 893 (1975 census).
Area: 75 000 miles² *195 000 km².*
Languages: Arabic.
Religions: Muslim.
Capital city: Sana'a, population 150 000 (1974 est).
Other principal towns: Hodeida 100 000; Ta'iz 100 000.
Highest point: Jebel Hadhar, 12 336 ft *3760 m.*
Principal mountain ranges: Yemen Highlands.
Head of State: Lt-Col Ibrahim Muhammad al-Hamadi (b. 1943), Chairman of the Military Command Council.
Prime Minister: Abdul-Aziz Abdul-Ghani (b. 4 July 1939).
Climate: Very hot (up to 130 °F) and extremely humid on semi-desert coastal strip. Cooler on highlands inland (average maximum of 71 °F in June) with heavy rainfall and winter frost. Desert in the east.
Crops: Millet, sorghum, barley, qat, coffee, cotton, fruit.
Monetary unit: Yemeni riyal. 1 riyal = 100 fils.
Denominations:
Coins 1, 5, 10, 25 and 50 fils.
Notes 1, 5, 10, 20, 50 riyals.
Exchange rate to US dollar: 4.54 (February 1976).
Political history and government: Formerly a monarchy, ruled by an hereditary Imam. Army officers staged a *coup* on 26–27 Sept. 1962, declared the Imam deposed and proclaimed a republic. Civil war broke out between royalist forces, supported by Saudi Arabia, and republicans, aided by Egyptian troops. The republicans gained the upper hand and Egyptian forces withdrew in 1967. A Republican Council, led by a Chairman, took power on 5 Nov. 1967 and announced a new constitution (which did not permit political parties) on 28 Dec. 1970. This provided for a unicameral legislature, the Consultative Assembly of 179 members (20 appointed by the Council and 159 elected for 4 years by general franchise on 27 Feb.–18 Mar. 1971). On

13 June 1974 power was seized by army officers who suspended the constitution, dissolved the Assembly and established a Military Command Council. On 19 June 1974 the new regime published a provisional constitution which, for a transitional period, gives full legislative and executive authority to the Command Council, whose Chairman has the powers of Head of State. The Council appoints a Cabinet, headed by a Prime Minister, to perform administrative duties.

Telephones: 5000 (1972).
Daily newspapers: 6 (1970).
  Total circulation: 56 000.
Radio: 250 000.
Length of roadways: 1025 miles *1650 km.*
Universities: 1.
Expectation of life: Males 41·4 years; females 43·3 years (1965–70).
Defence: Military service: three years. Total armed forces 32 000 (1975). Defence expenditure 1974–5 $58 million.
Wildlife: Ibex, oryx, civet cat.
Cinemas: 20 (1971).

THE PEOPLE'S DEMOCRATIC REPUBLIC OF YEMEN

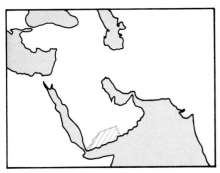

Official name: Al Jumhuriya al-Yaman al-dimuqratiya ash-Sha'abiya.
Population: 1 590 275 (1973 census); 1 657 000 (1975 est).
Area: 111 075 miles² *287 683 km².*
Languages: Arabic.
Religions: Muslim.
Capital city: Aden, population 264 326 (1973).
Other principal town: Al Mukalla 25 000.
Highest point: Qaured Audilla, 8200 ft *2499 m.*
Head of State: Salim Ali Rubayyi (b. 1934), Chairman of the Presidential Council.
Prime Minister: Ali Nasir Muhammad Hasaniya (b. 1944).
Climate: Summer extremely hot (temperatures over 130 °F) and humid. Very low rainfall (average less than 3 in per year). Winter can be very cold in high areas.
Crops: Sorghum, millet, cotton.
Monetary unit: Yemeni dinar. 1 dinar = 1000 fils.
Denominations:
  Coins 1, 2½, 5, 25, 50 fils.
  Notes 250, 500 fils, 1, 5, 10 dinars.
Exchange rate to US dollar: 0 3454 (February 1976).
Political history and government: Formerly the British colony of Aden and the Protectorate of South Arabia. Became independent, outside the Commonwealth, on 30 Nov. 1967 as the People's Republic of Southern Yemen. Power was held by a revolutionary movement, the National Liberation Front, now the National Front (NF).

The interim legislative authority was the NF's Supreme General Command. Since 22 June 1969 executive power has been held collectively by a Presidential Council (3 members in 1975), which appointed a Cabinet to administer the country. A new constitution, adopted on 30 Nov. 1970, gave the country its present name and provided for the establishment of a unicameral legislature, the Supreme People's Council (SPC). A Provisional SPC, inaugurated on 14 May 1971, has 101 members, including 86 elected by the NF's General Command and 15 elected by trade unions. It appoints members of the Presidential Council and the Cabinet. The ruling NF absorbed two smaller parties in 1975 and is now the country's only political organisation. Democratic Yemen is divided into 7 governorates.

Telephones: 9 876 (1973).
Daily newspapers: 3 (1971).
  Total circulation: 1600.
Radio: 150 000 (est).
TV: 27 000 (1970).
Length of roadways: 1150 miles *185 km.*
Universities: 1.
Expectation of life: Males 41·4 years; females 43·3 years (1965–70).
Defence: Military service: conscription (term unknown). Total armed forces 18 000 (1975). Defence expenditure (1972): $26 million.
Cinemas: 19 (seating capacity 20 000) in 1971.

YUGOSLAVIA

Official name: Socijalistička Federativna Republika Jugoslavija (Socialist Federal Republic of Yugoslavia).
Population: 20 522 972 (1971 census); 21 350 000 (1975 est).
Area: 98 766 miles² *255 804 km².*
Languages: Serbo-Croatian, Slovenian, Macedonian.
Religions: Eastern Orthodox, Roman Catholic, Muslim.
Capital city: Beograd (Belgrade), population 746 105 (1971).
Other principal towns (1971): Zagreb 566 224; Skoplje (Skopje) 312 980; Sarajevo 243 980; Ljubljana 173 853; Split 152 905; Novi Sad 141 375.
Highest point: Triglav, 9393 ft *2863 m.*
Principal mountain ranges: Slovene Alps, Dinaric Mts.
Principal rivers: Dunav (Danube) (1770 miles *[2848 km]*) and tributaries (Drava, Sava (584 miles *[940 km]*), Morava, Varder.
Head of State: Marshal Tito (b. Josip

Broz, 25 May 1892), Federal President.
Head of government: Džemal Bijedić (b. 17 Apr. 1917), President of the Federal Executive Council.
Climate: Mediterranean climate on Adriatic coast (dry, warm summers; mild, rainy winters). Continental climate (cold winters) in hilly interior. In Belgrade average maximum 37 °F (January) to 85 °F. (July), minimum 27 °F (January, February) to 61 °F (July). Rainiest months are April, May, June, December (each 9 days). In Split, average maximum 57 °F (January) to 87 °F (July, August) minimum 39 °F (January, February) to 68 °F (July), rainiest month is December (11 days). Absolute maximum temperature 46,2 °C (*115·2 °F*) Monstar, 31 July 1901; absolute minimum −37,8 °C (−*36·0 °F*), Sjenica, 26 Jan. 1954.
Crops: Maize, wheat, potatoes, sugar beet, grapes.
Monetary unit: Yugoslav dinar. 1 dinar = 100 para.
Denominations:
  Coins 5, 10, 20, 50 para, 1, 2, 5 dinars.
  Notes 5, 10, 50, 100, 500 dinars.
Exchange rate to US dollars: 18.08 (February 1976).
Political history and government: Yugoslavia was founded on 1 Dec. 1918 as a kingdom under the Serbian monarchy. Invaded by German and Italian forces on 6 Apr. 1941. Resistance was divided between royalists and Partisans, led by the Communist Party under Marshal Tito. Their rivalry led to civil war, won by the Partisans, who proclaimed the Federal People's Republic of Yugoslavia, with Tito as President, on 29 Nov. 1945. A Soviet-type constitution, establishing a federation of 6 republics, was adopted on 31 Jan. 1946. Yugoslav leaders followed independent policies and the country was expelled from the Soviet-dominated Cominform in June 1948. A new constitution, promulgated on 7 Apr. 1963, introduced the country's present name. Since 29 July 1971 national leadership has been held by a collective Presidency (led by Tito), elected by the Federal Assembly. The present constitution, which increased decentralisation, was adopted on 21 Feb. 1974. Legislative power is vested in the bicameral Federal Assembly, comprising a Federal Chamber of 220 members (30 from each of the 6 republics and 20 each from the two autonomous provinces within Serbia) and a Chamber of Republics and Provinces, with 88 members (12 from each Republican Assembly and 8 from each Provincial Assembly). Members are elected for 4 years by delegates in each Republic or Province, themselves elected by universal adult suffrage, with voters grouped according to their place of work. The collective Presidency has 9 members, the President and one each from the Republics and Provinces. The Federal Assembly elects the Federal Executive Council, led by a President, to be the administrative branch of government. The only authorised political party is the League of Communists of Yugoslavia, led by Tito, which controls political life through the Socialist Alliance of the Working People of Yugoslavia. The League's main policy-making body is the Presidium's Executive Bureau, with 13 members.

Telephones: 1 142 883 (1975).
Daily newspapers: 25 (1974).
  Total circulation: 1 852 000.
Radio: 4 081 000 (1974).
TV: 2 784 000 (1974).
Length of roadways: 61 125 miles *98 372 km.*
Length of railways: 6412 miles *10 319 km.*
Universities: 15.
Adult illiteracy: 16·3% (males 7·9%; females 24·2%) in 1971.

Expectation of life: Males 65·30 years; females 70·14 years (1970–71).
Defence: Military service: Army and Air Force 15 months; Navy 18 months. Total armed forces 230 000. Defence expenditure 1975 $1705 million.
Wildlife: Deer, chamois, wolf, fox, hare, deer, hamster, rabbit, lizard, jackal.
Cinemas: 1393 (seating capacity 480 000) and 30 part-time (capacity 26 306) in 1972.

ZAIRE

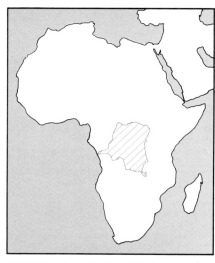

Official name: La République du Zaïre.
Population: 24 222 000 (1974 est).
Area: 905 365 miles² *2 344 885 km²*.
Languages: French, Lingala, Kiswahili, Tshiluba, Kikongo.
Religions: Animist, Roman Catholic, Protestant.
Capital city: Kinshasa (formerly Léopoldville), population 1 990 717 (1974 est).
Other principal towns (1974): Kananga (Luluabourg) 596 954; Lubumbashi (Elisabethville) 401 612; Mbuji-Mayi 334 725; Kisangani (Stanleyville) 297 829; Bukavu 180 633.
Highest point: Ngaliema (Mt Stanley), 16 763 ft *5109 m* (first climbed 1900).
Principal mountain ranges: Chaîne des Mitumba, Ruwenzori.
Principal rivers: Zaïre (Congo), Ubangi, Kasai.
Head of State: Lt-Gen Mobutu Sese Seko (b. 14 Oct. 1930), President.
Climate: Tropical. Hot and humid in Congo basin, cool in highlands. In Kinshasa (Léopoldville), March and April hottest (71 °F to 89 °F), July coolest (64 °F to 81 °F) and driest, April and November rainiest (16 days each). Absolute maximum temperature 41,0 °C (*105·8 °F*) at Yahila; absolute minimum. −1,5 °C (*29·3 °F*), Sakania, 11 Jan. 1949.
Crops: Cassava, maize, rice, groundnuts, palm oil and kernels, coffee.
Monetary unit: Zaire. 1 zaire = 10 000 sengi or 100 makuta.
Denominations:
Coins 10 sengi, 1, 5 makuta.
Notes 10, 20, 50 makuta, 1, 5, 10 zaires.
Exchange rate to US dollar: 0.50 (February 1976).
Political history and government: Formerly the Belgian Congo, independent as the Republic of the Congo on 30 June 1960. Renamed the Democratic Republic of the Congo on 1 Aug. 1964. Power was seized on 24 Nov. 1965 by army officers, led by Lt-Gen Joseph-Désiré Mobutu (from January 1972 called Mobutu Sese Seko). The

new regime, with Mobutu as President, was approved by Parliament on 28 Nov. 1965. A new constitution, approved by referendum, was adopted on 24 June 1967. The country's present name was introduced on 27 Oct. 1971. Mobutu was elected President by popular vote on 31 Oct.–1 Nov. 1970 and inaugurated for a 7-year term on 5 Dec. 1970. Under a 1974 amendment, the President's term of office is reduced to 5 years. A unicameral National Legislative Council of 244 members, led by Mobutu, was elected by acclamation for 5 years on 2 Nov. 1975. The President appoints and leads the National Executive Council, a cabinet of State Commissioners with departmental responsibilities. Since 1970 the only authorised political party has been the *Mouvement populaire de la révolution* (MPR) or People's Revolutionary Movement. The highest policy-making body is the MPR's Political Bureau of 20 members (1976), who nominate the President. The Bureau has a Permanent Committee of 10 members who assist the President. The country comprises 8 Regions, each headed by an appointed Commissioner, and the city of Kinshasa, under a Governor.
Telephones: 26 274 (1975).
Daily newspapers: 13 (1970).
Total circulation: 200 000 (est).
Radio: 100 000 (1972).
TV: 7100 (1971).
Length of roadways: *c.* 90 100 miles. *c. 145 000 km.* (1971).
Length of railways: 3215 miles. *5174 km.*
Universities: 1 (three campuses).
Adult illiteracy: 84·6% (males 70·8%; females 97·2%) in 1955–8.
Expectation of life: Males 40·4 years; females 43·6 years (1965–70).
Defence: Military service: voluntary. Total armed forces 43 400. Defence expenditure 1974 $104 million.
Wildlife: Monkeys, apes (including chimpanzee and gorilla), elephant, lion, leopard, jackal, crocodile, hippopotamus, buffalo, antelope. Parrots, stork, ibis, tern, hawk, heron.
Cinemas: 34 (seating capacity 13 600) in 1970.

ZAMBIA

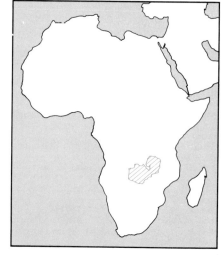

Official name: The Republic of Zambia.
Population: 4 056 995 (1969 census); 4 751 000 (1974 est.).
Area: 290 586 miles² *752 614 km²*.
Languages: English (official), Nyanja, Bemba, Tonga, Lozi, Lunda, Luvale.

Religions: Roman Catholic, Protestant, Animist.
Capital city: Lusaka, population 415 000 (1974).
Other principal towns (1974): Kitwe (incl Kalulushi) 314 000; Ndola 222 000; Chingola 202 000; Mufulira 136 000; Luanshya 119 000; Kabwe (Broken Hill) 95 000; Livingstone 58 000.
Highest point: 6210 ft *1893 m*.
Principal mountain ranges: Muchinga Mts.
Principal rivers: Zambezi and tributaries (Kafue, Luangwa), Luapula.
Head of State: Dr Kenneth David Kaunda (b. 28 Apr. 1924), President.
Prime Minister: Elijah Haatukali Kaiba Mudenda (b. 6 June 1927).
Climate: Hot season September–November, rainy season November–April, winter May–September. Day temperatures 80 °F to 100 °F in hot season, sharp fall at night. Average annual rainfall from 25 in in south to 50 in in north. In Lusaka, average annual minimum 64 °F, maximum 88 °F, average rainfall 33 in.
Crops: Maize, sorghum, cassava, groundnuts, sugar cane, tobacco.
Monetary unit: Zambian kwacha. 1 kwacha = 100 ngwee.
Denominations:
Coins 1, 2, 5, 10, 20 ngwee.
Notes 50 ngwee, 1, 2, 5, 10, 20 kwacha.
Exchange rate to US dollar: 0.6435 (February 1976).
Political history and government: Formerly the British protectorate of Northern Rhodesia, an independent republic and a member of the Commonwealth since 24 Oct. 1964. A one-party state was proclaimed on 13 Dec. 1972 and inaugurated by a new constitution on 25 Aug. 1973. Legislative power is held by the unicameral National Assembly, with 135 members (10 nominated by the President and 125 elected for 5 years by universal adult suffrage, with up to three candidates per constituency). There is also an advisory House of Chiefs (27 members) to represent traditional tribal authorities. Executive power is held by the President, elected by popular vote at the same time as the Assembly. He appoints a Cabinet, led by a Prime Minister, to conduct the administration. The sole authorised party is the United National Independence Party (UNIP), led by the President. The highest policy-making body is UNIP's Central Committee (25 members), to which the Cabinet is subordinate. Zambia is divided into 9 provinces, each administered by a Cabinet Minister.
Telephones: 67 962 (1975).
Daily newspapers: 2 (1972).
Total circulation: 77 000.
Radio: 100 000 (1972).
TV: 21 000 (1973).
Length of roadways: 21 725 miles *34 963 km.*
Length of railways: 1359 miles. *2187 km.*
Universities: 1.
Adult illiteracy: 52·4% (males 38·5%; females 65·4%) in 1969.
Expectation of life: Males 41·9 years; females 45·1 years (1965–70).
Defence: Military service: voluntary. Total armed forces 5800. Defence expenditure 1974 $78 million.
Wildlife: Monkeys, baboons, lion, cheetah, hyena, leopard, serval, civet, mongoose, pole-cat, jackal, otter, elephant, giraffe, hippopotamus, antelopes (many varieties), ant bear, pangolin, hedgehog, fruit bat, over 150 species of reptiles. Many varieties of birds.
Cinemas: 28 (seating capacity 13 400) and one drive-in (1971).

A

A, A₂ Vitamins, 43
Abdication Act, 1936, 107
Abdul-Ghani, Abdul-Aziz, 242
Aberdeen, Earl of, 119
Aberdeen, University of, 90
Abidjan, 201
aborigines, 146
absolute speed (light), 141
Abu Dhabi, 233
accidents, road, 131
Accra, 194
acetylenes, 159
Achernar, 141
Aconcagua Mountain, 75, 78, 80
Act of Settlement, 107
Addington, Henry, 119
Addis Ababa, 190
Adelaide, 175
Aden, 243
Adhara, 141
Aelfred, King, 56
Aelfric, 56
aerolite, 144
Aeta, 145
Afghanistan, Kingdom of, 172
Africa: area, 73
  ethnology, 145–6
  glaciers, 79
  mountains, 76
  overland distance, 72
agates, 66
Ahmedabad, 198
Ainu, 145
air, 70
aircraft, 133
Aire River, 86
airlines, major, 134
airports, major, 133
Alabama, 233
Alaska, 74, 233
  area, 74
  glaciers, 79
Albania (People's Republic), 172
Albany (N.Y.), 236
Albert Nile River, 80
Alberta, 181
Aldebaran, 141
Alderney, Island, 88, 90
Aleutian Trench, 75
alexandrites, 65
Alfred the Great, 104
Algara, R., 80
Algeria, Republic of, 172–3
Algiers, 172
Allegheny River, 82
alloys, 160–1
Alpha Centauri, 141
  Crucis, 141

alphabets,
  Greek, 59
  Russian, 59
Alphonse XIII Canal, 137
Alpine people, 146
Alps, 77
  highest peak, 77
  length, 77
Altair, 141
altocumulus clouds, 71
altostratus clouds, 71
aluminium compounds, 160
Amazon, River, 80
ambers, 66
America (continent)
  area, 73
  ethnology, 145
  see also Central, North
  South America
  (country) see United States
  of America
Amerinds, 145
amethysts, 65
'Amman, 203
Amphibia, 20
Amsterdam, 213
Amu-Dar'ya River, 82
Amur River, 81
Andaman and Nicobar Is., 145
Andaman Sea, 72
Andean civilization, 147
Andes, 75, 80
  highest peaks, 75
  length, 80
Andorra, 173
Andorra la Vella, 173
Andromeda, 141
Angel Falls, 83
Angevins, the, 105
Anglesey, 88
Anglo-Saxons, 104
Angola, 173
Anguilla (Leeward Is.), 169
animals, 14–26
  British mammals, 23–6
  longevity, 26
  size, 26
  speed, 26
Anjou House of, 105
Ankara, 231
Annapolis (Md.), 235
Anne, queen of England, 113
Anne of Cleves, queen of England, 111
anniversaries, 10–13
annular eclipses, 143
Antarctic Ocean, 72
Antarctica, 73
  area, 73
  Australian territory, 170
  British territory, 169
  mountains, 77
  New Zealand
    dependencies, 170

overland distances, 73
  see also South Pole
Antares, 141
anthropology, 145–7
  see also man, ethnology
Antigua, 169
Antipater of Sidon, 134
Apia, 242
Apollo, statue of, 134
apothecaries' measures, 150
aquamarines, 65
Arabia: area, 74
Arabian Desert: area, 74
Arabic civilisation, 147
Aral' skoye More, 83
Arctic, see North Pole
Arctic Sea: area, 72
Arcturus, 141
area formulae, 149, 162
  British units, 149
  metric conversions, 173–4
Argentina, 173–4
Argun, River, 81
Arizona, 234
Arkansas, 234
Arkansas River, 82
Artemis, Temple of, 134
Arthur, King, 104
artists, European, 46–7
Ascension Island, 170
ascorbic acid, 159
Asia: area, 73
  ethnology, 145
  glaciers, 79
  overland distances, 73
Asquith, Herbert Henry, 120
assizes, the, 126
asteroids, 144
Aston, University of (Birmingham), 91
astroblemes, 144
astronauts, 142
astronomy, 141–5
  radio, 145
Asunción, 217
Atacama Desert: area, 74
Athabasca, Lake, 83
Athens, 194
Atlanta (Ga.), 234
Atlantic Ocean, area, 72
  depth, 72
atmosphere, 70
  chemical elements, 70
atom bomb, 161
atomic numbers, 154–6
atomic, sub-particles, 151–2
atomic weights, 154–6
Attlee, Earl, 120
Augusta (Me.), 235
Aurora Australis, 70
Aurora Borealis, 70
Austin (Texas), 237

Australia, Commonwealth of, 174–5
  area, 73
  dependencies, 170
  ethnology, 146
  overland distances, 73
Australian Antarctic Territory, 170
Australian Desert: area, 74
Australoids, 146
Austria, Federal Republic of, 175
authors, British, 56–9
avalanches, 67
Aves, 20–1
aviation, 134
avoirdupois measures, 150
Avon, 93–4
Avon, Earl of, 120
Avon, River, 86
Aztecs, 145

B

B, B₁, B₂, B₆, B₁₂ Vitamins, 43
Babylon, Hanging Gardens of, 134
Babylonic civilization, 146
bacteria, 28
Baffin Island: area, 73
Baghdad, 199
Bahamas, 175–6
Bahrain, 176
Bairiki (Gilbert Islands), 170
balance of payments, (1965–75), 126
Baldwin, Stanley, 120
Balfour, Arthur James, 120
ball lightning, 68
Baltic sea: area, 72
  depth, 72
Bamako, 209
Bangalore, 198
Bangkok, 229
Bangladesh, 176
Bangui, 183
Banjul, 192
bank
  notes see currency, 122–3
  rate, 123
Bank of England, 122, 123
bank holidays, 8
Bann, River, 86
Barbados, 176
Barbuda (Leeward Is.), 169
Barking, 97
Barnard's Star, 142
Barnet, 97
barometric pressures, 70
barons, 107
Basse-terre (St Christopher,

Leeward Is), 170
Bath, Earl of, 118
Bath University, 91
Baton Rouge (La), 235
Battle of Hastings, 105
Baudouin, king of the Belgians, 177
Beaconsfield, Earl of see Disraeli, Benjamin, 120
Beaker Folk, 146
Beaufort scale, 68
Beaverhead River, 80
Bede, Venerable, 56
Bedfordshire, 93, 94
Bedouins, 146
Beethoven, Ludwig van, 52
Beirut, 205
Belfast, Queens University of, 91
Belgium, Kingdom of, 177
Belgrade, 243
Bellatrix, 142
Belmopan, 169
Benin, 177
Bering Sea: area, 72
  depth, 72
Berkshire, 93, 94
Berlin, 192
Berlioz, Louis Hector, 53
Bermuda, 169
Berne, 227
Beta Centauri, 141
Beta Crucis, 141
Betelgeuse, 141
Bexley, 97
Bhutan, 177
binary system (mathematics), 164
  eclipses, 143
birds, British, 20–2
Birmingham, University of, 91
Bismark (ND), 236
Bjorken, B., 152
Black Sea: area, 72
  depth, 72
Blois, House of, 105
blood Jasper, 66
bloodstones, 66
blue moon, 68
Boadicea, Queen, 104
Bogotá, 185
boiling points (elements), 154–6
Boise City (Idaho), 234
Boleyn, Anne, queen of England, 111
Bolivia, Republic of, 177–8
Bolton, John G., 145
Bombay, 198
bones, human, 41
Bonn, 193
Borders, 93–4
Borneo: area, 73
Boston (Mass), 235

OTHER
GUINNESS SUPERLATIVES
TITLES

FACTS AND FEATS SERIES

Air Facts and Feats, *2nd ed.,* John W. R. Taylor, Michael J. H. Taylor and David Mondey

Rail Facts and Feats, *2nd ed.,* John Marshall

Tank Facts and Feats, *2nd ed.,* Kenneth Macksey

Yachting Facts and Feats, Peter Johnson

Plant Facts and Feats, William G. Duncalf

Structures—Bridges, Towers, Tunnels, Dams . . ., John H. Stephens

Car Facts and Feats, *2nd ed.,* Anthony Harding

Business World, Henry Button and Andrew Lampert

Music Facts and Feats, Robert and Celia Dearling with Brian Rust

Animal Facts and Feats, *2nd ed.,* Gerald L. Wood

GUIDE SERIES

Guide to Freshwater Angling, Brian Harris and Paul Boyer

Guide to Mountain Animals, R. P. Bille

Guide to Underwater Life, C. Petron and J. B. Lozet

Guide to Formula 1 Motor Racing, José Rosinski

Guide to Motorcycling, *2nd ed.,* Christian Lacombe

Guide to French Country Cooking, Christian Roland Délu

Guide to Bicycling, John Durry

OTHER TITLES

English Furniture 1550–1760, Geoffrey Wills

English Furniture 1760–1900, Geoffrey Wills

The Guinness Guide to Feminine Achievements, Joan and Kenneth Macksey

The Guinness Book of Names, Leslie Dunkling

Battle Dress, Frederick Wilkinson

Universal Soldier, Martin Windrow and Frederick Wilkinson

History of Land Warfare, Kenneth Macksey

History of Sea Warfare, Lt.-Cmdr. Gervis Frere-Cook and Kenneth Macksey

History of Air Warfare, David Brown, Christopher Shores and Kenneth Macksey

The Guinness Book of Records, *23rd ed.,* edited by Norris D. McWhirter

The Guinness Book of 1952, edited by Kenneth Macksey

CHECK LIST OF THE 158

	COUNTRY	CONTINENT	ACHIEVED SOVEREIGNTY
77.	JORDAN	ASIA	22 MAR. 1946
78.	PHILIPPINES	ASIA	4 JULY 1946
79.	INDIA	ASIA	14–15 AUG. 1947
80.	PAKISTAN	ASIA	14–15 AUG. 1947
81.	BURMA	ASIA	4 JAN. 1948
82.	SRI LANKA (Ceylon before 1972)	ASIA	4 FEB. 1948
83.	ISRAEL	ASIA	14 MAY 1948
— 84.	KOREA (North)	ASIA	9 SEPT. 1948
= 84.	KOREA (South)	ASIA	15 AUG. 1948
86.	GERMAN DEMOCRATIC REPUBLIC	EUROPE	7 OCT. 1949
87.	LIBYA	AFRICA	24 DEC. 1951
88.	YEMEN (North)	ASIA	26 SEPT. 1952
89.	CAMBODIA (Khmer Republic 1970–5)	ASIA	9 NOV. 1953
90.	LAOS	ASIA	21 JULY 1954
91.	VIETNAM	ASIA	29 DEC. 1954
92.	SUDAN	AFRICA	1 JAN. 1956
93.	MOROCCO	AFRICA	2 MAR. 1956
94.	TUNISIA	AFRICA	10 MAY 1956
95.	GHANA	AFRICA	7 FEB. 1957
96.	MALAYSIA	ASIA	31 AUG. 1957
97.	GUINEA	AFRICA	2 OCT. 1958
98.	CAMEROON	AFRICA	1 JAN. 1960
99.	TOGO	AFRICA	27 APR. 1960
100.	MADAGASCAR	AFRICA	26 JUNE 1960
101.	ZAÏRE (formerly Congo (Kinshasa))	AFRICA	30 JUNE 1960
102.	SOMALIA	AFRICA	1 JULY 1960
103.	BENIN (Dahomey before 1975)	AFRICA	1 AUG. 1960
104.	NIGER	AFRICA	3 AUG. 1960
105.	UPPER VOLTA	AFRICA	5 AUG. 1960
106.	IVORY COAST	AFRICA	7 AUG. 1960
107.	CHAD	AFRICA	11 AUG. 1960
108.	CENTRAL AFRICAN REPUBLIC	AFRICA	13 AUG. 1960
109.	CONGO	AFRICA	15 AUG. 1960
110.	CYPRUS	ASIA	16 AUG. 1960
111.	GABON	AFRICA	17 AUG. 1960
112.	SÉNÉGAL	AFRICA	20 AUG. 1960
113.	MALI	AFRICA	22 SEPT. 1960
114.	NIGERIA	AFRICA	1 OCT. 1960
115.	MAURITANIA	AFRICA	28 NOV. 1960
116.	SIERRA LEONE	AFRICA	27 APR. 1961
117.	WESTERN SAMOA	AUSTRALIA	1 JAN. 1962